Your active listening experience has begun.

Welcome to Prentice Hall's UNDERSTANDING MUSIC, FOURTH EDITION music appreciation program. With a focus on the music of the Western tradition in its social, historical, and global contexts, this new edition addresses students as readers and listeners ready to encounter music through a lively text and interactive activities. Read on to find out how!

THE ART OF LISTENING

■ UNDERSTANDING MUSIC's unique and independent chapter on *The Art of Listening* guides the listener moment-by-moment through five short works, each illuminating different musical elements, techniques, and vocabulary. These activities lay a solid foundation of listening work throughout the remainder of the book.

■ The *Fundamentals* chapter and the *Listening* chapter are carefully coordinated to provide a supportive framework to enhance the listening experience.

LISTENING GUIDES

■ Clear and easy to follow, the *Listening Guides* explain form and structure, texture, instrumentation, and musical motives.

■ Special moments such as surprising gestures, unexpected key changes, or departures from conventional form are highlighted.

■ Exact timings and CD track numbers are supplied to identify important structural points within each work.

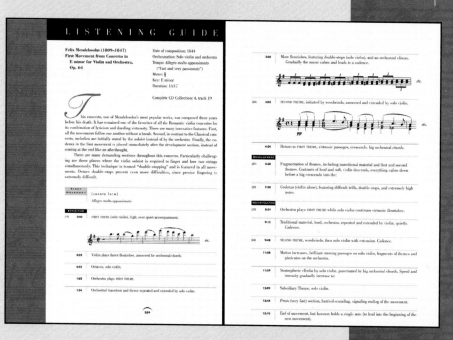

Sample excerpts from the text, CD-ROM, and video are accurate as of press time and reduced from their original size. © 2005 Pearson Prentice Hall, Upper Saddle River, NJ 07458

active

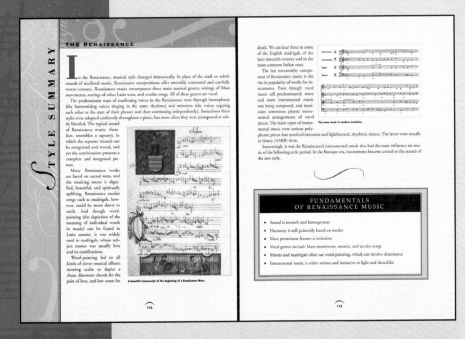

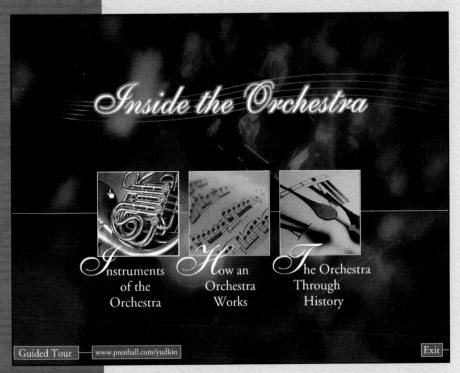

STYLE SUMMARY

This descriptive feature concisely encapsulates the key elements of a particular style period. Each *Style Summary* captures the essence of the musical style of each historical period and lists the musical elements central to each style.

INSIDE THE ORCHESTRA

New to the Fourth Edition, *Inside the Orchestra* beautifully illustrates how the orchestra—musicians and instruments—has grown and evolved throughout the history of music. Both the CD-ROM and Instructor Video include a section tied to this feature to enhance students' understanding.

STUDENT CD-ROM AND INSTRUCTOR VIDEO

Bound at no additional cost into each new copy of UNDERSTANDING MUSIC, FOURTH EDITION, this instructive new CD-ROM is a student's seat in the orchestra!

It consists of three video segments:

■ *Instruments of the Orchestra* is a preliminary introduction to the various instrument families;

■ *How an Orchestra Works* offers an informative guided video tour of Mozart's orchestra and a sampling of how these instruments work together;

■ *The Orchestra Through History* presents live performances of orchestral works from five different historical periods.

The CD-ROM is accompanied throughout by text. It also links to quizzes in the Companion Website™ at *www.prenhall.com/yudkin*. And, for the instructor's convenience, we provide the video portion of this student CD-ROM on videocassette for use in the classroom.

discovery

INSIDE THE ORCHESTRA
Table of Contents

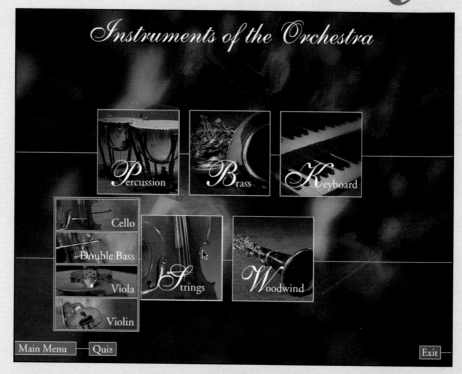

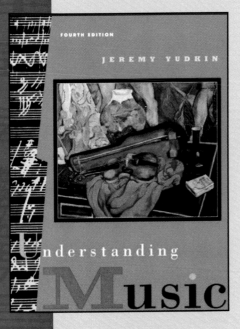

FOURTH EDITION

JEREMY YUDKIN

Understanding

Music

active teaching and learning resources

■ **Annotated Instructor's Edition (AIE) (0-13-150552-1)**
The AIE provides a wealth of helpful teachings tips, suggestions for classroom exercises, parallel pieces, historical comments, etc., printed in the margins of the text. Annotations appear only in the AIE and are designed to shorten preparation time and enliven classroom presentations.

■ **NEW! Inside the Orchestra Instructor Video Cassette (0-13-150561-0)**
Free to adopting instructors, the video contains all of the video from the *Inside the Orchestra* Student CD-ROM and is perfect for in-class activities.

■ **NEW! MusicNotes (0-13-150560-2)**
MusicNotes is Prentice Hall's one-stop resource for students to keep their course notes, their listening activities, and information in order. Easy to use and portable, *MusicNotes* includes listening guides with space on each page for note taking.

■ **The UNDERSTANDING MUSIC, FOURTH EDITION Companion Website™ at *www.prenhall.com/yudkin***
The Companion Website™ greatly enhances students' understanding with online study resources that reinforce comprehension of key concepts from the book, and listening exercises to round out their music experience.

■ **7-CD Complete Set (0-13-150564-5)**
Includes all the works analyzed in the text.

■ **3-CD Student Set (0-13-150563-7)**
Includes the most important musical pieces covered in the text.

■ **Expanded Repertoire Custom Compact Disc**
The UNDERSTANDING MUSIC recording program is enhanced by the edition of a customizable compact disc. Contact your local Prentice Hall sales representative for more details.

■ **Films for the Humanities Historical Videotape**
Produced exclusively for UNDERSTANDING MUSIC, this sixty-minute compendium presents a wealth of brief film extracts for classroom use.

■ **Instructor's Manual with Tests (0-13-150551-3)**
This resource provides a list of objectives, classroom activities and multiple choice, true-false, and essay format test items.

■ **TestGen EQ for Microsoft™ Windows or Macintosh® (0-13-150554-8)**
This test generator is designed to help create personalized exams, with maximum flexibility in producing and grading tests and quizzes.

■ **Films for the Humanities Video Library (0-13-150559-9)**
Available free to qualified adopters, this library contains 75 videos on a wide range of topics. Ask your local Prentice Hall sales representative for details.

■ **Ask your Prentice Hall sales representative about these Course Management Solutions, available with this text:** WebCT™, Blackboard™, and CourseCompass™ or visit *www.prenhall.com/demo.*

TO ORDER THE STUDENT EDITION OF THIS TEXT FOR CLASSES, CONTACT YOUR BOOKSTORE USING ISBN 0-13-150548-3.

FOURTH EDITION

Understanding Music

JEREMY YUDKIN

BOSTON UNIVERSITY

PEARSON

Prentice Hall

Upper Saddle River, NJ 07458

Library of Congress Cataloging-in-Publication Data

Yudkin, Jeremy.
    Understanding music / Jeremy Yudkin.—4th ed.
        p.   cm.
    Includes bibliographical references (p.) and index.
    ISBN 0-13-150548-3 (main textbook)
    1. Music appreciation. 2. Music—History and criticism. I. Title.
MT6.Y86U53 2004
780—dc22

                                    2003068954

Editorial Director: *Charlyce Jones Owen*
Acquisitions Editor: *Christopher T. Johnson*
Editorial Assistant: *Evette Dickerson*
Marketing Manager: *Sheryl Adams*
AVP/Director of Production and Manufacturing: *Barbara Kittle*
Managing Editor: *Joanne Riker*
Production Editor: *Joe Scordato*
Production Assistant: *Marlene Gassler*
Permissions Supervisor: *Ron Fox*
Manufacturing Manager: *Nick Sklitsis*
Manufacturing Buyer: *Benjamin D. Smith*
Creative Director: *Leslie Osher*
Interior and Cover Design: *Ximena P. Tamvakopoulos*

Cover Art: *Suzanne Valudon (1867–1938/French), "The Violin Box"*
(La Boîte à Violin), 1923. Oil on canvas. Musée d'Art Moderne de la Ville
de Paris, France / Giraudon Paris / SuperStock
Director of Image Resources: *Beth Boyd*
Image Permission Coordinator: *Nancy Seise*
Composition: *Stratford Publishing Services*
Printer/Binder: *The Courier Companies*
Cover Printer: *Phoenix Color Corp.*

Credits and acknowledgments borrowed from other sources and reproduced, with permission, in this textbook appear on pages 484–487. Beethoven's handwritten sketches for the Fifth Symphony used with permission of Gesellschaft der Musikfreunde, in Wien.

Pearson Education LTD.
Pearson Education Singapore, Ptd. Ltd
Pearson Education, Canada, Ltd
Pearson Education—Japan

Pearson Education Australia PTY, Limited
Pearson Education North Asia Ltd
Pearson Educacion de Mexico, S.A. de C.V.
Pearson Education Malaysia, Pte. Ltd

10 9 8 7 6 5 4 3 2 1
Student Edition ISBN 0-13-150548-3
AIE   ISBN 0-13-150552-1

"Music is the expression of the deepest

part of our souls. It expresses what

words and paintings cannot. And for

true understanding, music requires

careful attention and the engagement

of the intellect . . ."

J. Y.

Jeremy Yudkin was born in England and educated in England and the United States. He received his B.A. and M.A. in Classical and Modern Languages from Cambridge University and his Ph.D. in Historical Musicology from Stanford University. He has taught at the Palo Alto Community Adult School, San Francisco State University, the Ecole Normale Supérieure in Paris, Harvard University and, since 1982, at Boston University's School for the Arts and the Tanglewood Music Center. A recipient of fellowships from the National Endowment for the Humanities, Boston University's Society of Fellows, the Camargo Foundation, and the Marion and Jasper Whiting Foundation, he has written articles for the *Journal of the American Musicological Society*, the *Journal of Musicology*, the *Musical Quarterly*, *Musica Disciplina*, and *Music and Letters*, and contributed to several volumes of essays. His research specialties include the Middle Ages, early Beethoven, and jazz studies. A noted lecturer, Professor Yudkin has given talks and presented papers across the United States and in Europe and Russia. He is the author of six books on various aspects of music and music history, including *Music in Medieval Europe* (Prentice Hall, 1989) and *Discover Music* (Prentice Hall, 2004).

Dr. Yudkin is also an accomplished clarinetist, photographer, gardener, and soccer player. He and his wife, who is a teacher of French, have two children.

CONTENTS

Nowadays there is more music in our lives than at any previous time in history. Music surrounds us as we buy food or clothes, drive our cars, sit in the park, or jog down the street. Much of this is our own choice: we have radios in our cars, portable cassette players on our belts. Some of it may be unwanted: our neighbor's stereo, for example, or a "boom box" on the beach. Some of it we actually do not notice. There is so much noise in our daily environment that the music playing in elevators or stores sometimes simply merges with the surroundings.

In addition to the sheer *quantity* of music around us, there is a wider range of music available than ever before. We can listen to jazz, reggae, Vivaldi, Beethoven, or country ballads. Twenty-first-century technology has presented us with an unparalleled wealth of musical possibilities. The very idea that a one–hundred-member symphony orchestra can be heard with crystal clarity and rich resonance in our own bedrooms would have startled most of the composers in this book.

The consequences of this situation are (like the consequences of most technological advances) both good and bad. It is a wonderful thing to be able to go to a record store and buy a recording of a piece of music composed hundreds of years ago or thousands of miles away. But the ubiquitous nature of music today has also had negative consequences on the role that music plays in our society. For most of our history, music was rare; it therefore had more importance in people's lives. The composition and performance of music required deliberation and effort. Whether it was the commissioning of a symphony by an aristocratic patron or the playing of a country dance by peasants, music was performed with care and listened to with attention—it was never without significance.

The result of all this is that we have lost the art of listening.

Music is the only one of the three great arts—literature, the visual arts, and music—which can be absorbed without attention, passively. Music can surround us while we concentrate on other things; it can even be there in the background, entirely unnoticed.

This is not true of painting. To appreciate a painting we have to give it some of our attention. We have to study the forms and colors, the balance and proportions of its overall design. We may admire its style and technique, its humor, vigor, or despair. A good painting shows us objects or people or *life* in a new light. A great painting affects us profoundly and leaves us changed. Few people have seen Picasso's *Guernica* and not been deeply moved.

Literature has the same demands and the same rewards. We must pay attention to a book or a play. They cannot merely fill the room while we vacuum or accompany us while we jog or shop. And the effort of attention is repaid. A good book resonates in our own lives; a great book changes us forever.

Music, too, is the expression of the deepest part of our souls. It expresses what words and paintings cannot. And for true understanding, music requires careful attention and the engagement of the intellect, just as painting and literature do.

But even careful listening is not enough. Music is the expression of people in society. And, like the other arts, music is formed in a historical and social context. In the eighteenth century, for example, European music was the reflection of a hierarchical and orderly society, influenced by the ideals of the Enlightenment. Much eighteenth-century music, therefore, is carefully ordered and balanced, organized in a framework of fixed and widely accepted formal patterns. How can we truly understand this music if we do not know the forms used by composers of the time? It would be like reading Hawthorne's *The Scarlet Letter* without understanding the attitude of seventeenth-century New England puritans towards adultery; or reading Shakespeare without knowing the meaning of blank verse.

Like literature, music has its rules of grammar and its rhetorical effects. Without understanding the grammar and rhetoric of music, we experience it as a sensation and little else. By learning about the social context and the structural language of music, we can experience it to its fullest. We can hear the passion of Beethoven, the brilliance of Bach, the wit and genius of Mozart. We can understand how a jazz musician can weave compelling improvisations, seemingly out of thin air. We can engage with music at its deepest level. And like a great painting or a great book, it will change us forever. It will fill our lives with beauty and joy. It will deepen our understanding of what it means to be human.

It is with this philosophy in mind that I have come to write *Understanding Music*. I believe today's college students taking music appreciation courses want to learn "how" to listen to music—how to *hear* music, if you will—as more than just a combination of sound and melody. To this end, I have written a book that will be sensitive to the needs of today's students, a book that will guide them carefully and methodically through the art of listening itself, as well as one that will teach them the power of music as a form of human communication, and in doing so will transform the student from a passive recipient to an active participant. Unique in its design, approach, and content, *Understanding Music*

offers students a global approach, an explanation of the richness and diversity of the European tradition, a focus on listening, a thoughtful selection of works for study, a discussion of patrons and audiences, careful consideration of the role of women in creating music, and an enlightening treatment of the history of popular music. Listening to music is one of the great pleasures of human existence. I believe strongly that it is our vital task to demonstrate to our students that with a little effort, knowledge, and concentration, that pleasure can be immeasurably enriched.

Special Features of Understanding Music

New! *Inside the Orchestra* Videotape and CD-ROM

Bring an orchestra to the classroom every day! In this three-part program, students encounter the instruments of the standard orchestra; learn how the parts of the orchestra fit together; and study an orchestra as it performs five representative works from the Baroque Era to the Twentieth Century. "Inside the Orchestra" boxed readings in the text trace the evolution of the orchestra and provide additional context for understanding the video material.

Available to teachers as a 60-minute videotape, and to students as a CD-ROM bound FREE into each copy of *Understanding Music*.

Focus on Listening

Understanding Music has a complete and independent chapter on the Art of Listening. This chapter stresses the importance of active listening as a vital commitment on the part of the students. It guides them moment-by-moment through five short works, each of which illuminates different musical elements, techniques, and

vocabulary for the listening experience. These activities lay a solid foundation for the students' listening work throughout the remainder of the book. The Fundamentals chapter and the Listening chapter are carefully coordinated to provide a supportive framework for the listening experience.

Timed Listening Guides

The Listening Guides are clear, easy to follow, and illuminating. Form and structure, texture, instrumentation, and musical motives are explained, and special moments, such as surprising gestures, unexpected key changes, or departures from conventional form are highlighted. Each Listening Guide is supplied with exact timings and CD track numbers to identify important structural points within each work.

End-of-Chapter Style Summaries

These sections focus on the essence of musical style for each historical period. The Style Summaries also contain boxes that list the musical elements central to each style.

CULTURAL AND SOCIAL CONTEXT

Music does not occur in a vacuum. Throughout the book, music is presented in the context of its social and historical milieu. In addition, each chapter contains a special box that discusses the changing role of patrons and audiences in the history of music.

SERIOUS CONSIDERATION OF MUSIC AS A WORLDWIDE PHENOMENON

The book opens with a short chapter entitled Music Around the World. The main focus of the book is on music of the European tradition, but this focus is both explained and put into context by a look at music as a global phenomenon.

PROPER CONSIDERATION OF POPULAR MUSIC

Popular music is treated not just as a token but as a cultural phenomenon in its own right. The history of popular music is surveyed from its beginning until the present, and due weight is given to musical, cultural, and commercial considerations.

FLEXIBILITY

This book lends itself to great flexibility. It has been used effectively in courses of one quarter, one semester, and two semesters. Sample syllabi for all these applications are given in the Instructor's Resource Manual.

SUPPLEMENTARY MATERIALS FOR INSTRUCTORS AND STUDENTS

RECORDING PACKAGES

The recordings that accompany the book come in two available packages: (1) A **Student Collection** of three CDs which contains most of the important works covered in the text. (2) A **Complete Collection** of seven CDs containing all the works analyzed in the text. All the CDs are tracked not just for the beginnings of works or movements, but also at internal points so that instructors and students can instantly find important moments within a piece.

EXPANDED REPERTOIRE CUSTOM COMPACT DISC

The *Understanding Music* recording program has been enhanced by the addition of a new CD that can be cus-

tomized to the preferences of the individual instructor. With dozens of works of recorded music from which to choose, instructors can tailor the *Understanding Music* listening experience to their unique specifications. When packaged with the text the CD is FREE. Certain limitations do apply. Contact your local Prentice Hall representative for more details.

ANNOTATED INSTRUCTOR'S EDITION (AIE)

The AIE provides a wealth of helpful teaching tips, suggestions for classroom exercises, parallel pieces, historical comments, etc., printed in the margins of the text. The annotations appear only in the Instructor's Edition of the book and are of tremendous help in shortening preparation time and enlivening classroom presentations.

LISTENING GUIDES GENERALLY CONTAIN THE FOLLOWING FEATURES:

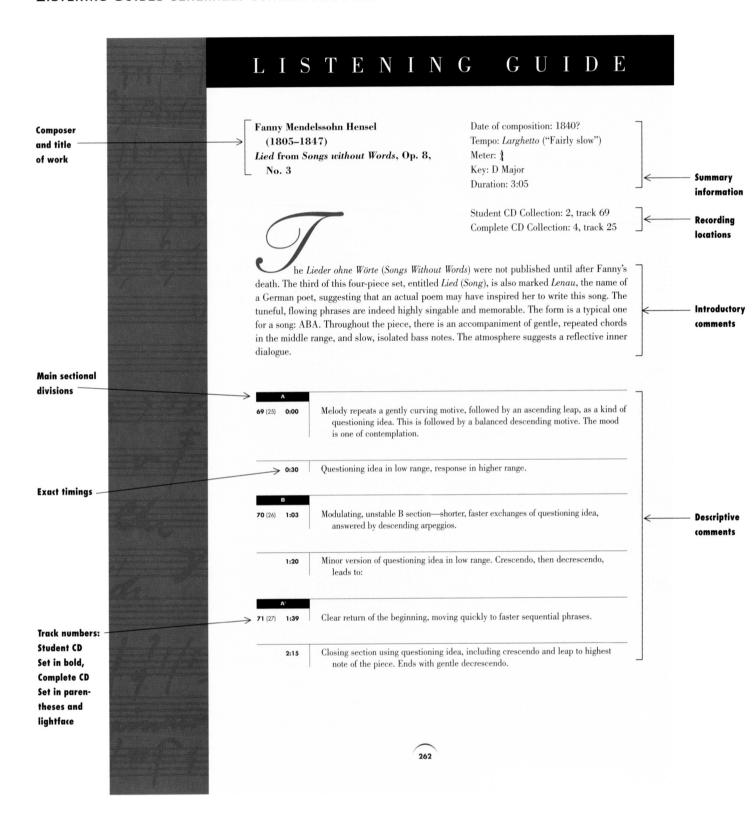

Composer and title of work

LISTENING GUIDE

Fanny Mendelssohn Hensel
(1805–1847)
Lied from *Songs without Words*, Op. 8,
No. 3

Date of composition: 1840?
Tempo: *Larghetto* ("Fairly slow")
Meter: ¾
Key: D Major
Duration: 3:05

Summary information

Student CD Collection: 2, track 69
Complete CD Collection: 4, track 25

Recording locations

*T*he *Lieder ohne Wörte* (*Songs Without Words*) were not published until after Fanny's death. The third of this four-piece set, entitled *Lied* (*Song*), is also marked *Lenau*, the name of a German poet, suggesting that an actual poem may have inspired her to write this song. The tuneful, flowing phrases are indeed highly singable and memorable. The form is a typical one for a song: ABA. Throughout the piece, there is an accompaniment of gentle, repeated chords in the middle range, and slow, isolated bass notes. The atmosphere suggests a reflective inner dialogue.

Introductory comments

Main sectional divisions

A		
69 (25)	**0:00**	Melody repeats a gently curving motive, followed by an ascending leap, as a kind of questioning idea. This is followed by a balanced descending motive. The mood is one of contemplation.
	0:30	Questioning idea in low range, response in higher range.

Exact timings

B		
70 (26)	**1:03**	Modulating, unstable B section—shorter, faster exchanges of questioning idea, answered by descending arpeggios.
	1:20	Minor version of questioning idea in low range. Crescendo, then decrescendo, leads to:

Descriptive comments

A'		
71 (27)	**1:39**	Clear return of the beginning, moving quickly to faster sequential phrases.
	2:15	Closing section using questioning idea, including crescendo and leap to highest note of the piece. Ends with gentle decrescendo.

Track numbers:
Student CD
Set in bold,
Complete CD
Set in paren-
theses and
lightface

262

MUSICNOTES: A NOTE-TAKING COMPANION NEW!

This handy companion reproduces Listening Guides from the text and provides ample room for note-taking. It is packaged FREE with all copies of *Understanding Music.*

FILMS FOR THE HUMANITIES HISTORICAL VIDEOTAPE

Produced by *Films for the Humanities* exclusively for *Understanding Music,* this sixty-minute video compendium presents a wealth of short film extracts for classroom use. Each film clip illustrates and illuminates a particular topic from the text. Margin notes found throughout the Annotated Instructor's Edition alert the instructor to the availability of each video item. A complete table of contents and descriptions of each item are provided with the tape. This Companion Videotape is available only to instructors who have adopted *Understanding Music* for their classes.

COMPANION WEBSITE™ (WWW.PRENHALL.COM/YUDKIN)

The *Understanding Music* Companion Website™ greatly enhances students' understanding. Through a variety of on-line multiple choice and essay questions, critical listening exercises, and links to pertinent websites around the world, students are able to reinforce their comprehension of key concepts from the book.

For the Fourth Edition, the website offers activities that test students' understanding of the concepts introduced in the *Inside the Orchestra* CD-ROM and videotape.

OTHER TEACHING AND LEARNING RESOURCES

To facilitate the teaching and learning processes, *Understanding Music* is accompanied by an **Instructor's Resource Manual,** filled with helpful items, including tests; and the **Computerized Testing Files,** available for Windows and Macintosh. *Understanding Music* is supported by three course management programs: BlackBoard™, WebCT™, and Prentice Hall's own CourseCompass™.

ACKNOWLEDGMENTS

I would like to thank my publisher, Bud Therien, who talked me into taking on this project in the first place, and who since that time has demonstrated a commitment to the subject and its importance far beyond professional necessity. He has been for decades a zealous promoter of the Arts at Prentice Hall, and the company is lucky to have him. The music editor is Christopher Johnson, and his keen intelligence, worldliness, and friendship have been invaluable to me. He is a superb colleague, and we have worked closely together on this and other projects for many years. His assistant is Evette Dickerson, who brings joy and authenticity to everything she touches. Joe Scordato is the hardworking, extraordinarily efficient, and responsive production editor. He and all the people mentioned above are both dedicated professionals and wonderful human beings.

A group of scholars and teachers provided invaluable guidance at the outset of the project. Their ideas formed the initial impetus to think clearly and consistently about the challenges that lay ahead. Since that time, many experts in the field have given of their time and knowledge to review all the elements of the book and its accompanying materials. They come from all across North America, and their comments, criticisms, and suggestions have been invaluable. They include Courtney Adams, Franklin and Marshall College; Hugh Albee, Palm Beach Community College; Marci Alegant, McGill University; James Anthony, Towson State University; Graeme Boone, Ohio State University; Gregory D. Carroll, University of North Carolina at Greensboro; Donald L. Collins, University of

Central Arkansas; Liane Curtis, Cambridge, Massachusetts; Barbara Harbach, Washington State University; John M. Heard, Louisiana Technical University; James Henry, Duke University; H. Wiley Hitchcock, Brooklyn College (Emeritus); Edward Hotaling, University of Central Florida; Douglas A. Lee, Vanderbilt University; Dale Monson, Brigham Yong University; Claire Nanis, University of Delaware; Charles Postlewate, The University of Texas at Arlington; Julia Ehlers Quick, South Carolina State University; Jane Reeder, Chattanooga State Technical Community College; Andrea Ridilla, Miami University; Thomas Riis, University of Colorado; Michael E. Scott, Shelby State Community College; Barry M. Shank, East Carolina University; Gary Sudano, Purdue University; Jewel T. Thompson, Hunter College-City of New York; Stephen Valdez, University of Oregon; Bertil H. van Boer, Western Washington University; Paul Verrette, University of New Hampshire; Michael Votta, Duke University; Rodney Waschka, North Carolina State University; and Steven Moore Whiting, University of Michigan, Ann Arbor.

Professor Liane Curtis helped with comments and timings for several Listening Guides. Professor Graeme M. Boone of Ohio State University read the chapter on jazz and offered helpful criticism. The Instructor's Resource Manual by Professor Jennifer Wolfe has been extremely carefully thought out and is most helpful. Professor Wolfe and Professor van Boer provided most of the resourceful annotations for the Annotated Instructor's Edition.

I have relied on many books by other scholars in the preparation of this text. They include Mark C. Gridley's *Jazz Styles: History and Analysis,* Charles Hamm's *Yesterdays: Popular Song in America,* William Malm's *Music Cultures of the Pacific, the Near East, and Asia,* Bruno Nettl's *Folk and Traditional Music of the Western Continents,* Bruno Nettl, et al.'s *Excursions in World Music,* Lewis Porter and Michael Ullman's *Jazz: From Its Origins to the Present,* Leonard G. Ratner's *Classic Music: Expression, Form, and Style,* Maynard Solomon's *Beethoven,* David P. Szatmary's *Rockin' in Time: A Social History of Rock-and-Roll,* and Piero Weiss and

Richard Taruskin's *Music in the Western World: A History in Documents.*

My thoughts on music and insights into musical works have benefited through the years from discussions with many friends and colleagues: Kofi Agawu, Rebecca Baltzer, Jonathan Berger, Tom Binkley, Evan Bonds, Patrick Botti, Larry Chud, Bill Crofut, John Daverio, Gene Drucker, Joe Dyer, Margot Fassler, Cathy Fuller, Jan Herlinger, H. Wiley Hitchcock, Bill Hopkins, George Houle, Andrew Hughes, David Hughes, Michel Huglo, Peter Jeffrey, James Johnson, Lewis Lockwood, Yo-Yo Ma, William Mahrt, Tim McGee, Holly Mockovak, Roger Norrington, Edward Nowacki, Leonard Ratner, Edward Roesner, Emilio Ros-Fabregas, Lee Rothfarb, Joel Sheveloff, Norman Smith, Arnold Steinhardt, Peter Swing, Judith Tick, Michael Tree, Roye Wates, Christoph Wolff, Craig Wright, Neal Zaslaw, and many others.

Several graduate students (some of whom are now professors in their own right) provided considerable assistance along the way. They include Jim Davis, Todd Scott, Simon Keefe, and John Howland. My assistant in the production of the second edition was Zbigniew Granat and, for the third, Lisa Scoggin. I am grateful to them both.

It would be impossible to mention here all those professors, instructors, students, reviewers, authors, performers and critics who have taken the time and trouble to comment on the first three editions of this book in the sincere desire to see it improved in the fourth. Those friends and colleagues from universities, four-year colleges, two-year colleges, and community colleges throughout North America whose contributions have substantially aided in the revision of this book include: Joseph Akins, Chattanooga State Technical Community College; Alexandra Amati-Camperi, University of San Francisco; Jack Ashworth, University of Louisville; Mark Evan Bonds, University of North Carolina; Pierre Bouchard, University of La Valle, Quebec; Donald L. Collins, University of Central Arkansas; David Green, Southeast Missouri State University; Douglas A. Lee, Vanderbilt University; Sterling E. Murray, West Chester University; James Parsons,

Southwest Missouri State University; Ron Penn, University of Kentucky; Heather Platt, Ball State University; June Reeder, Chattanooga State Technical Community College; Andrea Ridilla, Miami University; Patty Roy, Chattanooga State Technical Community College; Paul Schultz, University of Puget Sound; Elaine Sisman, Columbia University; Gary Sudano, Purdue University; Phillip Todd, University of Kentucky; Paul Verrette, University of New Hampshire at Durham; Paul Vogler, Chattanooga State Technical Community College. Reviewers for this Fourth Edition include: Robert Aubrey, University of Mississippi; Jean Bynum, Enterprise State Junior College; John Chiego, University of Memphis; James Douthit, Bloomsburg University; Suzann Rhodes Draayer, Winona State University; Sean Gallagher, Harvard University; A. C. "Buddy" Himes, University Louisiana; Jonathan Kulp, University of Louisiana; Dennis Ritz, Shippensburg University; Harris Saunders, University of Illinois at Chicago; William Shepherd, University of Northern Iowa; Ed Smaldone, Queens College; Richard Thorell, Indiana University; Thomas Trimborn, Truman State University; and Albin Zak, University of Michigan. I thank them all.

I would also like to thank all my students, both graduate and undergraduate, music majors and other majors, young and not so young, at Boston University, Harvard University, the Tanglewood Music Center, the Moscow and St. Petersburg Conservatories, and the École Normale Supérieure in Paris, who seemed to enjoy listening to my ideas and who offered many of their own.

J. Y.

*T*his book is as engaging as it is informative. I particularly like Jeremy Yudkin's lively presentation of an extraordinary amount of fascinating musical information within a broader historical and cultural context. Through this book Professor Yudkin conveys not only a wealth of knowledge, but also the message that music can be a uniquely rewarding medium of personal expression. It will surely encourage readers, students, and music lovers alike to become active participants in their musical experiences, whether as performers or listeners.

Yo-Yo Ma

Music Around the World

INTRODUCTION TO THE STUDY OF MUSIC

Much of this book focuses on the music of the European and American "high-art" tradition, because it is of such astounding richness, value, and complexity. We will also examine the fascinating history of jazz, rock, folk, and other types of popular music that grew up in the same cultural context. Music, however, is an art or an activity that appears in all cultures around the world. Each nation, each ethnic group, each tribe develops its own music and preserves its own musical traditions.

Our study of the rich and ancient store of mostly European music is made possible by the existence of written records that stretch back over a thousand years. But in most of the rest of the world, musical traditions are oral. Music is not written down, but transferred from one person to another, and from one generation to the next, simply by "word of mouth." One person learns the music by hearing someone else perform it; an older person teaches it to a younger person.

In most cases, in cultures around the world, it is very difficult to determine how old a musical tradition may be. Without written records, a culture's sense of history can stretch back no more than a few hundred years. There is also no way of knowing how the music of an oral tradition may have changed over the generations. Some cultures regard their musical heritage as sacrosanct and try to keep the music of the past more or less intact. Others regard music as part of the living present and continuously adapt the music of the past to conform to their current needs: This kind of music will be in a constant state of change.

It would be a mistake to assume that the music of an unfamiliar small tribe or society is "purer" or more "natural" than our own. The music of the European tradition also began as an orally transmitted art; it was kept alive for centuries by word of mouth.

Nor should we imagine that music of other cultures is nothing but an unadulterated representation of the soul of that people since time began. Representative it may be, because music reflects the society that performs it. But certainly not since time began. There is very little music in the world that has not undergone change and influence from outside forces. Native American music continues to bear traces of its people's origin across the Bering Strait in East Asia. Music in Africa has for centuries been affected by outside influences: from Indonesia, India, and Europe. In Brazil, one hears a mixture of music from West Africa and Portugal. In the Philippines, traditional dance is accompanied by music of Spanish origin. And in western Nigeria, the Yoruba people have mingled a native singing style with guitar music borrowed from Ghana. We may wish that the situation were simpler and more "authentic," but life, and the history of the world, are not like that. People adapt their music to their own

Decorated manuscript of written music from medieval Europe.

Elsner, Jacob. Ascension. At the bottom animals singing. Page from a Gradual ("Geese Book"), Nuremberg, 1507. M.905, Vol.I, f.186. The Pierpont Morgan Library, New York, N.Y., U.S.A. The Pierpont Morgan Library/Art Resource, NY

ideas of what they like, not to other people's views of what they "should" like.

The greatest influence today on music around the world is that exerted by Western classical and popular music. In Japan and China and India and Korea and Singapore, orchestras play symphonic music of the European tradition, and young Asian musicians are trained in the styles and techniques of Western classical music. In West Africa, *juju* music borrows influences from American country music, soul, reggae, and disco. In France, cafés and restaurants in the smallest villages are filled with the recorded sounds of English and American rock. In the Middle East, modern popular songs merge the sounds of Western pop with indigenous rhythms and singing styles.

One of the richest tapestries of musical culture is found in Israel, where the music of native-born Jews and Arabs mingles with that of Jews from Iraq, Latvia, Romania, Holland, Ethiopia, and the Yemen, as well as the music of Christian Arabs and Christians from Armenia and Russia.

In addition to this colorful tangle of music from all over the world, Israeli Arabs and Jews have created a modern Israeli music: dance songs or pop songs with a Western beat and harmonies sung in ornamented, intense, Middle Eastern style.

It has often been said that music is a universal language, that it transcends boundaries of nation and race.

Left: Arab street scene in Jerusalem.

Left: Two nuns in Jerusalem on Palm Sunday.

Far Left: An elderly Orthodox Jew in Jerusalem.

**Right: A Chinese girl
practicing the violin.**

**Far Right: A Cajun
practice session in
Louisiana.**

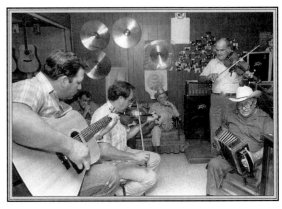

This is true, but only in a very specific sense. The fact that there *is* music seems to be universal: Every known human group has music.

But for each culture, music has a slightly different meaning. It takes different forms in different cultural groups. Even the definition of music differs from cul-ture to culture. Some cultures don't even have a word for music, for it is integral to their experience of the world, whereas others use many different words to distinguish among several types of music.

Music reflects the society that creates it, and each society creates the music that it wants. This sounds obvious, yet it is important, because it reminds us that in order to understand a culture's music, we need to understand the culture itself.

Perhaps, then, we could say that if music is not a universal language, it is universal, *like* language. Music, like language, is an accomplishment that distinguishes us as humans. Linguists tell us that there are more than 5,000 languages spoken in our world. It would not be surprising to discover that there are just as many types of music. And learning to understand the music of another culture is not very different from learning the language of another culture.

MUSIC AS A REFLECTION OF SOCIETY

Each culture, then, possesses its own musical language, which reflects its own traditions, concerns, and activities; and to begin to understand the music of another culture, we need to understand something of the nature of its cultural systems and the role that music plays in them. This is just as true of Western culture. To begin to understand music of the Middle Ages, or eighteenth-century opera, we will need to understand something of the cultural background of the West.

In other cultures, music plays very different roles. Among the Mandinka of Gambia and Senegal, for instance, there is a highly specialized type of professional musician known as the *jali*. The jali is both the historian of the tribe and the official singer of praises. The significance of this role will not become clear to us until we understand how Mandinka society operates.

Mandinka society is based upon a rigid class system. And class is determined by lineage. A person who has the right family background enjoys considerable social status and may choose among a variety of professional jobs. However, someone from a working-class family is required to take a job as an artisan, a carpenter, or a metalworker. Members of the working class are looked down upon by other members of the tribe.

Because family background is so important in determining people's lives, family history is entrusted to the jali, who specializes in historical knowledge. His job as historian and singer of praises, therefore, is of paramount importance. When hired to perform, he can evoke the noble ancestry of a patron, thereby enhancing that person's standing in society. Or, he can turn praise into insult and innuendo, thus damaging a person's social status. The jali is even called upon to de-

termine questions of inheritance, because he alone is familiar with the intricacies of genealogy.

This brief description, though by no means complete, allows us a deeper appreciation of Mandinka music. It explains the central role of solo singing in the society, the declamatory nature of the texts, the repetitive but highly flexible style of accompaniment (to accommodate the varying texts), and the formal nature of the performances. An analysis of the music would need to go into far more detail than this, but such an analysis could not even legitimately begin without a basic understanding of the social context in which the music is made. In turn, understanding the music can provide significant insights into the culture of which it is a part.

THE UNITED STATES: A TEST CASE

Now that this is clear, let's take a look at music in the United States today as a reflection of its culture. We'll describe the situation as though we were anthropologists looking at an unfamiliar tribe. This will help us focus on the kinds of questions we might ask about music in the rest of this book.

Let us start with classical music. In the United States, we note that classical music is treated as something of an elitist activity. Performances are very formal: Members of the audience sit listening very quietly until the end of each piece. Most of the music that is performed in classical-music concerts was composed in past centuries. The society treats the music of the past

Left: Opening night at the Metropolitan Opera House in New York City.

Far Left: A *jali* **from Gambia.**

Right: A roller skater listening to music.

Far Right: The audience at a rock concert.

with great reverence: there is a written musical tradition stretching back over a thousand years, though most of the music that is performed is between 100 and 250 years old. Concerts often feature the same pieces by many of the same composers, from one concert to another and from one year to the next.

In addition to classical music, people in the United States listen to many other types of music. There seems to be a distinction by class and age among these different types. Most young people listen to rock music, although some of them may also be interested in classical music. Classical music seems to be regarded as more of a "high-class," intellectual form of music than rock, which is far simpler and less formal. Young people listen to rock mostly in a convenient recorded format, either in their own rooms or as they walk about. Often they, too, listen to the same pieces over and over again. Many of the songs are about love or sex. Concerts of rock music are very informal: The audience may talk or sing or shout during the concert, but the music is often played so loudly that this doesn't matter. Some of the famous performers of rock music are financially re-

warded by the culture in a manner completely out of proportion to most other members of the society.

Our anthropological survey would also note that another type of informal music-making often occurs in cafés, bars, and nightclubs, as well as in concerts. This music is called jazz. Performers don't play from written music and often seem to make up what they play during a performance. Audiences for this type of music tend to be small. Many famous jazz performers are of African ancestry.

In classical and rock music (and increasingly in jazz), women are becoming more and more accepted by the society as music-makers. This was not always the case, and the society is changing rapidly in its view of women in music-making.

Many other types of music occur in the United States. Each ethnic group has a distinctive traditional music that helps to foster its separate identity. Religious groups are often distinguished by their music. Some large public events are marked by the singing of nationally known songs.

What does this "anthropological" description tell us about the society? It tells us that American culture is extremely diverse, divided as it is by age, class, ethnicity, and race. Divisions by gender role are gradually being erased. We learn that a very ancient musical tradition has been carefully preserved, and new music is constantly being produced. It is clear that the society is undergoing rapid change, because audiences for classical music are made up mostly of older people, whereas most young people embrace newer popular styles. As a result, rock music has become a highly competitive branch of the country's commerce. Change is also evident in the way each of the many different subgroups of the society—defined by race, ethnicity, age, social class, and the like—uses a very small segment of the total musical culture to reinforce its own separate identity. This seems to suggest a sense of anxiety within the society as a whole and a fragmentation of the society away from homogeneity toward a multiplicity of separate groups. There are, however, some national songs that help all the people feel unified, at least for brief moments.

Obviously there are many more things to say about music in the United States, but this brief glance in the

manner of an anthropologist teaches us two important things. The first is that the way music functions in a society is an important indicator of the way that society is formed and operates. The second is that whereas American society may regard music in a particular way, another society may see things very differently. Indeed, all the accepted notions in American society about music—the use of music primarily for entertainment, the naturalness of a schism between popular and classical music, the existence of a fixed repertory of ancient masterworks, and the use of music to divide groups as well as to reinforce the sense of membership within a group—all these notions are taken for granted by most Americans but are not necessarily found in the music of other cultures. Even such a deeply ingrained concept as the idea that music should be enjoyable to hear may not form a part of another culture's views. We must re-

alize that every culture views music in its own way—and that way may be very different from our own.

WORLD MUSIC: VIEW FROM A SATELLITE

For the purposes of our discussion, it is possible to divide the world into two large areas, each encompassing a dizzying array of different musical cultures, yet each containing certain unifying features. The first of these areas is made up of South, Central, and North America; Europe; and the entire portion of Africa that lies beneath the Sahara desert (often called sub-Saharan Africa). Music from this area has profoundly influenced the development of Western culture, and in turn, for the last several hundred years, Western culture has exercised a strong influence throughout these regions of the world.

The second area is made up of North Africa, the Middle East, the Far East, central and southern Asia, the Pacific Islands, New Zealand, and Australia. Broadly speaking, this area has been influenced by the religions and civilizations of Asia and the Middle East, though, as in the previous area, there exist a large number of identifiably indigenous musics.

Left: Singing of the national anthem at a baseball game.

Below: A scene from a Chinese opera.

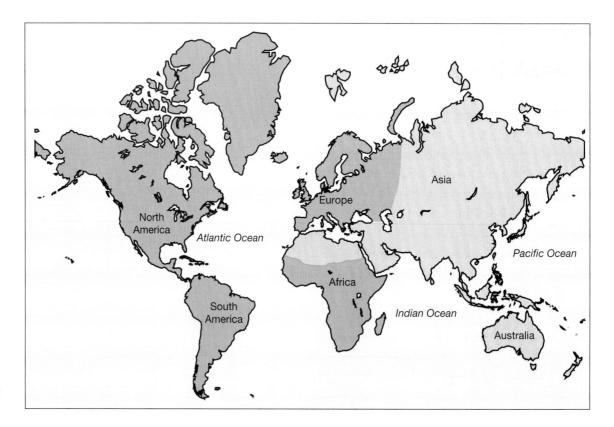

The two broad musical areas of the world.

These two large areas, although broadly different, have some things in common. Both contain cultures that have developed a sophisticated, "classical" repertory of music, played primarily by professional musicians. And both contain nonliterate cultures whose music is not written down or regulated by theory but is generally performed by most of the members of the society. Music of the second type is sometimes known as tribal music.

In both areas, there are also two types of music that lie somewhere between these two extremes. These we may call folk and popular music. Folk music exists in sophisticated societies alongside classical music and continues to be performed in rural areas away from the educated, usually urban, elite. It is often several generations old. Examples occur from China to Peru to Wales. In addition to folk music, most cultures that have developed a classical system of music also have a flourishing popular-music industry. This music tends to be ephemeral (a hit may last only a few weeks), commercial (designed to sell), and aimed at a broad, generally urban, audience. This is as true in India, for example, as it is in Finland or Argentina or any number of other countries.

WHAT TO LISTEN FOR IN MUSIC AROUND THE WORLD

Some of the general characteristics of world music have been discussed above, but let us summarize them here.

1. Much of the music around the world is part of an oral tradition. It is not written down but passed along the generations by memory.
2. All cultures use both voice and instruments.
3. Music is a reflection of a culture. To understand the music, we need to understand the role it plays in that culture.

There are some more detailed observations we can make about music that lies outside the European-American classical tradition, and we shall consider them now. These have to do with the nature of the music itself, its various melodic and rhythmic structures, and its textures, as well as the types of sound found among the different singing styles and instruments in use around the world. We shall also consider the context in which music appears in different cultures, the participation of women, and differing attitudes toward time and duration. But let us first look at attitudes toward music of the past. In the following pages, we shall take the music of the European-American tradition as a point of comparison, not to make value judgments but simply because for many of us it is the most familiar.

ATTITUDE TOWARD MUSIC OF THE PAST

We have already noted that in the United States, much of the music played in concerts dates from hundreds of years ago. Because most music in other cultures around the world is not written down, a different attitude exists with regard to music of the past. In some cultures, for example, there are a number of works from the past that serve as a basis for improvisation. In India and Japan, for instance, although there is a repertory of classical music that is fairly fixed, there are also some traditional pieces that serve as the framework for learned improvisations by highly trained master musicians. In other countries, music is regarded as a living, flexible artifact, constantly open to change. In these cultures, the music is constantly being reinvented, so that, in a sense, music of the past doesn't really exist: It is constantly turning into music of the present.

TEXTURE

The texture of most music around the world is very different from that of European classical music. Starting in the twelfth century, European music became more and more focused on polyphony—music that contains two or more composed lines. As a result, of course, harmony—the chords formed by these lines—also became a central concern. The works composed in Europe and the United States over the last several hundred years are highly organized, very sophisticated complexes of sound, often involving large numbers of people playing different musical lines on different instruments, all of which blend into a dense, unified, polyphonic whole, whose direction is guided by harmony.

Music of other cultures has focused on different aspects of musical style, and as a result the texture is very different. With significant exceptions, particularly in Africa, most other music has only one tune, or melody, sounding at a time, often with a rhythmic accompaniment of considerable interest. The essence of this music is therefore very different, and our way of listening to it must therefore be consciously modified. In some cultures, several different performers play the same melody, but each in his own way. The result is simultaneous, slightly varying, interweaving strands of a single tune.

MELODY

Although a great deal of European-American classical music contains beautiful melodies, we could not say that melody is the central focus of the music or that

Left: A violinist and singer in India.

the music explores melody to the fullest. During the Middle Ages, European music was primarily text and melody, and European and American folk song still concentrates upon melodic interest. However, for most of the music of the cultivated Western tradition, melody has become a secondary concern.

In many musical styles around the world, melody is of paramount interest. The prevailing musical texture, with its focus on a single line, helps in this regard. The *essence* of the music is in the melody. In Iran, a trained singer will improvise on a melodic pattern, exploring all possible aspects of the pattern in high notes and low notes, varying the quality of her voice, and using a wide range of ornamental flourishes. An Indian player of the *sitar*, a long-necked, resonant lute, weaves sinuous melodic lines above and around a constant fixed drone. A Japanese master of *shakuhachi*, an end-blown bamboo flute played solo, bends pitches, plays notes "between the notes," and generally explores every melodic possibility available to him.

RHYTHM

Many musical styles are highly complex in rhythm. Rhythmically, it has to be said, Western music—classical and popular alike—is rather dull. Most pieces use the same beat or meter throughout. It was only in the second half of the twentieth century, and often under the influence of music from other cultures, that European and American composers regularly began to explore more intricate approaches to rhythm in their music.

By contrast, many musical styles around the world are extremely intricate in their rhythm. African drummers frequently produce several complex rhythms si-

multaneously. In Mexico, Venezuela, and Argentina, three-beat and two-beat meters alternate in catchy irregular patterns. In India, rhythm is raised to the level of a special art, and rhythmic patterns are established in Indian music theory. There are hundreds of these patterns, and an Indian drummer has to study for years to learn them all.

TONE COLOR: VOICES AND INSTRUMENTS

European-American classical music encompasses a wide range of instrumental and vocal sounds. A symphony orchestra boasts dozens of different instruments, and

An Indian master of the tabla or drums.

Excerpt from a majara, a type of North Indian drumming pattern that often occurs at the close of a phrase or entire work. The syllables below the notes refer to specific drumstrokes.

na ga dhet ta ka ra dha ti ra ki ta dha ti ra ki ta ta ka ta ti ra ki ta ta ka

ti ra ki ta ta ka dha tit dha ta ka ta dha tit dha ta ka ta dha tit dha

these can play singly or in large numbers of different combinations. Music of other cultures, however, often displays tone colors, vocal and instrumental, that are very different from anything heard in a symphony orchestra.

In many cultures, the ideal vocal sound is not smooth, flowing, and relaxed, as it is in the cultivated European tradition. Singers often use a very tense, strained technique. This is true of many Native American tribes. Or they may be able to produce two tones at once (in Tibet, Mongolia, Siberia), or sing in an extremely florid manner, with incredibly fast, clean runs and trills and ornaments (in Morocco, Saudi Arabia, Pakistan). The singers of some areas practice a yodeling technique, in which the voice moves rapidly between a regular singing voice and a high, artificial voice. This technique is practiced by the Swiss, the Pygmies of central Africa, and the Berbers of the Sahara. Even voice ranges can defeat expectations. Brazilian cowboys sing in harmony at the very top of their range, whereas female folk singers in Turkey sing in a low, throaty voice.

Instruments around the world produce a very wide variety of tone colors. The type of instruments a culture develops often depends on the raw materials available. In Africa, instruments are made of wood, animal skins, and animal horns, sometimes even of ivory. In China, Laos, Cambodia, Vietnam, and Indonesia, where metal has been a part of the culture for thousands of years, bronze instruments, such as gongs and chimes, are favored.

Some instruments, like the violin, have been adapted to local use under the influence of European culture. The violin, with various modifications, is a central part of the traditional music of India, Iran, and the Apache and Navajo tribes of the southwestern United States.

Musical instruments around the world can be classified into four groups: stringed instruments, including those that are plucked and those that are bowed; wind instruments, which are blown; and two types of percussion instruments, those whose sound is produced by hitting some material stretched over a hollow object (drums) and those whose sound is made by hitting, shaking, or waving a solid object (gongs, chimes, rattles,

scrapers, etc.). Each of these categories includes an enormous variety of instruments. Stringed instruments can be long or short, have one or many strings, and range in sound from very loud to exceedingly soft and delicate. Wind instruments range from the gigantic alphorn, designed to be heard over mountain ranges, to the dovelike tones of the small clay ocarina. Percussion instruments represent the largest number of instruments around the world. They can often be pitched— that is, they can produce a definite note rather than just a bonk or a clunk. Drums can occur in pitched or unpitched varieties, and xylophones, chimes, bells, and gongs can all produce specific pitches. Finally, we should say that in many cultures, percussion is produced

An ivory trumpet from Nigeria.

Apache violin or fiddle.

Four alphorn players in Switzerland.

Tiny clay ocarina.

without instruments. Rhythmic sounds and complex rhythmic patterns are made by clapping hands, slapping thighs, and stamping feet.

Some of the sounds produced by instruments of different cultures are very different indeed, even if the instrument is a familiar one. In South India, a violinist plays on an instrument that is indistinguishable from those used in a symphony orchestra, but the sound he or she produces is totally unlike that of symphonic music. The player sits cross-legged on the floor, and the violin is supported between the chest and the ankle. This allows the fingers of the left hand complete freedom to slide up and down the strings. Pitches are not clean and distinct but flexible, loose, and joined by slides. The *hardingfele*, or Norwegian fiddle, is a violin that has been adapted to folk culture. It has extra strings that are not bowed but vibrate when the fiddle is played. The sound is highly resonant and penetrating.

Many instruments are completely independent of any Western equivalent, and their tone color is very distinctive. An instrument in widespread use in Africa is the *mbira* (pronounced "mmm-beera"), often translated as "thumb piano." The mbira has thin metal strips fastened to a small wooden box or gourd and is held in both hands while the thumbs pluck the strips. The sound is soft, buzzy, watery, plunky. The buzz is often enhanced by means of metal bottle-tops loosely at-

Above: Dancers in Zaire.

Left: South Indian violinist.

tached to the wood. In Eastern Europe, a short woodwind instrument known as a *shawm* is played in public places such as the marketplace or the town square. It is extremely loud and piercing and can be heard at a considerable distance.

The most dramatic illustration of the importance of tone color in instrumental playing is given by the *didjeridoo* of the Australian aboriginal people. This is a long, wet, hollowed-out eucalyptus branch, played like a trumpet. The didjeridoo can produce only two pitches, but the subtlety of the instrument lies in its tonal qualities. A skilled player can produce upwards of nine or ten different tone colors on his instrument. For these so-called primitive people, quality of musical sound outweighs quantity.

MUSICAL CONTEXT

In many regions of the world, music is part of a ceremony or a group activity. Studying the music without considering its context can provide half the picture, if that. The most frequent appearance of music around the world is in combination with dance. Think, for example, of the ubiquity of the samba and the tango both as dance and as musical genres in the Caribbean and South America. And in some African cultures, music is regarded primarily as an accompaniment to dance. But there are many other contexts in which music plays a role. In

Right: Xylophone.

Musser, a Division of The Selmer Co.

Africa, rhythmic group songs are also widely used to fa- cilitate work. In Japan, music is used as a central part of traditional theater, as vital expression at ritual Shinto cer- emonies, and to demonstrate a refined upbringing on the part of Japanese girls. Native American tribes use music to accompany gambling games, contact guardian spirits, conduct the medicine-bundle ceremony, cure ill- nesses, and distinguish among age and sex groups.

ATTITUDES TOWARD
THE PARTICIPATION OF WOMEN

The place of women is closely defined, and often se- verely restricted, in most cultures around the globe. In particular, the role of women in music-making is often carefully delineated. In a great many communities, women do not take part in musical activities, these be- ing reserved for men. In Japanese Kabuki theater and Chinese traditional opera, for example, female roles are sung by men.

In other communities, women participate as singers or dancers, but instruments are seen as inappropriate for them. (This is not very different from jazz in North America: there have been many female jazz singers, but almost all the instrumentalists have been men.) South Indian classical dances are danced by women, though only men play in the accompanying instrumental group. In Islamic countries, where most music is regarded with suspicion, and women's roles are strictly defined, women traditionally sing only wedding songs. In Korea, how- ever, both women and men sing the *japka* narrative songs, and among the Pwo Karen people of northern Thailand, both women and men sing the funeral songs.

A unique form of matriarchy is practiced by the Tuaregs of the Sahara. The men wear veils, and only the women know how to read and write. Women are the instrumentalists in this culture and do most of the singing. Men, however, are permitted to sing love songs at special communal gatherings.

TIME

One final facet of music that differs greatly among cultures is time. In twentieth-century European and

13

The Tuaregs of the Sahara.

American society, the length of a musical performance is highly conventionalized. A classical music concert is designed to take almost exactly two hours, including a 15- or 20-minute intermission. The concert starts at 8 P.M., so that members of the audience can have a meal beforehand, and it ends at 10 P.M., so that people do not get to bed too late. Rock concerts can run longer, but more or less the same limits apply.

Even in Western society, these conventions change from one era to the next. In the late eighteenth and early nineteenth centuries, for example, concerts could last much longer. When Beethoven presented his Fifth and Sixth Symphonies in 1808, they were on the same program with his Fourth Piano Concerto, his Mass in C, a solo vocal piece, and a work for piano, chorus, and orchestra. The concert lasted more than four hours.

But in other cultures, ideas about the length of a musical event can be very different. The Peyote ceremony of many Native American tribes consists of an entire night of singing. The religious Hako ceremony of the Pawnee lasts for several days. And the Navajo curing ceremony continues over a period of nine days and nights and includes hundreds of different songs. Even this does not exhaust the possible durations of musical ceremonies among certain peoples. The Pygmies, for example, who enjoy a deep and spiritual relationship with the forest in which they live, have developed a ceremony in which they sing to the forest every night over a period of several months.

In almost every facet of its existence, then, music is regarded in different ways among the various peoples of the world: in the melody, rhythm, tone color, and texture of the music itself; in the context in which music is performed; and in attitudes toward music of the past, the participation of women, and the duration of a musical event. As we have seen, even the definition of what music is can differ from one culture to the next. As human beings, we vary widely in our understanding of the meaning of music and the role it plays in our lives. Yet music is one of the great human accomplishments that we all share.

LISTENING TO MUSIC FROM AROUND THE WORLD

By now, you have some basis for listening to some examples of music from around the world. These will be chosen primarily to illustrate the enormous variety of kinds of music and attitudes toward music that exist on our planet. In all cases, we shall consider cultural context as well as musical content. The first two examples come from the Eastern half of our world, the third from the Western half. We shall listen first to solo music for the Japanese shakuhachi, then to the sounds of the Indonesian *gamelan* orchestra, and finally to mbira music from Africa.

JAPANESE SHAKUHACHI MUSIC

Ancient Japanese music dates back at least to the early Middle Ages and continues to the sixteenth century. In this feudal period, rival warlords established their own courts and fought for power, and the indigenous

Left: Scene from Japanese Noh theater.

Top Right: Performance of Japanese *Bunraku* theater.

Bottom Right: Male actor in a Japanese *Kabuki* performance. Two *shamisen* players are visible behind.

Shinto religion was joined by Buddhism, imported (together with the system of writing) from China. The music includes religious chant for the Buddhist liturgy, choral singing for observances of the Shinto religion, medieval courtly orchestral music known as *gagaku* ("elegant music"), and music for the Noh theater, which combines singing, dancing, and instrumental playing. The Noh theater, in particular, is a genre derived from the medieval *samurai* period. It is highly stylized, elegant, and formal. It reflects the samurai's philosophy of simplicity, submission to Buddha, and personal enlightenment.

In addition to this ancient repertoire, there is a body of "classical" music from Japan's Edo period, which lasted from 1615 to 1868. It is called "Edo" because the ruling clan at that time moved the capital of the country to Edo (modern-day Tokyo). This was a period of relative peace and prosperity after the military strife of the samurai era, and a prosperous middle class developed in the cities. The colorful music of this period is a reflection of this new audience.

Music from the Edo period is both theatrical and instrumental, and of Japan's classical music it is Edo music that is mostly heard today. Two types of theatrical music developed: music for the Bunraku puppet theater and music for Kabuki theater. *Bunraku* is akin to Western opera, except that there is only one (very versatile) performer. Kabuki theater is played by an all-male cast, includes dancing as well as lively traditional drama, and is accompanied by three different instrumental ensembles.

The purely instrumental music of the Edo period includes both small-group music and solo music. The traditional small ensemble is made up of a singer and three instruments: a *shamisen*, which is a three-stringed, long-necked lute; a *koto*, which is a delicate, 13-stringed plucked zither; and the shakuhachi

Listening Sketch for Shakuhachi Music
Koku-Reibo (**A Bell Ringing in the**
   Empty Sky)

Duration: 4:27

Student CD Collection: 1, track 1
Complete CD Collection: 1, track 1

*T*he shakuhachi is a bamboo flute with five finger holes and is blown from one end. Its name means "one and eight-tenths," because in Japanese measurement the shakuhachi has the length of one and eight-tenths *shaku* (a shaku is roughly a foot).

Music for the shakuhachi has a profound, mystical quality. The instrument was used as part of religious ceremony by Zen Buddhist monks in the seventeenth century, and it has been said that a single note of the shakuhachi can bring one to the state of nirvana (perfect blessedness).

The piece that we shall hear is one of the oldest in the repertory, dating back to the seventeenth century. It is called *Koku-Reibo* (*A Bell Ringing in the Empty Sky*). The title refers to the death of Zen monk Fuke-Zenji, who used to walk around ringing a small hand-bell. On his death, the sound of his bell could be heard getting fainter and fainter as it ascended into the clear blue sky. This and other ancient shakuhachi compositions are regarded as sacred and to be played only by great masters.

Playing the shakuhachi takes great skill, requiring an enormous amount of control and subtlety of expression. The musician performing here, Nyogetsu Seldin, has studied the traditional art of the shakuhachi for thirty years. He studied with Kurahashi Yodo Sensei in Kyoto and is now a Grand Master of the instrument.

The music is riveting. It demands all of your attention, because it depends on such minute details. There are only a few notes, but the variety of sounds is amazing. The player uses slides between notes, shadings of color and sound, variations of intensity, and carefully controlled gradations of volume to produce an atmosphere that is truly mystical. Our excerpt ends after only a few minutes, but the entire composition lasts more than 15 minutes. Listen to the excerpt very carefully, and listen to it several times. Each time you will hear something new. The music will capture your imagination in an entirely new way.

bamboo flute. But there also exist repertories of exquisite solo music for koto or shakuhachi alone. These repertories have been passed down the generations by means of oral tradition. Many, many years of dedicated learning, careful listening, and self-discipline are required to become a master of the koto or the shakuhachi. (**See Listening Guide above.**)

Japanese folk music is made up mostly of songs, sung unaccompanied in a high, tense voice, but there are also folk dances. The folk music of Japan reflects the culture's strong, early influences from China.

Popular music in Japan is highly varied, ranging from folk-inspired melodies to Western pop and rock styles. Indeed, much popular music played now in

Japan is imported from the United States and England, reflecting the current Japanese fascination with the West. Many young musicians today are also trained in Western classical music, and Japanese composers write symphonic music that is a blend of the Western symphonic idiom and traditional Japanese elements.

Let us summarize the ways in which Japanese music has responded to the changing nature of its society over time.

1. *The feudal period:* Music from this period includes both Buddhist chant and Shinto songs and prayers, together with courtly instrumental music and Noh theater.

2. *The Edo period:* Music becomes more urban and middle-class, involving entertaining stage works as well as instrumental compositions for master musicians.

3. *The modern period:* Music becomes more focused on popular song and begins to show Western popular and classical influences.

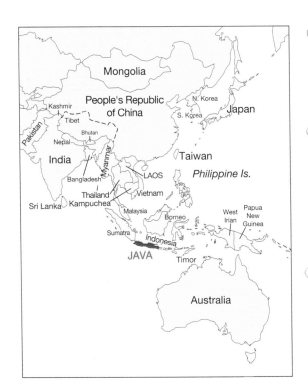

GAMELAN MUSIC FROM THE INDONESIAN ISLAND OF JAVA

In Indonesia, traditional music is played on a group of instruments made up primarily of metal percussion. This small orchestra is known as a **gamelan** (an Indonesian word meaning "musical ensemble"). A gamelan includes a wide variety of instruments. Among them are metal xylophones of three pitches: high, medium, and low. There are also two sizes of bronze bowls, which rest on cords in a wooden frame; bowls of different shapes produce different tone qualities. Gamelans also include a series of gongs (*gong* is another Indonesian word), one approximately three feet in diameter, with a very powerful sound, and several sizes of smaller ones. There are also skin drums, wooden percussion instruments, and sometimes flutes, a bowed two-string fiddle, and a plucked string instrument. The sound of the gamelan is unique, with its highly varied metallic sounds, its wide range from the deep gong to the highest xylophone, and its complex of interlocking parts. **(See Listening Guide on page 18.)**

When you see a gamelan in performance, you will notice something very ceremonial about it. The players sit cross-legged on the floor, as do players in much Eastern music. The instruments, with their elaborately carved and painted cases, are spaced about the floor in a carefully organized manner. And the performers treat their instruments with great respect. Gamelan orchestras are often owned by wealthy patrons, and some of the ensembles have names (such as "Dark Cloud" or "Thunder of Honey").

The gamelan in Indonesia is regarded with reverence. This derives partly from its association with ancient religious ritual, partly from its representation of royalty. Shoes must not be worn when playing the gamelan, and it is considered disrespectful to step over an instrument. Some ancient gamelans are regarded as possessing special spirituality and are presented with ritual offerings of food, flowers, and incense.

Religious and secular power is invested in gamelan

> Javanese gamelan is comparable to only two things: moonlight and flowing water. It is pure and mysterious like moonlight; it is always the same and always changing like flowing water. It is not a song. It is a state of being. — author Leonhard Huizinga

Map showing the Indonesian island of Java.

**Listening Sketch for
Javanese Gamelan Music**
Gangsaran - Bima Kurda - Gangsaran

Duration: 6:21

Student CD Collection: 1, track 2
Complete CD Collection: 1, track 2

G amelan music usually has picturesque or philosophical titles. In Javanese, *Gangsaran* means "achieving one's purpose," and *Bima Kurda* means "angry hero."

This composition mostly features metallic instruments—xylophones, bronze bowls, and gongs—but you will also hear at least two sizes of drum: a large bass drum and a medium-sized drum. Soon after the beginning, the music slows down for the main central section; it speeds up again toward the end. While the music is being played, a stylized dance is performed by two men: a drillmaster and a soldier. They utter occasional shouts and laughter, and twice they speak a ritual dialogue. The dialogue is as follows:

Drillmaster:	*Orang dua-dua!*	Hey you!
Soldier:	*Yaaah!*	Yes sir!
Drillmaster:	*Apa kita berani temen?*	Are you really brave?
Soldier:	*Yaaah, berani temen!*	Yes sir, I am!
Drillmaster:	*Haah, serobah!*	Then carry on!
Soldier:	*Inggih djadhaaaak, sendika!*	Yes, teacher, I obey! (laughs)

Here is an outline to follow as you listen to the music.

GANGSARAN			
Track 2 (2)	0:00	Regular rhythms, same note repeated.
	0:26	Music slows down.
BIMA KURDA			
3 (3)	0:40	Melody gathers interest, more notes are heard.
	0:55	Rhythm and melody become steady. Long section.
	2:35	Beginning of dialogue.
	2:57	Quiet section. Occasional shouts and laughter.
	4:20	Louder.
	4:36	Music gets faster again.
	5:18	Repeat of dialogue.
GANGSARAN			
4 (4)	5:32	Return of music from the opening section.
	6:15	Abrupt ending.

An Indonesian *gamelan*.

compositions too, which celebrate the spirituality and the political strength of princes. The pieces must be played with the appropriate reverent attitude, and the music should not be reproduced casually.

Gamelan music requires the cooperation of a large number of people, all of whom submerge their own personalities into the power of a unified whole. In this, perhaps more than in any other aspect, the Indonesian gamelan displays its link to a courtly, as well as to a spiritual, past.

AFRICAN DRUMMING AND MBIRA MUSIC

People in the United States and Europe tend to think of Africa as a single entity. This is, of course, an over-

simplification. The continent contains several hundred distinct ethnic groups, whose peoples are scattered widely across the national boundaries that were mostly established in colonial days.

The African diversity of social organization, language, ethnicity, race, and religion is mirrored in a great diversity of musical practices. Yet it is possible to make some generalizations that hold true.

First, there is a broad cultural division between North Africa and sub-Saharan Africa, which is mirrored in their musics. Music in North Africa (primarily Morocco, Algeria, Tunisia, Libya, and Egypt) is very similar in style to that of the Middle East, whereas music in the rest of the continent is more like what we think of as "African" music.

Second, it is possible to discover certain general characteristics within the music of sub-Saharan Africa, despite its enormous size and diversity. These include elements of context, style, aesthetics, and practice.

Let us try to summarize the elements that seem to bind together the peoples of sub-Saharan Africa, from the northwestern savanna region to the central rain forest to the cattle country of the Southeast.

1. Music is strongly associated with dance.
2. Instruments are numerous and widespread.
3. Sounds of percussion are heavily favored; these include drums as well as other percussion instruments.
4. Polyphonic (multiple) sounds predominate. These may involve several rhythms produced simultaneously or two or more melodies interwoven.
5. Melodies are made up of repetition, variation, and improvisation on short melodic fragments.

The two most widespread instruments in sub-Saharan Africa are the drum and the mbira. Drums come in many different sizes and forms. They include tall, single-headed drums, closed at the lower end; large, open-ended drums; small drums in an hourglass shape; two-headed drums with even-sized heads or with one small and one large head; and even a two-headed

African drum ceremony.

drum whose pitches can be changed by tightening or loosening the tension on the heads while the drum is being played.

African drumming is often extremely complex. A single drummer can produce an array of rhythms, as well as different notes and tone colors. Drumming ensembles are common: Several players of different-sized drums produce a dense, interlocking texture of multiple, simultaneous rhythms and notes.

Mbira music is no less complex. **(See Listening Guide on page 21.)** As mentioned previously, an mbira is an instrument made of a small wooden box or gourd with a row of thin metal strips attached to it. The strips are plucked by the thumbs of both hands. The mbira also comes in many different types, depending on the material of the resonating body, the size and number of the strips, and the objects (beads, shells, bottle tops) that are sometimes attached to the instrument to enrich the sound. The mbira is regarded as sacred by certain tribes. The Shona of Zimbabwe, for example, use it to summon the spirits of their ancestors.

Mbira music, like drum music, illustrates a very African view of music, which itself derives from a special sense of time. Mbira music and drum music are not frozen into "pieces" that can be reproduced more or less identically on

Map of present-day Africa.

Listening Sketch for Mbira Music
Mandarendare **(A Place Full of Energy)**

Duration: 5:32

Student CD Collection: 1, track 5
Complete CD Collection: 1, track 5

For the Shona, a people who make up most of the population of Zimbabwe and extend also into Mozambique, mbira music is mystical music that is used to communicate with the spirits of ancestors and guardians of the tribe. *Mandarendare* ("A place full of energy") is usually played at a dawn ceremony. The performer on this recording, Forward Kwenda, has been involved in keeping alive the musical traditions of the Shona people since he was a young boy. He says, "When I pick up my mbira, I don't know what is going to happen. The music goes by itself. It is so much greater than a human being can understand."

Although it sounds as though more than one person were playing on this piece, there is only one performer. Three distinct layers of sound can be detected: a deep, regular pattern in the bass and two interlocking lines above it. Although there seems at first to be constant repetition, careful listening will reveal slow, but constant, change. The tone quality is unusual; the notes are surrounded with a hiss or buzz that sounds to our ears like a sonic distortion. This hiss, which adds depth and complexity to the sound, is considered an essential element in mbira playing.

any given occasion. Each performance involves a lengthy combination of repetition and very gradual variation, so that the music may be seen as a *process* rather than as a piece. (Twentieth-century composers in the West have been heavily influenced by this African aesthetic.)

Mbira instrumentalists play a short melodic pattern over and over again. As time passes, they gradually weave slight changes into and around the melodic pattern, creating a variation. Each slightly different variation is also played over and over again before a new change is introduced. Change thus takes place over a long period of time.

This special conception of time may derive from the closeness to nature with which Africans have lived for so long. The world of the plains, the forests, and the jungle unfolds at its own pace, which is so different from the frenetic pace of modern urban life. Perhaps

The Zimbabwean musician Forward Kwenda with his mbira.

the music of African peoples is a reflection of this slow unfolding.

Like drum music, mbira music displays the African fascination with complex, multiple sounds. Because of the resonance of the instrument, each note played continues to sound for a while during the next few notes. Also, the attachment to the body of the instrument of beads or bottle tops, which vibrate or buzz slightly when the instrument is played, gives each note a rich, slightly hazy quality, like the moon on a misty night. An mbira melody, even on one instrument, is made up of the interlocking of two parts, one played by the right thumb, the other by the left. Often, however, mbiras are played in pairs or in groups, producing an even more complex web of sound. Finally, in some ceremonies, mbiras are accompanied by gourd rattles, handclaps, and the sounds of several people singing.

Conclusion

In this chapter, we have taken only a glance at several different cultures around the world, and we have seen how very different the music is in each of them. And yet from our glances we can make a few general observations. The first is that music is a reflection of the so-ciety that creates it. In order to understand the music, we need to understand something about that society. The second thing we have learned is that understanding the music can help us to understand the culture that produced it. The culture *forms* the music, and the music *represents* the culture.

Looking at the Japanese, Indonesian, and African cultures as briefly as we have, we begin to see how daunting a task it is to get a full picture of the meaning and significance of music in a particular cultural context. To understand even one type of music, in one corner of the world, requires a wide range of knowledge: historical and cultural background, specific listening skills, and a method for putting musical observations into words. Each type of music could fill a book on its own.

For most of *this* book, we will be examining music of the Western tradition, which has such a rich and lengthy written history that a thousand years of it can be explored in great detail. To do this, we will need a working vocabulary for talking about this music. We will need to examine just what skills are necessary for hearing a piece of music both as a whole and as a combination of elements. And we will need to work on a greater understanding of the culture surrounding the different historical periods of Western music.

FUNDAMENTALS

What exactly is music?

This sounds like an easy question. We all know music when we hear it. And yet on reflection, perhaps it's not so easy. People often ask a similar question about art. Is a Campbell's soup can art? How about a toilet seat? Both of these items have been displayed in art museums.

There is a difference between music and sound. Few of us would consider the unpleasant sounds of a bulldozer, a motorcycle, or a blaring car horn to be music. But we cannot simply say that unpleasant sounds are noise and pleasant sounds are music. Many of us enjoy listening to the pleasant sounds of nature, such as rain falling, the whistling of the wind, or the singing of birds, yet we would not call these sounds music. Even so, composers for hundreds of years have imitated the sounds of rain, wind, and birdsong in their works. Obviously, there is a *relationship* between sound and music.

It seems that we need to sense an element of human organization before we can call something music. The sound of a bird singing is one of the most beautiful sounds in nature, though we don't call it music. But when Beethoven writes notes in his Sixth Symphony that deliberately imitate the singing of a nightingale and a cuckoo, the sounds *become* music. In general, it is the deliberate organization of sounds by one person for other people to hear that creates music.

Composers rely upon certain elements and organizing principles in order to express their ideas in music. Indeed, each art has its own elements and organizing principles. In painting, there are important techniques of color mixture, theories of shape and balance, and methods of creating illusion (such as perspective) that have to be learned. In writing, we learn about vocabulary, grammar, syntax, and rhetoric. In music, the basics are more complicated, or maybe just less familiar, than in the other arts. But here they will be explained as clearly and straightforwardly as possible.

In order to discover what the fundamentals of music are, we'll learn first about some basic **elements**: sound and texture, pitch, interval, melody, harmony, scales, keys, chords, rhythm, and dynamics. We'll examine some of the **forms** that are used by composers to create musical structures such as songs and symphonies. We'll take a look at the **voice types** and the **instruments** that are featured most prominently in music. We'll briefly discuss **rehearsals** and **performances** of different types of music. And finally we'll consider **historical periods** and **individual style** in music.

THE ELEMENTS OF MUSIC

SOUND AND TEXTURE

The first thing that strikes you when you first hear a piece of music is the **sound**. Who or what is making the music? Is it a rock band with electric guitars and drums? A church choir with 50 voices? A fully blended symphony orchestra? Or a barbershop quartet with four men singing in close harmony? The kind of sound you hear will greatly influence the way you experience the music. Listen, for example, to the wonderfully stirring sound of this brass fanfare (MusicNote 1).

Another thing that affects your experience of the music is its **texture**. Texture is a word that describes the way in which different musical sounds are combined. One kind of texture, for example, is known as **monophony**. Monophony is a texture that involves melody with *no* accompaniment. This can be produced by one or more

MUSICNOTE 1

CD 1, track 6

Fanfare

(13 seconds)

people. A single person or a group of people all singing the same tune with no harmony or accompaniment (like a family in the car or the crowd at a baseball game) produces monophony. Monophonic texture means solo or unison singing or playing, as in Gregorian chant (MusicNote 2).

Homophony is music that moves by chords. The most common form of homophony, sometimes called **song texture**, involves a solo voice with chordal accompaniment, such as a folk singer accompanying herself on the guitar. Song texture can also be used to describe instrumental music, for example a solo instrument playing the melody with an accompaniment (MusicNote 3).

In pure **chordal homophony**, all parts move together, forming a succession of chords. A common example of chordal homophony is when the members of a choir sing together in harmony (MusicNote 4).

Polyphony, on the other hand, is music in which you can hear two or more distinct musical lines at once. This kind of texture is obviously more complex. Much Western classical music—a Beethoven symphony, for example—is at least partly polyphonic. If you listen carefully, you can hear several different musical lines at the same time (MusicNote 5).

MUSICNOTE 2
CD 1, track 7
Chant
(10 seconds)

MUSICNOTE 3
CD 1, track 8
Louis Armstrong
(18 seconds)

MUSICNOTE 4
CD 1, track 9
Madrigal
(10 seconds)

MUSICNOTE 5
CD 1, track 10
Beethoven Symphony
(22 seconds)

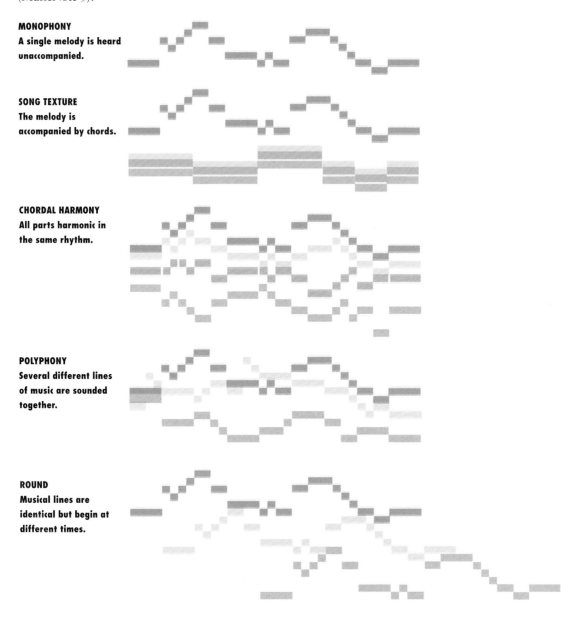

MONOPHONY
A single melody is heard unaccompanied.

SONG TEXTURE
The melody is accompanied by chords.

CHORDAL HARMONY
All parts harmonic in the same rhythm.

POLYPHONY
Several different lines of music are sounded together.

ROUND
Musical lines are identical but begin at different times.

You will sometimes hear the word **counterpoint** used in place of polyphony. A special kind of counterpoint is a **round** ("Row, Row, Row Your Boat"), in which the interweaving lines of music are actually the same but are fitted together to make a polyphonic whole (MusicNote 6).

These textures may be easier to remember if you consider them visually. In the diagram, a single melody is depicted in the various textures.

PITCH

If you press down the keys at either end of a piano, you will notice that one sound is high and the other is low. The difference between the two sounds is an extreme example of a difference in **pitch**.

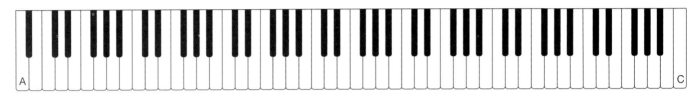

Sound is created through vibrations. When an object vibrates, the vibrations are picked up by our ears and transmitted to our brain as sound. The rate or **frequency** at which the object vibrates determines the pitch that we hear. The faster the vibrations, the higher the pitch. With a piano, for example, the high note at the top end has a frequency of 4,186 (that is, it vibrates 4,186 times per second), whereas the low note at the bottom end has a frequency of 27.5.

Most differences in pitch are not so extreme. Two adjacent notes on the piano might have frequencies of 185 and 196. The difference in the number of vibrations per second is only 11, but we can still hear a clear difference in pitch. Most of us can hear differences in pitch much smaller than this (as in an out-of-tune guitar), and some trained musicians can detect a difference of only one vibration per second.

NOTATION

To indicate their intentions, most composers of the Western tradition write down notes, or **notate** their music. Notes are written on a **staff** (plural: staves). Each staff has five lines:

Notes are placed on any of the five lines of the staff or in any of the four spaces. The pitch is indicated by the position of the round or oval part of the note, not by the stem.

In general, the higher a note appears on a staff, the higher it sounds. Examine this notation of "Take Me Out to the Ball Game," paying attention only to how high or low the notes appear on the staff.

Take me out to the ball game, take me out to the crowd.

You can see that the placement of the notes gives a very clear picture of which notes are higher and which are lower.

The symbol at the beginning of the staff is called a **clef**. A staff is not useful until it has a clef. One of two clefs is normally used: the **treble clef** (as in our "Ball Game" example) or the **bass clef**. High pitches are notated in the treble clef and low pitches in the bass clef.

Clef is the French word for "key," and the clef is the key to which notes are written where. In the treble clef, the central spiral encircles the line that represents the note G on the staff. In fact, the treble clef is derived from a fancy way of writing G (and is sometimes called the G clef). The two dots in the bass clef (or F clef) straddle the line representing the note F on the staff, and here the clef is made up of a stylized F.

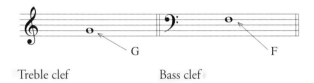

Treble clef   Bass clef

In speech or writing, the notes of music are referred to by letter names. The first seven letters of the alphabet are used: A, B, C, D, E, F, G. To indicate more notes, we simply use these letters over again: A, B, C, D, E, F, G, A, B, C, D, and so on. On each staff below, you will see two notes, E and A.

To find the names of the notes on the upper staff, you count either up or down from the G that is designated by the treble clef. (Remember to count lines *and* spaces.) The same applies to the bass clef: Simply count up or down from F.

You'll notice that the same name can be used for two entirely different pitches. We had an A on the treble staff, but we also used the letter A for one of the notes on the bass staff. These two notes are an **octave** (eight notes) apart. Notes that are an octave apart sound similar because they have multiples of the same frequency. The A at the top of the bass staff has a frequency of 220, and the A in middle of the treble staff has a frequency of twice 220, or 440, because it is an octave higher. Try playing these notes on the piano, or just try singing any two notes that are an octave apart (the first two notes of "Somewhere, Over the Rainbow" or "The Ball Game," for example).

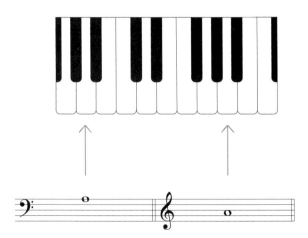

The range of notes covered in music is very wide, so each letter name is used many times. The piano, for example, covers more than seven octaves:

In fact, there are instruments that can play even lower than the piano, and some that can play even higher. To notate these notes on the staff—or, in fact, any notes that lie above or below the staff—various methods are used. One of the most common is the **leger line**.

Old   Mac - Don - ald   had   a   farm,   e - i - e - i - o.

The leger lines for "Old MacDon-" and "E-I-E-I-O" are used to indicate notes that lie too high to be marked on the staff itself. Similarly, notes that lie too low can be placed on leger lines below the staff. By counting up from the topmost staff line, A, you can see that "Old" is sung on a C.

Piano music is usually written with two staves (treble and bass) together, one for the right hand and one for the left. When these staves are put together they are called the **grand staff**. The note that lies on a single leger line in the middle of the grand staff is called middle C. This is the C you just saw in "Old MacDonald Had a Farm."

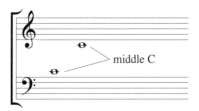

middle C

So far we have been dealing only with the white keys on the piano keyboard. The notation of the black keys is a little more complex. These notes are also put on the lines and spaces of the staff, but they are preceded by either a **sharp** sign (♯) or a **flat** sign (♭) to indicate that they are different from the white notes at the same place on the staff.

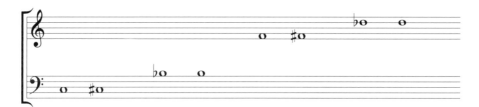

These sharp and flat signs indicate that the note is raised (sharped) or lowered (flatted). The black key located between C and D on a piano can be called either C-sharp or D-flat; it lies a half step above C and a half step below D. Now to understand the difference between a whole step and a half step, we will look briefly at the C-Major scale.

A **scale** is an ascending or descending group of notes. If you play all the white notes on the piano going up from middle C to the C above it, you've just created a scale—the scale of C Major.

The C-Major scale is made up of a series of half steps and whole steps. A half step is the distance between two consecutive keys of either color. The half steps in the C-Major scale, then, are those from E to F and from B to C—those with no intervening black key. A whole step is made up of two half steps, so the whole steps in the scale are those that straddle black keys—for example, from C to D or from A to B.

INTERVALS

The distance between any two pitches is called an **interval**. The closest possible interval is a **unison**. A unison is made up of two notes on the same pitch. This can happen on two different instruments, for example, or when two people sing the same note. After the unison, the other intervals are the **second**, **third**, **fourth**, **fifth**, **sixth**, **seventh**, and **octave**. You determine the name by counting the distance from one note to the next. (In music, you always count the first note as 1.) The interval from C to F, for example, is a fourth: C is 1, D is 2, E is 3, and F is 4. An octave, as we have seen, is the name for the interval between two successive notes of the same letter name (C to C, for example). Intervals can be either *successive* (one note sounded after the other) or *simultaneous* (the two notes sounded together).

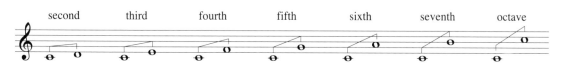

CONSONANCE AND DISSONANCE

The quality of sound of each of the intervals can be described in terms of **consonance** and **dissonance**. Generally speaking, an interval is consonant when the two notes sound pleasing or stable when played at the same time. The most stable, or most consonant, intervals are the unison, the fourth, the fifth, and the octave; the third and the sixth are also usually considered consonant.

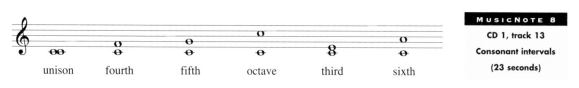

MUSICNOTE 8
CD 1, track 13
Consonant intervals
(23 seconds)

The intervals of a second, from C to D, and a seventh, from a C to the B, sound harsh. These intervals are dissonant. To our ears, dissonances sound unstable or "unfinished," whereas consonances sound stable and complete. The harsh dissonances of the second and the seventh seem to require resolution to a consonance. We can hear that the B in a C–B seventh seems to yearn for the C a half step above, which would turn the dissonant seventh into the

I n 1996 two Harvard psychologists demonstrated that four-month-old infants show a strong preference for consonant intervals and an aversion to dissonance. "Their reaction [to dissonance] is so clear," said Jerome Kagan. "It's like putting a drop of lemon juice on a one-day-old baby's tongue. Some actually had a facial expression of disgust."

very consonant octave. And the D in the C–D second wants to resolve up to a third or down to a unison—both consonances. (Unisons are rather hard to play on one piano!)

second resolving
to a third

second resolving
to a unison

seventh resolving
to an octave

Melody

If several individual pitches are played consecutively, then a **melody** is created. Melodies can be smooth and lyrical, or short, sharp, and jagged, or anything in between. We hear melodies every day: on the radio, on television, at school, and at work. Memorable melodies constitute an integral part of our lives. Every country, for example, has a national anthem, possessing a distinctive melody. Some melodies, like those in television ads or video games, stick in our heads even if we want to forget them. Popular melodies are an important element of all cultures. More often than not, we decide whether we like a piece of music purely on the basis of its melody.

A melody typically consists of different types of **melodic motion**. Melodic motion describes the spacing of notes in a melody. Most melodies contain a mixture of steps (either half steps or whole steps), leaps (movement to notes more than a step away), and repeated notes. The distinctive quality of an individual melody is determined by the combination of these three types of melodic motion.

The melody of "Happy Birthday to You" (see example) contains a mixture of steps, leaps, and repeated notes. It is very simple in construction and can be divided into four sections: 1, 2, 3, and 4. Each of these sections is called a **phrase**. A musical phrase is marked off by a tiny moment of repose at its end. If you sing "Happy Birthday," you will notice that the most appropriate points at which to take a breath are at the end of each phrase.

Hap-py birth-day to you; hap-py birth-day to you; hap-py

birth-day, dear read-er, hap-py birth-day to you.

The four phrases are very similar. Each is the same length. Each features almost exactly the same rhythm. The difference between the phrases is in the melodic motion. The first two are almost identical; the only difference is the size of one of the intervals. The first phrase has a fourth between "-day" and "to," whereas the second phrase has a fifth between those words.

The third and fourth phrases are more varied melodically. The third phrase has an octave leap at the beginning ("Happy BIRTH-"), which marks the high point of the entire melody, and then descends by thirds. And the fourth phrase starts higher than any of the others and descends to the last note of the melody. The fourth phrase has a feeling of finality to it, which is appropriate for the end of the melody.

"Happy Birthday" is an example of a melody that features phrases of identical length, unified by the repetition of a rhythmic pattern but given shape and contrast by differences in melodic motion. "America" (see example) has a much longer melody than "Happy Birthday" does, but it also contains phrases of equal length, and a repeated rhythm again unifies the melody. See how often you can find the same, or almost the same, rhythm in this melody.

My coun-try, 'tis of thee, sweet land of li - ber - ty,

of thee I sing. Land where my fa - thers died, land of the

Pil - grims' pride, from ev - 'ry __ moun - tain-side, let - free - dom ring!

MUSICNOTE 11
CD 1, track 16
"America"
(33 seconds)

This melody, however, is made up almost entirely of steps. In fact, if you don't count the intervals *between* phrases, the largest interval in the entire song is only a third. This interval (on "-try 'tis" and "-'ry moun-" and "let") sounds like a big leap when the rest of the melody is in stepwise motion. The word "let" also has the highest note. These two factors together create a strong climax for the words "let freedom ring!"

Another distinctive feature of this melody is its use of **melodic sequence** on the words "Land where my fathers died, land of the Pilgrims' pride." A melodic sequence occurs when a melodic pattern is repeated at a different pitch level, and it is a device used in many melodies. Here, the melodic pattern of "Land where my fathers died" is repeated a step lower for the words "land of the Pilgrims' pride." The musical sequence is matched by the similarity of the two lines of text. Both begin with the word "land," both have the same number of syllables, and the two lines rhyme ("died"/"pride"). Synergy between text and melody is a hallmark of memorable songs.

"Twinkle, Twinkle, Little Star" (see example) is an example of a melody that ends the same way it begins. Again, each phrase is the same length, and here, each phrase uses *exactly* the same rhythm. You will notice that the last two phrases are identical to the first two and that only the middle two provide any melodic contrast. This idea of melodic **contrast and return** is an extremely common device in music.

Phrase 1 — Phrase 2

Twin - kle, twin - kle, lit - tle star, how I won - der what you are,

Phrase 3 — Phrase 4

up a - bove the world so high, like a dia - mond in the sky,

Phrase 5 — Phrase 6

twin - kle, twin - kle, lit - tle star, how I won - der what you are.

MUSICNOTE 12
CD 1, track 17
"Twinkle, twinkle"
(25 seconds)

The melody of "Twinkle, Twinkle, Little Star" is made up primarily of repeated notes and descending steps, though there is a leap of a fifth at the beginning of the first phrase (and phrase 5). The range of the entire song is only a sixth, from a low of middle C to a high of A, making it an easy reach for most singers. The simple but satisfying structure, the repetitive rhythm, the limited range, and the pattern of repeated notes and stepwise melodic motion make this a favorite early song for children.

Melodic motion also contributes to a larger-scale aspect of melody, which is **melodic shape**. If you simply draw a line connecting the notes in a melody, you will get a visual picture of its melodic shape. We can also sense the shape of a melody with our ears. "Happy Birthday," for example, is made up of wave shapes, which gradually rise up to the highest note ("Happy BIRTH-") and then descend. "America" has extremely gentle waves (we might call them ripples) except for the last phrase. "Twinkle, Twinkle, Little Star" has two phrases (1 and 5) that rise rather suddenly, whereas all the rest of the phrases have a long, gradual descent. The overall shape of a melody has a very strong effect on whether the melody appeals to us or not.

"Happy Birthday," "America," and "Twinkle, Twinkle, Little Star" are simple melodies. Yet they exhibit the most important aspects of melody: division into phrases; a mixture of steps, leaps, and repeated notes; the use of sequence; the unifying role played by rhythm; and overall shape. These melodies have one other feature in common, one that is shared by almost every memorable tune: Each is dominated by a keynote, or tonic. An explanation of this aspect of melody must include a discussion of harmony, key, and tonality.

Harmony

Although melodies can be sung unaccompanied, most of them normally occur with accompaniment. Accompaniment adds depth and richness to a melody. The way in which this accompaniment is constructed is known as **harmony**. A composer can create different moods and feelings by changing the harmony in a piece of music.

A chord is formed when three or more different notes are played together. The intervals between these notes determine whether the chord is consonant or dissonant, stable or unstable.

The most common consonant chord is the **triad**, which consists of one primary note (called the "root") and two other notes, one a third above it and the other a fifth above it. This is the most frequently used of all chords.

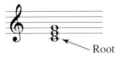

Both of the notes above the root form a consonance with the root, creating a very stable sound. If the notes are played one after another, rather than all at once, the result is not a chord but an **arpeggio**. An arpeggio is what you hear if you strum a guitar once very slowly.

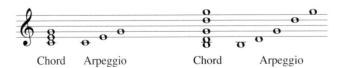

Chord   Arpeggio   Chord   Arpeggio

Sometimes composers will write a triad with the notes rearranged, so that the third or the fifth, or both, lie below the root. The resulting chords sound slightly different, but the root in each case remains C, because that is the note on which the triad was originally based.

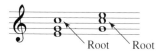

Triads can be built on any root. Triads built on G would look like this:

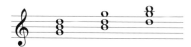

Other chords, which are variants of the basic consonant triad, imply subsequent movement to a *different* triad; in other words, the listener expects a chord change to follow. The most common of these is the **seventh chord**. This chord consists of a triad (for example, C, E, and G) with a flatted seventh (B♭) added.

You will notice a difference between the C-E-G sound of the first example in this section and the C-E-G-B♭ sound of this last example. The B♭ adds a dissonance to the basic triad because it creates the interval of a seventh with the C. Dissonant chords are unstable and seem to need resolution to a more stable chord. The B♭ in the seventh chord "leans" toward the A that is a half step below. But the note A is not a part of the C triad. Consequently, a change of harmony is required, based in this case on the root F, which has A as its third.

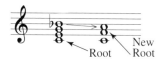

The relationship between the two chords in the example is an important one. Because the first chord requires the second as its resolution, the two chords can be said to belong together. To see why, we need to examine two further elements of music: key and tonality.

KEY AND TONALITY

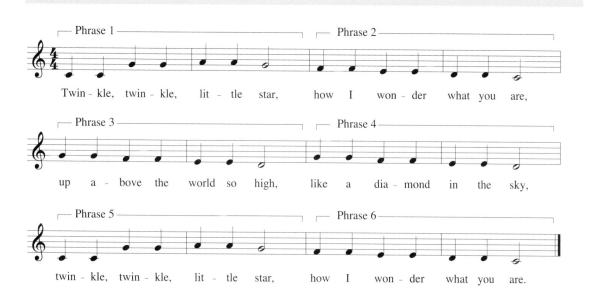

If you sing "Twinkle, Twinkle, Little Star" and stop at the end of phrase 4, the melody will sound incomplete. This happens because the melody needs to end on a C, the **tonic** or **keynote** of the piece. If you examine the melody, you will see that it begins and ends on the same note: C. If we were to change the melody to end on a different note (see below), its whole quality would change. Listen to these new versions of the melody and you will hear that the final note is not stable enough to end the piece. The only note that sounds right at the end of this piece is C.

MUSICNOTE 13

CD 1, track 18

Different endings for

"Twinkle, twinkle"

(44 seconds)

Because C is the keynote, "Twinkle, Twinkle, Little Star" can be said to be in the key of C. Music's ability to be molded by keys is known as **tonality**.

Now let's look again at the melody of "Happy Birthday."

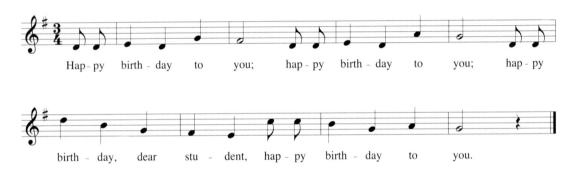

What is the keynote of this melody? The melody ends on G, so the keynote is probably G. (Most melodies end on their keynote.) If you try substituting any other note at the end of "Happy Birthday," you will find that the substitutions simply don't sound right; they don't give a sense of finality at the end of the song.

The keynote of "Happy Birthday" is G, so "Happy Birthday" is in the key of G, or simply in G. There are many different keys, and "Happy Birthday" could just as easily have been written in the key of B-flat, for example. Every key has a different series of notes associated with it. When you arrange the notes that belong to a particular keynote in their proper order, you create a **scale**.

Scales

A scale is more than just an ascending or descending group of notes. It is really a store of notes the composer draws from when writing a piece of music. A composer writing in the key of C Major mostly uses notes from the C-Major scale.

Let us reexamine the C-Major scale. As we saw before, this scale uses only the white notes from the piano. The first and last notes of the scale are C, and C is the keynote. But you can build a major scale on any keynote. What makes a scale major is not the keynote but the *pattern of intervals* between the notes.

Let's see what the intervals are in the scale of C Major. Look at the C-Major scale in the following example. The pattern of intervals going up is this: whole step, whole step, half step, whole step, whole step, whole step, half step.

whole step whole step half step whole step whole step whole step half step

Every major scale contains this pattern. If you use this pattern, you can build a major scale on any note. You will find that most major scales are not limited to the white notes. Try the scale of G Major. All you do is start on G and go up, keeping the same pattern of intervals. The pattern in shorthand is 1-1-$\frac{1}{2}$-1-1-1-$\frac{1}{2}$.

Start on G. Then go to A (a whole step from G), then B (a whole step from A), then C (a half step from B), then D (a whole step from C), then E (a whole step from D), then F♯ (a whole step from E), and finally G (a half step from F♯). You'll see that to keep the pattern, you have to use an F♯ instead of a plain F. So the scale of G Major looks like this:

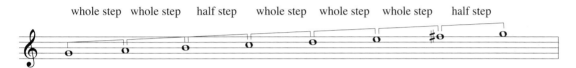

whole step whole step half step whole step whole step whole step half step

The same applies to any major scale: Just start on any note and keep the interval pattern exact. Try making some other scales. You'll see that some need quite a few sharps or flats.

There are two main types of scale: **major** and **minor**. Pieces that use a major scale are said to be in the major *mode*; pieces using a minor scale, in the minor mode. There is a difference in sound between the two modes. That difference is created by differences in the pattern of the intervals.

The minor scale still uses whole and half steps, but the arrangement is different. The pattern in the minor scale is this: whole step, half step, whole step, whole step, half step, whole step, whole step. The easiest minor scale is A minor, because it has no sharps or flats.

whole step half step whole step whole step half step whole step whole step

But just like the major scale, a minor scale can be built on any note. Here's D minor, with the same pattern of intervals (1-$\frac{1}{2}$-1-1-$\frac{1}{2}$-1-1).

whole step half step whole step whole step half step whole step whole step

As you can see, D minor needs one flat. Try building other minor scales. For example, try building C minor. You'll see that C minor needs *three* flats: B♭, E♭, and A♭.

Major-key pieces usually sound different from minor-key pieces. Pieces in a major key usually sound bright, positive, or cheerful, whereas pieces in a minor key sound more serious, even a little sad. Notice the difference in the sound of "Twinkle, Twinkle, Little Star" if we change it from C Major to C minor.

MUSICNOTE 14

CD 1, track 19
"Twinkle, twinkle"
in a minor key
(16 seconds)

Twin - kle, twin - kle, lit - tle star, how I won - der what you are.

Composers sometimes use different versions of the minor scale. The basic one we have been looking at is called the **natural minor**; the two other forms are called the **harmonic minor** and the **melodic minor**. Each has a slightly different interval pattern. The melodic minor scale is slightly different ascending and descending.

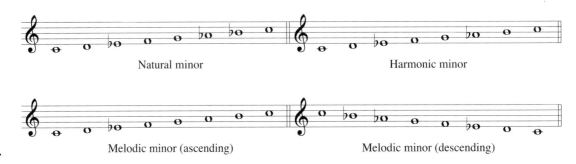

Natural minor   Harmonic minor

Melodic minor (ascending)   Melodic minor (descending)

Composers sometimes use other scales, including the **pentatonic scale** (a scale with only five notes) and the **chromatic scale**, which moves entirely by half steps. Music that uses many half steps *in addition to* those in the scale is also called chromatic.

KEY SIGNATURES

When we constructed the G-Major scale above, we needed an F♯ to keep to the pattern. If a composer were to write a piece in G Major, he or she would have to write a sharp sign every time an F♯ was required. If the piece were in C minor, the composer would have to write three flats all the time. Instead of doing that, composers usually write a **key signature** at the beginning of each line of music. This indicates to the performer that *whenever* the relevant notes appear, they should be sharped or flatted. The key signature for G Major shows an F♯, indicating that whenever an F appears, it should be sung or played as F♯. The key signature for C minor has three flats, showing that whenever B, E, or A appears, it should be flatted.

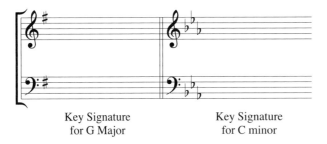

Key Signature   Key Signature
for G Major   for C minor

Occasionally, a composer will want to use a note different from those indicated by the key signature. In these cases, the composer writes a sign immediately in front of the note in question. The sign may be a sharp (♯) or a flat (♭), or it may be a **natural** (♮), which shows that the note is neither sharp nor flat. The natural sign temporarily cancels out any sharp or flat on that note. These individual signs are called **accidentals**.

Every key signature is shared by one major and one minor key. G Major and E minor, for example, *both* have one sharp: an F sharp. The difference is that the keynote of G Major is G, whereas the keynote of E minor is E. The major and minor keys that feature the same key signatures are called **relative** major and minor. E minor is known as the **relative minor** of G Major. E♭ Major is the **relative major** of C minor. Sometimes composers write part of a major piece in the relative minor, or the other way around. The difference in mode provides variety to the piece, but the common key signature provides unity.

When musicians see a key signature, they know what key a piece of music is in. If they see three flats, they can tell that the piece is either in E♭ Major or in C minor. Other factors—looking at the final chord, just listening to the *sound*—will tell them whether it's the major or the minor key.

CHORDS

We have examined the most common consonant chord, the triad (root + third + fifth). Triads, like scales, can be either major or minor. The third of a major triad is a major third—two whole steps—above the root; in a minor triad, it is a minor third, or 1½ steps. Listen to these chords and pay special attention to the difference in sound between major and minor.

major   minor   major   minor   major   minor   major   minor

Each key has a series of chords associated with it. The chords are formed by constructing triads on each of the seven notes in the scale. The most important of these is the **tonic chord**, built on the keynote. This chord is sometimes called the I chord, because the keynote is the first note of the scale. More often than not, a piece will begin and end with the tonic chord, thereby establishing the key at the beginning of the piece and reaffirming it at the end.

The **dominant** chord (chord V) in a key is second in importance to the tonic chord. It is built on the fifth note of the scale, so the dominant chord in C Major is built on G (root + third + fifth = G-B-D). Because the dominant chord in any key always contains the seventh note in the scale (B in this case), it sounds as though it requires resolution back to the tonic chord. Listen to the chords in each example. You'll hear how the V chord seems to want to go back to the I chord again. Some pieces use only these two chords throughout.

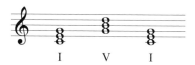

I   V   I

> **MUSICNOTE 15**
> CD 1, track 20
> I–V–I chords in C Major
> (11 seconds)

The effect of the I–V–I progression is the same whether it is played in C Major or any other key.

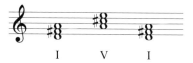

I   V   I

> **MUSICNOTE 16**
> CD 1, track 21
> I–V–I chords in D Major
> (12 seconds)

CADENCES

Cadences in music are like punctuation in grammar. They provide stopping points in the flow of the discourse. Stopping points in grammar have varying degrees of strength. A period marks the end of a sentence. A comma marks off a phrase. A semicolon provides both closure and continuity. Cadences perform these same functions in a musical context.

There are three main types of cadence: the authentic cadence, the plagal cadence, and the half cadence. Each consists of a different progression of two chords.

The chord progression we just examined is an **authentic** or **full cadence**. An authentic cadence consists of a V chord followed by a I chord. It is used to mark the end of sections in a composition or the end of the entire piece.

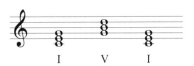

I   V   I

MusicNote 17

CD 1, track 22

Authentic cadence

(9 seconds)

The **plagal cadence**, on the other hand, features a IV chord (known as the **subdominant** chord) and a I chord. If you play these two chords consecutively, you will notice that the cadence is not as strident and forthright as the authentic cadence. Indeed, the plagal cadence is often called the "Amen" cadence, because it is frequently used to close hymns or liturgical pieces.

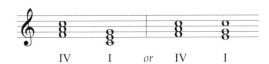

IV   I   *or*   IV   I

MusicNote 18

CD 1, track 23

Plagal cadence

(14 seconds)

The authentic and plagal cadences both end on a tonic chord (I). Both, therefore, can be used by composers to end pieces. The **half cadence** ends on the dominant (V) chord, though, so it lacks the finality of the authentic and plagal cadences. It may be preceded by a IV chord or a I chord; in either case, it provides a pause at the end of a musical phrase, but not an actual ending. It leaves the listener with the sense that there is more music to come.

I   V   *or*   IV   V

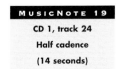

MusicNote 19

CD 1, track 24

Half cadence

(14 seconds)

Rhythm

If a melody is sung without its rhythm, it immediately loses much of its essence. Rhythm is as fundamental to music as pitch, possibly even more so. Rhythm is built into our bodies as heartbeats, or as the motion of our limbs in walking. Rhythm is one of the most important distinguishing features in music.

BEAT

If you are listening to music and find yourself tapping your finger on the table or your foot on the floor, then you are following the **beat**. You respond to the regular pulse of the music, a pulse that is easy to discern. If you tap a steady, even rhythm while singing "Happy Birthday," the rhythm that you tap is the beat. Try it a couple of times.

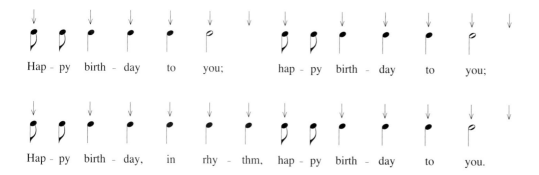

Hap - py birth - day to you; hap - py birth - day to you;

Hap - py birth - day, in rhy – thm, hap - py birth - day to you.

You will notice that on the syllable "-py" of "Happy," there is a note in the actual rhythm but no accompanying beat. This is because the two syllables of "Happy" are contained in the same beat. On the other hand, when you sing "you," the note is held for two beats. All the other syllables receive one beat each.

In the case of "Happy Birthday," the beat corresponds to one quarter note. This is not always the case, but in most music the quarter note is the usual "unit of beat." A quarter note is written like this: (♩). A half note is equivalent to two quarter notes and looks like this: (♩). A whole note is equivalent to four quarter notes and looks like this: (o). But there are smaller note values than a quarter note, too. An eighth note is notated with a small flag on the stem: (♪). There are two eighth notes in a quarter note. A sixteenth note has two flags on the stem: (♬). There are four sixteenth notes in a quarter note. And the smallest usual note value is a thirty-second note. This has three flags on the stem, and there are eight of them in a quarter note. Thirty-second notes are quite rare.

Corresponding to all these note values are **rests**, which indicate units of pause or silence in a piece of music. Each type of rest (whole rest, half rest, etc.) has its own notation symbol to designate it on the page.

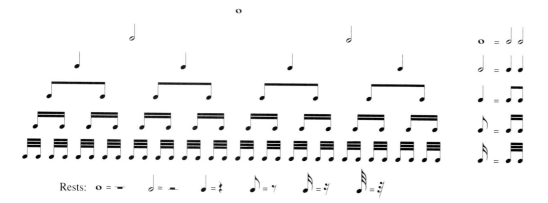

Rests:

The most difficult thing in the world to write is a rest. — Joseph Haydn

If the beat is steady, each row of this chart would take the same amount of time to play. You can see just how fast thirty-second notes might be!

M E A S U R E & M E T E R

When musicians say that a certain melody or theme is in two-, three-, or four-"time," they are referring to the number of beats in a **measure**. In most music, every measure in the piece has the same number of beats. The measures are marked off by **bar lines** (small vertical lines through the staff). If there are three quarter-note beats in a measure, then we say that the **meter** is $\frac{3}{4}$: the upper number (3) indicates that there are three beats in a measure; the lower number (4) indicates the type of note that constitutes a beat—in this case, a quarter note. If there are four quarter-note beats in a measure, the meter is $\frac{4}{4}$. And $\frac{3}{8}$ means three eighth-note beats in a measure.

Duple meters are those, such as $\frac{2}{4}$ or $\frac{4}{4}$, whose upper number (the number of beats) is divisible by 2. Duple meters sound firm and solid. Marches are always in duple meter. **Triple** meters, such as $\frac{3}{4}$ or $\frac{9}{8}$, tend to be graceful or flowing.

There is one other meter you are likely to come across fairly frequently, and that is $\frac{6}{8}$ (six eighth notes to a measure). The eighth notes are divided into two groups of three (♪♪♪ ♪♪♪). A $\frac{6}{8}$ meter has a very special feel to it. Melodies in $\frac{6}{8}$ such as "Row, Row, Row Your Boat," often have a gentle, lilting, slightly swinging quality.*

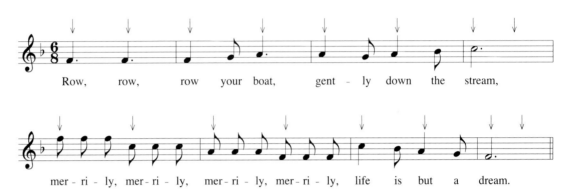

The eighth notes are sung in two groups in each measure, and again the first beat of the measure gets the most stress. (There is also a light stress at the beginning of the second group.) Some of the best-loved melodies are in $\frac{6}{8}$ meter. They include "Rock-A-Bye Baby," "Take Me Out to the Ball Game," and "Ring Around the Rosie." Can you think of any others?

The meter of a piece of music is always given right at the beginning (after the key signature). This indication is sometimes called the **time signature**. The chart below shows some of the most common time signatures.

METER	EXPLANATION	EXAMPLE
$\frac{4}{4}$	Four quarter notes in a measure	"When the Saints Go Marching In"
$\frac{2}{4}$	Two quarter notes in a measure	"Yankee Doodle"
$\frac{3}{4}$	Three quarter notes in a measure	"Happy Birthday to You"
$\frac{6}{8}$	Six eighth notes in a measure	"Row, Row, Row Your Boat"

Sometimes a melody contains notes that seem to come ahead of the beat. When this happens, the rhythm is said to be **syncopated**. Tap your foot or your finger lightly as you sing through the first lines of Stephen Foster's "Camptown Races," paying special attention to the rhythm of the last two measures.

MUSICNOTE 20

CD 1, track 25

(1) as written

(2) unsyncopated

(3) as written again

(33 seconds)

These measures are syncopated. Instead of placing "dah" directly on the beat, Foster placed it ahead of the beat, making for a much livelier rhythm. Try it again, and see how the syncopation pushes the melody along. Now try singing "dah" a little later, right on the beat. See how dull and plodding it sounds?

Syncopation makes you "feel" the rhythm physically, and as a result it is a device frequently found in dance music and jazz. It gives the music a rhythmic drive it would not otherwise have.

---

* A dotted note is half again as long as it would be without the dot. Thus, if a quarter note has two eighth notes, a dotted quarter note has three.

T E M P O

A composer almost always indicates the speed, or **tempo**, at which a piece should be played. This can be done in one of two ways or sometimes in both.

The first way is to use a general tempo indication at the beginning of a piece. These indications often appear in Italian, and the most common are listed below. You'll notice that some of them indicate the character or *spirit* in which the piece is to be played as well as the speed.

Largo	Broad
Adagio	Easy
Andante	At a walking pace
Moderato	Moderate
Allegro	Fast
Vivace	Lively
Presto	Very fast

The second way to indicate tempo is by means of a **metronome marking**. A metronome is a machine that ticks at a specified tempo. The composer might indicate, for example, ♩ = 60, or ♩ = 96. This means that the quarter notes should be played at the rate of 60 per minute (one every second) or 96 per minute. Performers often check their metronomes before practicing a piece, to get a clearer idea of what tempo the composer intended.

Musicians realize, however, that music is a living, breathing thing and not a machine. A metronome speed is rarely maintained exactly throughout a piece. It is usually used only as a guide. Some musicians prefer the Italian words, which have more character and flexibility than the strictly precise metronome markings.

Dynamics

Volume is an intrinsic part of the character of most music. A composer can play on your emotions with a melody that ebbs and surges in volume; likewise, there is no quicker way to get an audience's attention than with a sudden volume change. In fact, Haydn's "Surprise" Symphony—a 30-minute work—gets its nickname from a sudden loud chord that takes about two seconds to play.

The levels of loudness and softness in music are called **dynamics**, and they are mostly indicated by a simple system of three letters: **p**, **m**, and **f**, which represent the Italian words *piano* (soft), *mezzo* (medium), and *forte* (loud). The letters are combined to create a wide variety of dynamic markings.

p	piano	*soft*
pp	pianissimo	*very soft*
mp	mezzo piano	*medium soft*
f	forte	*loud*
ff	fortissimo	*very loud*
mf	mezzo forte	*medium loud*

When composers want to indicate that a change in volume is gradual, they may use the term **crescendo** for a gradual increase in volume, and **decrescendo** or **diminuendo** for a decrease. Usually these terms are abbreviated (*cresc.* and *dim.*). More often, crescendos and decrescendos are indicated by the marks ⟨ and ⟩.

In the following example, the music begins quietly. After a couple of measures, it becomes moderately loud, and then gradually fades away.

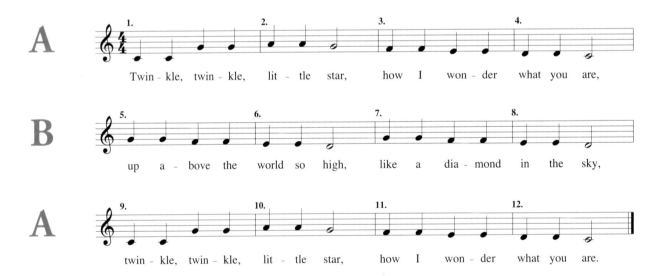

Musical Form

Music, like the other arts, needs structure. At the beginning of this chapter, we said that deliberate organization was a defining element of the arts. A book is written in words that are made up of letters and arranged into sentences. Sentences are organized into paragraphs. And the whole book is itself divided into sections or chapters. Similarly, musical flow is carefully organized: into notes, chords, phrases, sections, movements, and entire works. Structure is vital to music. It enables us to make sense of what we hear.

The organizing structure of a piece of music is known as its **form**. We can look at form in music in quite short pieces. Let us look again at "Twinkle, Twinkle, Little Star." You will notice that the first four measures are repeated in measures 9–12. We can label both of these parts "A." (Using letters makes musical analysis much simpler.) Measures 5–8, however, are markedly different from measures 1–4, so we can label that section "B."

This melody may therefore be described as being in ABA form, otherwise known as **ternary form**. This is the most frequent form in small units such as melodies and themes. But ternary form is also quite common on a far larger scale in music. It often occurs within a **movement** (a large, separate section of a musical work). Occasionally, composers even use a type of ABA form for an entire composition. People seem to find the idea of departure-and-return musically very satisfying. Sometimes the A section returns slightly modified; the form is then indicated as ABA'.

When we listen to a substantial piece of music, such as a movement from a symphony or a sonata, we hear individual melodies, keys, and rhythms in relation to the piece's large-scale form. The form gives meaning to the content and establishes hierarchies among melodies, keys, and rhythms. If a section of music is heard at the beginning of a piece, for example, and then heard again toward the end, the later appearance will remind us of the earlier one. The section will sound new the first time and familiar the second, so even if the repeat is exact, the music will have a different quality to our ears. Moreover, the **reprise** or **return** (that is, the second A section) affirms the important role played by that particular section of the music. This is true even if the return of the A section is modified. In that case, if we are listening carefully, we notice the subtle differences in the music the second time around.

Ternary form may appear, therefore, at two levels: either in small units such as themes and melodies or as the form of an entire movement or piece. The idea of departure-and-return lies behind many of the forms we shall encounter as this book progresses.

Binary form focuses on the idea of contrast. There are two sections, A and B, both of which are usually repeated to make the pattern AABB. Even in binary form, however, there is sometimes a brief thematic reprise of the A section *within* (and toward the end of) the B section.

Sonata form, employed as the structure for many large movements, uses both the idea of contrast and the idea of departure-and-return. There is a large opening section, which contains two contrasting smaller units. This entire larger section recurs, modified, after a middle section that itself contrasts with the outer sections in harmony, tonality, atmosphere, and presentation of thematic material.

Theme-and-variations form involves the idea of contrast by variation. A theme is presented and then played several more times, but each time it recurs, it is varied in some way: in melody, rhythm, dynamics, tempo, or harmony. On each occasion, the theme is recognizably different and yet recognizably the same.

Two forms basic to jazz and rock are **12-bar blues** and **32-bar AABA form**. Both of these depend upon repeated patterns of chord progressions.

Vocab for quiz in E-mail

MAKING MUSIC: VOICES

Singing is one of the most widespread ways of making music. Almost all people sing, whether they can carry a tune or not. People sing in the shower, walking along the street, driving their car, or just lying in bed. Others whistle or hum all the time: These are varieties of singing.

Singing can be done alone or in groups. Working people around the world have devised ways of singing together that help them work, lighten their loads, and create a sense of togetherness. Songs can also create a sense of national identity. Every country has its own national anthem. On a smaller level, songs can confirm a sense of belonging to a recognizable group. In the 1960s, if you listened to the latest rock music, you were in the "in group." Everyone else was considered "square." In a way, of course, things are still the same today.

Songs can also evoke a strong sense of nostalgia. People often have only to hear a tune to recapture the entire atmosphere of a past moment or period in their lives.

Some music allows quite informal standards of singing. Family sing-alongs, folk songs, and most rock songs are like this. Jazz singing, however, is quite specialized. Jazz singers use their voices in very special ways, with "slides" between notes and with "bent" or "blue" notes; and some singers perfect a kind of singing that uses nonsense syllables (called "scat" singing), in which the voice is used as a kind of very flexible instrument.

Singing classical music also takes a great deal of training. The voice must be carefully controlled for pitch and dynamics. Breathing has to be developed so that long phrases can be sung. And singers have to learn how to sing clearly in several different languages.

In folk, rock, and jazz, singers are simply divided into men's and women's voices. In classical music, however, there are several voice classifications, depending on the range of the voice. The high women's range is known as **soprano**; the low women's range is called **alto** or **contralto**. The high men's range is called **tenor**, the low men's range **bass**. There are two intermediate voice ranges as well. A voice between soprano and alto is known as **mezzo-soprano**; a voice between tenor and bass is known as **baritone**.

It is possible for men to make their voices go higher artificially. This type of singing, sometimes called falsetto, is hard to control, but it can be perfected with much practice, and the resulting voice type is known as countertenor.

	WOMEN	MEN
High:	Soprano	Tenor
Medium:	Mezzo-Soprano	Baritone
Low:	Alto	Bass

Far Right: The group Manhattan Transfer.

MAKING MUSIC: INSTRUMENTS

Above: Bone flute from prehistoric times.

Playing instruments also has a very long history. Prehistoric humans probably banged on hollow logs or rocks to make music. Flutes made of animal bone have been found dating from many thousands of years ago.

Around the world, people have devised many ways of creating musical instruments. In the Caribbean, instruments called steel drums are made from used oil barrels. In Africa, a musical bow is made from a stick, a string, and a gourd. In the Middle East, a type of double reedpipe is made from unequal lengths of narrow bamboo cane.

Apart from the way they are made, what most distinguishes one instrument from another is the **tone color**, or **timbre**, of the sound it makes. A flute playing a certain pitch sounds very different from a guitar playing exactly the same pitch.

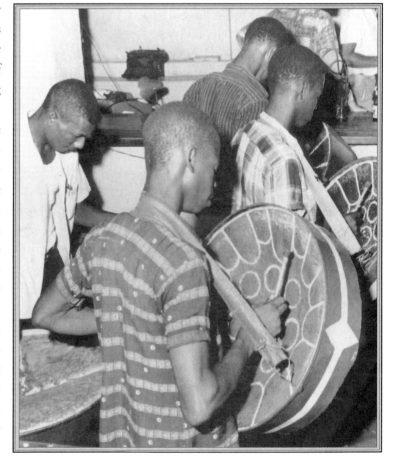

Right: Steel drums being played in the Caribbean.

Most instruments are designed to be played with others. Instruments can play together in small or large groups. Examples of small groups include a rock band, a jazz combo, or a chamber group. **Chamber music** is classical music played by a small group of instruments. This can range from a single violin and a piano, to a **string quartet** (two violins, one viola, and one cello), to up to eight or ten instruments. The most common example of a large group of highly varied instruments playing together is an orchestra.

Far Left: Musical bow from Africa.

Left: A Classical string quartet.

THE ORCHESTRA

The term "orchestra" is used loosely to describe any large group of instrumental musicians playing together at one time. It generally refers to a classical group, though some jazz bands call themselves orchestras. The size of a classical orchestra can vary considerably, depending on the work being played. A Mahler symphony may require close to 150 players, whereas only 20 or 30 are needed for the performance of a Mozart or a Haydn symphony.

Composers first began to write for what we identify as an orchestra in the Baroque era (1600–1750). A large number of new instruments have been introduced since then, and the orchestra has grown considerably in size. The trumpet (with valves), trombone, tuba, clarinet, harp, double bass, piccolo, English horn, bass clarinet, and contrabassoon, as well as numerous percussion instruments, have been incorporated into the orchestra since the mid-eighteenth century. As a result, nineteenth- and twentieth-century composers have had progressively more sounds and orchestral textures at their disposal. Experimentation with new instruments has continued but mostly in the fields of rock and jazz.

The instruments of the modern orchestra are divided into four groups: strings, woodwinds, brass, and percussion. Orchestral scores (written music for orchestras) normally follow these groupings.

STRINGS

There are four **string** instruments that are permanent members of the orchestra: violin, viola, violoncello (cello), and double bass. The violin is the smallest and the highest in pitch; the viola is slightly larger than the violin and consequently lower in pitch; the cello plays in the tenor and baritone ranges; and the double bass is the largest and the lowest in pitch of all the string instruments.

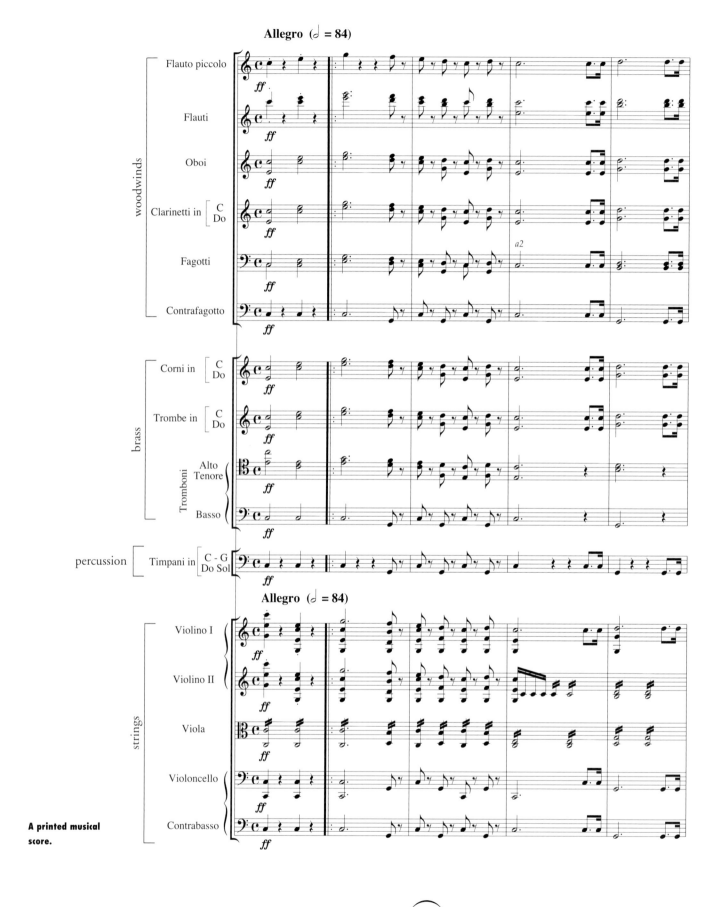

A printed musical score.

All four instruments are related, and their appearance and construction are similar. The handcrafting of string instruments is a demanding and time-consuming art. Some of the most beautiful, in sound and appearance, are quite old. The most famous (and most valuable) come from the seventeenth and eighteenth centuries.

The **violin** is small enough to be held under the chin by the performer as it is played. It is one of the most versatile instruments of the orchestra: It has a wide range and is very expressive. For these reasons, a great deal of music is written for solo violin. But the most recognizable violin sound is that of many violins playing together in an orchestra.

The versatile violin.

The **viola** is played in the same manner as the violin, but it is slightly larger, deeper in pitch, and mellower in sound. The viola does not usually play as many solo melodies as the violin, yet its dark tone quality is an essential component of the string section of an orchestra. The viola usually plays in the middle range, filling in harmonies and enriching the sound. It is fascinating to note how many great composers have been viola players. Perhaps it shows that composers are more interested in exploring the inner workings of music than in being the star of the show.

The rich, romantic sound of the **cello** is very special. It has been explored extensively by great nineteenth-century composers such as Beethoven, Tchaikovsky, and Brahms. The cello is quite large, so it is held between the knees rather than under the chin. A spike protruding from the bottom of the instrument helps to support the weight.

The largest and deepest member of the string family is the **double bass**. Whereas a cellist always plays sitting down, the double bass player either stands in place or sits on a high stool. Although the double bass cannot be played with as much agility as the cello, it provides a firm harmonic bass for the string section and for the entire orchestra. When many double basses are playing low, the sound is remarkable.

All four string instruments are usually played with a bow made of horsehairs stretched on a stick. The hairs are drawn across the strings, producing the sustained, intense sound that is characteristic of string instruments. The player's hand holds the bow, and the way he or she draws the bow across the strings determines the character of the sound: its tone color and its dynamics. The fingers of the other hand control the pitch of the sound. There are four strings, each tuned to a different note, and the player can change the pitch on any of the strings by pressing it down on the **fingerboard** at a certain point ("stopping" the string). It is extremely difficult to find the exact position on the string for each note while at the same time controlling the speed and pressure of the bow. String instruments are among the hardest to learn.

A beautiful bass.

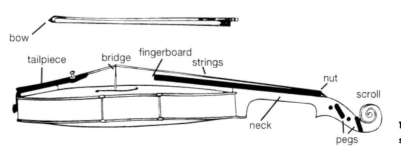

bow
tailpiece
bridge
fingerboard
strings
nut
scroll
neck
pegs

The main parts of a string instrument.

Hey, students! Musicians always like to make fun of viola players. For a great collection of jokes, check out "Viola Jokes" on the Internet.

The legendary Pablo Casals playing cello.

An orchestral harpist.

Other techniques have been developed to increase the sound possibilities of string instruments. They can be played **pizzicato**—that is, by plucking the strings with the fingers instead of using the bow. Sometimes a small device is placed on the **bridge** to dampen the sound slightly: This is called a **mute**. The fingers that are stopping the strings are often rocked back and forth against the fingerboard to make the pitch waver slightly. This is called **vibrato**. It is used to make the playing more expressive.

There are more violins in a modern symphony orchestra than any other instrument, usually between 24 and 32. They are divided into two groups: first violins and second violins. There is no difference between the instruments, but the first and second violins often play different musical lines. You can see the difference when you watch an orchestra, because all the first violinists move their bows together in one pattern, while the seconds are often bowing in a different pattern. The principal first violinist, who sits immediately to the left of the conductor, is known as the **concertmaster** (or **concertmistress**), and it is this person who determines the bowings, fingerings, and many other aspects of orchestral performance and personnel.

There are other instruments that must be classified as string instruments because they have strings, but these are always played by plucking and never by bowing. They include the harp and the guitar.

The **harp** is often seen in expanded orchestras. Some very big pieces call for two or more harps. The instrument has 42 strings that are graduated in size, and sharp and flat notes are obtained by pressing down pedals. The many strings allow the harpist to play **glissando**, a technique whereby the player runs his or her fingers across the strings in quick succession, creating an evocative, ethereal sound.

The **guitar** has six strings, and the sound is delicate and light. The guitar is strongly associated with music of Spain and Latin America, but it is widely used around the world, mostly for solo playing or to accompany singing. Very rarely, however, you will see the guitar in an orchestra, and there are some guitar concertos, in which the guitar has an extended solo part accompanied by the orchestra.

The string section is the largest of the four principal groups of the orchestra. The individual instruments complement each other perfectly. Many composers, such as Mozart and Tchaikovsky, have written pieces for strings alone (*Eine kleine Nachtmusik* and *Serenade for Strings*). Other great compositions for strings alone include Vaughan Williams's *Fantasy on a Theme of Thomas Tallis* and Albinoni's *Adagio*. The *Adagio for Strings*, by the American composer Samuel Barber, is also a most beautiful and moving piece.

Woodwinds

The flute, oboe, clarinet, and bassoon are the standard **woodwind** instruments in the modern orchestra. All are played by blowing through a reed or through a mouthpiece attached to the main body of the instrument. As with the strings, the woodwinds are divided into smaller subsections (flutes, oboes, etc.). Unlike the large individual string subsections, each woodwind subsection usually has only two to four players. In orchestral works, the woodwind instruments receive the most solo passages.

The **flute** was originally made of wood and is therefore classified as a woodwind instrument. Nowadays, however, it is usually metal. Most flutes are made of silver, but some famous flute soloists play gold or even platinum flutes. The instrument is held sideways, and sounds are produced by blowing across a hole in the mouthpiece, according to the same principle used in blowing across the top of a bottle. Different pitches are produced by moving the fingers on holes and keys.

The flute is famous for its bright, liquid upper notes and its haunting lower notes. It has a wide range and can be played very fast. The **piccolo**, a small version of the flute played in exactly the same way, is an octave higher than the flute and sounds very brilliant, even shrill.

The **oboe** and the **bassoon** are played by blowing through a double reed made of cane. Two small pieces of cane are tied together, and they vibrate against each other. The suave yet edgy quality of the oboe made it a favorite among eighteenth- and nineteenth-century composers. Two oboes playing together (with a bassoon playing the bass) are often used to contrast with the much smoother strings. Because the oboe varies little in pitch, the other instruments usually tune to it. Before a classical concert, when the concertmaster gives the signal for tuning, you can listen carefully and hear the pitch being given first by the principal oboist.

Whereas the oboe and the flute are among the highest-sounding instruments of the orchestra, the bassoon is one of the lowest. It is a large instrument and uses much larger double reeds than the oboe does. Its length is disguised, because it is made of a tube doubled back on itself. If it were straight, it would be more than nine feet long. The bassoon has a full, rounded, vibrant sound in its low **register** (area of sound) and a strange, rather haunting sound in its high register. The most famous example of a bassoon playing high is at the opening of Stravinsky's *The Rite of Spring*.

Left to Right: piccolo, flute, clarinet, bass clarinet, oboe, English horn, bassoon, contrabassoon.

The **English horn** is neither English nor a horn. It is really a low oboe, pitched a fifth lower than the standard oboe. The English horn has a rich, evocative sound. It is one of the most distinctive instruments of the orchestra. Perhaps for that reason, it is used quite rarely. Its most well-known appearance is in the slow movement of Dvořák's *New World* Symphony.

The **contrabassoon** is the lowest woodwind instrument of all. It plays an octave lower than the bassoon and is a very large instrument. It is made of a tube doubled back on itself twice. Unwound, it would stretch to 18 feet!

The **clarinet** is the most versatile of all the woodwinds. For this reason, perhaps, it is the only orchestral woodwind instrument that has been consistently successful in jazz. Mozart was said to

Far Left: bassoonist; Left: oboe player.

Right: Flutist James Galway playing a solid gold flute; Far Right: A wooden piccolo.

have adored the sound of the clarinet. It is played with a single reed, also made of cane, which is attached to the mouthpiece. The clarinet has a very wide range of nearly four octaves and three distinct registers. In the low register, it sounds rich and melancholy; in the middle register, it is singing and warm; in the high register, it is piercing and shrill.

Clarinet soloist.

The **bass clarinet** plays an octave lower than the standard clarinet; it has a wonderfully rich, buttery sound. The **E♭** clarinet is smaller and higher than the standard clarinet. It is bright and piercing and often used in bands.

Other woodwind instruments that have their main existence outside an orchestra are the saxophone and the recorder. The **saxophone** is, like the flute, made of metal, and like the clarinet it has a single reed. Saxophones come in many sizes. The most common are the alto and tenor, though soprano, baritone, and bass saxophones have also had their proponents. The saxophone is a fairly new instrument (invented in the mid-nineteenth century by Adolphe Sax), and it has not yet found a permanent niche in the classical orchestra. The saxophone is used mostly in jazz, where its smooth, flexible, melodious quality works particularly well.

The **recorder** was a favorite instrument in the sixteenth, seventeenth, and eighteenth centuries. It also comes in different sizes, the most common being the soprano and alto recorders. Because the recorder's sound is quite soft, its place in the orchestra was taken over in the eighteenth century by the more versatile flute. Recorders are fine instruments for children, because they are fairly easy to play at a basic level. Advanced recorder playing, however, is not at all easy.

Brass

The French horn, trumpet, trombone, and tuba are **brass** instruments. All four require the player to blow through a brass mouthpiece, which can be detached from the main body of the instrument. The vibrating medium in brass instruments is the player's lips. Composers tend to use brass instruments sparingly, because they produce considerable volume and can overwhelm all the other instruments in the orchestra. Yet the strident, extroverted character of brass instruments is balanced by a much-underrated warm, mellow quality.

Different notes are obtained on brass instruments not only by tightening or slackening the lips in the mouthpiece but also by changing the length of the tube that has air going through it. On the French horn, trumpet, and tuba, this is done by using the fingers to press down various combinations of three valves. On the trombone, however, the length of the tube is changed by means of a slide: One length of tubing is slid over another, varying the overall length.

Each of the brass instruments has its own distinctive sound. The **French horn**, often known simply as the horn, is often associated with "outdoor" sounds like hunting calls, though it also has a warm, mellow quality. The **trumpet** is the highest-pitched brass instrument. Composers often take advantage of its bold, strident quality in fanfare-like passages, though a trumpet playing quietly can sound delicate and mysterious. The **trombone** sounds very powerful and grand, sometimes even frightening. As with the horn, however, it has the potential to produce a rich, smooth, and mellow sound. Both the trumpet and the trombone are favored in jazz ensembles. The **tuba** is to the brass section what the double bass is to the string section—the lowest-pitched instrument and the supporting bass. It gives added weight to the brass section. Its sound is deep and round.

When a whole choir of brass instruments is playing together, the sound is like no other. It can range from introspective and religious (as in the slow movement of Mahler's Second Symphony) to utterly overwhelming. In fact, Berlioz's Requiem Mass calls for *four* brass choirs playing from four different corners of the hall.

Above: A row of French horns.

Above: The bell of a trombone and the valves of a trumpet.

Left to Right: 1) Clockwise from Top Left: French horn, tuba, trombone, trumpet. 2) Tuba player. 3) Trombone player.

PERCUSSION

Percussion instruments are those that involve hitting or shaking. They can be divided into two categories: those that produce pitched (tuned) sounds and those that produce unpitched sounds. Pitched percussion include timpani, xylophone, glockenspiel, and celesta.

The **timpani** have been an important feature of the symphony orchestra since the late eighteenth century. Two, three, or sometimes four of these large drums are arranged in a semicircle around the player. They are sometimes called kettledrums because they are made of copper. Timpani have a skin stretched across the top (this used to be animal skin but is now usually made of plastic), and each drum is tuned to a different (low) pitch. They are played either with soft padded sticks or with hard wooden ones. Timpani can sound like distant thunder (as in Berlioz's *Symphonie fantastique*). They can also sound superhuman (as in Richard Strauss's *Also sprach Zarathustra*, better known as the main theme of the film *2001: A Space Odyssey*) or military (in some of Haydn's symphonies). Often, however, they are used simply to reinforce the beat and the bass.

Above: Three timpani being played.

Far Right: 200-year-old pair of timpani from England.

The **xylophone** and the **glockenspiel** are very similar to each other. Each has two sets of bars—like the black and white keys of a piano—played with two hard sticks. The glockenspiel bars are made of metal and therefore produce a bright, luminous sound. The xylophone's bars are made of wood, so the sound is more mellow.

The **celesta** is based on the same principle as the previous two instruments, but it looks like a tiny upright piano. The hammers that strike the metal bars are controlled from a small keyboard. The sound of the celesta is tinkling, delicate, and sweet. You can hear it used most effectively in the "Dance of the Sugar-Plum Fairy" in Tchaikovsky's ballet *The Nutcracker*.

Untuned percussion instruments include snare drum, bass drum, triangle, and cymbals. The **snare drum** has strings attached to its underside, which sizzle or rattle when the drum is struck. The sound is dry and crisp. The **bass drum** is large and is suspended on its side. It gives a deep thump. The snare drum and the bass drum are prominently featured in jazz combos and marching bands and occasionally in classical music as well. The snare drum is the most conspicuous instrument in Ravel's *Bolero*.

The **triangle** is made of metal and is played with a metal beater. Its high, hard noise can be heard above a full symphony orchestra.

Cymbals come in many different sizes. Orchestral cymbals are usually a pair about 15 inches in diameter and are struck together. The crashing sound can last for several seconds. A jazz drum set often has several cymbals, either singly or in pairs. In jazz combos, the drum set is the heart and backbone of the music.

Right: A triangle player.

KEYBOARD INSTRUMENTS

The most important keyboard instruments are the piano, the harpsichord, the organ, and the synthesizer. The **piano** is the best-known solo instrument, but it can also appear with an orchestra. This happens in one of two ways. In a **piano concerto**, the piano takes a starring role in front of the orchestra. But occasionally the piano appears as just another orchestral instrument, adding one more tone color to the already enormous array of orchestral colors. Twentieth-century composers often use the piano in this way.

The piano can claim to be both a string instrument and a percussion instrument. Each key on the keyboard activates its own hammer. The hammer strikes the piano's strings inside the instrument, and a note is sounded. The harder the pianist strikes a key, the louder the sound. This ability to control dynamics so directly gave the piano its original name, *piano e forte*, which is Italian for "soft and loud."

The most important predecessor of the piano was the **harpsichord**. The harpsichord was the fundamental instrument of the Baroque era (1600–1750). It was used in symphonies, in operas, in chamber music, and as a solo instrument. Although the harpsichord may look quite similar to the piano from the outside, its internal mechanism is quite different in that there are no hammers. Pressing a key causes the string to be plucked. Regardless of how hard the key is pressed, the string is plucked in the same manner and produces the same dynamics. The sound of the harpsichord is delicate and dry, though full chords can be quite loud. There is a great deal of beautiful harpsichord music from the seventeenth and eighteenth centuries, ranging from the exquisite pieces of French composers to the brilliant compositions of Bach.

Today, people often play these pieces on

Far Left and Above: A modern "grand" piano, showing the heavy metal frame needed to support the weight and tension of the strings.

the piano, but using the harpsichord allows the music to sound the way the composers originally intended.

The **organ** is sometimes called the "king of instruments." Organs range in size from tiny, portable models to the enormous instruments found in large halls or churches. Air is propelled through pipes, and the route the air takes is controlled from a keyboard. Large organs can have hundreds of pipes and even two or three keyboards ("manuals"). They usually have a pedal keyboard for the lowest notes, which is operated by the player's feet. For this the player wears special shoes.

Left: Harpsichords, like this late sixteenth-century Italian instrument, often had decorated cases. The frame is light and wooden.

Not all organs are built the same way. Various designs are used to create different sets of pipes, each producing a different quality of sound. Pipes may be made of a variety of materials, in a variety of shapes, and with or without reeds. Big organs have many different sets of pipes. Each set is made accessible from the keyboard by special control buttons known as stops. This is where we get the expression "pulling out all the stops." As a result of this array of stops, the sound of the organ is very rich. There is nothing like the full, resonant sound of the organ played in a large church. Some of the greatest organ

Above: A superb sixteenth-century organ in a French cathedral.

Above Right: Console of the organ at the Cathedral of St. John the Divine in New York City, showing the four manuals, stops, and pedals.

music was written by Johann Sebastian Bach, who was himself an organist.

Another instrument that can imitate sounds is the **synthesizer**. This is an electronic instrument, usually with a keyboard, that can be programmed to imitate the sound of almost any other instrument. The synthesizer can also modify sounds or create completely new ones. The synthesizer has revolutionized the recording and film industries. It can be made to sound very much like a full orchestra or like a single electric guitar. Synthesized film soundtracks are very common. It is far less ex-

Imaginative inventors have always been attracted to musical instruments. Above: A seaweed horn made from different lengths of dried kelp, played by its inventor, Bart Hopkin.

pensive to use one synthesizer than to hire a conductor and an orchestra for several days! Nothing can replace the excitement of live music-making, however, and as long as there are people who have the discipline and dedication it takes to learn how to sing or to play an instrument, there will always be concerts, chamber music, jazz clubs, and rock bands.

REHEARSALS

The amount of rehearsal time that goes into music differs greatly according to the type of music involved. Jazz, for example, depends a great deal upon **improvisation**: people making up the music as they go along. Nonetheless, creative improvisation takes a great deal of practice. You have to know your instrument very well, and you have to be able to hear harmonies and listen carefully to what the other members of the group are doing. But there is a certain informality to much jazz that takes away the need for much joint rehearsal.

A musician marking up a score in a rehearsal.

Rock music takes quite a bit of studio time, but much of the work in making a recording nowadays is done by the engineers. Most recorded rock is "manufactured" in the studio by engineers mixing different tape tracks, adding synthesized sounds, and manipulating the overall result. For the performers, however, getting each individual track right can take some time.

Classical concert music takes an enormous amount of rehearsal. Much more time is spent rehearsing for a concert than actually presenting it. A typical orchestral musician will work for nine $2\frac{1}{2}$-hour periods a week, of which two-thirds are devoted to rehearsals. In addition, of course, the musician is expected to practice his or her instrument and learn new music.

The sayings of Eugene Ormandy, conductor of the Philadelphia Orchestra for over 35 years, have become legendary. His conducting was flawless, but his English (Ormandy was born in Hungary) needed more rehearsal. Some gems:

"Why do you always insist on playing while I'm trying to conduct?"

"He's a wonderful man, and so is his wife."

"Even when you're not playing, you're behind my beat."

"It is not as difficult as I thought it was, but it is harder than it is."

"Percussion a little louder!" (But Maestro, we don't have anything to play.) "That's right, play it louder!"

Left: A conductor coaxes expression out of his orchestra.

During rehearsals, the conductor and orchestra will rehearse the pieces to be featured on that week's program, deciding questions of tempo, tuning, dynamics, balance among the instrumental groups, and interpretation. This last factor is what distinguishes one performance of a piece of music from another: whether to slow down a little here, speed up a little there, pause for a moment between sections, allow the brass section to let rip in the last movement, and thousands of other tiny details. There is much more to a conductor's job than just "beating time!"

In addition, if the conductor is the permanent music director of a particular orchestra, he or she has to decide on the orchestra's program several years ahead of schedule, choose guest soloists to play or sing with the orchestra, and hire or fire orchestra members.

Attending a rehearsal is one of the most fascinating ways of learning about orchestral music. You hear the music several times; you see which ways the conductor decides to shape the music; and you learn what these changes can do to the overall effect. Most orchestra rehearsals are private, but many orchestras have taken to offering inexpensive seats for occasional "open rehearsals," to which the public is invited.

EMOTION IN MUSIC

Music involves communication and the expression of feelings. The composer communicates by means of the written notes, and the performer communicates by interpreting those written notes for an audience. Performers often get deeply involved with the feelings they are trying to convey. In 1773, a famous pianist was described as follows:

> After dinner he played until nearly 11:00 at night. During this time, he grew so animated and possessed, that he not only played but looked like one inspired. His eyes were fixed, his jaw fell, and drops of sweat fell from his face.

Nowadays, performers can also be carried away by the strengths of their feelings. Conductors grunt and moan, violinists often close their eyes and sway, rock guitarists thrash at their guitars. Sometimes these emotions can seem theatrical, but a great performer can seem genuinely in touch with the deepest impulses of the soul and convey these feelings directly to the audience.

Yo-Yo Ma is immersed in the music he's making.

Itzhak Perlman and Jean-Pierre Rampal concentrate on their playing.

PERFORMANCES

Concerts have an air of excitement about them that can never be matched by a record. Whether it is a rock concert, a jazz performance, a song recital, or a full-dress classical concert, there is something special about hearing people create "live" music. Music *needs* performance to bring it alive.

Many rock concerts are as much stage shows as they are musical performances. Makeup, clothes, dancing, and often elaborate stage machinery help create the special atmosphere. In part, too, that atmosphere is created by the sheer volume of sound, from the audience as well as from the band. In the past, people didn't realize how damaging these loud volumes could be. Many rock musicians are now wearing earplugs during performances. Unfortunately, some of them (and some of their audience) are wearing hearing aids instead, because their hearing has been permanently damaged by exposure to excessive volumes.

Orchestra concerts are more formal affairs. The musicians wear formal dress, and members of the audience are often quite dressed up too. The audience is expected to be quiet during the performance, and appreciation is usually expressed as polite applause. Occasionally, at the end of a concert, if the applause continues, the musicians may play an "encore." This was originally supposed to be a repeat of one of the pieces from the concert, but nowadays it generally takes the form of an additional short piece.

Opera performances are even more formal. Members of the audience often wear full evening dress. An opera tells a story, and that story is usually not sung in English. So if you go to an opera, it will help a great deal to read the story line first, so that you will know what's going on. Opera fans can be as passionate about their favorite singers as rock fans are. At the end of a performance, some opera stars are showered with roses or, more decorously, presented with bouquets of flowers.

Jazz concerts are usually much less formal. Often they are held in a club, where the audience may be eating and drinking during the performance, and where music is a *part* of the experience, rather than the *focus*

Sonny Rollins plays at the 1993 Newport Jazz Festival.

of the experience. Since the forties, though, jazz has also been presented in concert halls and festivals, where audiences are more likely to give the artists their undivided attention.

In many countries around the world, music is more integrated into the life of society, and the concept of a concert is quite alien. In many parts of Africa, music is used to mark important stages in an individual's life. In the Middle East, a shepherd will pass the time in the rocky hills by playing his flute. In China and Japan, music is the accompaniment for sacred ceremonies and stylized traditional theater. In some rural communities in Latin America, music and dance are reserved for special annual feasts and festivals. But in every culture of the world, in whatever format or environment it is performed, music is regarded as special magic.

Historical Periods and Individual Style

Above: Ancient Greek musical fragment.

Right: Cave painting from Lascaux, dating from about 12,000 years ago.

History is a strange affair. If we contemplate the present, we don't really consider it history. And yet after a while, of course, it turns into history. Similarly, people 100 years ago didn't think of themselves as living in a historical period. They were just living.

Time simply continues. It is an artificial construct to organize time into years and centuries and especially into historical periods. But it is useful. It gives us a sense of clarity and perspective to know the dates of Moses or Jesus or John F. Kennedy, or to be able to discuss "The Middle Ages" or "Romanticism."

Of course, people in the eleventh century didn't think they were living in the Middle Ages; they just went about their daily lives, as we do. And in the nineteenth century, nobody said, "Okay, time for Romanticism to begin!" It's only in retrospect that we can distinguish different historical periods because certain characteristics set them apart.

When we study painting, sculpture, architecture, literature, and music, these period labels are useful because we feel that the arts in some ways *reflect* the

historical period in which they are created. A painting of the Virgin Mary from the Middle Ages has very different aims and expresses very different things from a painting of a nude in 1830.

The history of Western music is much shorter than the history of art or literature. The great epics of Homer, the *Iliad* and the *Odyssey*, appear to date from nearly 3,000 years ago. And cave paintings have been discovered in France and Spain that are about 20,000 years old. We can imagine that people must have sung and played music that long ago, but unfortunately we have absolutely no trace of it. If music is not written down, it tends to disappear, for it is a *sounding* art.

Right: Musical notation from 11th-century Europe.

There are a few fragments of written music from ancient Greece and Rome, but not enough to be able to reconstruct whole pieces. The earliest manuscripts of whole pieces date from the Middle Ages, starting about the ninth century, though they contain music that seems to have been around for a few hundred years already. The main historical periods in music of the European tradition are given here, with approximate dates for each:

Middle Ages	*450* ~~400~~–1400
Renaissance	*1450* ~~1400~~–1600
Baroque	1600–1750
Classic	1750–~~1800~~ *1820*
Romantic	*1820* ~~1800–1900~~ *1885*
Twentieth Century	*1885* ~~1900~~–2000

The word **style** in music is used somewhat ambiguously. First, it is used to describe those characteristics that set apart the music of one historical period from another. We speak about the style of Baroque music or the style of Classic music. But the word is also used to describe the individual style of one particular composer. No composer works in a vacuum: His or her music will be recognizably of the period in which he or she lived. And yet, especially for a great composer, the music will also have some special features that set it apart from the music of other composers of the time. Mozart, for instance, used the language of mid- to late eighteenth-century Classicism; and yet there are things about the works of Mozart that mark them as unmistakably his. Throughout this book, we will try very carefully to balance these two aspects of style: the historical and the individual.

First, however, we need to consider the special kind of listening that true musical appreciation requires. Listening to music seems like a simple matter, but it really isn't. The kind of listening that brings out all the richness and complexity of great music is a real art. That is why the next chapter is entitled "The Art of Listening."

*L*et's hurry, because before you know it the Renaissance will be here and we'll all be painting!—Woody Allen in the "medieval" segment of *All You Ever Wanted to Know about Sex but Were Afraid to Ask.*

THE ART OF LISTENING

When all is said and done, the most important part of the musical experience is *listening*. There are many ways of listening to music. One of the most common is a passive kind of listening, the kind we do when music is playing as we are doing something else: eating at a restaurant, talking at a party, reading a book. There is even a kind of unconscious listening—on some movie soundtracks, for example, or in supermarkets, when the music creates a particular mood without our focusing on how or why.

The kind of listening this book encourages is a conscious, active, *committed* kind of listening, in which we really concentrate on everything that is happening, just as we would when reading a great work of literature. This kind of listening takes a great deal of concentration. It also offers very special rewards.

The previous chapter, on the fundamentals of music, presented some of the building blocks of the art of music; it also introduced you to some of the vocabulary that musicians and educated listeners use to talk and *think* about music. We shall use some of this vocabulary in what follows because it provides a clear means of describing what we hear. However, much of what we experience in listening to great music cannot be described in words, and this is the magic of music. It expresses things that cannot be expressed any other way.

The first and most important thing to know about listening to music is that you have to listen to a work several times to appreciate what is in it. Imagine reading a Shakespeare sonnet. The first time you read it, some of the meaning comes across, but a great deal is missed. Each successive reading provides you with greater insight into the thoughts and feelings expressed, the rhythm and sound of the words, the interplay of form and meaning. The words remain the same, but your understanding of them changes. The same is true of music. A great composition repays repeated hearings, and some of the greatest works reveal something new every time you listen.

This type of *active listening* is not easy at first. It takes practice. The secret of enjoying music, especially complicated and unfamiliar music, lies in your willingness to listen to a work more than once, and in the quality of your concentration as you listen.

In this chapter, you will be introduced to five very different pieces of music. Each one has something special about it, and the way we talk about each piece will differ according to the type of music under discussion. In each case, however, we shall try to capture something of the essence of the work: what makes it special, what sorts of feelings it expresses, and how it does so.

These questions call for a variety of approaches. We shall have to rely on some technical vocabulary; we shall give some historical background; we shall draw attention to significant events in the flow of the music. The clearest way to present much of the material is by means of a *Listening Guide*. This is a kind of road map. You can follow it as you go along, and it will point out significant features in the journey. The listening guides are timed so that you can check your perceptions against your watch or the timer on your CD player. Each listening guide will begin with some formal information about the piece—title, instrumentation, tempo, meter, and the like—to which you can refer at any time. Normally, a listening guide will then give some general observations about the piece, including historical and biographical context, and some of the important features to recognize as you listen.

In describing the music, we shall use technical vocabulary you have learned in the previous chapter. These words will be highlighted. So if you come across a word or a concept you have forgotten, just turn back a few pages to Chapter 2: Fundamentals.

SOUND, RHYTHM, AND TEXTURE

The first piece we shall listen to is a fanfare for brass instruments written by the French composer Paul Dukas, who lived from 1865 to 1935. As we listen to the fanfare, we will pay special attention to elements of sound, rhythm, and texture, but additional factors will also be considered. (**See Listening Guide on page 62.**)

Paul Dukas (1865–1935)
Fanfare from *La Péri*

Date of composition: 1912
Orchestration: 3 trumpets, 4 French
    horns, 3 trombones, tuba
Duration: 2:22

Student CD Collection: 1, track 26
Complete CD Collection: 1, track 26

*D*ukas composed ballets and operas as well as symphonic, choral, and chamber works. He is perhaps best known for his symphonic work *The Sorcerer's Apprentice*, which you can hear in the Mickey Mouse episode of Walt Disney's film *Fantasia*. The fanfare we will hear was written as the introduction to a ballet; it is scored for three trumpets, four horns, three trombones, and tuba.

The first thing you will notice is the **sound**. There is nothing quite like the sound of several brass instruments playing together. What is special, too, is the difference between the bright, extroverted sound when they play loudly and the slightly mysterious sound when they play softly. In this piece, the composer also takes advantage of the contrast between the high instruments (trumpets), the mid-range instruments (horns), and the low instruments (trombones and, especially, tuba).

The next is the **rhythm**. The rhythm is, for the most part, exciting and vigorous. In the middle of the piece, there is a more relaxed rhythm.

Other elements to notice are the contrasts of **dynamics**, the prevailing **texture**, and the overall **form**. The dynamics start out loud (*forte*, or ***f***); the middle section moves down to *mezzo forte* (medium loud, ***mf***) and then crescendos to *fortissimo* (very loud, ***ff***) for the final section. The prevailing texture is **homophonic** — mostly the instruments play in the same rhythm at the same time. Occasionally there is some **counterpoint**, with the horns taking one melody and the other instruments playing a contrasting line.

The overall form is a very common one in music: ABA form. There is an opening section, A, which presents the main ideas of the piece; then a contrasting middle section, B; then a return to the ideas of the opening. In this piece, the composer brings back a shortened, slightly varied version of the opening at the end. This, too, is a common technique. We usually indicate this with an A'; so the most accurate representation of the form of this piece is ABA'.

A 26 (26)	**0:00**	Full group, ***f*** (loud), homophony
	0:13	New idea, horns; counterpoint from other instruments
	0:23	Second idea moves to trumpets, rounded off by full group, cadence
	0:50	Back to horns, again rounded off by full group, cadence
B 27 (27)	**1:20**	Middle section, quieter (*mf*), more sustained, smoother
	1:40	Faster rhythm, crescendo to:
A' 28 (28)	**1:48**	Modified return of opening, ***ff***, leading to final cadence with trumpet flourish

MUSIC AND WORDS, KEY, DISSONANCE

The next work we shall study is a song by the Viennese composer Franz Schubert. Schubert lived in the early nineteenth century, when an artistic movement known as Romanticism was taking hold in Europe. This movement concentrated on feelings and the expression of subjective emotion. Schubert specialized in German songs; during his short lifetime, he composed no fewer than 600 of them.

The song we shall listen to is called *Gretchen am Spinnrade* (*Gretchen at the Spinning Wheel*). It describes the feelings of a young woman who sits by the window spinning as she laments the absence of her lover. The song is based on a poem by Schubert's contemporary, the German poet Johann Wolfgang von Goethe. But Schubert has not simply taken the poem and set it to music. He has added layers of meaning to what was al-

A portrait of the composer Franz Schubert, painted in 1825.

ready an expressive work of art. He has done this partly by slight changes and rearrangements of the text, but mostly by musical means: melodic, harmonic, and rhythmic. The voice is accompanied by a piano, which adds greatly to the available musical resources. The song is not just a musical version of the poem; it is a new work of art, intense and full of meaning. (**See Listening Guide below.**)

LISTENING GUIDE

Franz Schubert (1797–1828)
Song for voice and piano,
 Gretchen am Spinnrade
 (Gretchen at the Spinning Wheel)

Date of composition: 1814
Text by Johann Wolfgang von Goethe
Tempo: *Nicht zu geschwind* ("Not too fast")
Meter: ⁶⁄₈
Key: D minor
Duration: 3:37

Student CD Collection: 1, track 29
Complete CD Collection: 1, track 29

This song was written by Schubert when he was just 17 years old. It was only his second published work, though he had already composed more than 100 pieces. The text, in short four-line stanzas, contains the words of a young woman yearning for her lover. Schubert repeats some of the words of the last stanza for dramatic and emotional intensity.

The music for the voice is similar for each stanza and yet subtly different. Continuity is provided by the rippling piano part, which represents Gretchen's spinning wheel turning as she sings. A very effective **key change** can be heard at the beginning of the fourth stanza. Schubert changes from D minor (the key of the piece) to F Major (the relative major key) when Gretchen describes the manly physical characteristics of her lover. A magical moment occurs at the end of the fifth stanza on the words "Und ach, sein Kuss!" ("And oh, his kiss!"). For the only time in the whole song, the spinning wheel stops, as Gretchen is overcome by emotion, and two very **dissonant** chords are heard. Only reluctantly after that does the motion of the piano resume.

In the last stanza, the highest note in the song is heard on the word "vergehen" ("die"). This happens twice. And at the very end, Schubert unexpectedly repeats only the first two lines of the refrain, as the music gets very quiet, and the song ends, seemingly up in the air, with our feelings stirred up, not completely resolved.

29 (29) **0:00** | [S p i n n i n g   w h e e l   s t a r t s   u p — p i a n o]

REFRAIN

0:02 | *Meine Ruh' ist hin,*   My peace is gone,
| *Mein Herz ist schwer,*   My heart is heavy,
| *Ich finde sie nimmer*   And I will never again
| *Und nimmermehr.*   Find peace.

STANZA 1

0:22 | *Wo ich ihn nicht hab'*   Wherever he is not with me
| *Ist mir das Grab,*   Is my grave,
| *Die ganze Welt*   My whole world
| *Ist mir vergällt.*   Is turned to gall.

STANZA 2 | [voice gets higher]

0:36 | *Mein armer Kopf*   My poor head
| *Ist mir verrückt,*   Is crazed,
| *Mein armer Sinn*   My poor mind
| *Ist mir zerstückt.*   Is shattered.

REFRAIN | [voice resumes original range]

0:54 | *Meine Ruh' ist hin,*   My peace is gone,
| *Mein Herz ist schwer,*   My heart is heavy,
| *Ich finde, ich finde sie nimmer*   And I will never again
| *Und nimmermehr.*   Find peace.

STANZA 3

1:14 | *Nach ihm nur schau' ich*   I look out the window
| *Zum Fenster hinaus,*   Only to see him,
| *Nach ihm nur geh' ich*   I leave the house
| *Aus dem Haus.*   Only to seek him.

Form, Dynamics, Tempo, Meter, Cadences, and Key

Our next piece can help you appreciate how dynamic contrasts and changes of key combine to shape the form of a musical work. It is a movement from a symphony by Wolfgang Amadeus Mozart, one of the most brilliant composers of eighteenth-century Europe. The symphony was written in 1772, when Mozart was only 16 years old! (**See Listening Guide below.**)

Mozart as a teenager.

LISTENING GUIDE

Wolfgang Amadeus Mozart (1756–1791)
Minuet and Trio from Symphony No. 18
in F Major, K. 130

Date of composition: 1772
Orchestration: 2 flutes, 4 horns,
   Violins I and II (*this means the two
   groups of violins in the orchestra*),
   violas, cellos, double basses
Meter: $\frac{3}{4}$
Key: F Major
Duration: 2:05

Student CD Collection: 1, track 32
Complete CD Collection: 1, track 32

ballroom dance

The first thing to note about this piece is that it is a minuet; that is, it conforms to the spirit and form of a favorite eighteenth-century ballroom dance. Minuets were graceful and elegant dances, and the minuet style often appeared as one of the **movements** in symphonies (orchestral works) of the Classic era.

Minuets are always in triple **meter** and in moderate **tempo**. They also have a fixed repetition scheme. You will be able to hear the pattern of repeated sections in Mozart's minuet, and you can practice counting three **beats** per **measure** while you listen.

Every minuet is in **binary form**. There are always two sections, A and B, and each is repeated, making the pattern AABB. Usually the first minuet is followed immediately by a second minuet (called the trio), which is also in binary form (CCDD). Then the first minuet is played again, sometimes without repeats.

Therefore the overall pattern of the symphonic minuet is AABB/CCDD/AABB (or AABB/CCDD/AB). It is easy to see that across the binary scheme there is actually a *ternary* pattern, with a large-scale ABA form:

contrasting section

Minuet	Trio	Minuet
A	**B**	**A**
AABB	CCDD	AABB (or AB)

This pattern is quite clear in most minuet movements. There is a **cadence** (closing sound) at the end of each section, so you can hear the repeats. Each section is also usually quite short.

The challenge for the *composer* in writing a minuet and trio is to find the right balance between contrast and continuity. The trio is sandwiched between appearances of the minuet. The composer has to give the trio a little contrast, to make it interesting, and yet still make it sound as though it belongs in the sandwich.

The best way to keep track of all these things in the movement is to listen to it now with the timed listening guide. If you glance at the timer on your CD player or at your watch while you are listening, you'll be able to follow the structure more easily.

We have provided three listening guides for this same piece, each one of which focuses separately on a couple of different elements so that you can get them very clear in your mind. The first points out the **form** of the piece, with its repeated sections, the **instruments** that are used, and the **dynamics**. The second shows you how to notice **tempo** and **meter**. The third concentrates on **cadences** and **keys**.

Listening Guide 1

Listen for the repeated sections, the instruments, and the dynamics.

MINUET			
A 32 (32) **0:00**	First section of minuet. Begins with a graceful melody played softly by the strings; flutes and horns join in for loud ending.
A **0:09**	Repeat of the first section of the minuet.
B **0:18**	The second section of the minuet. Full orchestra, continuing loud.
B **0:27**	Repeat of the second section.

TRIO	
C 33 (33) **0:37**	First section of trio. Contrast of rhythm and texture, soft strings; answered by loud phrase including the flutes.
C **0:51**	Repeat.
D **1:04**	Second section of trio. Whole orchestra, loud; answered by a quiet phrase that gets louder at the end.
D **1:17**	Repeat.

MINUET	[The minuet is played again, exactly as before.]
A 34 (34) **1:29**	First section.
A **1:38**	Repeat.
B **1:47**	Second section.
B **1:56**	Repeat.

Now, before you go on to the second listening guide, listen to the piece with the first one a couple more times, just to make sure you've got it straight.

Listening Guide 2

This time we'll focus on tempo and meter.

If you tap your foot or your finger on each strong beat in this piece, you'll be tapping your foot about once every second. Try doing that for a while as you listen. Once you are secure about that, try tapping three times as fast. It's not hard. Just keep tapping along until you are coordinated with the music. With a little practice, you can get good at both kinds of tap and even switch between them in the middle of the piece.

Now all you need to know is that the slower tap is measures and the faster tap is beats. The *speed* of the beats is tempo, and the *number* of beats in a measure is meter. We have about three beats per second, which is medium-fast, and we have three beats per measure, which means that the piece is in triple meter.

MINUET		
A 32 (32) 0:00	First section. (Try tapping.)
A 0:09	Repeat.
B 0:18	Second section. (Keep going).
B 0:27	Repeat.

TRIO		
C 33 (33) 0:37	First section. (The *notes* are longer here, but the tempo and the meter stay exactly the same).
C 0:51	Repeat.
D 1:04	Second section.
D 1:17	Repeat.

MINUET		
	[whole minuet repeated]
A 34 (34) 1:29	First section.
A 1:38	Repeat.
B 1:47	Second section.
B 1:56	Repeat.

Notice as you do this tapping business that the tempo and the meter remain constant all the way through the movement from beginning to end. This is extremely common in many kinds of music.

Listening Guide 3

This listening guide focuses on key and cadences.

One of the hardest things for nonspecialists to listen for in music is key. Key is a bit like color in a painting. The color gives a painting a particular quality. Most paintings do not use only one color. Similarly, a piece of music does not usually stay in the same key the whole time, though most pieces end in the key in which they began. Often, they move to a different key in the middle and return to the original key at the end. Both the minuet and the trio in Mozart's movement do that. The minuet begins in F Major and moves to C Major (the **dominant** of F) in the middle before returning to F at the end. The trio begins and ends in C Major and moves to G Major (*its* dominant) in the middle.

The best way to hear this is to listen especially hard at the cadences where the musical sections end.

MINUET			
A 32 (32)	0:00	First section. Begins in F Major, ends in C Major.
A	0:09	Repeat.
B	0:18	Second section. Returns to F Major, ends in F.
B	0:27	Repeat.

TRIO			
C 33 (33)	0:37	First section. Begins in C Major, ends in G Major.
C	0:51	Repeat.
D	1:04	Second section. Starts in G Major, returns to C.
D	1:17	Repeat.

MINUET		[whole minuet repeated]
A 34 (34)	1:29	First section. F, moves to C.
A	1:38	Repeat.
B	1:47	Second section. Returns to F and ends in F.
B	1:56	Repeat.

Try this a few times, and notice how the keynote is different at the end of the different sections.

By now you should have listened to this little piece at least a dozen times, and you've probably learned a great deal about how classical music works. Don't worry if you didn't get it all. These things take time. You need to listen to a piece many, many times to appreciate all its subtleties. Take a break from this one. Then listen to it again a few more times tomorrow with the three listening guides. And a few more times the day after that…

BEATS, METER, FORM, AND TONE COLOR

The next piece we shall study is quite different, but it will give you some more practice in counting beats, listening for meter, and hearing form. Almost all music has form: It is form that gives music shape and coherence. This is no less true of jazz, pop, and rock than it is of classical music. **(See Listening Guide on page 70.)**

One of the basic patterns of both jazz and popular song is known as 32-bar AABA form. This form is based on a group of 32 measures, divided into four eight-measure phrases and organized in the format AABA:

A	eight-measure phrase
A	repeat
B	new eight-measure phrase
A	repeat of first phrase

Literally thousands of pop and rock songs, as well as countless jazz compositions, are based on this pattern. The 32-bar pattern can be repeated as many times as necessary, depending on the number of verses in the song.

Benny Harris (1919–1975)
Crazeology

Date of composition: 1947 (recorded 1994)
Performers: Daniel Ian Smith (tenor saxophone)
    and Mark Poniatowski (bass)
Tempo: Fast
Meter: $\frac{4}{4}$
Key: B-flat
Duration: 5:17

Student CD Collection: 1, track 35
Complete CD Collection: 1, track 35

The music we shall listen to is an instrumental composition written in 1947 by the jazz trumpeter Benny Harris, but presented here in a 1994 version by Daniel Ian Smith and Mark Poniatowski. With jazz, more than most other music, a new performance is really a new composition, because so much is left up to the performers. This is a piece in bebop style, played here by tenor saxophone and double bass. *Bebop*, or *bop*, is a term used to describe a style of jazz that grew up in the 1940s. It is characterized by small combos, a fast tempo, and lively, free improvisation. In this performance, we also have a fascinating example of contrast in tone colors. The tenor saxophone has a flexible, fluid, slightly unfocused sound and a wide range, whereas the double bass played pizzicato (plucked) is low, rhythmic, and dry.

The first thing to do is to listen to the piece and count beats. You may find yourself starting with a fairly slow pulse, but if you listen carefully you will end up tapping your foot or finger quite fast. Remember: The beat is the smallest unit of repeated pulse.

Next, try counting *measures* (each group of four beats). They go by quite fast—about one per second. You might get adventurous and tap beats with your finger and measures with your foot. You should end up with four beats per measure. This means that this piece is in $\frac{4}{4}$ meter, or four quarter notes to a measure.

After a while, you should be able to count measures quite comfortably. Some people find it easier just to count aloud and forget the tapping. Count in eight-measure units, four beats to a measure (*one*-two-three-four, *two*-two-three-four, *three*-two-three-four, etc.). After you get to *eight*, start again with *one*.

Once you are comfortable with the beat, you should be able to follow the structure of the entire piece with the timed listening guide. Each section of the AABA form, both A and B, has eight measures.

The other thing the listening guide will show is how the piece is divided into eight choruses, each in AABA form, as well as how the entire piece is framed by identical first and last choruses, played in unison (the two instruments playing the same notes). The inner choruses are improvised—that is, made up on the spot—using the original chord pattern as a foundation.

CHORUS 1

A 35 (35)	0:00	Unison; elaborate syncopated phrases
A	0:10	Unison; repeat
B	0:21	Unison; shorter leaping phrases; more key changes
A	0:31	Unison; repeat of A

CHORUS 2

A 36 (36)	0:40	Melody and accompaniment (song texture); swinging rhythm and
A	0:51	free-flowing improvisation
B	1:01	
A	1:11	

CHORUS 3

A	1:21	Continuation…
A	1:31	
B	1:41	
A	1:51	

CHORUS 4

A 37 (37)	2:02	Bass solo; improvisation with snatches of opening melody
A	2:11	
B	2:21	
A	2:32	

CHORUS 5

A 38 (38)	2:41	Continuation, with slides, chords, and twangs…
A	2:50	
B	3:00	
A	3:11	

CHORUS 6

A 39 (39)	3:19	Sax answered by bass ("call and response"), four measures each
A	3:28	
B	3:38	
A	3:47	

CHORUS 7

A	3:57	Continuation (progressively more elaborate)
A	4:07	
B	4:16	
A	4:26	

CHORUS 8

[repeat of Chorus 1]

A 40 (40)	4:36	Unison
A	4:46	Unison
B	4:56	Unison; shorter phrases
A	5:06	Unison

Texture, Chromaticism, and Word-Painting

The last composition we shall listen to in this chapter dates from the sixteenth century. This was an exciting period in European cultural history, a period generally known as the Renaissance. Painting, literature, architecture, and music flourished in an atmosphere of peace and prosperity. (See Listening Guide below.)

The country at the forefront of the Renaissance was Italy, and the piece we shall study was written by an Italian woman known as Maddalena Casulana. She was quite a prolific composer and wrote both sacred and secular music; she also sang and played the lute.

Italian Renaissance painting of a female lutenist.

Orazio Gentileschi (Florentine, 1563–1639), "The Lute Player," c. 1612/1620. Oil on canvas 1.435 × 1.288 (56 1/2 × 50 3/4). Photograph © 2000. Ailsa Mellon Bruce Fund. Board of Trustees, National Gallery of Art, Washington, D.C.

LISTENING GUIDE

Maddalena Casulana (c. 1540–c. 1590)
Madrigal, *Morte, te chiamo* (*Death, I Call on You*)

Date of composition: 1570
Small choir
Tempo: Slow
Meter: $\frac{4}{4}$
Duration: 1:38

Student CD Collection: 1, track 41
Complete CD Collection: 1, track 41

One of the favorite genres of Italian music in the Renaissance was the madrigal, a composition for a small number of voices, usually on some set theme such as the beauty of nature or the pain of love. Casulana's piece is among the latter; it explores one of the ideas common in love poetry: Since love causes so much sorrow, why not die? The madrigal is set in the form of a dialogue between the poet and Death.

All the musical voices take part in the dialogue, and the madrigal begins with one voice alone, gradually adding the others one at a time. The poet's perturbed state of mind is reflected in the shifting harmonies and **chromaticism**. The music begins contrapuntually; the central section ("You cannot? Why not?"/"Do it!" "I shall not!") is quite agitated, whereas the last line is set more calmly in **homophony**. There is a kind of musical in-joke in the setting of the Italian words "Sì fa!" and "Non fa!" for which the composer uses the notes B and F ("si" and "fa" in the do-re-mi system).

The excellent performance here is by a student group, the Butler University Madrigal Singers.

41 (41)	0:00	*Morte, te chiamo.*	Death, I call on you.
		[one voice enters at a time]	
		"Che voi? Ecco m'appreso."	"What do you want? Here I am."
		[all together; change of harmony]	
	0:21	*Prendi m'e fa che manchi il mio dolore.*	Take me, and make an end to my grief.
		[voices move lower]	
		"Non posso."	"I cannot."
	0:34	*Non poi? Perchè?*	You cannot? Why not?
		[quick dialogue]	
		"Perch'in te non regna il core."	"Because your heart no longer reigns in your body"
		[more homophonic]	
	0:43	*Sì fa!*	Do it!
		"Non fa!"	"I shall not!"
		[alternating duets]	
		Fatte'l' restituire,	Then give me back my heart,
		[cadence]	
	0:52	*Chè chi vita non ha non può morire.*	For a person who has no life cannot die.
		[smoother homophony]	
	1:03	[last four lines repeated]	

Maddalena Casulana has created a composition in which expression and form are in perfect balance. The shifting harmonies and chromaticism reflect the meaning of the words, while the textural changes and repetition create both variety and unity and provide closure at the end. She has communicated feelings to the listener that could not have been communicated in any other way than by the structural and expressive power of music.

The five pieces we have studied in this chapter—the Dukas brass fanfare, the Schubert song, the Mozart minuet, Benny Harris's *Crazeology*, and the Casulana madrigal—are all very different. They are different in date, style, type of musical composition, language, instrumentation, and emotional content. Their composers, too, are very diverse. Yet the works all have one thing in common: They all use the language of music to communicate. In addition, they all reveal greater and greater depth and provide more and more pleasure as a result of active and committed listening.

A Lesson in Music

Play the tune again: but this time
with more regard for the movement at the source of it
and less attention to time. Time falls
curiously in the course of it.

Play the tune again: not watching
your fingering, but forgetting, letting flow
the sound till it surrounds you. Do not count
or even think. Let go.

Play the tune again: but try to be
nobody, nothing, as though the pace
of the sound were your heart beating, as though
the music were your face.

Play the tune again. It should be easier
to think less every time of the notes, of the measure.
It is all an arrangement of silence. Be silent, and then
play it for your pleasure.

Play the tune again; and this time, when it ends,
do not ask me what I think. Feel what is happening
strangely in the room as the sound glooms over
you, me, everything.

Now,
play the tune again.

—ALASTAIR REID

THE MIDDLE
AGES: 400–1400

For the sake of convenience, historians today usually divide the Middle Ages into two periods: an early period, from 400 to 1000, and a later period, from 1000 to 1400. In the early Middle Ages, most of Europe was covered with forests. Most of the countries we know today did not exist. A small number of noble families controlled much of the land, and most of the rest of the population worked in near servitude. A highly organized system of power, called the feudal system, held everyone in its grip. The serfs owed their allegiance to the landowners, the landowners to the local lords, the lords to the king.

As time went on, the land was gradually cleared and small villages were established. By the later Middle Ages, some of these villages had grown into towns, and a more centralized economic system had evolved. The towns were magnets for trade and commerce and for many of the people from the countryside. The streets were filled with peddlers and beggars, children playing, and wagons rumbling through. Shopkeepers set up tables to display their wares and tried to attract the attention of wealthy merchants as they passed.

In Europe as a whole, some of the noble families became particularly powerful, and gradually the boundaries of many of the European countries were established more or less as we know them today. The rise of a middle class—represented by bankers and traders, merchants and shippers—helped to break down the feudal system.

For many people, life in the Middle Ages was not pleasant. They were serfs—virtually slaves—and spent their lives working in miserable conditions. Wars were frequent, and whenever one occurred, all the serfs controlled by the local lords were forced to take part. There were no vaccines or antibiotics, so most diseases and infections that we regard today as minor inconveniences were fatal.

But the image that people have nowadays of the Middle Ages as the "Dark Ages" is incomplete. The spread of Christianity brought with it the spread of learning. Literature and scholarship were kept alive by monks in their isolated monasteries all over Europe. Gradually, education became more widespread, and universities were established in towns all the way from England to Hungary. As well as being centers of trade and commerce, the new towns were centers of cultural exchange. The arts flourished: Music, painting, poetry, sculpture, and architecture all brought forth remarkable achievements.

Medieval Technology

We tend to think of technology as belonging exclusively to our modern world. And yet medieval technological innovations were at least as inventive and influential as those of today. ✦ In the sixth century, the invention of a heavy wheeled plow enabled millions of acres of Europe to be cultivated, leading to increased food production and a significant growth in population. In the eighth century, the development of safer oceangoing ships encouraged the Viking raids from Scandinavia and changed the racial, cultural, and linguistic makeup of Europe. The invention of the stirrup in the tenth century enabled soldiers to fight from horseback and led to the formation of the powerful class of knights. ✦ In the later Middle Ages, the rate of technological innovation increased dramatically. From the twelfth century came the spinning wheel, the wheelbarrow, and the mechanical clock; from the thirteenth century, compasses, windmills, and eyeglasses; from the fourteenth century, plate armor and gunpowder for war, paper and fixed-type printing for peace. ✦ Medieval cathedrals are monuments to the technological brilliance of medieval times. They are triumphs of engineering; many of them are still standing, tall and imposing, centuries after later buildings have collapsed.

In the Middle Ages, most artistic endeavor was inspired, encouraged, and paid for by the Church. And in each important town, the place where all the medieval arts were concentrated was the cathedral. Medieval cathedrals are marvels of architecture; their doorways and outer walls were graced by superb sculptures; paintings and tapestries adorned their inner walls; and every day the cathedrals were filled with music.

GENERAL CHARACTERISTICS OF MEDIEVAL MUSIC

A huge quantity of music has survived from the Middle Ages. The earliest written examples come from the eighth or ninth century, but much of the music dates from even earlier. This earlier music must have passed from generation to generation by means of an oral tradition. By the year 1000, an enormous amount of medieval music had been composed and was being performed throughout Europe.

Because one of the unifying characteristics of the Middle Ages is the influence of Christianity, it is not surprising that this is also one of the unifying characteristics of medieval music. Most of the surviving music from the medieval period is designed for use in the Christian (Roman Catholic) liturgy. This music is known as **liturgical music**. In addition, there are other pieces used for ceremonies that had a partly religious element, such as processions and coronations. Most of this music is vocal music. The melodies are very smooth and flowing.

Besides religious vocal music, there were probably many other kinds of music as well—folk songs, work songs, dances, and instrumental pieces. We know this from visual evidence in illustrated manuscripts and from poems and books written at the time. Very little of this music, however, has survived in notation. Those pieces we do have are fascinating, with irregular phrase lengths and lively rhythms.

By the later medieval period, two innovations were emerging. One was the rise of written **secular song** ("secular" means "nonreligious"), and the other was the rise of polyphony—music with more than one line or part sounding at a time. Both of these innovations had vital consequences for the entire later history of Western music. The idea that composers could devote their attention to topics outside religion—such as love, political loyalty, or dancing—broadened the scope of music immensely. And polyphony gave rise to harmony, which is one of the main features that distinguishes most Western music from that of other cultures.

Our survey of medieval music is therefore divided into two parts. Part One discusses liturgical chant, and Part Two looks at music of the later Middle Ages—secular song and polyphony.

THE MUSIC OF THE MIDDLE AGES

PART ONE: PLAINCHANT

The vocal music for church services from the early period of the Middle Ages is known as **plainchant**. Many people call it "Gregorian chant" after the famous Pope Gregory I, who lived from about 540 to 604. During the early Middle Ages, from about 400 to 1000, thousands of chants were composed. **(See Listening Guide on page 79.)**

Plainchant is monophonic—that is, it has only one line of music sounding at a time. Several people may be

A medieval depiction of Pope Gregory. The Holy Spirit (in the form of a dove) is whispering chants in his ear; Pope Gregory, in turn, is dictating the chants to a scribe.

Pope Gregory VII (1073–85), previously Hildebrand; c. 1021–Salerno 25.5.1085. Gregory VII and a scribe. Book illustration, contemporary. Leipzig, University Library. Photo: AKG London

There are also other ways in which plainchant is varied. It can be varied in the number of singers—with shifts between a solo singer, a small group of singers, and a whole choir. Or it can be varied according to the way the text is set. The text setting may be **syllabic**, with one note for every syllable of the text, or it may be **melismatic**, with a large number of notes sung to a single syllable; or it may be something in between. This middle style, with a small number of notes per syllable of the text, is known as **neumatic**. Most well-known songs today are syllabic ("On Top of Old Smoky," for example). But the Beatles' song "Not a Second Time" starts out quite neumatically. And you may be familiar with the carol "Angels We Have Heard on High," which includes a long melisma on the first syllable of the word "Gloria."

Finally, the most important element of variety in plainchant is given to it by the melodic system in which it is written. This is the system of **modes**. The modes are like colors used in painting. They give richness and variety to the music. There are four main modes in the medieval system, which end, respectively, on D, E, F, and G. All D-mode chants have a similar sound because of the characteristic series of intervals that occur in that mode. The difference in sound

singing that one line in unison, but still only one note is sounded at a time. It may seem very limiting to have music restricted to one line, but in fact plainchant is extremely varied. It ranges from very simple melodies, centered primarily on a single pitch, to highly elaborate ones, with long, flowing lines.

Syllabic.

On top of Old Smo - ky, all cov - er'd with snow,

Partly neumatic.

You know you made me cry— I see no use in won - drin'

why I cried for you.

Melismatic.

Glo - - - - - - - - - - - ri - a

Kyrie (plainchant)

Men's choir
Duration: 2:06

Student CD Collection: 1, track 42
Complete CD Collection: 1, track 42

*T*his is a chant from a medieval Roman Catholic Mass. It is one of many settings of this text. Although most of the Mass was in Latin, the words to the Kyrie are in Greek. There are three statements in the text: "Kyrie eleison—Christe eleison—Kyrie eleison" ("Lord, have mercy—Christ, have mercy—Lord, have mercy"). And each of these three statements is sung three times. There is great symbolism in this repetition scheme: the number three represented the Trinity, and three times three was considered absolute perfection.

Corresponding to the three statements of the text, there are three phrases of music. The whole piece begins and ends on G, so it is in the G mode, Mixolydian. As in painting, however, a composition may have a mixture of colors, and there are hints of the Phrygian mode in the first phrase, which ends on E. The shape of the melody is very carefully designed. The first phrase is the shortest and moves in waves. The second phrase starts high, and the motion is mostly descending. The last phrase is in the form of an arch and starts and ends on the same note (G). At the top of the arch, the music reaches up to the highest note in the whole piece. The last time the third statement of the text is sung, the music changes slightly, with the addition of three notes to the beginning of the phrase.

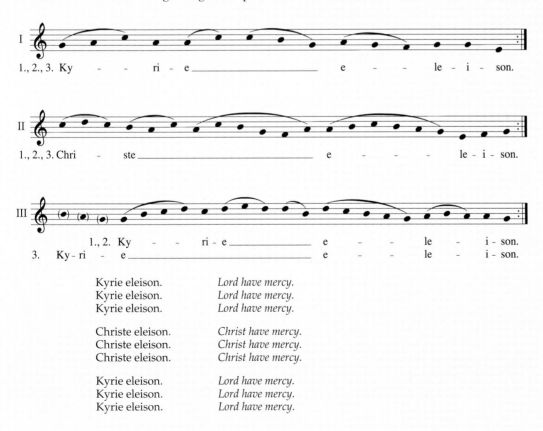

Kyrie eleison.   *Lord have mercy.*
Kyrie eleison.   *Lord have mercy.*
Kyrie eleison.   *Lord have mercy.*

Christe eleison.   *Christ have mercy.*
Christe eleison.   *Christ have mercy.*
Christe eleison.   *Christ have mercy.*

Kyrie eleison.   *Lord have mercy.*
Kyrie eleison.   *Lord have mercy.*
Kyrie eleison.   *Lord have mercy.*

A medieval manuscript from the fifteenth century, showing the music for a Kyrie, with an illumination of monks and a choirboy singing.

folk songs are Dorian. You can hear the special evocative quality of the Dorian mode in a song such as "Scarborough Fair," better known by the words of its refrain, "Parsley, sage, rosemary, and thyme."

The pattern of intervals in E-mode pieces is different. So chants composed in that mode sound different from those composed in the D mode. And the same is true for F-mode and G-mode pieces, because of their characteristic pattern of intervals.

The chart on the next page gives names and the patterns of these four main medieval modes. You will notice that the modes are given with their notes descending, whereas the scales we have looked at were shown in ascending form. This is because most medieval melodies descend to their keynote, giving the music a feeling of relaxation at the end, whereas many later melodies end with a more intense rise to the top of the scale.

This system of modes is very important. It is the basis upon which the music of the Middle Ages is built, and it is this system that makes the world of medieval plainchant so colorful, so rich, and so appealing.

Why does plainchant sound the way it does, with its serene, otherworldly character? The first reason has to do with rhythm. The music flows along without a clearly defined rhythm and with no regular pattern of strong or weak beats. The second reason for the sound of plainchant is the nature of the modes. The modes are very subtle. The colors they impart to the music are not stark or strong: they are gentle pastels. They lack the intense drive of modern scales or keys. Finally, because there is only one musical line, the listener can concentrate entirely on the shape and direction of the melody. Indeed, plainchant is the greatest repository of pure melody in the whole history of Western music and has been called "one of the great treasures of Western civilization."

between the modes is like the difference in sound between major and minor scales. The D mode (usually called the Dorian), from top to bottom, has a whole step, a half step, three whole steps, a half step, and a whole step. None of the other modes has exactly that pattern, so no other mode has the same sound. Many

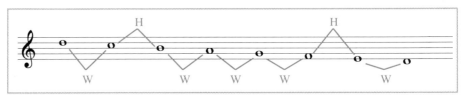

The Dorian mode.

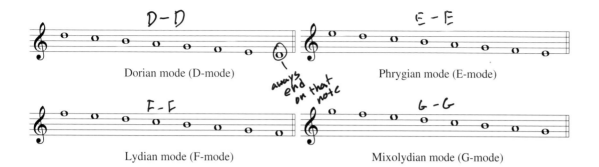

Dorian mode (D-mode)

always end on that note

Phrygian mode (E-mode)

Lydian mode (F-mode)

Mixolydian mode (G-mode)

PART TWO: SECULAR SONG AND POLYPHONY

SECULAR SONG

The rise of secular song can be dated to the twelfth century, when the troubadours were active. Troubadours were poet-musicians who composed songs for performance in the many small aristocratic courts of southern France. (In northern France, such musicians were called *trouvères*.) Troubadours and trouvères wrote their own poetry and music, and the subjects they favored were love, duty, friendship, ceremony, and poetry itself. The primary topic was love. The poems address an idealized vision of a woman, who is remote and usually unattainable. (Most of the troubadours were men.) The lover pines away and pleads for some sign of favor, however slight. There are also a few songs by women troubadours about men, written in the same manner.

This topic is sometimes called "courtly love," because it derived from a conventional code of manners that flourished in the aristocratic courts of the Middle Ages. But it had enormous influence on the whole history of Western love poetry. Eight centuries of love songs, up to and including those of the twentieth century, have been influenced by the conventions and vocabulary of courtly love.

As an example of troubadour music, we shall listen to a song, *A chantar*, by Beatriz de Dia. **(See Listening Guide on page 82.)**

POLYPHONY

It took some time before medieval composers began to be interested in polyphony. The plainchant and secular

Performance of Medieval Music

One of the fascinating things about medieval music is the set of questions it poses for performers today. Plainchant is difficult enough to re-create. But at least we know the context in which it should be sung (a religious service); we know who should be singing (a small choir); and we know that it should usually be sung unaccompanied (that is, without instruments). With secular song, many questions are unresolved. The original manuscripts of the music tell us very little about how to perform it. They provide the words and the notes, but that is all. ◆ There is still a great deal of controversy among modern scholars and performers about the question of accompaniment for medieval secular songs. Some people feel that the songs should be performed as they appear in the manuscripts—that is, with no accompaniment at all. Others point to the elaborate descriptions and pictures of instruments in medieval manuscripts and suggest that performers must have improvised instrumental accompaniments for so sophisticated a repertory.

Beatriz de Dia (late twelfth century)
Song, *A chantar*

Date of composition: c. 1175
Duration: 5:21

Student CD Collection: 1, track 43
Complete CD Collection: 1, track 43

Most of the troubadours of the Middle Ages were men, but a few women troubadours are known. Contrary to popular belief, women in the early Middle Ages enjoyed considerable freedom and political equality. Many of them in all social classes were involved in music,
either as patrons, as composers, or as performers. The powerful and charismatic Eleanor of
Aquitaine was a great patron of the arts.

Beatriz de Dia, often known as the Comtessa de Dia (Countess of Dia), lived in the late
twelfth century. Her medieval biography says that she was the wife of the Count of Poitiers and
the lover of a well-known nobleman, who was himself a troubadour. It also states that she was
the composer of "many good songs." Only a small number of her poems survive, and only this
one has music.

Like almost all the secular songs of the Middle Ages, this one is **strophic**: The same music is repeated for all the stanzas of the poem. The language is that of the south of France; it is
known as Occitan, sometimes called Provençal. The poem has five stanzas and a brief two-line
ending known as a *tornada*.

Beatriz de Dia addresses her lover, who has scorned her, and expresses her pain at his
treating her so badly. It is difficult to gauge the depth of true feeling in this song, because the
topic of unrequited love was a highly conventional one in troubadour poetry. Yet beneath the
convention, the blending of words and music produces a song of great beauty.

Each line of poetry has its own musical phrase. The first phrase ends with an ornamented
half cadence (a cadence that leaves more to be said) on E; the second with a full cadence on D.
These two musical phrases are repeated for the third and fourth lines of the poetry. The next
two lines are joined and are set higher in the range; they end with the E cadence. The last line,
on the other hand, uses the whole musical phrase of lines 2 and 4 with its D ending. The pattern is summarized here:

Line 1	Phrase A
Line 2	Phrase B
Line 3	Phrase A
Line 4	Phrase B
Lines 5 and 6	New higher phrase, with A ending
Line 7	Phrase B

Each stanza uses the same arrangement. This pattern gives a rounded feeling to the melody as a whole and a sense of increased intensity before the close. We shall listen to two stanzas.

In this performance, the singer is accompanied by a **vielle** (a bowed instrument—you can see one in the medallion at the top of this listening guide) and a low wooden flute, which provide an introduction and a close to the song as well as some links between stanzas. They are joined for the *tornada* by lute and drum.

43 (43)　**0:00**　| 　[v i e l l e p r e l u d e]

S T A N Z A   1

　　　　　　[v i e l l e a c c o m p a n i m e n t]

0:25　　*A chantar m'er de so q'ieu no voldria,*　I must sing, whether I want to or not.
　　　　　Tant me rancur de lui cui sui amia,　I feel so much pain from him whose
　　　　　　　　　　　　　　　　　　　　　friend I am,
　　　　　Car eu l'am mais que nuilla ren que sia;　For I love him more than anything.
　　　　　Vas lui nom val merces ni cortesia,　But neither grace nor courtesy has any
　　　　　　　　　　　　　　　　　　　　　effect on him,
　　　　　Ni ma beltatz, ni mos pretz, ni mos sens.　Nor my beauty, my decency, or my
　　　　　　　　　　　　　　　　　　　　　intelligence.
　　　　　C'atressim sui enganad'e trahia　I am despised and betrayed,
　　　　　Cum degr'esser, s'ieu fos desavinens.　As though I were worthless.

1:50　　[f l u t e i n t e r l u d e]

S T A N Z A   5

　　　　　　[v i e l l e a c c o m p a n i m e n t]

3:01　　*Valer mi deu mos pretz e mos paratges,*　My decency and my ancestry have
　　　　　　　　　　　　　　　　　　　　　their value,
　　　　　E ma beutatz e plus mos fis coratges,　As do my beauty and the depth of
　　　　　　　　　　　　　　　　　　　　　my heart.
　　　　　Per q'ieu vos mand lai on es　So I send to your noble home
　　　　　　vostr'estatges
　　　　　Esta chansson que me sia messatges:　This song: let it be my messenger!
　　　　　E voill saber, lo mieus bels amics gens,　And I want to know, my fair friend,
　　　　　Per que vos m'etz tant fers ni tant　Why you are so savage and cruel
　　　　　　salvatges,　　　　　　　　　　to me.
　　　　　Non sal si s'es orguoills o mals talens.　I don't know: is it pride or ill will?

T O R N A D A

　　　　　　[l u t e a n d d r u m j o i n i n s o f t l y]

4:18　　*Mas aitan plus vuoill li digas,*　But I want even more for you to tell
　　　　　　messatges,　　　　　　　　him, messenger,
　　　　　Q'en trop d'orguoill ant gran dan　That pride has been the downfall of
　　　　　　maintas gens.　　　　　　　many people!

5:01　　[f l o r i d e n d i n g]

Right: The original medieval manuscript of *Viderunt Omnes*.

Some medieval song manuscripts have very detailed pictures of musical instruments.

Above: We see a lute and a *rebec* (a high bowed instrument).

Below: Two wind instruments with uneven pipes.

song repertories were entirely monophonic, and the subtleties of melodic construction and the text/music relationship in these genres satisfied the musical aims of medieval composers for centuries. Only gradually did the idea of *combining* different notes in music gain popularity in the Middle Ages.

The idea of composing music with two or more independent musical lines first arose in the tenth century and really took hold about 1200, when there was a sudden explosion of polyphonic liturgical composition. The polyphony of this time is striking in its power and grandeur. Compositions of two, three, and even four voices were written to celebrate the major feasts of the church year. At a time when the cycle of life revolved around the church calendar, feasts such as Christmas and Easter must have been spectacular and vivid occasions. People spent days or even weeks preparing for the special celebrations that surrounded the feast days themselves. In the dress that was worn, in the meals that were prepared, in the brief escape from the constant burden of work, these days must have had special significance for the majority of medieval society. It is not surprising, therefore, that such days were marked by very special music.

Paris was the place where the most significant amount of polyphony was composed in the twelfth and thirteenth centuries. Paris was one of the primary centers of the late medieval world. The kings of France had their palaces in Paris. The first university in the Middle Ages was established in Paris, and Paris was a hub of commercial activity for the whole of Europe.

In the center of Paris, on an island in the middle of the river Seine, stood a huge cathedral, newly built about 1200. It was a magnificent sight. Indeed, it still is. Visitors to Paris still visit Notre Dame Cathedral, for it remains one of the great architectural marvels of Europe.

To match the splendor and beauty of this cathedral, and to celebrate the main feasts of the church year, two composers created the first great collection of polyphony in the history of Western music. Their names were Leonius and Perotinus, and we know little about either of them. They probably were officials at the cathedral in some capacity. Leonius was the older of the two and started the collection. Perotinus added to it and extended the range and scope of the music.

The collection of compositions by these two men is known as the *Magnus Liber Organi* (*Great Book of Polyphony*). This book contains a series of elaborate polyphonic compositions for the main feasts of the church year. These compositions are based directly on the ancient plainchants for those feasts. The music may contain several independent musical lines, but one of them is always the original chant melody. Among the most famous of the pieces written for the Cathedral of Notre Dame is the four-voice *Viderunt Om-*

nes by Perotinus, based on the plainchant of the same name. This chant is sung right in the middle of the Mass on Christmas. **(See Listening Guide on page 86.)**

Perotinus set some portions of the chant polyphonically for solo singers. The rest of the chant, sung by the choir, stays monophonic. So the piece has an alternation of performing forces (soloists–choir), but it also has an alternation of polyphonic and monophonic textures.

But there is even more to it than that. First, the textural contrast is reinforced by a rhythmic contrast. The monophonic (choir) sections are sung in the traditional way, in a free, smooth, essentially rhythmless style, whereas the polyphonic (soloist) sections are marked

The magnificent Cathedral of Notre Dame in Paris.

Perotinus (c.1170–c.1236)
Viderunt Omnes **(four-voice polyphony
for the Cathedral of Notre Dame)**

Date of composition: 1199
Solo singers and choir
Duration: 4:42

Student CD Collection: 1, track 44
Complete CD Collection: 1, track 44

The listening guide brings together all the elements of the preceding discussion. The text is given, with indications specifying whether it is sung in chant or in polyphony. In the polyphonic section, the contrast between sustained-tone and rhythmic accompaniment is marked. Note also the intricate intertwining of the three upper voices over the two different styles of the lower voice. The rich harmonies, the unrelenting rhythmic drive, and the sheer scope of the piece show how magnificent and awe-inspiring a piece of music from 800 years ago can be. (Here only a portion of the overall work is given; the entire piece lasts for nearly 12 minutes.)

POLYPHONY

44 (44)	**0:00**	(soloists)	*Vi-* (sustained-tone)	[rhythmic upper voices throughout]
	0:57	(soloists)	*de-* (sustained-tone)	
	1:25	(soloists)	*runt* (sustained-tone)	[dissonant opening; brief cadence for end of word]
	2:29	(soloists)	*om-* (rhythmic/sustained-tone)	
	3:40	(soloists)	*nes* (sustained-tone)	[strong dissonance just before cadence]

[cadence]

MONOPHONY

45 (45)	**3:46**	(choir)	*fines terrae salutare Dei nostri. Jubilate Deo omnis terra.*	[smooth plainchant]

[cadence]

Viderunt omnes fines terrae salutare Dei nostri. Jubilate Deo omnis terra.	All the ends of the earth have seen the salvation of our God. Praise God all the earth.

by very clear-cut rhythms. In addition, there are contrasts within the polyphonic sections themselves. Parts of these sections have extremely long, sustained notes underpinning them; other parts have faster notes in the lower voice, which move almost as quickly as those in the upper voices.

Below is a sample of this kind of polyphony, showing some of these elements: a bottom voice starting with a sustained tone but turning more rhythmic, a somewhat more complex middle voice, and an extremely elaborate upper voice.

The remarkable thing about this music is the fact that, despite its variety and density, it retains all of the original plainchant embedded in it. All the words are still there, and all the original notes are retained in the lower voice. The composition is a complex and sophisticated edifice, but it is built entirely on the foundation of an ancient structure. This is entirely appropriate, for the music was designed for a cathedral that was one of the glories of the new Gothic age but was erected on the site of a Paris church many centuries old.

LATE MEDIEVAL POLYPHONIC SONG

By the 1300s, the two main developments of the later Middle Ages had become fused: Secular songs were set to polyphony—often in delicate settings of great sophistication. France and Italy were the two areas at the forefront of the art of polyphonic song at that time. In France, the master composer was Guillaume de Machaut (c. 1300–1377).

Machaut is one of the first composers about whom we know quite a few biographical details. He was educated at Rheims, an important town in north-eastern France. Soon he became quite well known as an administrator, a poet, and a composer. He held positions at the courts of some of the most prominent members of the French ruling aristocracy, including Charles, Duke of Normandy, who later became King Charles V of France. Machaut also was an administrator of the cathedral at Rheims. He died in his late seventies after a busy and productive life.

A great deal of Machaut's work survives. He wrote many long poems and was probably the author of the poems for his own songs. He wrote some sacred music, but most of Machaut's pieces are polyphonic secular songs.

Machaut's musical style is both subtle and intense. The music is full of little rhythmic and melodic motives that tie the composition together and form beautiful melodies. The rhythm is very fluid and depends upon a constant interplay between duple and triple meters. Machaut often uses chromatic notes (unexpected sharps and flats) to make the sound more colorful. **(See Listening Guide on page 88.)**

In Italy, the musical style was rather different from that in France. Italian music tended to concentrate on florid vocal display. It was more lively, and often more down-to-earth. A favorite kind of Italian song was known as the **caccia**. The name is a play on words. *Caccia* means "hunt," and the songs are often about outdoor hunting scenes. But *caccia* also means a musical *round*, in which the voices sing the same music but begin at different times. This gives the impression of a

> **M**usic is a science that would have us laugh and sing and dance.
> —**Guillaume de Machaut**

Di ———   xit   Do-   mi-   nus

Late twelfth-century polyphony in the style of Perotinus.

Guillaume de Machaut (c. 1300–1377)
Secular song (rondeau)
Doulz Viaire Gracieus

Date of composition: Mid-fourteenth
  century
Voice, lute, and recorder
Duration: 2:00

Student CD Collection: 1, track 46
Complete CD Collection: 1, track 46

This short piece is a good example of Machaut's style. It is a setting of a poem that has a two-line refrain (printed in italics). The refrain comes at the beginning and the end, and its first line comes in the middle of the poem too. This kind of poem is known as a **rondeau**.

The music sounds very simple but is actually quite complex. There are only two sections of music, which alternate in setting each line of the poetry. The first section is five measures long, the second section seven. This contrasts with later music, where the number of measures in each phrase or section tends to be much more regular. A short descending passage on the lute joins the sections together.

There are other aspects of this music that seem unusual to a listener of today. Although the prevailing **meter** of the piece is triple, there are several places where the music moves in duple meter. **Bar lines** were not used in medieval music (although we print them today for the sake of clarity), so the meter could be much more flexible. Also, many of the notes are **chromatic**: even the opening chord contains two sharps. And although the first section ends on G, which leads you to expect that the whole piece will end on G, the final cadence is on B♭.

The voice is accompanied by two instruments: a recorder below the voice and a **lute** above. (A lute is a plucked instrument similar to a guitar.) Although the accompanying parts are quite independent, all three lines together create interesting harmonies, and there is a brief echo among them at the beginning of the B section.

This kind of carefully constructed polyphony, as well as the overall gentle beauty of the piece, are typical of Machaut's music and of fourteenth-century French music in general.

46 (46)	0:00	*Doulz viaire gracieus,*	*Sweet, gracious countenance,*
	0:12	*De fin cuer vous ay servy.*	*I have served you with a faithful heart.*
	0:30	Weillies moy estre piteus,	Take pity on me,
	0:42	*Doulz viaire gracieus;*	*Sweet, gracious countenance;*
	0:55	Se je sui un po honteus,	If I am a little shy,
	1:07	Ne me mettes en oubli.	Do not forget me.
	1:25	*Doulz viaire gracieus,*	*Sweet, gracious countenance,*
	1:38	*De fin cuer vous ay servy.*	*I have served you with a faithful heart.*

The medieval cathedral of Chartres in France.

melody chasing itself. Italian caccias are great fun. They usually have two voices singing the text, with an accompanying instrumental third part. The scenes are realistic and lively, and the voices usually indulge in some kind of dramatic dialogue, often with cries and shouts.

THE END OF THE MIDDLE AGES

At the end of the fourteenth century, the two distinct musical styles of France and Italy began to merge. There were many reasons for this. There was more commerce between the two areas, and political alliances were formed. In some of the Italian city-states,

French was spoken at court, and French was also used for official documents and scholarly writings. But the most important reason for the merging of the two musical styles was the split in the papacy starting in 1378.

For centuries, the popes had lived in Rome. But popes were not always Italian by birth, any more than they are today. And when a Frenchman was elected pope at the beginning of the fourteenth century, he decided to set up his papal residence in Avignon in the south of France. Succeeding popes continued to live in the palace at Avignon, but political factions arose that insisted upon the election of an Italian pope. There were riots in Rome, and some of the cardinals engineered the election of a rival pope. From 1378 to 1417

The Medieval Audience

At the beginning of this book, we defined music as sounds organized for people to hear. Without an audience, music has no meaning. And throughout the ages, music has changed as the audiences for it have changed. ¶ In the Middle Ages, there were two main kinds of audience for serious music: human and divine. For plainchant and the elaborate polyphony woven around it, the clearly intended audience was God. Much sacred music was sung in monasteries, where there was no congregation at all. The monks were singing because it was their primary duty to sing to God. ¶ The other main audience for the music that has survived from so many centuries ago was made up of a small aristocratic elite. These were the queens and kings, dukes and duchesses, and lords and ladies of the numerous small courts scattered across Europe, who listened to music as a pastime. The secular songs of the Middle Ages were designed for their ears and reflected their interests: courtly love, noble exploits, and hunting expeditions. ¶ For the remaining 90 percent of the population, we can only guess about their musical interests and experiences. The work songs, nursery rhymes, tavern music, and lullabies of the Middle Ages have disappeared from our collective memory along with the people who enjoyed them.

The palace of the Popes in Avignon, France.

(a period known as the Great Schism), there were two popes ruling simultaneously, one in Rome and the other in Avignon.

The papal court at Avignon was notoriously corrupt and immensely wealthy. A great deal of money was spent on bribes, banquets, clothes, furniture, paintings—and music. Many composers were supported by the court, and both French and Italian composers lived there and were able to learn from one another.

The result of this intermingling of composers in a place of such influence and prestige was a fusing of the French and Italian styles in music. This affected both sacred and secular music. The new international style was the basis for a new period of musical history—a period known as the Renaissance.

STYLE SUMMARY

Music in the Middle Ages was extremely varied. We have to remember that we are dealing with nearly a thousand years of history—from the year 400 to about 1400. Most of the music that survives from this period is plainchant—melodies ranging from very simple to very complex, but all of them designed to be sung by a group in unison, with no harmony and no accompaniment. This music is based on the modes, which are different from our modern scales and which give the melodies a sound that is fascinating and slightly exotic, as though we were listening in on another world.

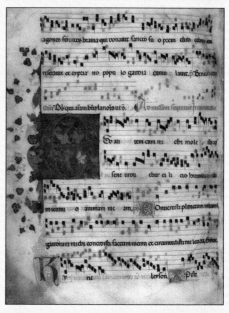

A manuscript of plainchant from the Middle Ages.

From about 1100, a culture arose of secular songs, mostly love songs. These songs, which are strophic, express an idealized vision of the beloved. The songs and the poems on which they are based started the whole tradition of writing and singing about love, a tradition that has carried through to Romantic poetry and even to many of the pop songs of today.

We have many pictures and descriptions of instruments from the Middle Ages, but we do not know exactly how and when they were used. We can only guess that instrumental music must have been very common and that instruments often must have been played to accompany vocal music.

In the last part of the Middle Ages, polyphony was developed, and polyphonic settings were made both of plainchant melodies and of secular songs. Some of the polyphonic chant settings are very grand, impressive works, in three or four voices, with detailed, complex upper parts and a lower part of almost architectural strength. The polyphonic secular songs, on the other hand, are fine, sophisticated pieces, based on subtle poetry and displaying delicate, interweaving musical lines.

FUNDAMENTALS OF MEDIEVAL MUSIC

✦ The music is based on modes, not modern scales

✦ Plainchant is sung in unison, with neither harmony nor accompaniment

✦ Stylized courtly love songs became popular

✦ Instruments were many and varied

✦ Polyphony was invented

THE RENAISSANCE:
1400–1600

LIFE AND TIMES IN THE RENAISSANCE

The dates historians assign to the European Renaissance vary greatly, depending on whether art, music, or literature is under discussion. For music, the Renaissance is generally regarded as beginning about 1400 and ending at 1600.

"Renaissance" means "rebirth." The term is used to indicate that during this period there was a revival of interest in the humanistic values of classical Greece and Rome. In fact, people in the Renaissance deliberately modeled themselves after the ancient Greeks and Romans—in their feeling of individual and collective responsibility, in their embracing of education, and, most important, in their sense of the enduring human value in the arts. As a result, the Renaissance was a time of remarkable accomplishments.

There were three notable changes from the climate of the Middle Ages. First, there was more focus on individual achievements. Second, people began to show more interest in the real world than in spirituality. And third, the growing ease of travel and the spread of printed books led to a widespread mingling of cultures.

These three facets of life in the Renaissance are reflected in the artistic accomplishments of the time. Artists and sculptors concentrated on the dignity of the individual human figure: Portraits of rulers exude self-confidence and splendor. And painters developed the techniques of perspective, three-dimensional representation, and working with oils, with which the most detailed effects of light and shade could be rendered naturally. The works of Renaissance painters such as Michelangelo and Leonardo da Vinci are still famous nearly 500 years later.

Renaissance architects throughout Europe used buildings from antiquity as models for their new buildings. Florence Cathedral, St. Peter's Basilica in Rome, Fontainebleau castle in France, and the palace of Charles V in Spain show how the Renaissance style became an international style. Columns and rounded roofs replaced the soaring, spiky look of medieval architecture.

St. Peter's Basilica in Rome.

Leonardo da Vinci in a self-portrait.

Courtesy of the Library of Congress

Literary masters of the age included Petrarch of Italy, Cervantes of Spain, Rabelais of France, and Shakespeare of England. In the works of these writers, a new emphasis on self-expression and on the worth of the individual is clearly felt.

The world of science, largely ignored by Europe in the Middle Ages, became a major focus of the European Renaissance. Inventions and scientific discoveries were impressive in quantity and scope. The most important of these was the invention, in 1450, of printing—a development as revolutionary in its time as the computer has been in ours. The rapid increase in the number of available books had an incalculable effect on education, as well as on the fame of individuals, the spread of scientific knowledge, and the growth of internationalism. Toward the end of the Renaissance, the invention of the telescope and the microscope changed forever the way people looked at the world.

People began to feel more in control of their own destinies than they had in the Middle Ages. Scholars pursued both literary and scientific studies. Many of the great figures of the Renaissance were highly educated and knowledgeable in all known fields—hence our modern phrase "Renaissance man (or woman)." The perfect example of the true Renaissance man was Leonardo da Vinci, who was a brilliant painter, sculptor, musician, engineer, and scientist.

New branches of Christianity were founded in this era. The Protestant movement known as the Reformation was begun by the German theologian Martin Luther, and the Anglican movement was founded when King Henry VIII of England refused to accept the supremacy of the pope in Rome.

In many ways, the Renaissance must have been an exciting time in which to live. New lands were discovered and explored, including much of the Far East, the coast of Africa, and North and South America. By the sixteenth century, there was enormous economic and commercial expansion throughout Europe, and a larger middle class was formed. Members of the middle class were also interested in learning and culture, and the growth of education and the new availability of books helped them achieve their goals.

Music played an important role in Renaissance society. Most educated people could either play an instrument or sing written music. People were not considered socially accomplished if they did not have some musical training. And an evening's entertainment usually included some kind of musical performance.

Music printing, which became widespread in the sixteenth century, greatly increased the amount of available music. Amateur music-making became more and more common.

The professional musicians included composers and performers. Many more individual musicians found jobs at court, and many towns supported musicians as public employees. Although very few women achieved careers as composers, some women began to be included in the ranks of performing musicians, and some of them were highly paid and became internationally known.

Sixteenth-century painting showing full modeling of the face and figure and detailed texture of the clothing.

Maria de Medici. Painting, Renaissance, 16th c. Bronzino, Agnolo (Agniolo di Cosimo) (1503–1572). Oil on poplar wood. Kunsthistorisches Museum, Gemaeldegalerie, Vienna, Austria. Art Resource.

Next to the Word of God, music deserves the highest praise.
—Martin Luther

A Renaissance painting reveling in the new-found technique of perspective.

As with the other cultural achievements of the Renaissance, music reached great heights. Some of the most beautiful compositions in the history of Western music were composed during this period, and the greatest musical works of the Renaissance match the finest works of literature, painting, and architecture in their depth and beauty.

GENERAL CHARACTERISTICS OF RENAISSANCE MUSIC

Renaissance music is distinguished from late medieval music in one important way: The overall sound is much smoother and more homogeneous, with less contrast. This change in sound is the result of a change in compositional technique. The highly contrasting and independent lines of late medieval polyphony were replaced by a new polyphonic style based on imitation.

Imitation is a form of polyphony in which all the musical lines present the same musical phrase one after the other. As each line enters, the previous ones continue, so there is a constant sense of overlapping. This technique can be much more varied than it sounds. The strictest kind of imitation is a round, in which all the voices sing exactly the same thing in turn. But often, imitation is much freer than that. In free imitation, only the first few notes of a melodic phrase are sung by each entering voice; the voices then continue freely.

Even though the *style* of music in the Renaissance was very different from that in the Middle Ages, the predominant types of composition were the same. They were these: (1) liturgical music (music for church services, usually Mass settings), (2) motets (settings of Latin texts that are sacred but not liturgical), and (3) secular songs.

Strict imitation (round).

Free imitation.

MUSIC IN THE EARLY RENAISSANCE

The early Renaissance saw a merging of the individual musical characteristics of the different European countries into an international style. Composers throughout Europe began to write similar music—polyphonic, often imitative, and concentrated primarily in the three main types: Mass, motet, and secular song. The foremost composers of the time were John Dunstable of England and Guillaume DuFay of France. Their careers show how the musical style of the Renaissance crossed national boundaries. Dunstable was born in England in 1390 and died there in 1453, but he spent nearly 15 years in France at the height of his career. DuFay (c. 1400–1474) was born in northern France but traveled extensively throughout Europe and spent many years in Italy. He was therefore exposed to the very different musical styles of northern and southern Europe and played an important role in bringing about a fusion of the two in his own music.

Both Dunstable and DuFay and the many other composers who flourished in the early Renaissance wrote music of great beauty and sophistication. Their polyphonic Masses were often unified by musical phrases that reoccur in different movements; their motets are based on Latin texts often taken from the Bible or designed to celebrate an important civic event; and their secular songs are usually three-part gentle love songs in French or Italian.

THE RENAISSANCE MASS

A Roman Catholic Mass as it was celebrated in the 1400s was a long service, with many different readings and prayers, ceremonies and processions, and a large amount of music. Through most of the Middle Ages, all of this music had been sung in plainchant. It was only with the advent of polyphony in the twelfth and thirteenth centuries that some parts of the Mass began to be sung polyphonically. Gradually, composers began to concentrate on those sections of the Mass that remained the same, regardless of the day, feast, or season. There are five of these sections—the Kyrie, Gloria, Credo, Sanctus, and Agnus Dei—and they are known collectively as the Ordinary of the Mass. The tradition of setting these five sections to music began in the fourteenth century and has continued through the Renaissance to the present day. **(See Listening Guide on page 99.)**

The principal musical characteristic of a Renaissance Mass is polyphony, usually imitation. The flexibility and variety of approach displayed by composers in the fifteenth and sixteenth centuries in using this one compositional technique is remarkable.

THE MID-RENAISSANCE

During the middle part of the Renaissance, the technique of unifying a composition by the use of imitation became fully established. Composers also experimented with ways of linking the five different sections of the Ordinary by drawing the musical material for them from a single source: a piece of plainchant or even a popular song of the day. The source melody usually appears in the tenor voice (the third musical line from the top in a four-voice piece), but the other voices are often derived from it as well.

Josquin Desprez in a sixteenth-century woodcut.

IOSQVINVS PRATENSIS.

JOSQUIN DESPREZ (C. 1440–1521)

Josquin Desprez was the most versatile and gifted composer of the mid-Renaissance. He was from northern France and spent much of his career there, as well as at some of the cathedrals and courts of Italy. During his lifetime he became quite famous, and rich noblemen were eager to hire him for their households.

Josquin composed prolifically in the three main genres of Renaissance music: Masses, motets, and secular songs. He brought the Renaissance technique of musical imitation to new heights of clarity and flexibility.

As an example of Josquin's style, we shall study one of his Mass settings: the *Pange Lingua* Mass, composed toward the end of his life. **(See Listening Guide on page 100.)** This composition is known as the *Pange Lingua* Mass because all five movements of the Mass are based on the plainchant hymn *Pange Lingua Gloriosi*. Before examining Josquin's polyphonic Mass setting, let us look at the plainchant that provided the basis for it.

JOSQUIN'S *PANGE LINGUA* MASS

In his Mass based on the *Pange Lingua* hymn, Josquin took almost all of his musical ideas from the plainchant. Remarkably, each vocal line in every section of the Mass is derived from the chant in some way or another. But it is the way in which he uses the musical material that demonstrates the composer's talent and that enabled Josquin to create a completely new composition from the ancient chant.

In the first place, of course, Josquin's Mass is polyphonic. It is written for four voice lines: sopranos, altos, tenors, and basses. Second, the Mass—unlike the chant—has rhythm (plainchant is usually sung with all the notes equal in length). Every musical phrase has a rhythm especially created by Josquin to fit the words of

> *J*osquin is master of the notes; others are mastered by them.
> —Martin Luther

the Mass. Josquin also molds and varies his phrases by adding notes to or modifying notes from the chant melody. His composition is in five movements, using all five sections of the Ordinary.

The Mass is by no means a lesser piece because of its dependence on earlier melodic material. Indeed, it is precisely in the molding of a well-known original that Josquin shows his ingenuity. The *Pange Lingua* Mass not only stands alone as a composition reflecting the individual genius of its composer. It also is colored throughout with the presence of a sacred tradition, not only in the words of the Mass itself but also in the music and the words of the hymn that stands behind the Mass—a hymn that would have been very familiar to Josquin's audience. The words of the original hymn are not sung in Josquin's Mass, but they would have been called to mind by his audience when they heard the strands of the hymn's melody woven into the polyphony.

Three characteristics of Josquin's special musical style can be heard clearly in this work:

1. Josquin has given each short segment of the music its own **point of imitation**, a musical passage that presents a single tiny musical phrase imitated among the voices. For each new segment of the music, the phrase is different. Each voice states the phrase in turn, and then a cadence follows. The number of statements, the voices that present them, the number of measures between them—all these things may vary.

2. Usually the music is controlled by **overlapping cadences:** The next group of voices begins its statements just as the first group comes to a cadence. This provides articulation for the music while allowing the forward motion to continue.

3. The imitation is usually paired imitation: One pair of voices begins the imitation and another pair answers.

Thomas Aquinas (1225–1274)
Plainchant hymn, _Pange Lingua_

Date of composition: Thirteenth
  century
Choir
Duration: 2:24

Student CD Collection: 1, track 47
Complete CD Collection: 1, track 47

Pan - ge lin - gua ___ glo - ri - o - si   Cor - po - ris my - ste - ri - um, ___

San - gui - nis - que pre - ti - o - si,   Quem in mun - di - pre - ti - um ___

Fruc - tus ven - tris ge - ne - ro - si   Rex ef - fu - dit ___ gen - ti - um.

same music repeated
for all the stanza

The _Pange Lingua_ hymn was written by Thomas Aquinas, one of the foremost scholars and theologians of the late middle ages. The hymn is strophic: All four stanzas are sung to the same music. Each stanza has six lines, and they seem to fall into pairs. The chant is in the E (Phrygian) mode, but the only line to end on the E is the last one. This gives the music a sense of continuity until the end. The chant is almost entirely syllabic, and the text urges praise for the miracle of Christ's birth and death.

→ 1 note per syllable

We shall listen to all four stanzas, but what is important here is the _music_; therefore, the entire text is not given. Remember: All four stanzas have exactly the same music.

47 (47)	0:00	Stanza 1	("_Pange lingua …_")
	0:33	Stanza 2	("_Nobis datus …_")
	1:04	Stanza 3	("_In supremae …_")
	1:39	Stanza 4	("_Verbum caro …_")
	2:12	"Amen"	

Josquin Desprez (c. 1440–1521)
Kyrie from the *Pange Lingua* Mass

Date of composition: c. 1520
Sopranos, altos, tenors, basses
Duration: 2:51

Student CD Collection: 1, track 48
Complete CD Collection: 1, track 48

A ll three of the characteristics listed on page 98 may be heard in the opening Kyrie of Josquin's *Pange Lingua* Mass. Let us first look at the phrase that provides the material for the first point of imitation:

This phrase is derived from the first phrase of the plainchant hymn. Notice, however, that Josquin adds a short turning passage between the last two notes to provide intensity and drive to the cadence. Notice, too, the rhythm that Josquin has applied to the notes. It starts out with long notes (which stress the characteristic E–F–E half step of the Phrygian mode) and increases in motion until just before the end. The *meter* of this music is also very flexible. Composers of this era did not use measures or bar lines (as you can see from the facsimile of the original shown below). This creates a very fluid sound without the regularly recurring accents that occur in later music.

illuminated manuscript

The movement as a whole has three main sections:

1. Kyrie eleison.
2. Christe eleison.
3. Kyrie eleison.

Each section begins with a new point of imitation, and all are derived from the original hymn. The "Christe" section is based on the third and fourth lines of the hymn, the final "Kyrie" section on the fifth and sixth lines. Toward the end of the last section, Josquin again adds new rhythmic material to create a strong drive to the final cadence.

48 (48)	**0:00**	*Kyrie eleison*	(Based on opening of hymn melody.) Tenors and basses; cadence overlaps with entry of altos. Sopranos enter before final cadence.
	0:45	*Christe eleison*	(Based on lines 3 and 4 of hymn melody.) Paired imitation, overlapping entries.
	2:02	*Kyrie eleison*	(Based on lines 5 and 6 of hymn melody.) Sopranos, altos, tenors, basses enter in turn; increase in activity before final cadence.

THE LATE RENAISSANCE

The sixteenth century was a time of remarkable musical achievements. The balance, beauty, and exquisite sound of imitative polyphony were fully explored by composers throughout Europe. In addition, composers began to use more homophonic texture in their compositions. There are few greater contrasts than that between the individual strands of imitative polyphony and the solid chordal texture of homophony, and Renaissance composers from Josquin onward took full advantage of this contrast. They alternated and interwove the two styles in their compositions to achieve ever greater variety of texture and to give expressive emphasis to the words.

In fact, this increasing focus on expressing the meaning of the words marks the progression of music during the Renaissance. During the sixteenth century, the combination of a high degree of technical accomplishment and a new interest in text expression led to the creation of some of the most beautiful works in the history of music. Masses, motets, and secular songs were created by composers throughout Europe: in France and Germany, the Netherlands, Spain, Poland, and England. But probably the main center of musical activity in the sixteenth century was Italy.

Italy was the focal point of the Roman Catholic movement known as the Counter-Reformation, which began partly in reaction to the Protestant Reformation and partly as the result of a genuine desire to reform the Catholic Church from within. The Counter-Reformation had important consequences for music, as we shall see.

One technical change that may be noticed in late Renaissance music is the sound of the last chord at the end of sections. Until this time, final chords contained

Patronage

Music costs money. Composers have to make a living, and so do performers. In the days before public concerts, ticket sales, and commercial recordings, music had to be financed by patrons (supporters). During the Renaissance, most patrons were wealthy aristocrats who could afford to employ musicians at their courts or palaces. Musicians were on the staff at these courts just like doormen, dressmakers, cooks, and other servants. ¶ Some wealthy aristocrats employed several composers at once. In the later part of the fifteenth century, the duke of Milan appointed the great composer Josquin Desprez to his staff, although he already had four other composers on the payroll. ¶ Sometimes patrons had to pay handsomely to hire the most famous musicians. When Josquin left Milan, he moved to the court of the duke of Ferrara. He was hired in 1503, against the advice of the duke's private secretary, who urged the duke to hire a composer named Isaac instead. "Isaac gets on better with his colleagues and composes more quickly," he wrote. "It is true that Josquin is a better composer, but he composes only when he feels like it and not when he is asked. Moreover, Josquin is demanding 200 ducats, while Isaac will take 120." The duke decided to go first-class, and Josquin got his 200 ducats.

only the "perfect" intervals (octaves and fifths). But in the late Renaissance, composers began to think that final chords should present the fullest sound possible and therefore should include the third, as well as the root, the fifth, and the octave of the chord. You can clearly hear the difference between a piece that ends with the open sound of an octave and a fifth and a piece that ends with a full chord.

THE COUNTER-REFORMATION AND THE MUSIC OF PALESTRINA

The Counter-Reformation was not primarily concerned with music, but music played a role in the deliberations of the church reformers. In 1534 the reformer Paul III was elected pope, and in 1545 he convened the Council of Trent, a council of cardinals that met from time to time over a period of about 20 years to discuss needed reforms in church administration and liturgy.

Music was discussed only during the last two years of the council. Many complaints were heard:

- ✧ secular songs were being used as the basis for sacred compositions;
- ✧ singers had become too theatrical and were distracting people from the liturgy; and
- ✧ polyphony had become too complicated and florid, obscuring the sacred words.

The council considered banning polyphony altogether, thinking that a return to plainchant was the best solu-

tion. In the end, however, the cardinals agreed that, in addition to the traditional chants, polyphonic music could be used in church, provided that the words could be heard clearly and the style was not too elaborate.

The composer whose music most clearly represents these ideals is Giovanni Pierluigi da Palestrina (c. 1525–1594). Like many people during the Middle Ages and the Renaissance, this man took his name from his home town. He was born in Palestrina, 40 miles from Rome, and was sent to Rome as a choirboy to study and sing. He spent most of his life there at some of the city's greatest musical institutions, including the Sistine Chapel (the private chapel of the pope).

The purity, serenity, and perfection of Palestrina's music have made him the most highly regarded composer of late Renaissance choral music. The principal characteristics of his style are balance, control, evenness, clarity, and perfect text setting. The overall effect conveyed by Palestrina's music is achieved by careful control of two primary elements: the structure of the individual melodic lines and the placement of dissonance.

In the structure of the individual melodic lines for his polyphonic pieces, Palestrina adhered strictly to the following guidelines:

- a. The motion of the line is primarily stepwise, with very few leaps.
- b. If there is a leap, it is small and is immediately counterbalanced by stepwise motion in the opposite direction.
- c. The rhythmic flow is not rigid or regularly accented, but is shifting, gentle, and alive.

Agnus Dei from *Pope Marcellus* Mass

A — gnus — De — i

The second primary element in Palestrina's style is his careful control of dissonance. His music has some dissonances (for without them, the music would be very bland indeed), but they appear only under partic-

ular circumstances. Usually, they are short passing notes or are off the beat. When dissonances do occur on the beat, they are always prepared and immediately resolved.

Four hundred years after Palestrina, the composer Charles Gounod observed: "This severe, ascetic music is as calm and horizontal as the line of the ocean, monotonous by virtue of its serenity; antisensuous; and yet it is so intense in its contemplativeness that it verges sometimes on ecstasy."

Two of six voice parts—Agnus Dei from *Pope Marcellus* Mass

1., 2.   Passing-tone dissonance of a second.
3., 4.   On-the-beat dissonance of a seventh, immediately resolved to a sixth.
5.   Passing-tone dissonance of a seventh.

It might be thought that such a highly disciplined approach to composition would lead to dull, constricted music. On the contrary, Palestrina's music is so inspiring that it has been taken as a model of perfection for all those wishing to imitate the grace and beauty of Renaissance polyphony. In this case, as so often in artistic endeavors, strict formal rules produced masterpieces of great and lasting value.

Palestrina was a superbly gifted and resourceful composer, and despite the rigor of his approach, he found many ways to introduce variety into his music. In the first place, there is a constant interplay between counterpoint and homophony. And within the sections of counterpoint, Palestrina draws on an almost limitless variety of methods. The imitative entries among the voices can vary in distance, number of entries, voice pairings, and even pitch. Different points of imitation can even be introduced at the same time—something that never happened in Josquin's music. And through it all, the text sounds clearly, with its natural rhythm perfectly conveyed.

Palestrina wrote more than 100 settings of the Mass and several volumes of secular songs, but perhaps his most impressive achievement is the composition of 250 motets. Motets could be written on almost any sacred text: biblical stories, passages from the Psalms, and so on. Almost always, composers chose expressive texts with elements of drama or mystery, and they matched the words with music of remarkable intensity or poignancy. **(See Listening Guide on page 105.)**

THE RENAISSANCE MOTET

The Renaissance motet usually has four voice parts. It is entirely vocal and is usually sung by a small choir rather than by soloists. All the voices sing the same text—a sacred text—in the same language, almost always Latin. Finally, the music may be imitative or homophonic and is usually a mixture of the two.

Motets often have very expressive words. Renaissance composers tended to write richer and more unusual music for motets than they did for the fixed liturgical texts of the Mass. As a result, the music of Renaissance motets is often highly expressive, with a sensitive and compelling approach to the meaning of the text.

THE RENAISSANCE SECULAR SONG

The Renaissance secular song evolved in two phases. In the fifteenth century, secular songs (songs with nonsacred texts) were not very different from those of the late Middle Ages (those of Machaut, for example). And an international musical style had been adopted in most countries. But in the late Renaissance, several European countries developed their own distinct national styles for secular songs.

The most influential of all these countries was Italy, and the distinctive type of secular song that developed there was the **madrigal**. Madrigals are secular vocal pieces

Giovanni Pierluigi da Palestrina
(c. 1525–1594)
Motet, *Exsultate Deo*

Date of composition: 1584
Sopranos, altos I, altos II, tenors, basses
Duration: 2:24

Student CD Collection: 1, track 49
Complete CD Collection: 1, track 49

The motet *Exsultate Deo* was first published in Palestrina's fifth book of motets in 1584. This book contains 21 motets written for five voices. The text is from Psalm 81. Palestrina uses only the first three lines of the psalm, the text of which is given here.

Exsultate Deo adiutori nostro,	Sing out in praise of God our refuge,
iubilate Deo Iacob.	acclaim the God of Jacob.
Sumite psalmum et date tympanum,	Raise a melody; beat the drum,
psalterium iucundum cum cithara.	play the tuneful lyre and harp.
Buccinate in neomenia tuba,	Blow the trumpet at the new moon,
insigni die sollemnitatis vestrae.	and blow it at the full moon on the day
	of your solemn feast.

There is a word painting …

In his setting Palestrina concentrates only on these exuberant opening verses of the psalm, rather than the fierce later ones. The music is bright and joyful, filled with dotted rhythms and running eighth-note patterns, which help to enliven the work. In addition, the composer uses some word-painting, such as on the opening word "Exsultate," where the musical line rises triumphantly.

Ex - sul - ta ———— te   De — o

With five independent musical lines, the number of possible combinations is large, and Palestrina constantly varies the texture of his music. The clearest examples of this variation are when the sopranos drop out briefly, leaving only the lower voices, or (on the words "psalterium iucundum"—"tuneful lyre") when only three voices are sounding. *Exsultate Deo* is full of imitation, but Palestrina points up the entrance of new lines of text by having them sung homophonically by a pair of voices, which adds an underlying structure to the work as a whole. Cleverly, he departs from this technique towards the end of the motet on the words "Buccinate" ("blow") and "tuba" ("trumpet"), where there is very close imitation, suggesting the echoing of the turmpet blasts.

This performance is by the choir of Christ Church Cathedral, Oxford, England. The choir, which has been in continuous existence since the early sixteenth century, is made up of the same distribution of voices as it was originally: sixteen boys and twelve men. So all the high voices you hear are those of boys.

Christ Church Cathedral choir.

49 (49)	**0:00**	*Exsultate Deo adiutori nostro,*	Sing out in praise of God our refuge,	[Imitation in pair of upper voices alone; rising line on "Exsultate."]
	0:11			[Pair of lower voices. Cadence in all five voices; overlaps with:]
	0:28	*iubilate Deo Iacob.*	acclaim the God of Jacob.	[Many entries, suggesting a crowd "acclaiming."]
	0:37			[Lower voices.]
	0:49	*Sumite psalmum et date tympanum,*	Raise a melody; beat the drum,	[Quite homophonic, becoming more imitative. Note dotted rhythm on "tympanum."]
	1:04	*psalterium iucundum cum cithara.*	play the tuneful lyre and harp.	[Elaborate flowering of the voices on "iucundum" ("tuneful").]
50 (50)	**0:00**	*Buccinate in neomenia tuba,*	Blow the trumpet at the new moon,	[Multiple echoes on "Buccinate;" homophonic climax on "neomenia"]
	0:13			[Running echoes on "tuba."]
	0:23	*insigni die solemnitatis vestrae.*	and blow it at the full moon on the day of your solemn feast.	[Slower, lower, more "solemn."]

for a small group of singers, usually unaccompanied. The favorite topics were love, descriptions of nature, and sometimes war or battles. The music for madrigals mingles chordal and imitative textures and sensitively reflects the meaning of the text. The Italian madrigal became so influential in the course of the sixteenth century that composers of many other nationalities wrote madrigals in Italian, and some composers in England copied the style and wrote madrigals in English.

THE MADRIGAL

As we have seen, matching the words of the text with a musical setting that expresses their meaning was a primary concern of late Renaissance composers. The madrigal is the musical genre that demonstrates this most colorfully.

The madrigal flourished in the courtly atmosphere of Italian aristocratic families. The poetry is serious and elegant, with a sonorous beauty of its own. And the music is carefully designed to reflect the text.

Composers used a variety of techniques to bring out the meaning of the words they set. In general, the same mixture of chordal textures and imitative polyphony is used in madrigals as in motets, but composers went much further in their search for direct expression. If the text had words such as "rising," "flying," or "soaring," then the music would have fast upward scales. "Peace" and "happiness" might be set to sweet major chords, "agony" and "despair" to wrenching dissonances. In fact, contrasts of this kind—between happiness and despair, for example—often appeared in madrigal texts within the same poem. This contrast is known as *antithesis*, and it presented ideal musical opportunities for madrigal composers. A sigh might be represented by sudden, short pauses—to be followed by long flowing lines evoking the elation of love.

In the "Listening" chapter, we heard *Morte, te chiamo*, a sixteenth-century madrigal by Maddalena Casulana that demonstrates these points (pages 72–73). It had a serious text, about love, life, and death, which was clearly expressed by the music. It also had contrast of textures, expressive dissonances, and antithesis.

The madrigal became immensely popular during the sixteenth century and survived well into the seventeenth. Composers strove for ever greater intensity of expression, and the late madrigalists managed to wring every ounce of feeling from each nuance of the text. The technique of depicting the meaning of words through music is known as **word-painting**.

Toward the end of the sixteenth century, a fascination with madrigals had taken hold in England. Italian madrigals sometimes appeared in English translation. One set

Musical Borrowing

The idea that originality is the most important characteristic of a composer is a very modern one. For most of music history, composers borrowed freely from one another. Imitating another composer was considered a mark of respect. ◆ During the Renaissance, composers made widespread use of previously existing material for their works. This included plainchant, popular songs, other people's compositions, and sometimes earlier pieces of their own. Palestrina, one of the greatest composers of the Renaissance era, was a frequent borrower from the works of other composers. Scholars have traced compositions by at least 10 other composers among the building materials of Palestrina's works. ◆ Occasionally you can trace the metamorphosis of the same piece from a chant to a motet to a Mass. For example, Palestrina wrote a motet based on the chant *Assumpta Est Maria*. The motet weaves the original notes of the chant into a beautiful polyphonic whole. Later, Palestrina wrote an entire Mass based on his motet, using the musical fabric of the motet as the basis for an impressive, new, large-scale composition.

was published in 1590 under the title *Italian Madrigalls Englished*. But English composers also wrote their own madrigals with English texts. These were often lighter in tone and more cheerful than their Italian counterparts.

The title page to Thomas Morley's *A Plaine and Easie Introduction to Practicall Musicke*, printed in 1597.

In his book, Morley provides a detailed description of the way to write a madrigal. He then concludes: "Keeping these rules, you shall have a perfect agreement and, as it were, an harmonical consent betwixt the matter and the music, and likewise you shall be perfectly understood of the auditor what you sing, which is one of the highest degrees of praise which a musician in dittying can attain unto or wish for."

The guiding force for the development of English madrigals was Thomas Morley (1557–1602), a gifted composer, author of an important textbook on music, and owner of the monopoly on music printing for the whole of England. Morley published more madrigals than any other English composer and established a style that was followed by most other English madrigalists.

We shall listen to a pair of extremely short madrigals by Thomas Morley from a collection he published in 1595. Both are for two voices rather than the conventional four. The first (*Sweet Nymph Come to Thy Lover*) is for two women; the second (*Fire and Lightning*) is sung by two men. They make a wonderfully pleasing and varied pair. (**See Listening Guide on page 109.**)

After the work of the late Italian and English madrigalists, the Renaissance polyphonic style had run its course. It had produced works of great beauty and variety, but new composers had new ideas. Their interest in text expression remained paramount, but they felt that new ways had to be found to allow the words to dominate the music. These new ways were the foundation of a new musical style in the seventeenth century, the Baroque style, in which instrumental music became more and more prominent. Let us examine the origins of the style in the rise of instrumental music in the Renaissance.

THE RISE OF INSTRUMENTAL MUSIC

During the Renaissance, instrumental music became more and more popular. A wide range of instruments was in use, from the loud, extrovert trumpets to soft, delicate strings and recorders. Compositions ranged from serious contrapuntal works to lighthearted dances.

One of the former types was the **canzona**, and the master of the canzona was Giovanni Gabrieli (c. 1555–1612), who was an organist and composer at St. Mark's Church in Venice. St. Mark's had two choir lofts facing each other, and Gabrieli took advantage of this to place contrasting groups of instruments in the two lofts, creating an early version of stereo sound. (**See Listening Guide on page 110.**)

The Importance of Dancing

The following extract comes from a dance treatise published in 1859. The treatise is cast as a dialogue between student and teacher.

Student: Without knowledge of dancing, I could not please the damsels, upon whom, it seems to me, the entire reputation of an eligible young man depends.

Teacher: You are quite right, as naturally the male and female seek one another, and nothing does more to stimulate a man to acts of courtesy, honor, and generosity than love. And if you desire to marry, you must realize that a mistress is won by the good temper and grace displayed while dancing. And there is more to it than this, for dancing is practiced to reveal whether lovers are in good health and sound of limb, after which they are permitted to kiss and touch and savor one another, thus to ascertain if they are shapely or emit an unpleasant odor as of bad meat. Therefore, apart from the many other advantages to be derived from dancing, it becomes essential to a well-ordered society.

The largest category of instrumental music during the Renaissance was dance music, since dancing was one of the favorite forms of entertainment. The music was usually binary in form (AABB) and followed the characteristic tempos and rhythms of each dance type. Dances were frequently performed in pairs, contrasting slow with fast, or duple meter with triple meter. (**See Listening Guide on page 111.**)

Thomas Morley (1557–1602)
Two English Madrigals

Date of composition: 1595

Two sopranos (*Sweet Nymph Come to Thy Lover*); two baritones (*Fire and Lightning*)

Duration: 2:31

Student CD Collection: 1, track 51
Complete CD Collection: 1, track 51

*T*he texts for these short pieces were probably written by Morley himself. Each one contains picturesque images, which the music captures beautifully. The first madrigal, *Sweet Nymph*, presents a nightingale, a favorite image for composers. The second, *Fire and Lightning*, is lively and frenetic, with a kicker at the end. Both are primarily imitative, with very close imitation in some sections to liven up the proceedings or intensify the sound. The very last line of *Fire and Lightning* is suddenly homophonic to draw attention to the sting at the end. This last line also exploits antithesis ("fair"/"spiteful") to make its effect.

Both madrigals have such short texts that there are many repetitions of each phrase, and you will hear many instances of word-painting. The fine performances here are by students Sarah Pelletier and Suzanne Ehly, sopranos, and faculty members William Sharp and Mark Aliapoulios, baritones, of the Boston University School for the Arts.

51 (51)	0:00		Sweet nymph come to thy lover,	Imitation.
	0:12		Lo here alone our loves we may discover,	Touches of homophony on "Lo here alone."
	0:20		(*Repeat of first two lines*)	
	0:39		Where the sweet nightingale with wanton gloses,	Imitation; high notes and close harmony on "gloses" [trills].
	0:49		Hark, her love too discloses.	High notes, very close imitation, especially last time through.
	1:03		(*Repeat of last two lines*)	
52 (52)	0:00		Fire and lightning from heaven fall	Lively; very close imitation.
	0:08		And sweetly enflame that heart with love arightful,	Smooth descending scales on "sweetly."
	0:16		(*Repeat of first two lines*)	
	0:31		Of Flora my delightful,	Scales in opposite direction on "delightful."
	0:45		So fair but yet so spiteful.	Last time through: homophonic, close pungent harmony, dissonance on "spite-," incomplete sound on "ful."
	0:47		(*Repeat of last two lines*)	

Giovanni Gabrieli (c. 1555–1612)
Canzona Duodecimi Toni

Date of composition: 1597
Two brass choirs
Duration: 3:53

Student CD Collection: 1, track 53
Complete CD Collection: 1, track 53

This work by Giovanni Gabrieli is divided into several sections and contrasts two brass "choirs," which are heard in dialogue. As in Josquin's *Pange Lingua* Mass, the music is pushed forward by overlapping cadences, one choir beginning as the previous choir ends. Sometimes the two choirs play together. The piece features dynamic contrasts of loud and soft, which are characteristic of late Renaissance and early Baroque music. A special effect involving dynamic contrast is "echo," in which the exact repetition of a phrase at a lower volume suggests distance.

The canzona is full of varied rhythmic patterns, but the most pervasive is the "canzona rhythm," LONG-short-short (♩ ♪ ♪), which you will hear throughout the piece, in fast and slow tempos.

INTRO		
53 (53)	**0:00**	Fairly slow, medium loud, both brass choirs; canzona rhythm is prominent.

SECTION 1		
54 (54)	**0:15**	Faster tempo, same musical motive and rhythm, faster tempo, homophonic, Choir I.
	0:20	Choir II, growing louder.
	0:27	Both choirs, loud, featuring flourishes by trumpets in imitation; cadence.

SECTION 2		
55 (55)	**0:43**	Second motive, quieter, mostly homophonic, echoes, passages of imitation between choirs, lively rhythms; cadence.

SECTION 3		
56 (56)	**1:26**	Third motive, loud, mostly homophonic, echoes, both choirs.
	1:43	Trumpet flourishes, cadence.
	1:49	Canzona rhythm; close imitation, cadence.

SECTION 4		
57 (57)	**2:10**	Fourth motive, quiet, canzona rhythm, lots of imitation between choirs, cadence.
	2:35	Multiple echoes, from loud to soft, between choirs; crescendo ...
	3:02	Final motive, both choirs loud, leading to big climax.

Tielman Susato (fl. 1543–1561)
Ronde and Saltarelle

Date of composition: 1551
Recorders and percussion
Duration: 1:52

Complete CD Collection: 1, track 58

This example is a dance pair written by the Flemish composer and publisher Tielman Susato. The *ronde* and *saltarelle* are both binary. On the repeats, the melody is occasionally ornamented with trills and decorative figures.

The two dances contain the same melody, but the ronde has duple meter, whereas the saltarelle is triple; the effect is very different in each case.

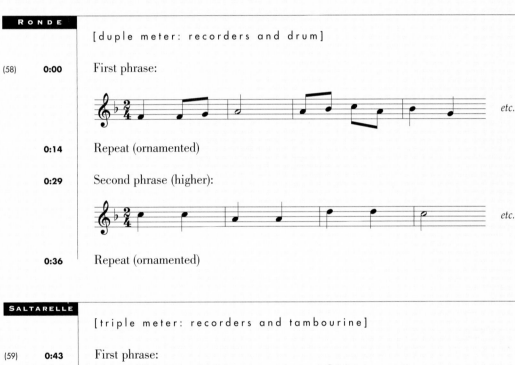

RONDE		[duple meter: recorders and drum]
(58)	**0:00**	First phrase:
	0:14	Repeat (ornamented)
	0:29	Second phrase (higher):
	0:36	Repeat (ornamented)

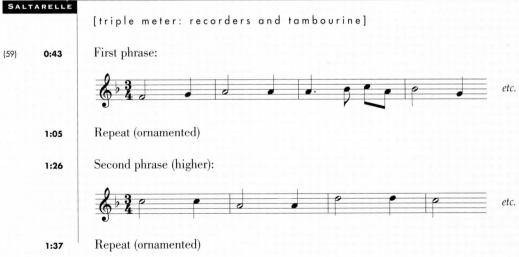

SALTARELLE		[triple meter: recorders and tambourine]
(59)	**0:43**	First phrase:
	1:05	Repeat (ornamented)
	1:26	Second phrase (higher):
	1:37	Repeat (ornamented)

In the Renaissance, musical style changed dramatically. In place of the stark or subtle sounds of medieval music, Renaissance compositions offer smoothly contoured and carefully woven textures. Renaissance music encompasses three main musical genres: settings of Mass movements, settings of other Latin texts, and secular songs. All of these genres are vocal.

The predominant ways of combining voices in the Renaissance were through homophony (the harmonizing voices singing in the same rhythms) and imitation (the voices copying each other at the start of their phrases and then continuing independently). Sometimes these styles were adopted uniformly throughout a piece, but more often they were juxtaposed or sub-tly blended. The typical sound of Renaissance music, therefore, resembles a tapestry, in which the separate strands can be recognized and traced, and yet the combination presents a complete and integrated picture.

Many Renaissance works are based on sacred texts, and the resulting music is dignified, beautiful, and spiritually uplifting. Renaissance secular songs such as madrigals, however, could be more down to earth. And though word-painting (the depiction of the meaning of individual words in music) can be found in Latin motets, it was widely used in madrigals, whose subject matter was usually love and its ramifications.

Word-painting led to all kinds of clever musical effects: running scales to depict a chase, dissonant chords for the pain of love, and low notes for

A beautiful manuscript of the beginning of a Renaissance Mass.

death. We can hear these in some of the English madrigals of the later sixteenth century and in the more common Italian ones.

The last noteworthy component of Renaissance music is the rise in popularity of works for instruments. Even though vocal music still predominated, more and more instrumental music was being composed, and musicians sometimes played instrumental arrangements of vocal pieces. The main types of instrumental music were serious polyphonic pieces that involved imitation and lighthearted, rhythmic dances. The latter were usually in binary (AABB) form.

The same music in modern notation.

Interestingly, it was the Renaissance's instrumental music that had the most influence on music of the following style period. In the Baroque era, instruments became central to the sound of the new style.

FUNDAMENTALS OF RENAISSANCE MUSIC

+ Sound is smooth and homogenous

+ Harmony is still primarily based on modes

+ Most prominent feature is imitation

+ Vocal genres include Mass movements, motets, and secular songs

+ Motets and madrigals often use word-painting, which can involve dissonance

+ Instrumental music is either serious and imitative or light and dancelike

THE BAROQUE ERA: 1600–1750

The word "baroque" began as a term of disapproval. In the seventeenth century, it was used by philosophers to describe tortuous forms of argument, and by jewelers to describe oddly colored or misshapen pearls. The word was first applied to music in the eighteenth century. In 1768, the French philosopher Rousseau defined Baroque music as that in which

the harmony is confused, full of modulations and dissonances; the melody is harsh and unnatural; the intonation is remote; and the motion is constrained.

Nowadays the term is not used disapprovingly. The creative works of the seventeenth and early eighteenth centuries are now recognized for their grandeur, depth, and technical mastery. The Baroque period, after all, is the age of the writers Milton, Racine, and Molière; the artists Rembrandt and Velázquez; and the composers Bach, Handel, and Vivaldi.

LIFE IN THE BAROQUE ERA

The Baroque era was a period of absolute monarchs. They were called absolute monarchs because they had total control over every aspect of their realms: the economy, the content of books, the style of art, and even life and death. The model for absolute monarchy was set by Louis XIV, who raised the power of the king to unparalleled heights. He regarded himself as synonymous with the whole nation of France. "I *am* the state," he said.

In many parts of Europe, life was characterized by a strict social hierarchy, rigid laws, and elaborate codes of dress and manners. The political instability and wars that had dominated Europe for so many years gave way to a period of international peace and economic expansion. There may have been political repression, punitive taxation, and gross social inequities, but there were no major wars, and rulers supported the arts as expressions of their cultivation and learning.

During the seventeenth and eighteenth centuries, a radical change took place in philosophical and scientific thinking. Aided by new technological developments, scientists began to test their ideas by measurement and mathematical analysis rather than by relying on preconceived notions. The foremost scientist of the age was Sir Isaac Newton, who discovered the principle of gravity, developed calculus, and determined that white light is made up of all the colors of the spectrum.

The discoveries of Newton and other scientists had a profound effect on philosophers, who began to search for comparable principles to apply to human life and society. They began to apply the techniques of mathematical analysis to human thought.

Order and organization were valued above all else in society and in the arts. Baroque artists thought that the emotions could be objectively classified and that art could be designed to arouse specific emotions in its audience. Indeed, Baroque art displays a fascination with states of emotion: grief, religious ecstasy, joy, passion, despair. Baroque artists studied these emotional states and strove to represent them. In art and architecture, Baroque works evoke intense reactions. They involve the viewer immediately. Portraits stress the grandeur and personality of their subjects; sculptures depict fleeting moments of emotional intensity; buildings radiate opulence, strength, and rhythmic order.

The most impressive building of the Baroque period is surely the palace of Versailles, built by Louis XIV in the mid-1600s. It is breathtakingly grand and symmetrical, with more than a thousand rooms, including one hall lined entirely with mirrors. The effect of grandeur continues outside, where the geometrically organized landscape—with its long rows of trees, pools, and elegant gardens—extends for miles.

> There are only six simple and primitive passions, that is, wonder, love, hatred, desire, joy, and sadness. All the others are composed of some of these six.
> —René Descartes (1646)

Right: Gianlorenzo Bernini's sculpture *Apollo and Daphne* (1625) depicts the very moment at which she is transformed into a tree.

Giovanni Lorenzo Bernini, Apollo and Daphne. Villa Borghese Gallery, Rome. Archivi Alinari/Art Resource, NY.

Far Right: A Baroque painting of the palace and gardens at Versailles.

Jean-Baptiste Martin, "Bassin du Dragon et de Neptune." Photo: Arnaudet/Lewandowski. Chateaux de Versailles et de Trianon, Versailles, France. Reunion des Musées Nationaux/Art Resource, NY.

Below Right: Self-portrait by Rembrandt as an old man.

Rembrandt Harmensz van Rijn (1606–1669). Rembrandt, self-portrait at old age. Oil on canvas. National Gallery, London, Great Britain. © Photograph by Erich Lessing. Erich Lessing/Art Resource, NY.

In all Baroque art, contrast and illusion are the dominant forces. Painters discovered the dramatic possibilities of strong contrasts between light and shade. In Rembrandt's portraits, light falls generously on the subject's face, while the background falls away in the gloom.

Illusion was a favorite device. Paper was decorated to resemble dense marble; doors and windows were painted onto walls; scenes creating the effect of outdoor vistas were drawn inside false window frames. Painted ceilings offered special opportunities for spectacular effects: The ceilings seem to open up to the heavens, with whirling clouds and cherubs leaping out of the sky.

Comparable characteristics are found in Baroque music. Baroque composers set out to portray specific states of emotion, and they created contrast and illusion through the use of dynamics and contrasting performing groups.

The emphasis on contrast can be heard most clearly in the concerto. Concertos are built on the idea of contrast—between the entire orchestra and a small group, or between the orchestra and a single instrument.

Dynamic contrasts also achieve illusion. In Baroque instrumental music, the same phrase is often played first loud and then soft. This echo effect gives the illusion of space and distance. Instruments sometimes give the illusion of being other instruments: a flute may play a trumpet fanfare.

Audiences in the Baroque Era

The Baroque era was an important period of transition from the time of small, elite, aristocratic audiences to that of a wider concertgoing public. The trend began in Italy with a new musical invention: opera. Public opera houses were built in Venice and Rome about the middle of the seventeenth century. In the 1670s the first public concert series was organized in London. Toward the end of the Baroque period, similar public concerts began to be held in France (in 1725) and Germany (in the 1740s). ¶ These concerts were funded by subscription. People would sign up for the series, and the organizer could then use the collected money to hire the performers, rent the hall, print programs, and the like. This might be regarded as the first move in the gradually emerging trend from individual patronage to "group patronage." ¶ Some Baroque composers arranged subscription concerts for their own benefit. George Frideric Handel gave many concerts of his own music and made a considerable amount of money during his lifetime. He was also very generous: He inaugurated the idea of giving annual performances of his *Messiah* for charity. A contemporary wrote that *Messiah* "fed the hungry, clothed the naked, fostered the orphan, and enriched succeeding managers of oratorios, more than any single musical production in this or any other country." Handel's *Messiah* performances were very popular. At the 1750 performance, there wasn't enough room for the large audience, despite the request in the announcement that "Gentlemen are desired to come without swords, and the Ladies without hoops."

GENERAL CHARACTERISTICS OF BAROQUE MUSIC

The Baroque era lasted only 150 years, somewhat shorter than the Renaissance and a fraction of the length of the Middle Ages. In spite of this, it is the first period of our musical history that is featured with any frequency in today's concert halls or on radio programs. Even then, only the last half-century of the Baroque era, the period of Bach and Handel and Vivaldi, is generally represented. It is logical, then, to divide our examination of Baroque music into two parts: the early Baroque (1600–1700) and the late Baroque (1700–1750). In fact, this division corresponds to actual musical events, because the early Baroque was the period in which stylistic trends were established, while the late Baroque was the time of the well-known masters and of fixed musical forms.

The early Baroque was a period of excitement and experimentation. The composers of the early 1600s combined expressiveness with great originality. The greatest invention of the age was opera, which displayed the best of all contemporary arts. It featured elaborate stage machinery, gorgeous costumes, and beautiful stage sets. All this was combined with moving stories, expressive acting, and dramatic music.

Early Baroque music was designed to be emotional. Both vocal and instrumental works were written to evoke specific states of mind. Certain melodic turns and harmonic patterns came to be associated with particular feelings. Composers experimented with ways to make music imitate the irregularity, the rise and fall, of impassioned speech.

At the same time, contrary tendencies can be seen in early Baroque music. There was a tendency toward more rigid formal design. Composers began to use bar lines to organize their music into regular metric groupings. And modern tonality began to evolve from the modal system of earlier music.

As the Baroque period progressed, organization and control began to replace experimentation. The forms used in opera and in instrumental music became standardized. The rigid hierarchy of society was reflected in opera plots, which often revolved around the effect on people of a powerful ruler's whims. The growth of tonality, with its carefully organized sequence of keys and harmonic patterns, may also be seen as a mirror of the Baroque social order.

With the Baroque fascination for structure and organization came the development of fixed musical forms. The chief vocal forms of the early Baroque were the opera and the cantata. **Operas** were large-scale productions, expressive and elaborate. They immediately became extremely popular. Great rulers and aristocratic families built their own private theaters for the performance of opera, and opera houses sprang up across Europe.

Cantatas were, in effect, very short unstaged operas: They were written for instruments and one or two voices and portrayed a single scene or situation. Some of the later **church cantatas** (notably those of Bach) were based on liturgical themes and were performed in church on Sundays, but the earlier **chamber cantatas** were secular in nature, telling stories of love lost and found, of nymphs and shepherds. They were perfect for performance in a salon or a small music room.

During the Baroque period, instrumental music gained greatly in importance. Instruments began to take on the shape and sound of their modern counterparts, and instrumental technique began to rival the brilliant speed, expressiveness, and control of the famous opera singers of the day. The most important instrumental forms of the Baroque era were the concerto, the sonata, and the dance suite.

Concertos are based on contrast. Their texture is formed by the interplay between a small group (or soloist) called *solo* and a large group called *ripieno*. The resulting instrumental dialogue allowed Baroque composers to create considerable drama within a purely instrumental form.

Sonatas are chamber works, smaller in scale than concertos and less dependent on contrast. Numbers could range from two or three instruments to a small handful, but a sonata was always designed for a group smaller than an orchestra.

Dance suites were originally designed exclusively to accompany dancing. An evening's entertainment often consisted of a series, or "suite," of contrasting dances, usually in binary form. Later, the dance suite became one of the most popular independent instrumental genres of the late Baroque.

The spread of the Protestant movement had an important influence on music. The most distinctive musical feature of a Protestant service was the **chorale**, a hymn with a steady rhythm and simple tune, usually sung in unison by the whole congregation. Chorale tunes, often dating from the Renaissance or even earlier, found their way into many types of Baroque music, including organ pieces and church cantatas. Another form of sacred music was the **oratorio**. This is a large-scale work like an opera, but it is based on a sacred story, and it is not staged. Instead, a narrator sings the story, and other singers sing the words of people in the story. Similar to the oratorio is the **Passion**, a composition based on the gospel account of the last days of Jesus.

Late Baroque music is characterized by rhythmic vitality. The driving rhythmic pulse of a Vivaldi concerto and the brilliantly organized harmonic motion of a Bach fugue are manifestations of the late style. Again, the vitality is given strength through order and control. But it would be a mistake to think that the emotions that were present in early Baroque music were suppressed in the late period. They were more organized and more formally presented, but they still constituted an essential part of the musical experience.

Stylistically, all Baroque music has one very notable characteristic: a strong bass line. This line not only forms the harmonic underpinning for Baroque music but also provides a strong foundation for the rhythmic momentum often present in music of the time. But whether the upper parts of a Baroque composition have strong rhythmic drive or extended expressive melodies, the bass part is always the driving force, both harmonically and rhythmically. Since the bass line is almost never silent in a Baroque composition, it is known as the **basso continuo** ("continuous bass"), or sometimes just **continuo**. The basso continuo part is usually played by a combination of a keyboard instrument, such as a harpsichord, and a low melody instrument, such as a cello or a bass viol. Whatever the genre, you can recognize a Baroque piece by the strength and powerful sense of direction of its bass line.

THE EARLY BAROQUE (1600–1700)

We saw earlier that the beginning of the Baroque period was a time of experimentation and excitement. Composers were trying out new ideas, and there was a great deal of discussion about music and the way it should be written. Some adhered to the Renaissance ideal of many-voiced polyphony, with its careful shaping of melodic lines and strict control of dissonance. Others felt that music should be subservient to the text, and that the rules of counterpoint and dissonance should be disregarded if they did not serve the primary aim of expressing the text. These composers favored a new song style known as **monody**, a type of music written for [*solo voice*] solo voice and basso continuo that imitated the natural rhythms of impassioned speech. Monody was composed for both sacred and secular texts; in all cases, the single voice part ranges freely and flexibly above the bass.

One of the early composers of monody was Francesca Caccini (1587–c.1640). She was the principal composer at the court of Tuscany, in northern Italy, and was multi-talented: she could also sing brilliantly, write poetry in both Latin and Italian, and play three different instruments, all equally well. The following brief extract (see below) from one of her sacred songs shows how free and rhapsodic the voice can be in monody. *Maria, dolce Maria*, composed in 1600, expresses the composer's joy in pronouncing the name of Mary.

In the end, both types of music—monody and traditional Renaissance-style polyphony—existed side by side. The most daring experiments in the new compositional style were carried out by a group of composers in Italy and led to the development of a completely new musical genre: opera. Among these composers was a man who was clearly the greatest composer of his age. His name was Claudio Monteverdi. Monteverdi made great contributions in two distinct historical periods. He lived a long life—from 1567 to 1643—and his life cut across the convenient boundaries that historians like to create out of the past. Monteverdi wrote many pieces in Renaissance style, especially madrigals, but he was also the first great opera composer of the Baroque era.

MONTEVERDI AND THE FIRST GREAT OPERA

The first great opera in the history of Western music was Monteverdi's *Orfeo*, written in 1607. The opera is based on the ancient Greek myth of Orpheus and Euridice.

THE STORY OF THE OPERA

Orpheus ("Orfeo" in Italian) and Euridice are in love. Shepherds and nymphs sing and dance together. Suddenly the revelries are interrupted by a messenger who announces that Euridice has been bitten by a snake

Francesca Caccini, *Maria, dolce Maria*

Voice: Ma - ria, dol - ce Ma - ri - a, no - me so - a - ve tan - to
che a pro-nun-ci- ar ti in pa-ra-di - s'il co - re. No - me
sa - cra - t'e san - to che'l cor m'in-fiam - mi di ce -
le - ste a-mo - re.

"Mary, sweet Mary, a name so sweet that in saying it my heart is in paradise. A name so sacred and holy that my heart is aflame with heavenly love."

and is dead. Orpheus, a musician, is grief-stricken and decides to travel to the underworld to bring Euridice back to life. The king of the underworld is moved by Orpheus's plea and allows Euridice to return, but on one condition: that Orpheus not turn back and look at her. On their journey, Orpheus becomes anxious and steals a glance at his beloved. She disappears forever.

Monteverdi sets this story with a wide variety of music. There are madrigal-like choruses, dances, and instrumental interludes. But the most striking style of all is called **recitative**, which developed out of the early experiments with monody. Recitative is designed to imitate as closely as possible the freedom and expressiveness of speech.

Recitative is always sung by one singer with accompanying basso continuo. It is very flexible, for it follows the changing meanings of the text, with the bass line supporting the voice and providing punctuation. It can be very simple or quite elaborate and songlike. It is designed to mirror, moment by moment, the emotional state of the singer. In all of his music, but especially in his recitatives, Monteverdi displays the talent that all great opera composers have in common: the ability to capture and reflect the feelings of the human soul. "The modern composer," he said, "builds his works on the basis of truth." **(See Listening Guide on page 122).**

OPERA IN THE SEVENTEENTH CENTURY

In Baroque opera, a distinction gradually arose between those portions of the recitative that were lyrical and songlike and those portions that were more straightforward and conversational. The lyrical part came to be known as **aria,** and the conversational part kept the old name of recitative. Arias were usually written in set forms, with a fixed pattern of repetition, whereas recitatives were freer in form and quite short. The sparse accompaniment and flexible style of recitative made it ideal for setting dialogue and quick interchanges

An Argument over the Future of Music

About 1600, composers and music theorists engaged in a furious debate over the direction that music should take. The most important figures involved were Giovanni Artusi, a prominent Italian music theorist, and the illustrious composer Claudio Monteverdi. They were on opposite sides of the debate. Artusi believed in the conservative Prima Pratica ("First Practice"), whereas Monteverdi was an adherent of the more progressive Seconda Pratica ("Second Practice"). Supporters of the Prima Pratica believed that all composers should adhere to the strict rules of composition adopted by the great composers of the late sixteenth century, most notably Palestrina. Composers should not break those rules regardless of the text they were setting. The slogan "Harmony is the ruler of the text" therefore became Artusi's battle cry. ✦ Monteverdi, however, believed that in passages with very expressive text, the rules could be broken to make the music more intense. He reversed Artusi's slogan to claim that "Text is the ruler of the harmony." In return, Artusi said that Monteverdi and other modern composers had "smoke in their heads" and that their compositions were "the product of ignorance."

Claudio Monteverdi (1567–1643)
Orfeo's recitative, Euridice's recitative,
**   chorus of nymphs and shepherds,**
**   and instrumental ritornello**
**   from the opera *Orfeo***

Date of composition: 1607
Tenor and soprano solo, chorus,
    instrumental ensemble and basso
    continuo
Duration: 3:55

Student CD Collection: 1, track 58
Complete CD Collection: 2, track 1

The following scene comes from the first act of the opera, in which the love of Orfeo and Euridice is celebrated. In his lyrical recitative "Rosa del Ciel ..." ("Rose of Heaven ..."), Orfeo expresses his passion for Euridice and his happiness that she returns his feelings. Euridice, responding to Orfeo's proclamation of love, affectionately pledges her heart to him in a declamatory passage ("Io non dirò ..."—"I shall not say ..."). A chorus of nymphs and shepherds follows with a celebratory dance ("Lasciate i monti ..."—"Leave the hills ..."), and the scene is closed by an instrumental ritornello.

Monteverdi uses a variety of forms and musical means to depict this pastoral setting. Both Orfeo and Euridice sing in a free, expressive recitative. The melody imitates the rhythms and the inflections of speech and mirrors the meaning of the text. In Orfeo's part, for instance, Monteverdi accentuates significant words such as "fortunato amante" ("happy lover") or "Mio ben" ("My love") by means of rising phrases and matches the musical rhythm with the rhythm of the words:

"fe-li-cís-si-mo" ("happiest")   [♪♪♪♩♪♪]
"sos-pi-rá-i" ("I sighed"); "sos-pi-rás-ti" ("you sighed")   [♪♪♩♩]

In Euridice's recitative, the composer uses similar lively motives for the words "gioir," "gioia," and "gioisca" ("rejoicing," "rejoice," "enjoys"); employs wide leaps to represent "Quanto" ("How much"); and provides the words "core" ("heart") and "Amore" ("Love") with soothing cadences.

The choral dance consists of two sections: The first, in duple meter, is based on imitative phrases that evoke the movement of dancers; the second provides a distinct contrast, since it is set in triple meter and its texture is completely homophonic. The instrumental ritornello that ensues is a faster dance, which adds variety and brings closure to this short and happy scene.

[soft arpeggiated chords in continuo]

58 (1) 0:00

Rosa del Ciel, vita del mondo, e degna	O Rose of Heaven, life of the world,
Prole di lui che l'Universo affrena,	And worthy offspring of him who rules the universe,

[voice becoming more animated]

0:25

Sol, ch'il tutto circondi e'l tutto miri	Sun, you who surround and watch everything
Da gli stellanti giri,	From the starry skies,

[rising melody]

0:34

Dimmi, vedesti mai	Tell me, have you ever seen
Di me più lieto e fortunato amante?	A happier or more fortunate lover than I?

[gentle cadence]

0:45

Fu ben felice il giorno,	Blessed was the day,
Mio ben, [loving phrase] *che pria ti vidi,*	My love, when first I saw you,

0:56

E più felice l'ora	And more blessed yet the hour
Che per te sospirai,	When first I sighed for you,
Poich'al mio sospirar tu sospirasti.	Since you returned my sighs.

[sighing phrases]

1:15

Felicissimo il punto	Most blessed of all the moment
Che la candida mano,	When you offered me your white hand,
Pegno di pura fede, a me porgesti.	As pledge of your pure love.

[many notes]

1:34

Se tanti cori avessi	If I had as many hearts
Quant'occh'il Ciel eterno, e quante chiome	As the eternal sky has eyes, and as many as these hills
Han questi colli ameni il verde maggio,	Have leaves in the verdant month of May,

1:45 [one "full" note]

Tutti colmi sarieno e traboccanti	They would all be full and overflowing
Di quel piacer ch'oggi mi fa contento.	With the joy that now makes me happy.

[soft cadence]

EURIDICE

[soft lute chords]

59 (2)   **2:09**

Io non dirò qual sia   I shall not say how much

[happy phrases]

2:15   *Nel tuo gioir, Orfeo, la gioia mia,*   I rejoice, Orfeo, in your rejoicing,

2:21   *Che non ho meco il core,*   For my heart is no longer my own

2:27   *Ma teco stassi in compagnia d'Amore;*   But stands with you in the company of Love;

["lui" emphasized]

2:35   *Chiedilo dunque a lui, s'intender brami,*   Ask of *it* then, if you wish to know,

2:42   *Quanto lieto gioisca, e quanto t'ami.*   How much happiness it enjoys, and how much it loves you.

[soft cadence]

CHORUS

[happy imitation, duple meter]

60 (3)   **2:59**

Lasciate i monti,   Leave the hills,
Lasciate i fonti,   Leave the streams,
Ninfe vezzose e liete,   You charming and happy nymphs,

[same music]

3:09   *E in questi prati*   Practiced in dancing,
Ai balli usati   And in these meadows
Vago il bel pie rendete.   Move your pretty legs.

[change of key, homophony, triple meter]

3:18   *Qui miri il Sole*   Here the Sun
Vostre carole   Sees your dances,
Più vaghe assai di quelle,   More beautiful yet than those

[same music]

3:26   *Ond'a la Luna*   Which the stars dance
La notte bruna   To the light of the moon
Danzano in Ciel le stelle.   In dusky night.

INSTRUMENTAL RITORNELLO

3:33   Faster; recorders, strings, basso continuo

between people in the drama, while arias were reserved for contemplative or passionate moments when the composer wanted to explore the full emotional content of a situation. Recitative usually had simple basso continuo accompaniment; the arias were usually accompanied by full orchestra. The most common forms for arias were ABA form (the B section providing a contrast) and ground bass form, in which a single phrase in the bass is repeated over and over again while the voice sings an extended melody above it.

Henry Purcell and English Opera

While music flourished in Italy, the state of music in England was highly fragmented because of an unstable political situation. The Civil War, which raged from 1642 to 1649, ended with the beheading of the constitutional monarch, Charles I. There followed a period called the Commonwealth, in which the Puritan ethic reigned. As a result, most musical positions were abolished, and theaters and opera houses were closed. In 1660, the son of Charles I returned from exile in France and assumed the throne as Charles II. His return, known as the Restoration, brought with it a rebirth of musical life in England.

Henry Purcell at the age of 36 (the year he died).

The most talented English composer of the late seventeenth century was Henry Purcell, who lived from 1659 to 1695. He held the important position of organist at Westminster Abbey in London and was one of the most prolific composers of his day. In his short life, Purcell wrote a large amount of vocal and instrumental music, including sacred music for the Anglican church, secular songs and cantatas, and chamber music for various combinations of instruments, as well as solo harpsichord music. His best-known work is a short opera called *Dido and Aeneas,* written in 1689.

Dido and Aeneas is a miniature masterpiece. It is based on a part of the great epic poem from antiquity, the *Aeneid* of Virgil. It tells the story of the love affair between Dido, Queen of Carthage, and Aeneas, a mythological Trojan warrior, and it ends with Aeneas's departure and Dido's death. There are three acts—with arias, recitatives, choruses, dances, and instrumental interludes—but only four main singers are required, together with a very small orchestra of strings and harpsichord. The whole opera takes only an hour.

The most famous aria from *Dido and Aeneas* is Dido's lament. Dido has been abandoned by Aeneas and has decided to kill herself. She expresses her determination, her grief, and the pathos of her situation in a deeply moving musical framework. The lament is a ground bass aria—that is, the entire melody is set over a repeated pattern in the bass. **(See Listening Guide on page 126.)**

Sonata and Concerto

Along with the invention of opera, the other major development in the early Baroque was the rise of instrumental music. And the most important instruments were those of the violin family.

Some Italian towns specialized in the making of violins, violas, and cellos, and some makers became very famous. The instruments of Antonio Stradivari and Giuseppe Guarneri are considered the finest ever produced. A genuine "Strad" can be worth several hundred thousand dollars.

The favorite genres of violin music in the last part of the seventeenth century were the sonata and the concerto. A **sonata** was a chamber piece of several contrasting movements, written for a small number of instruments. It could be a **solo sonata**, for a single instrument with basso continuo, or a **trio sonata**, for two instruments and basso continuo. The basso continuo was usually made up of a harpsichord and a low string instrument, such as a cello. The cello would play the bass line and the harpsichord would double the bass line in the left hand and play chords or melodic figures in the right, frequently improvising over the

Gustav Holst, the twentieth-century English composer, called Purcell's *Dido and Aeneas* "the only perfect English opera ever written."

The beauties and graces that are practised on the violin are so great in number that they force listeners to declare the violin to be the king of instruments.
—From a book of instruments published in 1673.

Henry Purcell (1659–1695)
Dido's lament from the opera
  Dido and Aeneas

Date of composition: 1689
Voice, strings, and harpsichord
Duration: 4:07

Student CD Collection: 1, track 61
Complete CD Collection: 2, track 4

The aria is introduced by a short recitative ("Thy hand, Belinda …") that sets the stage for the emotional intensity of the aria. The recitative has a sparse accompaniment that moves steadily downward, reflecting Dido's grief.

Immediately after this recitative, the ground bass for the aria is heard alone. It is worth looking closely at this phrase, not only because it occurs so many times in the aria (11 times in all), but also because it is very carefully constructed, and the overall effect of the aria depends upon it.

The first important element of this phrase is the fact that it descends chromatically (that is, by half steps). This chromatic descent immediately establishes a sad mood, which continues throughout the piece.

The next thing to notice is the rhythmic shift in the third and fourth measures of the phrase. This is a very subtle shift, but it is very important: it gives the bass line extra interest.

Finally, the ground bass pattern that Purcell establishes for this aria is five measures long, which is quite unusual. Most musical phrases are made up of four or eight measures. But Purcell chose this irregular length deliberately. It sets up a tension in the music, which contributes to the overall sense of strain and grief. It also enables Purcell to allow the vocal line more freedom as it floats over the ground bass. Throughout the aria, the endings of the ground bass pattern and the endings of the vocal phrases sometimes coincide and sometimes are independent. As the intensity increases, the vocal line becomes freer and freer from the constraint of the bass pattern. At the end of the aria, the voice and the ground bass cadence together, and the orchestra provides a short conclusion that is in keeping with the overall mood of the piece.

There are few words in this aria, but, as in most opera arias, they are repeated for dramatic effect. Arias are designed not to convey information or to further the plot but to explore an emotional state. The aria lasts much longer than the opening recitative. It is worth listening to this piece several times to appreciate the skill with which Purcell created it.

RECITATIVE			
61 (4)	0:00	Thy hand, Belinda, darkness shades me,	[slowly descending voice throughout the recitative]
	0:19	On thy bosom let me rest.	
	0:29	More I would, but Death invades me:	
	0:40	Death is now a welcome guest.	[minor chord on "Death;" dissonance on "welcome guest"]
	0:54	[beginning of ground bass: quiet, slow, descending chromatic line heard throughout aria]	
ARIA			
62 (5)	1:08 (1:43)	When I am laid in earth,	[ground bass pattern begins again on "am"]
	1:20 (1:55)	May my wrongs create	[no pause between these two lines]
	1:27	No trouble in thy breast.	[voice falls on the word "trouble"]
	(2:02)	[repeat]	
63 (6)	2:17	Remember me, but ah! forget my fate.	[much repetition; highly expressive rising lines; last "ah" is particularly lyrical]
	2:42	[several repeats]	
	3:30	[cadences of voice and ground bass coincide]	
64 (7)	3:32	[quiet orchestral closing; conclusion of chromatic descent]	
	4:02	[final cadence with trill]	

bass. As in other Baroque music, a strong bass line remained a characteristic feature of Baroque chamber music.

Both the solo sonata and the trio sonata had several contrasting movements. If the movements were based on dance rhythms, the sonata was known as a **sonata da camera** ("chamber sonata"). The movements of a **sonata da chiesa** ("church sonata") were more serious in character.

Apart from the sonata, the favorite form of instrumental music in the Baroque era was the **concerto**. This was a larger composition, meant for performance in greater spaces such as public halls, and it involved solo players and an orchestra.

The Italian word "concertare" has two meanings. It means to struggle or fight; it also means to cooperate. Both of these contrary meanings are present in a concerto, in which a solo player or a group of solo players is contrasted with an entire orchestra. Sometimes soloists and orchestra all play together, sometimes separately. Sometimes they play contrasting music, sometimes the same music. This dramatic balance and contrast of opposing forces is the essence of the concerto.

The concerto emerged about the end of the seventeenth century. The earliest concertos had a small group of soloists contrasting with the whole orchestra. This type of concerto is known as a **concerto grosso** ("large concerto"). The usual solo group was made up of two violins with basso continuo, but other instrumental groups were possible. The orchestra consisted of violins, violas, cellos, and basso continuo.

The **solo concerto** developed later. In a solo concerto a single soloist is contrasted with the whole orchestra, and the element of drama becomes particularly striking. It was the rise of the solo concerto that led to an increase in technically demanding playing and the **virtuoso** or "show-off" element that has been a characteristic of concertos ever since.

The composer who first brought Italian violin music to international prominence was Arcangelo Corelli (1653–1713). In his compositions, Corelli expanded the technique of violin playing, using repeated notes, fast scales, and double stops (playing more than one string at a time). He once wrote that the aim of his compositions was to "show off the violin." He concentrated entirely on violin music, writing only sonatas and concertos. Corelli was one of the first composers to become famous exclusively from instrumental music, and his compositions were highly influential throughout the remainder of the Baroque era and beyond. **(See Listening Guide on page 129.)**

FRENCH MUSIC

During the seventeenth century, while England was still racked by civil war, France was ruled by one of the most powerful monarchs in European history. Louis XIV reigned for an unusually long time, from 1643 to 1715, and his tastes governed French life for the entire second half of the seventeenth century and well into the eighteenth. Fortunately, Louis XIV was an avid supporter of the arts, and French music flourished under his patronage.

Louis XIV loved to dance, and one of the most important influences on French music was dance. It was featured prominently in French opera and French instrumental music throughout the seventeenth century. By the 1700s, French dances, which were elegant and dignified in their steps, had influenced instrumental music across the whole of Europe. One of the most popular French dances, the minuet, even became established as one of the standard movements of the eighteenth-century Classic symphony.

Dance influenced music in France in two ways. First, French opera included a great deal of ballet. Seventeenth-century French operas were splendid affairs, with elaborate scenery, large choruses, and frequent interludes for dancing. The most important composer of French opera was Jean-Baptiste Lully (1632–1687), the king's music director. Lully's ballet scenes were so popular that the dances from his operas were often played as independent suites. This popularity gave impetus to another trend that had begun late in the Renaissance: the use of dance forms purely as independent instrumental music.

All Europe knows what a Capacity and Genius the French have for dancing and how universally it is admired and followed.
—Luigi Riccoboni

Louis XIV himself!

Hyacinthe Rigaud (1659–1743). Louis XIV, King of France (1638–1715). Portrait in royal costume (the head was painted on a separate canvas and later added). Oil on canvas, 277 × 194 cm. Louvre, Dpt. des Peintures, Paris, France. © Photograph by Erich Lessing. Erich Lessing/Art Resource, NY.

Arcangelo Corelli (1653–1713)
Trio Sonata, Op. 3, No. 7, for two violins
**   and basso continuo**

Date of composition: 1689
Key: E minor
Duration: 5:46

Complete CD Collection: 2, track 8

Corelli composed two types of trio sonatas. Chamber (*da camera*) sonatas featured a series of dances. Church (*da chiesa*) sonatas were divided into four movements: slow-fast-slow-fast. The sonata featured here is of the church type. It is written for two violins and basso continuo (chamber organ with cello). The basso continuo group is always present, supporting the two violins as well as supplying a third independent voice.

Notice how Corelli introduces slight changes throughout each movement while keeping the musical ideas very much the same. In this way, each movement is unified, yet continually evolving.

I. GRAVE	("slow and serious")
(8) **0:01**	Motive (slow descending line):

	The motive is stated several times, one measure apart, in this order: first violin, second violin, continuo. End of phrase is marked by a long chord.
0:22	Motive is repeated at different pitch level (dominant key).
0:45	Accompanied duet (violins), imitation, similar motive but much longer. The interweaving of the violins creates many expressive dissonances.

1:24	Slow cadence.

II. ALLEGRO	("fast")
(9) **1:40**	Rapidly moving trio, fugal treatment. New motive is a "wedge" shape, ending with fast notes. Several short sections, based on "wedge" motive.

2:20	Cadence.

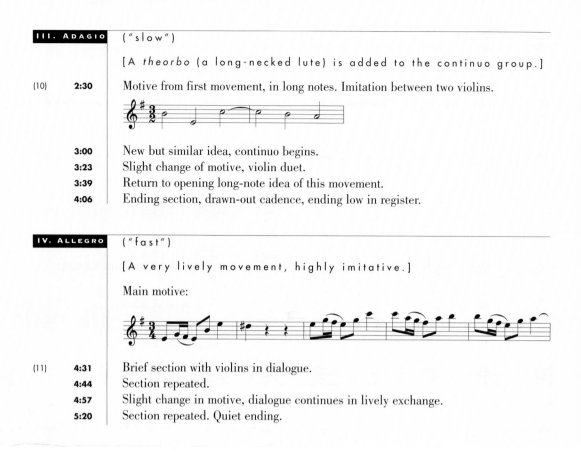

III. ADAGIO	("slow")
	[A *theorbo* (a long-necked lute) is added to the continuo group.]
(10) 2:30	Motive from first movement, in long notes. Imitation between two violins.
3:00	New but similar idea, continuo begins.
3:23	Slight change of motive, violin duet.
3:39	Return to opening long-note idea of this movement.
4:06	Ending section, drawn-out cadence, ending low in register.

IV. ALLEGRO	("fast")
	[A very lively movement, highly imitative.]
	Main motive:
(11) 4:31	Brief section with violins in dialogue.
4:44	Section repeated.
4:57	Slight change in motive, dialogue continues in lively exchange.
5:20	Section repeated. Quiet ending.

There were many different kinds of French dance in the seventeenth century, each with its own meter, rhythm, and characteristic melodic style. The most important is the minuet, a triple-time dance in moderate tempo, but there are many more. Each has its own special character.

A series of dances for instrumental performance is known as a dance *suite*. Usually, all the dances in the suite are in the same key, so that the variety of music resulting from the different types of dance can be unified. Composers of instrumental suites included François Couperin (1668–1733), known as *le grand* ("the great"), and Elisabeth-Claude Jacquet de la Guerre (1667–1729), who enjoyed the patronage of Louis XIV himself and was one of the first women to publish widely in French music and to be recognized for her achievements during her own lifetime.

The Main French Baroque Dances

DANCE	METER	TEMPO	DESCRIPTION
Allemande	Duple	Moderate	Continuous motion
Bourrée	Duple	Moderate to fast	Short, distinct phrases
Courante	Triple	Moderate to fast	Motion often in running scales
Gavotte	Duple	Moderate to fast	"Bouncy" sound
Gigue	usually 6/8	Fast	Lively, often imitative
Minuet	Triple	Moderate	Elegant
Sarabande	Triple	Slow	Stately; accent often on second beat

A grand ball at the French court.

THE LATE BAROQUE (1700–1750)

We mentioned before that the Baroque period as a whole can be divided into two phases: the early Baroque (1600–1700) and the late Baroque (1700–1750). In the early Baroque period, the main styles and genres were established; in the late Baroque, the fixed musical forms flourished in the hands of the Baroque masters who have become so popular today: Vivaldi, Bach, and Handel.

LATE BAROQUE OPERA

Opera continued to flourish in the late Baroque period. Other countries developed their own operatic traditions as well, but the favorite type of opera throughout Europe was Italian opera, and the main form of Italian opera was **opera seria** ("serious opera"). This had become quite stylized by the late Baroque period. The plots were often standard. Usually they were based on some story from ancient history and involved dramatic situations, two pairs of lovers, and a prince or king who resolves the situation in the end. There were always three acts, and the music was built around a constant alternation between recitatives and arias.

Recitatives were still used for carrying forward the plot. They were simple, fast, speechlike, and accompanied only by basso continuo.

Arias were the main reason people went to the opera. They provided the opportunity for the great singers of the time to display their talents. Every opera contained three or four arias for each of the main characters. At these moments, the action would stop, and the aria would explore the emotion created by the story: grief, rage, love, despair, and so on.

The standard form for opera arias continued to be ABA form. The mood was established in the first A section. Then the B section was sung as a contrast, usually in a different key or tempo. After the B section, the A section was repeated, with the same words and the same music but considerably ornamented with improvised figures, runs and scales, high notes, dramatic pauses, and the like. It was here that a singer could really show off his or her talent, vocal agility, and taste (or sometimes lack of it!).

THE LATE BAROQUE CONCERTO

By the beginning of the eighteenth century, the concerto had also become fixed in form. Composers con-

A Baroque instrumental concert. Notice the central position of the basso continuo players.

"Court concert at Prince Bishop of Luettich at Seraing Palace" (with violoncello of Prince Bishop Cardinal Johann Theodor of Bavaria). Painting, 1753, by Paul Joseph Delcloche (1716–1759). Oil on canvas, 186 × 240.5 cm. Munich, Bayerisches Nationalmuseum. Photo: AKG London.

tinued to write both concerti grossi (for small group and orchestra) and solo concertos, but the solo concerto became more and more popular. Instruments such as the flute, the oboe, and the trumpet began to be featured in solo concertos. Composers even began to write concertos for keyboard instruments. This was quite revolutionary, because the role of keyboard instruments in concertos had previously been restricted to the basso continuo.

There were many concerto composers active at this time, but the undisputed master of the concerto in the late Baroque period was Antonio Vivaldi.

ANTONIO VIVALDI (1678–1741)

Vivaldi's father was a violinist at St. Mark's in Venice, where Gabrieli and Monteverdi had made their careers, and Antonio learned music at an early age. Like many young men in the Baroque era, Vivaldi trained for the priesthood as well. Because of his red hair, he earned the nickname "The Red Priest." Illness prevented him

viola, and even mandolin. But most of his concertos are for one or more violins.

By the time of Vivaldi and the late Baroque period, concerto form had become clearly established. There are usually three movements, in the pattern fast-slow-fast. The first movement is usually an Allegro. The second movement usually has an expressive, slow melody that sounds like an opera aria. The third movement is a little faster and livelier than the first.

The first and third movements of a Baroque concerto are in **ritornello** form, which exploits the contrast

from continuing his priestly duties, however, and he soon began the job that would carry him through the remainder of his career: He was appointed director of music at the Ospedale della Pietà in Venice. This was a residential school for orphaned girls and young women, which combined basic education with religious training and placed a strong emphasis on music.

Vivaldi wrote a large amount of music for the Ospedale. The girls gave frequent concerts, and people traveled from all over Europe to hear them play. Among the composer's works are solo and trio sonatas, oratorios, sacred music, and nearly 600 concertos! Vivaldi wrote so much music that some of it has still not been published, and many of his pieces have not been heard since he first wrote them.

Vivaldi must have been inspired by the special talents of the young women in his school, because several of his concertos are for instruments that were then not normally thought of as solo instruments: small recorder, clarinet, bassoon,

Portrait of Vivaldi in his mid-forties.

Picture of a concert at the Ospedale della Pietà in Venice, where Vivaldi spent most of his career. The girls are playing behind the screen of the organ loft.

Vivaldi was himself an accomplished violinist. A young German law student saw him playing in 1715 and recorded in his diary: "Vivaldi played an improvization that really frightened me. I doubt anything like it was ever done before, or ever will be again."

133

between the solo instrument(s) and the orchestra in a highly organized way. *Ritornello* is the Italian word for something that returns. The ritornello in a concerto is an orchestral passage that constantly returns. Between appearances of the ritornello, the solo instrument plays passages of contrasting material, which are known as episodes.

At the beginning of a movement in ritornello form, the orchestra plays the entire ritornello in the tonic, or home key. During the body of the movement, the ritornello often will appear only in partial form and will be in different keys, but at the end it will return in its entirety in the tonic key. The solo episodes occur between these appearances. (See accompanying diagram.)

Perhaps the most famous of Vivaldi's concertos today are a group of four concertos known as *The Four Seasons*. They were published in 1725, when Vivaldi was 47 years old. They show Vivaldi's wonderful sense of invention in the concerto medium and his extraordinary flexibility within this seemingly rigid form.

These are solo violin concertos; but in several of the solo episodes, other instruments from the orchestra join in, so that the sound sometimes approaches that of a concerto grosso. There is also constant variety in the handling of the ritornello form, both in the keys employed for the partial returns and in the choice of which part of the ritornello is used. Finally, the *Four Seasons* concertos are an early instance of **program music**—music that is designed to tell a story.

For *The Four Seasons*, Vivaldi wrote four concertos, one for each season of the year. At the head of each concerto, Vivaldi printed a poem describing the season. Beyond that, Vivaldi actually wrote lines from the poem directly into the musical score, so that each musical phrase for the instrumental players is directly tied to the poetic descriptions. For example, there are pas-

sages for thunder and lightning, for a dog barking, for birds singing. But even apart from the poetic texts, the concertos are wonderful examples of the late Baroque violin concerto in their own right. (**See Listening Guide on page 135.**)

The Baroque concerto may seem rather rigid, with its set pattern of movements and its strict ritornello form, but, like pieces such as Vivaldi's *Four Seasons* show, it could be handled with great flexibility to produce music of variety, color, and contrast.

Vivaldi's music was heard and his influence felt not only in his native Italy but throughout Europe. Vivaldi's concertos were studied in great detail and closely imitated by another of the great masters of the late Baroque era: Johann Sebastian Bach.

JOHANN SEBASTIAN BACH (1685–1750)

One of the most influential musicians of all time, and certainly one of the greatest composers in the history of music, was Johann Sebastian Bach. His mastery of musical composition is so universally acknowledged that the date of his death is used to mark the end of the entire Baroque era.

Bach's whole career was spent in one region of Germany. He moved from one small town to another as job opportunities arose. The last part of his life was spent in the somewhat larger town of Leipzig.

Bach did not see himself as an artistic genius, but rather as a hard-working craftsman. He wrote most of his music to order, or to fulfill the requirements of a job. During his life, he was not widely known outside the relatively small circle of his family and acquaintances, and he traveled very little. He never wrote an opera, although that was the most popular

COMPLETE RITORNELLO	EPISODE 1	PARTIAL RITORNELLO	EPISODE 2	PARTIAL RITORNELLO	EPISODE 3	COMPLETE RITORNELLO

TONIC → OTHER KEYS → TONIC

Antonio Vivaldi (1678–1741)
First Movement from Violin Concerto,
    Op. 8, No. 1, *La Primavera* ("*Spring*"),
    from *The Four Seasons*

Date of composition: 1725
Solo violin, strings, and harpsichord
Duration: 3:34

Student CD Collection: 1, track 65
Complete CD Collection: 2, track 12

*L*ike most late Baroque concertos, Vivaldi's *La Primavera* has three movements: fast-slow-fast. Both of the fast movements are in ritornello form and are in a major key (E Major). The slow movement has a long, lyrical melody and is in the minor. In both of the outer movements, instruments from the orchestra join the soloist in some of the solo episodes, giving the impression of a concerto grosso. Both movements are also full of echo effects. The orchestra is made up of first and second violins, violas, cellos, basses, and harpsichord. Like all the *Seasons*, "Spring" is headed by a poem in the form of a sonnet. A sonnet has eight lines of poetry followed by six lines. The six lines are divided into two groups of three. Vivaldi uses the first eight lines for the first movement and the two groups of three for the next two movements.

First movement
(First eight lines of the poem):

> Spring has arrived, and full of joy
> The birds greet it with their happy song.
> The streams, swept by gentle breezes,
> Flow along with a sweet murmur.
> Covering the sky with a black cloak,
> Thunder and lightning come to announce the season.
> When all is quiet again, the little birds
> Return to their lovely song.

The first movement is written in the bright and extroverted key of E Major. The ritornello is made up of two phrases, both of which occur at the beginning of the movement; all the other times, only the second half of the ritornello is played. Between these appearances, the solo violin plays brilliant passages, imitating birdsong and flashes of lightning. Sometimes it plays alone, and sometimes it is joined by two violins from the orchestra.

ALLEGRO	["fast"]	
65 (12) **0:00**	"Spring has arrived, and full of joy"	[Ritornello in tonic, first half, loud and then soft]
0:15		[Ritornello in tonic, second half, loud and then soft]

	0:32	"The birds greet it with their happy song."	[Trills; three solo violins alone, no basso continuo]
	1:08		[Ritornello in tonic, second half, once only, loud]
	1:16	"The streams, swept by gentle breezes, Flow along with a sweet murmur."	[Quiet and murmuring]
66 (13)	1:41		[Ritornello in dominant, second half, once only, loud]
	1:49	"Covering the sky with a black cloak, Thunder and lightning come to announce the season."	[Fast repeated notes; flashing runs and darting passages]
67 (14)	2:17		[Ritornello in C# minor, second half, once only, loud]
	2:25	"When all is quiet again, the little birds Return to their lovely song."	[Long, sustained, single note in bass; rising solo phrases, trills again]
	2:43 3:10		[Buildup to: Ritornello in tonic, second half twice, first loud and then soft]

View of Leipzig in Bach's time. The spire of St. Thomas's Church is at the center.

musical genre of the time, because his jobs never required it.

The first jobs Bach held were as church organist in the small towns of Arnstadt and Mühlhausen near his birthplace. At the age of 23, he married and found a better position at the court of the Duke of Weimar, first as organist and later as leader of the orchestra. He stayed there for nine years (until 1717), leaving finally when he was turned down for the position of music director. The Duke of Weimar was so angry at Bach's decision to leave that he had him put in jail for a month!

But Bach got the position he wanted at the court of a nearby prince. The Prince of Cöthen was young, unmarried, and an enthusiastic amateur musician. He kept a small orchestra of his own and made Bach music director. Here, Bach was very happy. He was well paid, he could write a range of varied music, and he was highly regarded by the prince.

In 1720, when Bach was 35, his wife Barbara died. He was married again the following year to a young singer, Anna Magdalena, who, like Bach, was employed at the court of the Prince of Cöthen. Over the years, Bach and his wives had twenty children. Eleven of them died in childhood, as was common in those days, but nine grew to adulthood, and four became famous composers in their own right.

Bach might have stayed at Cöthen for the rest of his life, but the prince also married at this time, and his

and direct a new church cantata for every Sunday and feast day of the year. He was also head of the music school attached to St. Thomas's and was responsible for teaching Latin, composition, playing the organ, maintaining all the instruments, and preparing the choirs for the services at the three other main churches in Leipzig.

In 1747, Bach was asked to visit Frederick the Great, the powerful and autocratic King of Prussia. Like Louis XIV of France, Frederick loved music and employed several well-known musicians at his court. He also played the flute and composed a little flute music. One of Johann Sebastian Bach's sons, C. P. E. Bach, was the harpsichordist at Frederick's court. It was the younger Bach who was considered the more up-to-date

The sole surviving portrait of Johann Sebastian Bach.

Stadtgeschichtliches Museum Leipzig

new wife did not like music. The prince's support for Bach and his activities diminished, the orchestra was dismissed, and Bach started looking for a new job.

At this time, the town of Leipzig—a relatively large town with a university, two theaters, and a population of 30,000—was looking for a music director for its St. Thomas's Church. This position involved responsibility for all the town's church music, including that of St. Thomas's and three other churches.

The town council interviewed several musicians and finally settled on Bach as its third choice. (The first choice, composer Georg Philipp Telemann, turned them down, and the second man on the list was not permitted to leave his current post.) But third choice or not, Bach happily accepted the position and moved with his growing family to Leipzig in 1723, when he was 38 years old. He was to remain there for the rest of his life.

Bach was extremely busy in Leipzig. There were several aspects to his job, all of which he fulfilled cheerfully and efficiently. He was required to compose, rehearse,

A contemporary engraving of St. Thomas's Church and its school (left), where Bach worked for the last twenty-seven years of his life.

Frederick the Great playing the flute at a concert in his palace. Bach's son, C. P. E. Bach, is seated at the harpsichord.

composer. Johann Sebastian was known affectionately, but not very respectfully, as "Old Bach." By the middle of the eighteenth century, his music was regarded as old-fashioned and too complicated.

Bach died in 1750, leaving an unparalleled legacy to the musical world. Audiences ever since have been attracted to Bach's music for its careful organization, clear tonal direction, expressive nature, and intellectual brilliance. Bach himself saw his music as a means of supporting his family, instructing his fellow human beings, and glorifying God. For his sons and for his second wife, Anna Magdalena, he wrote books of short keyboard pieces. One book of organ pieces was written "for the instruction of my fellow men." And at the end of many of his compositions, he wrote the letters "S. D. G.," which stand for "Soli Deo Gloria" ("For the Glory of God Alone").

Bach was also exceedingly modest. Toward the end of his life, he said, "I was obliged to work hard. But anyone who is equally industrious will succeed just as well." Family man, teacher, good citizen, humble and pious spirit, Johann Sebastian Bach was also one of the musicians in history on whom we can unhesitatingly bestow the title "genius."

Musical Imitations

Bach's roles as teacher and performer during his years at Leipzig were extremely time-consuming. In addition, he was required to compose regularly. To save time, Bach sometimes reworked existing compositions (both his own and those of other composers) into new pieces. This process has come to be known as "imitation" technique. ✦ "Imitations" can be found both in Bach's instrumental and in his vocal compositions. One of Bach's crowning achievements, written near the end of his life, is the Mass in B minor, much of which consists of movements from his earlier cantatas. Bach welds a diverse range of compositions into a magnificent whole. One scholar has said that the B minor Mass demonstrates that Bach's technique of imitation, adaptation, and compilation must itself be accepted as "a creative act almost on a par with what we normally think of as 'original composition.'" ✦ In 1729, in addition to all his other activities, Bach was appointed director of the Collegium Musicum in Leipzig. During his years directing the Collegium, Bach produced 14 harpsichord concertos. Only one of these, however, was an original work. Most of them are brilliant reworkings of violin concertos by another great eighteenth-century composer: Antonio Vivaldi.

A Musical Offering

In May 1747, Bach traveled to Potsdam, near Berlin, to visit Frederick the Great of Prussia. He displayed his extraordinary skills of improvisation in the presence of the king, and as a result Frederick presented him with a theme to be used as the basis for a composition. When heard alone, the theme seems extremely unpromising. ✦ It is a testimony to Bach's brilliance as a composer that on his return home, he managed to work this theme into an extended and impressive series of pieces, which he entitled *A Musical Offering* and sent with a florid dedication to Frederick the Great. ✦ *A Musical Offering* consists of two fugues, 10 canons (rounds), and a trio sonata. Each of the 13 pieces uses Frederick's theme. The unity that this provides is complemented by the wide variety of canonic procedures employed. These include conventional canons, a canonic fugue, a canon in contrary motion, puzzle canons, and a "crab" canon, in which one player starts at the beginning of the piece and works forward, while the other starts at the end and works backward! Bach's skill and ingenuity in *A Musical Offering* confirm his status as the greatest composer of counterpoint in the history of music.

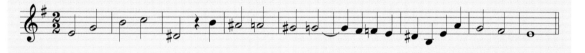

Bach's Music

Bach wrote in all the Baroque era's major musical genres, with the exception of opera. His works range from the monumental to the miniature, and they include both sacred and secular music. Every piece is marked by the same careful and faultless construction, the same unerring sense of direction and timing. The Baroque values of rhythmic drive and emotional intensity are vividly present in his compositions. His simple chorale harmonizations are magisterial models for students of harmony. Bach was also an unparalleled master of counterpoint, and composers ever since have studied his works to learn how to combine independent musical lines with conviction and clarity.

The types of music Bach wrote at different periods in his life depended on the kind of job he held at the time. In his early years, he primarily wrote organ music. At the court of the Prince of Cöthen, Bach mostly wrote for keyboard, or for orchestra and other instrumental groups. During the Leipzig years, he produced a large amount of church music, as well as more instrumental compositions.

Bach's Organ Music

Bach's organ music is extremely varied. It includes settings of Lutheran chorales, organ trio sonatas, and preludes and fugues. The chorales are either set in harmony for organ or used as the basis for a series of variations. In the organ trio sonatas, the right hand plays one line, the left hand plays another, and the pedals of the organ are used for the basso continuo.

The prelude and fugue contrast a free type of music

He did not write opera

Johann Sebastian Bach (1685–1750)
Prelude and Fugue in E minor

Date of composition: before 1708
Solo organ
Duration: 4:13

Complete CD Collection: 2, track 15

*B*ach, both an accomplished organist and an accomplished composer, makes full use of the organ in his Prelude and Fugue in E minor as well as in his other organ works. In the Prelude and Fugue in E minor, Bach displays the capabilities of both the foot-operated pedal keyboard (which plays the lowest-sounding notes) and the hand-operated keyboard (known as a "manual"). Organs usually have more than one keyboard on which the performer can play different sounds. Changes in timbre can also be produced by pulling and pushing on knobs (known as "stops"). These stops may be used not only to change timbre but also to add an additional line in parallel octaves to the notes (particularly in the pedal keyboard). The common phrase "pulling out all the stops" comes from organ playing.

Changes in timbre are quite evident in this recording. In the Prelude, the first long pedal low note is pure, simple, and flutey. Then the organist pulls out a stop to make the subsequent pedal notes richer and fuller. In the fugue, the organist uses the stops to set up what seem like two different instruments, one with an oboe-like sound and one with a clarinet-like sound. These instruments then compete with each other throughout the piece.

The theme or subject in the fugue is characterized by a special rhythm (dit diddle-DEE, dit diddle-DEE) that makes it easily recognizable.

PRELUDE		
(15)	0:00	Free-flowing music over sustained, soft, low pedal
	0:23	Timbre change; fanfare-like music with flourishes
	0:46	Pedal line alternating with keyboards
	0:55	Switches to top line answered by other voices
	1:10	Music gets "chunky," almost like a slow polka
	1:27	"Chunks" separated by climbing pedal line
	1:44	Pedals and manuals combine for full ending of Prelude

(16)	2:08	First entry of fugue subject (dit diddle-DEE, dit diddle-DEE); instrumental effects created by different stops
	2:14	Second entry of subject (slightly lower)
	2:25	Third entry (high); the other lines are still playing
	2:34	Fourth entry
	2:45	Fifth entry (!) on pedals (in octaves)
	2:54	Change of texture; intervening passage with sixteenth notes
	3:07	Low entry; pedals return to accompany
	3:24	High section with entries spaced out
	3:37	Light section; no pedals
	3:58	Final entry on pedals; the big finale

with a very strict type. The prelude (sometimes called "toccata" or "fantasia") is a rambling, improvisatory piece of the kind that organists play to fill in time before, during, or after a church service. The **fugue** is a carefully worked-out polyphonic composition, that uses a theme (or "subject") that occurs in all the voices, or musical lines, in turn. It begins with a single voice playing the subject unaccompanied. As the second voice brings in the fugue subject, the first one continues playing—and so on, until all the voices are sounding independently. A fugue may have two, three, or four voices. After visiting Frederick the Great, Bach wrote one fugue that has six voices.

Bach was a master of counterpoint, and the fugue is the most demanding type of counterpoint to write. (**See Listening Guide above.**)

BACH'S KEYBOARD, INSTRUMENTAL, AND ORCHESTRAL MUSIC

During his years at the Cöthen court, Bach produced a large amount of music for solo keyboard, other solo in-

struments, and small orchestra. In this music particularly, Bach melded the characteristics of Italian, French, and German styles. Italian music had rhythmic drive and brilliance. French music favored dance forms and ornament. German music was serious and contrapuntal. Bach drew on all these elements to produce an individual style that was the high point of the Baroque era.

Bach wrote much solo music, perhaps inspired by the fine players at the prince's court. There are suites and sonatas for solo violin and solo harpsichord, suites for solo cello, and a suite for solo flute. He also composed several sonatas and trio sonatas.

From the Cöthen years come a large number of orchestral compositions. These include some suites for orchestra, as well as several concertos, including the famous *Brandenburg* Concertos. (**See Listening Guide on page 142.**)

BACH'S VOCAL CHURCH MUSIC

During Bach's stay in Leipzig, he wrote hundreds of cantatas for church services, as well as several other

Johann Sebastian Bach (1685–1750)
First Movement from *Brandenburg*
  Concerto No. 2 in F Major

Date of composition: 1721
Instruments: Solo recorder, oboe, horn,
  and violin; with strings and continuo
Tempo: *Allegro*
Key: F Major
Duration: 5:12

Complete CD Collection: 2, track 17

$\mathcal{B}$ach completed the six *Brandenburg* Concertos for the Margrave of Brandenburg in 1721. They show a fusion of national styles, as well as Bach's brilliant mixture of melody and counterpoint.

The *Brandenburg* Concerto No. 2 is in three movements (fast-slow-fast), contrasting solo and ripieno (full ensemble) groups. Bach also explores coloristic possibilities within the solo group (recorder, oboe, horn, and violin) in various combinations of solos, duets, trios, and quartets throughout. Although this piece is often played with flute and trumpet, the word "flute" usually meant recorder in Bach's time, and an early manuscript copy of the score calls for "either trumpet or horn."

The first movement features three rhythmic motives, which combine to form the ritornello:

  a. mixture of eighth notes and sixteenth notes:

  b. eighth notes, triadic:

  c. sixteenth notes, running:

The ways in which these ideas are re-combined, sorted and re-sorted, and moved from one instrument to another, and the ways in which Bach organizes his harmonies and textures are nothing short of astounding.

I		[opening section]
(17)	**0:00**	Ritornello (Tonic: F Major), motives "a," "b," and "c" together
	0:20	Violin solo
	0:25	Ritornello
	0:31	Duet (violin and oboe)
	0:37	Horn solo
	0:41	Duet (recorder and oboe), followed by horn
	0:51	Duet (horn and recorder)
	0:57	Continuation
II		[second section]
(18)	**1:12**	Solo quartet, accompanied by continuo, based on "c"
	1:22	Sequences (fragment of "b"), horn answered by oboe; harmonic modulation
	1:40	Dynamic "echoes" (loud sections followed by soft); based on "a" and "c"
III		[episode]
(19)	**2:07**	Continuing to modulate, steady eighth notes in bass, reaching:
	2:22	Ritornello in B-flat Major
	2:32	Duet (recorder and violin), joined by oboe and horn
(20)	**2:53**	Ritornello, C minor; motive "c" now prominent on top
	3:03	Another harmonically unstable section
	3:16	More sequences between horn and oboe, modulating to:
	3:24	G minor, ritornello
	3:35	Constant changes of texture and harmony (basses get motive "a"!); cadence

IV		[closing section]
(21)	4:24	Surprise! Everyone in unison on motive "a"; back to home key of F Major
	4:35	Another surprise! One last harmonic excursion
	5:02	Return to original texture
	5:07	Return to original key and ritornello

important sacred vocal pieces. These include motets, Passions, and the Mass in B minor, which is regarded as one of the greatest traditional Mass settings that has ever been composed.

Bach wrote two Passions for the Lutheran churches of Leipzig. (A third is rumored to exist but has never been found.) A **Passion** is a musical setting of the story from the Gospels of the death and resurrection of Jesus. Bach based one setting on the account in the Gospel of St. John, and the other setting on the account in the Gospel of St. Matthew. Although Bach's musical legacy is full of masterpieces, the *St. Matthew Passion* is universally regarded as one of the most monumental musical masterpieces of all time. It is a huge composition, lasting some three hours, for solo singers, two choruses, one boys' choir, two orchestras, and two organs, and it runs the gamut of human emotion, from grief to awe to despair to spiritual transcendence. With this work alone, Bach shows us how music can reflect and deepen the meaning of human existence. **(See Listening Guide on page 146.)**

GEORGE FRIDERIC HANDEL (1685–1759)

Although Handel's life overlapped Bach's almost exactly, their careers were remarkably different. As we have seen, Bach lived a quiet, busy life in one small region of Germany. By contrast, Handel traveled extensively and became an international celebrity. Al-

though the central musical genre of the Baroque era was opera, Bach wrote no operas. Handel's career was built on the nearly 40 operas he wrote, mostly for the London stage. Bach was a family man; Handel never married.

Handel was born in Halle, a small town in Germany. His family was not musical, and his father wanted him to study law. He was so obviously gifted in music, however, that he was allowed to study with the music director and organist of the local church. He learned to play the organ, the harpsichord, and the violin, and he studied counterpoint and composition. Handel studied law at the University of Halle for only a year and then left for Hamburg, which was the main center of opera in Germany. He joined the opera orchestra there as a violinist and harpsichordist. At the age of 19, Handel composed his first opera, which was performed at the Hamburg opera house.

Because most operas at this time were Italian operas, Handel decided to travel to Italy, to the center of operatic activity. At 21, he was still only a young man, but he scored a phenomenal success there.

After three years in Italy, Handel was appointed music director to the Elector of Hanover, back in Germany. This was a well-paid position, but Handel was restless. He kept requesting leaves of absence to travel to London, which was fast becoming one of the most important musical centers in the world. In 1712, Handel was granted a short leave to London, which he greatly overstayed, ultimately turning it into a lifelong visit.

Portrait of Handel in his middle years.

Anonymous. Portrait of G. F. Handel. Civico Museo Bibliografico Musicale Rossini, Bologna, Italy. Giraudon/Art Resource, NY.

Handel did write operas

INSIDE THE ORCHESTRA CD-ROM

The Baroque Orchestra

It was during the Baroque period that the symphony orchestra as we know it today began to form. This was the period of great stringed instrument makers and performers, and music began to be composed for groups of string players: violinists, violists, cellists, and bassists. The court of King Louis XIV in the seventeenth century featured a famous string group known as "The Twenty-Four String Players of the King." Throughout the history of the orchestra it has been a body of strings that has formed the core of the sound. Other instruments quickly became common in Baroque orchestras. Since the bass line is so important in Baroque music, a keyboard instrument, usually a harpsichord, plays along with the basses. Sometimes a bassoon (or a pair of bassoons) does, too. And high wind instruments are often used in addition to the strings. The most frequent are a pair of oboes and a pair of horns. These have their own special sound: Oboes have a rich, incisive, edgy quality that adds intensity to the smooth sound of the strings. And horns, with their round and sometimes stirring sound, fill out the middle timbre of the orchestra. You can hear a Baroque orchestra most clearly in the Monteverdi, Purcell, Bach (*Brandenburg* Concerto), and Handel (*Giulio Cesare*) extracts featured in this chapter.

A perfect example of the Baroque orchestra is Handel's Overture to the "Water Music". You can watch a live performance of this work in Segment 3 of your *Inside the Orchestra* CD-ROM.

Johann Sebastian Bach (1685–1750)
St. Matthew Passion (excerpt)

Date of composition: c. 1727
Soprano, tenor, and bass voices,
  chorus, orchestra, and basso
  continuo
Duration: 8:07

Student CD Collection: 2, track 1
Complete CD Collection: 2, track 22

*T*his excerpt from Bach's *St. Matthew Passion* shows the composer's mastery at achieving a fusion of seriousness and expressiveness suitable to the biblical text. The role of narrator for the Gospel story is performed by the "Evangelist" (tenor), who sings in recitative with a simple continuo accompaniment. The words of Jesus (bass) are "haloed" by lush string accompaniment. The chorus portrays the responses of the 12 disciples. This happens most effectively when Jesus predicts that one of them will betray him, and they ask, "Lord, is it I?" (If you listen very carefully, you will hear 11 questions. The voice of the twelfth disciple—Judas—is missing.)

A soprano soloist begins this excerpt in an aria that beautifully reflects the situation (Jesus as the sacrifice for all) that is ultimately the focus of the entire work. And the whole section is rounded off in peace and contemplation by the plain but moving harmonies of the final chorale.

1 (22) 0:00	[orchestral introduction]	

SOPRANO		
	[aria]	
2 (23) 0:31	*Blute nur, blute nur*	Only bleed, only bleed,
	Blute nur, du liebes Herz,	Only bleed, you dearest heart.
	[repeat text four times; answering phrases on flutes and violins; motion throughout in orchestra]	
1:19	[orchestral interlude]	
3 (24) 1:51	[change of key, similar accompanying figures as A section]	
	Ach! ein Kind das du erzogen,	Ah! a child that you raised
	das an deiner Brust gesogen,	and nursed at your breast
	droht den Pfleger zu ermorder,	has become a snake
	denn es ist zur Schlange worden;	and bites the one who cared for it;
2:21	[repeat, varied]	
3:00	[orchestral passage from beginning]	
4 (25) 3:32	*Blute nur, du liebes Herz* ... [repeated exactly as beginning]	
4:20	[orchestral closing passage]	

EVANGELIST		
	[simple basso continuo accompaniment]	
5 (26) 5:00	*Aber am ersten Tage der süssen Brot*	Now on the first day of the feast of unleavened bread
	traten die Jünger zu Jesu und sprachen zu ihm:	the disciples came to Jesus and said to him:

CHORUS

[noble, serious tone]

5:10

Wo, wo, wo willst du, dass wir dir
bereiten, das Osterlamm zu essen?
Wo willst du, dass wir dir bereiten das
Osterlamm zu essen?

Where, where, where will you have us
prepare for you to eat the Passover?
Where will you have us prepare for you
to eat the Passover?

EVANGELIST

[recitative]

5:36

Er sprach:

He said:

JESUS

[accompanied recitative—violins form a "halo" around the
words of Jesus]

6 (27)   5:39

Gehet hin in die Stadt zu
einem und sprecht zu ihm:
Der Meister lässt dir sagen:
Meine Zeit is hier,
ich will bei dir die Ostern halten
mit meinen Jüngern.

Go to the city to a certain
man and say to him:
The Master says to you:
My time is here,
I will keep the Passover at your house
with my disciples.

EVANGELIST

[recitative—simple basso continuo accompaniment]

6:08

Und die Jüngern täten, wie
ihnen Jesus befohlen hatte,
und bereiteten das Osterlamm.
Und am Abend satzte er sich
zu Tische mit den Zwölfen,
Und da sie assen, sprach er:

And the disciples did as
Jesus had commanded,
and prepared the Passover.
And at evening he sat at the
table with the twelve,
and as they ate, he said:

JESUS

[accompanied recitative]

6:32

Warlich, ich sage euch:
Eines unter euch wird mich verraten.

Truly, I say to you:
One of you will betray me.

["halo;" dissonance and intensity on "betray"]

EVANGELIST

[recitative]

6:50

Und sie wurden sehr betrübt
Und huben an, ein jeglicher
unter ihnen, und sagten zu ihm:

And they became very troubled
and they spoke, each one
of them, and said to Him:

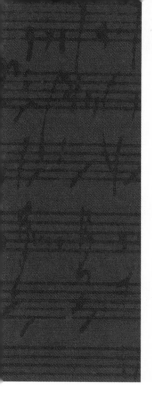

[fast, panicky music]

7 (28) **6:59**

Herr, bin ichs? bin ichs? *bin ichs? bin ichs?*	Lord, is it I? Is it I? Is it I? Is it I?
Herr, bin ichs? bin ichs? *bin ichs? bin ichs?*	Lord, is it I? Is it I? Is it I? Is it I?
Herr, bin ichs? bin ichs? bin ichs?	Lord, is it I? Is it I? Is it I?

[calm setting of final chorale]

7:11

Ich bins, ich sollte büssen,	I should bear all of it,
an Händen und an Füssen	my hands and feet tethered
gebunden in her Höll;	in the bonds of Hell;
Die Geiseln und die Banden	the scourges and shackles
und was du ausgestanden,	that You endured
das hat verdienet meine Seel'.	so that my soul might be delivered.

He made important contacts in London and soon became the favorite of the queen. An embarrassing situation arose two years later, when the queen died, and the Elector of Hanover, Handel's former employer, whose generosity he had exploited, became George I of England. It is said that Handel won his way back into favor by composing his famous *Water Music* suite for a party King George was having on the river Thames. Whether or not this story is true, the king employed Handel again, as he had in Hanover; he was given a sizable salary and was soon composing, conducting at court, and teaching the king's granddaughters. Certainly the king and Handel had much in common. They were both foreigners in England, and they both spoke English with a strong German accent. A contemporary writer made fun of Handel's accent by reporting that one day when there was only a small turnout for one of his concerts, Handel said to the musicians, "Nevre moind; de moosic vil sound de petter."

Handel spent the remainder of his career in London. He was an amazingly prolific composer, a clever politician, and a tough businessman. He made and lost a great deal of money, loved food and drink, and had a quick temper and a broad sense of humor. A contemporary said that "no man ever told a story with more

humor than Handel." He was at the center of English musical developments (and rivalries) for 40 years. And in the end, he became an institution. The British people today still regard Handel as an English composer. He is buried in Westminster Abbey—an honor reserved for great English notables such as Chaucer, Queen Elizabeth I, and Charles Dickens.

During his London years (from 1712 until his death in 1759), Handel was involved mainly with opera and oratorio, though he wrote a great deal of other music as well.

Italian opera was very fashionable in London until the 1730s, when public taste began to change. It was at this time that Handel turned his attention to oratorio.

The idea of a musical Bible story sung in English appealed to the English audience. Oratorio was also much less expensive to produce than opera. It was sung on the concert stage and required no costumes, no complicated machinery or lights, and no scenery. Handel's first oratorio was *Saul*, produced in 1739. But his first real success came with *Messiah* in 1741. This soon became his most popular work and remains one of his most frequently performed compositions today. After this, Handel's oratorios became the mainstay of the London concert scene. They were performed during Lent, when opera was not allowed anyway, and they

The writer Dr. Samuel Johnson called Italian opera an "exotic and irrational entertainment." Another critic dubbed it "nonsense well-tun'd."

attracted large audiences, especially from the prosperous middle class, which had always regarded Italian opera with suspicion or disdain. A special feature of Handel's oratorio performances was the appearance of the composer himself playing organ concertos during the intermission.

Toward the end of his life, Handel became blind, but he continued to perform on the organ and to compose by dictation. When he died, 3,000 people turned out for his funeral. He had become a British citizen many years earlier, and the British people had taken him completely into their hearts.

HANDEL'S MUSIC

Handel's music is attractive and easy to listen to. It appeals to a wide range of people because it sounds simple and tuneful. Handel's is the "art that hides art." The skill and brilliant craftsmanship of his music are hidden under the attractive exterior.

Curiously, most people today do not know the compositions on which Handel spent most of his time and for which he was best known in his own day: his Italian operas. These portray events of dramatic and emotional intensity. The main musical forms are the standard ones of opera seria: recitative and aria.

As you read earlier, Baroque arias are usually built in ABA form, with ornaments on the return of the A section. This kind of aria is known as a **da capo** ("from the beginning") aria, because after the B section the composer simply has to write the words "da capo" in the score, and the singer can improvise the embellishments for the repeat of the A section.

Handel's opera *Giulio Cesare* (*Julius Caesar*) was written in 1724 at the height of his involvement with opera. It is based on the story of Caesar and Cleopatra in Egypt. In the opera, Caesar falls in love with Cleopatra and joins forces with her against Ptolemy, King of Egypt. (Baroque operas are full of women controlling men by means of their sexual attractiveness.) In the end, Ptolemy is defeated and Cleopatra is crowned Queen of Egypt.

The excerpt we shall study comes from the third act of the opera, during a temporary setback for Caesar.

After a shipwreck, he is cast up on the shore where his army has been defeated in a battle. He laments his defeat, the loss of his troops, and his separation from Cleopatra.

Handel here deliberately manipulates the conventions of opera seria in order to inject more drama and realism into the situation. What the audience would expect at this point in the opera is a recitative followed by an aria. What Handel does is to begin the scene with "breezy" music—wafting figures on the strings that are appropriate to Caesar's words later in the scene when he calls upon the breezes to soothe him. Then comes recitative *accompagnato*, recitative that is accompanied

GEORGE FREDERICK HANDEL Esq.
born February XXIII. MDCLXXXIV.
died April XIV. MDCCLIX.   *L.F.Roubiliac inv.'et sc.*

The monument to Handel in Westminster Abbey in London.

Oratorio:
no scenery
no costume
Sang on the concert stage

George Frideric Handel (1685–1759)
***Giulio Cesare*, Act III, Scene 4**

Date of composition: 1724
Voice, strings, and continuo
Tempo: *Andante*
Key: F Major
Duration: 9:29

Complete CD Collection: 2, track 29

(29)	0:00	[Orchestral introduction]		"Breezy" music

RECITATIVE

0:46	*Dall' ondoso periglio salvo mi porta al lido il mio propizio fato.*	From the dangerous sea my lucky destiny safely takes me to the beach.	
	Qui la celeste parca non tronca ancor lo stame a la mia vita!	Here heavenly fate has not yet cut the thread of my life!	
1:11	*Ma dove andrò e chi mi porge aita?*	But where shall I go and who will bring me help?	[Recitative becomes louder and more pronounced (martial rhythms)]
	Ove son le mie schiere?	Where are my armies?	
	Ove son le legione,	Where are my legions,	
	Che a tante mie vittorie il varco apriro?	that opened the way to so many victories?	
1:31	*Solo in queste erme arene*	On these solitary sands	[Suddenly quiet]
	al monarca del mondo errar conviene.	only the King of the World is at home.	[Loud again]

ARIA

(30)	1:54	*Aure, aure, deh per pietà*	Breezes, breezes out of pity,	["Breezy" music returns]
		Spirate al petto mio,	Blow on my body,	
		Per dar conforto, O Dio!	To comfort me, O God!	
		Al mio dolor.	In my pain.	[Many repetitions]
	3:11	[Entire text repeated]		
	3:59	[Brief orchestral interlude]		
(31)	4:11	*Dite, dite dov'è*	Tell me: where is she,	[Minor key; contrasting musical figures for B section]
		Che fà l'idolo del mio sen?	Where is the idol of my life?	
		L'amato e dolce ben di questo cor.	Beloved and sweet object of this heart.	

4:52	*Ma d'ogni intorno i' veggio*	But all around me I see,	[Interruption: faster and agitated]
	Sparse d'arme e d'estint,	Strewn with weapons and corpses,	
	L'infortunate arene,	These unfortunate beaches,	
	Segno d'infausto annunzio al fin sarà.	An ill omen of my end.	

(32) 5:12	*Aure, aure, deh per pietà*	Breezes, breezes out of pity,	[Return of "breezy" music for repeat of A section]
	Spirate al petto mio,	Blow on my body,	
	Per dar conforto, O Dio!	To comfort me, O God!	
	Al mio dolor.	In my pain.	

| 7:08 | [Orchestral conclusion] |

Castratos

Castrato singers were exceedingly popular in the Baroque period. These were men who had been surgically castrated before puberty, so that they would retain the high voices of childhood but grow to have the vocal power and agility of adults. Although this practice was regarded as abhorrent by most people at the time, it was widely performed, especially among poor families. Few of these men made important careers, but one or two became musical superstars and acquired great fame and fortune. ✦ In the early eighteenth century, the most famous castrato was named Farinelli. A critic described his remarkable prowess: "The first note he sung [*sic*] was taken with such delicacy, swelled by minute degrees to such an amazing volume, and afterwards diminished in the same manner to a mere point, that it was applauded for a full five minutes. Indeed he possessed such powers as never met before, or since, in any one human being."

Hospital for the Maintenance and Education of exposed and deserted young Children.

THIS is to give Notice, that towards the Support of this Charity, the Sacred Oratorio, called,

MESSIAH,

Will be performed in the Chapel of this Hospital, under the Direction of George Frederick Handel, Esq; on Thursday next, the 27th inst. at twelve o'clock at Noon precisely; and, to prevent the Chapel being crouded, no more Tickets will be delivered than it can conveniently hold; which are ready to be had of the Steward of the Hospital; at Arthur's Chocolate-house in St. James's Street; at Batson's Coffee-house in Cornhill; and at Tom's Coffee-house in Devereux Court, at Half a Guinea each. T. COLLINGWOOD, Secretary.

An English writer in the eighteenth century complained that the opera house was more of a social than a musical event: "There are some who contend that the singers might be very well heard if the audience was more silent, but it is so much the fashion to consider the Opera as a place of rendezvous and visiting that they do not seem in the last to attend to the music."

by the orchestra to create a more dramatic effect. Finally, the aria starts, with its "breezy" music. All goes conventionally for a while; the A section of the aria continues. Then comes the B section ("Dite, dite dov'è,"—"Tell me, tell me where she is"). But at the point where everyone in the audience would expect the return of the A section (remember, the standard format is ABA), Handel interposes another accompanied recitative ("Mà, d'ogni intorno,"— "But all around me"), which dramatically reflects Caesar's state of mind at his unfortunate situation. It is as though Caesar's reflections are suddenly interrupted by the terrible sight of his surroundings. Handel breaks through the operatic conventions of his time to make his music correspond naturally to the psychological realism of the story. (**See Listening Guide on page 150.**)

Today, Handel's popularity rests mainly on his oratorios. And even in his own time, the oratorios appealed to a very wide public. Why have they always been so popular? First, and most important, the words are in English. Even in the eighteenth century, much of the audience for Italian operas couldn't understand most of the words. Second, the stories are from the Bible (mostly the Old Testament), which was familiar to everyone in those days. Behind the stories, there were political implications as well: references, for example, to the military triumphs and prosperity of Georgian England. Finally, oratorios were less of an aristocratic, snobbish, social event than operas and thus had wider appeal.

The music of Handel's oratorios is vigorous and appealing. It is not so different from the music of his operas. There are recitatives and arias, just as there are in operas. But the main difference is in the choral writing.

Choruses are very rare in late Baroque opera, but they are central to Handel's oratorios. Some of the greatest moments in the oratorios come in the choral pieces, when the chorus comments on the action or summarizes the feelings of the people. Perhaps the best known of Handel's choruses is the "Halleluyah" chorus from *Messiah*.

Messiah was composed in 1741 and soon became the composer's most famous work. It was written in the unbelievably short time of just over three weeks. As he was composing it, Handel said, "I did think I did see all Heaven before me and the great God himself."

Messiah is in three parts, which last some 2½ hours altogether. The music is made up throughout of recitatives, arias, and choruses. The famous "Halleluyah" chorus closes Part II. (**See Listening Guide on page 153.**)

Handel was also an accomplished composer of instrumental music. His two most famous instrumental suites are the *Water Music* and *Music for the Royal Fireworks*.

Handel's music is less complex than that of Bach, with more focus on melody than on counterpoint, and he deliberately appealed to a wider audience than had been traditional. Music was becoming less the preserve of the wealthy and more the delight of everyone who cared to listen.

George Frideric Handel (1685–1759)
"Halleluyah" Chorus from *Messiah*

Date of composition: 1741
Chorus and orchestra
Duration: 3:49

Student CD Collection: 2, track 8
Complete CD Collection: 2, track 33

The "Halleluyah" chorus comes as the climax of Part II of *Messiah*. In it Handel displays extraordinary ingenuity in combining and contrasting all the possible textures available to him: unison, homophonic, polyphonic, and imitative. In setting the word "Halleluyah" itself, he also uses a tremendous variety of different *rhythms*. Finally, much of the strength of the movement comes from its block alternation of simple tonic and dominant harmonies, as well as its triumphant use of trumpets and drums. The jubilant feeling is immediately evident and is a direct reflection of the text: "Halleluyah" is a Hebrew word that means "Praise God."

The text itself is treated in two ways:

1. Declamatory statements (e.g., "For the Lord God omnipotent reigneth") characterized by longer note values and occasional unison singing.
2. Contrapuntal responses (e.g., "forever and ever, halleluyah, halleluyah"), characterized by faster notes, and offering musical and textual commentary on the declamatory statements.

The "Halleluyah" chorus falls into nine relatively symmetrical sections, each featuring a single texture or combination of textures.

8 (33)	**0:00**	Instrumental opening ("pre-echo").

HOMOPHONIC

[Two phrases, each with five statements of "Halleluyah." Notice the changing rhythms.]

0:07	First phrase, tonic.
0:16	Second phrase, dominant.

UNISON

[With homophonic "halleluyah" responses: "For the Lord God omnipotent reigneth."]

0:25	First phrase, dominant.
0:37	Second phrase, tonic.

POLYPHONIC

9 (34)	**0:49**	Statement by sopranos, tonic.
	0:56	Statement by tenors and basses, dominant.
	1:05	Statement by tenors and altos, tonic.
	1:14	Short instrumental interlude.

[With noticeable change in dynamics: two phrases, one soft (*piano*), one loud (*forte*).]

1:16   *piano:* "The kingdom of this world is become …"

1:27   *forte:* "… the kingdom of our God and of His Christ."

IMITATION

[Four entries, "And He shall reign forever and ever."]

10 (35)   **1:38**   Basses, tonic.

1:43   Tenors in counterpoint with basses, dominant.

1:49   Altos in counterpoint with basses and tenors, tonic.

1:55   Sopranos in counterpoint with all other voices, dominant.

UNISON

[Three declamatory statements ("King of Kings and Lord of Lords") against homophonic responses ("forever and ever, halleluyah, halleluyah"), each at a different pitch, moving higher and higher.]

11 (36)   **2:01**   Sopranos and altos, answered by other voices.

POLYPHONIC

[Two statements of "And he shall reign forever and ever," against contrapuntal responses ("and he shall reign . . .").]

2:42   Basses, dominant.

2:48   Sopranos, tonic.

UNISON/ HOMOPHONIC

[Combination of unison and homophonic textures—"King of Kings" . . . ("forever and ever") "and Lord of Lords" . . . ("halleluyah, halleluyah").]

2:54   Tenors, answered by other voices.

HOMOPHONIC

[Statements by all voices.]

3:03   "And He shall reign forever and ever."

3:10   "King of Kings and Lord of Lords" (twice).

3:19   "And he shall reign forever and ever."

[Final statement of "King of Kings and Lord of Lords."]

3:26   Tenors and sopranos, answered by other voices.

3:34   Pause; one final drawn-out homophonic statement: plagal cadence (IV–I).

STYLE SUMMARY

It was during the Baroque era that many elements of what we recognize today as "classical" music were formed. These include regular patterns of meter and a formalized hierarchy of keys and chord progressions. Instrumental music came to be regarded on a par with vocal forms, and two influential instrumental genres—the sonata and the concerto—were established.

The great new musical invention of the Baroque era was opera. Opera brought together all the arts, combining carpentry and painting (for the scenery), costume design, dramatic acting, instrumental music, and, of course, beautiful singing, into one superb spectacle. The main topics of Baroque opera were stories from Classical antiquity—from Greek and Roman myths or history. And the principal vocal forms used in opera were recitative and aria.

Recitatives are relatively simple, with sparse accompaniment and with flexible and irregular rhythms designed to imitate speech. They are designed for dialogue and for moving the story along. Arias occur when the action stops and a character expresses his or her emotional reaction to the situation. Arias are lyrical and expressive; they can be about love or rage or grief, and they are the emotional high points of the music.

The most common form for arias is ABA form. The central (B) section offers a contrast, and the return of the A section can provide an opportunity for the singer to ornament the melody. In the Baroque period, audiences liked to hear high voices on the great arias, so the male roles were usually sung by castratos, whose voices were as high as those of the women.

The development of instrumental music was helped along by the great skill of the Italian makers and players of stringed instruments, especially the violin. Sonatas and concertos for violins are the most important instrumental works of the Baroque era. Sonatas were composed for one violin and basso continuo (solo sonata) or for two violins and basso continuo (trio sonata). Since the basso continuo is usually played by both a keyboard and a low stringed instrument, the solo sonata is performed by three players and the trio sonata by four.

Concertos exploit the Baroque love of contrast. They employ many different types of contrast, between loud and soft, fast and slow, and fiery and lyrical; however, the most important contrast is between the sound of the solos and that of the whole orchestra. There may be a small group of solo players (usually from two to four) or a single soloist. In the outer (first and third) movements of a Baroque concerto, the contrast is made explicit by using ritornello form.

An early print of an aria from Purcell's *Dido and Aeneas*.

The same aria in a modern score.

In the Baroque period, clear national differences in musical style were evident. Instrumental music for strings as well as opera were particularly favored in Italy. France developed music influenced by the dance: French operas contained many ballet scenes, and instrumental suites were made up of a series of movements in different dance styles. German music incorporated two important elements: the Lutheran chorale and a love of counterpoint. Chorales are found in organ works, church cantatas, and Passions. The undisputed German master of counterpoint, whose skill was displayed throughout his enormously productive and varied career, was Johann Sebastian Bach.

Finally, in England, another German composer, George Frideric Handel, apart from composing many Italian operas, also established a very English genre, the English oratorio. Oratorios are based on Biblical stories. They often set the words of a narrator, with other singers singing the roles of the principals in the story; there is also a chorus to represent groups of people. Oratorios, however, are not staged: they are sung in concert performances. The most famous English oratorio, *Messiah,* is unconventional in many respects: it has no narrator; the singers do not sing roles; and it doesn't tell a story. Rather, it is a series of descriptions and contemplations, set to exquisite arias, recitatives, and choruses.

From the earliest Italian opera—through instrumental suites, sonatas, and concertos; secular and sacred cantatas; organ works; and Passions—to the English oratorio, Baroque music is enormously expressive, colorful, and varied. Even with all of its variety, Baroque music has one unifying stylistic trait: the basso continuo. With a lute or keyboard instrument playing a constant chordal accompaniment and one or more low stringed instruments doubling the keyboard's lowest line, a Baroque piece is instantly recognizable from the power and momentum of its bass line. The Baroque era might easily be called the "Basso Continuo Era."

FUNDAMENTALS OF BAROQUE MUSIC

- ✦ Instrumental music is as important as vocal music
- ✦ Opera was invented, with vocal forms divided between recitative and aria
- ✦ Unifying feature of all Baroque music is the basso continuo
- ✦ Principal vocal genres are opera, cantata, and oratorio
- ✦ Principal instrumental genres are sonata, suite, and concerto
- ✦ The music is organized by hierarchy of chords and keys (tonal harmony)

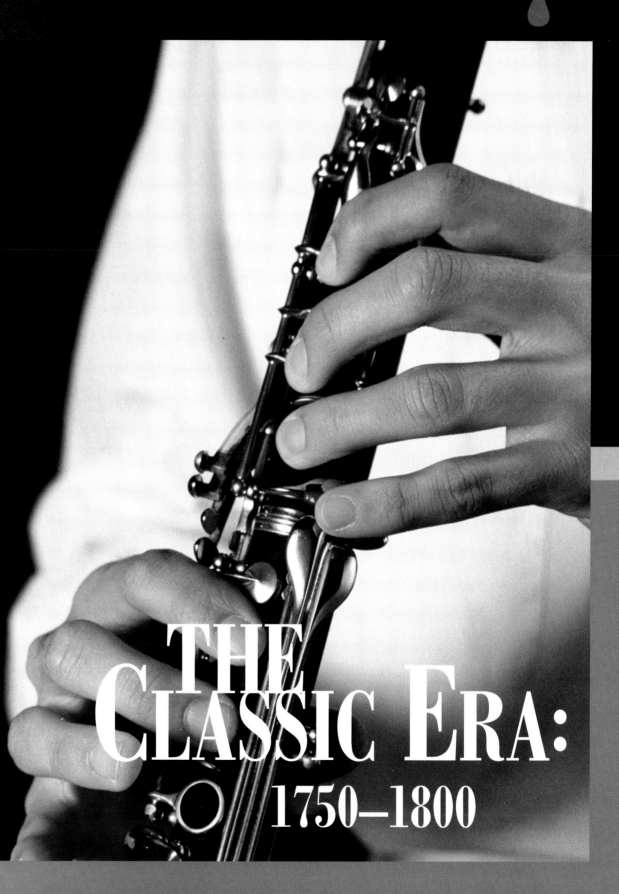

THE CLASSIC ERA:
1750–1800

The term "classic" is usually used to describe something that has an appeal both very broad and very long-lasting. A novel may be described as a classic, and so may a movie or a car. This means that the novel, the movie, and the car continue to attract enthusiasts long after they first appeared. It also means that they appeal to a wide range of people.

Both of these things are true of Classic music. The music of the greatest composers of the Classic era has been popular with audiences ever since it was written. Indeed, the masterpieces of Classic music were the first works in musical history that stayed in the concert repertoire long after they were first composed. Before that time, a piece was usually performed once or twice and then set aside.

What is it about Classic music that has given it such enduring appeal? Before we can answer that question, we need to consider the social and political climate of Europe in the middle of the eighteenth century.

FROM ABSOLUTISM TO ENLIGHTENMENT TO REVOLUTION

Top: Voltaire in 1718.
Bottom: Jean-Jacques Rousseau.

The eighteenth century was a time of profound social and political change. It began with the death in 1715 of Louis XIV of France, the most powerful absolute ruler in Europe, and it ended with two of the most significant revolutions in modern history: the American War of Independence (1775–83) and the French Revolution (1789–94).

The whole period was colored by the philosophical movement known as the Enlightenment. This movement was led by the great French philosophers Voltaire and Rousseau, who both died in 1778; it attempted to apply the principles of scientific objectivity to issues of social justice. The Enlightenment favored the human over the divine, reason over religion, and clarity over complexity. Its adherents tried to improve education, eliminate superstition and prejudice, and break down the rigid class structure that separated people from one another.

Although these changes were slow in coming, some of the rulers of the time were influenced by the ideas of the Enlightenment. Frederick the Great of Prussia and Emperor Joseph II of Austria, for example, were both regarded as "enlightened" monarchs (at least in comparison with their predecessors). Both men were also strong supporters of the arts. Frederick the Great, whom we have mentioned briefly already, played the flute and employed some of the most accomplished musicians of the day at his court. Joseph II, an amateur cellist, was a great patron of music and literature. In Vienna, which was the capital of the Holy Roman Empire and the place where Joseph held court, all the arts flourished. With names such as Haydn, Mozart, and Beethoven in the list of its citizens, Vienna was by the end of the century the musical center of Europe.

Enlightenment ideals reached their high point in Vienna in the 1780s and 1790s, but many other parts of Europe were affected as well. Throughout the century, England had a thriving economy and a rich and varied cultural life. Members of the middle class increasingly claimed free expression and leisure time as their own. In France, the reign of Louis XIV was succeeded by those of Louis XV (1715–74) and Louis XVI (1774–89). The powerful central authority

Right: Vienna in 1783.

Europe in 1750.

Left: Frederick the Great
of Prussia.

Right: Emperor Joseph II
of Austria.

wielded by Louis XIV gradually eroded, and his successors became corrupt and increasingly out of touch with popular sentiment. The reign of Louis XVI ended in the turmoil of the French Revolution, which had as its slogan the rallying cry of the Enlightenment: "Liberty, Equality, Brotherhood!" Louis XVI was guillotined by his own people in the middle of Paris on January 21, 1793.

The execution of Louis XVI.

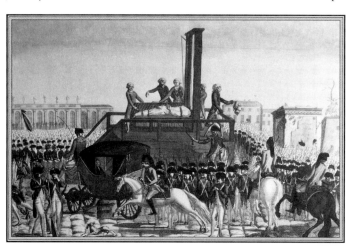

Brotherhood was the concept behind many new organizations founded in the eighteenth century. Chief among these was Freemasonry, founded in England in 1717. The Masons were—and are—an international secret society of mutual support and social charity. Freemasonry cut across the boundaries of class and profession. It spread quickly through Europe and America, and its ranks included kings, writers, composers, and politicians. Famous Freemasons of the eighteenth century were Joseph II, the great German poet Johann Wolfgang von Goethe, Mozart, and George Washington.

The idea of brotherhood did not include women, however. And because their roles were narrowly defined by society in this as in other eras, few women became monarchs, well-known writers, or famous composers. Important exceptions were Maria Theresa, ruler of Austria from 1740 to 1780, and Catherine II ("Catherine the Great") of Russia, who ruled from 1762 to 1796. One of the greatest novelists of the late eighteenth century was Jane Austen (1775–1817),

Rousseau, an "enlightened" philosopher, wrote in 1758: "Women, in general, possess no artistic sensibility. The celestial fire that ignites the soul . . . the inspiration that consumes . . . the sublime ecstasies that reside in the depths of the heart are always lacking in women's writings. Their creations are as cold and pretty as women themselves."

whose masterpieces include *Pride and Prejudice* and *Emma*. But the author's name did not appear on the title pages of her books when they were published, and she received very little public recognition during her own lifetime. Similarly, there were women who composed music but did not have their works published. Anna Amalie, the Duchess of Saxe-Weimar, wrote German operas and chamber music and was highly influential in bringing together intellectuals, poets, and musicians at her court, but her own music was never published.

Women's influence in all other areas of musical life was, however, great. They were accomplished music teachers, singers, instrumentalists, authors of instruction manuals, patrons, and organizers of musical life. Marie Lieszcinska, who married Louis XV in 1725, inaugurated an important concert series at Versailles, which attracted the leading musicians of the day. This tradition was continued by Madame de Pompadour in mid-century and by Marie-Antoinette of Austria, the wife of Louis XVI, after 1770.

In the later part of the century, society's attitudes toward women began to broaden, and women took a more public role in European musical life. Some became professional performers, others both composers and performers. Julie Candeille (1767–1834) was an opera singer, pianist, harpist, and composer. She made her performing debut at the age of 16 as piano soloist in a concerto; the following year, she played a concerto of her own composition. During her life, she published many of her own works. Her greatest success came in 1792–93, when her comic opera *Catherine* became a hit in Paris, and she sang while accompanying herself on the piano in more than 150 performances. The opera received numerous revivals during the next 20 or 30 years. A great deal more research, publishing, and performance work remains to be done to restore women's music in the Classic era to its rightful place.

The Musical Public

Changes in class structure in the eighteenth century had far-reaching effects on music. The flourishing economy created a large and prosperous middle class, whose members began to feel they were entitled to the same privileges and cultural diversions previously reserved for the aristocracy. The eighteenth century saw the rise of the public concert—a new idea at the time, because until then music had usually been performed in private courts or salons. Beginning in France about 1725, the idea quickly spread. We have already seen how Handel changed the focus of his activities from the aristocratic opera to the middle-class oratorio after the success of *Messiah* in 1741. By the end of the century, public concerts were the primary musical forum in London, Paris, Vienna, Prague, and countless other cities and towns across Europe.

The vast increase in the number of musical consumers affected other areas of music, too. Music publishing became a profitable business, and music publishers sprang up in many cities.

Middle-class men and women also wanted to learn to play music themselves. They arranged lessons for themselves and their children and bought musical instruments to play at home.

The social changes of the eighteenth century also affected the status of performers and composers. Although many musicians were still supported by powerful rulers or wealthy aristocrats, some could begin to make a living on their own as the century progressed.

Women making music at home.

Pietro Longhi (1702–1785). The House Concert. Around 1760. Oil on canvas, 50 × 62 cm. Pinacoteca di Brera, Milan, Italy. © Photograph by Erich Lessing. Erich Lessing/Art Resource, NY.

This gradual change is exemplified by the life of the composer Joseph Haydn. He spent most of his career in the employ of a wealthy prince, but toward the end of his life he became independent, living off the sale of his music, traveling abroad, and taking charge of his own financial and artistic affairs.

Even the type of music composed in the Classic era was affected by the new musical public. The complex rhythms and counterpoint of Baroque music, with its heavy bass line and emotional intensity, were no longer in fashion. Music was now designed to appeal to a broader public. It had to be lighter, clearer, and more accessible. It had to be easier to listen to and easier to play. This was the era of several new genres, including the *divertimento*—a piece played as a "diversion"—and comic opera. A common musical language developed, one that could be understood by a broad range of society. Within this language—the "classic" language of music—enormous amounts of music were composed. All of it is pleasant and accessible. Occasionally a genius would come along and use this same language to produce masterpieces of enduring significance.

> I am issuing by subscription a work consisting of six quartets . . . written in a new and special way [for] the great patrons of music and the amateur gentlemen.
> —Joseph Haydn

GENERAL CHARACTERISTICS OF CLASSIC MUSIC

Balance and proportion, clarity and accessibility: These are the primary features of Classic music. It is designed to be "easy on the ear." Yet that does not mean it cannot also be very beautiful, very moving, and very profound. Mozart once wrote to his father that his latest compositions would appeal to the most experienced listeners and to amateurs alike. The experts would appreciate all the subtleties, and the amateurs would be pleased "without knowing why."

Classic music was a reaction to the complexity of Baroque music. Classic music usually has just a melody and an accompaniment, and the accompaniment is light and simple. Imitative counterpoint is used only rarely, and then only for special effect. The melodies are pleasing and tuneful—the kind you can hum or whistle as you go through the day. Mozart was delighted when he was told that everyone on the streets of Prague was singing the tunes from his latest opera.

There are some technical aspects to the special sound of Classic music. The first is simple and has to do with the length of melodic phrases. Classic music is usually made up of two- or four-bar phrases, rather than the long lines common in Baroque music. This makes the music clear and balanced. These phrases are usually arranged into patterns of opening and closing phrases. A two- or four-bar opening phrase is immediately followed by a two- or four-bar closing phrase, creating a symmetrical pattern. This pattern makes the music easy to follow and establishes a sense of regularity in the mind of the listener.

> **M**elody **is the main thing.**
> —Joseph Haydn

The second technical aspect of Classic music is its harmony. The harmony of Classic music is generally simple, logical, and clear. Classic composers do not usually go very far afield in their harmonies. They tend to stick to relatively straightforward keys, and they do not often use strange or dissonant chords.

Finally, the effect of Classic music depends a great deal on its accompaniment. Gone is the powerful basso continuo of the Baroque. In its place, we find a simple "walking bass" (in which the bass line moves mostly by step, in even notes and with a regular rhythm) or little bustling accompanying figures that keep the rhythm lively.

Two examples of "walking bass."

Lively, rhythmic accompanying figures.

A special development of the Classic era was the "Alberti bass," named after the composer Domenico Alberti (1710–1740). This is an accompaniment made up of a continuously moving pattern of short notes. The accompanying chords are broken up into separate notes played one after the other, not together, to keep the texture light and lively.

Accompanying chords broken into "Alberti bass."

These three features—the balanced phrases, the simple harmony, the light accompaniment—help to give Classic music its special sound and to provide a framework for its tuneful, pleasing melodies.

GENRES OF CLASSIC MUSIC

Several musical genres were popular in the Classic era. The most important of these were opera, symphony, string quartet, and sonata. Some composers wrote in other genres, too. Mozart, for example, composed many beautiful piano concertos and some string *quintets*. But on the whole, composers stayed within the conventional genres. Notice that these genres are secular. Although composers still occasionally wrote sacred works such as Masses and oratorios, these forms are far less common in the Classic era, reflecting a shift in society's makeup and interests.

Operas were staged in the palaces of a few very wealthy aristocrats or in the public opera houses of big cities such as Prague, Paris, or Vienna. Symphonies also were performed in aristocratic courts or at the public concerts springing up all over Europe. String quartets and sonatas, with their smaller ensembles and more intimate sound, were designed for private gatherings—in an aristocratic salon or in the living rooms of middle-class music lovers.

Let us look briefly at how the opera, the symphony, the string quartet, and the sonata developed in the Classic era.

OPERA

We have seen that opera was the Baroque art form *par excellence*. It combined a story with artwork, costumes, illusion, and best of all, superb singing. But during the late Baroque period, some people began to criticize Baroque opera as artificial. They complained that the plots were always about mythological or historical figures rather than about real people and real situations; that the music was too heavy and complex; and that the stage sets, with their elaborate scenery and complicated machines for simulating battles and shipwrecks, were too involved. The arias, with their obligatory repeats (the *da capo* aria form, you remember, is ABA), were criticized for two reasons. First, the repeat of the opening section interrupted the continuity of the story. Second, singers abused the convention of embellishing the music on its repeat by showing off and drawing attention to themselves rather than to the plot. Finally, what could be more unnatural than a castrato—a man singing with a woman's voice!

This attack on Baroque opera was another sign of the changing social structure of the eighteenth century. Baroque opera was the province of the aristocracy; what was demanded was a style of opera that would appeal to everyone. It should be about real people in everyday situations.

The result of these attitudes was the development of a new type of opera called *comic opera*. Comic opera became very popular in the Classic era. It featured simpler music, down-to-earth characters, and an amusing plot.

In Italy comic opera was known as *opera buffa*, in France it was called *opéra comique*, and in Germany it was known as *Singspiel*. In French and German comic opera, the dialogue is spoken instead of being set to music, though there are still arias. The most famous early example of Italian comic opera is Pergolesi's *La Serva Padrona* (1733). Even the title is meant to be comical: It really means "The Servant Girl Who Became Mistress of the House." The opera is about a clever servant girl who tricks her master, a rich old bachelor, into marrying her. The story was designed to appeal to an age in which rigid class barriers were being called into question.

LISTENING GUIDE

Giovanni Pergolesi (1710–1736)
Opera, *La Serva Padrona*
(Duet from Act I)

Date of composition: 1733
Orchestration: 2 singers, harpsichord, and strings
Duration: 4:23

Complete CD Collection: 2, track 37

La Serva Padrona (*The Maid as Mistress*) is often referred to as the first example of opera buffa (comic opera). It is divided into two acts and features only two principal roles:

Serpina (literally "little snake"), a maidservant, and
Uberto, a bachelor, Serpina's master.

The plot is a simple one. Uberto, bothered by Serpina's insolent behavior and attitude, orders his servant (Vespone) to find him a suitable wife (to teach Serpina a lesson). Serpina (aware of Uberto's scheme) plays along and informs Uberto that she also is to be wed. She talks Vespone into playing the part of her fiancé, an army captain. She reports that her fiancé demands a dowry from her master or he will not marry her. Furthermore, if her fiancé cannot marry her, then Uberto must—or be cut to ribbons by the captain's sword. Uberto is ultimately tricked into marrying Serpina.

The following excerpt is a duet that comes at the end of the first act and features amusing exchanges between Serpina and Uberto. She insists that he marry her, and he is equally adamant that he will not.

The musical language is appropriately simple, with many repeats, and it is easy to follow. Notice the comic interchange between the principals: "no, no … si, si," etc. Toward the end of the scene, the words are repeated from the beginning, but the text is broken up to suggest an even more spirited exchange. Each stanza uses exactly the same arrangement, so you can listen to this structure several times in the course of the song. This pattern gives a rounded feeling to the melody as a whole and a sense of increased intensity before the close.

(37)	0:00	[lively orchestral introduction, strings and harpsichord; dynamic contrasts, short repeated phrases.]

SERPINA

0:17	*Lo conosco, lo conosco* *a quegli occhietti,* *a quegli occhietti* *Furbi, ladri, ladri, malignetti.*	I can see it, I can see it in your eyes, in your eyes: You're a cunning, scheming, naughty old man.
0:27	*Che sebben voi dite "no, no, no"* *Pur m'accennano di "si, si, si, si, si."*	You keep saying "no, no, no," but you really mean "yes, yes, yes, yes, yes."

UBERTO

[same melody]

0:38	*Signorina, signorina,* *v'ingannate, v'ingannate!* *Troppo, troppo, troppo, troppo* *in alto vi volate!*	Miss, miss, you're wrong, you're wrong! Too high, too high, too high Your ambitions fly! [loud, "flying"]
0:49	*Gli occhi ed io vi dicon "no, no, no"* *Ed è un sogno questo "si, si, si, si, si."*	Both my eyes and I say "no, no, no" and you're dreaming if you hear "yes, yes, yes, yes, yes."

SERPINA

[new key]

1:00	*Ma perché, ma perché?*
	Non son graziosa?
	Non son bella e spiritosa?
	
	Su, mirate leggiadria, leggiadria.
	
	Ve' che brio, che maesta, che maesta!
		But why, but why? [expressive]
		Am I not graceful? [graceful]
		Am I not beautiful
		  and spirited? [spirited]
		Just look how elegant,
		  how elegant! [elegant]
		What panache! [with panache]
		What dignity! What
		  dignity! [dignified]

UBERTO

[dark, rising chromatically]

1:28	*(Ah, costei mi va tentando quanto va che* *me la fa.)*	(Ah, she must be testing me to see how long I can resist.)

SERPINA

1:36	*(Ei mi par che va calando, va calando.)* *Via, Signore!*	(I think he's weakening, weakening.) [lightly] Decide then, Sir!

UBERTO

1:42	*Eh, vanne via!*	Get out!

SERPINA		
	[decisive]	
1:45	*Risolvete!*	Decide!

UBERTO		
1:47	*Eh, matta sei!*	You must be mad!

SERPINA		
1:49	*Son per voi gli affetti miei,* *E dovrete sposar me,*	All my feelings are for you. You must marry me.
1:52	*dovrete, dovrete, dovrete,* *sposar me!*	You must, you must, you must, marry me!

UBERTO		
1:52	*Oh, che imbroglio, ch'imbroglio,* *ch'imbroglio, egli è per me!*	Oh, what a mess, what a mess, what a mess I've gotten into!
2:00	[Instrumental interlude, dynamic contrasts, back to tonic key and text of opening. Music is changed, though, and dialogue more broken up.]	

SERPINA		
(38) 2:07	*Lo conosco a quegli occhietti* *furbi, ladri, malignetti.*	I can see it in your eyes, you cunning, scheming, naughty old man.

UBERTO		
	[sternly]	
2:16	*Signorina, signorina, v'ingannate.*	Miss, miss, you're wrong.

SERPINA		
2:22	*No, no, no, no,* *che sebben voi dite "no,"* *pur m'accennano di "si."*	No, no, no, no, you keep saying "no," when you mean to say "yes."

UBERTO		
2:32	*V'ingannate!*	You're wrong!

SERPINA		
2:35	*Ma perché, ma perché?* *Non son bella, graziosa, spiritosa?*	But why, but why? Am I not beautiful, graceful, spirited?

UBERTO		
2:46	*(Ah, costei mi va tentando.)*	(She's testing me.)

SERPINA		
2:51	(Va calando si, si.)	(He's weakening, yes, yes.)
	Ve'che brio, che brio, che maestà, che maestà!	See what panache I have! What panache! What dignity! What dignity!

UBERTO		
	[minor key]	
(39) 3:03	(Quanto val, quanto val, Quanto val che me fa la.) Laralla, laralla, la la la la la la la.	(She's just seeing how long I can resist.) Laralla, laralla, la la la la la la la.

SERPINA		
3:11	Via, signore, resolvete!	Decide then, Sir!

UBERTO		
3:12	Eh, vanne via. Eh matta sei!	Get out! You must be mad!

SERPINA		
3:16	Son per voi gl'affetti mei,	All my feelings are for you.

UBERTO		
3:16	Signorina, v'ingannate!	Miss, you're wrong!

SERPINA		
3:19	E dovrete si, si!	You must, yes, yes!

UBERTO		
3:22	Signorina, no, no!	Miss, no, no!

SERPINA		
3:24	E dovrete sposar me!	You must marry me!

UBERTO		
3:24	Oh, che imbroglio egli è per me!	Oh, what a mess I've gotten into!
3:26	(Quanto va, quanto va, quanto va che me la fa!)	(She's just seeing how long I can resist.)

SERPINA		
	[with long pauses]	
3:31	Non son bella, graziosa, spiritosa?	Am I not beautiful, graceful, spirited?

UBERTO

3:41

La la la, la la la.	La la la, la la la.

SERPINA

3:43

Ve'che brio, ve che brio!	What panache I have! What panache!

UBERTO

Oh, che imbroglio, oh, che imbroglio!	Oh, what a mess, oh, what a mess!

SERPINA

3:50

(Va calando, si, si.)	(He's weakening, yes, yes.)
Son per voi, son per voi,	All for you, all for you,
Son per voi gl'affetti miei.	My feelings are all for you.

UBERTO

Signori-, signori-, signorina, matta sei!	Miss … miss … Miss, you must be mad!

SERPINA

3:56

E dovrete si, si.	You must, yes, yes.

UBERTO

3:58

Signorina, no, no!	Miss, no, no!

SERPINA

Si, si!	Yes, yes!

UBERTO

No, no!	No, no!

SERPINA

4:03

Si, si dovrete, dovrete, dovrete sposar me, sposar me!	Yes, yes, you must, you must, you must marry me, marry me!

UBERTO

Oh, che imbroglio, ch'imbroglio, ch'imbroglio egli è per me, egli è per me!	Oh, what a mess, what a mess, what a mess I'm in, I'm in!

Stamitz

SYMPHONY

The most important genre of instrumental music in the Classic era was the symphony. Indeed, the origins of the symphony date from the beginnings of the Classic era, about 1730, and the symphony grew to maturity in the hands of the great Classic masters Haydn and Mozart.

The symphony began life as an introductory piece to Italian opera. At the beginning of the eighteenth century, Italian operas were usually preceded by an **overture**—an instrumental introduction in three short movements: fast-slow-fast. The Italian name for this type of opera overture was *sinfonia*. The music of these overtures was unrelated to the music of the operas they introduced. Gradually these instrumental pieces achieved independent status and were played in concert performances. The idea of independent symphonies spread rapidly, and soon composers from Italy to Germany to England were writing symphonies with no connection to opera.

The most important center of symphonic composition and performance in the early Classic era was Mannheim in Germany. Here was a wealthy court, which supported the largest and most accomplished orchestra in Europe. The concertmaster and conductor of the Mannheim orchestra was Johann Stamitz (1717–1757), who was famous for his rigorous discipline. Stamitz was also a prolific composer who wrote more than 60 symphonies. These symphonies established the norm for the Classic symphony for the remainder of the eighteenth century.

Stamitz expanded the fast-slow-fast pattern of the Italian *sinfonia* to a four-movement scheme. The first movement is fast and serious, the second movement slow and lyrical, the third movement graceful and moderate in tempo, and the last movement very fast and lively. This pattern of movements became standard for the symphony throughout the Classic period.

Stamitz also established the basic structure of the Classic orchestra, which had three main instrumental groups: strings, woodwinds, and (sometimes) trumpets and drums. The string section consisted of two groups of violins ("first violins" and "second violins"), as well as violas, cellos, and double basses. The woodwind section had either two flutes or two oboes, plus two horns. Only bright, ceremonial symphonies used trumpets and timpani.

In the later Classic period, the orchestra was augmented slightly, particularly in the woodwind section. Composers often used both flutes *and* oboes. Bassoons were employed to fill out the low sounds of the woodwind section, and in the late eighteenth century clarinets also became popular.

A composer could choose the number and types of instruments in a particular work to achieve different effects. If a composer wanted a delicate sound, he or she might write for strings, one flute, and two horns. A fuller, richer sound could be obtained with the strings plus all the woodwind instruments. And for a really festive piece, trumpets and drums were added.

In actual performance, the size of the string section varied according to the financial resources of the sponsor. In rich cities or aristocratic courts, there could be as many as 12 first violinists, 12 second violinists, six viola players, eight cellists, and four double bass players. In smaller orchestras, there were only three or four first violins, three or four second violins, two violas, two cellos, and one double bass.

CHAMBER MUSIC

The increase during the eighteenth century in the number of middle-class householders who were interested in music brought about an increase in the demand for music that could be performed at home. Because this music is designed to be played in smaller rooms, it is usually known as chamber music. It includes duets, trios, and quintets for various instrumental combinations, but the most important types of chamber music during this period were the string quartet and the sonata.

The string quartet developed about the middle of the eighteenth century. It involves four string instruments: two violins, a viola, and a cello. This grouping had great appeal for Classic composers, and many of the finest works of the eighteenth century are written

> It is an army of generals.
> —Charles Burney on Stamitz's Mannheim orchestra

> If only Salzburg had clarinets! You have no idea what a wonderful sound they make.
> —Mozart to his father in 1776

for string quartet. The string quartet provides an ideal balance between high and low instruments. The first violinist plays the principal melody while the second violinist plays the accompanying figures. Meanwhile, the violist fills in the harmony in the middle, and the cellist provides the bass line. The instruments cover a wide pitch band from high to low. The smooth, high, silvery sounds of the two violins are balanced by the drier, throatier quality of the viola and the strong, rich tones of the cello. Because all the instruments belong to the same family, they blend perfectly together.

Works for string quartet closely followed the pattern of symphonic works. They usually had four movements: the first fast and serious, the second slow and lyrical, the third graceful, and the fourth lively.

Sonatas could be written either for a keyboard instrument alone or for a keyboard instrument with another instrument such as a violin or a flute. Until about

1775, the predominant keyboard instrument was the harpsichord. By the last part of the eighteenth century, the piano, invented early in the century, began to replace the harpsichord as the favorite keyboard instrument. The piano was capable of gradations of volume—that was why it was originally called the piano-forte ("soft-loud")—and it had a fine, delicate sound. Eighteenth-century pianos sounded very different from the large concert grand pianos of today. They were softer and lighter in the upper register, and more muffled and less resonant in the bass.

Keyboard sonatas often contain some of the most interesting music of Classic composers, because it was (and still is) common for composers to compose while sitting at the keyboard—to experiment with ideas, play them through, and see how they sound. Some keyboard sonatas, therefore, have an improvisatory effect, as though we were actually hearing the composer at work.

CONVENTION IN CLASSIC MUSIC

The eighteenth century was a time of strict social conventions. Dress codes were carefully followed. People wore powdered wigs, brocaded coats, and silver shoe buckles. There was an elaborate pattern of rules that governed social behavior—when to curtsy, when to bow, what to talk about. Even written communication was highly formalized.

So it is not surprising to learn that strict conventions were established for music, too. The instruments used for particular types of works, the number of movements, the approximate length of each movement—these were all fixed by convention. Yet the pattern of expectations in Classic music went further than that. Even the keys in which a composition might be written were governed by convention. Some keys were far more common than others, and each key was linked with a certain mood or atmosphere. D Major, for example, is ceremonious and bright, whereas F minor is strained and melancholy. One reason is that major keys sound brighter than minor keys. Another has to do with the tuning system and instruments of the time. Trumpets and drums could play particularly well in D Major, so that was the key often chosen for festive music. F minor, with four flats, was (and remains) a difficult key to play. In addition, more flat notes in a key tended to make the instruments of the time sound muffled and shadowy.

The most far-reaching convention in Classic music was the *form* in which a composer could write each individual movement of a composition. There were only a few forms used in Classic music, and composers adhered to them most of the time. The most important of these are sonata form, aria form, minuet-and-trio form, and rondo form. We shall look at each of these in turn, but before we do, let us consider the importance of convention in Classic music.

Today, nothing seems more important to us than originality. We look for it in our own work, in the books we read, the paintings we look at, the music we listen to. The cult of originality, however, is a recent phenomenon. In the eighteenth century, writers, artists, and composers were respected not for the originality of their work but for its quality. Between about 1730 and 1800, hundreds of composers wrote tens of thousands of symphonies. From this enormous quantity of music, the works of Haydn and Mozart stand out, not because they are original, but because they demonstrate the most skill, the greatest resourcefulness, and the widest range of expression. Haydn and Mozart were the greatest composers of the age not because they ignored convention but because they used it to better advantage than anyone else.

FORMS OF CLASSIC MUSIC

SONATA FORM

The most important single-movement form in Classic music is **sonata form.** This form was used for almost all first movements of Classic instrumental music. Although it is called **sonata form**, it was used for the first movements not only of sonatas, but also of symphonies, string quartets, and many other genres. For that reason, it is sometimes known as "first-movement form." But sonata form became so popular in the Classic era that it was often used for other movements as well.

Sonata form is an intellectually demanding form, and composers used it for their most serious ideas. That doesn't mean it has to be difficult to listen to. As with any art form, however, it takes practice to become familiar with the ways in which it is organized. Once we understand sonata form, many of the secrets of Classic music are revealed to us.

Sonata form has three sections: the **exposition**, the **development**, and the **recapitulation**. The exposition begins in the tonic key and presents the opening material of the piece. Then it moves to a second key (usually the dominant or the relative major) and presents new material in that key. The exposition ends with a clear cadence. In Classic sonata-form movements, the exposition is normally played twice.

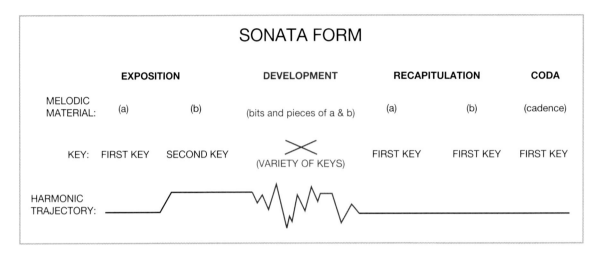

The development section explores many different keys. It usually moves quickly from key to key, has a great deal of counterpoint or sequence, mixes up short phrases of the previous material, and is generally quite turbulent. The development leads dramatically into the recapitulation, usually without an intervening cadence.

The recapitulation brings back all the music of the exposition, but with one crucial change: *The material that was previously presented in the second key is now played in the home key, so that the movement can end in the key in which it began.* Sometimes there is a short additional section added to the end of a sonata-form movement just to round it off. This short section is called the **coda** (literally "tail").

The preceding diagram summarizes these main features of sonata form.

The most important place to listen carefully in a sonata-form movement is right at the beginning. If you remember the sound of the beginning of the exposition, you will be able to recognize the recapitulation when it comes, because it brings back the same music. Also, with practice, you will be able to recognize the development section, partly because it changes key frequently and partly because it contains a great deal of turbulence—as though the material of the exposition

had been thrown into a blender and was being cut up and tossed around.

ARIA FORM

Aria form is simple, and we have discussed it before in the context of opera. Classic composers often used it for the second, slow movement of a sonata, a symphony, or a string quartet. This movement is designed to be lyrical and songlike. Aria form is ABA, with a slow, lyrical opening section (A) that is often in triple meter. This is followed by a contrasting central section in a new key (B), which sometimes has slightly faster notes. Finally, the opening section (A) is repeated, often decorated or slightly modified. Slow movements are often in aria form, but they sometimes follow sonata form or theme-and-variations form.

MINUET-AND-TRIO FORM

Minuet-and-trio form is the standard form for third movements in sonatas, symphonies, and string quartets, although it is often omitted from piano sonatas. The minuet was originally a Baroque court dance in moderate triple meter. Gradually it became an instrumental form and made its way into Classic music. We analyzed a Classic minuet and trio in the Listening

---

ARIA FORM

A (melody and key)   B (new melody, new key)   A (repeated, often embellished)

chapter of this book. In the Classic era, a minuet and trio simply means two minuets played in the pattern Minuet–Trio–Minuet. The trio usually presents some kind of contrast to the minuet—in instrumentation, texture, dynamics, or key.

The minuet itself is in two parts, each of which is repeated: AABB. The trio has the same pattern: CCDD. Then the first minuet is played again (often without repeats). The whole scheme of a minuet-and-trio movement looks like this:

MINUET	TRIO	MINUET
AABB	CCDD	AABB (or AB)

The most important characteristics of a minuet-and-trio movement are:

1. It is always in 3/4 meter.
2. It has a moderate tempo.
3. It is always in ternary form (minuet–trio–minuet).
4. It always has some kind of contrast in the trio.

Rondo Form

Rondo form was often used for the last (fourth) movement of symphonies, string quartets, and sonatas. Rondos are usually fairly fast, with a lively or catchy tune that keeps on returning or coming round again (hence "rondo"). In between appearances of the tune (sometimes called the refrain or **main theme**) come **episodes** of contrasting material. Thus, if we designate the main theme as A and the contrasting episodes with other letters, we have:

ABACADA

Sometimes composers used the first episode again just before the last appearance of the refrain:

ABACABA

This makes a particularly symmetrical kind of rondo.

FOUR-MOVEMENT STRUCTURE

Movement	Form	Key
I	Sonata	Tonic
II	Aria or Sonata or Theme and Variations	Dominant or Subdominant or Relative minor
III	Minuet and Trio	Tonic (Trio is sometimes in a different key)
IV	Rondo or Sonata	Tonic

SUMMARY

Let us summarize this overview of the main forms of Classic music. The most common and most serious form is sonata form. First movements are nearly always in sonata form. Second movements are often in aria form: ABA. Minuet-and-trio form is the usual form for third movements. Last movements are often in rondo form.

These are the main forms for the standard four movements of most Classic instrumental music, and you will find listening guides for each of these forms in this chapter. There are variants of this pattern, however. For example, Classic concertos had only three movements: sonata form, slow, and rondo. Also, in the other genres, sonata form was sometimes used for movements in addition to the first. It is not uncommon for the slow movement of a Classic composition to be in sonata form, and sometimes composers used sonata form for the last movement also. Some compositions reverse the position of the slow movement and the minuet and trio, putting the minuet second and the slow movement third.

THE EARLY CLASSIC PERIOD

Although the end of the Baroque era is generally given as 1750 (the date of Bach's death), the origins of the Classic style date from earlier than that. Starting about 1730, a new musical style began to appear that was lighter, more accessible, more varied, and less demanding. The name given to this musical style at the time was *galant*, which we might translate as "fashionable" or "up-to-date." Two of the composers involved in this stylistic change were Bach's sons: C. P. E. Bach, who was at the court of Frederick the Great in Berlin, and J. C. Bach, who made his career in London. Other important composers of this early Classic style were Johann Stamitz in Mannheim and Giovanni Battista Sammartini (1701–1775) in Italy.

These composers rejected the dense contrapuntal style of the late Baroque era in favor of music that was lighter in texture, easier to listen to, and more varied. Early Classic music has far more variety than Baroque music. There are frequent changes of texture, of dynamics, of instrumentation. The phrases are shorter, and each phrase may be quite different from the one that precedes it.

Many early Classic compositions have three movements instead of four because the minuet did not become a standard feature of sonatas and symphonies until the second half of the eighteenth century.

THE CLASSIC MASTERS

The masters of the Classic style were Haydn and Mozart. Since their own time, these two composers have been regarded as the most accomplished among a large number of highly skilled musicians active in the second half of the eighteenth century. Both men were extraordinarily prolific, completing many hundreds of superb compositions during their lifetimes. Although the musical language and techniques they used were common throughout Europe at the time, their individual abilities were so remarkable, their grasp of harmony, form, and expression so assured, and their melodic invention so rich that they stand out from their contemporaries. Both men were so fluent in music and created so many masterpieces that they may rightly be regarded as among the greatest geniuses of the age.

Above: Haydn at 60.

Thomas Hardy, *Joseph Hayden (Franz Joseph), Composer*, 1792. Painting London (active 1778–1801). London, Royal College of Music. AKG London.

Below: Mozart at 33.

FRANZ JOSEPH HAYDN (1732–1809)

Anyone can see that I'm a good-natured fellow.
—Haydn

Haydn was born in a small village in Austria. His father was a wheelmaker—an important trade in the eighteenth century—and Haydn was one of 12 children. There was much music-making at home and in the village, and Haydn displayed an early talent for music. At the age of eight, he was accepted as a choirboy at St. Stephen's Cathedral in Vienna, the biggest city in the Austrian empire. Here he stayed until he was 18, when his voice changed. (In those days, the onset of puberty

The Classic Orchestra

By the time of the Classic period, the orchestra had inherited certain traits from the Baroque, but it also featured new ones. The main body of the orchestra is still formed by the strings: perhaps eight to twelve violins (divided into two groups), four violas, two or three cellos and a double bass or two. (These numbers can be greater or lesser depending on the occasion for which the music was written or the financial resources of the sponsoring organization). But now there is a clearer and more separate role for the wind instruments. Instead of playing along with the strings, they have more clearly defined music of their own. The wind section is formed of flutes, oboes, bassoons, and horns, usually in pairs. Toward the end of the eighteenth century clarinets also were featured. A composer such as Mozart, with his subtle and refined sense of sound, would assign very distinctive roles to the winds. One flute might join the violins in a slow movement to add luster to their song. A pair of oboes and a bassoon might be featured in the Trio section of a Minuet. And often the winds play passages of their own to contrast deliberately with the strings. In line with the Classic desire for symmetry and clarity, the balance of the strings and the winds is more clearly organized. Finally, for festive occasions, or for a symphony that the composer wanted to make stirring or more extrovert, the orchestra could feature trumpets and timpani. You can immediately hear the difference between an orchestra with trumpets and drums and one without.

A perfect example of the Classic orchestra is Mozart's Second Movement of the Clarinet Concerto. You can watch a live performance of this work in Segment 3 of your *Inside the Orchestra* CD-ROM.

Haydn in full dress.

Edouard Jean Conrad Hamman, Portrait of Joseph Haydn. Engraving. Bibliothèque Nationale, Paris, France. Giraudon/Art Resource, NY.

> I was never so devout as when I was at work on *The Creation.* —Haydn

Haydn's Contract

When Haydn was appointed to the Esterházy court, his contract was very specific about his duties. He was required to dress "as befits an honest house officer in a princely court," that is, with brocaded coat, powdered wig, white stockings, and silver buckles on his shoes. He was to be in charge of all the musicians, serve as an example to them, and "avoid undue familiarity with them in eating and drinking or in other relations, lest he should lose the respect due to him." He was responsible for looking after all the music and the instruments. And he was required to compose music as the prince demanded, and forbidden to give away or sell copies of his music or compose for anyone else "without the knowledge and gracious permission of his Serene Princely Highness." ✦ Haydn was quite content with this arrangement. He said later: "My Prince was happy with all my works; I received approval; I could, as head of an orchestra, make experiments in my music. I was cut off from the world: there was no one to confuse or annoy me, and I was forced to become original."

for both boys and girls was many years later than it is today.)

While he was at the cathedral, he had learned to play the harpsichord and the violin, so for the next 10 years (about 1750 to 1760) Haydn made a living giving harpsichord lessons and playing in local orchestras. During this time, he lived in a small room in an apartment building in Vienna. Luckily for him, some of the grander apartments were occupied by people who became very useful in furthering his career. One was Pietro Metastasio, the most famous poet and opera librettist (opera text writer) of his time; Metastasio introduced Haydn to many prominent figures in the musical world. Another was a woman who was the head of one of the most prominent aristocratic families of the time. Her name was Maria Esterházy, and the Esterházy family was to play a significant role in Haydn's life and career.

In 1761, Haydn was hired as assistant music director to the household of Prince Paul Anton Esterházy. The prince had a sizable retinue of servants, including a small orchestra of about 12 players. Haydn was responsible for composing music on demand, supervising and rehearsing the other musicians, and caring for the instruments.

Prince Paul Anton died in 1762 and was succeeded by his brother Nikolaus. Prince Nikolaus Esterházy was an avid music lover who spent a great deal of money on his court and entertainment. In the countryside, Prince Nikolaus built a magnificent palace that had two large music rooms and two small theaters for opera. He called this palace Esterháza after the family name.

In 1766 Haydn was promoted to music director at Esterháza. He was responsible for directing all the music at the palace. There were usually two full operas as well as two big concerts given each week. Extra concerts were put on whenever an important visitor came to the palace. Music was performed at meals, and the prince had chamber music played in his own rooms almost every day. Haydn wrote much of this music himself.

Over the course of his lifetime, Haydn wrote about a dozen operas, more than 100 symphonies, nearly 70

Left: The palace of Esterháza, where Haydn spent most of his life.

Below: The music room in the palace of Esterháza.

string quartets, more than 50 keyboard sonatas, and a large amount of choral music, songs, and other chamber music. Haydn stayed in the service of the Esterházy family until 1790, when Prince Nikolaus died. The new prince, Nikolaus II, did not like music and disbanded the orchestra. Haydn, now nearly 60, moved back to Vienna.

By this time, his work was internationally known, and he traveled twice to London—first from 1791 to 1792, then from 1794 to 1795. For his visits to London, Haydn wrote his last 12 symphonies, brilliant and fascinating works, which were performed there to wild public acclaim. They are known as the *London* Symphonies.

In his late years, back in Vienna, Haydn wrote mostly string quartets and vocal music. His quartets are varied and masterful, covering the entire range of expression from playfulness to profundity. The vocal works include six Mass settings for chorus and orchestra and the two great oratorios of his last years, *The Creation* (1798) and *The Seasons* (1801).

Haydn died in 1809 at the age of 77. His reputation transcended even national disputes. Vienna was under siege by the French army at the time, but Napoleon posted a guard of honor outside Haydn's house to pay homage to the greatest composer of the age.

Haydn's Music

For a long time, Haydn's music was regarded as genial and lively, and much of its depth, wit, and brilliance went unnoticed. This was because only a few of his compositions were performed regularly at concerts. Nowadays, however, much more of Haydn's music is being performed, and the extraordinary range of his achievement is being recognized.

His operas are full of beautiful music—lyrical, inventive, and moving. His symphonies range from ceremonious public works with trumpets and drums to compositions of great delicacy, charm, and even tragedy. The string quartets explore an enormous range of expression, with a masterful handling of the intimate medium and brilliant writing for the four instruments. The early quartets usually give most of the melodic material to the first violin, but in the later quartets the other instruments are more fully integrated, with each of the four players contributing much to the discourse. When the great German poet Goethe compared a string quartet to a conversation among four equally interesting individuals, he must have been thinking of the Haydn quartets.

The Haydn Masses are noble, grand structures, combining a conservative choral style appropriate to the traditional texts with his own individual orchestral

LISTENING GUIDE

Franz Joseph Haydn (1732–1809)
Minuet and Trio from Symphony No. 45
in F-sharp minor

Date of composition: 1772
Orchestration: 2 oboes, 2 horns, violins I and II, viola, cello, double bass
Tempo: *Allegretto* ("Moderately fast")
Meter: $\frac{3}{4}$
Key of movement: F♯ Major
Duration: 4:53

Student CD Collection: 2, track 12
Complete CD Collection: 2, track 40

*W*e studied a fairly simple minuet and trio in the Listening chapter at the beginning of this book. This movement is more fascinating and complex. Understanding its many levels can take dozens of repeated hearings, and yet it is also graceful and lively, and a pleasure to listen to.

Among the standard features of minuet form and style—a fixed pattern of repetition, triple meter, moderate tempo—Haydn has incorporated several others that make this particular minuet unique. The most striking is the amount of contrast he has written into this piece. There is contrast of dynamics, texture, instrumentation, and key.

The first—contrast of dynamics—is evident from the outset. In the first section of the movement, which takes only about 13 seconds to play, Haydn changes dynamics four times. These dynamic contrasts are reinforced by textural contrasts: Haydn tends to use monophony or very thin counterpoint for the quiet passages and thick polyphony for the loud. For this first section the instrumentation also follows suit. We hear violins alone in the quiet passages and the whole orchestra playing when the music is loud. All these contrasts continue throughout the piece. As for contrast of key, there is a move to the dominant key for sections B and C and a sudden and unexpected shift to F-sharp *minor* in the middle of the D section.

In some ways it seems as though Haydn is deliberately trying to confuse his listeners. Usually in minuet movements the form is easy to hear. But in this movement, the form is quite difficult to hear. Haydn tries every trick in the book to confuse us. He does this by (1) putting the strong cadences in the wrong place, (2) using linking phrases across the section divisions, (3) syncopating the rhythm, and (4) using internal repetitions. For example, he repeats some of the A section inside the B section and so on (this is known as *rounded binary*).

There is more. In his internal repetitions of the rounded binary form (repeating A inside B, and C inside D), instead of repeating exactly, Haydn rewrites the music each time.

Let's look at the D section first, since that is the easiest one. The D section contains a shortened restatement of C. Haydn actually repeats only the first half of C (compare 1:41–1:56 with 2:33–2:40). But if you listen closely, you will hear that Haydn has actually rewritten the passage to make it sound fresh. In its first appearance, the instrumentation involves only the two horns, with a tiny touch of strings at the end. In its restatement, oboes, horns, and all the strings play the music.

The rewriting of the A section within the B section is even more subtle. Compare 0:00–0:14 with 0:49–1:05. Listening carefully, you'll find many differences involving dynamics, phrase lengths (including the length of the whole passage), and instrumentation. Haydn is really trying to keep his audience on their toes!

The best way to untangle all of this is by means of the timed listening guide. If you glance frequently at your watch or CD timer while you are listening, follow the listening guide carefully, and listen to the piece several times, you'll be able to get some sense of what a brilliant and sophisticated composer Haydn really was.

MINUET			
A	12 (40) **0:00**	The first section of the minuet, in F♯ Major. Graceful dancelike character; full of contrasts; syncopation. Ends with quiet linking passage on violins alone.
A	**0:14**	Repeat of first section of the minuet.
B (+**A'**) 13 (41) **0:30**		The second section of the minuet, longer than the first. Dominant key (C♯ Major). Short loud passage, longer quiet syncopated passage on strings alone. Then a crescendo into a restatement (A') of the first section of the minuet (0:49).
B (+**A'**)	**1:05**	Repeat of entire second section, including its restatement of A.
TRIO			
C	14 (42) **1:41**	First section of trio. Rising phrase for horns, graceful answering phrase for violins.
C	**1:56**	Repeat.
D (+**C'**) 15 (43) **2:11**		Second section of trio, longer than the first. Back to tonic key (F♯ Major). Divided into three parts: beginning, with descending phrases in horns; (2:21) oboes replace the horns, sudden shift to F♯ *minor*; (2:33) shortened restatement (C') of the first section of the trio.
D (+**C'**)	**2:40**	Repeat of entire second section of trio, including its restatement of C.
MINUET			
		[The entire minuet is repeated exactly.]
A	16 (44) **3:10**	A section.
A	**3:24**	Repeat of A section.
B (+**A'**)	**3:39**	B section, including restatement of A.
B (+**A'**)	**4:14**	Repeat of B section with restatement of A.

and symphonic brilliance. And Haydn's two oratorios, *The Creation* and *The Seasons*, display a wit and a liveliness together with the kind of exquisite pictorial writing that never fails to captivate audiences. In *The Creation*, for example, which describes the creation of the world, Haydn begins with a depiction of Chaos, in which darkness and void are represented by murky harmonies and unsettled rhythm. On the last word of the choral proclamation "And there was *light!*," there is a loud, radiant climax on a C-Major chord. Both *The Creation* and *The Seasons* contain cleverly realistic musical descriptions of nature: a cooing dove, a flashing storm, a slithery worm.

In the middle of Haydn's career at Esterháza, in the early 1770s, there was an interesting change of style that affected his string quartets, piano sonatas, and symphonies. Quite suddenly, some of Haydn's works began to display a mood of melancholy and longing that had not been there before. Haydn experimented with this style by writing several compositions in un-

usual minor keys, with sudden changes of dynamics, remote harmonic excursions, and burdened, intense, slow movements. We shall listen to a movement from one of Haydn's symphonies from this period. Possibly because the prince did not react favorably to the new style, Haydn abandoned it after a few years. **(See Listening Guide on page 178.)**

All of Haydn's pieces adopt Classic formal procedures. Nevertheless, Haydn showed great ingenuity in exploiting the fixed forms of Classic music for his own expressive purposes. One device that he invented was the "false recapitulation." You remember that in sonata form, the opening music of the movement comes back again—after the development section—with the same melody and harmony that it had at the beginning. Haydn sometimes liked to play games with the expectations of his audience by *pretending* to start the recapitulation in the middle of the development section. The music of the opening of the movement is played, leading us to think that the recapitulation has started.

LISTENING GUIDE

Franz Joseph Haydn (1732–1809)
Fourth Movement from String Quartet,
Op. 33, No. 2, in E-flat Major

Tempo: *Presto* ("Very fast")
Meter: $\frac{6}{8}$
Key: E♭ Major
Duration: 3:08

Student CD Collection: 2, track 17
Complete CD Collection: 2, track 45

This movement is in the form of a rondo. There is a catchy main theme, which constantly returns in the course of the movement. Between appearances of the main theme are passages of contrasting material known as episodes. In this rondo Haydn adopts the following form, with A as the main theme and B, C, and D as the three episodes:

A B A B A C A B A D A Coda

Haydn has written this movement in the attractive and bouncy meter of 6/8 and in a fast tempo, which makes the music particularly lively and fun. But the joke comes in the final measures, as the listener has no idea where the ending really is.

A 17 (45) **0:00**	Main theme.
0:06	Repeat.
B **0:12**	First episode.
A **0:28**	Main theme.
B **0:34**	Repeat of first episode.
A **0:50**	Main theme.
C 18 (46) **0:57**	Second episode, many key changes.
A **1:25**	Main theme.
B **1:31**	First episode again.
A **1:48**	Main theme.
D **1:54**	Third episode.
2:13	Pace slows down, anticipation, then:
A **2:23**	Main theme again.
CODA **2:30**	Final cadence?
19 (47) **2:32**	Sudden change of texture and tempo.
2:45	Final cadence?
2:46	Main theme, broken up into four separate phrases.
2:58	Ending?
3:01	First phrase of main theme!

Mozart at the age of 7.

Lorenzoni, Pietro Anton (attributed to). Young Mozart wearing court-dress. 1763. Mozart House, Salzburg, Austra. Erich Lessing/Art Resource, NY.

But then the harmonies change, the development continues, and we realize we've been tricked. A little while later, the true recapitulation occurs.

Haydn liked to play other kinds of tricks on his listeners. In 1781 he published a set of six string quartets, which have come to be called the "Joke Quartets." The quartets contain serious music and emotionally expressive passages, but there are many witty moments, too: cadences in the "wrong" places, oddly shaped melodies, and unexpected rhythms. At the end of the second quartet of the set (Opus 33, Number 2), there is a "false ending." The music seems to stop, suddenly moves on, stops again, and then seems to begin again. Then the movement ends. **(See Listening Guide on page 180.)**

This kind of manipulation of audience expectations could occur only in a period in which formal procedures were strict. When there are no rules, breaking the rules is no fun!

Even today, much of Haydn's music is only rarely performed. But as time goes on, and more of his compositions become familiar, we realize that Haydn was one of the most versatile and gifted composers of his time.

WOLFGANG AMADEUS MOZART (1756–1791)

For most listeners, Mozart's music is easier to appreciate than Haydn's. Compared with Haydn, Mozart wears his heart on his sleeve. His music is more colorful, more intense.

Mozart was born into a musical family. His father,

> I pay no attention whatever to anybody's praise or blame. . . . I simply follow my own feelings.
> —Mozart, in a letter to his father

Leopold Mozart

Leopold Mozart is often mentioned only in relation to his illustrious son, Wolfgang Amadeus Mozart. This is a little unfair, because he was a distinguished performer, composer, author, and music theorist in his own right. ♦ In 1756, Leopold published a treatise entitled *Versuch einer grundlichen Violinschule* (*Essay on a Fundamental Violin Method*), designed partly as an aid for teaching the violin and partly as a discussion of musical performance and analysis. It represents one of the most important contributions to music theory in the mid-eighteenth century. ♦ Unfortunately, a large number of Leopold's compositions remain unresearched, uncatalogued, and unpublished. Those that are documented include Masses, symphonies, di-

vertimenti, partitas, serenades, and a wide variety of chamber music. Much of Leopold's music exhibits a strong naturalistic tendency and employs instruments such as bugles, bagpipes, the hunting horn, the hurdy-gurdy, and the dulcimer. Leopold sometimes asks for dog noises, human cries, pistol shots, and whistles! ♦ Leopold composed little after 1762. This sudden decrease in productivity can be attributed to the huge amount of time he devoted to teaching his son and to the numerous tours of Europe they undertook together in an attempt to promote Wolfgang's extraordinary talents. In short, Leopold sacrificed his own considerable career to further that of his son. No one was better qualified to recognize Wolfgang's gifts than his own father.

Leopold, was a distinguished violinist and composer who held the post of deputy music director at the court of the Prince-Archbishop of Salzburg in Austria. He was also the author of an important book on violin-playing.

He decided to devote his career to promoting the abilities of young Wolfgang. Wolfgang was uniquely, breathtakingly gifted. His father piously referred to him as "this miracle God has caused to be born in Salzburg."

Mozart was born in 1756. By the age of four, he was already displaying amazing musical ability. At six, he had started to compose and was performing brilliantly on the harpsichord. For the next ten years, his father took him on journeys to various courts, towns, and

Portrait of the Mozart family from about 1780. Mozart plays a duet with his sister, while his father listens, and his mother is remembered in a painting behind them.

Painting, Baroque, 18th Century. Johann Nepomuk Della Croce, *The Mozart Family* (1780–1781). Oil on canvas. 140 × 186 cm. Mozart House, Salzburg, Austria. Erich Lessing, Art Resource.

principalities around Europe, where he played for noblemen, princes, and even the Empress of Austria, Maria Theresa.

These constant travels in his formative years had a valuable effect on the young boy. Mozart's principal teacher at this time was his father, but he absorbed other

The Boy Genius

Mozart's genius as a child caused such a sensation in London that he was examined and tested by a scientist. The scientist wrote a report attesting to Mozart's musical ability and age. The proof that he was indeed a boy and not a midget came at the end of a rigorous series of musical examinations:

While he was playing to me, a cat came in, upon which he immediately left his harpsichord, nor could we bring him back for a considerable time. He would also sometimes run about the room with a stick between his legs for a horse.

Engraving from Leopold Mozart's *Violin Method*, published in 1756, the year of Wolfgang's birth.

The city of Salzburg, Mozart's birthplace, in the mid-eighteenth century.

musical influences like a sponge. Wherever he went, he picked up the musical style of the region and of the prominent local composers.

From all these sources and from his own teeming imagination, Mozart fashioned an individual style. By the time he was eight, Mozart had already had some music published. By 10, he was writing symphonies. At 14, he had produced his first full-length opera. By the time he was 17 years old, when he and his father returned home to Salzburg to try to find Wolfgang a job, he was a mature and fully formed creative artist.

Finding Mozart a job was not easy. The Prince-Archbishop of Salzburg was an autocratic ruler, and his patience had already been tried by the constant leaves of absence of his deputy music director (Mozart's father). The archbishop agreed to employ Mozart, but only in a junior position. Mozart wrote a fair amount of music in these years, but both he and his father felt that Salzburg was too stifling for him. After a few years, Mozart traveled again to try to find a position elsewhere. This time he traveled with his mother, since his father could not afford to leave his post for any more trips. He went to Munich, Mannheim (where Stamitz's great orchestra was centered), and Paris. But in none of these places was a job forthcoming. Most of Mozart's prospective employers thought he was too young and too talented ("overqualified" is the word we would use today) for a normal position. Indeed, any music director would have been threatened by this brash and brilliant youngster. In Paris he encountered not only disap-

The ending of Mozart's dedication to Haydn: "I remain with all my heart, dearest friend, your most sincere friend."

Title page of Mozart's six string quartets dedicated to Haydn.

pointment but also tragedy: his mother died. He wrote to his father and sister:

> I hope that you are prepared to hear with fortitude one of the saddest and most painful stories....I can only judge from my own grief and sorrow what yours must be.

Although Mozart was given a promotion upon returning to Salzburg, he was still unsatisfied. In 1780 he accompanied the archbishop on a visit to Vienna.

SEI
QUARTETTI
PER DUE VIOLINI, VIOLA, E VIOLONCELLO,
Composti e Dedicati
al Signor
GIUSEPPE HAYDN
Maestro di Cappella di S.A.
il Principe d'Esterhazy & &
Dal Suo Amico
W. A. MOZART
Opera X.
In Vienna presso Artaria Comp.
Mercanti ed Editori di Stampa Musica,
e Carte Geografiche.

Composers and Patrons in the Classic Era

Music patronage was at a turning point when Mozart went to Vienna in the last part of the eighteenth century. Many patrons of music continued to be wealthy aristocrats. Haydn's entire career was funded by a rich prince. Mozart's father and, for a time, Mozart himself were in the employ of another prince. But when Mozart went to Vienna in 1781, he contrived to make a living from a variety of sources. In addition to performances at aristocratic houses and commissions for particular works, Mozart gave piano and composition lessons, put on operas, and gave many public concerts of his own music. ¶ The eighteenth century saw a considerable rise in the number and availability of public concerts. Three types were common: charity concerts to raise money for local poorhouses and orphanages; subscription concerts, for which tickets were sold in advance; and benefit concerts, at which composers played for their own profit. Music was becoming more and more the province of the general public, and composers less and less the servants of the rich.

Mozart was outraged when he was forced to eat in the servants' quarters and infuriated when the archbishop refused to let him go to the houses of other aristocrats who had invited him to perform for them. Mozart angrily demanded his release from the archbishop's employ and received it, as he wrote to his father, "with a kick on my ass from our worthy Prince-Archbishop."

Thus began the freelance career of one of the most brilliant musicians in history. At first Mozart supported himself by giving piano lessons. He also wrote several sonatas for the piano and some piano concertos. Piano music was very popular in Vienna. Mozart had some success with a German comic opera he wrote in 1782 called *The Abduction from the Seraglio* (so called because the action takes place in a Turkish *seraglio*, or harem). Also in 1782 he married his landlady's daughter, a young soprano named Constanze Weber. His father, to whom he continued to write regularly, disapproved strongly of the marriage.

For the next few years, Mozart was highly successful. He undertook a set of string quartets that were designed to emulate those of Haydn, and he dedicated them in a warm and heartfelt style to the older master. We know the two composers met a few times at string quartet parties. Haydn played the violin, Mozart the viola.

In these years Mozart won great fame—and made quite a lot of money—by means of piano concertos. Between 1784 and 1786, he wrote 12 piano concertos. This was a fine opportunity for him to appear before the Viennese public as both composer and pianist, because he played the solo parts in the concertos himself. The concertos were very successful, and Mozart was at the height of his career.

Gradually, however, Mozart's popularity began to wane. The Viennese were always eager for some new sensation, and Mozart had been around for a while. In addition, the city was undergoing a recession, and concert dates and composing contracts were hard to come by. Mozart's correspondence from the late 1780s is full of letters requesting loans from friends, and, despite his dislike of authority, he made attempts to find a secure position at the Viennese court.

Mozart did not write many new symphonies during this period, but in the summer of 1788, in the space of about eight weeks, he wrote three symphonies in a row. These last three symphonies, Nos. 39, 40, and 41, are the culmination of his work in the genre. They are very different from each other, but all three are richly orchestrated, enormously inventive, and full of subtle details that repay frequent rehearings.

Perhaps the greatest achievement of Mozart's last years is represented by his operas. Mozart had been interested in opera since his boyhood travels to Italy. He had already written several youthful pieces and, since coming to Vienna, both an opera seria (serious Italian opera) and a German comic opera. Now, in what would be the last five years of his life, he completed five great operas. The best known of these are *The Marriage of Figaro* (1786), *Don Giovanni* (1787), and *The Magic Flute* (completed in the year of his death, 1791). These operas are all very different, but in each of them Mozart displays his remarkable understanding of human nature in all its richness. In Figaro, he depicts with the finest subtlety the urgent adolescent sexuality of a servant boy and the deeply moving despair of a neglected wife. In *Don Giovanni*, Mozart explores the richly human traits of determination, pride, grief, comedy, and seduction. In *The Magic Flute*, the themes are noble ambition, marital harmony, and pure love. In Mozart's hands, these ideals and emotions are transformed from the conventions of the opera stage into the deepest expression of human feelings.

In November of 1791, while he was working on a Requiem Mass (Mass for the Dead), Mozart became ill. And on December 5, at the age of 35, with half a lifetime of masterpieces still uncomposed, Wolfgang Amadeus Mozart died.

Mozart's Music

Mozart's music is a remarkable combination of the accessible and the profound. As Mozart wrote to his father, his music appeals to experts and amateurs alike. Another reason so many people are so attached to Mozart's music is its extraordinary breadth. There is an

> I swear before Almighty God that your son is the greatest composer I know either in person or by reputation.
> —Haydn to Mozart's father

Musical Forgeries

The fame of Haydn and Mozart and other great composers has led to great excitement whenever one of their music manuscripts turns up in an attic or an old desk drawer. Sometimes these documents are authentic. But often they are forgeries, and some of them are good enough to fool even the experts (for a while). In 1994, some "newly discovered" Haydn piano sonatas, authenticated by a world-renowned Haydn scholar and due for performance at Harvard University's Music Department, were declared to be fakes. ✦ The name of one of the great composers on the title page virtually guarantees a favorable reception for a work. For nearly a hundred years, a well-known symphony was thought to be by Mozart (his "37th Symphony"). It was hailed by critics as "typical of the master." But when the symphony turned out to be not by Mozart at all but by a less famous contemporary of his, critics immediately described it as "obviously not on a par with the work of the master." The work hadn't changed—it was the same music!—only people's preconceptions had changed.

Autograph manuscript of a work for voice and piano by Mozart. Notice the speed and clarity of Mozart's handwriting.

incredibly wide range of music to choose from—more than 800 compositions, from the lightest little comic pieces to works that explore the great themes of human existence: life and death, love, tragedy, romance, despair and hope.

Mozart wrote in all the main genres of Classic music: opera, symphony, string quartet, and sonata. He wrote solo concertos for a wide variety of instruments: violin, flute, oboe, clarinet, bassoon, and horn. But for his own instrument, the piano, he composed more than 20 concertos, which are among his greatest masterpieces. We shall listen to a slow movement from one of these piano concertos. **(See Listening Guide on page 188.)**

Mozart wrote dozens of sonatas, both for solo piano and for combinations of instruments, including piano, strings, and winds. He also composed many great string quartets. In addition to these works, Mozart wrote several string quintets, in which an extra viola is added to the two violins, viola, and cello of the string quartet. This makes the music richer and the counterpoint fuller.

Mozart also greatly enriched the expressive power of opera. In *The Magic Flute, Don Giovanni,* and *The Marriage of Figaro,* Mozart transcends convention by portraying people in all their psychological complexity.

Of *The Magic Flute:* "This opera . . . is the only one in existence that might conceivably have been composed by God."
—Neville Cardus, music critic, 1961

O Mozart, immortal Mozart, how many, how infinitely many inspiring suggestions of a finer, better life have you left in our souls!
—Franz Schubert

Wolfgang Amadeus Mozart
(1756–1791)
Second Movement from Piano Concerto
No. 21 in C Major, K. 467

Date of composition: 1785
Orchestration: Solo piano, flute,
  2 oboes, 2 bassoons, 2 horns, and
  strings
Tempo: *Andante* ("Moderately slow")
Meter: $\frac{4}{4}$
Key of movement: F Major
Duration: 7:46

Complete CD Collection: 2, track 48

ozart wrote this piano concerto in the space of 27 days, a period during which he also taught private students, entertained his father, held a string quartet party that included Haydn, and played in about a dozen private and public concerts. One of Mozart's best-known piano concertos, No. 21 follows formal conventions, containing three movements: *Allegro maestoso*, *Andante*, and *Allegro vivace assai*. From this fast-slow-fast format, we'll examine the lyrical middle movement. The movement displays the powerful influence of opera on eighteenth-century instrumental music: It employs wonderfully singable melodies and uses aria form (ABA). Underneath all the melodies throughout the movement we hear the *pizzicato* bass and the pulsating lapping of triplet (three-in-a-beat) notes.

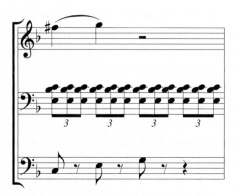

SECTION A		[divided into three parts, two of which are repeated by the piano]
(48)	**0:00**	(1) The meter is a slow 4/4, but the triplet subdivision of the beat is heard in the repeated pulses of the accompaniment. Muted violins play the gentle theme, which rises in waves and then descends to a sighing figure.
	0:31	(2) A contrasting phrase is marked by sudden dynamic changes and dramatic downward leaps; winds enter to articulate this moment. Another downward leap leads to a long series of upward leaps that gradually descend and are offset by oboes. The mood is one of suspension and weightlessness.
	1:13	(3) The section ends with a pair of balanced phrases on oboe and violins, the second of which is joined by flute and bassoons.
	1:43	The piano enters and repeats the first two sections, (1) and (2), of the preceding material. The underlying triplets are played by the left hand of the piano, the melody by the right. Although this is a repeat of previously heard material, the differences in tone quality render it striking and fresh.
	2:35	Triplet accompaniment moves into section B (minor key) with no repeat of part (3) of section A.
SECTION B		
(49)	**2:37**	This section is designed as a contrast with section A. It is more freely structured and introduces some new melodic ideas. It begins in D minor (the relative minor), but it modulates frequently.
	2:44	The piano is still playing, but now faster and more energetically.
	3:15	The "weightless" material that ended part (2) of section A is recalled, leading into idea (3).
	3:41	Now the piano (with violins) states idea (3)—the paired phrases—from section A. A striking moment! Listen also to the rich parts for accompanying woodwinds.
	4:03	Sustained woodwinds, strings, and piano exchange phrases.
	4:51	A passage reminiscent of the "weightless" phrases of (2) leads to the return of section A.

SECTION A'

| (50) | **5:24** | The return of section A is recognizable, but it is altered by being in a different key. It is also ornamented, much as a singer would ornament the return of the A section in an aria. And parts of the ideas come in a slightly different order. (Mozart always made simple things more interesting.) |
| | **7:20** | Return to the tonic key. A brief new melody is heard using repeated notes. The triplet accompaniment ends the movement. |

Even in his purely instrumental works, Mozart wrote music that flouted convention. He created works of great depth and seriousness for "background music" at garden parties. He wrote slow movements of heartbreaking simplicity for his piano concertos. Often he used counterpoint to intensify his music in places where counterpoint was not usual. And his melodies often have passages that are chromatic (moving by half steps) at a time when most composers wrote melodies that are entirely diatonic (using only notes from the scale). Finally, Mozart's music often passes briefly into the minor mode, even in major-mode passages, which creates added depth and emotional resonance. It is like the shadow of a small cloud passing over a sunny meadow.

Only a very small number of his works use a minor key as the tonic. Among these is the Symphony No. 40 in G minor, written in 1788. **(See Listening Guide on page 191.)**

Although Mozart's music is richer, more versatile, and more varied than most eighteenth-century music, it does use the same basic conventions as other music of the time. The instruments are the same, the forms are the same, and the primary genres that Mozart cultivated are the same. But Mozart's music speaks deeply to more people, covers a wider range of feeling, and resonates with more human significance than that of almost any other composer before or since. In that sense, Mozart's music is truly "classic."

A scene from a production of Mozart's opera *The Magic Flute*.

Wolfgang Amadeus Mozart
    (1756–1791)
First Movement from Symphony No. 40
    in G minor, K. 550

Date of composition: 1788
Orchestration: Flute, 2 oboes, 2 clar-
    inets, 2 bassoons, 2 horns, and
    strings
Tempo: *Allegro molto* ("Very fast")
Meter: ²⁄₂
Key: G minor
Duration: 8:16

Student CD Collection: 2, track 20
Complete CD Collection: 3, track 1

*I*n the space of eight weeks during the summer of 1788, Mozart completed three large-scale symphonies. Though there was no reason for him to have known this, they were to be his last. Perhaps he intended them to be published and performed together.

The G-minor Symphony, the middle one of the three, is one of Mozart's best-known works, representing one of his greatest achievements in the symphonic realm. It is marked by perfect balance and control, a wealth of harmonic and instrumental color, and a brilliant use of formal structure.

The first movement is a superb example of these characteristics. In it, Mozart takes advantage of the dramatic possibilities of sonata form, while also playing with its conventions for expressive purposes. The basic structure of sonata form is easy to hear, but we can also see how Mozart *manipulated* the form to surprise and delight his listeners. There are many examples, but the most obvious one is the way he leads us to expect the recapitulation at a certain point, only to pull the rug out from under us.

You should first listen to the piece a few times simply to enjoy the fine expressive writing—the brilliant balance between loud and soft, woodwinds and strings, descending and ascending phrases, and minor and major keys. Notice, too, how Mozart spices up the sound with chromatic passages and surprise notes. Next, listen for the structure, the basic template of sonata form, which is so clearly articulated in this movement. The next couple of times, listen for how Mozart plays with this structure (and with his audience's expectations) for expressive purposes. Finally, try putting all these things together and listen for them all at once.

Don't stop listening after that, however. For you may find, as many of the most experienced listeners do, that you will hear something new in this movement every single time you listen to it. And there are three other movements in this symphony ... three other symphonies in the group ... dozens of other symphonies by Mozart.

EXPOSITION		
		[timings for the repeat are in parentheses]
20 (1)	**0:00**	Opening theme: violins, quiet, G minor; closed by full orchestra, loud.
22 (3)	**(2:02)**	

Allegro molto

Violins I & II

p

0:24 **(2:27)**		Restatement of opening theme, woodwinds added, beginning modulation to second key.
0:34 **(2:37)**		Energetic bridge passage, loud, full orchestra, preparing for second key. (Central to this passage is a strong rising figure, which appears later in the movement.)

Violins I & II

0:50 **(2:53)**		Cadence in new key (B♭–relative major).
21 (2) **0:52** **(2:56)**		Second theme, also quiet, smooth alternation of strings and woodwinds, quite chromatic.

Violins   Clarinets   Violins

1:10 **(3:14)**		Odd surprise notes.
1:20 **(3:23)**		Cadence.
1:27 **(3:31)**		Spinning-out section (clarinet, bassoon, strings).
1:47 **(3:50)**		Ending passage, loud, whole orchestra.
2:00 **(4:04)**		Final cadences of exposition.
22 (3) **2:02**		(Exact repetition of entire exposition.)

DEVELOPMENT

23 (4) **4:09**		Many key changes, by means of first theme dropping down.
4:23		A "blender" passage, in which the themes are cut up and tossed around; whole orchestra, loud.

24 (5)	4:52	Music gets quiet … quieter (we are expecting the recapitulation … but:)
	5:09	Suddenly loud (we've been fooled: no recapitulation here).
	5:19	Another preparation, quiet woodwind descent (watch out: is this real … ?)

RECAPITULATION

25 (6)	5:24	YES! (But notice how Mozart sneaks it in ever so quietly.) All goes normally here, though there are some changes from the exposition.
	5:57	New material, loud, whole orchestra (sounds like it's left over from the development). It uses the rising figure from the opening bridge passage (shown above at 0:34).
	6:29	Back on track …
26 (7)	6:40	Second theme: quiet, winds and strings, this time in tonic key (G minor).
	6:58	Surprise notes.
	7:05	New material.
	7:14	Back on track …
	7:21	Spinning out.
	7:44	Music opens out to:

CODA

27 (8)	7:53	Confirming tonic key, floating, quiet.
	8:03	Repeated definitive cadences, loud.
	8:09	Three final chords.

STYLE SUMMARY

Classic music presents a notable contrast from that of the Baroque era. Classic music is lighter, more delicate, with simpler harmonies and clearer textures. The most obvious difference is in the bass. We pointed out in the style summary of the previous chapter that a Baroque piece's most characteristic feature is the strength and powerful sense of direction of its bass line. (This is usually played in chamber music by at least two instruments, a keyboard and a low stringed instrument, and in orchestral music by a keyboard and all the low strings.) In Classic music, the accompaniment is usually much lighter, with the chords broken up into patterns or with the bass notes more separated, with some "air" between them.

Second, Classic music tends to stick to simpler harmonies, usually staying within the home key or using closely related keys, without some of the dissonant chords sometimes used for expressive effect in Baroque music. A standard pattern of key relationships within a movement or among the movements of a work became clearly established in this period.

Third, Classic music uses a symmetrical arrangement of musical phrases. Phrases tend to be two or four measures long and to be arranged into pairs. This symmetry is used as the basis for simple, attractive melodies.

Finally, the ruling force in Classic music is convention. Convention governs the number of movements in a piece, the forms in which they are cast, and the tempos at which they are played. The key relationship among movements is set by convention, as is the order and approximate length of the key areas within movements. Individual keys are associated with particular moods and even with particular instruments.

The most important musical genres of the Classic era are opera, symphony, and chamber music—especially the string quartet and sonata. Symphonies and chamber works follow a four-movement format: a moderately fast first movement, a graceful or lyrical slow movement, a minuet and trio, and a fast final movement. The first, third, and last movements are usually in the tonic key. The slow movement might be in the dominant key (V), the subdominant key (IV), or the relative minor key (vi). Sonata form is used in the first movement. Aria form, theme and variations form, or sonata form in the second; minuet-and-trio form in the third; and either rondo or sonata form in the fourth.

In concertos, the convention is that the piece should contain only three movements: moderately fast, slow, and fast. Historically, concertos did not take on the minuet-and-trio movement of the symphonic format. The piano became one of the principal solo instruments featured in Classic concertos.

The last page of music Mozart wrote before his death.

The instrumentation in symphonies was for a small group of wind instruments, sometimes trumpets and drums, and a full string section. The instrumentation in chamber music was either for piano alone or for one to four instruments (usually strings) and a piano. Sometimes a small group of wind or stringed instruments played together without piano. A favorite combination of the Classic period was the string quartet (two violins, viola, and cello).

Operas on serious subjects continued to be composed; however a new, more down-to-earth, more realistic type of opera known as comic opera became popular. Mozart used to mingle types of opera. He introduced comic scenes into serious operas and generally broke out of the conventional mode, producing works of extraordinary variety and psychological insight.

The same music in a modern score.

The absence of the basso continuo in Classic music created the opportunity for a much lighter, more transparent texture, more freedom in instrumental writing, and a more accessible style. This was music for nonexperts as well as for connoisseurs.

FUNDAMENTALS OF CLASSIC MUSIC

- ✦ The music is more accessible, with shorter, symmetrical phrases, simpler harmony, and easier tunes

- ✦ No basso continuo

- ✦ Texture is more transparent

- ✦ Principal genres are opera, symphony, and chamber music, though concertos (especially for piano) are also popular

- ✦ New genres are piano concerto, comic opera, and string quartet

- ✦ The music is largely ruled by convention (number of movements, form and structure of movements, keys, harmony)

BEETHOVEN

Sometimes there are composers who simply do not fit conveniently into pigeonholes or our conveniently constructed time periods. We say that the Classic era in musical style ended about 1800 and that the Romantic era began about the same time. But there is one composer whose life spanned that boundary by about a quarter century in either direction and whose individuality was so strong that he simply cannot be labeled. That composer was Beethoven.

Beethoven grew up at a time when both Haydn and Mozart were still alive and actively composing. The music he heard and studied was strictly Classic in style. But he died in 1827, well into the nineteenth century, when Romanticism was in full flower.

Like all great artists who live at a time of change, Beethoven was both a beneficiary of that change and partly responsible for it. He took the forms, procedures, and ideals that he had inherited from the Classic era and developed them beyond their previously accepted limits. He brought Classic genres—symphony, concerto, sonata, string quartet—into the nineteenth century and transformed them into the vehicles of musical expression for a new age. He burst through the boundaries of Classic restraint to create works of unprecedented scope and depth. He enlarged the orchestra, changed musical structure, added a chorus to the symphony, and told

narratives with some of his purely instrumental works—all things that had wide-ranging repercussions for a century and more. Finally, he invested instrumental music with a personal subjectivity and with the stamp of his own extraordinary personality in such a way that music was never the same again. He was both the child of one era and the founding father of another. That is why Beethoven has a chapter of his own.

The history of Beethoven is tantamount to an intellectual history of the nineteenth century.
—Karl Dahlhaus

Portrait of Beethoven at the age of 49.

Ludwig van Beethoven, portrait by Joseph Karl Stieler, 1820. Beethoven–Haus Bonn.

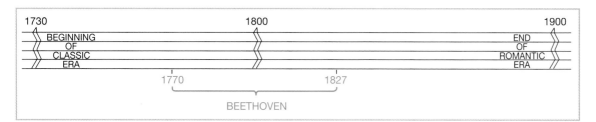

BEETHOVEN'S LIFE

Beethoven is perhaps the most famous musician of all time. Ever since his death in 1827, he has been revered as the principal figure in the history of Western music. His influence on later composers was enormous, to the extent that many of them actually found his accomplishments intimidating.

Who was this man?

The only composer's name over the stage of Symphony Hall (built 1900) in Boston.

Beethoven's Early Life

Ludwig van Beethoven was born in 1770 into a family of musicians. Both his grandfather and his father were professional musicians at the court of the Elector (the local ruler) in the German town of Bonn. His grandfather was highly respected, but his father became something of a problem at the court because he was an alcoholic. As a teenager, Beethoven was put in charge of the family finances and started a job at the court. He studied organ and composition and helped look after the instruments. About the same time, he began to write music, mostly songs and chamber works.

In 1790, an important visitor passed through Bonn. This was Haydn, on his way to London for the first of his successful visits. He met the young Beethoven and agreed to take him on as a student when he came back from London to Vienna. In 1792, Beethoven moved to Vienna to study with the great master. He was 22; Haydn was 60.

Apparently the lessons did not go well. Haydn was old-fashioned and a little pompous, Beethoven rebellious and headstrong. But Beethoven was a formidable pianist, and he soon found support among the rich patrons of the arts who lived in Vienna. Prince Lichnowsky gave him board and lodging at his

> Though I had some instruction from Haydn, I never learned anything from him.
> —Beethoven

palace, in return for which Beethoven was to compose music and play the piano at evening parties . . . at least that was the arrangement. In fact, Beethoven hated being dependent and often refused to play. But the prince was very tolerant; he finally set Beethoven up with his own apartment so that he could work as he pleased.

In the early years, Beethoven wrote mostly keyboard and chamber-music pieces. As time went on, however, he decided to start composing in the larger musical forms of the day—string quartet, piano concerto, and symphony. By the time Beethoven was 32, he had written—among other works—piano sonatas, a great deal of chamber music, a set of six string quartets, three piano concertos, and two symphonies. The string quartets, concertos, and symphonies owe a great debt to Haydn and Mozart.

But Beethoven's music was already starting to show signs of considerable individuality. The First Symphony deliberately begins in the wrong key, before turning to the right one. The Third Piano Concerto features a powerful unifying rhythm. And the last movement of one of the early string quartets has a deeply expressive slow introduction entitled *La Malinconia* (*Melancholy*).

Beethoven had every reason to feel melancholic at this time of his life. For it was in 1802 that he discovered the tragic truth that was to haunt him for the rest of his life: He was going deaf. He contemplated suicide but, overcoming his despair, decided that his first responsibility lay with his music. He had to produce the works that were in him.

His disease progressed gradually. It took some years for him to become totally deaf, and there were periods when normal hearing returned. But by 1817, Beethoven could not hear a single note, and his conversations were carried on by means of an ear trumpet and a notebook slung around his neck. His deafness eventually prevented him from performing and conducting, but he continued to compose until the end of his life. He could hear everything inside his head.

THE HEROIC PHASE

The middle period of Beethoven's life was marked by a vigorous concentration on work and the sense of triumph over adversity. For these reasons, it is often called the "heroic" phase. "I will seize Fate by the throat," he said. This was also a period of extraordinary productivity. In the ten years between 1802 and 1812, Beethoven wrote six more symphonies, four concertos, five more string quartets, an entire opera, some orchestral overtures, and several important piano sonatas as well as other pieces of chamber music.

The music Beethoven wrote during this time is strong and muscular, with contrasting passages of great lyricism. This contrast exists *between* works (Symphonies Nos. 4, 6, and 8, for example, are gentle, whereas Symphonies Nos. 3, 5, and 7 are more powerful) and also *within* works. Some compositions build to aggressive climaxes and then move into moments of purest beauty and radiance. (The first movement of the Fifth Piano Concerto does this.) Like Mozart, Beethoven wrote his piano concertos to display his own virtuosity, but soon his deafness prevented him from playing in public, and he became increasingly introverted and antisocial. He was sometimes seen striding around the countryside without a coat or a hat, ignoring the weather and muttering to himself.

The most striking thing about the compositions from the heroic phase is their length. From the Third Symphony on, Beethoven was writing works much larger in scope than those of his predecessors. The Third Symphony has a first movement that is by itself as long as many complete symphonies of Haydn and Mozart.

During this phase, Beethoven became very famous. His works were regarded as strong and patriotic at a time when his homeland was at war with France. He even wrote some overtly political pieces, such as

Beethoven's Personality

Beethoven is often portrayed as a wild, aggressive individual, intolerant in the extreme, and prone to violent fits of rage. There is an element of truth to this image of the composer, though it hardly does justice to the complex nature of his personality. ✦ He lived at a time when the established hierarchy of European society was in question, and he held ambivalent views toward authority. When he was asked to play in aristocratic homes, he insisted that no one be in the same room with him. He hated the idea of conforming to fixed social etiquette. His deafness, naturally enough, also made him more withdrawn and unsociable. ✦ There were many contradictory strands to Beethoven's personality. At times he was warm and welcoming; on other occasions he could be cold and hostile. He was a loner, yet he enjoyed the company of a number of intimate friends. He appeared content to work in his cramped quarters in Vienna, yet he relished long walks in the countryside and often spent summers in country villages. He often expressed the desire for a tranquil home life, yet he never married. Perhaps we should expect such contradictions from a genius as extraordinary as Beethoven.

I must confess that I live a miserable life…. I live entirely in my music. —Beethoven, in a letter to a friend, 1801

a *Battle* Symphony—complete with brass fanfares and cannon fire—to celebrate an early victory of the Duke of Wellington over Napoleon. He also became quite wealthy. His music was published and performed more than ever, and his income from these sources as well as from aristocratic and royal patrons was substantial.

PERSONAL CRISIS AND HALT TO PRODUCTIVITY

After the extraordinarily productive years of the heroic phase, Beethoven found himself embroiled in a family crisis, which robbed him of his creativity for several years. In 1815 came the death of Beethoven's brother, who left his widow and Beethoven with joint custody of his son—Beethoven's nephew, Karl. This caused Beethoven great turmoil and distress. Having never married himself, he yearned often for a normal family life, with a wife to comfort him and a child of his own. He once said to a friend that such intimacy was "not to be thought of—impossible—a dream. Yet… I cannot get it out of my mind."

To be thrust suddenly into a position of paternal responsibility for a child and into close contact with a young woman completely undermined Beethoven's equilibrium. He threw himself into a series of devastating legal battles with his brother's widow to obtain sole custody of Karl. The conflict dragged on for years, sapping Beethoven's energy and destroying his peace of mind (not to mention that of the boy and his poor mother). Ultimately, Beethoven won the legal battles (he had powerful friends), and Karl came to live with him. The relationship was a stormy one, however, because Beethoven was appallingly strict and possessive. At the age of 19, Karl pawned his watch, bought two pistols, and tried to kill himself. This action, from which Karl soon recovered, brought some sense back to the situation. Karl was allowed to return to his mother's house, and he escaped from Beethoven's domination by joining the army.

Beethoven's funeral procession in Vienna. There were 20,000 people in attendance at this event.

LATE YEARS

After the most intense period of the battle over Karl, Beethoven only gradually regained his productivity. The most important works of his late years are the last three piano sonatas, the Ninth Symphony, and a series of string quartets. The piano sonatas are remarkable pieces, unusual in form and design, and most moving in their juxtaposition of complexity and simplicity. The Ninth Symphony, finished in 1824, continued Beethoven's tradition of breaking barriers. It is an immense work with a revolutionary last movement that includes a choir and four vocal soloists. This was unheard of in a symphony at this time, although many later composers imitated the idea in one way or another. The text for the last movement of the Ninth Symphony is a poem by the great German poet Schiller: the *Ode to Joy*. It is a summation of Beethoven's philosophy of life: "Let Joy bring everyone together: all men will be brothers; let all kneel before God."

Beethoven's last three years were devoted entirely to string quartets. In this most intimate of genres, he found a medium for his most personal thoughts and ideas. Many people have found Beethoven's late string quartets to be both his greatest and his most difficult music. Yet there are moments of tenderness and great

beauty, as well as passages of dissonant harmonies and rhythmic complexity, and some of the most profound music in the Western tradition. Beethoven died on March 26, 1827, at the age of 56, leaving an indelible mark on music and the way it has been experienced by listeners ever since.

BEETHOVEN'S MUSIC

Beethoven's music has always represented the essence of serious music. In the twentieth century, people who know of only one classical composer know of Beethoven. And his music is played more, written about more, and recorded more than the music of any other composer in the world.

His music is appealing, moving, and forceful. It reaches something inside us that is elemental. It has a unique combination of the simple and the complex, the emotional and the intellectual. We recognize, on hearing it, that it comes from the spiritual side of a man, but also from a man who was entirely, and sometimes painfully, human.

There are some stylistic traits in Beethoven's music that might be regarded as his "fingerprints"—traits that can be instantly recognized and that mark the music

> I shall hear in Heaven.
> —Beethoven's last words

Beethoven's Work Habits

As Beethoven grew older and withdrew more and more from society, he became wholly absorbed in his art. He would habitually miss meals, forget or ignore invitations, and work long into the night. He himself described his "ceaseless occupations." Beethoven felt the strongest urge to produce the music within him, and yet he suffered the same creative anxiety as lesser mortals: "For some time past I have been carrying about with me the idea of three great works .... These I must get rid of: two symphonies, each different from the other, and also different from all my other symphonies, and an oratorio .... I dread beginning works of such magnitude. Once I have begun, then all goes well." ✦ We are fortunate in possessing many of the sketchbooks in which Beethoven worked out his musical ideas. They present a vivid picture of the composer at work.

> In his final illness, Beethoven is reported to have said: "Strange—I feel as though up to now I have written only a few notes."

A page from one of Beethoven's manuscripts.

Beethoven, to a violinist who complained of the difficulty of playing a certain passage: "When I composed that, I was conscious of being inspired by God Almighty. Do you think I can consider your puny little fiddle when He speaks to me?"

as unmistakably his. These include the following: (1) long powerful *crescendos* that seem to carry the music inexorably forward, (2) themes that sound exactly right both quiet and very loud, (3) *dramatic* use of Classic structures such as sonata form, and (4) sudden key changes that nonetheless fit into a powerful harmonic logic.

The most famous of Beethoven's compositions come from the middle part of his life: the heroic phase. These include Symphonies Nos. 3–8, the middle string quartets, Piano Concertos Nos. 4 and 5, the Violin Concerto, and the opera *Fidelio*. Some of the pieces are actually *about* heroism: The Third Symphony is entitled the *Eroica* (*Heroic*), and *Fidelio* (*The Faithful One*) displays the heroism of a woman who rescues her husband from unjust imprisonment. As

a result, much of this music is strong, dramatic, and powerful.

But there is another side to Beethoven: the lyrical side. Some of the middle symphonies are very tuneful and smoothly contoured, like the Sixth Symphony, known as the *Pastoral*. And even in the more dramatic pieces, there are often contrasting passages of great tenderness. One of the secrets of Beethoven's style is the way he juxtaposes strong and tender passages within the same work.

Less well known are the compositions from Beethoven's early period. These include pieces that he wrote before moving to Vienna and some compositions from his first years in that city. Some are deliberately modeled on the works of his great forebears, Haydn and Mozart; others already show signs of re-

Music Critics

During the latter part of Beethoven's life, music journalism began to appear. Daily newspapers started to carry articles and reviews of music, and journals devoted to music were established. Then, as now, critics were not always well disposed toward new music. Here are a few early reviews of Beethoven's compositions: ✦ On the overture to Beethoven's opera *Fidelio*: "All impartial musicians and music lovers were in perfect agreement that never was anything as incoherent, shrill, chaotic, and ear-splitting produced in music." ✦ On the Third Symphony: "It is infinitely too lengthy. . . . If this symphony is not by some means abridged, it will soon fall into disuse." ✦ On the Fifth Symphony: ". . . a sort of odious meowing." ✦ On the Ninth Symphony: ". . . crude, wild, and extraneous harmonies." ". . . ugly, in bad taste, cheap." ✦ On the late music: "He does not write much now, but most of what he produces is so impenetrably obscure in design and so full of unaccountable and often repulsive harmonies that he puzzles the critic as much as he perplexes the performer." ✦ On all his music: "Beethoven always sounds to me like the upsetting of bags of nails, with here and there also a dropped hammer."

Beethoven's Orchestra

Beethoven grew up during the Classic period, so the orchestra he used in his early years was the one that he inherited from Haydn and Mozart: a string section made up of violins, violas, cellos, and basses; a wind section featuring pairs of flutes, oboes, clarinets, bassoons, and horns; and an occasional group of trumpets and drums. Beethoven enlarged this orchestra during his lifetime just as he expanded the boundaries of form and personal expression. For the last movement of his Fifth Symphony, Beethoven adds a piccolo, a contrabassoon, and three trombones. A piccolo and trombones appear also in the Sixth Symphony; and the Ninth Symphony of Beethoven's last years calls for the usual complement of strings and winds, plus piccolo, contrabassoon, two extra horns, three trombones, triangle, cymbals, and bass drum. After Beethoven, the orchestra, like almost everything else he touched, was expanded to encompass ever-greater areas of expression.

A perfect example of Beethoven's orchestra is Beethoven's First Movement of the Sixth Symphony ("Pastoral"). You can watch a live performance of this work in Segment 3 of your *Inside the Orchestra* CD-ROM.

markable originality. There are songs, piano pieces, and much chamber music.

Finally, there are the works from the last part of Beethoven's career. These are all very different, and there are fewer of them. They include the Ninth Symphony, the *Missa Solemnis*, the late piano sonatas, and the last five string quartets. Beethoven's late music is very rich. There is a sense of great depth juxtaposed with an extraordinary, almost heartbreaking, innocence and simplicity. In his last years, Beethoven was no longer concerned with drama and heroism but with pursuing the path of his own creativity, wherever it might lead. Some of the music from this period is demanding and difficult to

listen to, but with repeated hearings it can provide listeners with a lifetime of enjoyment and reward.

LISTENING EXAMPLES

To get an idea of the range of Beethoven's achievement, we shall listen to compositions from each of the three main periods of his life. The first is a set of variations on a theme, written by Beethoven in 1790 for solo piano. Next we shall study the whole of the Fifth Symphony, perhaps the most famous of Beethoven's compositions. It was written in 1807–8, right in the middle of the heroic phase. Finally, we shall listen to one movement from a late piano sonata, to see how profound and compelling Beethoven's late music can be.

> A giant goblin crossing time and space.—E. M. Forster in *Howard's End,* describing the Fifth Symphony

Beethoven at about the time he wrote the Fifth Symphony.

Ludwig van Beethoven, miniature by Christian Horneman, 1802. Beethoven-Haus Bonn, Collection H. C. Bodmer.

LISTENING GUIDE

Ludwig van Beethoven (1770–1827)
Six Easy Variations on a Swiss Tune in F Major for Piano, WoO 64

Date of composition: 1790
Tempo: *Andante con moto* ("Fairly slow but with motion")
Meter: $\frac{4}{4}$
Key: F Major
Duration: 2:47

Student CD Collection: 2, track 28
Complete CD Collection: 3, track 9

This is one of many sets of variations that Beethoven wrote in his early years. Variations on melodies are an easy way for a composer to learn his or her craft, since the tune and the harmony already exist and all the composer has to do is think of ways to decorate or vary them.

The little Swiss tune that Beethoven uses as the basis for this composition is very simple and attractive. Underlying its simplicity, however, is an interesting quirk: It is made up of unusual phrase lengths. This is probably the feature that attracted Beethoven to the theme in the first place. Instead of the usual four-measure phrases, this tune is made up of two three-measure phrases answered by a phrase of five measures.

This phrase structure, as well as the skeleton of the tune and its harmony, are carried through all the six variations. Beethoven uses triplets, march rhythms, dynamic changes, eighth notes, sixteenth notes, and even the minor key to decorate and vary the music; however, if you play the recording of just the theme a few times first, before listening to the variations, you will be able to follow its outline throughout the piece.

THEME	[*Andante con moto*—"Fairly slow but with motion"]
28 (9) **0:00**	The theme is simple and pleasant. Notice how it ends very much as it begins.

VARIATION 1	
0:23	Beethoven introduces triplets (three notes to a beat) in both the right and the left hand.

VARIATION 2	
0:40	The melody is mostly unchanged in the right hand, but the left hand has jerky, marchlike accompanying rhythms.

VARIATION 3	
29 (10) **1:02**	This variation uses the minor key, and Beethoven indicates that it should be played "smoothly and quietly throughout."
1:28	The last part of this variation is repeated.

VARIATION 4	
1:48	Back to the major and loud again. Octaves in the right hand, triplets in the left.

VARIATION 5	
2:04	The fifth variation is mostly in eighth notes with a little syncopation and some small chromatic decorations.

VARIATION 6	
2:26	Dynamic contrasts, sixteenth-note runs, and trills mark the last variation, which ends with a two-measure coda to round off the piece.

BEETHOVEN'S FIFTH SYMPHONY

Beethoven's Fifth Symphony was written in the middle of his heroic period, when the composer was in his late thirties. It is his most famous piece and probably the most famous symphony ever written. The music is taut and expressive, and unified to an unusual degree. The opening four-note motive, with its short-short-short-LONG rhythm, pervades the whole symphony in one form or another. There is a cumulative sense of growth right from the beginning of the first movement to the end of the last movement, and many commentators have noted the feeling of personal triumph that this gives. Underlying this feeling is the motion from C minor to C Major. Symphonies almost always end in the key in which they begin, but Beethoven's Fifth starts out tense and strained in C minor and ends up triumphant and exuberant in C Major. Beethoven also adds several instruments to the orchestra for the last movement, to increase the power and range of the music and add to the sense of triumph.

The feeling of unity in the symphony is reinforced by two further techniques. Instead of being separate, the last two movements are linked, with no pause between them. And Beethoven actually quotes the theme of the third movement in the last movement, thus further connecting them.

All these things—the progression from minor to major, the larger orchestra, the linking of movements, the reference back to earlier movements toward the end—were new to symphonic music at the time and had an enormous influence on later composers throughout the remainder of the nineteenth century.

In the Fifth Symphony, Beethoven set the stage for an entirely new view of music. Music was now seen as the expression of a personal and subjective point of view, no longer as the objective presentation of an artistic creation. This new view was the basis of Romanticism.

LISTENING GUIDE

Ludwig van Beethoven (1770–1827)
Symphony No. 5 in C minor

Date of composition: 1807–8
Orchestration: 2 flutes, 2 oboes, 2 clarinets, 2 horns, 2 trumpets, timpani, strings
Duration: 33:06

Student CD Collection: 2, track 30
Complete CD Collection: 3, track 11

FIRST MOVEMENT

Tempo: *Allegro con brio* ("Fast and vigorous")
Meter: $\frac{2}{4}$
Key: C minor
Form: Sonata-Allegro
Duration: 7:26

The first movement of Beethoven's Fifth Symphony is dense and concentrated. There is not a note or a gesture too many in the whole movement. The exposition begins with a short-short-short-LONG motive that colors almost every measure of the movement.

The second theme is announced by a horn call. The theme itself starts quietly and smoothly, but underneath it, on cellos and basses, the initial rhythmic motive quietly makes itself heard. Quickly another climax builds, and the exposition ends with the whole orchestra playing the original motive together.

During the development section, the horn call that introduced the second theme is gradually broken down into smaller and smaller elements until only a single chord is echoed quietly between the strings and the woodwinds. Then the recapitulation brings back the music of the movement's first part with crashing force. A short coda brings the movement to a powerful conclusion.

Throughout the movement, long crescendos (from *pianissimo*, **pp**, to *fortissimo*, **ff**) and short passages of quiet music (*piano*, **p**) serve to increase the intensity and drive. The overall effect is one of great power and compression.

EXPOSITION		
30 (11) **0:00** (1:25)		*First theme* Opening motive is played **ff** by the strings and clarinets in octaves and then repeated a step lower.

0:06 (1:31)	Sudden **p**, strings immediately develop opening motive.
0:14 (1:39)	Crescendo and loud chords lead to a high sustained note in the violins.
0:18 (1:44)	*Transition* Opening motive, **ff**, played only once by full orchestra. Sudden **p**, further development of the opening motive by strings. Strings gradually crescendo and ascend. Reiterated timpani notes, sudden stop.

0:43	Horn-call motive, _**ff**_.
(2:08)	

| **31** (12) **0:46** | _Second theme_ |
| **(2:11)** | |

A contrasting gentle melody, _**p**_, relative major key (E♭ Major), accompanied by a version of the opening motive in the lower strings.

| **0:58** | Crescendo and ascent lead to another new melody: a jubilant theme, _**ff**_, in the |
| **(2:23)** | violins, played twice. |

Violins

| **1:15** | Woodwinds and horns rapidly descend, twice; then a cadence in E♭ minor, using |
| **(2:40)** | the rhythm of the basic motive. Pause. |

| **32** (13) **1:25** | (Entire exposition is repeated.) |

DEVELOPMENT

33 (14) **2:50**	Opening motive in horns, _**ff**_, in F minor, echoed by strings.
	Sudden _**p**_, basic motive developed by strings and woodwinds.
	Another gradual ascent and crescendo, leading to forceful repeated chords.

3:25	Horn-call motive in violins, _**ff**_, followed by descending line in low strings, twice.
	Pairs of high chords in woodwinds and brass, _**ff**_, alternating with lower chords in strings, _**ff**_.
	Sudden decrease in volume, alternation between single chords, key changes.
	Sudden _**ff**_, horn -call in full orchestra; return to alternation of wind and string chords, _**pp**_, with key changes.
	Sudden _**ff**_, opening motive repeated many times, leading back to recapitulation.

34 (15)   **4:08**   *First theme*

         Opening motive, ***ff***, in tonic (C minor), full orchestra.
         Opening motive developed, strings, ***p***, joined by slow-moving melody on one oboe.
         Oboe unexpectedly interrupts the music with a short, plaintive solo.

         4:39   *Transition*

         Development of opening motive resumes in strings, ***p***.
         Gradual crescendo, full orchestra, ***ff***, repeated timpani notes, sudden stop.
         Horn-call motive, ***ff***, in horns.

35 (16)   **5:02**   *Second theme*

         Contrasting gentle melody, ***p***, in C Major (the *major* of the tonic!), played
            alternately by violins and flutes. (Basic motive accompanies in timpani when
            flutes play.) Gradual buildup to the return of:
         Jubilant string theme, ***ff***, in violins, played twice.
         Woodwinds and horns rapidly descend, twice, followed by a cadence using the
            rhythm of the opening motive. Then, without pause, into:

36 (17)   **5:52**   Forceful repeated chords, ***ff***, with pauses.
         Horn-call motive in lower strings and bassoons, along with flowing violin melody,
            f, in tonic (C minor).
         Descending pattern, violins, leads to:
         6:17   A completely new theme in the strings, rising up the minor scale in four-note
            sequences.

         Four-note fragments of the new theme are forcefully alternated between woodwinds
            and strings.
         A short passage of fast, loud, repeated notes leads into a return of the opening
            motive, ***ff***, full orchestra.
         Suddenly ***pp***; strings and woodwinds develop the motive for a few seconds.
         A swift and dramatic return to full orchestra, ending with ***ff*** chords.

Tempo: *Andante con moto* ("Fairly slow but with motion")
Meter: ⅜
Key: A♭ Major
Form: Modified Theme and Variations
Duration: 10:32

*T*he second movement is lyrical and reposeful in contrast to the first movement, but there are passages of great strength and grandeur. The movement is cast as a theme and variations, but it is unusual because there are *two* themes instead of one. The first theme, which is very smooth and songlike, comes at the beginning on the low strings: violas and cellos, accompanied by *pizzicato* (plucked) basses.

The second theme is introduced softly on the clarinets and bassoons but is suddenly transformed into a blazing fanfare. Then come several variations on both of the themes, with changes of mood, instrumentation, and structure. Even the central section of the movement and the coda are based on the two themes.

The coda contains striking dynamic contrasts and ends with a big crescendo to the short final cadence.

---

37 (18) **0:00** | *Theme A*

Lyrical melody in tonic (A♭ Major), first presented by violas and cellos, ***p***.
　　Accompaniment in basses, pizzicato.

Violas, Cellos

0:26 | Melody is continued by woodwinds, concludes with alternation between woodwinds and strings.

---

38 (19) **0:59** | *Theme B (in two parts)*

(1) A gently rising theme in the clarinets, ***p***, in the tonic.

Clarinets

	1:15	Clarinet theme is taken over by violins, ***pp***. Sudden crescendo forms a transition to: (2) A brass fanfare in C Major, ***ff***. Violins continue this theme, ***pp***. Slow sustained chords and a cadence in the tonic key form an ending to Theme B.
39 (20)	**2:14**	*Variation 1(A)* Theme A, varied, in the tonic, again on the violas and cellos, ***p***, enhanced by a smooth, continuously flowing rhythm, and with long notes from the clarinet.

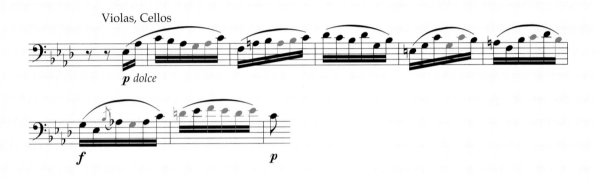

		(Note that Variation 1A contains all the notes of the original Theme A. These notes are printed in black in the example above.) Again, a conclusion with an alternation between the violins and woodwinds.
40 (21)	**3:05**	*Variation 1(B)* The B theme—clarinet part as well as fanfare part—is presented with a more active accompaniment. The concluding sustained chords, ***pp***, are now accompanied by quick repeated notes in the cellos, and ended by a brighter cadence.
41 (22)	**4:11**	*Variation 2(A)* Theme A, varied, again enhanced by a smooth, flowing rhythm, but twice as fast as the first variation, and with long notes from the woodwinds. This embellished melody is repeated by the violins, ***pp***, in a higher register.
	4:47	Then the embellished melody is played by the cellos and basses, accompanied by powerful repeated chords. The variation ends on two rising scales, leading to a high sustained note.

42 (23) **5:12**		*Central Section*

42 (23) **5:12** *Central Section*

Sudden **pp**, repeated string chords accompany a short, delicate phrase based on Theme A and played by the clarinet, bassoon, and flute in turn. This blossoms into a woodwind interlude, leading to a return of:

6:12 Brass fanfare from Theme B, **ff**, with timpani rolls, in C Major.
A short repeated motive in the strings, **pp**, leads to:
Staccato passage in the woodwinds based on Theme A,
  but in A♭ minor.
Ascending scales in the flute and strings, crescendo, into:

43 (24) **7:43** *Variation 3(A)*

Climactic restatement of melody from Theme A by the full orchestra, **ff**. (Violins play melody, while woodwinds work in imitation with violins.)
The end of the first section of the melody is accompanied by rising scales in the strings and woodwinds.
Once more, a conclusion with an alternation between the violins and the flute.

C O D A

44 (25) **8:36** Faster tempo, single bassoon, **p**, plays a passage based on the beginning of Theme A, with comments from a single oboe.
Rising melody in the strings, crescendo.

9:04 The original tempo resumes. Flute and strings, **p**, again play the last section of Theme A, but the violins poignantly extend the final phrase. Cadence in tonic.

9:43 Another variation of the first phrase from Theme A, clarinets, **p**.
First three notes of Theme B (fanfare part), played repeatedly in the low strings, outlining the tonic chord. Gradually builds in intensity and leads to a cadence by the full orchestra, **ff**.

THIRD MOVEMENT

Tempo: *Allegro* ("Fast")
Meter: ¾
Key: C minor
Form: Scherzo and Trio, with Transition
Duration: 5:34

The third movement is quite remarkable. It is in the form of a scherzo and trio. Structurally, this is the same thing as a minuet and trio, but the character of a scherzo is different: it is usually faster and more vigorous. And in this case, there are also some striking changes in the traditional structure. The movement begins hesitantly, but suddenly the horns come blasting in with a repeated-note figure that is taken up by the whole orchestra:

The figure sounds familiar, and we recognize that it combines two features from the first movement: the opening short-short-short-LONG motive and the horn call in the middle of the exposition. In the trio section, a low, scurrying passage on cellos and basses is taken up in turns by other instruments in an imitative section that has the quality of an informal fugue.

It is at the return of the scherzo that the main surprises start. Instead of repeating the scherzo music literally, Beethoven changes the atmosphere entirely. The music is played very quietly by plucked strings and soft woodwinds. The whole effect is mysterious, hushed, and a little ominous.

Also, instead of ending the movement after the return of the scherzo, Beethoven adds a transitional passage that continues the atmosphere of mystery, hesitancy, and questioning. Gradually the hesitant fragments take on more and more motion and get louder and louder until they build to a tremendous climax leading directly into the fourth movement.

SCHERZO	
	[with several internal repetitions of phrases, but no overall repeats]
45 (26) **0:00**	Short rising unison melody in cellos and basses, unaccompanied, **_pp_**, in the tonic (C minor).

	Strings and woodwinds conclude the phrase. Pause.
0:08	Cellos and basses repeat and extend their melody. Same concluding phrase in the woodwinds and strings.

| 0:19 | Sudden **ff**, horns state a powerful repeated-note melody based on the opening short-short-short-LONG pattern from the first movement. |

Horns

| | This repeated-note melody is developed by the strings and winds, changing key, **f**. |

| **46** (27) **0:37** | The first melody is restated by the cellos and basses and answered by strings and woodwinds. Pause.
This is resumed and developed. It intensifies, changing keys rapidly, and leads to: |

| **0:59** | The repeated-note melody in the tonic, played by the full orchestra, **f**.
Volume decreases, dialogue between strings and woodwinds, **p**. |

| **1:29** | A sprightly, graceful theme in the violins, **p**, accompanied by offbeat chords in the woodwinds. |

| **1:41** | The scherzo concludes with cadence chords in the short-short-short-LONG rhythm. |

TRIO

| **47** (28) **1:47** | *Trio Section A* |

Scurrying melody, unaccompanied, in the cellos and basses; in C Major, **f**.

Cellos, Basses

| | This develops in the style of a fugue and quickly comes to a cadence. |

| **2:01** | *Trio Section A* (exact repeat) |

48 (29)	**2:16**	*Trio Section B*

After a couple of humorous false starts, the fuguelike theme continues, *f*, accompanied by a syncopated, leaping melody in the woodwinds. As the sound builds, a portion of the "fugue" theme is stated by the full orchestra, leading to a cadence.

	2:42	*Trio Section B* (altered)

The section begins again, but now the music dwindles down from the winds to a pizzicato melody in the cellos and basses, leading to a return of the scherzo.

RETURN OF SCHERZO

49 (30)	**3:11**	The original minor melody returns, *pp*, but the answering phrase is stated by winds alone. Pause. The repeat of the melody is played by bassoons and pizzicato cellos and is answered by pizzicato strings. Pause.

	3:30	The powerful horn melody appears, eerily and *pp*, on pizzicato strings with occasional wind comments. Both themes are again combined and developed (the *pp* continues). The sprightly theme returns, *pp*, and without its former bouncing character. Cadence chords, *pp*, in the short-short-short-LONG rhythm, end the scherzo but also begin the next surprising passage.

TRANSITION TO LAST MOVEMENT

50 (31)	**4:17**	A low sustained string tone, *ppp*, accompanies ominous repeated notes in the timpani, *pp*.

	4:27	A violin melody, *pp*, based on the opening of the scherzo, is added to this suspenseful moment. As the melody rises in pitch, it changes from minor to major. There is a rapid crescendo on a sustained chord, leading without pause into the fourth movement.

FOURTH MOVEMENT

Orchestration: 3 trombones, a piccolo, and a contrabassoon are added to the orchestra for this movement.
Tempo: *Allegro* ("Fast")
Meter: $\frac{4}{4}$
Key: C Major
Form: Sonata
Duration: 11:27

$\mathcal{T}$he fourth movement is the triumphant conclusion to the symphony. It is in the bright and forceful key of C Major, and Beethoven now adds to the orchestra three powerful trombones, a deep, rich contrabassoon, and a high-flying piccolo. The overall atmosphere is one of triumph, glory, and exhilaration.

The movement is in sonata form. The exposition positively overflows with themes; there are four in all (two for each key area), each one bright and optimistic.

The development section concentrates on the third of these themes, which is tossed about in fragments among the instruments of the orchestra. We cannot help noticing that one pervasive fragment is very much like the opening short-short-short-LONG motive of the whole symphony.

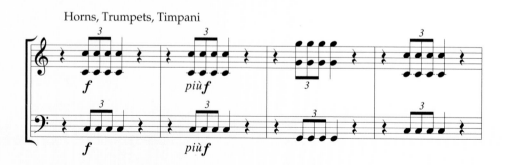

The development section builds up to a huge climax, and then suddenly Beethoven pulls off another amazing surprise.

Between the end of the development section and the beginning of the recapitulation, Beethoven places a brief reminiscence of the music from the scherzo. This, too, is most unusual. It is as though Beethoven is remembering the past in the midst of his triumph. But the hesitancy and doubt are swept away by the blaze of the orchestra.

The movement ends with one of the longest codas Beethoven ever wrote. It is forceful and definitive. Often it seems as though the music will end, only to get faster and faster and come to a cadence yet again and again. It is as though Beethoven cannot stop emphasizing his feeling of triumph.

EXPOSITION

51 (32) **0:00** *Theme 1*
         (1:54)

Electrifying marchlike melody, full orchestra, **ff**, with especially prominent trumpets. The first three notes spell out the tonic chord of C Major.

Trumpets

0:14 The rising staccato notes of the end of the melody are developed at length, with full
(2:06) orchestration, **ff**.

0:29 A descending scalar melody with off-the-beat accents leads to the transition theme.
(2:21)

---

52 (33) **0:34** *Transition Theme (Theme 2)*
         (2:26)

A new, forceful theme, **ff**, begins in the horns.

Horns

0:45 Transition Theme is extended by the violins, leading to a quick dialogue between
(2:38) woodwinds, violins, and low strings, and then:

---

53 (34) **1:00** *Theme 3*
         (2:52)

A light, bouncing melody in the violins (dominant key, G Major) with the short-short-short-LONG rhythm, incorporating triplets, contrasts of loud and soft, and a countermelody (colored notes in the example) that becomes important in the development section.

A frantic, **ff**, scalar passage in the strings, and two loud staccato chords, herald the entrance of:

---

54 (35) **1:25**
(3:18)

Closing Theme (Theme 4)

Theme 4, heard first in the strings and woodwinds:

Immediate repeat by the full orchestra, **f**, leading to repeated chords by the full orchestra and an ascending motive in the strings, **ff**, and directly into:

---

55 (36) **(1:54)**

(Repeat of Exposition)

DEVELOPMENT

[wide mix of keys]

56 (37) **3:48**

A long section concentrating on the recombination of the triplet motives of Theme 3, eventually accompanied by slowly ascending flute scales.

4:00

Theme 3's countermelody is now put in the spotlight, first by the lower strings and contrabassoon, then by the powerful new trombones, then by the strings and trombones in imitation, and finally by the full orchestra.

4:49

A long, gigantic climax leads to a real surprise:
We hear the short-short-short-LONG horn melody of the scherzo, **pp**, but on strings, clarinets, and oboes.
This reminiscence is swept away by a crescendo and the recapitulation.

57 (38) **5:52** | *Theme 1*

The marchlike melody is again stated in the full orchestra, ***ff***. Once again, the staccato notes at the end of the melody are developed at length, and descending scales lead into the Transition Theme.

6:26 | *Transition Theme (Theme 2)*

Theme 2 is stated in the horns and continued at length by the violins, as in the exposition.

6:55 | *Theme 3*

The triplet-dominated Theme 3 is stated essentially the same way as in the exposition, but with a fuller accompaniment and in the tonic key.

7:21 | *Closing Theme (Theme 4)*

Theme 4 is presented but slightly reorchestrated, leading to a long coda.

CODA

58 (39) **7:50** | The coda begins with further development of Theme 3 and its countermelody.

8:13 | After six staccato chords, the winds develop a variant of Theme 2 in imitation, ***p***.

8:35 | This is followed by rapid ascending piccolo scales.

8:45 | The variant of Theme 2 returns, this time in the strings, with piccolo trills and scales.
Then, an acceleration in tempo until:

9:12 | A very fast return to the first part of Theme 4 in the violins. The motive gradually climbs higher, as the full orchestra joins in.
There is a crescendo and fragmentation of the theme, leading to:

9:28 | Theme 1, full orchestra, ***ff***, but much faster.
It is quickly developed and comes to an extremely long ending passage of incessantly pounded chords, finally coming to rest on the single note C, played ***ff*** by the full orchestra.

BEETHOVEN'S LATE MUSIC

Beethoven's late music presents great challenges to performers and listeners alike. Certainly, the music is technically difficult to play, yet the true challenge comes in the understanding. The performer has to understand the music in order to play, and the listener has to be up to the challenge of understanding it, too.

There is great variety in the late works of Beethoven, but they share some characteristics: a combination of inner depth and outward simplicity; new approaches to multi-movement design; and a return to some of the techniques of his youth, such as song forms and theme-and-variations form.

To gain some idea of the variety and depth of this music, we shall listen to a piano sonata, one of the last three that Beethoven wrote. Remember that of all the instruments, the piano was closest to Beethoven's heart. These last three piano sonatas contain some of the most profound music that Beethoven ever wrote.

The ear trumpet that Beethoven began to use about 1816.

Beethoven's Piano-Playing

Before he started going deaf, Beethoven was known as one of the foremost piano virtuosos of his age. When he was only 21, a newspaper article described him as "one of the greatest of pianists." Another contemporary described his brilliance as an improviser: "In whatever company he might chance to be, he knew how to produce such an effect upon every hearer that frequently not an eye remained dry, while many would break out into loud sobs; for there was something wonderful in his expression, in addition to the beauty and originality of his ideas and his spirited style of rendering them." ✦ But by 1815, when Beethoven was almost totally deaf, the descriptions become heartrending: "On account of his deafness, there was scarcely anything left of the virtuosity of the artist which had formerly been so greatly admired. In loud passages the poor man pounded on the keys till the strings jangled, and in quiet passages he played so softly that whole groups of tones were omitted, so that the music was unintelligible."

Ludwig van Beethoven (1770–1827)
Third Movement from Piano Sonata in
E Major, Op. 109

Date of composition: 1820

Tempo: *Andante molto cantabile ed espressivo* ("Quite slow, very lyrical and expressive")

Meter: ¾

Key: E Major

Duration: 13:34

Complete CD Collection: 3, track 40

*T*his is the last movement of one of the last of Beethoven's piano sonatas, written just seven years before his death. It shows the remarkable freedom Beethoven felt in his compositions toward the end of his life. The sonata is completely untraditional in the form of each movement and in the order of its movements. The music itself contains abrupt changes of mood and ideas, as though the great composer were improvising at the keyboard. The whole composition transcends the accepted boundaries for the genre of the piano sonata, both in its architecture and in its emotional depth.

The three movements are *Vivace* ("Lively"), *Prestissimo* ("Very fast"), and *Andante molto cantabile ed espressivo* ("Quite slow, very lyrical, and expressive"). Already this is a radical break from the traditional arrangement of movements, which normally would be fast-slow-minuet-fast. But Beethoven departs from convention even more than this. The first movement (*Vivace*—"Lively") is interrupted twice by sections that are labeled *Adagio espressivo* ("Very slow and expressive"), and the last movement has, in addition to the detailed Italian tempo marking, a heading in German: *Gesangvoll mit innigster Empfindung* ("Songlike and with the innermost feeling"). Beethoven is using every means at his disposal to invest his music (and the performance of his music) with strong emotion.

THIRD MOVEMENT

Gesangvoll mit innigster Empfindung ("Songlike and with the innermost feeling"). *Andante molto cantabile ed espressivo* ("Quite slow, very lyrical, and expressive").

Toward the end of his life, Beethoven returned to some of the simple techniques of his youth. This movement is in the form of a theme and variations (the same form as the piano piece we just studied). But the spirituality and depth of feeling of this music belong exclusively to the late period of Beethoven's life. In scope, the movement dwarfs the preceding two. It lasts more than 15 minutes, twice the length of the previous movements put together. The theme has the remarkable combination of simplicity and profound feeling that is characteristic of Beethoven's late music. It is like a song of the soul. There are six variations that seem to explore the rich inner life of the theme and all its potential.

The theme is originally presented in two sections, both repeated. Each section is eight measures long, divided into two four-measure phrases. Some of the variations follow the scheme of the theme, with two sections, both repeated. But in some of the variations, the "repeats" of the sections are not really repeats but continue the process of evolution and further variation. Technically, these are known as "double variations." By 1820, Beethoven had composed more than 60 sets of variations, but with Opus 109 he invests the form with a completely new feeling of transfiguration, almost of ecstasy.

The first variation (again Beethoven marks the music *Molto espressivo*—Very expressive) explores the lyrical, dreamy side of the theme with wider-ranging music and rich harmonies. In the other variations, the character of the music changes, becoming faster and denser, and the outline of the theme itself becomes progressively more obscured, as its inner essence is revealed. But after the sixth and final variation, the theme returns even more simply than at its very first appearance. This final return of the theme (without repeats) is deeply moving. It sounds radiant and centered, as though it has been purified by the fire and passion of its experiences.

THEME		[dignified, profound]
(40)	**0:00**	First section.
	0:35	Repeat.
	1:10	Second section.
	1:46	Repeat.
VARIATION 1		[higher, more decorated, more rhythmic motion]
(41)	**2:13**	First section.
	2:43	Repeat.
	3:22	Second section.
	3:52	Repeat.
VARIATION 2		[a double variation: lightly delicate, beginning with repeated notes, steady rhythm, and trills, and opening out to syncopated chords]
(42)	**4:25**	First section: light and delicate.
	4:49	"Repeat" is varied again. First four-measure phrase: steady rhythm, gradually climbing. Second phrase: alternating syncopated chords.
	5:15	Second section: light and delicate again.
	5:39	"Repeat" continues the variation, also starting with steady phrases and ending with alternating chords.

VARIATION 3

[another double variation: lighthearted in tone; fast, louder, and in duple meter]

(43) **6:07** First section: staccato eighth notes ascending in right hand, descending sixteenths in left. Switch after four measures.

6:13 "Repeat" with increasing motion.

6:19 Second section: still fast, runs continuously into and through the "repeat."

VARIATION 4

[slower than the theme, two-part counterpoint, in $\frac{9}{8}$ meter]

(44) **6:32** First section: gentle, contemplative.

7:06 Literal repeat this time.

7:41 Second section: louder and more determined in the middle.

8:19 Repeat.

VARIATION 5

[another double variation: complex four-part counterpoint, duple meter]

(45) **9:02** First section: loud and determined, fast.

9:13 "Repeat," elaborated.

9:23 Second section: higher, still loud.

9:33 Elaborated "repeat."

9:43 *Extra* repeat, quiet.

VARIATION 6

[This is extraordinary music. Back to $\frac{3}{4}$. Another double variation—really a quadruple one!]

(46) **9:56** First section. The motion increases from quarter notes to eighths, to triplet eighths, to sixteenths.

10:30 "Repeat"—ever-increasing motion: thirty-second notes, and finally trills!

10:58 Second section: cascades of broken chords, rushing passagework, over a deep trilled bass note.

	11:23	In the "repeat," with the trill now *above* the rushing scales, the theme tolls out, syncopated, in the highest reaches of the piano.
	11:46	An added three measures of brilliantly gauged descent (both in pitch and in intensity), leading to:

RETURN OF THEME

[magically peaceful return to theme, even simpler than at first, and without any repeats]

(47)	**12:09**	First section.
	12:45	Second section.

This ending, with its return to purified simplicity, has much the same quality as the close of Milton's great poem *Samson Agonistes*, which speaks of God:

> His servants he with new acquist
> Of true experience from this great event,
> With peace and consolation hath dismiss'd,
> And calm of mind, all passion spent.

Around the world, the music of Beethoven has come to symbolize one of the high points of Western artistic achievement, on a par with the plays and poetry of Shakespeare or the paintings of Rembrandt or Picasso. Beethoven stands as a giant in our cultural history.

This impression is reinforced both by the power of his music and by the impression it gives of conquering life's adversities. Beethoven was wholly devoted to his work and regarded it as somehow sacred. In this way he changed the direction of music and society's attitude towards it for the next two hundred years.

Beethoven inherited the forms, genres, and conventions of the Classic era. He wrote symphonies, piano concertos, chamber music, piano sonatas, and other types of music just as Classic composers had done. And yet he invested these works with greater scope and power and with a greater sense of personal expression than his predecessors. His symphonies are longer and use more instruments than those of the Classic period. And for the last movement of his Ninth Symphony, Beethoven added four solo singers and a chorus.

With his loud music, Beethoven seems louder and more urgent than his predecessors. In his soft music, he seems to reach for deeper emotion.

Special characteristics of Beethoven's music include: insistent and driving rhythms; taut and muscular themes; long crescendos and powerful climaxes. But his music also features themes of great beauty and lyricism; passages of extraordinary lightness and delicacy; and a gentleness and spiritual depth that are unprecedented.

He expanded the orchestra in terms of loudness (trombones), high notes (piccolos), and low notes (contrabassoon). In his first movements, he turned sonata form from an expression of wit and aesthetic beauty to one of narrative and drama. His slow movements can plumb the depths

A page from Beethoven's handwritten score for the Ninth Symphony.

The same music in a modern printed score.

of human emotion. His third-movement scherzos range from sophisticated rhythmic play to grim humor. And his finales present moods of exuberance, triumphant exaltation, or spiritual transcendence. Beethoven also favored theme-and-variation form, which he used from his earliest learning days as a composer up to his very last works.

In a way, Beethoven single-handedly invented the idea of Romantic music and laid the groundwork for all our modern ideas of what a classical composer does and what his or her music means.

FUNDAMENTALS OF BEETHOVEN'S MUSIC

- ✦ Forcefulness and strength are balanced by emotional depth, gentleness, and lyricism
- ✦ Movements are longer
- ✦ Orchestra is expanded to include contrabassoon, trombones, and piccolo
- ✦ His music expresses personal feeling
- ✦ Sonata form used for expression of drama
- ✦ His music reaches unprecedented spiritual depth
- ✦ Beethoven wrote in all vocal and instrumental genres
- ✦ His music leads the way to Romanticism

THE NINETEENTH CENTURY

THE AGE OF ROMANTICISM

George Stephenson's "Rocket," one of the earliest locomotives.

The nineteenth century was a time of great change in Western society. The foundations of modern industry were laid during this period; political and social changes took place that were more far-reaching than ever before; and the arts reflected a new concern with subjectivity and inner feeling. All three of these aspects of the new era—industrialization, changes in the structure of society, and a new artistic spirit—had powerful effects on nineteenth-century music.

Industrial Europe, 1860.

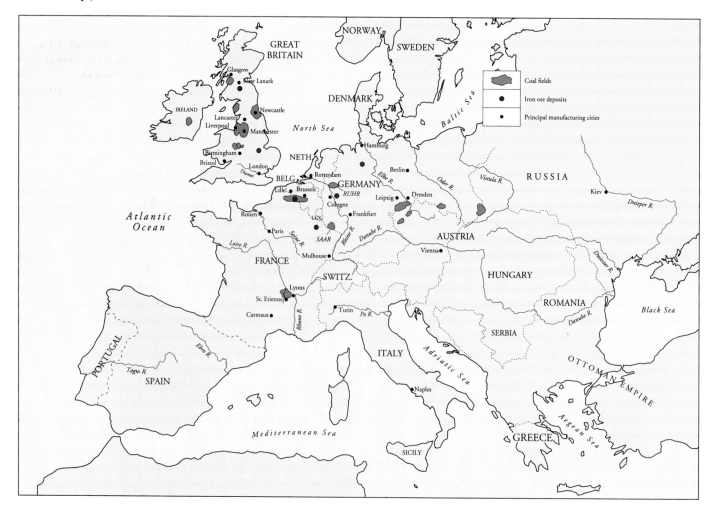

Come forth into the light of things, Let Nature be your teacher. One impulse from a vernal wood May teach you more of man, Of moral evil and of good, Than all the sages can.
—William Wordsworth

A nineteenth-century landscape by John Constable.

John Constable, *Hampstead Heath: Branch Hill Pond,* 1828. Oil on canvas. V&A/Art Resource.

THE INDUSTRIAL REVOLUTION

The Industrial Revolution began in England, where a long period of peace and prosperity encouraged expansion and innovation. Agriculture was highly efficient, leading to a tripling of the population between 1750 and 1850. Advances in mechanical engineering made possible the invention of power machines, used initially in the textile industry and then in mining, iron and steel production, and railways. And communications were revolutionized first by the railways and the inauguration of a cheap postal system, and then by the American inventions of the telegraph and the telephone.

All these technological advances spread rapidly throughout Western Europe and the United States. In many countries, especially Germany, new mining techniques led to the growth of the chemical industry.

Minerals could be used as the basis for new fertilizers, thus greatly increasing food production and hence population growth in industrialized societies. The French developed a process for bleaching cloth and a new loom for weaving patterns. And Americans were responsible for the sewing machine and a host of agricultural machines designed for the wide expanses of the continent. Toward the end of the century, the harnessing of electricity marked a new phase in the Industrial Revolution.

POLITICAL, INTELLECTUAL, AND SOCIAL CHANGES

Politically, the most important event for the nineteenth century was the French Revolution, which began in 1789 but whose aftershocks continued to be felt

A young woman working in a coal mine in the 1840s.

The heroic Napoleon Bonaparte, painted in 1800.

throughout Europe until 1848. By 1815, a general revulsion against the excesses of the Revolution and the dictatorship of Napoleon had set in across Europe.

Intellectuals and philosophers also reacted strongly against the Enlightenment, whose ideas were believed to have inspired the Revolution. In 1814 the French monarchy was reestablished, and in 1815 the leaders of the last campaign against Napoleon restored the old European balance of power and hierarchical systems of government.

This counterrevolutionary feeling inspired a reactionary movement that was the beginning of Romanticism. Writers, thinkers, and artists reacted against the rationalism and orderliness of the eighteenth century and yearned for a return to emotionalism, complexity, and traditional faith. God and nature were seen as more important than reason and science. Indeed, nature, with all its unpredictability and random profusion, became a central feature of the Romantic ideal. Like many other Romantics, the great English poet of Romanticism, William Wordsworth, deplored the destruction of the environment by the ravages of industrialization.

The French Revolution and the ensuing Romantic movement had further consequences in the nineteenth century. One of these was the growth of **nationalism**. Peoples throughout Europe began to foster their own national identities and rebel against outside domination. Nationalism remained a potent force on the political landscape throughout the nineteenth century.

Changes in the structure of society were very dramatic in this era. The Industrial Revolution created great wealth and an increased standard of living for some, while condemning many others to appalling work conditions in mines and factories.

Large numbers of women and children began to work outside the home. The hours were brutal. A factory worker testified to a committee of the English Parliament in 1832 that he and his entire family had to work from 3 A.M. until ten at night for a little more than three shillings a week. Women and children were paid half the wages of a man. Children were often used for pulling heavy coal carts through low mining shafts, and half of the workers in the textile mills of England, France, Belgium, and Germany were children.

Towns and cities appeared throughout the newly industrialized Europe and United States. Many people left their rural environments for crowded city slums and polluted city air. Living conditions and the dreariness of life in London in the nineteenth century are dramatically described in some of the novels of Charles Dickens.

In spite of the hardships and inequities of the times, the nineteenth century also saw the rise of some of the benefits of modern civilization. Medical advances were dramatic. The prevention of infection by antiseptic measures was begun, and Louis Pasteur saved countless lives by developing a rabies vaccine and inventing the process for the sterilization of milk (still called pasteurization in his honor).

It was a biological theory that was contained in one of the most revolutionary works of the century: Charles Darwin's *On the Origin of Species* (1859). Darwin argued that species evolved through the process of natural selection and that evolution was based on the concept of the "survival of the fittest." Darwin thought that the book might be of interest only to other scientists, but it sold out on the first day of its publication. Eventually it became one of the best known books in the world. The social consequences of Darwin's theory were enormous. In the first place, it engendered a conflict between orthodox religion and the theory of evolution, a conflict that has continued to this day. Second, it reinforced ancient beliefs that the poor were poor as a result of their own unfitness and inferiority, which played into the rigid hierarchies of class structure. Finally, and paradoxically, it also gave ammunition to those who believed in helping the less fortunate. The idea of charity, they argued, was also a result of the evolutionary process.

Darwinism and the plight of the new working class led to a vastly increased social consciousness. The nineteenth century saw the foundation of many charitable organizations, the birth of private philanthropy, the establishment of free public schools, and the development of the political ideals of socialism and communism.

In those days, socialism meant putting the good of the general population ahead of the private interests of the few.

The extreme form of socialist thinking found expression in the revolutionary ideas of Karl Marx (1818–1883). Marx predicted the 1917 Bolshevik Revolution, in which the workers would take over the government in a violent uprising. And in *Das Kapital* (1867) he argued that capitalism would eventually self-destruct.

The nineteenth century was also a time of colonial expansion, justified by the Darwin-inspired ideals of "helping" societies seen as poor, uneducated, and unenlightened. Africa, Asia, and the Pacific became networks of colonies ruled by different European countries; and the United States expanded westward,

ON

THE ORIGIN OF SPECIES

BY MEANS OF NATURAL SELECTION,

OR THE

PRESERVATION OF FAVOURED RACES IN THE STRUGGLE
FOR LIFE.

By CHARLES DARWIN, M.A.,

FELLOW OF THE ROYAL, GEOLOGICAL, LINNÆAN, ETC., SOCIETIES;
AUTHOR OF 'JOURNAL OF RESEARCHES DURING H. M. S. BEAGLE'S VOYAGE
ROUND THE WORLD.'

LONDON:
JOHN MURRAY, ALBEMARLE STREET.
1859.

The right of Translation is reserved.

The title page of one of the most influential books ever published.

It was a town of machinery and tall chimneys, out of which interminable serpents of smoke trailed themselves forever and ever, and never got uncoiled. It had a black canal in it, and a river that ran purple with ill-smelling dye, and vast piles of buildings full of windows where there was a rattling and a trembling all day long . . .
—Charles Dickens, *Hard Times*

Colonial Africa, 1880–1914.

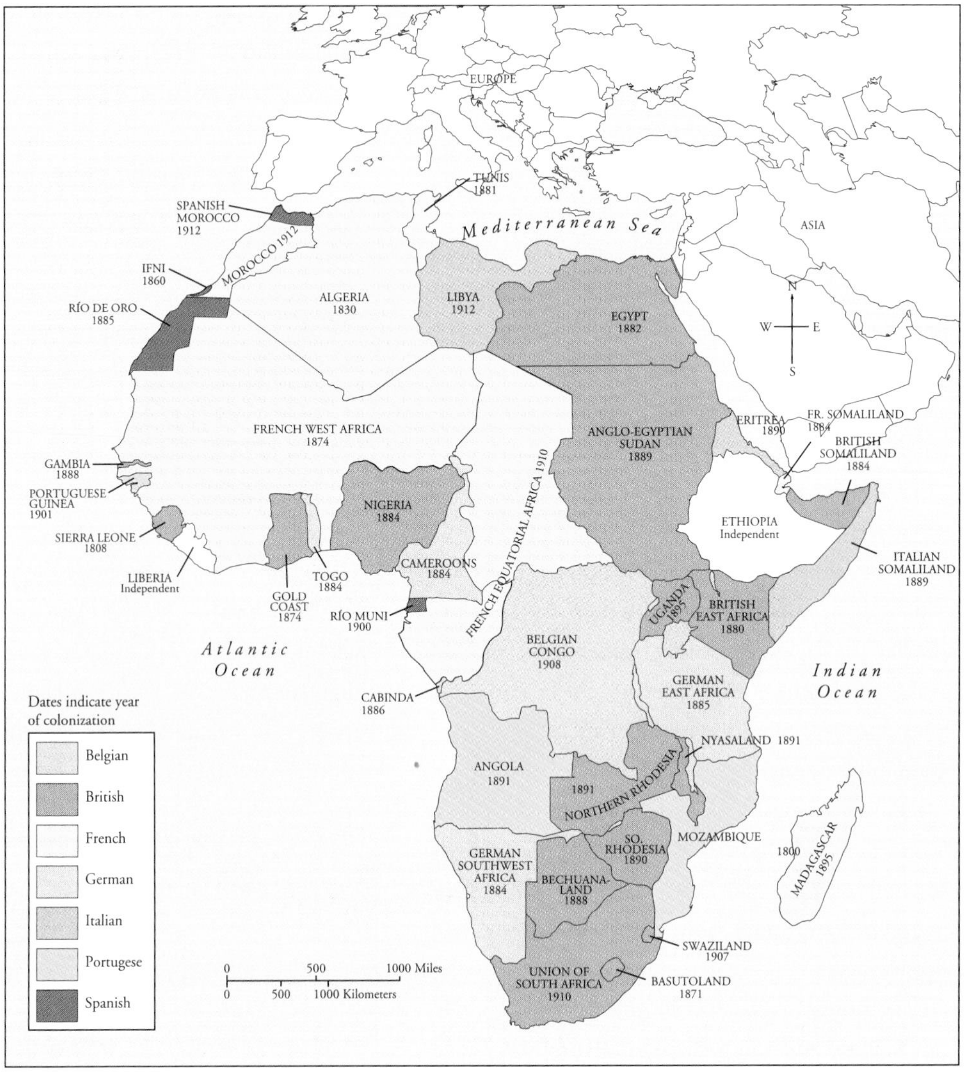

> A work of art must always be a free creation of the spirit.
> —Arrey von Dommer, music theorist

as well as to the south (Puerto Rico, 1898) and the north (Alaska, 1867). Colonialism played a role in the nineteenth-century obsession with the exotic, as foreign countries were explored and people began to get a sense of the diversity and richness of the world in which they lived.

THE NEW ARTISTIC SPIRIT

Romanticism was above all an artistic movement. It began in the last two decades of the eighteenth century with the literary works of the two great German writers Goethe (1749–1832) and Schiller (1759–1805).

Goethe was a poet, novelist, and dramatist—and the author of the single most influential literary work of the nineteenth century, his long dramatic poem *Faust*. Goethe's *Faust* summarizes the themes of Romanticism: life, death, faith, sin, individual insight, selflessness, and redemption. Goethe's play served as inspiration to many composers throughout the nineteenth century.

Another element in literary Romanticism was a renewed fascination with the past. Schiller wrote a series of dramas based on historical and legendary figures, including Joan of Arc, Mary Queen of Scots, and William Tell. And the popular Scottish novelist Sir Walter Scott wrote more than 30 historical novels.

Of all historical periods, it was the Middle Ages that most captured the imagination of the Romantics. The best known of Walter Scott's novels was *Ivanhoe* (1819), set in the days of the Crusades.

The evocative, faintly erotic scene of the burial of Atala by Anne-Louis Girodet.

Anne-Louis Girodet-Trioson, *Atalas Begräbnis*, 1808. Oil on canvas, 206 × 286 cm. Paris, Musée du Louvre. Archiv für Kunst und Geschichte, Berlin.

dieval history or legend. Shakespeare's works underwent an enormous revival in the nineteenth century.

In architecture, medieval Gothic cathedrals, many of which had been gradually falling into ruin, suddenly became a Romantic inspiration. Great cathedrals such as Notre Dame in Paris underwent extensive restoration, and the latest "modern" architectural style in the nineteenth century was known as "Gothic revival." Classical antiquity provided another

The mysterious, the supernatural, and even the macabre fascinated nineteenth-century readers. A favorite American author of the nineteenth century was the ghoulish Edgar Allan Poe (1809–1849). And in 1818, Mary Shelley (second wife of the poet) published the perennially popular story *Frankenstein*.

Romantic poets flung off the strict forms of eighteenth-century classicism and reveled in a new freedom of style. This was the time of the great (mostly English) Romantic poets: Wordsworth, Coleridge, Byron, Shelley, and Keats, as well as the American Longfellow.

The Romantics also developed a love affair with the works of Shakespeare. His plays were highly inventive, many of them in blank verse, freely flowing in structure, and often based on me-

Revival of ancient Greek architectural styles as displayed in the Supreme Court building, Washington, D.C.

> All art aspires to the condition of music.
> —Walter Pater

> It is scarcely credible that a separate romantic school could be formed in music, which is in itself romantic.
> —Robert Schumann

Upper Right: The Gothic-inspired British Houses of Parliament, built in Victorian times.
Lower Right: The Eiffel Tower in 1889—at 984 feet the highest building of its time.

Right: The highly Romantic *Eternal Springtime* by Rodin, 1884.

Rodin, Auguste (French, 1840–1917), *Eternal Springtime*, 1884. '53-26-1 Plaster, painted white, 26″ × 27-5/8″ × 16-5/8″. Philadelphia Museum of Art: Gift of Paul Rosenberg.

ogy produced works of monumental size, the most famous of which are the Brooklyn Bridge (1883), the Statue of Liberty (1886), and the remarkable Eiffel Tower (1889).

In painting, Romantic artists attempted to capture their view of the exotic, the irrational, and the sublime. The paintings of the French artist Delacroix were often set in foreign lands with scenes of violence. He said that the aim of art was not to depict reality but to "strike the imagination."

Nature inspired the great artist William Turner, in whose paintings natural scenes such as a mountain range or a storm at sea take on a power and a significance that reflect the human emotions of fear, awe, and wonder. In Turner's paintings, we can see the foundations of the later Impressionist movement.

Of all the arts, however, music was the most quintessentially Romantic. With its embracing of nature, nationalism, the exotic, the minute, and the monumental, with its focus on individual consciousness, and with its fascination with extremes of expression, Romanticism was a heady mixture, and music was considered the perfect vehicle for expression of all these feelings. The German author E. T. A. Hoffmann wrote

inspiration from the past, and from Jefferson's Virginia to Napoleon's Paris, buildings were constructed in the "Greek Revival" manner, with columns, triumphal arches, and huge rounded domes.

In the second half of the century, the technological advances of the Industrial Revolution had a powerful impact on both sculpture and architecture. Auguste Rodin's figures are triumphs both of new foundry techniques and of the Romantic spirit. The new technol-

Turbulence, passion, danger, and death are captured in Eugène Delacroix's painting of a lion hunt.

Eugène Delacroix, French (1798–1863), *Lion Hunt*, 1860/61. Oil on canvas. 76.5 × 98.5 cm. Mr. and Mrs. Potter Palmer Collection, © 1993 The Art Institute of Chicago, 1992.404.

A dreamy, evocative Romantic painting of 1834.

J. M. W. Turner, *The Golden Bough* (1834). The Core Collection, Tate Gallery, London/Art Resource, NY.

and parlors of middle-class audiences throughout the United States and Europe. The philanthropic attitude of the times also led to the establishment of free concerts for the "improvement" of the working class. Bandstands were erected in public parks, cheap seats were made available in concert halls, and performing groups traveled to less developed areas such as the American West.

in 1813 that music was "the most romantic of all the arts, for its only subject is the infinite."

MUSIC FOR ALL

During the nineteenth century, music became more and more a public concern. From the aristocratic salons of the rich, it moved into the concert halls

Concert halls were built in every town, and many cities had their own symphony orchestras. Music conservatories were founded to train professional musicians. And many music journals were founded, carrying articles and critiques about new compositions. These projects were supported by the businesspeople who were thriving in the wake of the Industrial Revolution.

In addition to public music-making, there was an enormous growth in private music-making at home.

The late nineteenth-century composer Max Reger once wrote to a critic who had just savaged his latest composition: "I am sitting in the smallest room in my house. I have your review in front of me. Soon it will be behind me."

An awe-inspiring, almost Impressionist, scene by William Turner.

Turner, Joseph Mallord William, English (1775–1851), *Slave Ship (Slavers Throwing Overboard the Dead and Dying, Typhoon Coming On),* 1840. Oil on canvas, 90.8 × 122.6 cm. (35-11/16 × 48-5/16 in.) unframed. Henry Lillie Pierce Fund, 19.22. Courtesy, Museum of Fine Arts, Boston. Reproduced with permission. © 2000 Museum of Fine Arts, Boston. All Rights Reserved. Gift of Joseph W., William B., and Edward H. R. Revere.

A bandstand erected in a public park, Edinburgh, 1886.

Industrialization had made pianos cheaper and more plentiful. Piano factories flourished in Germany, Austria, France, England, and the United States, and by the last part of the century, most middle-class homes boasted a piano in the parlor. An evening of parlor songs or informal chamber music became commonplace in Victorian times.

THE NEW SOUND

If you listen to an orchestral piece from the Romantic era, you will notice that it is very different in *sound* from a piece of music from the Classic era. This, too, is partly a result of social and technological changes. As concerts moved from small halls to larger ones and audiences increased in size, orchestras became bigger, and instruments were adapted so that their sounds would be louder and carry further. In contrast to the intense, focused sound of Baroque and Classic instruments, instruments in the nineteenth century were built for power. They were also built for speed. As a result of the new technology, nineteenth-century woodwind and brass instruments were equipped with complex key or valve systems whose primary aim was to facilitate fast fingerwork. New instruments were invented during the nineteenth century, especially instruments made of brass, such as the tuba and the saxophone.

Pianos, too, changed enormously during the nineteenth century. The small, delicate, wooden instruments known to Haydn and Mozart were replaced by larger and louder pianos. A new mechanism was invented, allowing for much more rapid playing and faster repetition of notes, and the range was greatly extended. In Mozart's day, the piano had a range of five octaves. By 1830, the range was over seven octaves (the standard range today).

Orchestras also increased in size. Whereas a Mozart symphony requires perhaps 25 or 30 players, a Brahms symphony needs 50 or 60 people, and some compositions, such as the Requiem Mass of Berlioz or Mahler's Second Symphony, call for an orchestra of more than 100 players.

Sound is also a matter of how an orchestra is used.

Apart from creating huge volume, a large orchestra can be used to produce a very wide range of different combinations of instruments. Romantic composers often used their orchestras as Romantic painters used their palettes: to create an almost infinite variety of colors and textures. The technique of manipulating orchestral sounds is known as **orchestration**, and many Romantic composers were brilliant and sensitive orchestrators.

Finally, the sound of a Romantic work depends upon a number of other factors, such as dynamics, tempo, melody, harmony, and form, which we shall consider separately.

DYNAMICS

In most Classic music, the range of dynamics does not go beyond *piano* and *forte*. In Romantic music, this range is vastly extended. Dynamics up to triple or even quadruple fortissimo (***fff*** and ***ffff***) are common, and indications of quietness often go down to triple pianissimo (***ppp***). There is even a famous passage in a Tchaikovsky symphony in which the composer calls for sextuple pianissimo (***pppppp***). Changes of dynamics are much more frequent and less predictable in Romantic music than in music of earlier times.

TEMPO AND EXPRESSION

The range of tempo also increased in Romantic music. Long, languorous, slow movements are common in the nineteenth century, whereas the favorite slow tempo in the eighteenth century had been a graceful, moderate, walking tempo (*andante*). Changes of tempo

A cozy scene of nineteenth-century middle-class music making.

Beethoven's piano.

The History of the Pianoforte, 1700–1860

About 1700, Bartolomeo Cristofori, an employee of the Medici Court in Florence, constructed the first working piano. The sound was similar to that of the harpsichord, and the instrument was called *gravicembalo col piano e forte* ("harpsichord with soft and loud"). The difference was that the strings of the new instrument were struck rather than plucked, so that gradations in volume could be achieved. If the pianist touched the keys lightly, the sound would be soft; if the pianist pushed them down hard, the sound would be loud. ✦ Piano makers flourished all over Europe in the second half of the eighteenth century. Andreas Stein (Augsburg, Germany) and Anton Walter (Vienna, Austria) used a type of action called the "Prellmechanik." With this system, each key received an escapement lever instead of a stationary rail. This system provided more control and accuracy of touch, though Stein's and Walter's pianos were very delicate in sound and unsuitable for any but the most intimate settings. Johannes Zumpe, a German maker who moved to England in 1760, produced instruments that provided a little more volume and dynamic variety. ✦ The first English grand piano action was devised and developed by John Broadwood about 1770 and patented by Broadwood's apprentice, Robert Stodart, in 1777. Iron bracing, introduced to the piano about 1800, allowed for heavier hammers, thicker strings, and greater string tension. As a result, considerably more volume and sustaining power could now be attained. ✦ By the mid-nineteenth century, the five-octave range of the eighteenth-century piano had been expanded, and the modern pattern of white natural keys with black sharps was adopted (previously it had been the other way around). In 1859, Steinway & Sons of New York took out a patent for an "overstrung" grand piano in which the strings were crossed inside the frame in a fanlike pattern. The huge frame of the Steinway grand piano could accommodate greatly increased string tension, which in turn resulted in the big, bright sound quality that characterizes the Steinway and other grand pianos to this day.

Manuscript of a Haydn symphony (left) compared with a Mahler manuscript calling for a huge orchestra (below).

within a movement are also much more frequent in the Romantic era. This creates a variety of moods inside a single movement, not just between individual movements of a work. And there is far more flexibility of tempo: A Romantic composition seems to ebb and flow as it goes along.

Composers' indications of tempo also became much more expressive. Before, simply the words *Allegro* or *Andante* had sufficed; now composers felt it necessary to indicate the emotional content of a piece by expressive indications. Markings such as *Allegro agitato* ("an agitated Allegro") or *Adagio dolente* ("a grieving Adagio") are often found, and the indication *espressivo* ("expressively") is scattered liberally throughout the pages of Romantic music.

MELODY

Romantic melodies are very different from Classic ones. In the first place, they are usually much longer. Also, they often have a "surging" or "yearning" quality about them, which makes them highly emotional. They may speed up or slow down slightly in the middle, to make them sound more spontaneous, and the dynamics often change as well. Some of the most famous Romantic melodies are intense and strong, but others are wistful, dreamy, or deeply sad. The primary aim was always expression of feeling.

HARMONY

One of the most important weapons in the Romantic search for expression was harmony. In a sense, eighteenth-century harmony had been used mostly for its functionality (one chord leading to the next, which leads to the next, which moves toward the cadence); Romantic harmony, on the other hand, is often also an

Tempo and expression markings in a nineteenth-century piano piece.

Più moto ed espressivo
dolce ma espr.

*("**More quickly and expressively**")*
("sweet but expressive")

From Brahms's *Intermezzo, Op. 117, No. 3*

A perfect example of Romantic melody—long (46 measures long!), emotionally charged, surging, ebbing and flowing, highly expressive.

From Rachmaninov's *Piano Concerto No. 2, first movement*

expressive device. Chords can create color and atmosphere, so more and more unusual chords are used, unexpected combinations appear, and **modulation** (movement among keys) is much more frequent. Toward the end of the century, composers even began to end their pieces in a different key from the one in which they had begun, which was a radical departure from centuries of convention. Chromatic melodies and harmonies become much more frequent, undermining the central, static sense of key that had always governed music. It was only a few years after the end of the nineteenth century that the entire system of tonality was called into question. This would not have been possible without the adventurous experimentation of the Romantics.

FORM

Along with the loosening of harmony came a loosening of form. Romantic pieces tend to blur the outlines of form rather than highlight them. In a Romantic composition it is often harder to "hear" the form than it is in a Classic piece. In part, this is because Romantic works are often much longer, making it more difficult to follow structural devices.

This blurring of formal outlines was deliberate. It corresponds to the change in Romantic poetry from strict forms to freer, more exuberant writing. Romantic composers wanted their music to be as expressive as possible, to represent the spontaneous flow of feelings rather than to display a carefully organized structure.

Formal templates are still used, of course. Great art is never without form. In most Romantic pieces, one can still detect arrangements such as sonata form, scherzo and trio, aria form, or rondo. But these are used with great flexibility, and the exact points of articulation in them can often be a matter of debate.

Even formal organization on the phrase level is less clear-cut in Romantic music: Phrases tend to flow into each other rather than to be separate and distinct. This is achieved by avoiding or undermining cadences. As a phrase reaches its conclusion, it may turn away from the expected cadence in a completely new direction.

Or the composer may make the beginning of a new phrase overlap the end of the old one.

PROGRAM MUSIC

One of the most important differences between Classic and Romantic music lies in the distinction between "program" and "absolute" music. **Program music** is music that tells some kind of story. It may be a love story, or it could be a different kind of narrative, such as a spiritual journey, or scenes from nature, or a child's reverie. **Absolute music** is the term for music that has no meaning outside the meaning of the music itself and the feelings it produces in its listeners.

The nineteenth century did not invent the idea of program music. Vivaldi's *Four Seasons* is a famous example of Baroque program music. But never before had so many composers been so concerned with tying their music to ideas, stories, or events outside the actual notes they were writing. Sometimes composers even published lengthy narratives to accompany performances of their works.

MASSIVE AND MINIATURE

We have noted before that many Romantic works are longer than their Classic counterparts. And some compositions are very long indeed. Some Romantic symphonies last nearly two hours. A Romantic opera can last four hours or more. And Wagner's cycle of operas, *The Ring of the Nibelungs*, is designed to be performed over four entire evenings!

This love of the massive, or monumental, also determined the size of orchestras, as we have seen. More and more instruments were added to orchestras, and larger numbers of the traditional instruments were used.

In contrast to the massive works of the Romantic era, there were some compositions that went to the opposite extreme, using delicate miniaturization. Most of

> I do not say that program music should not be written. But I do maintain that it is a lower form of art than absolute music.
> —Edward Elgar, English composer

these were works for solo piano, which could last less than a minute. Some of these piano miniatures were not programmatic and were simply called "Prelude" or "Waltz" or "Intermezzo" (meaning "interlude"), but many of them had programmatic titles like "Dreaming," "Why?," and "Poet's Love." The piano miniature was the musical response to the Romantic interest in intimacy and individualism.

FAVORITE ROMANTIC GENRES

Many of the same genres that had been popular in the eighteenth century continued into the nineteenth. Opera and symphony were the most extensive genres, calling as they did for large forces. After Beethoven's revolutionary Ninth Symphony, with its use of solo singers and choir in the last movement, other Romantic composers sometimes used voices in their symphonies, especially those written toward the end of the century.

Voice was the central component of two other Romantic genres: song and the Requiem Mass. These also display a contrast between intimacy and grandeur. Intimate solo song settings of Romantic poetry accompanied by piano were great favorites of the nineteenth century. And Requiem Mass settings often call for huge musical resources, including enormous orchestras, extra brass groups, solo singers, and large choruses. Their drama, subjectivity, and emotional appeal take the Romantic Requiems very close indeed to the style of Romantic opera.

Another favored orchestral genre was the concerto, which symbolized the highly Romantic notion of the individual against the group. Piano concertos were common, violin concertos even more so. But Romantic composers also chose other instruments to highlight in this way: cello, flute, clarinet, even viola.

Chamber music also was popular in the nineteenth century. After the string quartet, a particular favorite was the combination of piano and strings, as in a piano quintet (piano and string quartet). Composers also enjoyed writing chamber works for larger string groups—quintets, sextets, even octets—to obtain the rich sounds so typical of the Romantic ideal.

Solo piano works were very popular. Some composers continued to write piano sonatas in the usual three or four movements, but many composed more programmatic pieces, like the piano miniatures mentioned previously, or longer works with a series of short movements that tell a story or depict a series of scenes.

The link between program music and literature is particularly evident in a new genre: the **symphonic poem**. The symphonic poem is a relatively short orchestral work in one continuous movement, though it may fall into contrasting sections. Symphonic poems are always programmatic, though the source of the program need not be literary; it may be a painting or a scene from nature.

Finally, it is important to note that Romantic composers had a tendency to write music in what we might call "mixed genres." Romantic composers did not like to be constrained by conventions of genre, any more than they liked to be constrained by conventions of harmony, form, size, or duration. Many Romantic works do not fall conveniently into any one definition of genre, and some of them are fascinating precisely because they do not conform to expectations.

FAVORITE ROMANTIC INSTRUMENTS

The favorite Romantic instruments were probably the piano and the violin. The piano lends itself both to great intimacy and to great drama; the violin has a very wide range and possesses the potential for great lyricism. And yet there were other instruments that captured the Romantic imagination. Both the cello and the French horn—with their rich, expressive tenor range—were heavily favored by nineteenth-century composers. And for special effects, composers often turned to the English horn (tenor oboe) for its reedy, evocative sound.

THE INDIVIDUAL AND THE CROWD

Romantic writers and thinkers were fascinated by the notion of the individual—a single person's thoughts and feelings. It has been said that in Romantic poetry, the word "I" makes its first important appearance. And in the nineteenth century the idea of the starving artist, living in a tiny room, wholly dedicated to his art, first gained widespread currency.

Romantic poets often stress their sense of isolation, their separateness from the mass of humanity. This focus on the individual is reflected in the Romantic concentration on dramatic musical genres such as the concerto, which contrasts the individual and the group, and in its love affair with great performing musicians.

During the nineteenth century, some performing musicians became very famous. The great Italian violinist Nicolò Paganini (1782–1840) used to travel around the world, displaying his astounding virtuosity. Paganini could perform technical tricks on the violin that nobody else was able to achieve. And he had a flair for the dramatic. He used to cut partway through one or more of the strings on his violin before a performance so that they would snap while he was playing. To the amazement of his audience, he would complete the piece on the remaining strings. Paganini's technical brilliance was the inspiration for several composers in the nineteenth century, as we shall see.

Another great virtuoso performer was the pianist and composer Franz Liszt. Audiences treated him the way modern audiences treat rock stars: Women fainted and people mobbed the stage. Indeed, our hero-worship of performing musicians today is a direct holdover from the Romantic era.

WOMEN IN NINETEENTH-CENTURY MUSIC

The nineteenth century opened doors of opportunity to a wide range of people, and women were no exception. Music conservatories began to accept women for musical training, and although considerable prejudice remained, some women became famous as performers and composers during the nineteenth century. This is not to say that there was equal opportunity. Most orchestras were still composed entirely of men, and many people thought that it was "unseemly" for women to appear as professional musicians in public. Still, a large number of women played the piano or sang, and many performed in their own living rooms or at the homes of friends.

Some women played an important role behind the scenes in nineteenth-century musical life, either as hostesses of vibrant salons, where much music-making took place, or as wealthy patrons of the arts. Tchaikovsky, one of the most famous composers of the Romantic era, was supported privately by a very rich woman. Other composers relied heavily on their personal relationships with women, as supporters and lovers or as colleagues and critics. Among the most important women in the history of nineteenth-century music were Fanny Mendelssohn and Clara Schumann, and we shall look at their lives and contributions to music during the course of this chapter.

ROMANTIC SONG

Romantic songs are intimate miniatures. They are written for a single voice with piano accompaniment and are designed to be sung in private parlors rather than in large concert halls.

The setting of the song is always designed to mirror the meaning of the text, either with specific word painting or in general atmosphere. The greatest Romantic songs (and there are many great ones) add a level of richness and emotional depth to the poem considerably beyond that of the text alone.

Romantic songs may be either strophic or through-composed. **Strophic** songs are those that use the same music for each stanza of the poetry. **Through-composed** songs are those in which the music is

A daguerreotype (earliest type of photograph) of renowned violinist Paganini, taken shortly before his death in 1840. (The fingers of his left hand have been exaggerated, however.)

Everyone is talking of Paganini and his violin. The man seems to be a miracle. —Thomas Macauley, 1831

different for each stanza. Sometimes modifications or combinations of these forms may appear.

Although most Romantic songs stand on their own as self-contained works, composers sometimes linked together a group of songs to create what is known as a **song cycle**. A song cycle may present a series of songs that are woven together to make a narrative, or it may link several songs by presenting them as different facets of a single idea.

PART ONE: EARLY ROMANTICISM

In addition to Beethoven, five great composers were active in the first half of the nineteenth century: Franz Schubert, Hector Berlioz, Felix Mendelssohn, Fryderyk Chopin, and Robert Schumann. Also important were the women Clara Schumann (1819–1896) and Fanny Mendelssohn Hensel (1805–1847), though their achievements are harder to assess, as we shall see.

FRANZ SCHUBERT (1797–1828)

Schubert was the son of a Viennese schoolmaster and lived most of his life in Vienna. It is extraordinary to think that Schubert and Beethoven lived at the same time and in the same city and that they met only once.

The two men could not have been more different. Whereas Beethoven was proud, assertive, and difficult to get along with, Schubert was shy, retiring, and exceedingly modest, with a large number of good friends. Their music, too, is very different: Beethoven's dramatic and intellectually powerful, Schubert's gentle, relaxed, and lyrical, with a magical harmonic gift. Finally, whereas most of Beethoven's music was published during his own lifetime, only a small percentage of Schubert's enormous output was published while he was alive, much of it having to wait decades for publication. Schubert wrote more than 900 works in his very short life (he died at the age of 31), a level of productivity that surpasses even that of Mozart.

Schubert sang as a choirboy when he was young and also played the violin, performing string quartets with his father and brothers at home and playing in the orchestra at the choir school, where he came to know the symphonies of Haydn, Mozart, and Beethoven firsthand. Schubert's gift for composition was already evident, and when his voice changed, he left the choir and was accepted as a composition student by the composer at the Imperial Court in Vienna, Antonio

Franz Schubert.

Salieri. His father wanted Schubert to become a schoolmaster like himself; he tried briefly, but he was a poor teacher and soon gave it up. Schubert then embarked on his quiet career as a composer, living in Vienna and working every morning. He seemed to be a limitless fountain of music. "When I finish one piece," he said, "I begin the next." In the afternoons, he went to one or another of the Viennese cafés and spent time with his friends.

Schubert occasionally tried to win recognition by writing opera, the most popular (and lucrative) genre of his day; but although he composed many operas, they met with little success. He also applied for some important musical positions, with the same disappointing result. It seemed as though Vienna had room for only one brilliant composer, and the powerful figure of Beethoven cast a long shadow. In spite of these setbacks, Schubert's talent and modest personality won the affection of many people, who gave him moral and, occasionally, financial support. At one time, several of his friends banded together to pay for the publication of a group of his songs. Toward the end of his life, however, Schubert's essential loneliness often overcame him, and he despaired of achieving happiness. Some of Schubert's most profound works come from this period of his life.

In his last year, Schubert's productivity increased even further. Perhaps he knew that he did not have much time left. A month before he died, Schubert arranged to take lessons in counterpoint! "Now I see how much I still have to learn," he said. He died of syphilis on November 19, 1828. According to his last wishes, he was buried near Beethoven in Vienna. His epitaph, written by a friend, reads: "Here the art of music has buried a rich possession but even more promising hopes."

SCHUBERT'S MUSIC

"Everything he touched turned to song," said one of his friends about Schubert. Schubert's greatest gift was his genius for capturing the essence of a poem when he set it to music. In fact, his song settings seem to transcend the poetry that he put to music. The melodies he devised for the voice, the harmonies and figuration of the piano part—these turn mediocre poetry into superb songs and turn great poetry into some of the most expressive music ever written. During his pathetically short life, Schubert composed *more than 600* songs. These range from tiny poems on nature, to dramatic dialogues, to folklike tunes, to songs of the deepest emotional intensity. In addition to this enormous number and variety of individual songs, Schubert also wrote two great song cycles, *Die schöne Müllerin* (*The Pretty Miller-Maid*, 1824) and *Winterreise* (*Winter's Journey*, 1827). The first tells the story of a love affair that turns from buoyant happiness to tragedy; the second is a sequence of reflections on nostalgia, old age, and resignation. Both contain music of the greatest simplicity as well as the greatest sophistication. Whether expressing the joys of youthful love or the resignation of old age, Schubert's music goes straight to the heart.

Schubert's gift for lyricism influenced everything he wrote, even his instrumental music. He composed a great variety of music for solo piano and some wonderful chamber music. Apart from the innate lyricism of "everything he touched," two of his chamber works are actually based on songs he wrote. One is called the *Death and the Maiden* String Quartet, the other the *Trout* Quintet. Each has a movement that is a set of variations on a melody from one of those songs. (**See Listening Guides on pages 246 and 248.**)

Among the larger works are several operas, a number of choral works, and eight symphonies. The best known of Schubert's symphonies are his last two, the so-called *Great* C-Major Symphony (1828) and the *Unfinished* Symphony (Schubert completed only two movements).

From his tiny, moving, earliest songs to the expansiveness and grandeur of his late symphonies, Schubert's music is finally emerging from the enormous shadow cast by Beethoven. It is fascinating to contemplate how highly we would regard Schubert's music today if Beethoven hadn't been there at all.

"My peace is gone, my heart is heavy, and I will never again find peace." I may well sing this every day now, for each night, on retiring to bed, I hope I may not wake again; and each morning but recalls yesterday's grief.
—Letter of Franz Schubert, 1824, quoting from one of his own songs

Franz Schubert (1797–1828)
Song, *Die Forelle* (*The Trout*)

Date of composition: 1817
Voice and piano
Tempo: *Etwas lebhaft* ("Rather lively")
Meter: $\frac{2}{4}$
Key: D♭ Major
Duration: 2:10

Student CD Collection: 2, track 59
Complete CD Collection: 4, track 1

"The Trout," written to the poem of a German poet, Christian Friedrich Schubart, appeals to today's listeners just as it did to Schubert's contemporaries. Part of the song's charm lies in the composer's remarkable ability to depict the atmosphere of the poem by blending the melody with its accompaniment, both of which have an equal share in the musical interpretation of the poem.

The song begins with a piano introduction based on a "rippling" figure that evokes the smooth flow of a stream. This figure becomes the dominant feature of the accompaniment, over which the voice sings an animated and lighthearted melody.

The song represents a modified strophic form with an unexpected change of mood in the last stanza. The first two stanzas are sung to the same music simply because the scene remains the same: As long as the water in the stream is clear, the fish is safe. In the third stanza, however, when the fisherman grows impatient and maliciously stirs up the water to outwit the trout, the music becomes more agitated and unsettled. After the fish is finally hooked, the smoothing of the water's surface is represented by the return of the gentle "rippling" figure, which gives a sense of artistic unity and makes the song a highly organic work.

The subtlety of expression, the perfect matching of feeling to music, and the gentle pictorial touches all combine to make of this song a complete miniature masterpiece.

59 (1) **0:00**	Piano introduction based on the rippling figure.	

STANZA 1		
	[rippling accompaniment continues]	
0:08	*In einem Bächlein helle,*	In a limpid brook
	Da schoss in froher Eil'	In joyous haste
	Die launische Forelle	The whimsical trout
	Vorüber wie ein Pfeil.	Darted about like an arrow.
0:20	*Ich stand an dem Gestade*	I stood on the bank
	Und sah in süsser Ruh'	In blissful peace, watching
	Des muntern Fischleins Bade	The lively fish swim around
	Im klaren Bächlein zu.	In the clear brook.
	[last two lines repeated]	
0:39	Piano interlude	

[same music]

60 (2)   **0:45**

Ein Fischer mit der Rute	An angler with his rod
Wohl an dem Ufer stand,	Stood on the bank,
Und sah's mit kaltem Blute,	Cold-bloodedly watching
Wie sich das Fischlein wand.	The fish's flicker.

0:57

So lang' dem Wasser Helle,	As long as the water is clear,
So dacht' ich, nicht gebricht,	I thought, and not disturbed,
So fängt er die Forelle	He'll never catch that trout
Mit seiner Angel nicht.	With his rod.

[last two lines repeated]

1:17   Piano interlude

[sudden change of rhythm, harmony, and accompanying figures]

61 (3)   **1:23**

Doch endlich ward dem Diebe	But in the end the thief
Die Zeit zu lang. Er macht	Grew impatient. Cunningly
Das Bächlein tückisch trübe,	He made the brook
	cloudy, [diminished sevenths]
Und eh ich es gedacht,	And in an instant [suspense gaps
	in piano]

1:37

So zuckte seine Rute,	His rod quivered,
Das Fischlein zappelt dran,	And the fish struggled on it. [crescendo]
Und ich mit regem Blute	And I, my blood boiling, [earlier music
	returns]
Sah die Betrog'ne an.	Looked at the poor tricked creature.

[last two lines repeated]

1:58   Piano postlude

Franz Schubert (1797–1828)
Fourth Movement from Quintet in A
Major, D. 667 (*The Trout*)

Date of composition: 1819
Orchestration: Violin, viola, cello,
    double bass, piano
Tempo: *Andantino—Allegretto*
    ("Medium slow"—"A little faster")
Meter $\frac{2}{4}$
Key: D Major
Duration: 8:34

Student CD Collection: 2, track 62
Complete CD Collection: 4, track 4

Schubert chose the gentle theme from his song "The Trout" for a set of variations written for piano and strings. The original song was written in the key of D♭ Major, but here it is transposed to D Major, which is easier to play and more resonant on string instruments. Instead of the normal complement of strings (two violins, viola, and cello—the "string quartet" group), Schubert uses one each of violin, viola, cello, and double bass. This makes for a slightly more transparent texture and, of course, a deeper bass line.

The movement consists of the "Trout" theme and six variations. The theme is presented first, in a simpler form than in the song. It is played by the strings; the violin plays the melody while the other instruments provide a simple accompaniment. You can clearly hear the double bass, with its deep, rich tones. In the first three variations, the theme is heard successively in the treble, in an inner part, and in the bass with little modification. In the fourth variation, it is presented in the parallel minor key, D minor, and transformed, but it comes back again in recognizable form in the fifth variation in B♭ Major. In the closing variation, *Allegretto*, Schubert presents the theme in yet another version; this time he borrows the texture and the rippling accompanying figure directly from the original song.

The theme consists of two sections, the first of which is repeated. In the second section, after eight measures, a trill at the cadence leads to a four-measure extension before the close.

‖: 8 measures :‖ ‖ 8 + 4 measures ‖

THEME		Strings only.
62 (4)	**0:00**	First section.
	0:21	Repeat.
	0:43	Second section.

VARIATION I

In this variation, the theme is played by the piano and is slightly embellished. The strings weave an ornamentation around the melody with fast-moving triplets and trills. Listen here to the *pizzicato* bass.

63 (5)	**1:19**	First section.
	1:36	Repeat.
	1:53	Second section.

VARIATION II

Now the main melody is taken over by the viola, above which the violin plays ornaments in triple rhythm. The theme is complemented by short imitative phrases in the piano part.

64 (6)	**2:40**	First section.
	2:58	Repeat.
	3:15	Second section.

VARIATION III

This variation is dominated by the piano, which plays an uninterrupted flow of fast notes. The theme is played (rather ploddingly!) by the double bass and progresses steadily along this perpetual motion of the piano part.

65 (7)	**3:40**	First section.
	3:55	Repeat.
	4:10	Second section.

VARIATION IV

This variation bursts out loudly in the minor key, but the initial dramatic chords soon yield to a more playful section in triplets. The second half gradually becomes more and more calm, gently introducing the cello.

66 (8)	**4:33**	First section.
	4:49	Repeat.
	5:06	Second section.

VARIATION V

It is the cello that dominates the fifth variation, which is in B♭ Major but is also tinged with melancholy minor touches. The second section is extended to lead the music back to its home key, D Major.

67 (9)	**5:38**	First section.
	6:00	Repeat.
	6:21	Second section.

VARIATION VI

"A little faster." The music livens up for the final variation, which is marked by the rippling accompaniment that characterizes the original song. Violin and cello trade phrases, and the ripple brings the movement to a peaceful conclusion.

68 (10)	**7:16**	First section. Violin with piano.
	7:27	First section repeated. Cello with strings.
	7:40	Second section. Violin/piano.
	7:58	Second section repeated. Cello/strings, joined by piano for quiet ending.

My life is to me a deeply interesting romance. —Hector Berlioz

Berlioz on his prospects in medicine: "Become a doctor? Study anatomy? Dissect? Take part in horrible operations? Instead of giving myself body and soul to music?"

Hector Berlioz.

HECTOR BERLIOZ (1803–1869)

In nineteenth-century France, Romanticism was a vital force, defined by writers such as Madame de Staël, Chateaubriand, and George Sand; poets such as Lamartine and Vigny; novelists and playwrights such as Stendhal, Balzac, and Victor Hugo; and painters such as Anne-Louis Girodet and Eugène Delacroix. No less important than these literary and artistic figures was the French composer Hector Berlioz, who established music as central to the Romantic ideal.

Berlioz was the oldest child of a distinguished French doctor and his strictly religious Catholic wife. As a child Berlioz read widely; he also took music lessons and, on his own, studied music theory. And he began to compose music when he was a teenager.

His father wanted him to become a doctor, so Berlioz entered medical school in Paris. But he became more and more interested in music, and more and more horrified by what he saw as a medical student. He finally quit medical school against his father's wishes and supported himself by taking singing jobs and giving music lessons. Berlioz enrolled at the Paris Conservatory of Music as a composition student at the age of 23.

During the next few years, he wrote several compositions. He also had several first-time experiences that were to affect him profoundly: hearing some of the great Beethoven symphonies, coming across a French translation of Goethe's *Faust*, and encountering Shakespeare's plays. He also fell in love with an Irish actress, Harriet Smithson, who was touring with a Shakespearean acting company. All these experiences had lasting effects on his music.

During the 1830s, Berlioz composed two highly original symphonic works: *Harold in Italy*, which was inspired by a reading of the Romantic poet Byron's *Childe Harold*, and *Romeo and Juliet*, based on Shakespeare's play. He also wrote a powerful and expressive Requiem Mass, composed in memory of the national heroes of France.

In the 1840s, when Berlioz should have been approaching the peak of his career, he was generally spurned by the French establishment. His music was regarded as too innovative, his forms unconventional, his orchestration too demanding, and the emotionality of his music too direct. "They don't understand me," he said. But throughout the rest of Europe, Berlioz was more appreciated. The great Italian virtuoso Paganini sent him 20,000 francs out of the blue, and Wagner described *Romeo and Juliet* as a "revelation." He was often invited to conduct abroad, and other conductors, especially in Germany, scheduled performances of his music.

In the 1850s, despite his critics at home, Berlioz poured his energies into producing one of his greatest masterpieces, the five-act opera *Les Troyens* (*The Trojans*). Based on Virgil's *Aeneid*, it tells the story of the escape of Aeneas from Troy and his doomed love affair with Dido, the Queen of Carthage.

For the last part of his life, Berlioz was not in good health, and he felt bitter and depressed. He composed very little music but worked on his memoirs, which make fascinating reading today. Berlioz died in 1869, and his grave may be visited at Montmartre in Paris. In many ways, Hector Berlioz can be seen as the incarnation of the Romantic artist: brilliantly gifted, completely dedicated to his art, yet rejected by society and isolated during his lifetime.

BERLIOZ'S MUSIC

The most striking aspects of Berlioz's music are its color and atmosphere. He used the orchestra brilliantly, with great sensitivity to the myriad qualities of sound available from all the instruments. Some of his pieces call for enormous resources. The Requiem Mass is written for an orchestra of 140 players, a huge chorus, and four groups of brass and timpani placed at the four corners of the performing space. The *Te Deum* calls for a solo singer, a large orchestra, an organ, two choirs of 100 singers each, and a choir of 600 children!

But even more fascinating than these gigantic effects are those quiet places in the works of Berlioz where he conjures up an unforgettable atmosphere with completely original orchestration. In the Requiem, for example, he uses violas, cellos, bassoons, and English horns in simple, long phrases for a passage of penitence and introspection. And his *Symphonie fantastique* is full of wonderful atmospheric moments: an echoing song between solo oboe and solo English horn, the quiet rumble of distant thunder on four timpani, and an eerie, menacing march on muted horns and plucked double basses. **(See Listening Guide on page 252.)**

Berlioz's best known work is his *Symphonie fantastique* (*Fantastical Symphony*), which is also one of the

Berlioz composes by splashing his pen all over the manuscript and leaving the result to chance.
—Fryderyk Chopin

Instead of a musician, they have chosen a journalist!
—Anonymous remark in the Parisian paper *Revue des deux mondes* on Berlioz's election to the Institute of Music

most famous examples of Romantic program music. Like many other composers of program music, Berlioz felt ambivalent about tying a musical work to a specific verbal narrative. He wanted to explain the ideas behind his music to his audience, but he also felt that the music ought to be able to stand alone. For the first performance, he said that "the distribution of the program to the audience… is indispensable for a complete understanding of the work." Twenty-five years later, though, Berlioz said that one could dispense with distributing the program, keeping only the titles of the five movements. "The author hopes that the symphony by itself can provide musical interest independent of the dramatic purpose."

LISTENING GUIDE

Hector Berlioz (1803–1869)
First Movement from *Symphonie fantastique* (*Fantastical Symphony*)

Date of composition: 1830
Orchestration: Piccolo, 2 flutes, 2 oboes, 2 clarinets, 2 bassoons, 4 horns, 2 cornets, 2 trumpets, 2 timpani, violins I, violins II, violas, cellos, basses
Tempo: *Largo—Allegro agitato e appassionato assai* ("Broad—Fast, quite agitated and passionate")
Meter: $\frac{4}{4}$
Key: C minor (Introduction), C Major (Allegro)
Duration: 11:17

Complete CD Collection: 4, track 11

The *Symphonie fantastique*, Berlioz said, describes various situations in the life of a young musician. The young man falls desperately in love with a woman at first sight. The symphony depicts his dreams, despairs, and fantasies. Clearly the symphony is autobiographical.

The first movement is entitled "Reveries, Passions." It describes the young musician who sees for the first time a woman "who embodies all the charms of the ideal being he has imagined in his dreams." The woman is linked in his mind to a musical idea; Berlioz calls it an *idée fixe*, an idea that won't go away. The program continues: "The passage from a state of melancholy reverie (interrupted by moments of inexplicable joy) to one of frenzied passion, with its feelings of fury and jealousy, its return of tenderness, its tears, its religious consolations—all this is the subject of the first movement."

Berlioz has cast his first movement into an approximation of sonata form with a slow introduction. He deliberately blurs the outline of the form: The end of the exposition runs directly into the development, and the second theme comes back before the first in the recapitulation (and its treatment here still sounds "developmental"). The keys are vague rather than clear-cut. And the whole effect—with its constant changes of tempo, dynamics, and instrumentation—is surging, passionate, and free. Also, the *idée fixe*, the musical idea representing the beloved, permeates the whole movement: The theme of the slow introduction is like a "pre-echo" of this idea, the first theme of the Allegro *is* the *idée fixe*, and the second theme starts out very much like it too. The idea itself is the perfect embodiment of Romantic melody—long, flexible, yearning upward, falling back, hesitating, surging, retiring: It breathes as though alive. In this, one of his earliest works, Berlioz has taken a fixed Classic form and radically reinterpreted it to express the new Romantic spirit.

INTRODUCTION		
		C minor ("Melancholy Reverie")
(11)	**0:00**	Flutes and clarinets: repeated notes, ***pp***, ascending scale in oboes; held chord.
	0:09	Dreamlike melody on muted violins, then other strings.
(12)	**0:47**	Scooping melody in violins with pizzicato basses (faint pre-echo of *idée fixe*).

	1:14	Crescendo on low strings and held note.
	1:19	Staccato violin melody skitters upward, ***p***; addition of winds and lower strings, crescendo; melody climbs upward forcefully then slides down gracefully; quieter.
	1:36	Slow passage, flute, clarinet, horn, and strings, surging.

1:59		Dreamlike melody, slightly louder, now accompanied by rapid flutes and clarinets; crescendo, with climb and then gradual descent.
3:11		Suspense.
3:24		Two contrasting violin figures, alternating with pulsating wind chords, accompany a solo horn, then two horns; gradual crescendo.
4:14		Sustained chords swell to **ff**, and back to **pp**; alternating cadential figures on strings and winds, with loud punctuating chords, end the Introduction.

A<small>LLEGRO</small>

C Major ("Frenzied Passion")

E<small>XPOSITION</small>

(13)   **4:33**   *First Theme*

First theme (*idée fixe*) in violins with solo flute, first unaccompanied, then with repeated notes in low strings; striving upward, crescendo, agitated, then calming.

Transition

5:09	Brilliant rapid passage in strings leads to:
5:15	Short peaceful passage, flute, clarinet, horn.
5:21	Again, brilliant string passage, leading to:
5:27	Faster melody, flutes, clarinets.
5:33	Short, rapid motif in strings, crescendo, leads to:

Second Theme (E minor/G Major)

(14)   **5:41**   First part of theme (similar to *idée fixe*): flute and clarinet, quiet. Second part: strings, loud.

Flute, Clarinet

Violins I

dolce   *ff*   *sf*

Continuation, crescendo, leads directly into:

DEVELOPMENT

(15)   **5:54**   Low strings develop opening idea of *idée fixe*, answered by winds; big crescendo.

6:14   Fragments of second theme.

6:19   Chromatic rise and fall with crescendos, increasing in intensity.

6:41   Sudden stop and long pause.

6:44   Sustained horn note, *p*, accompanies leaping motif in strings.

6:52   *Idée fixe* returns in flute, clarinet, and bassoons, dominant key; leaping strings join in; crescendo.

7:24   Low descending continuation on bassoons and cellos, crescendo, full orchestra, merges into:

RECAPITULATION

[still sounds developmental]

Second Theme (C Major/G Major)

(16)   **7:52**   Second part of second theme by strings in imitation, *ff*, then strings and winds together.

	8:07	Peaceful passage, *p*, winds then strings over timpani roll; diminuendo, low strings.
	8:37	Solo oboe over strings, new long melody with expressive leaps; continuation is doubled by flute (both striving upward). Huge crescendo (with cornets and trumpets) to:
		First Theme (C Major)
(17)	**9:22**	Climactic return (faster) of *idée fixe*, *ff*, full orchestra (first appearance of piccolo), wild.
	9:44	Suddenly quiet, crescendo again to:
	9:53	Sudden relaxation—flute, clarinet, oboe, and bassoon overlap opening of *idée fixe*, *p*.
	10:05	Again sudden crescendo to:
	CODA	
(18)	**10:15**	Rapid syncopated melody, *f*, full orchestra, timpani strokes.
	10:21	Fast rising strings, followed by falling pizzicato strings and cadential chords.
	10:28	Chromatically descending strings and oboe, decrease in volume.
	10:40	Violins, alone, state opening of *idée fixe*, *pp*.
	10:51	Movement ends with alternating churchlike chords, *pp*; plagal cadence (IV–I); "religious consolations."

FELIX MENDELSSOHN (1809–1847)

Mendelssohn is one of the two composers in this chapter (the other being Gustav Mahler) who illustrate the uncomfortable position occupied by Jews in nineteenth-century Europe. His grandfather had been the famous Jewish philosopher Moses Mendelssohn. His father was a banker, a prominent member of German middle-class society. And his mother was also from a distinguished family; she was cultivated and very musical. In 1811 the Mendelssohn family was forced to flee from Hamburg to Berlin for political reasons, and when Felix was seven years old, his father had the children baptized; a few years later, his father converted to Christianity himself. Despite the increasing toler-

ance of nineteenth-century society, it was still easier to make your way in an "enlightened" age if you were not Jewish.

After that, the family enjoyed increasing prosperity and social status. The Mendelssohn home was a focal point for writers, artists, musicians, and intellectuals in Berlin society. Among the regular guests were the famous philosopher Hegel and the brilliant biologist Humboldt. Chamber concerts were held every weekend, and under the tutelage of their mother, Felix and his older sister Fanny soon proved to be especially gifted in music.

About Fanny we shall say more later. Felix was precocious in everything he undertook. At the age of 10, he was reading Latin and studying arithmetic, geometry, history, and geography. He played the piano and the violin, and he started music theory and composition lessons with a distinguished professor of music in Berlin. He began to compose, write poetry, and paint. Several of his early compositions were performed at the Sunday concerts in his parents' home.

As a youth, Mendelssohn was introduced to the most famous literary figure in Germany, Goethe, and a great friendship developed between the old man and the gifted teenager. Mendelssohn also traveled widely in Europe, either on holidays with his family or in the company of his father.

All of this time, Mendelssohn was composing prolifically. He had an extraordinary fluency and control. By the time he was 20 he had written more than 100 pieces.

Mendelssohn was very interested in music of the past. It was at the age of 20 that, together with a family friend who was a professional actor, he arranged for a performance of one of the great masterpieces of Bach that had not been heard for nearly a century—the *St. Matthew Passion*. The performance, with Mendelssohn conducting, was a landmark in the revival and appreciation of Bach's music in the modern era. "To think," said Mendelssohn, "that it should be an actor and a Jew who give back to the people the greatest of all Christian works."

Art and Life are not two different things.
—Felix Mendelssohn

Felix Mendelssohn about 1829.

In his twenties, Mendelssohn continued to perform as a conductor and a pianist, to compose prolifically, and to travel a great deal, in Italy, Scotland, and England. In 1835, he was appointed conductor of the Leipzig Gewandhaus Orchestra, where he worked hard to improve the quality of performances and the working conditions of the musicians. He revived many important works of the past and also championed the music of his contemporaries. When the score of Schubert's *Great* C-Major Symphony was discovered, the world premiere was given by Mendelssohn and his orchestra.

Mendelssohn was married in 1837, and the couple had five children. In 1843 he was appointed director of the Berlin Cathedral Choir and director of the Berlin Opera. He continued to divide his time between Berlin and Leipzig, and in the same year he was appointed director of the newly opened music conservatory in Leipzig. Despite all these activities, Mendelssohn continued to compose. Among the many works he wrote at this time were an opera, two large oratorios, symphonies, concertos, chamber music, and numerous pieces for solo piano.

In May of 1847, his closest friend and confidante, his sister Fanny, suddenly died. Felix was shattered. His last great work, the String Quartet in F Minor, Op. 80, was composed as a "Requiem for Fanny." He became ill and tired and could no longer conduct. A series of strokes in October led to his death on November 3, 1847, at the age of 38. Mendelssohn was buried in Berlin, near Fanny's grave.

Mendelssohn's Music

Mendelssohn was a composer who continued the Classic tradition in his works, while adopting some of the less extreme ideas of Romanticism. He wrote in most of the traditional genres of the Classic era, and the formal outlines of his works are clear and easy to follow. Mendelssohn maintained the greatest respect for the past—especially the music of Bach, Handel, Mozart, and Beethoven—and his music shows the influence of

these composers. His style is more transparent and lighter than that of many early Romantic composers, certainly less extroverted and smaller in scale than that of Berlioz; it ranges from lively and brilliantly animated to lyrical and expressive.

Mendelssohn's main orchestral works include five symphonies and several overtures. Many of these are programmatic, though only in a general sense: They do not tell a detailed story but evoke scenes and landscapes. The best known of these are the *Scottish* Symphony (Symphony No. 3), the *Italian* Symphony (Symphony No. 4), and the *Hebrides* Overture, all written after Mendelssohn's travels. The *Hebrides* Overture was inspired by his trip to Scotland and evokes a rocky landscape and the swell of the sea. Like many early Romantics, Mendelssohn read and admired Shakespeare, and another overture often performed today is the Overture to Shakespeare's *A Midsummer Night's Dream*. Listening to this piece, it is hard to believe it was written when the composer was only 17.

Mendelssohn also wrote several concertos, mostly for piano but also for violin. His Violin Concerto in E minor is certainly the most popular of all his works, because of its beauty and lyricism. (**See Listening Guide on page 259.**)

Mendelssohn's admiration for Bach and Handel led to his interest in choral writing. After the famous revival of Bach's *St. Matthew Passion*, Mendelssohn studied Handel's oratorios and composed two major oratorios of his own, *Elijah* and *St. Paul*. He also wrote a great deal of other choral music, and his sacred music includes works for Jewish, Catholic, Lutheran, and Anglican services.

His chamber music includes songs, string quartets, sonatas, and piano trios. Perhaps the most popular of these works is the Piano Trio in D minor. In addition, Mendelssohn wrote a large number of miniatures for solo piano; in the typical mold of early Romanticism, he called them *Songs Without Words*. They are gentle, delightful, and lyrical—expressive without being deeply profound. In these ways, they capture the essence of Felix Mendelssohn's music.

> E*ver since I began to compose, I have remained true to my starting principle: not to write a page because the public or a pretty girl wanted it a certain way, but to write solely as I thought best.*
> —Felix Mendelssohn

Felix Mendelssohn (1809–1847)

First Movement from Concerto in E minor for Violin and Orchestra, Op. 64

Date of composition: 1844
Orchestration: Solo violin and orchestra
Tempo: *Allegro molto appassionato*
 ("Fast and very passionate")
Meter: $\frac{2}{2}$
Key: E minor
Duration: 13:17

Complete CD Collection: 4, track 19

*T*his concerto, one of Mendelssohn's most popular works, was composed three years before his death. It has remained one of the favorites of all the Romantic violin concertos for its combination of lyricism and dazzling virtuosity. There are many innovative features. First, all the movements follow one another without a break. Second, in contrast to the Classical concerto, melodies are initially stated by the soloist instead of by the orchestra. Finally, the cadenza in the first movement is placed immediately after the development section, instead of coming at the end like an afterthought.

There are many demanding sections throughout this concerto. Particularly challenging are those places where the violin soloist is required to finger and bow *two* strings simultaneously. This technique is termed "double-stopping" and is featured in all movements. Octave double-stops present even more difficulties, since precise fingering is extremely difficult.

FIRST MOVEMENT	[sonata form]
	Allegro molto appassionato

EXPOSITION		
(19)	0:00	FIRST THEME (solo violin), high, over quiet accompaniment.

	0:32	Violin plays faster flourishes, answered by orchestral chords.
	0:52	Octaves, solo violin.
	1:02	Orchestra plays FIRST THEME.
	1:34	Orchestral transition and theme repeated and extended by solo violin.

| 2:06 | More flourishes, featuring double-stops (solo violin), and an orchestral climax. Gradually the music calms and leads to a cadence. |

| (20) | 3:03 | SECOND THEME, initiated by woodwinds, answered and extended by solo violin. |

| | 4:24 | Return to FIRST THEME, virtuosic passages, crescendo, big orchestral chords. |

DEVELOPMENT

| (21) | 5:38 | Fragmentation of themes, including transitional material and first and second themes. Contrasts of loud and soft, violin descends, everything calms down before a big crescendo into the: |

| (22) | 7:20 | *Cadenza* (violin alone), featuring difficult trills, double-stops, and extremely high notes. |

RECAPITULATION

| (23) | 8:54 | Orchestra plays FIRST THEME while solo violin continues virtuosic flourishes. |

| | 9:13 | Traditional material, loud, orchestra, repeated and extended by violin, quietly. Cadence. |

| (24) | 9:48 | SECOND THEME, woodwinds, then solo violin with extension. Cadence. |

| | 11:08 | Motion increases, brilliant running passages on solo violin, fragments of themes and pizzicatos on the orchestra. |

| | 11:59 | Stratospheric climbs by solo violin, punctuated by big orchestral chords. Speed and intensity gradually increase to: |

| | 12:09 | Subsidiary Theme, solo violin. |

| | 12:44 | *Presto* (very fast) section, hurried-sounding, signaling ending of the movement. |

| | 13:10 | End of movement, but bassoon holds a single note (to lead into the beginning of the next movement). |

FANNY MENDELSSOHN HENSEL (1805–1847)

Fanny was four years older than Felix, and they were very close throughout their lives. Fanny was a talented pianist and also a gifted composer, but her career as a composer illustrates the distance women still had to travel for equality of opportunity in the nineteenth century.

Her father strongly disapproved of the idea of her pursuing a career in music. Like many people of his time, he felt that a professional career was unsuitable for a woman. Amateur music-making was entirely acceptable—indeed, it was the province of a cultivated young woman—but making a living as a performer or a composer was out of the question. Even her brother Felix agreed with this view.

So Fanny led the more conventional life of a well-educated middle-class woman. At 24, she married Wilhelm Hensel, a painter and artist at the court in Berlin. Fanny had a son and ran the family household. She continued to play the piano, and after her mother's death she took over the organization of the famous Sunday concerts at her parents' home. She often played the piano at the concerts and directed a choral group that performed there. One day, at the age of 41, while rehearsing the chorus for a performance of a cantata composed by Felix, she had a stroke. She died that same evening.

Despite discouragement from her father and her brother, Fanny had composed a great deal. She wrote many songs, some cantatas and oratorios, chamber music, and small piano works, which, like Felix, she called *Songs Without Words*. (**See Listening Guide on page 262.**)

Some of her early songs were published in collections with pieces by her brother, though they carried Felix's name. After the death of her father, she did arrange for publication of one or two works under her own name.

Fanny Mendelssohn about 1830.

All in all, Fanny composed about 400 works, though most of them have never been published. They remain in manuscript in American and European libraries. In the last few years, with increasing focus on the contributions of women to the history of music, more and more of her works are being published and recorded. It is impossible to assess her true contributions or to compare her achievement with Felix's until her compositions have received the same attention as those of her brother.

**Fanny Mendelssohn Hensel
(1805–1847)**
Lied from *Songs without Words*, Op. 8,
No. 3

Date of composition: 1840?
Tempo: *Larghetto* ("Fairly slow")
Meter: $\frac{4}{4}$
Key: D Major
Duration: 3:05

Student CD Collection: 2, track 69
Complete CD Collection: 4, track 25

*T*he *Lieder ohne Wörte* (*Songs Without Words*) were not published until after Fanny's death. The third of this four-piece set, entitled *Lied* (*Song*), is also marked *Lenau*, the name of a German poet, suggesting that an actual poem may have inspired her to write this song. The tuneful, flowing phrases are indeed highly singable and memorable. The form is a typical one for a song: ABA. Throughout the piece, there is an accompaniment of gentle, repeated chords in the middle range, and slow, isolated bass notes. The atmosphere suggests a reflective inner dialogue.

A		
69 (25) **0:00**		Melody repeats a gently curving motive, followed by an ascending leap, as a kind of questioning idea. This is followed by a balanced descending motive. The mood is one of contemplation.
0:30		Questioning idea in low range, response in higher range.
B		
70 (26) **1:03**		Modulating, unstable B section—shorter, faster exchanges of questioning idea, answered by descending arpeggios.
1:20		Minor version of questioning idea in low range. Crescendo, then decrescendo, leads to:
A'		
71 (27) **1:39**		Clear return of the beginning, moving quickly to faster sequential phrases.
2:15		Closing section using questioning idea, including crescendo and leap to highest note of the piece. Ends with gentle decrescendo.

Music for the Middle Classes

The nineteenth century witnessed the rise, across Europe, of a large, primarily urban, middle class. Members of this class not only formed the largest audience for music, but also became music "consumers," buying sheet music of songs or chamber music for performances at home. An evening was not complete without a song recital or an amateur piano performance after dinner. Nineteenth-century novels, such as those of Eliot or Thackeray, are full of references to such performances, mostly by women. ¶ Composers, too, belonged mostly to the middle class. They were small entrepreneurs in their own right, negotiating fees with publishers and concert promoters. Many composers made a comfortable living from their music. They were also freer from the constraints of employers, such as the church or aristocratic courts, which often had dictated terms of style or content to composers in previous eras. The artistic freedom of composers in the nineteenth century was therefore the result of economic as well as aesthetic conditions.

FRYDERYK CHOPIN (1810–1849)

Portrait of Chopin at the age of 28 by the famous French painter Eugène Delacroix.

Eugène Delacroix (1798–1863). *Portrait of Frederic Chopin (1810–1860),* 1838. Oil on canvas, 45.5 × 38 cm. Louvre, Dpt. des Peintures, France. © Photograph by Erich Lessing. Erich Lessing/Art Resource, NY.

Chopin was the first of the great piano virtuosos in the Romantic era. Most composers before Chopin played the piano, and many of them actually composed at the keyboard, even if they weren't writing piano music. But after Beethoven, Chopin was the first important nineteenth-century composer to achieve fame as a performing pianist, and almost all his compositions are written for solo piano.

Chopin was born in 1810 to a French father and a Polish mother. His father taught French, and his mother taught piano at a school in Warsaw. Chopin began formal piano lessons at the age of seven, and his first composition was published the same year. At the age of eight, he gave his first public concert, and at the age of 15 he was sufficiently accomplished to play before Tsar Alexander I of Russia, who presented him with a diamond ring.

When Chopin was 19, he heard the great violinist Paganini play and was inspired to become a touring virtuoso himself. Most of his compositions at this time were designed for his own use. Chopin would improvise for hours at the keyboard and only occasionally write down what he had played. His music was often based on Polish dances such as the polonaise or the mazurka.

In 1830, Chopin completed two piano concertos, which he performed in public concerts, and toward the end of the year he left Poland, unaware that he would never see it again. From a distance he heard of the Warsaw uprising and the storming of Warsaw by the Russian army. From this time on, the Polish quality of his music deepened, and his compositions became more intense and passionate. A review stated: "Chopin has listened to the song of the Polish villager, he has made it his own and united the tunes of his native land in skillful composition and elegant execution."

In 1831, at the age of 21, Chopin settled in Paris, the center of European artistic activity. Soon he was caught up in the whirl of Parisian society, and his brilliant and poetic playing made him very much in demand in the city's fashionable salons. He had a wide circle of friends, including some of the great cultural figures of the time, such as Berlioz, Liszt, and the artist Delacroix.

In his late twenties, Chopin was introduced by Franz Liszt to Aurore Dudevant, a well-known novelist who published under the male pseudonym George Sand. They soon started living together, and the years they spent together were among the most productive of Chopin's life. He was often ill, however, displaying the first signs of the tuberculosis that would later kill him. George Sand looked after him devotedly, though Chopin was a difficult patient, and there is a rather unflattering portrait of him in one of her novels.

The relationship ended in 1847, after which Chopin's health rapidly deteriorated. He composed little but gave public recitals in London and Paris. It was reported that he was too weak to play louder than *mezzo-forte*. Chopin died in 1849 at the age of 39. At his request, Mozart's Requiem was played at his funeral.

CHOPIN'S MUSIC

The best way to think of Chopin's music is as poetry for the piano. In an English newspaper, he was once called a "musical Wordsworth." He wrote no program music, and almost all his works are for solo piano. The two piano concertos are really piano solos with rather sketchy orchestral accompaniment.

Chopin's style is entirely a personal one, as might be expected from one who improvised so freely. Most of his pieces are fairly short, and they fall into several categories. First there are the dances—polonaises, mazurkas, and waltzes. The **waltz** was fast becoming the favorite ballroom dance of the nineteenth century. Chopin managed to create enormous variety of mood with the basic format of this one dance. (**See Listening Guide on page 267.**) **Mazurkas** and **polonaises** are both Polish dances, and Chopin invested them with the spirit of Polish nationalism. Mazurkas are in triple meter with a stress on the second or third beat of the bar. Polonaises are stately and proud.

Chopin also wrote in free forms without dance rhythms: preludes, études, nocturnes, and impromptus. The **preludes** follow the pattern established by Bach in his *Well-Tempered Clavier*: There is one in each major and minor key. (**See Listening Guide below**.) **Étude** literally means "study piece," and each of Chopin's études concentrates on one facet of musicianship or piano technique. The **nocturnes** are moody, introspective pieces, and the **impromptus** capture the essence of improvisation ("impromptu" means "off the cuff").

The formal structure of these pieces is fundamentally simple, relying upon the ABA pattern common to aria or song form. However, Chopin usually varied the return of the opening section quite considerably, creating instead an ABA' structure.

In all these genres, Chopin wrote highly individual pieces, each one with an elegiac or rhapsodic quality, and each one expressive and pianistic—that is, perfectly suited to the special sound and capabilities of the piano. Chopin's works are carefully designed for the instrument of his day. They depend upon the new technology of the early nineteenth-century piano, which allowed the rapid repetition of single notes. The sound of the instrument was softer, less brilliant than it is today, and Chopin's melodies and chords exploited this quality. Often, the melodies are highly lyrical and dreamy, and the sustaining pedal allows widely spaced notes to blend together as chords in the left hand. Chopin's left-hand harmony is varied and expressive, and sometimes the main melody can appear in the left hand with the accompaniment above it in the right. There is often much delicate, rapid ornamentation in the right hand, with short free passages or runs or trills that add to the impression of improvisation. Finally, Chopin's written directions often call for a special expressive device called **rubato**. Literally, this Italian word means "robbed." Using this technique, the player keeps the tempo going in the accompaniment while the melody slows down slightly before catching up a moment later. Carefully applied, rubato can suggest the kind of expressive freedom that must have characterized the playing of Chopin himself.

> Compared with Berlioz, Chopin was a morbidly sentimental flea by the side of a roaring lion.
> —J. W. Davison

LISTENING GUIDE

Fryderyk Chopin (1810–1849)
Prelude in E minor, Op. 28, for Piano

Date of composition: 1836–39
Tempo: *Largo* ("Broad")
Meter: $\frac{2}{2}$
Duration: 2:27

Student CD Collection: 3, track 1
Complete CD Collection: 4, track 28

Chopin composed 24 preludes between 1836 and 1839. They follow the same idea as Bach's two sets of preludes and fugues, presenting all 24 major and minor keys of the scale system.

This particular piece features an ABA' structure. In the A section, an almost static melodic line is accompanied by steady chords that constantly descend. Notice the use of "neighbor" tones in the right-hand melody: the melody goes to an adjacent pitch and then

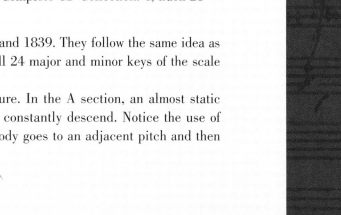

returns. The B section is marked by melodic arpeggios and has more rhythmic movement. The return of the A section is varied, and there is a wonderfully expressive silence before the end.

A SECTION		
1 (28) **0:00**	Opening melody. Focus is on descending left-hand accompanying chords. Upper neighbor tone is heard several times in right hand.
0:20	New note, melodic motion continues to descend.

B SECTION		
2 (29) **0:46**	More motion in melody and change in accompanying figures.
1:01	End of section, little flourish in melody, returning to:

A' SECTION		
3 (30) **1:07**	Variation of A.
1:22	More rhythmic activity in both hands.
1:25	Loudest section.
1:35	Feeling of stasis.
1:48	"Goal" reached.
2:01	Final chord?
2:04	Expressive silence.
2:09	Real final cadence (three chords).

Fryderyk Chopin (1810–1849)
Waltz in D-flat Major, Op. 64, No. 1,
for Piano Solo (*Minute* Waltz)

Date of composition: 1847
Tempo: *Tempo giusto* ("Exact tempo")
Meter: $\frac{3}{4}$
Duration: 1:47

Complete CD Collection: 4, track 31

his is the sixth of 14 waltzes Chopin wrote for the piano. Each one is based on the characteristic "ONE-two-three ONE-two-three" waltz rhythm, but each one is different.

The D♭-Major Waltz is known as the *Minute* Waltz because it is so short, though it actually takes about two minutes to play. Chopin marks it *Molto vivace—leggiero* ("Very fast and lively—light"). The opening theme, in which the melody seems to circle around itself, has been compared to a dog chasing its own tail. The overall scheme is ABCAB, with repetitions of melodic phrases within each section. This gives form to the delicate and swirling music.

A		
(31)	**0:00**	Around and around, right hand only.
	0:04	Waltz rhythm enters in left hand, right-hand melody in eighth notes.
B		
(32)	**0:12**	New melody, rapid key changes, continuing fast eighth notes.
	0:22	Repeat of B section.
C		
(33)	**0:33**	Lower melody in A♭, slower in effect (melody in half and quarter notes).
	0:48	Ornamented repeat; slow down.
	1:01	Trill, return to:
A		
	1:06	Around and around, opening music and melody.
B		
(34)	**1:19**	B section again; repeated.
	1:38	Very high descent to closing chords.

267

Clara and Robert Schumann.

Photograph of Clara & Robert Schumann, Museé d'Orsay, Paris. Reunion des Musées Nationaux / Art Resource, NY.

ROBERT SCHUMANN (1810–1856)

Of all the early Romantics, Robert Schumann was the most imbued with a literary imagination. He was born in 1810 in a small German town. His father was a bookseller, so the young boy had unlimited access to the popular Romantic writings of the day.

Schumann read voraciously and began to pour his feelings into poems and novels of his own, before finding a more suitable outlet in music. He played the piano well, though his exuberance outran his discipline.

"I was always a fiery performer," he said, "but my technique was full of holes."

After his father died, Schumann went to the University of Leipzig as a law student, but he had no interest in the subject. He drank heavily and spent his money on having a good time. While in Leipzig he met Friedrich Wieck, an eminent piano teacher, and Schumann took lessons from him.

A turning point in Schumann's career came (as it did for so many Romantic musicians) upon his first hearing the Italian virtuoso Paganini play a concert. He was entranced by the showmanship and hypnotic intensity of the great violinist and decided to become a piano virtuoso. He gave up his undisciplined life, enrolled as a full-time student of Friedrich Wieck, and took a room in Wieck's house in order to devote himself to constant practice. Unfortunately, Schumann took this to extremes, as he tended to do with everything. He overdid the practicing and permanently damaged his hand.

There was, however, a bright side to this episode: Schumann turned from performing to composing music, and he met Clara, Wieck's daughter, who was to become the love of his life. When Schumann moved in with the Wiecks, Clara was only 10 years old. But she was a brilliant pianist, and Wieck had the highest hopes for her. Clara could outplay Schumann, even though he was twice her age.

By the time Clara was 15, she was already a great pianist, astounding audiences at home and abroad. But her father suddenly noticed a cloud on the horizon: Clara and Robert were falling in love. This was not at all in the plans. His daughter had a career ahead of her and didn't need to get involved with a neurotic, obsessive student, 10 years her senior, who barely made a living. So he opposed the relationship with all the means at his disposal. He took Clara away on long tours, refused to let the couple meet, and even threatened to shoot Schumann if he tried to see Clara. During this long period, the two wrote secret letters to each other, and Schumann poured his feelings into his music. He described his F#-minor piano sonata as "a single cry of my heart for you," and Clara wrote to him that when she played, she played for him: "I had no other way of showing you what was in my heart."

In the end, the couple had no choice but to go to court to obtain the freedom to marry, and they were finally married in 1840, when Clara was 20 and Robert was 30. In that year, Schumann turned his attention to compositions for piano and voice. He was on fire with inspiration and composed no fewer than 140 songs, including three song cycles. His texts were taken from the great poets of Romanticism: Byron, Goethe, Heinrich Heine, and others. Schumann's wedding gift to Clara was a setting of *Du bist wie eine Blume*, Heine's poem comparing his love to the beauty of a flower.

If 1840 was Schumann's "year of song," 1841 was his "year of the symphony." The two settled happily into their home in Leipzig, with a music room each, and Clara wrote: "We enjoy a happiness such as I have never known before." Schumann had recently encountered a symphony by Schubert. He was overwhelmed, and Clara encouraged him to work on a symphony of his own. His Symphony No. 1 (*Spring* Symphony) was sketched out in four days. The first performance was given by the Leipzig Gewandhaus Orchestra with Felix Mendelssohn conducting.

Clara went on tour in 1842, and Schumann threw himself into a new passion: chamber music. He studied the string quartets of Haydn, Mozart, and Beethoven intensively. On Clara's return, he wrote three string quartets in five weeks, and by the end of the year had also completed a piano quintet, a piano quartet, and a piano trio.

About 1845, Schumann began to experience the fits of depression and illness that were to haunt him for the rest of his life. Composition now came only sporadically, and he had occasional nervous breakdowns.

In 1850, Schumann was appointed music director in Düsseldorf, but it soon became clear that his health and mental state were not sufficiently stable to allow him to perform his duties. Newspaper reviews became highly critical, singers refused to attend rehearsals, and

Schumann's assistant conductor had to take over concerts at the last minute. Schumann began to suffer from hallucinations.

On a rainy day in February 1854, Schumann left his house in his slippers and walked to the bridge over the Rhine. He stepped over the railing and threw himself into the water. He was pulled out by some fishermen and carried home. A few days later, he was committed to a mental institution.

With eight children, Clara could not long maintain her household alone. She began touring again, but in 1856 she was summoned back urgently by the doctors. "I had to go to him," she wrote in her diary. "I saw him between 6 and 7 in the evening. He smiled and with great effort put his arms around me. I shall never forget it. All the treasures in the world could not equal this embrace." Two days later Schumann died. He was 46.

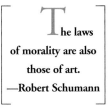

The laws of morality are also those of art.
—Robert Schumann

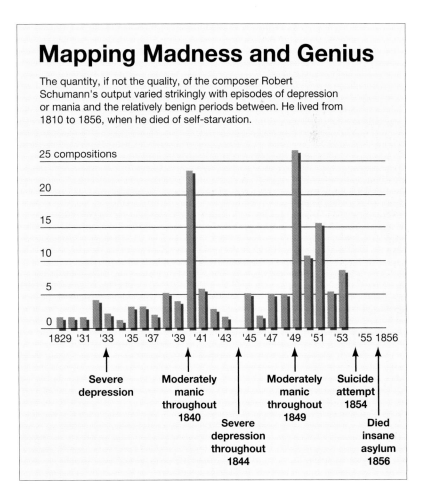

Mapping Madness and Genius

The quantity, if not the quality, of the composer Robert Schumann's output varied strikingly with episodes of depression or mania and the relatively benign periods between. He lived from 1810 to 1856, when he died of self-starvation.

25 compositions

Severe depression

Moderately manic throughout 1840

Severe depression throughout 1844

Moderately manic throughout 1849

Suicide attempt 1854

Died insane asylum 1856

SCHUMANN'S MUSIC

Schumann was a literary Romantic. Much of his music is inspired by literary references, and even when the inspiration is not literary, there is often some other programmatic reference to people or ideas.

His writing for piano, his own instrument, is masterly. The pieces for solo piano range from short works deliberately designed for children to **character pieces** (small programmatic movements) to large sonatas. Many of the character pieces are grouped together into cycles. One such cycle, *Carnaval*, contains musical portraits of Schumann himself, some of his friends, Chopin, Paganini, and the 15-year-old Clara Wieck. The piano parts for his songs are also very beautiful, playing an equal role with that of the voice. Many of the songs are also grouped into cycles, the most famous being *Dichterliebe* (*A Poet's Love*) and *Frauen-Liebe und Leben* (*Women's Lives and Loves*).

> *S*chumann is *the* composer of childhood.
> —Igor Stravinsky

Schumann wrote only one piano concerto. It is the complete opposite of the typical Romantic concerto. Rather than flashy and brilliant, it is restrained and tender—perhaps because it was written for his beloved Clara to play.

Two of Schumann's four symphonies have programmatic titles. The First Symphony is called the *Spring* Symphony, and the Third Symphony is called the *Rhenish* Symphony. (Rhenish means "on the Rhine.") He composed the latter immediately after taking up his appointment in the city of Düsseldorf, on the Rhine River. Like Berlioz's *Symphonie fantastique*, it has five instead of the normal four movements.

Schumann's chamber music is more Classical in form. There are fewer apparent programmatic references, but the music flows with intensity and charm. As with song and symphony, Schumann took hold of Classical genres and invested them with his own particular brand of Romantic imagination.

LISTENING GUIDE

Robert Schumann (1810–1856)
Träumerei (Dreaming), from
Kinderszenen, Op. 15, for Piano

Date of composition: 1838
Meter: $\frac{3}{4}$
Key: F Major
Duration: 3:00

Student CD Collection: 3, track 4
Complete CD Collection: 4, track 35

This selection comes from Schumann's *Kinderszenen* (*Scenes from Childhood*). It is a simple accompanied melody, in an ABA' structure. The beautiful melody features a fairly wide range, and its ascending contour characterizes all three brief sections. The slow tempo and the reiteration of the theme create a wonderfully "dreamy" atmosphere.

4 (35)   **0:00**   Melody is presented: first phrase:

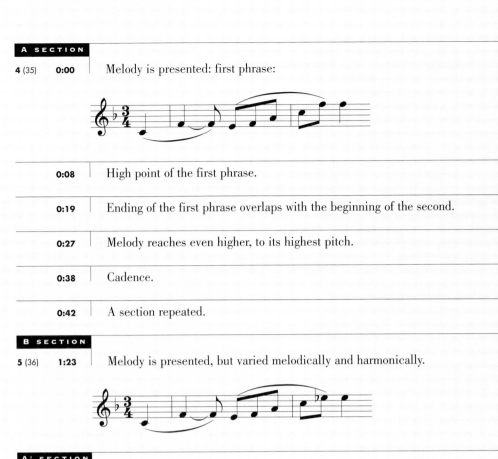

0:08   High point of the first phrase.

0:19   Ending of the first phrase overlaps with the beginning of the second.

0:27   Melody reaches even higher, to its highest pitch.

0:38   Cadence.

0:42   A section repeated.

B SECTION

5 (36)   **1:23**   Melody is presented, but varied melodically and harmonically.

A' SECTION

6 (37)   **2:03**   Melody is restated.

2:31   Large, rolled chord under the highest pitch of melody ("signal" that the piece will end soon).

2:45   Ending cadence.

CLARA SCHUMANN (1819–1896)

The first part of Clara Schumann's life, from the age of 10 to the age of 36, was closely bound up with that of Robert Schumann and has already been partly described. There is no doubt that she both loved and admired her husband. He in turn was deeply in love with her and depended heavily on her for emotional support. Robert encouraged her performing career, but in their relationship his composing certainly took precedence over hers.

Her musical career was nonetheless a remarkable one. She benefited from her father's close attention to her musical education. At the age of nine, she first per-

formed in public; two years later, she gave her first complete solo recital.

By the time she married, at the age of 20, Clara Schumann had an international reputation as a concert pianist. She had received many honors and was admired by Goethe, Mendelssohn, Paganini, and Chopin. Clara was renowned for playing everything from memory and for her poetic touch and seriousness of intent. She had also composed a considerable number of works by this time, and several had been published.

During her married life, Clara continued to perform and compose, although we must remember that in 14 years she had eight children. She submitted all her compositions to her husband for his criticism, and

Clara Schumann in her later years.

> The only woman in Germany who can play my music.
> —Chopin, speaking of Clara Schumann

> To me, Schumann's memory is holy.
> —Johannes Brahms

Clara Schumann

Clara Schumann's life reflects the changing attitudes toward women in nineteenth-century society. She made a successful career as a professional pianist, though she was one of only very few women to do so. She managed this despite running a household and raising a large number of children. Her own ability to compose was clearly compromised by her marriage to one of the foremost composers of the age as well as by society's views, which were changing only slowly. She wrote in her diary: "I once thought that I possessed creative talent, but now I have given up this idea. A woman must not desire to compose. Not one has been able to do it, so why should I?" ✦ That was over a hundred years ago. It takes a long time for attitudes to change.

she clearly regarded him as the greater talent. By the time of his death, she had published 20 or 30 compositions of her own; several others remained unpublished. Her works include character pieces for piano, songs, some chamber music, and a piano concerto, which was completed when she was 15 years old. Perhaps her best-known work is her Piano Trio in G minor, Op. 17, written in 1846. Mendelssohn regarded the piece highly, and it was widely performed in the nineteenth century. (**See Listening Guide on page 273.**)

After Robert Schumann's death, Clara continued to perform and to teach, though she wrote no more music. She maintained a heavy schedule, doubtless to support her large family. Clara continued to appear in public into her seventies and promoted her husband's music by performing it as much as possible. She also helped prepare a complete edition of his works for publication.

Throughout this latter half of her life, Clara was the friend and confidante of Johannes Brahms, a composer 14 years her junior. Brahms had been a protégé of Schumann's, and the three musicians had been close. Brahms was especially supportive during the last terrible years of Schumann's illness. Brahms and Clara remained good friends. He often sent her drafts of his work for her en-

couragement and criticism. Brahms, however, remained a bachelor, and Clara never remarried.

Clara Wieck Schumann was an important figure in the history of nineteenth-century music. The daughter of a famous teacher, she became the wife of one remarkable composer and the lifelong friend of another. She was the inspiration for some of the greatest music of the century. And in addition to all this, she had a brilliant career as a pianist and piano teacher and was herself a gifted composer.

Clara Schumann died on May 20, 1896, at the age of 77, while her grandson played Robert Schumann's music at the piano.

Clara Schumann (1819–1896)
Third Movement from Trio in G minor
for Piano, Violin, and Cello

Date of composition: 1846
Tempo: *Andante* ("Quite slow")
Meter: 6/8
Key of movement: G Major
Duration: 5:19

Complete CD Collection: 4, track 38

Clara Schumann's Trio in G minor dates from shortly after the birth of her fourth child. Published in 1847, the four-movement work is a Romantic reflection of the Classic heritage in its structure. The expansive first and fourth movements employ sonata form, and the middle two movements reverse the ordering of the conventional four-movement arrangement: The scherzo is the second movement, and the thoughtful, melancholy, slow movement is the third.

This slow movement, marked *Andante*, is in ABA' song form. It reflects the Romantic period's fascination with warm, lyrical melodic lines and the expression of heightened contrasts in emotion.

As we have come to expect with the various ABA forms, the sections show contrast, and the modified A section returns enriched by the experience of the B material.

A		
(38)	0:00	The opening melody is slow, songlike, and pensive, with regular phrase-lengths. But tension and a subtle restless quality are created by the pattern of using dissonances on strong beats, resolving on weak beats. Also, while the steady accompaniment keeps up the regular 1-2-3 grouping, the melody gently pushes against this pattern with its grouping by twos.

| 0:37 | The melody is taken up by the violin, with the piano energizing the accompaniment with sixteenth notes while the cello plays pizzicato on the weak third beats, adding to the rhythmically unsettled quality. |

| 1:12 | Finally, the cello takes the melody while the violin plays a rich harmony. The short subphrases here rise to a dramatic high point, while the piano accompaniment still emphasizes the third beat. |

B

più animato ("more animated")

| 1:48 | This section, in E minor, is darker, agitated, and more intense: the melody uses faster note values with jerky rhythm. The strings play staccato, with brusque chords in the piano. |

Più animato

| 2:01 | The melody moves to the cello. |

| 2:13 | A brief contrasting phrase in the violin, smoother, and in the major. |

| 2:29 | Return to the agitated figure from the beginning of the B section; then the piano returns to the minor key. |

| 2:50 | Assertive statement of agitated melody in piano with heavy chords in the cello. |

| 3:00 | The agitation subsides as the rhythmic values slow and the material becomes smoother. |

A'

| (39) 3:18 | The cello begins with the original melody, accompanied by rocking piano arpeggios. Back to G Major. |

| 3:50 | Without repetition, the first phrase moves directly into what corresponds to the last phrase of the original A section, with the roles of the instruments now reversed; the violin has the melody in its rich lower register. |

CODA

| 4:19 | New material gently transforms the agitated fast rhythmic values of the B section; conclusion with peaceful arpeggios and harplike, ascending rolled chords. |

PART TWO: MID-ROMANTICISM

By the middle of the century, the main aspects of musical Romanticism had become established: Music should represent human emotions to the utmost, and it must tell a story or express an idea that is profound, resonant, or uplifting. A favorite term of the Romantics was "sublime," which means grand, beyond normal experience, awe-inspiring.

During the mid-Romantic period, from the 1850s to the 1870s, the most important musical genres were solo piano works, symphonic program music, and opera. The most important composers were Franz Liszt, Giuseppe Verdi, Richard Wagner, and Pyotr Ilyich Tchaikovsky.

WORKS FOR SOLO PIANO

Solo piano music appealed to the Romantics for its focus on the individual. Audiences could concentrate on both the expression of individual emotions and the technical prowess of a great performer. This was the period during which the idea of the performer-hero first took hold, an idea that is still current today (witness our fascination with stars of both the rock and the classical worlds). The great piano performer of the mid-Romantic period was Liszt.

SYMPHONIC PROGRAM MUSIC

Symphonic program music followed two paths during the 1850s and 1860s. The first was that of the programmatic symphony. This path had been made secure by the earlier success of Berlioz's *Symphonie fantastique*. In several movements, usually three to five, the programmatic symphony is a full-length symphony, with each movement depicting an episode in the narrative.

The second path was that of the symphonic poem, the successor to such works as Mendelssohn's *Hebrides* Overture. The symphonic poem, as we have said, is a single-movement self-contained work, also for orchestra and also programmatic. Liszt was the greatest composer of symphonic poems and programmatic symphonies in the mid-Romantic era, though several other composers followed his lead in later decades.

OPERA

During the nineteenth century, there were three national schools of opera: the French, the Italian, and the German. All three had roots going back at least 150 years, and all three had distinct national identities by the time of the mid-Romantic period.

French opera had two very different genres, each with its own style and even its own opera house. The first was **grand opera**, which incorporated lofty subject matter and spectacular staging, including ballet, choruses, and crowd scenes. The second was **opéra comique** (comic opera), with a much smaller cast and orchestra, simpler musical style, and more down-to-earth plots with humorous or romantic (love) interest. A technical distinction between grand opera and comic opera was that in grand opera the dialogue was set in accompanied musical recitative, whereas in comic opera the dialogue was spoken.

By the 1850s and 1860s a new, highly popular operatic genre had evolved in France, one that stood between grand opera and comic opera. It was known as **lyric opera**. Lyric opera was melodious, as its name implies; its primary subject matter was tragic love; and its proportions lay somewhere between the spectacular and the skimpy. The greatest lyric opera is *Carmen*, written by Georges Bizet (1838–1875). *Carmen* represented a turning point in the history of opera. With its realistic plot, down-to-earth characters, and turbulent passion, it set the stage for a new, more pointed approach to opera (known as **verismo**, or "realism") toward the end of the nineteenth century.

> All nineteenth-century music wishes it were opera.
> —Alvah Felix

The Romantic Orchestra

We have seen how Beethoven expanded the Classic orchestra to include more, and more unusual, instruments, including piccolo, trombones, bass drum and other percussion. Beethoven's influence was felt by those who followed. Just three years after Beethoven's death, Berlioz, in his *Symphonie fantastique,* writes for all the usual instruments, plus many others, as well as piccolo, English horn (a kind of tenor oboe), extra bassoons, extra horns, cornets (shorter, military-style trumpets), trombones, bass drum, snare drum, cymbals, bells, and two harps. And by the end of the century, Mahler was calling for an orchestra of one hundred and twenty players, with *eight* horns, *four* each of all the woodwinds, as well as piccolo, English horn, and bass clarinet, *four* trombones, a bass tuba, *six* timpani, and *twelve* other percussion instruments. Throughout the nineteenth century, the core of the orchestra remained the string section, but more and more players were featured even there, with thirty or forty violinists and correspondingly large numbers of violists, cellists, and bassists. This larger orchestra perfectly suits the style of Romantic music, with its long flowing melodies, rich harmonies, and focus on storytelling and drama. All these instruments can do many things other than simply make a louder sound. When all the instruments are playing, of course, the sound is huge, but the Romantic orchestra also gave composers the opportunity to use a wide array of individual instruments to create special effects and paint pictures with an almost limitless variety of colors.

A perfect example of the Romantic orchestra is Smetana's *The Moldau.* You can watch a live performance of this work in Segment 3 of your *Inside the Orchestra* CD-ROM.

Italian opera was dominated by the achievements of one man: Giuseppe Verdi. He was preceded, however, by three important Italian operatic composers: Rossini, Donizetti, and Bellini. Rossini's gifts were best suited to comic operas, and the most famous of these is his *The Barber of Seville* (1816). Donizetti wrote both comic and serious operas, whereas Bellini composed only serious operas. Bellini's best-known opera is *Norma* (1831).

The central figure in **German opera** was Wagner, who created some of the most significant masterpieces of the entire nineteenth century, and whose powerful personality made him a major artistic figure of his time. We shall study Wagner's contributions, both positive and negative, to Romantic culture. Wagner was influenced by the operas of Carl Maria von Weber (1786–1826), especially *Der Freischütz* (*The Magic Marksman*, 1821), with its supernatural and heroic subject matter and heavy emphasis on the role of the orchestra.

NATIONALISM

The existence of distinct national styles in Romantic opera was one facet of an important movement in nineteenth-century music. This movement was known as **nationalism**, and it coincided with important political events in Europe.

After the Napoleonic Wars ended in 1814, European countries began to assert their independence and to stress national identity. Italy, which had previously been organized into several city-states, republics, and provinces, was finally unified under a constitutional monarchy in 1870. (See map on page 278.) A single German empire was created out of a collection of separate states in 1871. There were rebellions of the Polish people against the ruling Russians, and of the Czechs against their Austrian rulers. Norway gained independence from Sweden, and Finland struggled for independence from Russia. In Russia itself, a sense of national identity was fostered by writers such as Dostoevski and Tolstoi. In America, the Civil War was fought partly to preserve a single national identity.

The nationalist movement was reflected in the arts. In each country, the local language was fostered, books of national poetry were published, and intellectuals turned with increasing interest to the folk tales, dances, and songs of their native heritage. Operas were based on national legend or history and were written in the native language. Folk tunes appeared in symphonic music, and the rhythms of folk dances were used in chamber works. Some composers became famous national symbols. Verdi, who often wrote barely disguised political protests into his operas, was regarded as a national hero by his countrymen.

FRANZ LISZT (1811–1886)

Franz Liszt was born in 1811 in Hungary. His father was an administrator and court musician at the Esterházy palace, where Haydn had spent most of his career. Liszt first learned to play the piano with his father. When the family moved to Vienna, he studied composition with the eminent court composer Salieri, who had previously taught Schubert and Beethoven. At the age of 11, Liszt gave his first concert, and a year later he played in public again. The great Beethoven was in the audience and, after the concert, kissed the young boy on the forehead.

When Liszt was 13, the family moved to Paris, and he began to tour Europe as a piano virtuoso. His incredible technique amazed audiences everywhere, and by his late teens he had become famous as a showman. His striking looks, flamboyant manner, and reputation as a womanizer did not hurt his career a bit.

At the age of 20, he heard the great violinist Paganini for the first time. Liszt was enormously impressed and vowed to attain the same level of mastery on his own instrument. This he did, and he was soon known as the "Paganini of the piano." Liszt's fingers were unusually long and thin, and he could easily play consecutive tenths (a very wide stretch of an octave plus two notes). He soon became the greatest pianist of

A smasher of pianos.
—Clara Schumann on Liszt

He has an excessively tall and thin figure and a pale face with sea-green eyes that shine with quick flashes like waves in flame . . . He appears uneasy and distracted, like a ghost about to return to the underworld.
—Marie d'Agoult on Liszt

Unification of Italy, 1859–1870

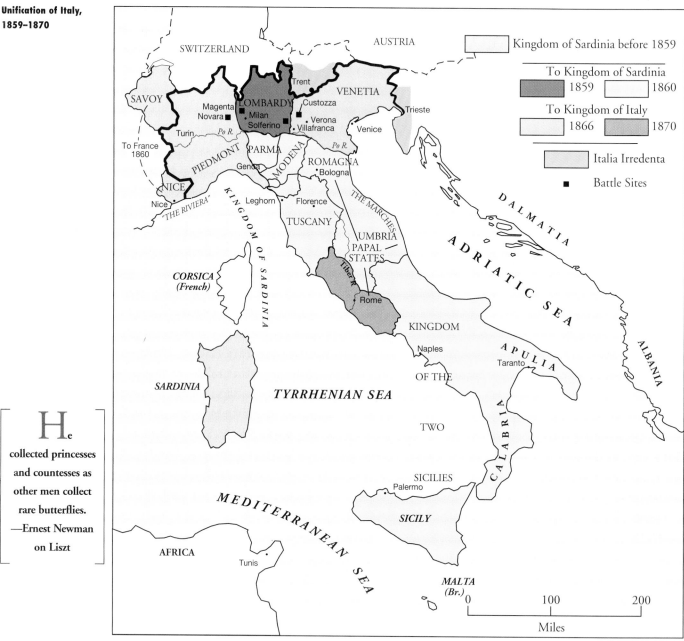

Kingdom of Sardinia before 1859

To Kingdom of Sardinia
1859 1860

To Kingdom of Italy
1866 1870

Italia Irredenta

■ Battle Sites

> H_e collected princesses and countesses as other men collect rare butterflies.
>
> —Ernest Newman on Liszt

his age and may well have been the greatest pianist of any age.

Over the next few years Liszt developed great friendships with Berlioz and Chopin. He also began living with the Countess Marie d'Agoult, a novelist who published under the name Daniel Stern. She left her husband to live with Liszt, and together they had three children (one of whom, Cosima, later left *her* husband to live with Wagner). They traveled frequently around Europe, and he continued to perform to ever more enthusiastic crowds and to compose prolifically.

In 1842, Liszt settled in Weimar, Germany, where he had been appointed music director and could devote

A typically Romantic painting of Liszt at the piano. Those listening (from left to right) are the great figures of nineteenth-century music and literature: the poet Alfred de Musset, authors Victor Hugo and George Sand, fabled violinist Paganini and composer Rossini, and (seated) author Marie d'Agoult, Liszt's common-law wife. The entire scene is dominated by the almost surreal figure of Ludwig van Beethoven.

performer who devoted himself to the music of others, a composer whose works range from the flashy and brilliant to the quietly searching.

LISZT'S MUSIC

Together with Wagner, Liszt is regarded as one of the most avant-garde composers of the mid-Romantic era. He experimented with unusual harmonies and chords, and in some cases he seemed to ignore the rules of traditional harmony altogether.

himself to conducting and composing. After his relationship with the Countess ended in 1844, Liszt began an affair with a Russian princess. Between 1848 and 1858, with her encouragement, he completed most of the compositions upon which his fame as a composer now rests. The most important of these are 12 symphonic poems and two programmatic symphonies, as well as a large number of works for solo piano.

In 1861, Liszt suddenly resigned from his position at Weimar and went to Rome to begin religious studies. After four years he became a member of the church hierarchy and was officially known as an *abbé*. He now undertook several religious compositions, writing psalm settings, Masses, and an oratorio.

Toward the end of his life, Liszt turned again to compositions for solo piano and completed some remarkable pieces that anticipate the shifting harmonies and Impressionism of the early twentieth century. Liszt died in 1886 while visiting the new opera house at Bayreuth for some performances of Wagner's operas.

With his extraordinary personality, Liszt stood at the center of Romanticism. He was a complex of contradictions: a diabolical figure who sought spiritual solace in the Church, a flamboyant and narcissistic

Liszt's piano music is quite varied. Much of it is extremely difficult to play. Schumann once said that there were only "ten or twelve people in the world" who had the technical ability to play Liszt's music. Berlioz said that the only person who could play it was Liszt himself. Runs and rippling octaves surround the melody; cascades of notes tumble from top to bottom of the keyboard; often it sounds as though there must be more than one person playing. Liszt's *Transcendental Études* contain some of the most difficult piano music ever written. We shall hear one of these studies in a moment. (**See Listening Guide on page 281.**)

One of Liszt's masterpieces is the superb Piano Sonata in B minor, written in one long movement. It has three themes, which are stated at the outset and reappear in different forms throughout the piece. This technique is known as **thematic transformation**. Liszt used it in many of his other compositions.

A number of Liszt's piano pieces are in dance forms, including waltzes, mazurkas, polonaises, and Hungarian dances. Liszt's contribution to the beginning of nationalism in music was a large body of Hungarian music, including the well-known *Hungarian Rhapsodies*.

Finally, a great proportion of Liszt's piano music is made up of transcriptions. A transcription is the "translation" of a piece of music from one medium to another. Liszt made hundreds of transcriptions of orchestral and operatic works, rewriting them for the piano. At a time when recording devices had not yet been invented, this practice made available the music of Bach, Beethoven, Berlioz, Wagner, and other composers to people in their own homes.

Liszt's orchestral music dates mostly from the 1840s and 1850s, when he was a conductor in Weimar. During that time, he wrote 12 symphonic poems and two symphonies. The best known of the symphonic poems are *Les Préludes* and *Hamlet*. *Hamlet*, a reflection upon Shakespeare's play, is one of the shortest of Liszt's symphonic poems but also one of the greatest. (**See Listening Guide on page 283.**)

Liszt's two symphonies are perfect examples of the power of the programmatic ideal in mid-Romantic music. His *Faust* Symphony represents the three main characters in Goethe's famous play. And Liszt's *Dante* Symphony is in three movements, corresponding to the three main parts of Dante's *Divine Comedy*.

Liszt influenced several generations of pianists and composers. His phenomenal technique and demanding piano writing expanded the boundaries of what was considered possible on the piano. His symphonic poems inspired other composers to write works in the same form. His Hungarian music contributed to the nationalistic movement. And his novel approach to harmony foreshadowed the great harmonic revolution of the twentieth century.

In 1836 an English pianist heard Liszt play in Paris and wrote: "Such marvels of skill and power I could never have imagined. In comparison with Liszt, all other pianists are children. Chopin carries you into a dream world, in which you would like to dwell for ever; Liszt is all sunshine and dazzling splendor, overcoming his listeners with a power that no one can withstand."

Critical Views of Liszt

During the twentieth century, the reputation of Liszt's music suffered a serious decline. The popularity of certain composers is partly a matter of fashion, and Liszt's reputation as a showman and his extroverted musical style did not fit with the cool rational climate of Modernism. Recently, however, musicians and audiences have begun to appreciate the seriousness behind the showmanship. Here are two views on Liszt's music, one from a nineteenth-century musical journal, the other by the celebrated pianist Alfred Brendel. ¶ "Composition indeed! Decomposition is the proper word for such hateful fungi, which choke up and poison the fertile plains of harmony, threatening the world with drought."— *Musical World*, 1855 ¶ "Liszt is the most underrated composer of the nineteenth century."—Alfred Brendel, 1991

Franz Liszt (1811–1886)
***Transcendental Étude* No. 10 in F minor**

Date of composition: 1839
Tempo: *Allegro agitato molto*
   ("Fast and very agitated")
Meter: $\frac{2}{4}$
Duration: 4:06

Student CD Collection: 3, track 7
Complete CD Collection: 4, track 40

precipitato

from Liszt *Transcendental Étude No. 10*

The *Transcendental Études* were first composed in 1826, when Liszt was 15 years old. But, as with much of Liszt's music, the works were revised and reissued later—in this case, 1839. Though the music was extremely difficult to perform in its earlier version, Liszt's revisions made it even more demanding. Number 10 in particular was described as being "ten times more difficult than before." Contemporaries of Liszt were amazed by this music and by Liszt's own performances of it. Berlioz said, "No one else in the world could approach being able to perform music of this kind."

In this work, Liszt explores every possibility of demanding piano technique, including doubled octave passages, rapid skips, intricate bass tracery, fast runs, massive chords, and widely separated hands. It also has some unusual harmonies and a great sense of *surging*, with occasional slightly quieter passages serving only to heighten the intensity of the remainder. The power and strength of the music are astounding. The seeming randomness and uncontrollable energy are actually carefully organized by sectionalization and repetition.

7 (40)	**0:00**	Starts quietly with fast descending runs.
	0:07	Crescendo, then quiet.
	0:14	Loud and wild.
	0:23	Descending runs again.
8 (41)	**0:26**	Surging melody in octaves in right hand, hectic passagework in left hand.
	0:53	Agitated alternation of short phrases.
	1:07	Heavy chordal melody in bass, fireworks in right hand.
	1:18	Suddenly quiet, surging melody again, crescendo.
9 (42)	**1:32**	Descending runs again.
	1:39	Slow down, quieter.
	1:41	Crescendo and speed up.
10 (43)	**1:51**	Surging melody again, crescendo.
	2:03	Moment of tenderness.
	2:18	Huge crescendo, massive climax.
	2:58	Alternating short phrases again.
	3:12	Heavy bass chords again.
	3:29	Contrary motion; stop.
	3:33	Coda. Speed up; alternation of very high and very low.
	3:55	Massive ending chords.

Franz Liszt (1811–1886)
Symphonic Poem, *Hamlet*

Date of composition: 1858; revised
    1876
Orchestration: 2 flutes, 2 oboes,
    2 clarinets, 2 bassoons, 4 horns,
    2 trumpets, 3 trombones, tuba,
    timpani, strings
Meter: $\frac{6}{4}$ $\left(\frac{3}{2}\right)$
Key: B minor
Duration: 13:55

Complete CD Collection: 4, track 44

This work, the last of Liszt's symphonic poems, testifies to the fascination the plays of Shakespeare continued to exert on nineteenth-century composers. Liszt originally wrote this piece in 1858 as a prelude to a performance of the play, but he revised it nearly 20 years later as an independent concert work.

The connection to Shakespeare's *Hamlet* is loose and evocative rather than very specific. The introduction, marked "Very slow and gloomy," evokes the melancholy mood of its hero. The central slow sections ("Sweet and expressive") are meant to suggest the presence of Ophelia, the daughter of the king's adviser, who is in love with Hamlet. This is interrupted by a fast reminiscence of many of the "Hamlet themes," presumably representing Hamlet's rejection of Ophelia ("Get thee to a nunnery!"). At the end, the gloomy mood returns, and a funeral march is heard. Since there are so many deaths at the end of Shakespeare's play, this music could refer to several people. Perhaps the most likely is Hamlet himself, who is killed in a duel with Ophelia's brother and given a military funeral.

Throughout the work, there is a constant, moody alternation between slow and fast passages. Tension is imparted by means of frequent low string tremolos and by constant changes of dynamics and tempo. The structure is deliberately unfocused, combining features of a loose overall ABA form with elements of sonata form (exposition, harmonic development, partial recapitulation).

MOLTO LENTO E LUGUBRE

["Very slow and gloomy"]

(44)	0:00	Muted horns, wind chords, timpani strokes, very quiet.
	0:39	A little faster, rising strings; winds and brass join in, louder.
	1:25	Winds and string chords alternate, changing harmonies.

	1:43	Loud, agitated, speeding up, sudden pauses.
	2:10	Low strings, marchlike rhythm, timpani.
	2:37	String tremolos, quiet; trombones, crescendo, timpani; quiet again.

ALLEGRO APASSIONATO ED AGITATO ASSAI

["Passionate, fast, and quite agitated"]

(45)	3:14	Rising theme on strings, crescendo; whole orchestra, faster, marchlike rhythm.
	3:30	Climax, descent in whole orchestra.
	3:56	Brass fanfares; striding forceful theme, based on march rhythm.
	4:32	Winds join in, then whole orchestra, very loud.
	5:00	Sudden pause.

DOLCE ED ESPRESSIVO

["Sweet and expressive"; (Liszt also writes in the score: "Peaceful, sounding like a passing shadow, and suggesting Ophelia")]

(46)	5:03	Sudden change of mood: slow, gentle, quiet woodwinds, then solo violin.
	6:03	Fast interruption of quiet section, with fragments of much of the previous "Hamlet music:" forceful theme, loud; rising theme; alternating chords; then bassoons, quietly.
	6:35	Return to slow, gentle, "Ophelia music:" winds, solo violin.

| (47) | 7:42 | Sudden key change to E♭! Tense. Rising strings, tremolos, punctuated by short chords; fanfares on trombones mixed with march theme; very loud short chords, dynamic contrasts. |

MOLTO LENTO E LUGUBRE

["Very slow and gloomy"]

| (48) | 9:50 | Return to gloomy music of introduction with muted horns and woodwinds. |

MODERATO—FUNEBRE

["Moderate tempo—funereal"]

(49)	10:26	Slow, sad, funeral march.
	11:20	Long, smooth, new theme on low strings, ending with slow chromatic descent.
	12:02	Funeral march returns.
	12:09	Tremolos, crescendos to loud climax; trombones.
	12:43	Very slow, low strings; timpani.
	13:29	Crescendo.
	13:34	Dissonant chord, winds.
	13:44	Two final pizzicato chords on strings and timpani, very quiet.

VERDI AND WAGNER

Both Giuseppe Verdi and Richard Wagner were born in 1813. Each transformed the operatic traditions he had received from the past to create new forms, and each became the musical symbol of his own country: Verdi for Italy, Wagner for Germany. In 1842 each composer had his first success. Wagner completed his first major masterpiece in 1850, Verdi in 1851. From then on, both composers turned out one great score after another, working fruitfully into old age. Wagner's last work was written when he was nearly 70, Verdi's as he approached 80. Together they made opera the central genre of mid-Romanticism.

GIUSEPPE VERDI (1813–1901)

In Italy today, Verdi symbolizes opera. His name inspires passionate declarations of affection, and many Italian shopkeepers, vineyard workers, professors, and politicians can sing Verdi arias by heart.

This adulation began when Verdi was still a relatively young man. He was born in a small village in northern Italy, where his father ran an inn. As a boy, he played the organ for services at the village church and conducted the town band in the small nearby town of Busseto. One of the wealthy merchants of Busseto took him into his own home and later sent him to Milan to study music.

Milan was the center of Italian opera and the home of the famous opera house called La Scala. Verdi resolved to become an opera composer. First he went back to Busseto and married his patron's daughter. He was 23, his new wife 16. Filled with hope, he returned to Milan and threw himself into composition. But tragedy struck. Within two years, the couple's two babies died; then Verdi's young wife, the girl he had romped with in the hills and fields of the Italian countryside, also died.

Verdi was overcome by depression and decided to compose no more. One night, however, the concert manager at La Scala made him take home a new libretto (opera text) called *Nabucco* (*Nebuchadnezzar*). According to Verdi's own account, the libretto first fell open on the chorus of the Jewish prisoners who mourn their native land by the waters of Babylon. "I was much moved," he said, "because the verses were almost a paraphrase from the Bible, the reading of which had always delighted me." He spent the whole night reading and rereading the libretto, and by the next day he was already working on his new opera. *Nabucco* was produced at La Scala in 1842 and was a great success. It brought Verdi fame throughout Italy, and by the end of the decade his name was known around the world.

Verdi followed *Nabucco* with a string of wonderful operas. During the next 11 years, he wrote 15 operas, including *Rigoletto* (1851), *Il trovatore* (1853), and *La traviata* (1853). By now Verdi was a wealthy man. He bought a country estate near his home town and lived the life of a country gentleman. He married his second

> **O**ur music differs from German music. Their symphonies can live in halls, their chamber music in the home. Our music resides principally in the opera house.
> —Giuseppe Verdi

Giuseppe Verdi.

wife, a singer who had starred in his early operas, and their deep and devoted relationship lasted for nearly half a century.

Verdi's pace of composition relaxed, but the depth and richness of his music only increased. He became more and more involved in the details of the libretto and the staging of his works. In the 1860s and 1870s he wrote three fine operas, including the great *Aida* (1871), which was commissioned to celebrate the opening of the Suez Canal.

Although he several times spoke of retirement, Verdi was persuaded in his seventies to tackle two Shakespearean projects. The results of this final surge of creativity were two of his greatest masterpieces: the tragedy *Otello* (1887) and the comedy *Falstaff* (1893). **(See Listening Guide on page 288.)**

During his life, Verdi became a national symbol. The chorus of Jewish prisoners in *Nabucco* lamenting the loss of their homeland was heard as a cry of the Italian people against their Austrian rulers. In other operas, a woman yearning for rescue or references to a free Italy were greeted with frenzy by audiences and provoked political demonstrations. Even Verdi's name became a rallying cry for the Italian nationalist movement. After independence in 1870, Verdi was named an honorary member of the new parliament. And when he died, at the age of 88, Italy declared a national day of mourning.

VERDI'S MUSIC

Verdi wrote in genres other than opera. There are several choral works, including a magnificent requiem. He also wrote several songs and a fine string quartet. But it is on his remarkable operas that his reputation rests. During his long life, he completed 28 full-length operas, among which are some of the best-loved operas in the world.

What is the secret of Verdi's success? First and foremost, the secret lies in his melodies. His gift for vocal writing has never been exceeded, and singers and listeners alike love his soaring vocal lines. The second special element is rhythm. Verdi specialized in writing stirring rhythms that can set the heart pounding. But finally, the true essence of a Verdi opera is in the human drama. Verdi constantly sought out dramatic situations, full of strong emotional resonance, violent contrasts, and quick action. He loved to explore the human emotional reaction to exciting or terrifying events.

As Verdi continued to compose, from the 1840s to the 1880s, his style became more fluid. In place of the set aria-and-recitative style of earlier Italian opera, Verdi tended more and more to create a continuing musical flow in which the drama could unfold naturally. What held this unfolding in place was the orchestra.

> I want subjects that are novel, big, beautiful, varied, and bold—as bold as can be.
> —Giuseppe Verdi

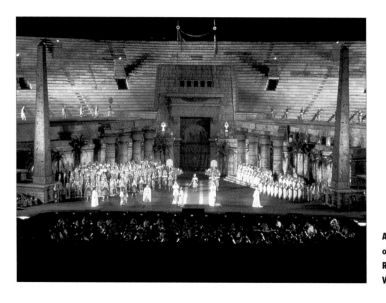

A spectacular production of Verdi's *Aida* in the Roman amphitheatre at Verona.

Throughout a story, Verdi's orchestra binds the voices together in duets, trios, and ensembles, keeps the action moving, and supplies rich and colorful harmonies to underpin moments of climax or poignancy. Verdi also uses the orchestra to sound out musical motives that have symbolic content or to refer to people in the story as the drama progresses. In these ways—his use of the orchestra for continuity and his fashioning of "reference" motives with specific meanings—Verdi approached the style of Wagner, though Wagner employed these techniques in very different ways, as we shall see.

LISTENING GUIDE

Giuseppe Verdi (1813–1901)
Otello **(Excerpt)**

Date of composition: 1887
Duration: 6:17

Student CD Collection: 3, track 11
Complete CD Collection: 5, track 1

*O*tello was the last of Verdi's tragic operas. Inspired by Shakespeare's play *Othello*, it has a libretto by Arrigo Boito (1842–1918).

Dramatic interest in this work lies not so much in the tragic plot as in the portrayal of human emotions. The story revolves around the evil deception of Iago, an ensign in the Venetian army. He is intensely jealous of the promotion of his friend Cassio to a high post. Iago is determined to rectify the situation by deceiving Otello that Cassio is having an affair with his wife.

Much of the musical interest in *Otello* (and in many of Verdi's operas) lies in the use of accompanied recitative, which is a flexible form halfway between aria and recitative, and perfect for catching the changing feelings of the participants in the drama.

The excerpt begins toward the end of Act II, where Iago cleverly tries to convince his commander (Otello) that his rival (Cassio) has romantic designs on Desdemona (Otello's new bride). The scene builds from the lightly accompanied opening and the representation of sleep-talk to a huge orchestral climax of sworn revenge.

11 (1)	**0:00**	[h o r n , s i n g l e n o t e]

IAGO

0:04	*Era la notte, Cassio dormia,* *gli stavo accanto.* *Con interrotte voci tradia* *l'intimo incanto.* *Le labbra lente, lente movea,* *nell'abbandono del sogno ardente;*	I watched Cassio the other night as he slept. All of a sudden he began to mutter what he was dreaming. Moving his lips slowly, very slowly, I heard him betray his secret thoughts;
0:40	*e allor dicea, con flebil suono:*	saying in a passionate voice:
0:48	*"Desdemona soave!* *Il nostro amor s'asconda,* *cauti vegliamo*	"My sweetest Desdemona! let us be careful, cautiously hiding our love,
1:02	*l'estasi del ciel tutto m'innonda!"*	our heavenly rapture!"
1:14	[m o r e a g i t a t e d o r c h e s t r a l a c c o m p a n i m e n t]	
1:16	*Seguia più vago l'incubo blando;* *con molle angoscia l'interna imago* *quasi baciando,*	Then he moved toward me and gently caressing the person in his dreams,
1:32	*ei disse poscia: "Il rio destino* *impreco che al Moro ti donò!"*	he said this: "Oh accursed fortune that gave you to the Moor!"
1:55	*E allora il sogno* *in cieco letargo si mutò.*	And after his dream, he went calmly back to sleep.

OTELLO

12 (2)	**2:17**	*Oh, mostruosa colpa!*	Oh, monstrous deed!

IAGO

	Io non narrai che un sogno…	No, this was only his dreaming…

OTELLO

2:22	*Un sogno che rivela un fatto…*	A dream that reveals the truth…

IAGO

2:25	*Un sogno che può dar forma* *di prova ad altro indizio.*	A dream that may support other evidence.

OTELLO

E qual?	What kind of evidence?

[a little slower; horn note]

IAGO

2:37

Talor vedeste	Have you ever seen
in mano di Desdemona	in Desdemona's hand
un tessuto trapunto a fior	a handkerchief decorated with flowers
e più sottil d'un velo?	and of the finest texture?

OTELLO

2:54

È il fazzoletto ch'io le diedi,	That is the handkerchief I gave her,
pegno primo d'amor.	It was my first gift to her.

IAGO

3:01

Quel fazzoletto ieri certo ne son	That same handkerchief I swear
lo vidi in man di Cassio.	I saw in Cassio's hand.

OTELLO

[agitated; furious]

13 (3)   3:13

Ah! mille gli	Ah! May God give the slave
donasse Iddio!	a thousand lives!
Una è povera preda al furor mio!	One is all too little for my revenge!
Iago, ho il cuore di gelo.	Iago, my heart is ice.
Lungi da me le pietose larve:	Rise, Vengeance, from your cave:
Tutto il mio vano amor,	my deepest love—
esalo al cielo—	I vow to heaven—
Guardami, ei sparve!	look, it's gone!
Nelle sue spire d'angue l'idra m'avvince!	I yield to tyrannous hate!

3:49

Ah sangue! sangue! sangue!	Oh blood! blood! blood!

[determined]

3:56

Si pel ciel marmoreo giuro!	I swear by yonder marble heaven!
Per le attorte folgori,	and the eternal stars above,
per la Morte e per l'oscuro mar	and the darkest sea below,
sterminator.	
D'ira e d'impeto tremendo,	Never shall my anger cease
presto fia che sfolgori questa man	until this hand
ch'io levo e stendo!	has brought about my revenge!

4:28

Non v'alzate ancor!
Testimon è il Sol ch'io miro;
che m'irradia e inanima,
l'ampia terra e il vasto spiro,
del Creato inter;
che ad Otello io sacro ardenti,
core, braccio ed anima s'anco
ad opere cruenti

No, wait!
Witness Sun, which illumines us:
Earth, on which we live,
you, ambient air that we breathe,
the Creator's breath;
witness that I eagerly give Othello
my heart, my hands, and my soul
to these bloody deeds.

5:01

s'armi suo voler!

Let him command!

OTELLO
& IAGO

[duet, rising to a powerful climax]

14 (4)   **5:07**

Si pel ciel marmoreo giuro!
per le attorte folgori,
per la Morte e per l'oscuro per mar
    sterminator.

I swear by yonder marble heaven!
and eternal stars above,
and the darkest sea below,

5:25

D'ira e d'impeto tremendo
presto fia che sfolgori questa man
ch'io levo e stendo;
presto fia che sfolgori questa man,
presto fia che sfolgori questa man

Never shall my anger cease
until this hand
has brought about my revenge;
until this hand,
until this hand

5:46

ch'io levo e stendo.

has brought about my revenge.

5:53

Dio vendicator!

God of vengeance!

[unaccompanied]

5:59

[loud orchestral postlude; brass and timpani; whole orchestra]

6:13

[End of Act II]

RICHARD WAGNER (1813–1883)

Richard Wagner is a perfect example of the contradictions inherent in genius. His importance as a composer was enormous, and his writings on music, literature, and politics exerted a tremendous influence on artistic and intellectual thought throughout the second half of the nineteenth century. Yet he was an appalling egoist, a home-wrecker, and an outspoken and virulent anti-Semite.

Wagner was born in Leipzig. His father died when Wagner was an infant, and when his mother married again, Wagner was educated under the influence of his stepfather, who was a writer and an artist. Wagner studied Shakespeare and Homer and was overwhelmed by hearing Beethoven. At Leipzig University he studied music, but, before completing his degree, left to take a job in a small opera house. For the next six years, Wagner learned about opera from the inside, as a chorus director and as a conductor. He married an actress, Minna Planer, and composed his own first operas. From the beginning, Wagner wrote his own librettos and was thus able to achieve remarkable cohesion between the drama and the music.

From the beginning, too, Wagner spent more than he earned. In 1839, he was forced to flee Germany rather than end up in debtor's prison. His passport and Minna's had been revoked, so they crossed the border at night and made a harrowing journey to Paris.

The two were extremely poor, and the Paris Opera would not accept Wagner's latest work, *Rienzi*, for production. He made a living by selling some music—and most of Minna's clothes! He also composed another opera, based on the folk tale of *The Flying Dutchman*.

Discouraged by his reception in Paris, Wagner suddenly received news that both *Rienzi* and *The Flying Dutchman* had been accepted for production in Germany. He was overwhelmed with gratitude and swore never to leave his native land again. The operas were a great success. At the première of *Rienzi* at the Dresden

opera house, Wagner "cried and laughed at the same time, and hugged everyone he met." At the age of 30, Wagner was appointed court conductor in Dresden.

The couple was financially comfortable for the first time, and Wagner was able to compose two more operas: *Tannhäuser* (1845) and *Lohengrin* (1848). In both operas, Wagner continued to base his librettos not on historical drama but on folk legend. *Tannhäuser* is the story of a medieval German troubadour; *Lohengrin* is based on Grimm's fairy tale of the Swan Knight of the Holy Grail.

After joining a failed coup against the monarchy in 1848, Wagner again had to leave the country. And despite his earlier vow, the next 12 years were years of exile. He and Minna settled in Zurich, and from this period date his most important writings: an essay called *The Art Work of the Future* (1849) and a book entitled *Opera and Drama* (1851). In these works, he called for a renewal of the artistic ideals of Greek antiquity, in which poetry, drama, philosophy, and music would be combined into a single work of art: the "complete art work," as Wagner called it. Music and words should be completely interwoven in a retelling of old myths, which could carry the resonance of profound human truth. This new type of opera was known as **music drama**.

Wagner spent the next 35 years fulfilling this vision. But before he did so, he revealed a far less attractive side of his personality by publishing a vicious anti-Semitic essay entitled *Jewishness in Music*. He attacked the music of Mendelssohn and other Jewish composers and went on to call for the removal of the entire Jewish community ("this destructive foreign element") from Germany.

Wagner next started composing the poetry and the music for the largest musical project of the entire Romantic period: his cycle of music dramas entitled *The Ring of the Nibelungs*. This was to be a series of four long operas based on medieval German legend, involving gods and goddesses, dwarfs and giants, and human heroes. The central symbol of the cycle is a

The French poet Baudelaire on Wagner's music: "I love Wagner, but the music I prefer is that of a cat hung up by its tail outside a window and trying to stick to the panes of glass with its claws."

The Ring *Cycle*

Wagner's *The Ring of the Nibelungs* is a cycle of four music dramas: *The Rhinegold, The Valkyries, Siegfried,* and *The Twilight of the Gods.* It represents one of the greatest achievements in the history of Western music. Its creation took Wagner more than 25 years. The four dramas together take more than 15 hours to perform. ◆ Wagner wrote the music *and* the poetry for *The Ring.* Although the poetry is itself an impressive achievement, it is the manner in which the music describes and illuminates the poetry that is most extraordinary. Wagner's dense network of **leitmotivs**—musical phrases associated with objects, characters, events, thoughts, and feelings—adds meaning to the text and offers psychological insights into the characters and the reasons behind their actions. ◆ *The Ring* explores universal and contradictory themes: love and hate, heroism and cowardice, good and evil, greed and selflessness, naïveté and unscrupulousness. Power, symbolized by the ring itself, is exposed as a corrupting force. The English playwright and critic George Bernard Shaw interpreted parts of *The Ring* as a political allegory of the oppressed masses in the nineteenth century. The German author Thomas Mann, a profound admirer of Wagner, considered the huge *Ring* cycle the equivalent of Émile Zola's cycle of novels or the epic Russian novels of Tolstoi and Dostoevski. Like those great literary masterpieces, *The Ring* is still powerfully relevant today.

magic ring made of stolen gold that dooms all who possess it.

Wagner set about this enormous task with no hope of performance. Halfway through, he broke off work to write two other operas unconnected to the Ring cycle: *Tristan and Isolde* (1859) and *The Mastersingers of Nuremberg* (1867). He was in the grip of an unstoppable creative urge. Speaking of these years later in life, he said: "The towering fires of life burned in me with such unutterable heat and brilliance that they almost consumed me."

He had affairs with other women: the wife of a French patron (her husband threatened to put a bullet through Wagner's head), the wife of a wealthy merchant who lent him money (she was the inspiration for *Tristan and Isolde*), and the new wife of a good friend, the conductor and enthusiastic Wagner supporter Hans von Bülow. Cosima von Bülow was the daughter of Franz Liszt, another loyal friend of Wagner's. The affair gradually deepened, and Wagner and Minna separated. But it was not until eight years later that Wagner and Cosima could be married, after overcoming the objections of both Liszt and Hans von Bülow. By then the couple had already had two daughters and a son. Cosima was 32, Wagner 57.

During these last eight years, Wagner had despaired of having his new operas produced, but his hopes were suddenly realized beyond his wildest dreams. In 1864 an 18-year-old youth ascended the throne of Bavaria as King Ludwig II of Bavaria. Having read Wagner's writings and admired his operas, King Ludwig was an ardent fan of Wagner's. He was also in love with Wagner. "An earthly being cannot match up to a divine spirit," the king wrote to Wagner. "But it can love; it can venerate. You are my first, my only love, and always will be."

For the rest of Wagner's life, his extravagant financial demands were met with unparalleled generosity by the young king. Wagner's work prospered. He was able to finish the gigantic *Ring* cycle, and he made plans for a new theater in which the four-evening event could be staged. These plans finally came to fruition in a new opera house in Bayreuth (pronounced "BYE-royt"), a small town in Bavaria.

On February 13, 1883, Wagner died of a heart attack. Since Wagner's death, his memory has inspired a cult. Worshippers make the pilgrimage to Bayreuth for the annual Wagner festival. Wagner societies exist in countries around the world. The Bayreuth Festival has been run by members of Wagner's family since his death.

The Bayreuth Festival

Wagner laid the foundation stone for his own *Festspielhaus* ("Festival Theater") in Bayreuth on May 22, 1872. Initially, money for the project was hard to come by. However, King Ludwig's generous financial assistance enabled the theater to be completed. The first production—the entire *Ring* cycle—took place in August of 1876. The next Bayreuth Festival did not take place until 1882. At a performance of *Parsifal* that year, Wagner conducted the final scene—his only conducting appearance at the theater. ¶ Since Wagner's death in 1883, the Bayreuth Festival has been run by members of Wagner's family. His widow and son,

Cosima and Siegfried, were in charge until they both died in 1930, whereupon Winnifred, Siegfried's widow, took over. The ensuing years, 1930–44, were clouded by Adolf Hitler's association with Winnifred and with Bayreuth. ¶ The Bayreuth Festival closed in 1944 as a result of the Second World War. It reopened in 1951 with extraordinarily successful productions of *Parsifal* and *The Ring*, directed by Wieland Wagner, the composer's grandson. Under Wieland, Bayreuth attained a new acceptability, distancing itself from its Nazi association. Wolfgang Wagner, another of Wagner's grandsons, assumed responsibility for the Festival in 1966, following Wieland's death.

Wagner's art is diseased.
—Friedrich Nietzsche

WAGNER'S MUSIC

Wagner's only important works are for the opera stage. His first two operas, *Rienzi* and *The Flying Dutchman*, are in the tradition of German Romantic opera, with grand scenes and with separate arias, duets, ensembles, and choruses. Already, however, we see Wagner writing his own librettos and concentrating on human beings as symbols of grand ideas. (Verdi, by contrast, concentrated on human beings for their expression of humanity.) By the time of *Tannhäuser* and *Lohengrin*, Wagner had developed his poetic skill and found fertile ground in ancient legend. His poetry is terse and powerful. In both operas, the individual items (aria, recitative, chorus) are less distinct in musical style, and there is much more musical continuity.

For the works up to *Lohengrin*, we can still use the term "opera"; the later works are music dramas. In the *Ring* cycle (made up of four music dramas: *The Rhinegold, The Valkyries, Siegfried*, and *The Twilight of the Gods*), Wagner developed his technique of continuity

to the fullest. The music is absolutely continuous, and the orchestra carries the main musical content. The voices sing in an **arioso** style (that is, halfway between speechlike recitative and lyrical aria), blending into the instrumental fabric. *Tristan and Isolde* and *The Mastersingers*, which Wagner composed in the middle of *The Ring*, and *Parsifal*, which he composed after it, also display this technique.

The orchestra is central to Wagner's music, and he wrote for a large one. He particularly enjoyed using brass instruments. He even invented a new musical instrument to cover the gap between the horns and the trombones. This instrument is known as a **Wagner tuba**. The orchestra of the *Ring* uses four of them. Their sound is rounder, a little deeper, and more solemn than that of the horns.

Musical continuity in Wagner's music dramas is also achieved through harmonic means. In this, too, Wagner was a revolutionary. Instead of ending each phrase with a cadence, he tends to melt the end of one phrase into the beginning of the next. And whereas most music of the time is clearly in a specific key, Wagner's music is tonally very ambiguous. Often it is so chromatic that it is hard to say which key is being used at any one point. In Wagner's *Tristan and Isolde*, for example, there seems to be no fixed key or clear-cut cadence until the very end of the work! This perfectly suits the sense of unfulfillment and longing that is the subject of the drama. **(See Listening Guide on page 296.)**

Finally, Wagner's music depends upon a technique that he himself invented (though it might be seen as the logical outcome of earlier musical developments). This technique is the use of **leitmotiv** (pronounced "LIGHT-moteef"). This is a German word that means **leading motive**. A leitmotiv is a musical phrase or fragment that carries associations with a person, object, or idea in the drama.

You may remember that Berlioz used a recurrent theme (*idée fixe*) to refer to the beloved in his *Symphonie fantastique*. And other composers used themes associated with particular characters in their operas. Wagner's leitmotiv technique is different. First, leitmotivs can refer to many things other than a person.

Leitmotivs in Wagner's music dramas are associated with a spear, longing, fate, and the magic ring itself. Second, Wagner's leitmotivs are flexible, undergoing musical transformation as the ideas, objects, or people change in the course of the drama. Finally, Wagner uses his leitmotivs like threads in a tapestry. They can be combined, interwoven, contrasted, or blended to create an infinity of allusions and meanings.

Wagner, the political revolutionary, revolutionized music by his brilliant writing for orchestra, by making the orchestra the central "character" of his dramas, and by his development of the leitmotiv technique. In addition, Wagner's continuity of writing and tonally ambiguous harmonic style laid the foundation for the completely new language of twentieth-century music.

LISTENING GUIDE

Richard Wagner (1813–1883)
Prelude and *Liebestod* from the Music Drama *Tristan und Isolde*

Date of composition: 1865
Orchestration: 3 flutes, 2 oboes, English horn, 2 clarinets, bass clarinet, 3 bassoons, 4 horns, 3 trumpets, 3 trombones, tuba, timpani, harp, violins I and II, violas, cellos, double basses; voice
Duration: 18:03

Complete CD Collection: 5, track 5

*L*ike most of Wagner's works, *Tristan und Isolde* is based on a medieval legend. Tristan and Isolde are lovers, and the opera is about their passion and final union in death. The Prelude and *Liebestod*, respectively the beginning and the end of the opera, are often excerpted from the work.

The Prelude introduces the main leitmotiv of the work, an upward-striving phrase that never quite resolves. This phrase saturates the whole Prelude, giving it a strong sense of urgency and yearning. In addition, there is a rising cello theme, closely based on the opening leitmotiv.

Although Wagner creates a feeling of constant flowing motion, the Prelude is also characterized by two other, opposing techniques: building short motives into long passages, and "deconstructing" the music into mere fragments. Although the music remains (barely) anchored to a tonal center, the harmonies are so chromatic that it also seems to float and surge freely above this anchor.

Liebestod ("Love-Death") comes at the very end of the opera. At the moment of reunion with Isolde, Tristan dies; she then also dies, joining him in the transcendence of death. Like the Prelude, *Liebestod* is based primarily on two leitmotivs: the "love-death" music heard when the voice enters, and the motive of "transcendental bliss" first played by the flutes a third of the way through.

Toward the end, the "yearning" leitmotiv from the very beginning of the Prelude recurs, but here, for the first time, it ends in harmonic resolution. It is as though only the final chords can resolve the urgent longing established at the outset of the work.

The large orchestra is used for delicate passages as well as for enormous climaxes. And the voice soars in and out and over the orchestral fabric, as though it were an additional special thread in the overall texture of the work.

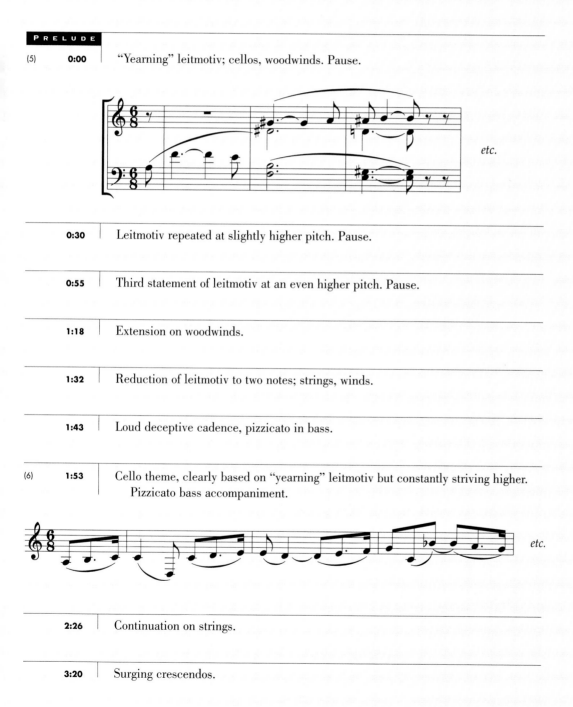

PRELUDE

(5)	0:00	"Yearning" leitmotiv; cellos, woodwinds. Pause.
	0:30	Leitmotiv repeated at slightly higher pitch. Pause.
	0:55	Third statement of leitmotiv at an even higher pitch. Pause.
	1:18	Extension on woodwinds.
	1:32	Reduction of leitmotiv to two notes; strings, winds.
	1:43	Loud deceptive cadence, pizzicato in bass.
(6)	1:53	Cello theme, clearly based on "yearning" leitmotiv but constantly striving higher. Pizzicato bass accompaniment.
	2:26	Continuation on strings.
	3:20	Surging crescendos.

(7)	**3:37**	Development of cello theme on woodwinds.
	4:03	Reduction of cello theme (strings and woodwinds).
	4:28	Surging; strings, horns, woodwinds.
	5:27	Further crescendos; long flowing section.
	6:29	Rising violin passages, getting increasingly intense.
	7:17	Climax and loud intense passage.
(8)	**7:48**	Orchestral climax, very loud; brass.
	7:58	Orchestra winds down.
(9)	**8:10**	Return to "yearning" leitmotiv.
	8:30	Repetitions of leitmotiv at higher pitches.
	9:09	Climax, followed by decrescendo.
	9:26	Fragments.
	9:52	Timpani roll, English horn, "yearning" leitmotiv.
(10)	**10:13**	Timpani; bass clarinet; "yearning" leitmotiv stripped down; quiet.
	10:31	Double basses only; ending with two pizzicato notes; very quiet.

LIEBESTOD

"Love-death" leitmotiv in voice, continues throughout section.

etc.

(11)	**0:00**	*Mild und leise wie er lächelt,*	How quietly and tenderly he smiles,
		[String tremolos; trombones]	
	0:16	*wie das Auge hold er öffnet,*	How sweetly he opens his eyes!
		seht ihr's, Freunde? Seht ihr's nicht?	Do you see, my friends? Do you not see?
		[Tremolos continue; horn]	
	0:41	*Immer lichter, wie er leuchtet,*	How brightly he shines,
		[Sudden crescendo, high notes on "leuchtet" ("shines")]	
	0:55	*stern-umstrahlet hoch sich hebt?*	How high he soars, surrounded by stars?
		[Harp; high on "hoch" ("high")]	
	1:10	*Seht ihr's nicht?*	Do you not see?
		Wie das Herz ihm mutig schwillt,	How valiantly his heart swells,
		[Loud]	
	1:25	*voll und hehr im Busen ihm quillt?*	Majestic and full, beats in his breast?
	1:41	*Wie den Lippen, sonnig mild,*	How his lips, soft and gentle,
		süsser Atem sanft entweht?	Exhale sweet, delightful breath?
		[Horns, woodwinds, "bliss" leitmotiv on flutes (continues throughout section)]	

etc.

	2:15	*Freunde! Seht! Fühlt und seht ihr's nicht?*	Friends! Look! Do you not feel it and see it?
(12)	**2:35**	*Höre ich nur diese Weise,*	Do I alone hear this melody,
		die so wundervoll und leise,	Which, so wondrously tender,
		[Sense of return to opening; surging]	
	2:58	*Wonne klagend, alles sagend,*	Softly mourning, saying all,
		mild versöhnend aus ihm tönend,	Gently forgiving, sounds from him,
		[Voice takes over "bliss" leitmotiv]	

	3:20	*in mich dringet, auf sich schwinget,*	Penetrates within me, rising up,
		hold erhallend um mich klinget?	Sweetly echoes and rings around me?

[Speeding up; crescendo]

	3:43	*Heller schallend, mich umwallend,*	Sounding yet more clearly, surrounding me,
		sind es Wellen sanfter Lüfte?	Are they waves of holy breezes?
		Sind es Wogen wonniger Düfte?	Are they clouds of wondrous fragrance?

[Repeated phrase in orchestra ... rising ever higher]

	4:08	*Wie sie schwellen, mich umrauschen,*	As they swell and roar around me,
		soll ich atmen, soll ich lauschen?	Shall I breathe them in, shall I listen to them?
		Soll ich schlürfen, untertauchen?	Shall I sip them, dive in among them?
		Süss in Düften mich verhauchen?	Sweetly expire amidst the fragrance?
		In dem wogenden Schwall, in dem tönenden Schall,	In the surging swell, in the ringing sounds,

[More and more agitated]

	4:40	*in des Welt-Atems wehendem All*	In the world's breath, encompassing everything,
		ertrinken, versinken	To drown, to sink

[Huge climax; decrescendo. Dramatic change of harmony]

(13)	**5:25**	*unbewusst höchste Lust!*	Unconscious—what utter bliss!

[Last word floats ... Slow. Decrescendo. "Bliss" leitmotiv very slowly leads to:]

	6:09	Return of "yearning" leitmotiv from Prelude

	6:24	Resolution chord

	6:31	Final chords

THE NATIONALIST COMPOSERS

In the opening pages of this chapter, we noted that one of the consequences of Romanticism was the growth of nationalism throughout Europe. We have seen how this affected some of the composers we have already discussed. Verdi's operas contain references to Italy's struggle for independence, and Verdi became a national hero. Wagner's music focused on a mythic and heroic German past, and he became a symbol of German ethnic pride.

But there were other composers whose music responded even more obviously to the nationalist movements in their own countries. These composers deliberately rejected the German and Italian dominance in instrumental music and opera and fostered national pride in their own native traditions. They did this in several ways. First, they wrote operas in their own native languages—languages that had not previously been used for opera, such as Russian or Czech. Second, they based operas and symphonic poems on stories from national folklore and on descriptions of native scenes of natural beauty. Finally, composers often wove their own countries' folk tunes into their compositions to give their music a distinct national identity.

The main nineteenth-century nationalist composers were to be found in Russia, Czechoslovakia, Scandinavia, Spain, and France. In the early twentieth century, nationalism also affected Hungarian, Polish, English, and American composers.

RUSSIA

The nationalist movement in music was first felt in Russia, where music had been dominated entirely by foreign influence. Starting in the middle of the nineteenth century, Russian composers began to write operas in their own language, on Russian themes, and they often based their librettos on literary works by the great Russian writers of the time. And in the second half of the century, a group of composers known as "The Mighty Handful" set out consciously to forge a native

musical tradition. Of these composers, the most stirring nationalist was Modest Mussorgsky (1839–1881), whose works include the opera *Boris Godunov*, based on a story by the Russian writer Alexander Pushkin; the series of pieces known as *Pictures at an Exhibition*, which describe paintings hanging in a gallery; and the symphonic poem *Night on Bald Mountain*.

BOHEMIA

Bohemia had been an independent kingdom until it was taken over by Austria. (For most of the twentieth century, it formed part of Czechoslovakia but is now a region in the Czech Republic.) The two principal Bohemian composers of the nineteenth century were Bedřich Smetana (1824–1884) and Antonin Dvořák (1841–1904). Smetana based his most famous opera, *The Bartered Bride*, on Bohemian folklore. Another well-known piece by Smetana is the symphonic poem *The Moldau*, which describes the flow of a river across the Bohemian countryside. It cleverly combines depictions of nature with feelings of national pride. (**See Listening Guide on page 302**.) Dvořák wrote symphonies, concertos, operas, choral works, and chamber music. Chief among these are the Ninth (*New World*) Symphony (which he wrote in America), the Cello Concerto, and his *Slavonic Dances* for orchestra. The *New World* Symphony combines American themes with Bohemian folk melodies. Dvořák hoped it would inspire American composers to become nationalists. "America can have her own music," he said.

MORAVIA

Moravia—formerly independent, then a part of Czechoslovakia, now a region of the Czech Republic—was the homeland of Leoš Janáček (1854–1928). Janáček collected authentic Moravian folk songs and was a great and innovative composer. His superb Czech operas and his two fine string quartets were written primarily in the 1920s.

SCANDINAVIA

Norway produced the most famous Scandinavian nationalist composer in Edvard Grieg (1843–1907).

Bedřich Smetana (1824–1884)
Symphonic Poem, *The Moldau*

Date of composition: 1874
Orchestration: Piccolo, 2 flutes, 2 oboes, 2 bassoons, 4 French horns, 2 trumpets, 3 trombones, tuba, timpani, bass drum, triangle, cymbals, harp, strings
Tempo: *Allegro commodo non agitato* ("Fast but comfortable and not agitated")
Meter: 𝄴
Key: E minor
Duration: 12:46

Complete CD Collection: 5, track 14

*T*he Moldau is a majestic tone poem that combines several components of Romanticism: it is descriptive program music, and it expresses an interest in nature and, above all, nationalism. The title of the work refers to a powerful river. This piece is part of a cycle, *Má Vlast* (*My Country*), which depicts six different scenes of Smetana's native Bohemia.

Smetana employs the rich color of a large orchestra: Note the use of harp, tuba, piccolo, bass drum, cymbals, and triangle. With this vivid palette he creates scenes of contrasting atmosphere. Smetana's program describes the river Moldau beginning from two small streams, growing in size, and then flowing through the countryside, in the moonlight, over rapids, and past an ancient castle, finally disappearing into the distance. These distinct scenes are clearly audible in the tone poem, and Smetana adds further description in the score. Throughout, the flowing water is suggested by smooth, slurred, stepwise melodies.

		THE TWO SPRINGS
		[This section acts as an introduction, a brief prelude before we actually reach the river.]
(14)	**0:00**	Smooth running line in the two flutes, ***p***, representing the two springs. Sparse accompaniment of pizzicato violins and high harp suggests delicate stream.
	0:40	The lower strings enter on a long-held dominant chord, building a feeling of expectation.

		THE RIVER
	1:00	Sense of arrival as the dominant chord resolves to the tonic, accented by pizzicato lower strings and triangle.
(15)	**1:06**	River theme, E minor, a songlike melody, smooth and stepwise, and with longer note values providing a gentle rocking motion. Swirling sixteenth notes act as accompaniment, adding to the depth of the river.

| (16) | 2:59 | The four horns play in chordal harmony, *f*; accented repeated notes; then a melody of up-and-down arpeggiation.
Winds and lower strings pick up the leaping arpeggiated melody, violins continue the flowing sixteenth notes. Decrescendo to repeated notes, leading into: |

PEASANT WEDDING

| (17) | 4:03 | Simple rhythms of the bouncing repeated notes and smooth, lilting pairs of notes evoke a country dance, *p*. Short phrases and homophonic texture, G Major. Repeated notes fade into: |

MOONLIGHT: DANCE OF THE WATER-NYMPHS (TRANQUILLY)

| (18) | 5:39 | Still in major key, *pp*; sustained chords. |

| (19) | 6:06 | High melody of even, stately half notes in muted violins. Accompaniment of sixteenth notes and graceful ascending harp arpeggios. Gradual increase in dynamics and level of activity; more instruments and new rhythms added. |

| | 7:46 | Crescendo, aggressive sounds, brass enter with staccato chords. Timpani rolls and trumpet fanfares accentuate the growing intensity. Accelerating runs of sixteenth notes lead into: |

| (20) | 8:38 | The return of the river theme. But the waters suddenly turn turbulent. |

THE RAPIDS OF ST. JOHN

| (21) | 9:29 | Ascending minor scales alternate in the low brass and low strings, *ff*. Jagged, piercing arpeggios in the piccolos. Both outline harsh dissonant chords. Timpani rolls and cymbal crashes of increasing speed suggest violently cresting waves. Gradual shortening of the phrase lengths adds to building intensity and leads to: |

| (22) | 10:43 | An accelerated return of the river theme, now in major, *ff*; the river is more powerful than ever. |

THE ANCIENT CASTLE VYŠEHRAD

| (23) | 11:13 | Chordal brass melody, harmonized by the full brass sections, *ff*; the tempo is stately and broad. |

| | 11:31 | Bright cadential chords, arpeggiated like a fanfare; the ending section is triumphal and in major. |

| | 12:02 | Final decrescendo, still with the rocking motion of the river theme, as the Moldau disappears in the distance, *pp*. Full orchestra for the strong closing chords, *ff*. |

Grieg specialized in piano miniatures inspired by Norwegian tunes. His well-known orchestral *Peer Gynt* Suite was written for the play of the same name by the Norwegian writer Henrik Ibsen. The Danish composer Carl Nielsen (1865–1931) was a highly individual composer, whose main works (operas, symphonies, and string quartets) belong to the first two decades of the twentieth century. The leading composer of Finland was Jan Sibelius (1865–1957). He wrote seven superb symphonies and a deeply emotional string quartet, but his most famous work is the symphonic poem *Finlandia* (1899), whose intense national flavor caused it to be banned by the foreign rulers in Finland, though it was an immense success throughout the rest of Europe.

SPAIN

The principal nationalist composers of Spain were Enrique Granados (1867–1916), Isaac Albéniz (1860–1909), and Manuel de Falla (1876–1946). Granados and Albéniz wrote piano suites in lively Spanish rhythms and with colorful melodies. De Falla is best known for his wonderful *Nights in the Gardens of Spain*, a series of three evocative and atmospheric pieces for piano and orchestra.

FRANCE

After the end of the Franco-Prussian War in 1871, a National Society for French Music was founded to encourage French composers. The most gifted of these were Camille Saint-Saëns (1835–1921) and Gabriel Fauré (1845–1924). Saint-Saëns' *Carnival of the Animals* for chamber orchestra is great fun; his Symphony No. 3 is a more serious work but also very attractive. Fauré wrote exquisite French songs to poems by some of the leading French poets of his day.

PYOTR ILYICH TCHAIKOVSKY (1840–1893)

The Russian composer Pyotr Ilyich Tchaikovsky wrote operas in Russian based on works of Russian literature and also made use of Russian folk songs—but he was not as committed a nationalist as some of his contemporaries. It may be partly for this reason that he achieved an international success.

Tchaikovsky was the son of a mining engineer and a mother of French extraction, to whom he was very close. He had piano lessons as a child and did some composing, but he turned to music as his main emotional outlet only after his mother died when he was 14. Tchaikovsky began to earn a living as a government clerk at the age of 19, but when the new St. Petersburg Music Conservatory was founded, he quit his job and entered the Conservatory as a full-time student. A family friend described him as "poor but profoundly happy" at having chosen music as a career. His talents were such that a year after graduating, he was appointed professor at the music conservatory in Moscow. From that time on, he devoted his life to music.

In Moscow he met many other composers and publishers and flourished in the lively atmosphere of the cosmopolitan city. He also traveled abroad. He wrote articles and a book on music and composed prolifically.

All this time, however, Tchaikovsky lived with a secret: He was gay. He was tormented by self-hatred and the fear of being exposed. In 1877, at the age of 37, he suddenly decided to get married. Partly he may have felt that this step might "cure" him of his nature; partly he may have thought he needed the cover. The marriage was an instant disaster. Tchaikovsky fled, attempted suicide, and had a nervous breakdown.

After some months of convalescence, Tchaikovsky gradually recovered and turned once more to music. Both his Fourth Symphony and his opera *Eugene Onyegin* date from this time, and both contain powerful reflections of his emotional state.

A strange turn of events helped to provide emotional and financial support for Tchaikovsky. A wealthy widow named Madame von Meck decided to become his patron. She said she would commission some pieces and provide the composer with an annual income. There was only one condition: The two must never meet. This suited Tchaikovsky perfectly, and for the next 13 years Madame von Meck and Tchaikovsky

From Tchaikovsky's review of a performance of Das Rheingold, *from Wagner's* Ring *cycle: "From the scenic point of view it interested me greatly, and I was also much impressed by the marvelous staging of the work. Musically it is inconceivable nonsense."*

carried on an intense personal relationship without ever seeing each other. They shared their innermost thoughts, but only by letter, and they wrote to each other every day.

Tchaikovsky was able to resign his teaching post, and he composed a great deal of music during those years. In 1890, Madame von Meck suddenly broke off the relationship and the patronage. No explanation was offered, though her family may have put pressure on her to direct her funds elsewhere. Tchaikovsky was deeply hurt, but by now he had a substantial income from his music, and the Russian czar had provided him with a life pension.

In his last years, Tchaikovsky wrote some of his best-known music, including a ballet entitled *The Nutcracker* and his Sixth Symphony, subtitled *Pathétique*. Tchaikovsky died in 1893, apparently of cholera, though it has been suggested that, threatened with public exposure of his homosexuality, he committed suicide.

TCHAIKOVSKY'S MUSIC

Tchaikovsky's music is highly emotional. It surges with passion and appeals directly to the senses. The range of expression is very great, from the depths of despair to the height of joy. There is sensuousness, delicacy, nobility, tenderness, and fire. *The Nutcracker* is one of the most popular ballet scores in the world, though it is followed closely by *Sleeping Beauty* and *Swan Lake*, both also by Tchaikovsky. The Fourth and Sixth Symphonies are deeply emotional utterances, and his operas, such as *Eugene Onyegin* and *The Queen of Spades*, though less well known, are powerfully dramatic works. Tchaikovsky also wrote three piano concertos as well as a violin concerto that enraptures audiences every time it is played.

Tchaikovsky used an orchestra of moderate size; he never went to the extremes of some other Romantic composers. But he was very interested in orchestral color. There is little in music to match the stirring brass fanfare at the beginning of the Fourth Symphony or the

Copyright

Before the first international convention on the issue of copyright, held in Berne, Switzerland, in 1886, composers' works were unprotected. There was little that famous composers could do to prevent "pirate" editions of their works from circulating. Unscrupulous publishers would simply get hold of a copy of the work and then print and sell copies of it. A fundamental principle was established at Berne, namely that a published work (including a musical one) is protected under copyright during the author's or composer's lifetime and for 50 years following his or her death; the principle has remained more or less intact to the present day. In addition, regarding musical works, a fee must be paid for each *performance* of a work, whether it be live or recorded.

Tchaikovsky in 1888.

> **R**epulsive and barbaric.
> —a Viennese newspaper on Tchaikovsky's Violin Concerto

paired clarinets at the beginning of the Sixth. For "The Dance of the Sugar-Plum Fairy" in *The Nutcracker*, Tchaikovsky contrasts the delicate shimmery sound of the celesta with the deep richness of a bass clarinet.

Tchaikovsky was a master of melody. Some of his tunes have become a part of the Western consciousness, featured in famous popular songs or as soundtracks to movies. He sometimes used folk tunes, but most of his melodies came from his own inexhaustible lyrical gift. Tchaikovsky was a Russian composer, as he always insisted, but his music speaks to millions of people as the expression of a human heart.

> **W**here words fail, music speaks.
> —Tchaikovsky, quoting the German writer Heinrich Heine

Pyotr Ilyich Tchaikovsky (1840–1893)
First Movement from Symphony No. 4
   in F minor

Date of composition: 1877–78
Orchestration: 2 flutes, 2 oboes,
    2 clarinets, 2 bassoons, 4 horns,
    2 trumpets, 2 trombones, bass
    trombone, tuba, timpani, strings
Tempo: *Andante sostenuto* ("Fairly slow
    and sustained")
Meter: ¾
Key: F minor
Duration: 18:43

Complete CD Collection: 5, track 24

Tchaikovsky's Symphony No. 4 is a powerful, impassioned work, written at the time of Tchaikovsky's disastrous marriage. The composer described it as a "musical confession of the soul." The first movement particularly has an enormous expressive range. Its two most striking elements are a powerful brass fanfare that opens the work (and returns to interrupt the music at crucial points) and a radical reinterpretation of Classic sonata form. Tchaikovsky described the brass fanfare as "inescapable Fate," and the whole movement as "a perpetual alternation between grim reality and dreams of happiness."

To mold the passion and intensity of his music, Tchaikovsky casts his first movement in a sonata form that has been forcefully reshaped. The development of the first theme occurs mostly *within* the exposition; the development section itself is correspondingly brief; and the recapitulation is foreshortened and condensed, leading to a frantically accelerated coda. At major structural points in this form (at the beginnings of the development, recapitulation, and coda), the Fate motive intrudes forcibly and inexorably. Finally, for this movement, Tchaikovsky adopts a highly unconventional key-scheme that traces a circle of minor thirds beginning and ending on F: F, A♭, C♭ (=B), D, and F. As a true Romantic, Tchaikovsky created his own individual blend of tradition and innovation as a vehicle for his most personal utterances.

EXPOSITION		
		First theme area [F minor]
(24)	**0:00**	Brass fanfare, **ff**, "Fate."

(25)	**1:22**	Waltzlike melody with hesitant cross-rhythms in violins and cellos; gradual descent and ascent; ***p***, crescendo to ***f***.
	1:47	Full emphatic statement of waltz melody leads to developmental section with overlapping statements.

	3:06	Full emphatic statement of waltz melody.
	3:36	More fragmentary versions of waltz melody.
	4:09	Full statement, strings with repeated sixteenth notes.
	4:37	Suddenly quiet, transition to:
(26)	**5:20**	*Second theme area* [A♭ m i n o r] Clarinet, rhythmically jumpy theme and fast, falling chromatic scales echoed by other winds.
	5:43	Jumpy theme again with new lyrical countermelody in cellos.
	6:34	[C♭ = (B)] ***pp***; timpani articulate gradual accelerando and crescendo; new lyrical idea in violins alternates with waltz melody in winds.
	7:13	Lyrical idea in flutes; waltz melody in strings; accelerando and crescendo continue.
(27)	**7:54**	Closing theme: bold descending arpeggios in strings linked by rising scales, accompanied by *rhythms* of waltz melody in brass.
	8:12	Descending arpeggios in brass.
	8:29	Closing material: waltz theme.

DEVELOPMENT

(28)	**9:02**	Fanfare idea, "Fate." Sounds like repeat of the exposition but moves directly into:
	9:21	Developmental treatment of waltz melody.
	9:55	Ascending version of waltz melody in cellos.
	10:02	Lyrical idea in cellos now as countermelody to waltz melody.
	10:27	Lyrical idea again.
	10:50	Long crescendo; building and gradually ascending.

(29)	**11:26**	Fanfare idea used developmentally.
	11:46	Fanfare, again, at higher pitch; illusion of ever-ascending pitch and growing intensity.
	12:14	Descending scales.

RECAPITULATION

		[D minor]
(30)	**12:18**	Fanfare returns, "Fate."
	12:30	Powerful return of waltz idea, decrescendo to:
(31)	**13:04**	Quiet return of second theme; jumpy rhythms in bassoon, followed by fast falling chromatic line.
	13:28	Lyrical idea in French horn as countermelody.
		[F minor]
	14:21	Lyrical idea and waltz melody alternate quietly; timpani articulates a long gradual crescendo and accelerando.
	15:31	Building intensely to:
	15:43	Closing material built on waltz theme.

CODA

(32)	**16:13**	Return of fanfare, "Fate," with timpani roll. [Slower tempo]
	16:36	New sustained ascending flute line.
	16:55	Sustained line moves to oboe; waltz rhythms build.
	17:13	Suddenly *pp* and quicker; waltz rhythms accelerate even more.
	17:36	Previous passage repeated.
	18:04	Tremolo version of waltz melody; conclusion with timpani rolls and heavy octave chords.

PART THREE: LATE ROMANTICISM

Toward the end of the nineteenth century, a new atmosphere reigned in Europe and the United States. Independence and unification brought more stability to many countries, and there were moves toward greater democracy, with monarchies being replaced by parliamentary governments. Free compulsory education led to a more educated public, and the early horrors of the sweat shops were gradually replaced by better working conditions. Commerce and industry were central preoccupations, and a more down-to-earth attitude replaced the dreamy fantasyland of high Romanticism. The movement known as Realism affected all culture, from the novels of Dickens, Flaubert, and Zola to the plays of Henrik Ibsen, the paintings of Gustave Courbet, and the philosophy of William James. Music was also affected, as we shall see. As the end of the century approached, a spirit of general dissatisfaction and uneasiness took hold.

The major composers of late Romanticism were Johannes Brahms, Giacomo Puccini, and Gustav Mahler. All these composers reflected the new atmosphere in different ways. Brahms found new force in the rigor of Classic and Baroque musical genres and forms. Puccini wrote dramatic realist operas of acute psychological insight. Mahler created a new synthesis of song and symphony in a mood tinged with resignation.

JOHANNES BRAHMS (1833–1897)

Johannes Brahms was born in Hamburg in 1833. His father was an orchestral and band musician; his mother came from a wealthy family and was 44 when Brahms was born, a fact that may have colored Brahms's later relationship with Clara Schumann, who was 14 years older than he.

Brahms was a child prodigy. He gave his first piano recital at the age of 10, and an American entrepreneur tried to book him for a concert tour of the United States, but his piano teacher refused. Brahms spent much of his youth playing the piano at bars and coffee houses; he also wrote pieces for his father's band. While still a youth, he was exposed to Hungarian gypsy music as a result of the flight of many nationalist rebels from Hungary after the Hungarian uprising of 1848. This led to a fascination with gypsy tunes and rhythms. Brahms also met the great violinist Joseph Joachim, with whom he developed a lifelong friendship. But the real turning point for Brahms came when he was 20 and he met Robert Schumann. Brahms played some of his own compositions for the great Romantic master in

Johannes Brahms as a young man.

Schumann's study. After a few minutes, Schumann stopped him and went to fetch Clara. "Now you will hear music such as you have never heard before," he said to her. During the time of Schumann's illness, Brahms and Clara Schumann became very close. Their friendship lasted until Clara's death 43 years later, one year before Brahms's own.

Throughout his life, Brahms compared himself, mostly unfavorably, with other great composers of the past, especially Beethoven. He said that he felt the presence of Beethoven as "the step of a giant over my shoulder." It took him 20 years to summon the courage to publish his First Symphony.

Brahms settled in Vienna, the imperial capital, where he made a name for himself as a pianist. "He plays so brightly and clearly," wrote Joseph Joachim. "I have never met such talent." He also worked as a conductor. Brahms lived a quiet, reserved life, and although he enjoyed the company of many friends, he also needed a great deal of solitude. He usually hid his feelings. Clara Schumann, who knew him better than anyone else, called him "a riddle." In his musical life, he was not pleased to be seen as a symbol of conservatism and the leader of an "anti-modern" movement in music. Wagner attacked him mercilessly in print, calling him a "street-musician," a "hypocrite," and a "eunuch."

Brahms deliberately avoided the innovative genres of modern music, such as the symphonic poem and music drama, preferring instead solo piano pieces, songs, choral works, chamber music, concertos, and symphonies. He continued to be conscious of the great achievements of the past. The last movement of his First Symphony makes a deliberate reference to Beethoven's Ninth, and the last movement of his Fourth Symphony uses a Baroque form and is based on a theme by Bach.

Throughout the years, Brahms continued to rely on Clara Schumann for advice and comments on his compositions. Her enormous enthusiasm undoubtedly bolstered his self-confidence. But in the spring of 1896 came terrible news: Clara had died of a stroke. Brahms traveled to Bonn to attend her funeral. On his return, he wrote one of his most beautiful works, the *Four Serious Songs* for piano and voice on texts that Brahms selected from the Bible. The fourth song, with a text from Corinthians, describes the immortality of love: "These three things endure: faith, hope, and love; but the greatest of these is love." A month after Clara's funeral, Brahms was diagnosed with cancer. He died on April 3, 1897, at the age of 64. Large crowds attended his funeral, and messages of sadness poured in from all over Europe. In the great port city of Hamburg, where Brahms had been born, all the ships lowered their flags to half mast.

BRAHMS'S MUSIC

Brahms was a Romantic who expressed himself in Classic and sometimes even Baroque forms; within these forms, his music is highly original. Brahms avoided the fashionable genres of Romantic music, such as opera and symphonic poems. And he wrote no program music, though he liked to hide references to women he admired in his compositions. He adored the human voice, and his Romantic songs follow directly in the line of Schubert and Schumann. The main themes of his songs are love, nature, and (toward the end of his life) death. He also set many folk songs to music. The most famous of these is the exquisite *Lullaby*, Op. 49, No. 4 (sometimes called "Brahms's Lullaby"). We shall listen to this work. (**See Listening Guide on page 312.**)

His four symphonies are masterpieces—the first and the fourth powerful and intense, the second and the third more lyrical and serene. We shall study a movement from the Fourth Symphony. (**See Listening Guide on page 313.**) The Violin Concerto stands with those of Beethoven, Mendelssohn, and Tchaikovsky as one of the great violin concertos of the nineteenth century. It is technically impressive, powerful, and lively, but it also has passages of great calm and beauty. Written for himself to play, Brahms's two piano concertos are also masterpieces. In all his orchestral works, Brahms used an orchestra not much bigger than Beethoven's, avoiding the huge, showy sounds of Wagner and Liszt. One characteristic of Brahms's style is his thick orchestral textures. He liked to "fill in" the sound between treble and bass with many musical lines, and to double melodies in thirds or sixths. He especially favored instruments that play in the middle range, such as clarinet, viola, and French horn.

This warmth of sound may be found in his chamber music as well. Because he was a fine pianist, Brahms wrote several chamber works for piano and strings, but he also composed some excellent string quartets. His love of rich textures is shown in the two string *quintets* and two string *sextets*. Toward the end of his life, after he had decided to give up composition, Brahms met a fine clarinetist who inspired several chamber works featuring the clarinet. In all these works there is passion, but the passion is mingled with resignation and an autumnal sense of peace. Brahms's solo piano music was written mostly for his own performance. The early pieces are strong and showy, but the later ones are much more delicate and extremely profound.

Brahms composed several choral works. The most important of these is the *German Requiem*, for soprano and baritone soloists, chorus, and orchestra, for which Brahms chose his own texts from the German Bible. It was not written for a religious service but for concert performance. Nevertheless, the music is sincere and deeply felt. Brahms was a man who did not believe in organized religion, yet he was privately devout and read every day from the Bible he had owned since childhood.

Brahms has been called a conservative composer because of his adherence to models from the past. Yet he was an innovator in many ways. His rhythms are always complex and interesting, with syncopation and offbeat accents and with a very frequent use of mixed duple and triple meters. His phrases are often irregular—expanded or contracted from the usual four- or eight-bar format. And he was a master of variation, in which something familiar is constantly undergoing change. Indeed, in Brahms's music there is very little exact repetition or recapitulation: the music seems to grow organically from beginning to end. Brahms himself was both complex and fascinating, and the same can be said of his music.

Because of the beauty and sweetness of his tone, Brahms called clarinetist Richard Mühlfeld *Fräulein Klarinette* ("Miss Clarinet"). He also described him as "the greatest artist there is on the instrument."

Johannes Brahms (1833–1897)
Wiegenlied (Lullaby), Op. 49, No. 4

Date of composition: 1868
Tempo: *Zart bewegt* ("Moving tenderly")
Meter: $\frac{3}{4}$
Key: E♭ Major
Duration: 2:07

Complete CD Collection: 5, track 33

Brahms wrote this, perhaps his most famous song, for the baby son of a woman who sang in his choir in Hamburg. It is strophic: The two stanzas are sung to the same music. The poem (an old German folk song) has three pairs of lines, but Brahms repeats the last pair to make a balanced four pairs, with four phrases of music, given four measures each. There are an additional two measures of piano introduction. Brahms uses every means at his disposal to create a peaceful musical setting for this lullaby. The vocal line is smooth and wafting; the piano part has transparent texture, a rocking, hazy rhythm, and extremely stable harmonies. There is the slightest intensification of the piano part in the second half of each stanza ("Morgen früh ... "/"Schlaf nun ... ").

9 (33)   **0:00** | [Two measures piano introduction, setting the mood]

STANZA 1

0:06

Guten abend, gut' Nacht,	Good night, good night,
Mit Rosen bedacht,	(Those covers) decorated with roses,
Mit Näglein besteckt,	Embroidered with carnations,
Schlupf unter die Deck.	Slip under them.

[ends high]

0:31

Morgen früh, wenn Gott will,	Tomorrow morning, God willing,
Wirst du wieder geweckt.	You will wake again.
Morgen früh, wenn Gott will,	Tomorrow morning, God willing,
Wirst du wieder geweckt.	You will wake again.

[ends low]

STANZA 2

[music repeated for second stanza]

1:05

Guten Abend, gut' Nacht,	Good night, good night,
Von Englein bewacht,	You are watched over by angels,
Die zeigen im Traum	Who will show you in your dreams
Dir Christkindleins Baum.	The Christ child's tree.
Schlaf nun selig und süss,	Sleep now, blessed and sweet,
Schau im Traum's Paradies.	And look at Paradise in your dreams.
Schlaf nun selig und süss,	Sleep now, blessed and sweet,
Schau im Traum's Paradies.	And look at Paradise in your dreams.

Johannes Brahms (1833–1897)
Fourth Movement from Symphony No. 4
  in E minor

Date of composition: 1885
Duration: 10:36
Orchestration: 2 flutes, 2 oboes,
    2 clarinets, 2 bassoons,
    contrabassoon, 4 French horns,
    2 trumpets, 3 trombones, timpani,
    full string section
Tempo: *Allegro energico e passionato*
    ("Fast, energetic, and passionate")
Meter: ¾
Key: E minor

Student CD Collection: 3, track 15
Complete CD Collection: 5, track 34

The fourth movement of Brahms's Symphony No. 4 is based on a regularly recurring eight-measure harmonic progression. This form is known as a *passacaglia*, a variation form that was popular with Baroque composers. Brahms's use of this form shows how he valued the musical past as a source of inspiration.

The repetitive harmonic element gives the movement a clear and accessible form, and the eight-measure patterns can be followed simply by counting. The harmonic progression is not repeated strictly each time but is used instead as a flexible point of departure. The variations range from pure harmonic chord progressions, as in the initial statement, to melodic ideas.

The initial presentation of the theme is bold, strong, and direct. Although this statement is primarily harmonic—a series of chords—it also has a powerful melodic element, a relentless ascending line that dramatically drops an octave just before the end. The theme begins in the tonic key and moves to the dominant in measure 6 before returning to the tonic. These features (the melodic line and the harmonic motion) are drawn on in the course of the movement, but the most fixed and unchanging feature is the length of the variations. The consistent use of the eight-measure pattern creates a movement of great strength.

In addition to this small-scale structural element, Brahms organizes the work by grouping the 30 variations into three large sections. The middle section contrasts with the outer sections; and the third section includes some varied restatements of earlier material. Thus the larger form of this movement is another manifestation of one that is by now very familiar: ABA', with Coda:

A	**B**	**A'**	**CODA**
Theme, and Variations 1–11	Variations 12–15	Variations 16–30	

Within these large groups, Brahms focuses our attention by grouping similar variations together. Variations that share related ideas are bracketed in the timed description that follows.

[minor key, 3/4 meter]

15 (34) **0:00** Theme. Strong, measure-long chords, ascending melodic line, brass and woodwinds. (Count the eight measures.)

0:16 *Variation 1*

Also chordal, with timpani rolls and string pizzicatos on the second beat of the measures.

0:30 *Variation 2*

Smooth melody with regular rhythmic values and smooth motion. Flutes join clarinets and oboes in a crescendo.

0:46 *Variation 3*

The regular rhythm of the melody is given a staccato articulation; brass is added.

1:01 *Variation 4*

The ascending melody of the theme is used as a bass line in the lower strings, while the violins introduce a new melody, featuring leaping motion and jumpy rhythms.

1:18 *Variation 5*

Violins elaborate this melody with faster rhythms; accompaniment thickens with arpeggios.

1:33 *Variation 6*

Rhythms become even faster and more intense, building to the next variation.

1:48 *Variation 7*

New melodic idea, with the violins strained in their upper register, and a new jumpy rhythm.

16 (35) **2:04**	*Variation 8*	
	Faster rhythms (sixteenth notes) used in violins, busy energetic feel; violins repeat a single high note while the flute plays a smoother melodic line.	

2:19	*Variation 9*	
	Suddenly loud; even faster rhythms (sixteenth-note triplets), violins swoop from high to low range; decrescendo with violins again on repeated note; descending chromatic scale in the winds.	

2:35	*Variation 10*	
	Calm exchanges of chords between winds and strings.	

2:53	*Variation 11*	
	More chord exchanges, but the violins elaborate theirs with faster, detached notes. Descending and slowing chromatic scale in the flute connects to solo of the next variation.	

B Section

[Here the new, slower tempo and meter (3/2) result in longer variations, although they are still eight measures. The descending chromatic scale that ended Variation 11 also ends Variations 13, 14, and 15.]

17 (36) **3:14**	*Variation 12*	
	Flute solo that restlessly ascends, gradually reaching into higher ranges, and then descends. Duple pattern in accompaniment emphasizes the new meter.	

3:57	*Variation 13*	
	Change to brighter E Major. Much calmer mood. Clarinet and oboe alternate simple phrases. Duple pattern in accompaniment continues, supplemented by long rising arpeggios in the strings.	

4:36	*Variation 14*	
	Trombones enter with chordal, hymnlike sound. Short rising arpeggios in the strings are the only accompaniment.	

5:17	*Variation 15*	
	Brass and winds continue rich chordal sound, with fuller string arpeggios, as in Var. 14. Descending line in flute, slows to a halt.	

[The return of the A material is bold and dramatic. The faster tempo has renewed drive and energy after the contemplative B section.]

| **18** (37) | **6:03** | *Variation 16* |

Repeat of the original statement of the theme, only joined in measure 4 by searingly high violins descending a scale. Back to E minor and 3/4.

| | **6:16** | *Variation 17* |

String tremolos crescendo and decrescendo while winds emphasize beats 2 and 3 of the 3/4 meter.

| | **6:27** | *Variation 18* |

String tremolos continue while winds and brass exchange a jumpy figure that builds in a rising melody.

| | **6:40** | *Variation 19* |

f; new staccato articulation as strings and winds alternate bold eighth-note gestures.

| | **6:53** | *Variation 20* |

Staccato figure builds in intensity, using faster triplet rhythm.

| | **7:05** | *Variation 21* |

Swift ascending scales in strings, ending with accented notes, alternate with brass unison attacks rising in pitch.

| | **7:18** | *Variation 22* |

p; syncopated quarter notes, creating a two-against-three feeling, are exchanged with staccato triplet figures.

| | **7:30** | *Variation 23* |

Suddenly *f*; theme in French horns, triplet figures build in strings and winds, ending in eighth notes moving by leaps.

| **19** (38) | **7:44** | *Variation 24* |

With its accents on beat 2, this variation recalls Var. 1 but is much more forceful, with heavy accents.

7:59	*Variation 25*	
	Here the soft melody of Var. 2 returns, now frenzied in intensity through the loud volume and string tremolos. Emphasis on beat 2 continues with brass and timpani repeated notes.	
8:12	*Variation 26*	
	The staccato quarter notes of Var. 3 are smooth and rich here, in the French horns, then moving to the oboes.	
8:25	*Variation 27*	
	Sustained chords in the high winds, with smooth arpeggios rising and falling in the violas and cellos.	
8:40	*Variation 28*	
	Sustained melody in winds becomes more active; faster arpeggios rise to violins and violas.	
8:53	*Variation 29*	
	Rising two-note figures in flutes, accompanied by syncopated string offbeats; ends with stepwise violin melody.	
9:07	*Variation 30*	
	Suddenly *f*; accented quarter notes, with offbeats; slight slowing and ever wider leaps in the violins; four additional measures outside of the theme move us into the Coda.	

CODA

20 (39) **9:29**	Based on melodic outline of theme; increasing tempo; high violin line accompanied by driving arpeggios and tremolos; two-note exchanges between high and low.
9:51	Trombones with two accented, compressed statements of the theme melody, punctuated by strings.
9:59	Violins crescendo; winds play theme statements answered by orchestra; strings and winds in a syncopated statement of the theme; vigorous descending arpeggios weight the concluding chords.

GIACOMO PUCCINI (1858–1924)

The greatest opera composer of the late nineteenth century was Giacomo Puccini. He grew up in Lucca, a medieval town near the coast of Italy. Puccini came from a family of musicians: His father, grandfather, great-grandfather, and great-great-grandfather were all composers. At the age of 14, he became the organist at Lucca, and he surprised the congregation by working the tunes of opera arias into his organ-playing during services. He was in love with opera, and after he saw a performance of Verdi's *Aida* at the age of 18, he decided to become an opera composer himself.

Puccini went to Milan, the opera capital of Italy; he spent many years there leading a typical student life, refining his composing skills, and soaking up opera. After graduation, he got his first break when he played and sang portions of one of his own works at a private party. An important impresario and the head of the largest publishing firm in Italy were at the party, and they were so impressed they decided to publish the opera and stage it. Puccini spent five years on his next opera, which was not a success.

Giacomo Puccini.

For both of these early works, Puccini had relied on other people's choice of libretto. Now he decided to choose his own. At 35, he produced the first of his string of immortal Romantic operas: *Manon Lescaut*, based on a French love story. It came in the same year as the last opera of the grand old man of Italian opera, Verdi. Immediately, Puccini was hailed as "the heir of Verdi." He was an overnight success, his fortune was assured, and his name traveled around the world. *Manon Lescaut* was followed by *La Bohème* (1896), *Tosca* (1900), and *Madama Butterfly* (1904), three of the most popular operas in the entire repertory. They are all cast in the new *verismo* (realist) mode of opera. *La Bohème* tells the story of a group of poor students and artists living in Paris; *Tosca* contains scenes of attempted rape, murder, execution, and suicide; and *Madama Butterfly* describes the pathetic death of a devoted Japanese geisha girl. But all three are also full of life, love, and passion.

Puccini's next opera, *La fanciulla del West* (*The Girl of the Golden West*, 1910), was given its premiere at the Metropolitan Opera House in New York. This is Puccini's "American" opera, set in the "Wild West," with saloons, guns, and a manhunt. For the premiere, the great Arturo Toscanini was the conductor, and the legendary tenor Enrico Caruso took the leading male role.

Puccini's last opera was *Turandot*, set in China and based on a Chinese folk story. It was not quite finished when Puccini died in 1924. A colleague completed the last two scenes, and the first performance was given in 1926 at the great opera house of La Scala in Milan. Puccini's death was declared a national day of mourning in Italy.

Before he died, Puccini wrote, "When I was born, the Almighty touched me with his little finger and said: 'Write operas—mind you, only operas!' And I have obeyed the supreme command."

PUCCINI'S MUSIC

Puccini's music never fails to stir the strongest emotions. It seems to have the ability to touch all who listen to it. His senses of timing, drama, and poignancy were perfect, and he was able to set a scene or a mood with just a few phrases of music. His melodies soar, and the vocal lines are buoyed up on waves of orchestral sound. A trademark of his style is the doubling or even tripling of the vocal lines by the orchestra, especially in the strings, so that the voices gain an almost luminous intensity. Puccini also wrote fresh and modern harmonies, with some strong dissonances and unexpected chord progressions, and these serve to heighten the drama. Sometimes he also employed unusual scales, such as the pentatonic scale, to suggest an exotic locale.

The action in Puccini operas is continuous, with short orchestral phrases woven together under the sung dialogue. For the most part, there is little distinction between recitative and aria, although in each of his operas there are some arias that are unforgettable. We shall listen to one of them: the exquisite, passionate, heartbreaking melody of an aria from *Madama Butterfly*. **(See Listening Guide below.)** "Without melody," said Puccini, "there can be no music."

LISTENING GUIDE

Giacomo Puccini (1858–1924)
Un bel dì (One Fine Day) from
Madama Butterfly

Date of composition: 1904
Duration: 4:32

Student CD Collection: 3, track 21
Complete CD Collection: 5, track 40

*M*adama Butterfly, one of Puccini's most beloved operas, premiered in 1904, at a time when American naval vessels frequented Japanese seaports. Oriental customs and exotic scenery provide the background for this tragic plot, which involves Benjamin Franklin Pinkerton (an American lieutenant) and Cio-Cio-San ("Butterfly," a young Japanese girl). Pinkerton has rented a Japanese house for a period of 999 years. Also in the rental package is his "betrothal" to Cio-Cio-San.

Looking at the marriage merely as a casual affair, Pinkerton proves to be unfaithful to his bride. His ship returns to America after the wedding, and he marries an American woman shortly thereafter. When he returns to Japan three years later with his American wife, the deeply loyal Cio-Cio-San, in grief and humiliation, kills herself.

Butterfly's aria *Un bel dì* comes near the beginning of Act II, as she tries to convince herself and her servant that her husband will return to her. You will hear gorgeous soaring melodies and exotic Oriental sounds in this superb *da capo* (ABA) aria. Listen to the doubling and sometimes tripling of the vocal line in the orchestra, which gives great richness to Puccini's wonderful lyricism.

A SECTION			
21 (40)	0:00	*Un bel dì, vedremo levarsi un fil di fuomo sull' estremo confin del mare.* *E poi la nave appare.* *Poi la nave bianca* *entra nel porto,*	One fine day, we'll notice a thread of smoke rising on the horizon of the sea. And then the ship will appear. Then the white vessel will glide into the harbor,

	0:50	*romba il suo saluto.*	thundering forth her cannon.
		Vedi? E venuto!	Do you see? He has come!
		Io non gli scendo incontro,	I don't go to meet him,
		Io no . . .	Not I . . .

B SECTION

22 (41)	1:18	*Mi metto lá sul ciglio del colle,*	I stay on the brow of the hill,
		e aspetto, e aspetto gran tempo,	and wait there, wait for a long time,
		e non mi pesa la lunga attesa.	but never weary of the long waiting.
		[m o r e m o v e m e n t]	

	1:44	*E . . . uscito dalla folla cittadina*	From the crowded city comes
		un uomo, un picciol punto,	a man, a little speck in the distance,
		[s l o w i n g d o w n]	

	2:00	*s'avia per la collina.*	climbing the hill.

	2:15	*Chi sarà? chi sarà?*	Who is it? Who is it?
		E come sara giunto,	And when he's reached the summit,
		che dirà? che dirà?	what will he say? What will he say?

		[s l o w e r , w i t h s o l o v i o l i n]	
	2:24	*Chiamerà "Butterfly"*	He will call "Butterfly"
		dalla lontana.	from a distance.
		Io senza dar riposta me	And I, without answering,
		ne starò nascosta,	will keep myself quietly concealed,
		un po' per celia,	a bit to tease him,
		e un po' per non . . .	and a bit so as not to . . .

A SECTION

23 (42)	2:52	*morire al primo incontro,*	die at our first meeting,
		ed egli alquanto in pena,	and then, a little troubled,
		chiamerà, chiamerà,	he will call, he will call,
		"Piccina mogliettina	"Dearest, little wife of mine,
		olezzo di verbena!,"	dear little orange blossom!,"
		i nomi che mi dava	the names he used to call
		al suo venire.	when he first came here.

	3:28	*Tutto questo avverrà*	This will come to pass,
		te lo prometto.	I promise you.

	3:34	*Tienti la tua paura,*	Banish your idle fears,
		io con sicura fede l'aspetto.	I know for certain he will come.

	3:48	[l u s h o r c h e s t r a l p o s t l u d e]	

	4:19	[f i n a l c h o r d s]	

GUSTAV MAHLER (1860–1911)

Gustav Mahler was the last great Romantic composer. In his work, Romantic song and the Romantic symphony come together in a final (somewhat nostalgic) triumph of late Romanticism. Mahler was born in Bohemia of Jewish parents and made his career in Germany and Austria. His musical talent was evident at an early age, and he gave his first public piano recital at the age of 10. Mahler lived near a military base, and when he was small he loved to listen to the marching bands. Band music and marches of all kinds show up constantly in Mahler's music. He also was attracted to folk poetry and songs.

As a student in Vienna, Mahler took many classes in history and philosophy as well as in composition. For the next 20 years, he made a living as a conductor. He had a large number of appointments in towns across Europe, most of them lasting for only a year or two. Mahler had tremendously high standards; he was autocratic and demanding of his musicians and uncompromising in his approach to the music. This did not endear him to administrators or to his players, but he gradually made a name for himself as a brilliant conductor, specializing in the works of Mozart, Beethoven, and Wagner. Mahler worked so hard that he had little time for composition, but gradually he developed a habit of composing during the summers, when the concert season was over. In this way, he managed to complete his first three symphonies, but people found them hard to understand.

The most important conducting position in Austria at that time was as music director of the Vienna Opera House. Mahler was by now the obvious choice for the job, but the fact that he was Jewish presented a formidable barrier in a city notorious for its anti-Semitism. He therefore had himself baptized as a Catholic and was appointed to the position in Vienna in 1897. Mahler's tenure there had its problems: He was unpopular with the players because he was so strict, and there was considerable resentment over his appointment, de-

spite his religious conversion. Mahler continued composing, and he completed several large-scale compositions during this time.

In 1902, when he was in his forties, Mahler fell in love with Alma Schindler, a talented young woman of 23. Mahler was as autocratic in his marriage as he was in his work, and the couple had difficulties, but the depth of their relationship was never in doubt. Alma Mahler later published books of memoirs about her life with Mahler and with her two later husbands, one a famous architect and the other a novelist.

In 1907, Mahler suffered three profound setbacks. The campaign against him in Vienna finally led to his resignation from his job; his five-year-old daughter died of scarlet fever; and it was discovered that Mahler himself had a heart condition. In 1908, in an attempt to change entirely the circumstances of his life, Mahler accepted two positions in New York. He was appointed music director of the Metropolitan Opera and conductor of the New York Philharmonic. Mahler was superstitious and afraid to finish his Ninth Symphony,

Gustav Mahler with his daughter Anna.

Alma Mahler

Gustav Mahler first met Alma Schindler at a dinner party in Vienna on November 7, 1901. Three weeks later he proposed to her, and on March 9, 1902, they were married in Vienna's Karlskirche. At Mahler's request and in spite of her considerable talent, Alma gave up composition after their marriage. She devoted herself entirely to her husband. Mahler's enormous productivity after their marriage can be attributed in no small measure to Alma's constant encouragement.

✦ Alma's *Gustav Mahler: Memories and Letters* paints an interesting picture of her husband. He is portrayed as egocentric and incapable of profound love for anyone but himself. How-ever, Mahler's letters to Alma and his adoration of his daughter Maria show us a different picture of his character. Nevertheless, Alma knew Gustav better than anyone else did; for this reason, her writings will always be important to scholars and lovers of Mahler's music.

✦ Before meeting Mahler, Alma had been in love with the artist Gustav Klimt and the composer Alexander Zemlinsky. After Mahler's death, she married the architect Walter Gropius in 1915 and the writer Franz Werfel in 1929. She was also the mistress of the painter Oskar Kokoschka. Alma outlived Gustav Mahler by 53 years and died in the United States in 1964, at the age of 85.

remembering that both Beethoven and Schubert had died after completing nine symphonies. Nonetheless, his Ninth was finished, and Mahler began working on his Tenth. But his worries turned out to be well founded. In 1911 he fell seriously ill. Mahler decided to return to Vienna, where he died at the age of 50, leaving the Tenth Symphony incomplete.

Mahler's Music

Mahler's music represents the last great achievement of the Romantic ideal. In it, he tried to capture "the whole world": nature, God, love and death, exaltation and de-spair. To do this, Mahler had to invent new musical genres and forms. Most of his work is closely connected to song. Four of his symphonies use voices as well as instruments, and song melodies find their way into many of his instrumental works. Mahler wrote some important **orchestral song cycles**, in which the typical Romantic song takes on a completely new guise: In place of piano accompaniment, Mahler uses the orchestra, hugely expanding the range of expressive possibilities.

Mahler was a radical innovator in many other ways. He had the most precise idea of what he wanted to express—and no fear of disregarding tradition to achieve this. "Tradition is a mess," he once said. His harmony is quite unorthodox, and he often ends a work in a key different from the one in which it began. We have seen that Beethoven was able to begin a symphony in a minor key and end it in the major, but actually changing the tonal center of a work was quite new. It gave a whole new meaning to the idea of long-range tonality. Some of Mahler's symphonies are longer than any that had come before, lasting 90 minutes or more.

Mahler was a brilliant and very subtle orchestrator. He had an exact idea of the sound he wanted to produce. He used enormous orchestras, and sometimes the effect is shattering; but the main reason he needed so many instruments was to achieve the widest possible range of tone colors. In the Third Symphony, he writes a solo for a very rare instrument: the posthorn, a small horn generally used on mail coaches. In the Second Symphony, he combines an English horn with a bass clarinet—an amazing and evocative sound. He was extremely meticulous about how he wanted his works to be played. Because he was a professional conductor himself, his scores are covered with exact instructions for almost every phrase of the music.

Most of Mahler's music is programmatic in some way. The slow movement of the Fifth Symphony is a testament of love for his wife, Alma. And the scherzo of the same symphony is a portrait of his children playing. Some of his programs are ambitious in the extreme, including representations of the creation of the world (Symphony No. 3) and the journey from life to death to resurrection (Symphony No. 2). **(See Listening Guide on page 324.)**

Throughout his music, there is a tinge of regret, of irony, even of deliberate distortion. A sense of yearning fills the pages of his work: a feeling of the impossible aims, the losses, the tragic undercurrent of human existence. If Mahler's musical impulse could be summed up in one musical phrase, it would look like this:

Try playing or singing these four notes. Notice how the phrase reaches up—only to fall back a little. Notice how the sense of striving overcomes the feeling of resolution. And notice (if you play the notes together as a chord) the slight dissonance, which sounds bittersweet and thoughtful. This is the essence of Mahler's music.

Mahler's music is full of quotations from Wagner, Brahms, Mendelssohn, and especially Beethoven. It is as though he were looking backward at the entire history of Romantic music. And this is appropriate, for he was its last and one of its greatest manifestations.

Gustav Mahler (1860–1911)
Fourth Movement, *Urlicht* (*Primeval Light*) from Symphony No. 2 in C minor (*Resurrection*)

Date of composition: 1888–94
Orchestration: Alto voice; 2 piccolos, 3 flutes, 2 oboes, English horn, 3 clarinets, 2 bassoons, contrabassoon, 4 horns, 3 trumpets, glockenspiel, 2 harps, and strings
Tempo: *Sehr feierlich, aber schlicht* ("Very ceremonial, but straightforward")
Meter: $\frac{4}{4}$
Key of movement: D♭ Major
Duration: 5:13

Student CD Collection: 3, track 24
Complete CD Collection: 6, track 1

The *Resurrection* Symphony is an enormous work, lasting nearly 90 minutes. It is in five movements, and it traces a spiritual journey from death to resurrection. In its sense of subjectivity and spiritual progression, it is reminiscent of Beethoven's Fifth Symphony. This parallel is made the more obvious by Mahler's choice of the same key, C minor, and by the move in the last movement to triumph (C major).

The fourth movement marks the beginning of Mahler's lifelong preoccupation with the blending of symphony and song. The movement is actually the setting of a song text, sung by a solo alto voice with the orchestra. It is entitled *Urlicht* (*Primeval Light*). The text's central message is contained in its eighth line: "Ich bin von Gott und will wieder zu Gott" ("I am made by God and will return to God"). Mahler said of this movement: "The stirring voice of simple faith sounds in our ears."

The melodic shape of the vocal line often follows the pattern described previously an upward curve followed by a slight fall. In addition, Mahler has composed the most remarkable instrumental music for this movement: quiet, stately, and richly orchestrated, with striking changes of key. The music does far more than accompany the words: It gives them new and profound meaning beyond their own power of expression.

SONG TEXT

O Röschen rot!	O red rose!
Der Mensch liegt in grösster Not!	Humanity lies in deepest need!
Der Mensch liegt in grösster Pein!	Humanity lies in greatest pain!
Je lieber möcht ich im Himmel sein!	I would rather be in Heaven!
Da kam ich auf einen breiten Weg;	Then I came upon a broad path;
Da kam ein Engelein und wollt mich abweisen.	Then came an angel, that tried to turn me away.
Ach nein! Ich liess mich nicht abweisen!	But no! I will not be turned away!
Ich bin von Gott und will wieder zu Gott!	I am made by God and will return to God!
Der liebe Gott wird mir ein Lichten geben,	Dear God will give me a light,
Wird leuchten mir bis in das ewig, selig Leben!	Will light my way to eternal, blessed life!

24 (1)	**0:00**	Begins with words of alto (*"O Röschen rot! "*), accompanied by low strings.
	0:22	Brass chorale: 3 trumpets, 4 horns, bassoons, contrabassoon.
	1:07	*"Der Mensch liegt in grösster Not!"* (strings).
25 (2)	**1:19**	Change of key. *"Der Mensch liegt in grösster Pein!"* (strings).
	1:32	Trumpets.
	1:37	*"Je lieber möcht ich im Himmel sein!"* Note upward swoop on *"Himmel"* ("Heaven").
	1:57	Repeat of previous line. Voice with oboe. Note curve of melodic line.
	2:16	Oboe and strings.
	2:49	Tempo marked: "Somewhat faster." Clarinets, harp, and glockenspiel.
	2:55	*"Da kam ich auf einen breiten Weg;"*
26 (3)	**3:02**	Solo violin, representing the "ich" ("I") of the poet (probably Mahler himself).
	3:14	Miraculous key change, very quiet: *"Da kam ein Engelein und wollt mich abweisen."* Fuller orchestration: piccolos, harps, strings.
	3:32	Back to slow tempo: *"Ach nein! Ich liess mich nicht abweisen!"* (tremolo strings, oboes)
	3:43	Higher: Repeat of previous line.
	3:55	Back to D♭: strings, horns, harp. *"Ich bin von Gott und will wieder zu Gott!"*
	4:03	*"Der liebe Gott, der liebe Gott,"*
	4:10	Very slow: *"wird mir ein Lichten geben,"*
27 (4)	**4:21**	*"Wird leuchten mir bis in das ewig, selig Leben!"* Note wondrous curve of melodic line and the muted violins shimmering *above* the voice on *"Leben"* ("Life").
	4:50	Muted strings, harps; dying away.

The largest proportion of the music played in concert halls today was composed in the nineteenth century. People nowadays seem to have the greatest affinity for music of that period. This means that there are a lot of composers to consider and many different stylistic trends to summarize for this chapter.

Beethoven set the tone for the century. Almost every composer that followed Beethoven attempted to match the force and depth of his music. Many copied his formal innovations. Others built on his style of molding music into personal revelation.

In this last aspect, music was the strongest representative of the new Romantic spirit. Composers wanted their works to express the inexpressible: the height of joy, the depths of despair, the transcendence of love. Compositions ranged from the tiniest miniatures for solo piano to works for the largest conglomeration of performing forces ever seen.

Instruments themselves changed. They became bigger and louder, and new instruments, such as the tuba and the saxophone, were invented. Favorite older instruments were the piano and violin, especially for solo playing. Many people in the growing middle class played the piano or chamber music at home, and great performers of the piano and violin became international stars. The warm sound of instruments that play in the middle range, such as French horn and cello, was also favored by composers. The range of dynamics in all music was widened, as was the range of expression. Above all composers wanted their music to be expressive.

This striving for expression led to other, more systemic changes. Melodies became longer and more flowing. Tempo, rather than being more or less fixed from the beginning to the end of each movement, became more fluid, allowing the music to ebb and flow as it went along. Harmony became more adventurous, with more and more unusual chords appearing and with more rapid changes of key. Chromatic notes became much more frequent. Later nineteenth-century works, in particular, seem far less fixed in their key centers than do those of the Classic era. Finally, Romantic composers liked to blur the formal outlines of their works; the organizing structure became less obvious and heightened the sense of spontaneity and continuity.

The second half of the century saw the widespread development of the symphonic poem, a one-movement symphonic work that tells a story. Indeed all such narrative music, or program music, was popular. Another central genre was Romantic opera, which also became far more fluid and continuous; much of the action

The first page of Mahler's handwritten score for the fourth movement of his Second Symphony.

unfolded in a style called *arioso* (singing which is between aria and recitative), and much of the feeling was portrayed in the orchestra.

The nationalist movement, which was primarily political and cultural, nonetheless strongly affected nineteenth-century music. Nationalist composers from Norway, Finland, Denmark, Russia, Bohemia, Moravia, Spain, France, and even the United States sought to portray national identity in their works. They incorporated folk themes and national dances in their music and set words for songs and operas in their own languages.

By the end of the century, the search for expression led to the final dissolution of the Romantic movement. Works could become no bigger, and the subject matter now ranged from murder, rape, and suicide to the creation of the world and life after death. Also, the system of tonality, with its ordered hierarchy of keys, had been stretched to the breaking point.

Romantic song, nineteenth-century symphony, and program music came together in the music of Gustav Mahler—music that has direct and strong links back to Beethoven, but that also stands poised at the end of an era. Three years after Mahler's death, Europe was engulfed in the flames of the First World War.

The same music in a modern printed score.

FUNDAMENTALS OF NINETEENTH-CENTURY MUSIC

- ✦ The size of musical works ranges from miniature to enormous
- ✦ Tempos are fluid and variable
- ✦ Melodies are longer, more flowing, and seemingly more spontaneous
- ✦ Forms are less structured and their outlines deliberately disguised
- ✦ Harmony pushes at the outer limits of tonality
- ✦ New instruments were invented, and older instruments were redesigned to make them louder and faster
- ✦ Brilliant individual performers on instruments such as the piano and violin ruled the concert stages
- ✦ New genres, such as the programmatic symphonic poem, became popular, and other genres, such as the symphony, were used for program music
- ✦ Operas are more continuous in their music, with much of the action set in *arioso* style; the subject matter ranges from grandiose to gritty and realistic

THE TWENTIETH CENTURY I: THE CLASSICAL SCENE

AN OVERVIEW

The twentieth century was a time of extraordinary contrasts. Technology reached dizzying heights of achievement. Radio, telephone, television, satellites, and computers radically altered both personal and worldwide communication. Travel was completely revolutionized. Medical science conquered many infectious diseases and invented complex surgical procedures for prolonging life.

But the twentieth century also displayed mankind's weaknesses, cruelty, and inhumanity at their worst. Two world wars decimated populations across Europe. World War II brought one of the most appalling instances of organized savagery in human history and introduced a new word, "genocide," into the language. The destructive power of military technology was displayed by the explosion of two atomic bombs on civilian populations in Japan.

Although science made impressive gains in the last century, its limitations became more apparent as the century waned. AIDS swept through populations of Africa, the Caribbean, Europe, Asia, and North America, seeming to represent a return to the incurable plagues of the Middle Ages. Short-sighted economic policies and commercial greed caused widespread destruction to the world's environment. And most damning of all, the richest and most wasteful countries of the world were not able to find a way to save millions of people in other countries from starvation. As the twentieth century gave way to the twenty-first, the contrast between its successes and its failures seemed particularly stark.

HISTORY AND THE ARTS, 1900–1939

In 1900, Europe and the United States were in a period of unusual stability, peace, and prosperity. Economic growth was strong, the standard of living was improving rapidly, and scientific breakthroughs contributed to health and comfort.

At this time, the movement known as Modernism began to affect all the arts: literature, painting, sculpture, architecture, and music. Modernism was a movement of self-conscious innovation. Artists, writers, intellectuals, poets, and painters reacted strongly to the accepted rules of the nineteenth century and created works of striking experimentation and revolutionary force. Composers rejected tonality, the harmonic basis of music since the seventeenth century, and adopted radically new harmonic structures.

In this period of excitement, experimentation, and optimism, the greatest composers were Debussy, Schoenberg, and Stravinsky. The works they created during the period were innovative and daring. Their brilliance matched the extraordinary accomplishments of the greatest poets and painters of the age.

World War I (1914–18) shattered this sense of optimism. In this long drawn-out conflict—ugly, brutal, and often senseless—40 million people died and 20 million were wounded. A sense of the devastation and despair caused by this war is given in the poems of Wilfred Owen, poems that were later used in the magnificent *War Requiem* of the English composer Benjamin Britten.

The period after the war was one of uncertainty and a gradual decline into new conflict. The Bolshevik revolution had given rise to the first Communist state, one of the most influential political developments of the whole twentieth century. The economic devastation of Germany led directly to Hitler's rise to power. In Italy, Mussolini founded the first Fascist state in Europe in 1922. A Fascist government was established in Spain after the Spanish Civil War of 1936–39.

During the 1920s, the United States experienced a period of prosperity. The war had strongly stimulated America's economy. American products were sold all over the world, and President Calvin Coolidge made his famous statement that "the business of America is business." A break in this upward spiral came with the Great Depression of 1929–33, which caused widespread unemployment and hunger. During the 1930s, President Franklin D. Roosevelt's policies instilled confidence in the nation and led to gradual economic recovery, the full impact of which was not felt until the new boom brought about by the outbreak of World War II.

In social terms, the period between the wars was one of turmoil and change. Women won the right to vote in 1920. Prohibition created an entire counterculture of bootleg liquor and organized crime. Many intellectuals, who today might be termed liberals, were attracted by the social ideals of Marxism.

The greatest composers of the period between the wars were still Schoenberg and Stravinsky (Debussy had died in 1918) but also included two students of Schoenberg—Berg and Webern—as well as Bartók in Hungary, Shostakovich in the Soviet Union, Britten in England, and Ives and Copland in the United States.

Below: President Roosevelt greets a crowd of well-wishers in 1933.

"Flapper" (fashionable young woman) on the cover of a magazine in the 1920s.

Courtesy of the Library of Congress.

1939 TO 2000

World War II (1939–45) broke out only 21 years after the end of the First World War. Thirty million people died; cities and towns in England, continental Europe, and the Far East suffered enormous and widespread damage; irreplaceable works of art and buildings, some of them dating back to the Middle Ages, were destroyed. The economy of Europe was in shambles, and the political map was highly uncertain. The Soviet Union and the United States emerged as the dominant powers of the postwar period, and Europe was divided by its allegiance to one or the other of these powers. Populations around Europe were uprooted, and many countries were flooded with refugees.

One of the magnets for refugees was the United States. Large numbers of people—including scholars, artists, writers, composers, and performing musicians—came from Europe to America. This influx made the United States the most prominent center of Western culture after the war.

From 1945 to the 1960s, two musical trends asserted themselves. The first was a tendency toward intellectualization. Music became so organized, so mathematical in its structure that many audiences turned away from classical music altogether. It seemed as though composers were writing only for other composers and were no longer interested in communicating to audiences.

The second trend in this period involved radical experimentation, parallel in some ways to the period about 1900. Composers experimented with music in every conceivable way, throwing out all the conventionally accepted norms of music-making. They put the compositional process into the hands of the performers. They challenged audiences and violated conventions of time, performing medium, and concert decorum. Most particularly, they experimented with *sound*. Conventional instruments were pushed to new limits, exotic instruments were introduced, and new instruments were invented. Most influential was the use of tape and then synthesizers and computers in the production of musical sounds. The foremost figures of this period were Pierre Boulez and John Cage.

Since the mid-1960s, a new movement was evident in Western culture, a movement called Postmodernism. It is a troubling term. If "modern" means up-to-date or the present, how can you have a period after the present? Indeed, literature, art, and music in the last few decades of the twentieth century were in a period of severe self-examination, which has continued into the opening years of the twenty-first century. From the start of Postmodernism, everything was cast

Refugees leaving the city of Königsberg with their last possessions after shelling by the Russian army in April 1945.

into doubt, including the worth and meaning of Western culture itself. Literary works struggled for identity. Paintings juxtaposed the old and the new in startling ways. Postmodern buildings became highly eclectic, combining an exaggerated variety of styles in a single unit. And music made a radical move away from the intellectualized compositions of the postwar period toward a new accessibility of style.

Composers began again to address their audiences. They borrowed ideas from rock music to appeal to a wider public. They expanded their frame of reference to include the rhythms, timbres, and harmonies of other countries. And many of them made a conscious return to traditional tonality, to provide an aural context and meaning that many Modernists had rejected.

GENERAL CHARACTERISTICS OF TWENTIETH-CENTURY MUSIC

Music of the twentieth century embodied more experimentation and diversity than in previous eras. Everything was called into question, including the tonal system upon which Western music had been based for centuries, and even the very idea of a concert itself. The length of compositions changed a great deal: Pieces could be very tiny or immensely long. All types of sound were used, and the distinction between sound and noise was often erased.

THE REPLACEMENT OF TONALITY

In the early years of the twentieth century, the Viennese composer Arnold Schoenberg invented a new system, which, he said, would free music from "the tyranny of tonality." This new system was the **twelve-**

Revolutionary composer Arnold Schoenberg in a photograph by Man Ray, c. 1930.

tone system, which treated every pitch as equal in significance to every other. The gravitational pull of a key center was replaced by a sense of complete openness. Rather than **atonality** (nontonality), Schoenberg preferred the term **pantonality** (all-tonality).

This new system opened the floodgates for a totally new approach to musical composition in the twentieth century. Completely new chord combinations could be used, and consonance and dissonance no longer had the significance of the past. In previous eras, consonance had implied stability, and dissonance instability, but now all kinds of dissonances could be used at any point in a piece. Dissonances could be piled on top of one another to produce new sounds. Composers used chords called **tone clusters**, in which a large number of adjacent pitches are all sounded at once. (On the piano, you can play a tone cluster by pushing down all the keys under your entire forearm.) Other methods of replacing tonality included new scales, polytonality, and nontriadic harmony.

Because tonality was based on a standard scale pattern, music based on new scale patterns had the effect of replacing traditional tonality. New scale patterns included the pentatonic scale, the whole-tone scale, and the octatonic scale.

The **pentatonic scale** has only five notes, usually in the following pattern:

Pentatonic Scale

second   second   minor   second   minor
third   third

The same pattern of intervals can be reproduced by playing only the black keys on the piano. (You can easily compose your own pentatonic melody this way. Just improvise on the black keys. The music will sound evocative and folklike.) Pentatonic scales had been around for a long time in many Asian musics and Western folk musics, but they were new to Western classical music.

The **whole-tone scale** has a whole step between each pitch and the next, and the scale has only six notes:

Whole-tone Scale

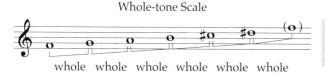

whole whole whole whole whole whole

Because there are no half steps in this scale, the sense of "pull" given by the last half step in the traditional octave scale is missing, and tonality is bypassed.

The last new scale developed by composers in the twentieth century was the **octatonic scale**. This has eight pitches *within* the octave, in a pattern of alternating whole and half steps:

Octatonic Scale

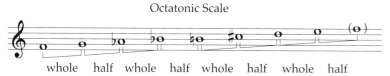

whole half whole half whole half whole half

As well as inventing new scales, composers sometimes turned to a system that had been in use *before* the establishment of tonality. This was the **modal** system, the basis of music during the Middle Ages and the Renaissance. The use of an old system made music sound new again and provided composers with a further alternative to tonality.

In addition to using new (or very old) scales, composers experimented with polytonality and nontriadic harmony. **Polytonality** means the simultaneous sounding of two or more keys at once. Both Igor Stravinsky and the American composer Charles Ives used polytonality. Ives once wrote a piece for two brass bands, each playing in a different key.

Nontriadic harmony means harmony that is not based on the triad, the standard basis for chords in conventional tonality. In the twentieth century, many composers experimented with alternative types of chord structure. The German composer Paul Hindemith, who emigrated to the United States in 1940

and was an extremely influential teacher, often used **quartal chords**, based on fourths instead of thirds.

Triad   Quartal

MELODY

Before the twentieth century, melody was generally smooth, balanced, and predictable. Pitches were usually closely connected, gaps were small, and phrases were balanced. In the twentieth century, melody often became erratic, with wide leaps, irregular rhythms, and unexpected notes. Phrase-lengths changed constantly. It was impossible to anticipate where a melody would go next.

RHYTHM

One of the greatest changes in twentieth-century music was in the use of rhythm. Rhythm was the one element of Western music that had remained relatively unexplored compared with the music of other cultures, such as Africa or India. In the twentieth century, composers began to adopt far more complex rhythms in their music. Sometimes they achieved this goal by calling for constantly changing meters in the course of a composition. For example, instead of remaining in 4/4 meter, a piece might have a measure in 3/4 followed by a measure in 6/8, then a 2/4 measure and so on. Sometimes composers adopted very unusual meters, such as 5/4 or 7/4, which give an unexpected beat to the music. And sometimes they grouped the notes *within* a regular meter in an irregular way. (See next page.)

Irregular metrical groupings in twentieth-century music.

Another way in which rhythms became more complex was by the use of rhythmic *freedom*. Composers frequently directed each individual performer to play at his or her own speed, thus creating a series of overlapping rhythms in place of one steady pulse. Finally, the advent of the computer allowed composers to manipulate rhythm in an infinite variety of complex ways.

Length

Until the last part of the nineteenth century, the length of most musical compositions had been quite standardized. Audiences knew what to expect when they went to hear a symphony or a chamber work. But in the twentieth century, this changed radically. Some pieces were no more than a few measures in length, lasting only seconds, whereas others went on for hours. Some compositions were designed to last *ad infinitum* (or until people's patience wore out!).

Tone Color and Sound

One final element that distinguished twentieth-century music from music of earlier eras was a heightened awareness of tone color. This became a central focus in music, both to provide more variety and interest and to create a new structural element. Webern's *Six Pieces for Orchestra*, for example, written in 1909, calls for an enormous orchestra, including a wide range of brass and percussion—but these forces are rarely used all at once, and the instruments play mostly alone or in small combinations, creating an immense variety of

sound. The piece *depends* upon the tone colors of specific instruments.

In addition, composers in the twentieth century called for greatly expanded playing techniques from instrumentalists. Wind players were asked to produce higher and higher pitches by means of special fingering and blowing techniques, and sometimes they were required to make squawking, squeaking, or chattering noises on their instruments. String players were asked to produce unusual glissandos (slides) on their strings, or to bang their instruments with their bows, or to pluck the strings so hard that they snapped against the fingerboard. And both string and wind players were called upon to produce **quarter tones**, pitches *between* the half steps.

Instruments that had never or only rarely been used in traditional orchestras—such as saxophones, bass clarinets, alto flutes, tenor tubas, and bass trombones—were now featured regularly. The greatest changes occurred in the percussion section. Previously, orchestral music had called for timpani, sometimes bass drum, and only very occasionally a snare drum, cymbals, or a triangle. Now, percussion sections were often large and varied, calling for a huge collection of instruments—including large and small cymbals, a whole array of drums of different sizes, tam-tams, bells, wooden blocks, whips, rattles, tambourines, bass drums, gongs, and melody percussion instruments, such as the xylophone, marimba, vibraphone, chimes, celesta, and glockenspiel.

Modern technology strongly influenced the sounds of twentieth-century music. At the beginning of the century, new electronic instruments were invented, including the **telharmonium**, an instrument that produces sound by means of electronic generators; the theremin, an instrument that can make oscillating streams of sliding sounds, like ghost noises; and the first electronic organ. Later, in the 1940s and 1950s, the advent of magnetic tape brought many new experiments in sound production.

In the latter half of the century, the production and control of musical sounds were revolutionized by the computer and the synthesizer. On the computer, all the various parameters of sound—pitch, dynamics, duration, timbre, even spatial positioning—can be controlled digitally. Synthesizers can both generate and control sound. Almost any sound can be produced, changed, combined, and controlled on a single small keyboard. Synthesizers can imitate any instrument, including an entire orchestra, or produce a whole array of artificial sounds. Much music of the later twentieth century—including both classical and popular music, whether live or recorded or on a film

soundtrack—would not have been possible without the synthesizer.

The theremin, one of the first electronic musical instruments.

THE BEGINNINGS OF CHANGE

As we have seen, the Modernist movement at the beginning of the twentieth century had an effect on all the arts. Painting, poetry, architecture, and music were in the grip of a revolutionary fervor, a feeling that the rules of the past could now be challenged in favor of new forms of expression. In music, the chief figures of this movement were Debussy, Stravinsky, and Schoenberg. Although they were all striking innovators, each contributed to this movement in his own particular way—Debussy in orchestral color, Stravinsky in rhythm, and Schoenberg in the invention of a new system to replace tonality.

IMPRESSIONISM AND SYMBOLISM

In the Modernist movement, which was centered in Paris, there were many parallels between music and the other arts. The most important movement in painting was known as Impressionism. Impressionist paintings are fresh, lively, and atmospheric. They revel in the play of light and color. Outlines are vague, and details are left to the viewer's imagination.

Parallel to the Impressionist movement in painting was the literary movement known as Symbolism. Symbolists attempted to convey ideas by suggestion rather than by direct statement.

Impressionism in music refers to a style of composition in which the outlines are blurred and there is a great deal of harmonic ambiguity, often created by whole-tone, pentatonic, or chromatic scales. Indeed, it was sometimes felt that music, with its natural fluidity, could create an Impressionist atmosphere more successfully than the other arts.

Monet's painting of Rouen Cathedral is vague, cloudy, and elusive.

Claude Monet (1840–1926), *The Cathedral of Rouen, façade*, circa 1892/94. Oil on canvas, 100.6 × 66 cm. Juliana Cheney Edwards Collection. Museum of Fine Arts, Boston/ Archiv für Kunst und Geschichte, Berlin.

CLAUDE DEBUSSY (1862–1918)

The composer whose music most closely parallels these developments was Debussy, who was also French and lived in Paris. He attended many of the first exhibitions of Impressionist painting and was a personal friend of several of the Symbolist writers.

Claude Debussy was a talented pianist as a child and was accepted as a student at the Paris Conservatory of Music at the age of 10. When he was 18, he began to study composition, and in 1884 he won the prestigious Prix de Rome, the highest award for French composers. One of the influences on his music was the distinctive sound of the Indonesian gamelan. (We heard an example of gamelan music in the opening chapter of the book.)

Debussy's most famous orchestral composition is the *Prelude to the Afternoon of a Faun* (1894), which is based on the poem by the Symbolist poet Mallarmé. The music is dreamy and suggestive, using a large orchestra primarily for tone color. Other orchestral pieces by Debussy include *Trois Nocturnes* (*Three Nocturnes*) and *La Mer* (*The Sea*). *Trois Nocturnes* has three sections, entitled "Clouds," "Festivals," and "Sirens." *La Mer* also consists of three sections, evoking sun and sea, the play of waves, and the sound of the wind on the water. Later, Debussy wrote his only opera, *Pelléas et Mélisande*, to a Symbolist play by Maeterlinck. **(See Listening Guide on page 337.)**

Debussy's piano music is highly varied and includes some of his greatest compositions. There are pieces of pure Impressionism, such as *Jardins sous la pluie* (*Gardens in the Rain*) or *La Cathédrale engloutie* (*The Sunken Cathedral*), but also humorous pieces, technical studies, and music for children. The best-known piece for children is *Golliwog's Cake-Walk*. Debussy also wrote some non-Impressionist chamber music, including a fine string quartet and sonatas for violin and piano, cello and piano, and flute, viola, and harp.

Debussy's music was little known until he was about 40. After the premiere of *Pelléas et Mélisande*, he became quite famous and traveled around Europe conducting performances of his work. He loved fine food and fancy clothes and as a result was often short of money. He had two wives and a mistress, though not all at the same time! Debussy died of cancer in his native Paris at the age of 56.

Claude Debussy in a portrait by Marcel Baschet, 1884.

Claude Debussy (1862–1918)
Prélude à l'après-midi d'un faune

Date of composition: 1894
Orchestration: 3 flutes, 2 oboes,
    English horn, 2 clarinets,
    2 bassoons, 4 horns, 2 harps,
    antique cymbals, strings
Duration: 11:10

Complete CD Collection: 6, track 5

Debussy's *Prelude to the Afternoon of a Faun* is an evocation of natural scenes, sense-impressions, and moods. It suggests the thoughts and feelings of a mythical creature of the forest, who is half man and half goat (not to be confused with "fawn"). He is half asleep in the hot sun and his mind dwells on sexual fantasies. He expresses his feelings by playing his panpipes.

Debussy matches the mood of the poem with sensuous, dreamy music that often swells up with emotion. He uses a large orchestra, with two harps but no trumpets, trombones, or timpani. The only percussion instruments are antique cymbals—very small cymbals that resonate quietly near the end of the piece. Other special orchestral colors are created by harp glissandos and horn calls played with mutes to make them sound far away. Most of the time, the strings play very quietly, and sometimes they use special effects, such as playing with a mute or bowing over the fingerboard, which creates a hushed tone. In this context of a piece that is mostly quiet, the few passages of crescendo sound emotional and surging.

The opening flute melody is sensuous, chromatic, and vague. This melody serves as the basis for much of the piece. It is shaped as a series of curves, gently rising and falling. Debussy deliberately modeled the shape of this melody on medieval plainchant, which he thought could serve as an inspiration for composers in the Modernist era.

The composition falls into three sections in an ABA pattern, though each section merges imperceptibly with the next, and the return of the opening A section is modified. One of Debussy's aims was to break down the clear formal outlines of traditional music.

A SECTION

[E Major]

(5)   0:00   Opening motive, (chromatic motion), dreamy and suggestive.

etc.

     0:24   Harp glissando, horns in dialogue.

     0:57   Flute motive again, quietly accompanied by the orchestra.

| | 1:15 | Horns play quick little figures. Oboe elaborates flute motive. |

	1:38	Orchestral crescendo, repeated chordal figures.
	1:57	Chordal figures reduce to clarinet.
	2:05	Harp signals a return of the flute motive.
(6)	2:22	Flute accompanied by rising harmonies.
	2:46	Harp plays under flute; flowing movement in orchestra. Cadence.
	3:27	Flute motive migrates to clarinet against ominous, slightly agitated orchestral accompaniment.
	3:35	Chromatic flourishes; dialogue between flute and clarinet.
	3:58	Oboe melody rides on top of the orchestra, beginning another orchestral crescendo.
	4:07	Full, flowing music, decrescendo.
	5:01	Clarinet floats above orchestral accompaniment, transition to new key and new section.

B SECTION

[Db Major]

| (7) | 5:24 | New motive (much slower and diatonic). |

338

	5:50	Crescendo.
	6:04	New motive becomes slow-moving melody for strings.
	6:14	Crescendo, decrescendo; music is constantly moving and pulsating.
	6:54	Horn melody in duet with solo violin, harp accompaniment.
(8)	7:23	Flute introduces abbreviated, slower form of the opening motive, at a slightly higher pitch; harp accompaniment continues.

	7:44	Oboe, faster motion with trill; lively conversation with other woodwinds.
	8:00	Oboe plays slow version of motive.
	8:22	English horn reiterates the oboe motive, with similar comments from the other woodwinds.

A¹ SECTION

[return to E Major]

(9)	8:40	Flute melody returns, along with E-Major tonality. Diatonic accompaniment against chromatic solos of the woodwinds.
	9:02	Antique cymbals.
	9:54	Ending chords; oboe melody; mixed orchestral colors.
	10:20	Single descending notes from harp. Brief nostalgic reminiscences of motive.
	10:59	Pizzicato (low strings).

PRIMITIVISM

Primitivism is the name given to a movement in painting at the beginning of the twentieth century. Artists were attracted by what they saw as the directness, instinctiveness, and exoticism of non-urban cultures. This was a time during which writers such as Sigmund Freud were exploring the power of instinct and the unconscious.

Among the painters of Primitivism were Paul Gauguin, Henri Rousseau, and Pablo Picasso. Again, the center of this artistic movement was Paris. Paul Gauguin was fascinated by "primitive" cultures and eventually went to the South Sea Islands to live and work among the islanders. His paintings are bold and bright, and they use symbols of cultural primitivism. Henri Rousseau's paintings are deliberately naive but highly imaginative. Their vivid scenes are not designed as representative of nature but as evocations of a state of mind. Pablo Picasso was one of the greatest painters of the twentieth century, and he changed his style many times during his lifetime. But in the early 1900s, he, too, was interested in Primitivism, and his painting *Les Demoiselles d'Avignon* (*The Young Women of Avignon*) is an example of this style. It is also a landmark in twentieth-century art. The painting is raw, primitive, and deliberately shocking. Its flat planes, deconstruction of the bodies, angularity of form, and especially the use of African masks for some of the faces had a revolutionary impact on the development of modern painting.

Paul Gauguin was fascinated by the inhabitants of the South Sea Islands. Is it the artist himself staring at the young nudes?

Paul Gauguin (1848–1903), *Contes barbares*. 1902. Oil on canvas, 130 × 89 cm. Essen, Museum Folkwang. Archiv für Kunst und Geschichte, Berlin.

IGOR STRAVINSKY (1882–1971)

The musical equivalent of Picasso was Stravinsky. He, too, lived a long life, evolved several distinct styles during his career, and had a lasting impact on twentieth-century culture.

Igor Stravinsky was born in St. Petersburg, Russia. His father was an opera singer, but he insisted that Igor study law at the university instead of music. Stravinsky used to compose on the sly. At the age of 21, he gave up law altogether and began formal music lessons with the great Russian nationalist com-

poser Rimsky-Korsakov. From his mentor, Stravinsky learned how to obtain vivid colors and strong effects from an orchestra.

In 1910, Stravinsky moved to Paris, at that time the undisputed center of European culture. Stravinsky was asked to produce some works for the Ballets Russes, a famous and influential ballet troupe based in Paris and headed by the great Russian impresario Serge Diaghilev. Stravinsky wrote three of his most important ballet scores as commissions for the Ballets Russes: *The Firebird* (1910), *Petrushka* (1911), and *The Rite of Spring* (1913). All three are inspired by the prevailing style of Primitivism. The primitive atmosphere in Stravinsky's music is enhanced by his use of **polyrhythms** (different meters sounding at the same time), **bitonality** (two different keys sounding at the same time), and **ostinato** (constantly repeated phrases).

The Rite of Spring, a composition of tremendous power and boldness, is one of the most revolutionary works of the twentieth century. It depicts the rituals of ancient pagan tribes, and it caused a riot at its first performance in Paris in 1913. The audience was profoundly shocked by the violent and overtly sexual nature of the choreography on stage as well as by the pounding rhythms and clashing dissonances from the orchestra. Soon thereafter, the work was recognized as a masterpiece. **(See Listening Guide on page 342.)**

Stravinsky lived in Switzerland during the First World War, and then returned to Paris in 1920. His most important compositions from this period took a different direction entirely. Smaller and more transparent, they relied on small groups of varied instruments and sometimes were influenced by the new music emanating from America—jazz. The jazz-influenced pieces from this period include *Ragtime* for 11 instruments (1918) and

Igor Stravinsky in 1925.

Stravinsky's music used to be original. Now it is aboriginal.
—Ernest Newman, 1921

Stravinsky looks like a man who was potty-trained too early, and his music proves it as far as I'm concerned.
—Russell Hoban

Picasso's revolutionary painting *Les Demoiselles d'Avignon* (1907).

Pablo Picasso, *Les Demoiselles d'Avignon.* Paris (June–July 1907). Oil on canvas, 8′ × 7′8″ (243.9 × 233.7 cm). The Museum of Modern Art, New York. Acquired through the Lillie P. Bliss Bequest. Photograph © 1998 The Museum of Modern Art. © 2002 Estate of Pablo Picasso/Artists Rights Society (ARS), New York.

Igor Stravinsky (1882–1971)
Le Sacre du Printemps (The Rite of Spring), **Opening Section**

Date of composition: 1913

Orchestration: Piccolo, 3 flutes, alto flute, 4 oboes, English horn, E♭ clarinet, 3 clarinets, 2 bass clarinets, 4 bassoons, contrabassoon, 8 horns, D trumpet, 4 trumpets, 3 trombones, 2 tubas, 2 timpani, bass drum, side drum, triangle, antique cymbals, strings

Duration: 8:50

Complete CD Collection: 6, track 10

*S*ome of Stravinsky's most memorable works were written for the Ballets Russes in Paris within 10 years before World War I. *Le Sacre du Printemps*, the third of a group of ballets (with *The Firebird*, 1910, and *Petrushka*, 1911), was finished in 1913. It features the largest orchestra ever used by Stravinsky and presents bold, daring, and often alarming moments that shocked the first audiences. *Le Sacre du Printemps* was one of the musical masterpieces that was visually realized in Walt Disney's animated feature *Fantasia*, as musical background to the creation of the world. See how your own imagination compares with that of the Disney classic, or even that of Stravinsky's own conception, which was a succession of tribal rites. Even without pictures, the music is brilliantly imaginative, colorful, and striking. Maybe even more so!

We will listen only to the first several minutes, beginning with a solo bassoon, playing in its eerie highest register:

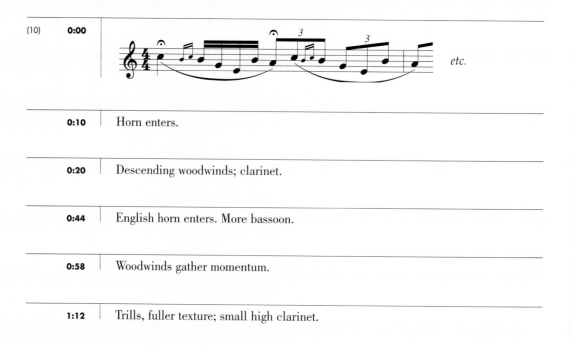

(10)	0:00	
	0:10	Horn enters.
	0:20	Descending woodwinds; clarinet.
	0:44	English horn enters. More bassoon.
	0:58	Woodwinds gather momentum.
	1:12	Trills, fuller texture; small high clarinet.

1:32	Bubbling bass clarinet.
1:45	Section comes to a close, trills in violins.
1:55	Small clarinet, interplay with English horn.
2:16	Flute response.
2:24	Oboe.
2:29	Small clarinet in high register.
2:47	Muted trumpet.
2:51	Begin orchestral crescendo.
3:01	Stop!
3:02	Bassoon reappears, high-register solo.
3:10	Clarinet trill, pizzicato strings, chords. Monotonous two-note figure starts and continues through the following:
(11) **3:34**	Pounding, steady orchestral chords, irregular accents.

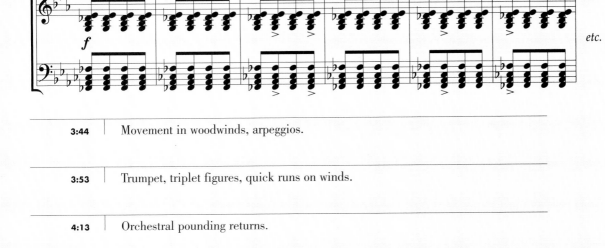

3:44	Movement in woodwinds, arpeggios.
3:53	Trumpet, triplet figures, quick runs on winds.
4:13	Orchestral pounding returns.

	4:22	Bass melody: bassoons interspersed with orchestra rhythms.
	4:32	Trombone, orchestral flashes of color.
(12)	4:53	Big brass chord; timpani; return of two-note figure; orchestral flashes.
	5:17	Horn melody.
	5:21	Flute response.
	5:28	Dialogue between flute and muted trumpet.
	5:36	Flutes enter, accompanied by other woodwinds; two-note figure continues.
(13)	5:53	Brass chords, parallel motion up and down; much louder now.
	6:09	Agitated strings; piccolo.
	6:17	Woodwind melody.
	6:27	Orchestral crescendo, with short blasts.
	6:53	Loud drum crashes, rhythmic activity increases over static accompaniment.
(14)	7:03	Brass chords.
	7:29	Triplet rhythms, horn calls, high flutes, dissonant wild trumpet calls, very fast strings punctuated by drum strokes.
	8:17	Clarinets in octaves, melody over flute trills.
	8:42	Pulse slows down to a low-pitched trudge.

Piano-Rag-Music (1919). Stravinsky was attracted to jazz because of its clear, clean textures and lively rhythms.

In 1920, Diaghilev invited Stravinsky to arrange some eighteenth-century music for a ballet called *Pulcinella*. Stravinsky took some chamber sonatas by Classic composers and not only orchestrated them but also subtly reworked them, transforming the Classic style into a modern idiom. He organized the accompanying figures into ostinatos, rewrote some of the harmonies to make them slightly more biting, and changed the phrase-lengths to make them slightly irregular. The result is a remarkable work that was also extraordinarily influential on the development of twentieth-century music. Indeed, *Pulcinella* ushered in a completely new compositional style known as Neo-Classicism.

STRAVINSKY AND NEO-CLASSICISM

Stravinsky's work on *Pulcinella* led him to a new consideration of Western musical traditions, and he used the past as a means of renewing the present. He said: "*Pulcinella* was my discovery of the past, the epiphany through which the whole of my late work became possible."

Neo-Classical composers in the twentieth century adopted ideas not only from the Classic period, but also from the Baroque era. In place of the big, wild, expressive orchestral sounds of the 1910s (like those in *The Rite of Spring*), the focus now was on formal balance, clarity, and objectivity. Many Neo-Classical compositions use small ensembles, and some of them have titles that deliberately recall Classic and Baroque genres, such as Concerto or Symphony.

As well as adopting the genres (concerto, concerto grosso, symphony) of eighteenth-century music, Stravinsky adopted their formal structures. In the music from his Neo-Classical period, you can find patterns that are like sonata form, theme-and-variations form, aria form, and rondo form. In no way, however, could one of Stravinsky's Neo-Classical compositions ever be mistaken for an original piece from the eighteenth century. Although the aesthetic of the past is clearly there, the style of the music has been updated and modernized. Harmonies are modern, accompanying figures are new, phrase-lengths are irregular, and the rhythm is lively, bouncy, even a little quirky. **(See Listening Guide on page 346.)**

In 1939, as Europe headed once again toward the catastrophe of a world war, Stravinsky moved to America. He settled in Los Angeles and was engaged by Hollywood to write some film scores. Unfortunately, none of these was ever completed. He did finish a Mass, as well as an opera called *The Rake's Progress* (1951). *The Rake's Progress* is the last composition of Stravinsky's Neo-Classical style and one of the finest.

After 1951 Stravinsky began to experiment with twelve-tone techniques and again radically changed his musical style. Many of his late compositions use twelve-tone methods of composition. They include an elegy for President John F. Kennedy (completed in 1964) and a Requiem written in anticipation of Stravinsky's own death. Stravinsky died in 1971, near the age of 90, having undertaken several stylistic shifts in his compositional career and having profoundly influenced the course of music during the greater part of a century.

STRAVINSKY'S MUSIC

Igor Stravinsky
USA 2c

As we have seen, Stravinsky's personal style underwent several changes during the course of his career. He wrote in the splashy, colorful orchestral style of the Russian nationalists, composed music with the force and power of Primitivism, adopted jazz techniques, invented a new musical style known as Neo-Classicism, and turned finally to twelve-tone techniques.

Stravinsky took ideas from the medieval, Baroque, and Classic periods, as well as from contemporary music. He wrote for almost every known musical combination, both instrumental and vocal, choral and orchestral, chamber and stage. His genres included opera, ballet, oratorio, symphony, concerto, chamber music, sonata, piano solo, song, chorus, and Mass.

And yet some things remained common to all of

Igor Stravinsky (1882–1971)

First Movement from Concerto in E-flat
  (***Dumbarton Oaks***) **for Chamber**
  Orchestra

Date of composition: 1938

Orchestration: Flute, clarinet, bassoon,
  2 horns, 3 violins, 3 violas, 2 cellos,
  2 basses

Meter: $\frac{2}{4}$

Key: E♭

Tempo: *Tempo giusto*

Duration: 4:11

Student CD Collection: 3, track 28

Complete CD Collection: 6, track 15

This concerto is from Stravinsky's Neo-Classical period, during which he imitated the clarity and transparency of earlier masters. It is scored for a chamber group of winds and strings, in three movements, and is known as *Dumbarton Oaks* because it was commissioned by some wealthy patrons of the arts whose home near Washington, D.C., had that name.

Stravinsky modeled the work after Bach's *Brandenburg* Concertos, which provided him with the inspiration for both the texture and the liveliness of the music. Compare the Bach extracts with those of Stravinsky:

etc.

FIGURE 1A: Bach, *Brandenburg* Concerto No. 6, first movement, mm. 1–2.

FIGURE 1B: Stravinsky, Concerto in E♭, first movement, mm. 15–16.

etc.

FIGURE 2A: Bach, *Brandenburg* Concerto No. 3, third movement, m. 1.

FIGURE 2B: Stravinsky, Concerto in E♭, first movement, m. 155.

A slow, chordal section recurs several times, functioning much like the ritornello of a Baroque concerto grosso. The piece is saturated with the lively rhythms and quirky sense of humor that are typical of Stravinsky, and it combines great clarity with pungent modern harmonies. Its jazzy swing and transparency of texture create a wonderful listening experience. The following comments just provide a few "signposts" along this delightful journey.

28 (15) **0:00**	Opening motive on strings and flute, with intriguing offbeats:	

0:18	Continuing on strings, with sustained dissonance on winds.

0:27	Syncopated development of opening motive (see "Bach figure," Figure 1A), with "rocket" phrase on clarinet.

0:35	Jazzy rhythms.

0:59	Short clarinet solo.

1:04	Fanfare: horns and bassoon.

	1:21	Clarinet again, followed by strings and bassoon.
	1:38	Crescendo: syncopated rhythmic figure in all parts except basses.
	1:52	Climax. Unison playing, winding down to:
29 (16)	**2:02**	An extended fugue on strings alone; violas, followed by violins, basses, and cellos.
	2:47	Louder, horns and strings, with fanfare.
	3:05	New melody in horns, with busy, bubbling accompaniment on bassoon and clarinet.
	3:26	Crescendo. Sixteenth-note figure in strings against cross-rhythms in winds. (See Figure 2B.)

	3:55	Ritornello: slow chords.

etc.

	4:11	Soft ending.

Stravinsky in later life.

rest or silence appears, to throw the rhythm off balance. He often used several different meters, one right after the other or even simultaneously.

Second, Stravinsky had an acute ear for tone color. He used unusual combinations of instruments to get exactly the effect he wanted, and he also used instruments in novel ways. *The Rite of Spring*, for example, begins with a bassoon, which is a low instrument, playing at the very top of its range, producing a strange, eerie sound. (This passage is used at the start of Walt Disney's *Fantasia* to suggest the beginning of Creation.)

Finally, Stravinsky's use of harmony was highly original. Much of his music is tonally based, and yet he often used *two* key centers instead of one. Another very characteristic harmonic effect is the use of an ostinato (repeated pattern) as an accompaniment. Above the ostinato, the harmonies may change, but the ostinato remains as a kind of tonal anchor.

Stravinsky used to compose carefully and consistently every day in his study, which was filled with the tools of his trade: paper, pencils, erasers, rulers, ink, scissors, and a large desk. He worked regular hours—"like a banker," he said. But his lasting legacy is his music.

Stravinsky's periods and compositional styles. First of all was his interest in rhythm. His rhythms are highly individual—catchy, unexpected, and fascinating. Stravinsky used syncopation with great effect, and often a short

EXPRESSIONISM

The links among the visual arts, literature, and music were particularly evident in one branch of Modernism that became popular during the years 1910–39. This was known as Expressionism, and it evolved during a time of growing fascination with the unconscious and people's inner feelings. Although the Expressionist movement had its exponents in Germany, Norway, and other countries, the center of activity was Vienna. It was here that Sigmund Freud lived and worked, developing his groundbreaking theories on the human psyche. It was here that the writers Arthur Schnitzler and Hugo von Hofmannsthal, the political visionary Theodor Herzl, and the painters Gustav Klimt and Oskar Kokoschka

revolutionized their own fields of endeavor. And it was in Vienna that the revolutionary musical world of Schoenberg and his students Berg and Webern was created.

The connections between painting and music at this time were particularly strong. In fact, Schoenberg himself was a talented painter. Both Expressionist painters and Expressionist composers attempted to focus on inner states of being and the evocation of extreme feelings. Today, their concentration on anguish, insanity, fear, hatred, and death may seem obsessive. But the movement was a reaction against what was perceived as the prettiness and superficiality of the Impressionists.

A nightmarish evocation by Kokoschka (1914).

Oskar Kokoschka (1886–1980), *Die Windsbraut*, 1914. Oil on canvas. 181 × 220 cm. Basel, Kunstmuseum. Archiv für Kunst und Geschichte, Berlin. © 1998 Artists Rights Society (ARS), New York/Pro Litteris, Zurich.

ARNOLD SCHOENBERG (1874–1951)

> I believe art is born not of "I can" but "I must."
> —Arnold Schoenberg

Photo-portrait of Schoenberg with three self-portraits.

© 1981 Richard Fish, Photographer.

The most important Expressionist composer was Arnold Schoenberg. He was also one of the most radically innovative composers of the century, for he evolved a completely new approach to musical harmony that has had a profound influence on all music written up to the present day.

Schoenberg was born in 1874 in Vienna to a poor Orthodox Jewish family. He took violin lessons as a boy but had no other musical training. He studied the works of Mozart, Haydn, and Beethoven as well as those of Brahms and Mahler, who were still very active in Vienna as Schoenberg was growing up.

Schoenberg began composing at about the age of eight. His early works, up to the age of about 25, continued in the Romantic tradition. But soon, Schoenberg started to take a different path.

He gradually came to feel that tonality—the centuries-old harmonic basis of music, with its carefully ordered hierarchy of keys and its feeling of a single, central key for each movement or work—had outlived its usefulness. And he began to develop a completely new system of musical organization. At first he called this system *atonality*—that is, a system *without* key. In Schoenberg's atonal works, the feeling of key is deliberately avoided. The music uses so many chromatic notes that no tonal center can be heard, as you can see in this line from his *Five Pieces for Orchestra*:

Schoenberg wrote many atonal pieces between 1908 and 1915. The most important of these are *Das Buch der hängenden Gärten* (*The Book of the Hanging Gardens*), 1908; *Five Pieces for Orchestra*, 1909; and *Pierrot Lunaire* (*Moonstruck Pierrot*), 1912. Schoenberg's atonal music was not well received. Yet he continued to struggle with the idea of writing music without tonality. "I feel that I have a mission," he said.

For the next several years, Schoenberg wrote no music at all. This period coincided with the First World War and the years after the war, and Schoenberg was facing a personal and intellectual crisis in addition to a national and political one. The problem was in the direction his music should take. Atonality freed music from the "straitjacket" of tonality, but it had no organizing principle. How can you structure a piece with no keys? So far he had solved the problem in two ways: Either the pieces were very short, or they were held together by a text.

Schoenberg gradually developed a solution to this problem, coming up with an idea that held composers in its grip for much of the remainder of the twentieth century. His idea was the **twelve-tone system.**

The twelve-tone system is an outgrowth of atonality, but it has a strict unifying principle. The composer uses all the available notes, instead of just some of them (there are twelve notes in an octave, counting all the half steps). But the notes are used in a strict order (established in advance by the composer), and this order must be followed throughout the piece.

Schoenberg first used his twelve-tone system in his *Five Piano Pieces* of 1923. From then on, he used the system (more or less strictly) in almost all his compositions. The most important of these are the gigantic *Variations for Orchestra* (1928), the extraordinary opera *Moses and Aaron* (1932), the Violin Concerto (1936), the Fourth String Quartet (1937), and the Piano Concerto (1942). The twelve-tone system allowed Schoenberg to write far more extended compositions than had been possible before.

During the time of these developments, Schoenberg was fortunate enough to have two brilliant and like-minded students. They were Alban Berg and Anton Webern, only about 10 years younger than he was. The three shared a great many of their ideas and wrote similar kinds of pieces, yet each composer developed his own distinct musical personality.

This was a dangerous period for Jews in Germany, however, and when the Nazis came to power in 1933, Schoenberg was summarily dismissed from his teaching job at the Academy of Arts in Berlin, along with the hundreds of thousands of other Jews around Germany who lost their jobs. As a result, Schoenberg

I am a conservative who was forced to become a revolutionary.
—Arnold Schoenberg

Schoenberg with students at his home, c. 1950.

© 1981 Richard Fish, Photographer.

Schoenberg and Atonality

By 1900, tonality had been a guiding feature in Western music for 300 years. It was the common denominator behind works by such diverse composers as Corelli, Bach, Mozart, Beethoven, Wagner, and Brahms. While musical forms, genres, styles, and idioms changed radically between 1600 and 1900, tonality remained a consistent musical element. Composers *assumed* that they were to compose tonally. ✦ By the late nineteenth century, the music of Wagner, for example, had become extremely dissonant. Schoenberg was profoundly influenced by the rich harmonic style of Wagner. But he believed that Wagner had taken chromaticism and dissonance as far as it could go in the tonal system. Schoenberg's solution was to abandon tonality—in his words, "to emancipate the dissonance"—in favor of atonality. ✦ An atonal piece contains none of the hierarchy among notes and chords always present in tonal music: Each of the twelve notes of the chromatic scale is equally important. By 1924, Schoenberg had developed his twelve-tone system to reflect this fundamental principle of equality. A melody in Schoenberg's twelve-tone style would state each of the 12 tones before any are repeated. It is easy to make up your own twelve-tone series. For example:

✦ All you do is add rhythm and you have a melody. The art lies in finding a series and a rhythm that work together:

✦ The twelve notes in their given order are referred to as a tone row. The use of a tone row was fundamental to nearly every work by Schoenberg after 1924.

✦ Schoenberg believed that his system was a logical, evolutionary step. Nowadays, it seems as though composers are moving away from this system (and from atonality in general) and are reverting once more to tonality. Whatever the future holds, Schoenberg's initial forays into atonality will always be considered one of the most radical and audacious innovations in the history of Western music.

embraced Judaism, from which he had lapsed at the age of 18, more firmly than ever. Many of Schoenberg's works—including the oratorio *Jacob's Ladder* (1922), the opera *Moses and Aaron*, and a setting of the *Kol Nidre* text from the Jewish liturgy (1938)—are based on Jewish themes. In addition, after the Second World War he wrote a cantata entitled A *Survivor from Warsaw* (1947), which relives the horror of the Warsaw Ghetto, in which more than 400,000 Jews were systematically murdered by the Nazis. The text is based on a personal account by one of the very few people who survived.

After Schoenberg was fired from his job in Berlin, he moved to the United States and settled in Los Angeles, where he taught at the University of California and took on private students as well. This was the period of his large-scale twelve-tone works, but he also wrote two "old-fashioned" tonal pieces for student ensembles.

Schoenberg died in 1951. During his life, his music was not much performed—and even since then, most audiences have found it difficult and inaccessible. But Schoenberg was highly influential in two ways: directly, because he was the teacher of Berg and Webern, each of whom turned out to be a great composer in his own right; and indirectly, because his development of the twelve-tone system affected an entire generation of composers who came after him.

SCHOENBERG'S MUSIC

Schoenberg's music can be divided into three periods: the early period, the atonal period, and the much longer twelve-tone period. During the early period, from the 1890s to 1907, Schoenberg wrote music in a late Romantic idiom. The pieces are passionate and intense; they range from the Piano Sonata (1894) to the programmatic string sextet *Verklärte Nacht* (*Transfigured Night*) (1899) to the enormous cantata *Gurre-*

lieder (written in 1901 and orchestrated in 1911). In these pieces, we can see an increasing use of chromaticism and a gradual dissolving of a central tonality. The music wanders further and further afield through many keys other than the central one.

In Schoenberg's middle period, from 1908 to 1915, he developed his idea of atonality. His most important atonal compositions either have a text (like *Das Buch der hängenden Gärten* and *Pierrot Lunaire*) or are quite short. **(See Listening Guide on page 354.)** The five movements of *Five Pieces for Orchestra*, although written for a huge orchestra, are dense and brief.

From 1923 until the end of his life, Schoenberg concentrated on twelve-tone composition. It is fascinating to notice how, at the beginning of his twelve-tone period, Schoenberg balanced his revolutionary ideas with very traditional forms. Many of the compositions from this time adopt the structures of eighteenth-century music, such as sonata form or minuet-and-trio form. It is as though Schoenberg felt the need to hang on to something familiar while he was striking off in such new directions! **(See Listening Guide on page 356.)** After the first few years, though, he was able to create works freer in form, such as the opera *Moses and Aaron* and the Piano Concerto. By the middle of the twentieth century, there were large numbers of composers who modeled their careers and their own musical styles on the work of this remarkable man.

In fact, it would be more accurate to say that almost no composer since Schoenberg has been able to ignore his accomplishments. The revolution he led—freeing up music from the tonal system—affected most musicians, by demonstrating a system that composers could either adopt or had to consciously avoid. For an entire generation, composers were required to justify writing music that was *not* twelve-tone. And even composers who avoided the twelve-tone system had available to them a vocabulary of sounds that could be called upon occasionally to enrich their overall language.

Arnold Schoenberg (1874–1951)
Madonna **from** *Pierrot Lunaire*

Date of composition: 1912
Orchestration: Voice; flute, bass
clarinet, viola, cello, piano
Duration: 1:47

Student CD Collection: 3, track 30
Complete CD Collection: 6, track 17

Schoenberg's *Pierrot Lunaire* sets 21 poems by Albert Giraud. The entire collection functions much in the same way as a song cycle, in that the individual movements share a single viewpoint—in this case, that of Pierrot, a deeply troubled clown who seems to have a fascination with the mysterious powers of the moon.

Pierrot Lunaire has been described as an *Expressionist* art form because it reveals the darker side of human nature. Just as the visual creations of artists such as Munch, Vlaminck, and Kokoschka abandon the familiar lines associated with beauty and form, *Pierrot Lunaire* similarly abandons tonality and normal singing style in favor of inner emotional expression.

A special feature of this work is found in the voice of the soloist, who does not sing these movements in the customary way. Instead, she *approximates* the written pitches, in an eerie effect that merges singing with speaking. This technique is called *Sprechstimme* ("speech-song").

The individual movements are accompanied by a small group of instrumentalists (who double on various woodwinds) and a pianist.

Madonna (No. 6) seems to be inspired by some of the more grotesque figures seen in large cathedrals, as well as Catholic ritual. The lyrics speak of blood, wounds, redness of the eyes, and so on, which are effectively rendered in Schoenberg's setting. Notice particularly the instance of word-painting on the word "Rise" (*Steig*) in the second stanza. Here Schoenberg writes the widest interval between two notes in the whole song. Notice also how expressively the words "blood" (*Blut*) and "sorrows" (*Schmerzen*) are presented.

30 (17)	0:00	[Flute, clarinet, cello (1 measure)]	

STANZA 1			
	0:03	*Steig, o Mutter aller Schmerzen,* *Auf den Altar meiner Verse!*	Rise, O Mother of all Sorrows, on the altar of my verses!
	0:18	*Blut aus deinen magern Bruesten* *Hat den Schwerten Wut vergossen.*	Blood pours forth from your withered bosom where the cruel sword has pierced it.

STANZA 2		
0:32	*Deine ewig frischen Wunden* *Gleichen Augen, rot und offen.*	And your ever-bleeding wounds seem like eyes, red and open.
0:42	*Steig, o Mutter aller Schmerzen,* *Auf den Altar meiner Verse!*	Rise, O Mother of all Sorrows, on the altar of my verses!
0:57	[Instrumental interlude; change in instrumental figures]	
1:09	*In den abgezehrten Haenden* *Haelst du deines Sohnes Leiche,* *Ihn zu zeigen aller Menschheit—*	In your torn and wasted hands holding thy Son's holy body, you reveal Him to all mankind—
1:23	*Doch der Blick der Menschen meidet*	but the eyes of men are turned away,
1:28	*Dich, o Mutter aller Schmerzen!* [Piano enters, loud and abrupt with cello]	O Mother of all Sorrows!
1:42	[Final chord, piano]	

355

Arnold Schoenberg (1874–1951)
Theme and Sixth Variation from
   Variations for Orchestra, Op. 31

Date of composition: 1928
Duration: 2:36

Student CD Collection: 3, track 31
Complete CD Collection: 6, track 18

*T*he second piece we will study by Schoenberg, *Variations for Orchestra*, Op. 31, employs Schoenberg's twelve-tone method, and features a tone row, the basic building block for twelve-tone music. The row is as follows:

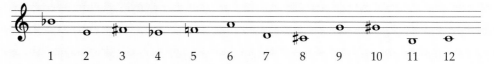

1 2 3 4 5 6 7 8 9 10 11 12

It is used four times to make up the theme. The theme itself is in ternary form, made up of the unusual and irregular phrases of five and seven measures. The main section is made up of twelve measures divided into five and seven. The middle section covers five measures, and the return of the main section is compressed into seven measures.

Even the accompaniment of the theme is numerically based. The first phrase, which consists of five notes, is accompanied by a five-note chord. The second phrase of four notes is heard against a four-note chord, and the following phrase of three notes is accompanied by a simple triad (three notes).

In this composition, Schoenberg uses a large orchestra. But the scoring is very spare, so that the effect is like chamber music in its texture. We shall listen to the theme and the sixth variation.

(Read the Listening Guide first, and then while listening.)

THEME	
	[Molto moderato ("Very moderate")]
31 (18) **0:00**	The first appearance of the row (cello melody, first twelve notes) presents the row in its ORIGINAL sequence:

O   1 2   3   4   5   6 7 8 9   10   11   12

| **32** (19) **0:12** | The continuation of the cello melody (next twelve notes) presents the row in RETROGRADE INVERSION (backwards and upside-down), beginning on the note G: |

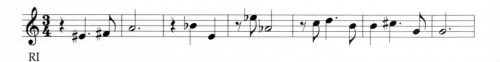

RI

33 (20)   **0:30**   The middle section of the theme is played as RETROGRADE ORIGINAL (the row backwards):

0:42   Gentle cadence.

34 (21)   **0:43**   The melody travels to the violins, which present the row in INVERSION (upside-down), beginning on high G:

1:04   The movement ends very quietly. Conclusion.

VARIATION VI

[Andante ("Quite slow")]

(This variation features several instruments playing the main theme, against varying combinations of instruments playing melodic figures derived from the row.)

35 (22)   **0:00**   Main theme, clarinets, answered by English horn and flute.

0:07   Continuation.

0:18   Main theme inverted, played by solo viola, answered by flute and horn.

0:26   Melodic fragments, all instruments.

0:31   Flute, short chromatic figure, followed by solo viola playing descending line in longer notes.

0:43   Main theme, clarinets.

0:51   More rhythmic movement, entire orchestra.

0:55   Muted trumpet chords.

1:07   Main theme, violins.

1:16   Faster motion.

1:28   Motion stops, movement ends.

SCHOENBERG'S STUDENTS

The two most famous students of Schoenberg were Alban Berg and Anton Webern. Both men began studying with Schoenberg in their late teens, and both became deeply absorbed in his pursuit of atonality and finally of the twelve-tone system. Despite this close association, however, each composer managed to keep his own individual musical personality, and each one's work is clearly distinguishable.

ALBAN BERG (1885–1935)

Berg was, like Schoenberg, born in Vienna, and he, too, had no formal training before he began writing music. He played the piano and wrote some songs. Berg was 19 years old and working as a government clerk when he saw Schoenberg's newspaper advertisement for students and signed up for private lessons. He

> Berg is the only one to have achieved large-scale development forms without a suggestion of "neoclassic" dissimulation.
> —Igor Stravinsky on Berg

Alban Berg (left) and Anton Webern in 1914.

studied with Schoenberg for six years, and the two men became close friends. Berg's early compositions are in the late Romantic style and include a piano sonata and several songs. His first atonal piece was the String Quartet, Op. 3, written in 1910. Just before the war, Berg completed his *Three Pieces for Orchestra.*

During World War I, Berg served three years in the army and worked in the Ministry of War, but he also managed to begin composing the first of his two great operas. *Wozzeck* was completed in 1922 and stands as the first atonal Expressionist opera. It is also one of the great operas of the twentieth century.

In 1925, Berg finished his *Kammerkonzert* (Chamber Concerto) for piano, violin, and 13 wind instruments. Hidden in the Chamber Concerto are musical references to the names of the three friends: Schoenberg, Berg, and Webern. The *Lyric Suite* was written in 1926. Originally for string quartet, it was later arranged for string orchestra by the composer.

In 1928, Berg began work on his second Expressionist opera, *Lulu*. The entire opera was complete, except for the orchestration of the third act, when Berg died in 1935 of an infected insect bite (this was before the discovery of antibiotics). Berg's widow refused to release his draft for the third act, and the opera was not performed in its entirety until 1979, after she had died.

Berg's last completed composition also comes from the year of his death. He broke off work on *Lulu* to write his Violin Concerto as a memorial to a young woman who had died. Manon Gropius was the 18-year-old daughter of Mahler's widow. Berg dedicated the work "to the memory of an angel."

BERG'S MUSIC

Of the three colleagues, Berg retained the strongest links with the past. He adopted atonality and twelve-tone technique but much more flexibly than either Schoenberg or Webern. You can find passages of tonal music in many of his compositions, and he never abandoned the Romantic idea of lyricism. His music is more passionate and emotionally intense than that of the other two composers.

Berg's experience of war is reflected in his opera *Wozzeck*. The opera tells the story of a poor, working-class soldier (Franz Wozzeck) who is bullied by his superiors, betrayed by Marie, the woman he loves, and beaten up by his rival. Driven to madness, Wozzeck murders Marie and then commits suicide. The drama is intensely emotional, and the music, like much of Berg's work, is both highly expressive and very tightly organized. Although the music is atonal, Berg uses tight, closed structures borrowed from the past: sonata form, rondo form, fugue, theme and variations, and many others. Berg's love of symmetry is also shown by the use of the same music for the end of Act I and the end of the entire opera. Later, we shall listen carefully to the climactic scenes of *Wozzeck*. **(See Listening Guide on page 360.)**

BERG'S *WOZZECK*

Wozzeck was begun during World War I and not completed until 1922. The story is based on a play called *Woyzeck* by the nineteenth-century German playwright Georg Büchner. (Berg saw the play in 1914.) But its tragic story of a soldier driven mad must have been given added depth by Berg's own experiences in the war.

The music that Berg crafted is brilliant, powerful, and enormously inventive; it is continuous within each of the three acts. Each act is divided into five scenes, but the scenes are connected by orchestral interludes. Berg came up with a brilliant way to unify each scene: The music for each one is an independent type of composition—theme and variations, march, sonata form, and so on. Stylistically, Berg borrowed from Wagner and Schoenberg. From Wagner he took the technique of the leitmotiv: Each character is associated with a particular musical idea. The Expressionist quality of the music owes much to Schoenberg's *Pierrot Lunaire*. The sounds are atonal, producing new combinations and colors. The palette is very wide, as Berg uses an enormous orchestra. The music is jagged, distorted, careening wildly between extremes: between very loud and very soft, between very

high and very low, between singing and talking. Perhaps the greatest extremes come in the vocal line: The singers use *Sprechstimme*, but they also use spoken words, flowing melody, screams, whispers, and folk tunes.

In Act I, we meet Wozzeck, a poor soldier who is tormented by nightmares. His captain persecutes him for no reason, and the army doctor uses him as a guinea pig in human experiments. In Act II, Wozzeck is driven mad by the woman he lives with, who sleeps with another man, and by his rival, who brutally beats him up. At the beginning of Act III, Wozzeck stabs Marie to death near a pond in the forest.

WOZZECK, ACT III, SCENE 3

In Scene 3, Wozzeck sits in a bar, trying to console himself with a drink and with the company of the barmaid, Margret. He persuades her to dance and sing a song. Suddenly she notices blood on one of his hands. People come out of the barroom shadows and surround Wozzeck. He manages to escape.

The music of the whole scene is dense and enormously varied, with a fascinating complexity of orchestral sounds, as well as vocal techniques ranging from speech to *Sprechstimme* to full singing. As Wozzeck escapes, the orchestral interlude before Scene 4 is wild and frantic.

WOZZECK, ACT III, SCENE 4

Wozzeck returns to the pond to hide the knife. He tries to wash the blood off his hands, but it seems to him that the whole pond is turning to blood. He drowns. The captain and the army doctor hear him drowning but leave him to his fate.

The music for this scene is designed as a series of *harmonic* variations. There are also powerful pictorial descriptions in the orchestra: the moon rising, the forest at night, the water welling over Wozzeck's head, the gradual ebbing of life.

The orchestral interlude that follows this scene is the longest and most emotional in the whole opera. Berg writes a deeply sympathetic lament for Wozzeck and his tragic existence. The music is purely Romantic; it is even fully in a key (D minor), which gives it a powerful

Alban Berg (1885–1935)
Wozzeck, Act III, Scenes 3, 4, and 5

Scene from a 1959 production of *Wozzeck*.

Date of composition: 1924

Orchestration: Piccolo, 4 flutes,
4 oboes, English horn, 2 E♭
clarinets, 4 clarinets, bass clarinet,
3 bassoons, contrabassoon, 4 horns,
4 trumpets, 4 trombones, bass
trombone, tuba, 2 timpani, bass
drum, side drum, tam-tams,
2 cymbals, triangle, xylophone,
celesta, harp, strings

Duration: 13:05

Complete CD Collection: 6, track 23

We begin listening in the middle of Act III. Wozzeck has just murdered his lover, Marie, and finds himself in a dimly lit tavern. Musical interest in the third scene is that of a rhythmic motive, heard first on the "honky-tonk" piano.

This rhythmic figure appears throughout the scene, representing the haunting memory of the murder. It is presented in many altered forms. Orchestral chords:

In dialogue:

In's Schwa - ben land, da ____ mag ich nit,

At Margret's discovery of blood on Wozzeck's hand:

A - ber was hast Du an der Hand?

And in the comments by the chorus:

Frei - lich ____ da ____ stinkt's nach ____ Men-schen-blut!

Throughout these three scenes, Berg's use of instrumental colors and texture is extraordinary. From the high, silvery celesta to the low trombones and tuba, he exploits the richest possible palette of sounds.

SCENE THREE		
(23) **0:00**	[Beginning of scene, "honky-tonk" piano—rhythmic motive]	

WOZZECK		
0:03	*Tanzt Alle;* *tanzt nur zu,* *springt, schwitz, und stinkt, es holt* *Euch doch noch einmal* *der Teufel!*	Dance, all of you; dance away, leap, sweat, and reek, for someday soon he'll fetch you, the Devil!
	[drinking down a glass of wine, shouting down to the pianist]	
0:17	*Ritten drei Reiter wohl an den Rhein,* *Bei einer Frau Wirten da kehrten* *sie ein.* *Mein wein ist gut, mein bier ist klar,* *Mein Töchterlein liegt auf der …*	Three riders came riding up to the Rhine, and went to my hostess to taste of her wine. My wine is good, my beer is clear, My daughter dear lies on the …
	[stopping]	
	Verdamnt!	Damn!
	[jumping up]	
	Komm, Margret!	Come, Margret!
	[dancing a few steps with Margret, then suddenly stopping]	
	Komm, setz Dich her, Margret!	Come, let's sit down, Margret!
	[pulling her onto his lap]	
	Margret, Du bist so heiss.	Margret, you're so hot.
	[letting her go]	
	Wart nur, wirst auch kalt werden! *Kannst nicht singen?*	But wait, you'll be cold one day! Can't you sing?

MARGRET		
	[rhythmic motive]	
1:11	*In's Schwabenland, da mag ich nit,* *Und lange Kleider trag ich nit,* *Denn lange Kleider, spitze Schuh,* *Die kommen keiner Dienstmagd zu.*	To Swabia I will not go, and nice long dresses I'll not wear, for nice long dresses, pointed shoes, do not belong to servant girls.

WOZZECK		
	[angrily]	
1:41	*Nein! keine Schuh, man kann auch* *blossfüssig in die Höll' geh'n!* *Ich möcht heut raufen, RAUFEN!*	No! Wear no shoes, for one can go to hell barefooted! Today I want to wrestle, WRESTLE!

MARGRET		
(24) 1:56	*Aber was hast Du and der Hand?*	But what is that on your hand?
	[rhythmic motive]	

WOZZECK		
2:03	*Ich? Ich?*	Me? Me?

MARGRET		
	Rot! Blut!	Red! Blood!

WOZZECK		
	Blut! Blut!	Blood! Blood!

MARGRET		
	Freilich! Blut!	Surely blood!

WOZZECK		
	Ich glaub', ich hab' mich geschnitten, da an der rechten Hand.	I think I must have cut it, there on my right hand.
	[Chorus enters]	
	[Wozzeck, Margret, and chorus overlap.]	

MARGRET		
(25) 2:26	*Wie Kommts denn zum Ellenbogen?*	How did it get on your elbow?

WOZZECK		
	Ich habs daran abgewischt.	I wiped my hand on it there.

CHORUS		
	Mit der rechten Hand am rechten arm?	His right hand wiped his right arm?

MARGRET		
	Puh! Puh! Da stinkt's nach Menschenblut!	Pew! Pew! It smells like human blood!

WOZZECK		
	Was wollt Ihr?	What do you want?
	Was geht's Euch Was geht's Euch an?	What is it with you?
	Bin ich ein Mörder?	Am I a murderer?

CHORUS		
	Freilich da stinkt's nach Menschenblut!	Surely it smells like human blood!
	[rhythmic motive]	
	Blut, Blut, Blut, da stinkt's nach Menschenblut!	Blood, blood, blood, it smells like human blood!

2:45 | *Platz! oder es geht wer zum Teufel!* | Off! Or someone goes to the Devil!

[Wozzeck runs out of the tavern; end of scene]

3:02 | [snare drum roll; brass climax]

[by the pond, scene of the crime]

(26) **3:19** | *Das Messer? Wo ist das Messer: Ich habs da gelassen. Näher, noch näher. Mir graut's. Da regt sich was. Still! Alles still und tot.* | Where is it? Where can the knife be? Somewhere here, I left it somewhere. I'm scared. There. Something moved. Quiet! All is quiet and dead.

[Celesta]

[trumpets, low trombones]

3:50 | *Mörder! Mörder!!* | Murder! Murder!!
Ha! da ruft's? | Ah, who cried?
Nein. Ich selbst. | No. It was me.

[discovering the corpse]

Marie! Marie! Was hast du für eine rote Schnur um den Hals? Hast Dir das rote Halsband verdient, wie die Ohr-Ringlein, mit Deiner Sünde?! Was hängen Dir die schwarzen Haare so wild?! Mörder! Mörder!! Sie werden nach mir suchen. Das Messer verrät mich! | Marie! Marie! What is that like a crimson cord round your neck? And was that crimson necklace a gift, like the golden earrings, the price of sin?! Why is your fine black hair so wild on your face?! Murder! Murder!! They'll soon be coming for me. That knife will betray me.

[slide on strings]

[discovering the knife]

Da, da ist's! | Here it is!

[throwing the knife into the pond]

So! da hinunter! | Down! to the bottom!

[bass tuba, trombones, contrabassoon]

Es taucht ins dunkle Wasser wie ein Stein. | It sinks through deep dark water like a stone.

[voice sinking]

[looking up at the moon; harp]

Aber der Mond verrät mich. Der Mond is Blutig. [solo violins] Will den die ganze Welt es ausplaudern?! Das Messer, es liegt zu weit vorn, sie findens beim Baden oder wenn sie nach Muscheln tauchen.

See how the moon betrays me. The moon is bloody. Must the whole wide world be shouting it?! That knife is too near the shore. They will find it when bathing, or when they are gathering mussels.

[wading into the pond]

Ich find's nicht.
Aber ich muss mich waschen. Ich bin blutig. Da ein fleck und noch einer.

I can't find it now.
I should wash myself. I am bloody. Here's a spot and here another.

[lamenting]

(27)   5:54   *Weh! Weh! Ich wasche mich mit Blut. Das Wasser ist Blut ... Blut ...*

Woe! Woe! I wash myself with blood. The water is blood ... blood ...

[slow rising strings, representing the water rising]

[He begins to drown. The Captain and the Doctor enter.]

CAPTAIN

6:20   *Halt!*   Stop!

DOCTOR

Hören Sie? Dort!   Do you hear? There!

CAPTAIN

Jesus! Was war ein Ton.   Jesus! What a sound.

DOCTOR

Ja, dort!   Yes, over there!

CAPTAIN

Es ist das Wasser im Teich. Das Wasser ruft. Es ist schon lange niemand entrunken. Kommen Sie, Doktor! Es ist nicht gut zu hören.

It is the water. The water is calling out. No one has drowned here for a long time. Come, Doctor! It is not good to hear.

DOCTOR

Das stöhnt, [clarinets, horn] als stürbe ein Mensch.

Groaning like a man dying.

Da ertrinkt Jemand!   Someone is drowning!

CAPTAIN

Unheimlich! [celesta and harp] Der Mond rot, und die Nebel grau. Hören Sie? jetzt wieder das Aechzen.

Eerie!
The moon is red, the mist grey.
Do you hear? Again that sound.

DOCTOR

Stiller, jetzt ganz still.   Quieter now. Now completely quiet.

[silence]

CAPTAIN

Kommen Sie! Kommen Sie schnell.   Come! Come quickly.

[timpani, basses; low harp]

7:48   [End of scene]

ORCHESTRAL INTERLUDE

[D minor]

(This is the only section in the entire opera that has a tonal center.)

---

(28)   **7:54**   Low strings and horns; orchestral crescendo.

8:48   Brass instruments are heard, followed by harp glissando.

9:12   There begins a series of orchestral crescendos. Trombones; horns.

9:53   The mood changes. Trumpets prominent.

10:24   Drumroll. More drumbeats.

10:30   Trombones.

10:57   Loud cymbal crash, slow descending dissonant orchestral chords, arriving again at D minor.

11:38   End of interlude.

SCENE FIVE

(This final scene is probably the most dismal of all. The simple children's melodies heard here are every bit as disturbing as the pounding rhythms heard in Scene 3.)

---

(29)   **11:39**   *Ringel, Ringel, Rosenkranz, Ringelreih'n'*   Ring-a-ring-a-rosie, all fall down!
                           Ringel, Ringel, Rosenkranz, Rin-   Ring-a-ring-a-rosie, all-

---

ONE OF THE CHILDREN

11:52   *Du, Kaethe! Die Marie ...*   You, Kathy! Do you know about Marie?

SECOND CHILD

Was ist?   What is it?

FIRST CHILD

Weisst' es nit? Sie sind   Don't you know? They've all gone out
schon Alle 'naus.   there.

[solo violin]

THIRD CHILD

[to Marie's son]

Du! Dein Mutter ist tot!   You! Your mother is dead.

[string harmonics]

MARIE'S SON

[not really paying attention, riding his play-horse]

Hopp, hopp. Hopp, hopp.   Hop, hop. Hop, hop.
Hopp, hopp.   Hop, hop.

[sticks]

SECOND CHILD

Wo ist sie denn?   Where is she then?

FIRST CHILD

Draus liegt sie, am Weg,   Out there, on the path,
neben dem Teich.   by the water.

THIRD CHILD

Kommt, anschaun!   Come! Let's go and look!

[clarinets]

MARIE'S SON

12:31   *Hopp, hopp. Hopp, hopp.*   Hop, hop. Hop, hop.
        Hopp, hopp.   Hop, hop.

[xylophone]

[Discovering he has been left alone, he stops, then follows after the others.]

12:43   Strange inconclusive finish and end of the opera.

[flutes, celesta, strings]

366

emotional appeal in the stark and jagged context of its atonal surroundings.

WOZZECK, ACT III, SCENE 5

Wozzeck and Marie have a little boy. He is playing in front of their house with some other children. They run off to see Marie's body, and he follows them naively, not understanding what has happened.

The music for this scene is finely drawn, with continuous running notes, throwing into relief the cruelty/innocence of the children. The scene does not end, it simply stops, providing no feeling of conclusion to the opera, only a sense of isolation and continuing horror.

ANTON WEBERN (1883–1945)

If Berg represented the link backward from Modernism to the past, Webern may be seen as the link forward from the first stage of Modernism to the second stage after World War II. Whereas Berg's music is lush, intense, and emotionally committed, Webern's is spare, abstract, and restrained.

The Migratory Bird (1941) from the *Constellations* series by Joan Miró.

Joan Miro, *The Migratory Bird*, from the Constellation series. Palma de Mallorca, May 26, 1941. Gouache and oil wash on paper, 18⅛ x 15" (46.1 x 38.1 cm). Private Collection. Pierre Matisse Gallery. © 2002 Artists Rights Society (ARS), New York/ADAGP, Paris.

Webern was born in Vienna, like Schoenberg and Berg. He came from a middle-class family and as a teenager was immersed in music; he played the piano and the cello and studied music theory in addition to composing many pieces. While he was at the university, Webern studied musicology and wrote a doctoral dissertation on the music of the Renaissance composer Heinrich Isaac. This close study of counterpoint had a strong influence on his own music. Like Berg, he took private composition lessons with Schoenberg.

Webern's death goes down in history as one of the many thousands of incongruous tragedies caused by war. In 1945, after the war had ended and American forces were occupying Austria, Webern went outside one night to smoke a cigarette and was shot by a jittery American soldier.

WEBERN'S MUSIC

Webern's music is extraordinarily concentrated and delicate. Everything is understated, and there is never an extra note. In this very finely sculpted atmosphere, the silences are as meaningful as the notes. In painting, a close parallel to Webern's music can be found in the *Constellations* series of Joan Miró, in which stars and tiny figures are carefully balanced with empty space throughout the canvas to create an overall effect.

Webern had an exact ear for precisely the sounds he wanted to achieve. He wrote detailed instructions all over his scores, indicating exactly how he wanted each tiny phrase to sound. It is a measure of the refinement of his music that although there is a whole spectrum of dynamics in his works, almost all of it lies between medium loud and very, very soft.

Most of Webern's compositions are quite short. Many movements last less than a minute, and some are as short as 20 seconds. Even the biggest works are only 10 minutes long altogether.

Webern used a great deal of imitative counterpoint in his music, like the Renaissance masters he studied. But in Webern's style, the counterpoint is atonal and,

> We must hail not only a great composer but a hero. Doomed to total failure, he still kept on cutting out his diamonds, his dazzling diamonds.
> —Igor Stravinsky on Webern

Anton Webern.

> Webern can say more in two minutes than most other composers in ten.
> —Humphrey Searle, English composer

Anton Webern (1883–1945)
Third Movement from *Five Movements*
**   *for String Quartet*, Op. 5**

Date of composition: 1909
Orchestration: 2 violins, viola, cello
Duration: 0:41

Student CD Collection: 3, track 36
Complete CD Collection: 6, track 30

he third movement of Webern's *Five Movements for String Quartet* is so short that even the tiniest gesture becomes significant. Also, Webern uses a wide range of articulations and special string sounds that throw every note into relief. These include

1. *am steg*, "at the bridge." This produces very scratchy, high-pitched sounds.
2. *pizzicato*, "plucked."
3. *arco*, "bowed."
4. *staccato*, "short, detached notes."
5. *col legno*, "with the wood." The strings are struck with the wood of the bow.

36 (30)	**0:00**	*staccato*, cello, short notes.
	0:01	*am steg*, violins and viola.
	0:03	*pizzicato*, violins and viola.
	0:04	*arco*, violins and viola.
	0:08	*arco staccato*, first violin and cello.
	0:10	*col legno*, violins and viola.
	0:16	*arco*, first violin; *pizzicato*, second violin, viola, cello.
	0:26	*arco*, cello; *pizzicato*, first violin and viola.
	0:30	*arco*, first violin; *arco staccato*, second violin, viola, cello.
	0:35	Loud finish, all instruments *staccato*, with two final *pizzicato* chords.

from the 1920s on, twelve-tone. The intervals are often sevenths and ninths, and there are many dissonances, but the texture is so light and transparent that the dissonances sound colorful rather than harsh.

In addition to his finely honed ear for dynamics, Webern possessed a keen awareness of very fine distinctions in instrumental sound. He calls for a great variety of tones and timbres, especially from string instruments, which are asked to play *pizzicato* (plucked), *sul ponticello* (bowed near the bridge), *con sordino* (with a mute), or *tremolo* (very rapid bowing on a single note), as well as combinations of the four. And each one of these instructions may appear over a phrase of just two or three notes.

Webern also had very specific instrumental sounds in mind when orchestrating. In fact, with Webern you get the feeling that he did not compose a piece and then orchestrate it; rather, the choice of instruments seems to

have been part of his conception from the beginning. And sometimes his choices are quite unusual: He wrote a set of songs for a singer, E♭ clarinet (a high-pitched, soprano instrument), and guitar. And his *Five Pieces for Orchestra*, Op. 10, is written for a small orchestra of 18 instruments, including chimes, cowbells, glockenspiel, harmonium, harp, guitar, mandolin, snare drum, bass drum, clarinet, French horn, trombone, violin, viola, and cello. On the other hand, even a conventional group like a string quartet sounds completely new in the hands of this delicate and masterful colorist. We shall listen to one of Webern's very short movements for string quartet. **(See Listening Guide on page 368.)**

In Webern's music, with its rarefied atmosphere and extreme concision, every note has meaning, every gesture is significant. The utmost attention is required from the listener. Nothing could be further removed from the soaring length of Romantic music.

OTHER COMPOSERS ACTIVE BEFORE WORLD WAR II: BARTÓK, SHOSTAKOVICH, BRITTEN, IVES, COPLAND

We have examined the music of the most influential composers up to the middle of the twentieth century, but, as always in a survey of this kind, several important names have been omitted. Here we shall look briefly at the music of some of those figures. Although none of them founded a school or had brilliant and influential students, each one wrote compelling music of profound significance. Among the five composers—Bartók, Shostakovich, Britten, Ives, and Copland—four different nationalities are represented.

BÉLA BARTÓK (1881–1945)

One of the most independent and original composers of the first half of the century was Béla Bartók. His work grew out of the nationalist movement of the second half of the nineteenth century. Bartók was born in

Hungary. As a student, he entered the Budapest Academy of Music, where he later became professor of piano. He toured extensively as a concert pianist. But he also spent a great deal of time in Eastern Europe, Turkey, and North Africa, recording and notating indigenous music, including songs and instrumental pieces. He ultimately published 2,000 tunes, notating as authentically as he could every inflection and detail of the performances he had heard.

In the 1930s, Bartók was able to spend more and more time on his own compositions. In 1940 he emigrated to the United States with his wife, who was also a concert pianist. The couple made a meager living playing concerts, and Bartók worked for the folk music collection at Columbia University. He was virtually unrecognized, however, and he wrote no new music.

In 1943, though very ill, Bartók was given an important commission by the music director of the Boston

Bartók at the age of 18.

Symphony Orchestra, Serge Koussevitsky, whose patronage helped support many struggling artists. The composition, known as the Concerto for Orchestra, was first performed in 1944. The belated recognition and the stimulus of working on the piece helped to revive Bartók's health and his spirits. He began to compose once again and almost finished three more major works before he died on September 26, 1945.

Bartók's music

Bartók had three simultaneous careers: as an ethnomusicologist (someone who studies indigenous musics), a concert pianist, and a composer. Each of the first two influenced the third. First, many of his compositions are colored by the rhythms and melodies of the indigenous music of Hungary (and Eastern Europe in general). Second, the piano is featured in many of his works.

Partly for his students at the Budapest Academy of Music and partly for his son Peter, Bartók wrote a long series of piano pieces that start out very simple and gradually increase in difficulty. The series is called *Mikrokosmos*. It is in six volumes, ranging from wonderful little pieces for beginners to extremely complicated works. Other Bartók piano compositions include three highly original piano concertos and a fascinating work, full of novel sounds, called *Sonata for Two Pianos and Percussion*, written in 1937.

Like Beethoven, Bartók reserved his most profound music for his string quartets. The six quartets span most of his career, the first dating from 1908, when he was 27, and the last from 1939, just before he left Hungary for the United States. Each quartet is a profound and brilliant example of his art.

The most famous of the works composed in America is the Concerto for Orchestra (1943). The title is a play on words, because concertos usually put the spotlight on a single instrument rather than on a whole orchestra. But the work was written to celebrate the brilliance of all the orchestra's players.

Bartók's musical style is very individual. It is also very profound. You always have the sense that Bartók was a man of great integrity and seriousness of purpose, although that doesn't mean his music is dull. On the contrary, his fast movements are often very exciting—both wild and passionate. And his slow movements range from pieces of delicate mystery to extremes of lyrical intensity.

LISTENING GUIDE

Béla Bartók (1881–1945)
**Fifth Movement (*Allegro molto*) from
String Quartet No. 4**

Date of composition: 1928
Orchestration: 2 violins, viola, cello
Duration: 5:38

Complete CD Collection: 6, track 31

*B*artók's Fourth String Quartet uses an "arch" form. The quartet has five movements, of which the first and the last are related, as are the second and the fourth; the central slow movement stands at the apex of the work. The last movement, which we shall hear, unleashes an almost barbaric energy. It is propelled by clashing chords, whirling melodies, and asymmetrical rhythms. A rough approximation of sonata form can be heard, with a first theme of great intensity, a second theme that is lighter and more graceful, a condensed and varied recapitulation, and a fast coda. The movement ends with the same heavy chords that ended the first movement. The dissonances in this quartet are extreme; look, for example, at the repeated loud chords that open the movement:

(31)	0:00	Violent, highly dissonant chords; cross-rhythms in cello.
	0:08	Rhythmic pattern established.
(32)	0:11	Heavy, brusque **first theme** (low).
	0:17	Answer, inverted (high).
	0:23	Rhythmic accompaniment continues; varied and expanded statements of first theme; continued loud.
	1:18	Cadential chords.
	1:22	Quieter transitional passage.
	1:38	Return of violent dissonant chords with cross-rhythms.
	1:55	Cadential passage; sudden ending; pause.
(33)	2:05	*pp*; muted arpeggios accompany **second theme**, light and graceful; answered by rhythmic cello phrase.
(34)	2:30	**(Development?)** Rhythmic phrase becomes central; soft and loud passages alternate; fragments of both themes combined.
	2:41	Pizzicato rising phrases against quiet scattered fragments.
	2:52	Crescendo to louder section; *pp*, crescendo again to two loud cadential chords; pause.
(35)	3:15	Condensed **recapitulation**, *ff*; first theme combined with violent chords.
	3:35	Continuation and expansion, *ff*.
	3:47	Loud folklike theme emerges.

3:55	Variant of folk theme in close canon; dissonant cadential chords.
4:09	Suddenly **pp**; close double canon, violins up, viola/cello down; gradual crescendo.
4:24	Reemergence of rhythmic phrase, then first theme, broken down and punctuated by dissonant chords.
4:39	Dissonant chords alternate with chords played *col legno* (with the wood of the bow).
4:46	Cello slide and recitative, with brief fragments on other strings.
5:04	Sustained harmonics lead into:
(36) **5:06**	**Coda;** faster, growing in intensity.
5:14	Rhythmic phrase, ***f***, close canon, descending in pitch; sudden stop.
5:25	Fragment and sustained harmonics.
5:31	Heavy closing chords.

In his harmony, too, Bartók was highly original. He mingled the modality that is present in much indigenous music with both chromaticism and tonality. You have the feeling that a key center is always present, giving the work a gravitational center, but it may be lost or disguised for long passages. Bartók used strict structures, like sonata form or ABA form, but in novel ways. And he invented new forms. One of his favorites was the arch form. In a five-movement piece, movements 1 and 5 correspond, and so do movements 2 and 4. Movement 3 is considered the apex of the arch. Bartók used this form with great effect in the Concerto for Orchestra and in his Fourth String Quartet, of which we shall hear the last movement. **(See Listening Guide on page 370.)**

DMITRI SHOSTAKOVICH (1906–1975)

Shostakovich was born just before the Russian Revolution and died 14 years before the collapse of Commu-

nism. He lived most of his life under the Soviet system, attempting to find a balance between creative freedom and the demands of a totalitarian state. His plight is movingly described in his memoirs, entitled *Testimony*, smuggled out of the Soviet Union and published in 1979. Because music in the Soviet Union was supposed to represent the policies of the state, Shostakovich often came in for official criticism. He had to withdraw several of his works from performance after they had been composed. Often he would write a piece and not even publish it. (And Shostakovich's terror was justi-

Portrait of Shostakovich, 1964.

fied. Under Stalin, 20 million people were murdered, including many artists, writers, and musicians.)

After Stalin's death, Shostakovich wrote his Tenth Symphony in 1953. This is one of his greatest works. It is highly expressive and personal, with a voice of grieving introspection.

By the time of his death, Shostakovich had composed 15 symphonies. He also wrote 15 string quartets, some of which are also intensely personal. The Eighth String Quartet, written in 1960, is particularly moving.

Shostakovich often used a short musical motive in his works to put his signature on them. Bach had done this in the eighteenth century: The letters B-A-C-H are all names of notes in German (B is B-flat, H is B-natural). Shostakovich's signature is based on his monogram "D. Sch." S is E-flat, so D-S-C-H in notes is D, E-flat, C, and B-natural. This musical signature is found in many works, especially the very personal Eighth String Quartet and the Tenth Symphony.

Shostakovich used traditional forms, such as the symphony and the string quartet, but he did so with great flexibility, expanding the number of movements, adding voices, and writing to a program. His language is intense, overlaying tonal areas with dense chromaticism or playing off highly dissonant chord structures with passages of great lyricism.

Like Bartók, Shostakovich was a composer who proved that tonality, updated, refreshed, and reinvented for the twentieth century, was still a highly viable means of expression.

Benjamin Britten (1913–1976)

Benjamin Britten was born in a small English country town in Suffolk. He was a child prodigy and began turning out compositions at the age of five. Later, he arranged some of these childhood pieces into the *Simple Symphony* (1934), which is one of his most attractive works. Britten's *The Young Person's Guide to the Orchestra* (1946) is designed to display all the different instruments of a symphony orchestra.

Britten was gay, and he lived with Peter Pears, a fine tenor singer, who remained his lifelong companion. During World War II, the couple was invited to America by the poet W. H. Auden, who was also gay and who had formed an artists' community in New York. But after only two years, Britten and Pears returned to England.

Peter Pears (left) and Benjamin Britten in 1949.

Then began the remarkable series of operas on which Britten concentrated for the next ten years. The first was *Peter Grimes* (1945), then came *Billy Budd* (1951), *Gloriana* (1953), written for the coronation of Queen Elizabeth II, and *The Turn of the Screw* (1954). In most of his vocal works, a central role is designed for tenor Peter Pears.

During the 1960s, Britten concentrated on two major projects. The first was the production of several cello works for the great Soviet cellist Mstislav Rostropovich, who had recently been allowed to travel from the Soviet Union and whose great artistry Britten admired.

The other project of Britten's from this time was the *War Requiem* (1961). This is certainly the most important achievement of Britten's career, and it stands as one of the great works of the century. Britten's *War Requiem* was written for the dedication of the new cathedral in Coventry, England, which had been constructed to replace the great medieval church destroyed

I always try to make myself as widely understood as possible; and if I don't succeed, I consider it my fault.—Dmitri Shostakovich

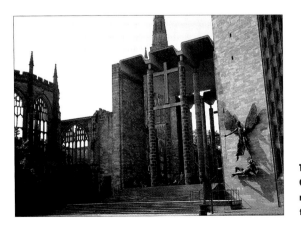

The new cathedral at Coventry, England, merged into the ruins of the old.

Benjamin Britten (1913–1976)
Sanctus **from** *War Requiem*

Date of composition: 1962
Duration: 9:52

Complete CD set: 6, track 37

Britten's *War Requiem* is a modern setting of the Catholic Mass for the Dead. Interspersed throughout the Mass are poems written by Wilfred Owen, who was killed in the First World War. These poems act as a kind of commentary on the different Mass movements. The work calls upon a large number of disparate musical forces: soprano soloist, chorus, boys' choir, organ, and orchestra for the Latin text; tenor and baritone soloists and instrumental chamber group for the English poems.

We will listen to the fourth movement, *Sanctus*. The Mass text appears unaltered in the original Latin and is set in musical styles appropriate to Gregorian chant (syllabic, neumatic, recitational, and melismatic), as well as in the Renaissance styles of imitative and free counterpoint. Owen's poetry (in English), in contrast to the ecclesiastical style of the Latin sections, uses operatic forms (recitative, aria, etc.) and is performed by a baritone soloist. There is a striking contrast between the exaltation of the *Sanctus* text and the profound despair of the poetry. The texts are as follows:

(Soprano soloist and chorus, with full orchestra):

Sanctus, sanctus, sanctus,	Holy, holy, holy,
Dominus Deus Sabaoth.	Lord God of hosts.
Pleni sunt coeli et terra gloria tua.	Heaven and earth are full of your glory.
Hosanna in excelsis.	Hosanna in the highest.
Benedictus qui venit	Blessed is He who comes
in nomine Domini.	in the name of the Lord.
Hosanna in excelsis.	Hosanna in the highest.

(Baritone soloist, with chamber orchestra):

After the blast of lightning from the East.
The flourish of loud clouds, the Chariot Throne;
After the drums of Time have rolled and ceased,
And by the bronze west long retreat is blown,

Shall life renew these bodies? Of a truth
All death will He annul, all tears assuage?—
Fill the void veins of Life again with youth,
And wash, with an immortal water, Age?

When I do ask white Age he saith not so:
"My head hangs weighed with snow."
And when I hearken to the Earth, she saith:
"My fiery heart shrinks, aching. It is death.
Mine ancient scars shall not be glorified,
Nor my titanic tears, the sea, be dried."

(37)	**0:00**	Beginning; vibraphone, glockenspiel, antique cymbals, bells, and piano; short crescendo. This group continues throughout the opening section.

	0:04	*Sanctus*, (syllabic).
	0:17	*Sanctus,*
	0:24	*Sanctus*, (melismatic).
	0:40	*Dominus Deus Sabaoth, Dominus Deus Sabaoth* (neumatic).
	1:00	*Sanctus*, (long melisma).

1:15	*Pleni sunt coeli et terra gloria tua* (recitative, beginning with orchestral sounds piling up, then parts of the chorus layered on top of one another in a large crescendo, then …)
1:53	Stop!

	[new section, jubilant feeling with brass fanfares]
1:55	*Hosanna in excelsis* (sopranos, altos, tenors) against *Sanctus* (basses, doubled by orchestral basses, fairly long section). Horns leap and trumpets blast. Becomes quieter.

		[lyrical with responses by chorus]
(38)	**3:11**	*Benedictus, benedictus qui venit in nomine, in nomine Domini, in nomine Domini, Benedictus qui venit, qui venit in nomine Domini* (long melisma), *qui venit in nomine* (neumatic) *Domini, Domini, Domini* (extremely long melismas).
	5:35	Stop!
	5:36	*Hosanna in excelsis* (sopranos, altos, tenors) against *Sanctus* (basses, doubled by orchestral basses). Brass fanfares; horn and trumpet calls, similar to previous *Hosanna*. Long crescendo, ending with big splash.
	6:15	Stop!

(39)	**6:17**	[new section, baritone solo]
		Single pitch heard on horn and low strings.

6:21	*After the blast of lightning from the East,* (recitative), harp glissando, flutes, lively woodwind figures.
6:36	*The flourish of loud clouds, the Chariot Throne;*
6:41	Harp glissando, lively woodwind figures.
6:46	*After the drums* (timpani roll) *of Time have rolled and ceased,* (harp glissando, woodwind figures), *And by the bronze west* (harp glissando) *long retreat is blown,* (woodwind figures, leading into …)

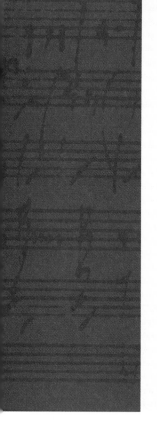

BARITONE

[New section, beginning with staccato strings, repeating woodwind motive]

7:21	*Shall life renew these bodies?* (snare drum taps, horn note) *Of a truth* (accompaniment continues) *All death will He annul, all tears assuage?* (more motion) *Fill the void veins of Life again with youth, And wash, with an immortal water, Age?* (climax)
7:53	Instrumental interlude (strings, oboe, insistent timpani strokes, continuing through:)
7:59	*When I do ask white Age he saith not so:*
8:11	(over soft high-pitched flute) *"My head hangs weighed with snow."*
8:24	Motion continues.
(40) 8:28	*And when I hearken to the Earth, she saith:*
8:40	(accompanied by woodwinds in long notes, and pizzicato strings, slow) *"My fiery heart shrinks, aching. It is death. Mine ancient scars shall not be glorified, Nor my titanic tears,* (slower) *the sea, be dried."*
9:29	Slow, descending, sparsely orchestrated tones, deeper and deeper, quieter and quieter … dying away …
9:52	End of movement.

during World War II. For this event, Britten mingled lamentation for Britain's war dead with a powerful call for peace. He alternates settings of the age-old, timeless Latin Mass for the Dead with settings of poems by Wilfred Owen, who had been killed a week before the end of the First World War at the age of 24. The *War Requiem* is richly varied and, with its expressive tension between the old and the new, both powerful and moving. We shall listen to a section of this work. **(See Listening Guide on page 374.)**

Britten's very individual sound is based on many factors: the directness and lack of pretension in the melodic lines, the common use of high tenor voice (this range seems to affect even his instrumental compositions), and an almost constant tension between conflicting tonalities. This can extend sometimes to clear instances of bitonality.

THE AMERICAN SCENE

The history of classical music in America reaches back to Colonial times, during which period the most significant composer was William Billings (1746–1800), a composer of rough-hewn (he called himself a "carver") and highly original settings of psalms and songs for unaccompanied chorus. His publication in 1770 of *The New-England Psalm-Singer* marked the appearance of the very first published collection of American music.

In the nineteenth century, the American tradition was kept alive in the South and the Midwest by means of "shape-note" books, in which pitches are indicated (for people who cannot read music) by simple signs such as small triangles, circles, and squares. One of the best-known of these shape-note hymn collections is *The Sacred Harp*, published in 1844. African-American spirituals were sung widely throughout the nineteenth century, although the first published collection of spirituals did not appear until 1867. And in the Midwest, one of the most original American composers, Anthony Heinrich (1781–1861, known as "the Beethoven of Kentucky") wrote elaborate and complex orchestral works descriptive of nature on the frontier.

But the rough-and-ready style of American music was soon overwhelmed by more "proper," European-trained composers. One of these was Lowell Mason (1792–1872), who wrote over a thousand hymn settings, some of which may still be found in Protestant hymnals.

About the beginning of the twentieth century, American music and music-making were still strongly influenced by the mid-nineteenth-century European tradition. The United States had not participated in the nationalist wave that swept through many other countries from the 1860s to the 1890s. During this period, America was absorbed by its own inner turmoil: the Civil War, the assassination of President Lincoln, and Reconstruction. American composers, mostly trained in Europe, paid little attention to the enormously varied indigenous music around them: African-American spirituals, New England hymn tunes, Native American songs and dances, the music of jazz bands, revival-meeting songs, and Irish-Scottish-English-American folk melodies. And the American public was interested only in imported music: Italian operas, Handel's English oratorios, and above all, German symphonies and chamber music.

Music was, however, becoming better established on the American scene. Conservatories of music were founded, concert halls were built, and music began to be taught as a serious discipline on university campuses. Most composers in the years around the turn of the century began or concentrated their careers in Boston. They included John Paine (1839–1906), who was the first professor of music ever to be appointed in the United States (at Harvard University); Edward MacDowell (1860–1908), a fine pianist as well as a composer; Horatio Parker (1863–1919), a choral composer on mostly religious texts; George Chadwick (1854–1931), a symphonist and American opera composer, who was for more than 30 years director of the newly founded New England Conservatory of Music in Boston; and Arthur Foote (1853–1937), whose best works are his beautiful solo songs and chamber music.

Boston was also the home of several women composers. They included Helen Hood, Mabel Daniels, Helen Hopekirk, and Margaret Lang, who was born in 1867 and died in 1972 at the age of 104.

Perhaps the best-known woman composer in Boston at the turn of the century was Amy Beach (1867–1944). She began her musical career as a concert pianist but also composed a wealth of important music, including a Mass, a piano concerto, an opera, a symphony, chamber music, piano works, and songs. She was the piano soloist in the first performance of her Piano Concerto (1899), which was premiered by the Boston Symphony Orchestra. Her symphony, entitled the *Gaelic Symphony* (1896) because it is based on Irish folk tunes, was also first performed by that orchestra and carries the distinction of being the first American symphony by a woman.

Today, although there are some attempts at an American music revival, little of this late nineteenth- and early twentieth-century music receives regular concert performance. Perhaps the inferiority complex vis-à-vis music from Europe has still not quite disappeared.

CHARLES IVES (1874–1954)

The first Modernist composer whose work was distinctively American was Charles Ives, who grew up in a small Connecticut town. He was the son of a bandmaster and music teacher whose approach to music was fun-loving and unconventional. Ives's father used to play tunes in two different keys at once, and he sometimes asked Charles to sing a song while he played the accompaniment in the "wrong" key on the piano. This open-minded and experimental approach stayed with Ives all his life.

Ives went to Yale as an undergraduate and then went into the insurance business, devoting his spare time to music. Over the next 10 years, he wrote an enormous quantity of music, while his business prospered, too. Although he lived until 1954, most of his music dates from before the First World War.

Ives's music is a remarkable, unique mixture. He was a radical experimentalist, who nonetheless believed in the values of small-town America. Most of his compositions are based on American cultural themes: baseball, Thanksgiving, marching bands, popular songs, the Fourth of July, fireworks, and American literature. Working alone, Ives developed some of the avant-garde innovations that would not take hold in the broader musical scene until the 1960s. He wrote music with

Charles Ives, composer and insurance agent.

An Old Testament prophet crying a New Mythology in the American wilderness.—David Woodridge on Ives

Charles Ives (1874–1954)
**Second Movement from *Three Places
in New England* ("Putnam's Camp,
Redding, Conn.")**

Date of composition: 1903–11
Orchestration: Flute/piccolo,
    oboe/English horn, clarinet,
    bassoon, 2 or more horns, 2 or more
    trumpets, 2 trombones, tuba, piano;
    timpani; drums; cymbals; strings
Duration: 5:38

Student CD Collection: 3, track 37
Complete CD Collection: 6, track 41

"*P*utnam's Camp" captures a child's impression of a Fourth of July picnic
with singing and marching bands. In the middle of the picnic, the boy falls asleep and dreams
of songs and marches from the time of the American Revolution. When he awakes, he again
hears the noise of the picnic celebration.

Ives's piece is a type of aural collage. Contrasting sounds and textures are overlaid and
connected. Moments of simplicity provide the listener with a point of repose and orientation
before one is thrown back into the vivacious tumult. The moments of thinner texture—when
one or a few instruments stand out with a clear and simple melodic idea—separate passages of
fervent, strident, jumbled polyphony. Although Ives combines every melody and every rhythm
very precisely, the effect is (and it is an effect he strove for) one of varying successions of vigorous, raucous noise. Audiences today delight in the energy of the work, and different ideas
surface with every rehearing.

37 (41)	**0:00**	*Introduction:* full orchestra with dissonant but rhythmically unified descending scales, leading to repeated notes; a vigorous marchlike pulse.
	0:10	*Allegro* ("quick-step time"): a bouncy, accessible melody accompanied by a regular thudding bass. The conventional harmonies contrast with the harsh introduction.
		Flutes and trumpets can be heard with competing melodies as Ives evokes the atmosphere of a chaotic festive event.
	0:47	After a fanfare by a single trumpet, the confused fervor of the different simultaneous events continues even more energetically, with strong melodies in trombones and trumpets, and heavy use of cymbals and snare drum.
38 (42)	**1:00**	Thinner texture and softer dynamics lead to parodied quotation of "Rally Round the Flag" and "Yankee Doodle," with:
	1:08	Disjunct melody in violins with conflicting piano and percussion, leading to:
	1:50	Softly throbbing cellos and basses, gradually slowing down, illustrating the child gradually falling asleep.
	1:55	Decrescendo, then quiet.

39 (43)	**2:06**	*Dream section:* Begins with an ethereal sustained high chord (the Goddess of Liberty), then continues with a legato but energetic melody (first flute, then oboe). But the regular pulse (percussion and piano) accompanying this melody accelerates and takes off on its own (the soldiers march off to pipe and drum). Different melodies in the violins, oboes, clarinets, and trumpets, in a number of different meters and keys, combine with a building tension. The conflicting pulse of the piano and snare drum against the slower pulse of the repetitive low strings can be clearly heard. This gradually dies down, and then:
40 (44)	**3:10**	A bold, new, brass melody emerges and leads to another section of conflicting melodies; simultaneously, "The British Grenadiers," a favorite revolutionary tune, is heard in the flutes.
	3:36	A strongly accented and repetitive tune ascends in the brass and starts another dense passage.
	3:57	*Awakening:* This comes to an abrupt halt (the boy suddenly awakes), and a lively tune is revealed in the violins (the boy hears children's songs in the background). This builds to another complex passage (different bands, songs, and games combine). Heavy, low rhythms and several meters combine. Fragments of lively string melody, "The British Grenadiers," and other tunes.
	4:47	Repeated notes in trumpets and brass cut in suddenly.
	4:54	Another swirl of melodies and rhythms, oscillating notes crescendo, frantic scales, as all the instruments push their dynamic limit, leading to the final jarring chord.

wild dissonances; Ives wrote a note to his music copyist, who had "corrected" some of the notes in his manuscript: "Please don't correct the wrong notes. The wrong notes are right." He wrote for pianos specially tuned in quarter tones; in his *Concord* Sonata he called for the pianist to use an elbow to press down notes and, in one place, a wooden board to hold down 16 notes at once. "Is it the composer's fault that a man has only ten fingers?" he asked. Ives's most famous composition is *The Unanswered Question* (1908), in which two different instrumental groups, sitting separately, play different music at the same time. And in his program piece called *Putnam's Camp*, the music depicts two marching bands passing each other, playing different tunes. (**See Listening Guide on page 378.**)

The music of Charles Ives was virtually unknown in its own time. It was only in the 1940s that Ives's work began to be performed, and only many years later that he began to be recognized as the first truly original American musical genius.

AARON COPLAND (1900–1990)

If Ives represents the avant-garde in American music, Aaron Copland represents a more mainstream approach. Copland was born into a Jewish immigrant family in Brooklyn and decided to become a composer at the age of 15. When he was 20, he went to Europe—specifically to Paris, where he studied with Nadia Boulanger.

Boulanger was perhaps the most famous composition teacher of the twentieth century. She was also a composer, pianist, organist, and conductor. She was extremely strict in her teaching, insisting that her

Composer, conductor, and author Aaron Copland conducting his own work at Tanglewood, Massachusetts.

students learn all aspects of music, including careful and detailed analysis of musical scores. A large number of American composers of the twentieth century studied with Boulanger, forming in this way a thorough and rigorous background for their own work.

When Copland returned from Paris in 1924, he decided to write works that would be specifically American in style. To do this, he drew on the most recognizably American musical style: jazz. And many of his compositions are marked by the syncopated rhythms and chord combinations of American jazz. One of these is the Clarinet Concerto (1948), which he wrote for the famous jazz clarinetist Benny Goodman.

Another way Copland strove to put America into his music was by the use of purely American cultural topics. His ballet suites *Billy the Kid* (1938) and *Rodeo* (1942) are cowboy stories, and *Appalachian Spring* (1944) depicts a pioneer wedding in rural Pennsylvania.

Appalachian Spring also demonstrates a third technique used by Copland to make his music sound American: quoting from folk songs, hymns, and coun-

try tunes. The fourth scene of *Appalachian Spring* sounds like country fiddling, and the seventh scene is a series of variations on the exquisite Shaker melody "Simple Gifts."

Finally, Copland made his music sound American by a rather more sophisticated technique. He used very widely spaced sonorities—deep basses and high, soaring violins—to evoke the wide-open spaces of the American landscape. In addition, he often used the interval of a fifth in his music, a very open-sounding interval, and his chord changes are slow and static, suggesting the more gradual pace of nature's clock. Copland said that he wanted to write music "that would speak of universal things … music with a largeness of utterance wholly representative of our country."

Two of Copland's more accessible and popular works are *Lincoln Portrait* and *Fanfare for the Common Man*, both composed in 1942. For the *Lincoln Portrait*, Copland arranged extracts from Lincoln's speeches and letters to be recited with orchestral accompaniment. The *Fanfare for the Common Man* is a wonderful piece; written for brass instruments and percussion, it is rousing and strong. Both works were composed to provide patriotic encouragement at a time of national anxiety. **(See Listening Guide on page 381.)**

Copland wrote books on music, gave lectures, conducted around the world, composed film scores, and was the mentor of such luminaries as Leonard Bernstein. Copland's leading position in the world of twentieth-century American musical life led to his being called "the dean of American music."

The Shaker song "Simple Gifts."

'Tis the gift to be sim-ple, 'tis the gift to be free, 'tis the gift to come down where you ought to be. And when we find our-selves in the place just right, 'twill be in the val-ley of love and de-light.

Aaron Copland (1900–1990)
Fanfare for the Common Man

Date of composition: 1942
Orchestration: 3 trumpets, 4 horns,
    3 trombones, tuba, timpani, bass
    drum, tam-tam
Duration: 3:36

Student CD Collection: 3, track 41
Complete CD Collection: 7, track 1

Perhaps today we might find Copland's piece more aptly titled *Fanfare for the Average American.* Certainly Copland did not consciously intend his "common man" to be conceived in terms of gender exclusivity. And although Copland's title does not mention any nationality, this piece has become almost a sound icon for America—specifically, for the spirit of the American pioneer, facing vast challenges and wide vistas, from the open prairie to outer space.

Much of the piece's bold, assertive mood comes from its instrumentation, as it is scored entirely for brass and percussion. The simplicity of its motives—using triads, fifths and octaves—gives an open, spacious quality to the piece.

41 (1)	**0:00**	Somber strokes on the bass drum, timpani, and gong (tam-tam); gradual decrease in volume.
	0:25	Fanfare idea in a steady, deliberate tempo—ascending triad; then the fifth outlining that same triad leads to a high note and a slower, descending arpeggio. Stark, unison trumpets.
	0:54	Timpani and bass drum.
42 (2)	**0:59**	Fanfare idea, louder, now harmonized with one additional contrapuntal line in the French horns.
	1:39	Tam-tam, timpani, and bass drum.
43 (3)	**1:50**	Accented low brass take up the fanfare, imitated by timpani, then by trumpets and French horns. Harmony expands richly to three and more chord tones. Rising fifth and octave intervals in timpani.
44 (4)	**2:38**	Another series of statements of the fanfare motive begins. This moves to a series of stepwise descents from the highest pitch of the piece.
	3:04	A contrasting harmonic area is introduced, but with the same rising fifth–octave motive.
	3:27	The work ends with a bold crescendo but an unsettled harmonic feeling, evoking a restless spirit, the spirit of exploration.

BUILDING BRIDGES

Much of Copland's music is the result of an attempt to bridge the gap between "serious" music and its audience. Two other American composers did this in different ways; these composers were George Gershwin and Leonard Bernstein.

GEORGE GERSHWIN (1898–1937)

George Gershwin was primarily a composer of popular songs and a jazz pianist. But he was also attracted to the world of the concert hall, and he wrote four works that reach across the cultural divide between popular and classical music. The first was *Rhapsody in Blue* (1924), a highly attractive and successful mixture of the jazz idiom and concert music, scored for solo piano and orchestra. Next came the jazzy Piano Concerto in F (1925). Both compositions were designed for Gershwin's own brilliant piano playing.

In 1928, Gershwin composed *An American in Paris*, a programmatic symphonic poem. The music is colorful, lively, and drawn from Gershwin's own experience in visiting Paris several times.

The last of Gershwin's works to bridge the gap between popular and classical music was by far the most ambitious: It was a full-length opera, in which Gershwin combined elements of jazz, church meetings, street cries, lullabies, and spirituals. The opera was *Porgy and*

LISTENING GUIDE

George Gershwin (1898–1937)
"Bess, You Is My Woman Now" from
  Porgy and Bess

Date of composition: 1935
Duration: 5:59

Complete CD Collection: 7, track 5

The boundaries between opera and musical are frequently blurred in the twentieth century, but Gershwin conceived of his work as an opera and envisioned its performance at the Metropolitan Opera in New York. To write it, he steeped himself in black culture, living on a small island in South Carolina and working with the Charleston writer DuBose Heyward (author of the original story *Porgy*) as the work was being planned.

"Bess, You Is My Woman Now" celebrates a moment of happiness in Porgy's struggle for the love of Bess. Porgy is portrayed as a straightforward, hardworking man with a physical handicap, who must compete with the rough gambler Crown and the smooth, sophisticated drug dealer Sportin' Life for Bess's affection.

The song's larger structure is of three varied stanzas, with a short refrain employed after the second and third. In the Listening Guide, lowercase letters attached to the phrases serve to identify related melodic ideas. The broad, sustained sweep of the "a" phrase, with its large leaps, is contrasted with phrases of faster rhythms and more scalar motion. Repeated notes and a declamatory style distinguish the simple, striking refrain; in its second appearance, it is expanded and serves as a conclusion.

The "togetherness" of Bess and Porgy is emphasized musically by their singing alternating stanzas with very similar music and wording, and by their singing a duet at the end of the extract. The Southern black dialect is imitated by the spelling and dropped consonants of the text. Gershwin's musical vocabulary includes many elements of jazz, including the slide and the "blue note" on "woman" and the syncopated rhythmic patterns on "you is, you is."

(5)	0:00	Solo cello leads to vocal entry.

STANZA 1			
		PORGY	
(6)	0:14	**a**	Bess, you is my woman now, you is, you is!
	0:27	**b**	An' you mus' laugh an' sing an' dance for two instead of one.
	0:41	**a'**	Want no wrinkle on yo' brow, no how.
	0:53	**c**	Because de sorrow of de past is all done done. Oh, Bess, my Bess, De real happiness is jes' begun.

STANZA 2			
		BESS	
(7)	1:23	**a**	Porgy, I's yo' woman now, I is, I is!
	1:36	**b**	An I ain' never goin' nowhere 'less you shares de fun.
	1:51	**a'**	Dere's no wrinkle on my brow, no how,
	2:03	**d**	But I ain't goin'! You hear me sayin', If you ain' goin', wid you I'm stayin'.
			[higher octave]
	2:20	**a"**	Porgy, I's yo' woman now, I's yours forever,

REFRAIN		
(8)	2:44	Mornin' time an' evenin' time an' summer time an' winter time.

PORGY

2:52		Mornin' time an' evenin' time an' summer time an' winter time,
3:01		Bess, you got yo' man.

STANZA 3

BESS

[Porgy sings a countermelody]

(9)	**3:15**	**a'**	Porgy, I's yo' woman now, I is, I is!

PORGY

Bess, you is my woman now an' forever.
Dis life is jes' begun.

3:27	**b**	An I ain' never goin' nowhere 'less you shares de fun.

Bess, we two is one now an' forever.

3:42	**a'**	Dere's no wrinkle on my brow, no how,

Oh, Bess, don' min' dose women.
You got yo' Porgy, you loves yo' Porgy,
I knows you means it, I seen it in yo' eyes, Bess.

3:54	**d**	But I ain't goin'! You hear me sayin',
		If you ain' goin', wid you I'm stayin'.

[slower]

4:10	**a"**	Porgy, I's yo' woman now, I's yours forever,

We'll go swingin' through de years asingin'.
Hmmm . . .

REFRAIN

(10)	**4:37**	Mornin' time an' evenin' time an' summer time an' winter time. Hmmm . . .
	4:46	Mornin' time an' evenin' time an' summer time an' winter time.

CODA

(11)	**5:03**	Oh, my Porgy, my man Porgy,
		My Bess, my Bess,

[voices declaim in harmony over "a" idea then over refrain in orchestra; long decrescendo]

5:24	From dis minute I'm tellin' you, I keep dis vow;
	Porgy, I's your woman now.
	Oh, my Bessie, we's happy now,
	We is one now.

[peaceful cadence with lowered leading tone]

Bess, which contains some of Gershwin's best-known tunes, including "It Ain't Necessarily So" and "Summertime." Many people know these songs, but not so many have heard the entire opera, which is one of Gershwin's greatest achievements. *Porgy and Bess* was completed in 1935. A year and a half later, the brilliant young composer was dead, cut off in the midst of his career by a brain tumor at the age of 38. (**See Listening Guide on page 382.**)

LEONARD BERNSTEIN (1918–1990)

The person who best represented American music and music-making in the second half of the twentieth century was also one of the most famous musicians in the world. His name was Leonard Bernstein, and he continued the tradition, started by Copland and Gershwin, of blending popular and "serious" styles. Like Copland and Gershwin, Bernstein was Jewish. Like them, he was a brilliant pianist and a prodigiously gifted all-round musician. Like Copland, Bernstein lectured and wrote books about music and loved to

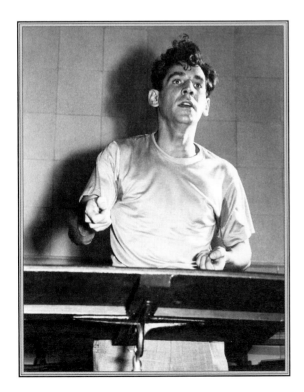

Passion, commitment, intensity—Leonard Bernstein conducting.

teach. Like Gershwin, Bernstein enjoyed fast cars, fancy clothes, and all-night parties.

Bernstein got his start in music at Tanglewood, where he became a protégé of the conductor and music patron Serge Koussevitsky. In 1943, Bernstein caused a sensation when he took over a New York Philharmonic concert as conductor on only a few hours notice. From then on, his career was assured.

Bernstein was enormously versatile, and he had the energy of three men. He used to sleep only two or three hours a night. He could have been a great pianist, a great conductor, or a great composer. Instead, he was all three.

As a pianist, Bernstein enjoyed playing everything from Mozart to Gershwin. As a conductor, Bernstein's career was unparalleled. He was for 10 years the permanent conductor of the New York Philharmonic, but he was in demand by orchestras all over the world. His conducting was manically energetic: He would throw his arms around, shake his fists, twist and cavort. Sometimes he would leap into the air to express his excitement. But underneath the showmanship, there was a profound musical intelligence.

As a composer, Bernstein was highly versatile. Like Stravinsky and Copland, he wrote ballet music. Bernstein also wrote musicals, including *On the Town* (1944), *Wonderful Town* (1953), and *Candide* (1956). His most successful musical, and his most famous composition, was *West Side Story*, written in 1957. An updating of Shakespeare's *Romeo and Juliet*, it tells the story of lovers separated by the gulf between rival gangs on Manhattan's West Side. The score is brilliant,

Leonard Bernstein in 1947.

combining jazz, snappy dances, and moving lyricism. Bernstein had an uncanny ability to write immensely moving music that seems simple and direct and completely hides the craft that went into it. **(See Listening Guide below.)**

In addition to ballets and musicals, Bernstein wrote gentle songs and delicate piano pieces, as well as big choral works, three symphonies, two operas, and a Mass. Multiple reconciliations are attempted in his *Mass*, written in 1971. It is a rock setting of the Catholic Mass with singers and orchestra; it is a concert piece that is designed to be staged; and some of the text is in Hebrew.

LISTENING GUIDE

Leonard Bernstein (1918–1990)
"Make Our Garden Grow"
  from *Candide*

Date of composition: 1956
Orchestration: 2 flutes, oboe, 2 clarinets,
    bass clarinet, bassoon, 2 horns,
    2 trumpets, 2 trombones, tuba, timpani
    and percussion, harp, strings
Duration: 3:58

Complete CD Collection: 7, track 12

The comic operetta *Candide* is based on the satire by the eighteenth-century author Voltaire. It was set in two acts by Lillian Hellman, with lyrics by Richard Wilbur, John Latouche, and Dorothy Parker, and first produced in 1956.

The comical story of Candide follows him through several countries as he searches for Cunegonde, the beautiful daughter of a European baron. The lovers were separated when they were "discovered" by her brother, who reported the incident to their father. The story recounts the wild and steamy escapades of Candide and Cunegonde as they go their separate ways but ultimately meet again somewhere in Turkey, where they adopt the "work ethic" philosophy, buy a small farm, and vow a life of simplicity.

This selection comes at the end of the production and features all the principal characters. The entire ensemble is joined by the chorus (in a moving unaccompanied section) toward the end of the dramatic finale.

The musical structure Bernstein adopts for this number is a fairly simple, strophic, song form. The overall tonal scheme outlines a dissonant augmented chord (C-E-A♭-C), which lends a strong sense of resolution to the final verse. This feeling of conflict resolved is also played out in the orchestral section.

		[C Major]
(12)	**0:00**	Orchestral prelude, (strong resolving dissonances).

CANDIDE

		[E Major]
	0:15	You've been a fool and so have I, But come and be my wife, And let us try before we die To make some sense of life.

We're neither pure nor wise nor good;
We'll do the best we know; [gentle]

0:57   We'll build our house, and chop our wood,
And make our garden grow, [climax]
And make our garden grow.

1:21   Orchestral interlude.

CUNEGONDE

[A♭ Major; same melody, more motion in accompaniment]

(13)   **1:30**   I thought the world was sugarcake,
For so our master said;
But now I'll teach my hands to bake
Our loaf of daily bread.

**CUNEGONDE
& CANDIDE**

[duet]

1:55   *Refrain:*

We're neither pure nor wise nor good,
We'll do the best we know;
We'll build our house, and chop our wood,
And make our garden grow,
And make our garden grow.

2:30   Orchestral interlude.

**PRINCIPAL
CHARACTERS**

[return to C Major—louder]

2:35   Let dreamers dream what worlds they please,
Those Edens can't be found.
The sweetest flow'rs, the fairest trees
Are grown in solid ground.

**WITH
CHORUS**

[unaccompanied voices; orchestra suddenly drops out]

Refrain:

(14)   **3:02**   We're neither pure nor wise nor good;
We'll do the best we know; [gentle]

3:14   We'll build our house, and chop our wood,
And make our garden grow, [high C in sopranos!]
And make our garden grow. [orchestra rejoins]

3:36   Huge orchestral climax.

3:46   Final cadence.

Audiences for Music in the Twentieth Century

Audiences for music expanded enormously in the twentieth century, largely as a result of new technology. The radio and the phonograph brought music to millions of people who would otherwise not have been able to hear it. The commercialization of popular music also brought with it an exponential increase in the number of people hearing music of all kinds, in dance halls and nightclubs as well as on radio and on recordings. From the earliest cylinders invented before the turn of the century to the compact discs and CD-ROMs of today, recording technology has turned music into a business worth billions of dollars. ¶ In this atmosphere of popularization, classical music, with its greater subtlety and deeper intellectual challenges, had to struggle for survival. The audiences for live classical music are still dwindling. Many orchestras have had to disband. Others have had to rely more and more on a small repertoire of orchestral "standards" to ensure a viable level of attendance. This, in turn, has turned most orchestras (as well as opera houses and chamber-music groups) into highly conservative organizations, rather than the places of excitement and experimentation they used to be. In Mozart's time, most performances were of new music; now they are mostly of old music. The 2,000-year-old tradition of Western music, with its treasury of musical masterpieces and proven ability to express the human soul in ways that words cannot reach, is at a turning point. Will it survive our new century?

Bernstein lived his life to the hilt. It always seemed he didn't want to miss anything. He was bisexual, smoked and drank to excess, and loved to surround himself with people. His charisma was magnetic. He managed to wring 72 years out of life, though he never stopped smoking, and suffered from severe emphysema. In the end, he simply dropped dead. In his passionate commitment and his manifold achievements, Leonard Bernstein personified American music for half a century.

AFTER THE WAR: MODERNISM, THE SECOND STAGE

Although the careers of many of the composers discussed earlier (e.g., Stravinsky, Shostakovich, Britten, Bernstein) continued well into the second half of the century, the ending of World War II marked a real turning point in the development of new music. It was a turning point for the Western world, of course. As societies struggled to recover from the enormous human loss and destruction of the war, economies boomed, and a new optimism reigned. In the 1950s, Americans enjoyed a higher standard of living than ever before, and in Europe, though recovery was much slower, gradual rebuilding and long-term prospects for peace led to increased hopes for the future. The birthrate multiplied, resulting in what has been called the "baby boom," whose effects (and ripple effects) continue to have an enormous influence on our society.

After the war, and especially in the fortunate Fifties and the radical Sixties, the arts flourished, and music entered the second stage of Modernism. This was a period of radical experimentation, expanding upon ideas set forth in the first stage and marked by two opposing tendencies: extreme control and complete freedom. The controls were established by a technique known as total serialism, which we will discuss. The outer fringes of the "freedom movement" allowed performers to play what they liked when they liked.

TOTAL SERIALISM

Before the war, the twelve-tone technique had been employed primarily by the Viennese trio Schoenberg, Berg, and Webern. After the war, many other composers in several different countries began to use the technique. But they felt that Schoenberg and his students had not gone far enough. If pitches can be organized into a strict sequence, then why not do the same with all the elements of music: dynamics, rhythm, tone quality, and so on? The twelve-tone technique had sometimes been called **serialism,** because it arranged the notes into a series; this new idea was therefore called **total serialism.**

The first composition based on total serialism was *Structures I* (1952) by the French composer Pierre Boulez. Born in 1925, Boulez was one of the most influential musical figures in postwar Europe. He was 20 when the war ended, and he possessed a formidable intelligence and a strong training in mathematics as well as in music.

> Just listen with the vastness of the world in mind. You can't fail to get the message.
> —Boulez on his own music

Pierre Boulez in 1966.

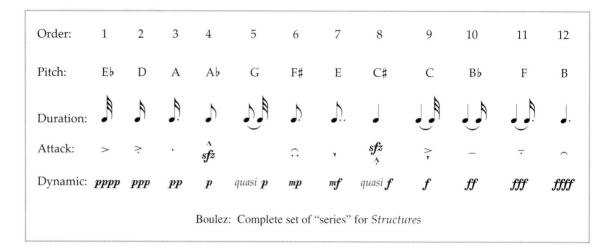

Order:	1	2	3	4	5	6	7	8	9	10	11	12
Pitch:	E♭	D	A	A♭	G	F♯	E	C♯	C	B♭	F	B
Duration:												
Attack:	>	⸝	·	sfz		⌢	˅	sfz	˃	—	ˉ	⌢
Dynamic:	*pppp*	*ppp*	*pp*	*p*	quasi *p*	*mp*	*mf*	quasi *f*	*f*	*ff*	*fff*	*ffff*

Boulez: Complete set of "series" for *Structures*

For *Structures I*, which was written for two pianos, Boulez made series for four different musical elements: pitch, duration, attack (the way the pianist strikes the note), and dynamics. These elements are all arranged into series numbered from 1 to 12. If you look carefully for a minute or two at the chart above, you will grasp this easily. The 12 available pitches are arranged in an order, starting E♭, D, A, A♭, and so on. Then durations (note lengths) are put in order, starting from the smallest duration (♪) and going all the way up to a dotted quarter note (♩.). These are also numbered from 1 to 12. Then Boulez lists 12 methods of attack, ranging from a very aggressive striking of the note to a very smooth legato. Finally, 12 dynamic levels are arranged, from *pppp* to *ffff*. This chart is then used as the basis for composing the piece. **(See Listening Guide on page 391.)**

Who Cares If You Listen?

The article by the American composer Milton Babbitt entitled "Who Cares if You Listen?" represents one extreme in a controversy that has raged for much of the twentieth century. On one hand is the view that composers should write what people want to hear: Audiences are consumers, and consumers can demand what they want. On the other hand, some of the greatest art has been created by people who were completely unappreciated during their own lifetime. Webern's music was almost never performed while he was alive; after his death, he became a catalyst for a whole generation of composers. Stravinsky's *Rite of Spring* caused outrage at its first performance; now it is considered one of the masterworks of the twentieth century. ✦ Who decides if a work is great? Other composers? Contemporary audiences? Posterity? ✦ During Bach's lifetime, he was considered an inferior composer to Telemann. Today, we hear Telemann's music as fluent but not profound. Who's right? People in the eighteenth century or people today? Will people change their minds *again* about Telemann in another 250 years? And will they necessarily be right because they are later? ✦ Nowadays composers care quite a lot if you listen. They are reaching out to audiences in remarkable new ways. But how many people are there left out there listening to contemporary classical music?

Pierre Boulez (b. 1925)
Structures I

Date of composition: 1952
Orchestration: 2 pianos
Duration: 3:26

Student CD Collection: 3, track 45
Complete CD Collection: 7, track 15

This piece demands a great deal of skill from the performers and considerable effort from the listeners. What at first might sound like a random, disjointed piano experiment is instead a precisely constructed work.

Numbers and mathematical principles have concerned composers for centuries, and Boulez has here extended the serial technique from a structured means of controlling pitches to a means of controlling every aspect of the music in a strictly rational way. What one hears in the piece, however, is a palette of shifting textures and contrasting panels of sound.

45 (15)	**0:00**	Sustained notes, use of extremes in range; although pitches overlap, few notes are struck simultaneously as chords.
	0:11	Pause, then quick articulations, some fast repeated notes.
	0:28	More held notes in low and middle range; a slight slowing.
	0:39	This section begins with a surprise—a chord—and has more use of simultaneously sounded pitches and thus a richer harmonic feel. The pulse moves forward and seems to gain momentum. Scattered notes leap about in the high and middle ranges.
	1:08	Low rumblings make a distinct line in that register.
	1:18	A series of stark, accented notes, moving deliberately in different registers; ends with staccato note.
46 (16)	**1:29**	Another held chord; return to a sustained texture, much slower and smoother, gentle and atmospheric.
	2:06	Sudden staccato chord moves into faster, more crisply articulated section.
	2:16	Another chord; others follow, repeated notes, playful quality.
	2:40	Pause; then held note in medium register leads to more sustained single notes; sustained notes contrast with staccato notes.
	3:08	Pause; then fast chords, gentle flourish of notes, fading away in a faint high range.

In practice, the method is used with some flexibility. Each series (pitch, duration, etc.) can be applied independently. And the entire series can be used backward or forward, even with the pitches transposed. The strange thing is that despite its strict and rigid compositional basis, the music sounds more or less random. The number of organizing elements is so large that it is very hard to *hear* the structure (let alone play it!).

Other composers who worked with total serialism in the 1950s were Karlheinz Stockhausen (b. 1928) in Germany, Luciano Berio (b. 1925) in Italy, and Milton Babbitt (b. 1916) in the United States. Audiences found the style difficult and unappealing and deserted concert halls in droves. But many composers felt that the music had its own validity, even if people didn't like it. And Milton Babbitt published a famous article that summarized this view. Its title was "Who Cares If You Listen?"

An important step for total serialism and for other experimental music was the development in the late 1950s of electronic music technology. The newly invented music synthesizer could produce precisely defined sounds. All aspects of a sound could be controlled—pitch, length, tone color, intensity, attack, and decay (the ending of a note)—and the performance of a work no longer needed a human being!

THE RADICAL SIXTIES: NEW SOUNDS, FREEDOM, AND CHANCE

In the 1960s, the United States and Europe underwent profound change. The "baby boomers" grew to adulthood, and experimentation was in the air. It was a time of unprecedented freedom in the areas of sex, drugs, social mores, and individual lifestyles, and this sense of radical experimentation was reflected in the music. This was the era in which popular music began to overwhelm the music of "serious" composers. And yet it was certainly in "serious" music that the most interesting musical experiments were being made.

The English conductor Sir Thomas Beecham was once asked if he had played any Stockhausen. "No," he replied, "but I have trodden in some."

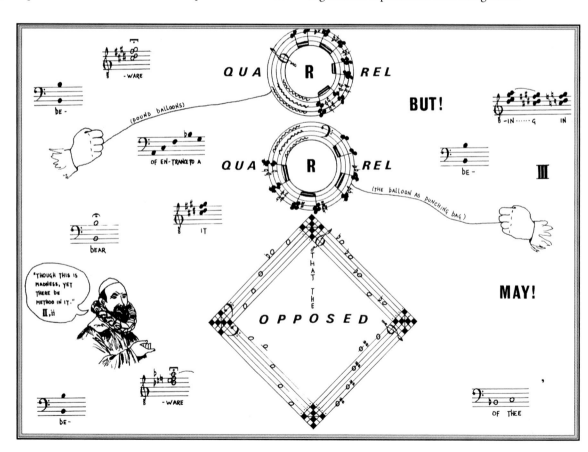

A "radical sixties" musical score (actually 1971) by Edwin London.

From the *Polonius Platitudes*, copyright 1971 by Edwin London.

NEW SOUNDS

Many of these experiments revolved around new sounds. The synthesizer, the tape recorder, and the computer made available to composers both new sounds and the ability to manipulate sounds in completely new ways. New sounds were also produced by an inventive and imaginative use of normal musical instruments. Composers began to call for a far more extended range of sounds from traditional instruments: squeaks, whines, and flutters from wind instruments, bonks and slides from string instruments. Modification of the piano became popular at this time, with nuts and bolts, plastic spoons, or pieces of paper inserted between the strings inside the piano or lying on top of the strings to create new sounds. And some of the more radical composers wrote fascinating pieces for large groups of instruments playing in quite novel ways.

The two most interesting composers working with sound textures in the 1960s were the Hungarian composer György Ligeti (b. 1923, last name pronounced *Li*ggety) and the Polish composer Krzysztof Penderecki (b. 1933, last name pronounced Pender*et*zki).

Ligeti worked with large blocks of sound, created by having the singers or instrumentalists sing or play a whole mass of adjacent notes at once. A block created in this way can then expand or contract like a wedge, often over considerable amounts of time.

Other musical shapes can also be created in sound—triangles, squares, and the like—though describing the shape doesn't begin to describe the musical effect, which is extraordinary. In Ligeti's 1961 orchestral piece *Atmospheres*, for example, there are sections in which the wide span of the block, sometimes covering as much as four octaves, remains fixed, but within the block the internal parts are constantly changing positions, creating a sense of continual motion within a static whole.

In Poland, Penderecki was working with very similar techniques. One of his most ambitious works was his *St. Luke Passion* for solo singers, chorus, and orchestra, written in 1965. In scope and orchestration and spiritual commitment, the work pays homage to Bach, but the sounds are very new. Penderecki has the chorus shout, whisper, and moan; the solo singing is wild and dramatic; and the orchestra uses massive sound blocks, with special instrumental effects.

Penderecki's most famous composition dates from 1960. It is written for a string orchestra composed of 24 violins, ten violas, ten cellos, and eight double basses, and it is entitled *Threnody* (which means a homage to the dead) *for the Victims of Hiroshima*. This is an incredibly powerful piece—lamenting, angry, and intense. Sometimes it seems even to assault the listener. Huge sound blocks are used, and the players produce a

LISTENING GUIDE

Krzysztof Penderecki (b. 1933)
Threnody for the Victims of Hiroshima

Date of composition: 1960
Orchestration: 24 violins, 10 violas,
     10 cellos, 8 double basses
Duration: 9:44

Complete CD Collection: 7, track 17

*P*enderecki's *Threnody* is a work of great power. The piece falls into six identifiable sections with an introduction, reaching a peak of intensity in section IV and finally fading, after a roar of sound, to nothingness at the end of section VI.

17 (17) **0:00**	High sustained pitches; at first two, then joined by others to produce a piercing effect.
0:18	Sound spreads and softens, some of the pitches waver and oscillate.
I	
18 (18) **0:38**	Sudden drop in volume, sound still high and sustained, but with some wavering.
0:49	Pizzicato and thumping on instruments; these percussive effects build in intensity and gradually (1:19) are replaced by high, brief squeaks and short runs and flourishes; these also build in rhythmic activity and intensity; some lower grunts are added (1:34); crescendo.
2:10	Suddenly calm and sustained. Unison pitch that spreads into a cluster and returns to a unison,
2:42	then fades; a faint distant pitch emerges, then another one, in a lower range; overlapping successions of single pitches enter, spread into a cluster, return to a unison and fade.
II	
19 (19) **2:53**	A high pitch enters; it crescendos gradually while lower pitches continue to enter beneath it.
3:02	High pitch spreads to cluster and returns to near-unison.
3:13	Sudden break; low, unfocused tone cluster.
3:27	Pause, then loud tone clusters enter at various pitch levels, and are sustained.
III	
20 (20) **4:03**	Instruments drop out, and sense of spreading is created as low instruments fall in pitch while high ones slide higher; decrescendo; sound seems to "disappear" at the outer edges of perception.
4:15	Beginning softly, instruments enter with short accented notes, gradually increasing in volume and becoming more sustained; builds to an intense level, then

IV		
21 (21)	**4:44**	violins drop out, leaving lower instruments exposed; they glissando, first downward in a cluster, then arrive at a unison (4:55), and decrescendo, the sound again gradually disappears. Long pause.
	5:45	Diffuse texture of plucking, thumps, extreme highs and low tremolos and glassy single pitches;
	5:56	calmer, fewer events;
	6:10	more activity, faster rhythms;
	6:56	sounds press higher,
	7:14	upward fast glissandos and quick thumping are added,
	7:26	occurring in an intense succession.
V		
22 (22)	**7:36**	High clusters are sustained, string basses make grunting sounds, intensity builds, clusters oscillate with vibrato; crescendo,
	8:02	then sound ebbs, sustained pitches take over with a dense, focused, sustained cluster, then fade away,
	8:10	revealing a lower, busy oscillating sound.
	8:21	Higher clusters reenter, and are joined by more low- and high-range clusters, active with various speeds of tremolos.
	8:39	Suddenly gentle, but still active and intense.
VI		
23 (23)	**8:52**	Entrance of a dense, broad wall of sound, thick and heavy. A very long decrescendo, finally fading into nothingness.

wide assortment of noises by knocking on the bodies of their instruments or by scraping the strings hard. Often the effects are strikingly similar to those produced by electronic means. Once you hear this piece, you will never forget it. **(See Listening Guide on page 393.)**

FREEDOM AND CHANCE

Both total serialism and the use of block sound textures require very careful control on the part of the composer. At the same time as these ideas were being explored, a completely opposite tendency was prevalent in music. This was a move *away from* control, in the direction of freedom for the performers, even to the point of leaving some musical matters to chance. Some scores have several pages of music for each of the performers, allowing them to choose which page they want to play and when. Others simply indicate time durations and give very general instructions: "As high as you can," or "Any sound repeated five times." And some scores simply give rough drawings or sketches on the page, abandoning musical notation altogether.

The idea of leaving musical events to chance was the main focus of a musical revolutionary named John Cage (1912–1992). Cage was born in Los Angeles, the son of an inventor. At the age of 22, he studied with Schoenberg—who told him he had no ear for music and would never make a composer. But Cage decided that music was too narrowly defined. "Everything we do is music," he said.

Cage invented the idea of the "prepared piano," with nuts and bolts and plastic spoons inside the lid. He asked performers to throw dice and toss coins to determine which parts of a composition would be played. He wrote a piece called *Imaginary Landscape No. 4* (1951) for 12 radios, all playing on different stations. He stood on stage smoking a cigarette and drinking a glass of water with a microphone attached to his throat, the loudspeakers turned up as high as they would go. Once, when invited to give a lecture, he read for hours from various scraps of newspaper. "If my work is accepted," he once said, "I must move on to the point where it isn't."

Cage erased the boundaries between deliberate and random, between a performance and a "happening," between music and noise. His most famous composition was written in 1952 and is entitled *4' 33"*. In it, the performer is instructed to sit at the piano for four minutes and 33 seconds and do *nothing*. The audience grows restless and finally starts listening to sounds inside and outside the hall—sounds of rustling, coughing, the buzz of the lights, police sirens—sounds that are not music. Or are they?

Cage was a leading member of the postwar avantgarde. He infuriated many critics, performers, and scholars, who thought he was destroying music, but his influence was vast, ranging from the painter Robert Motherwell to the rock group the Grateful Dead. "One need not fear," he once said, "about the future of music."

POSTMODERNISM

During the latter part of the twentieth century, artists began to question the continued viability of the Modernist movement. It had been unusually productive and long-lived: The feeling of innovation and experimentation had lasted from 1900 to the mid-1960s. Now some of its achievements were thrown into doubt. The meaning of art itself was no longer certain. Was a can of paint dropped on the floor "art"? How about graffiti on the subway?

During the century, people had become increasingly alienated from modern classical music. By the 1950s, audiences for new music were made up of tiny groups of specialists, mostly composers themselves. Concert organizations turned more and more to presenting the classics of the past. There was real validity to the claim that American symphony orchestras were turning into museums. The twelve-tone system and its later refinements produced music that was so arcane

The Twentieth-Century Orchestra

In the first part of the twentieth century, large orchestras were still in vogue. Stravinsky uses an immense orchestra for his remarkable work *The Rite of Spring* (1913), and Schoenberg required enormous forces for his *Variations for Orchestra* (1928). But these orchestras are used in revolutionary ways: Stravinsky's to create the effect of frightening primitive power, Schoenberg's to create very spare textures with a kaleidoscope of different colors. But there was also a reaction against the excesses of these performing groups and a return to the clarity and transparency of the smaller orchestras of the eighteenth century (Stravinsky's *Dumbarton Oaks* Concerto). In the second half of the twentieth century composers moved in two different but interrelated directions. They reconceived the ways in which traditional instruments could be played (in his *Threnody for the Victims of Hiroshima* Penderecki creates sounds both eerie and terrifying on fifty-two perfectly ordinary stringed instruments); and they used newly invented technology (audio tape, electronic keyboards, computers, and synthesizers) to create new sounds (Olly Wilson's *Sometimes*). Often, however, the new technology is used to imitate the sounds of a traditional orchestra. This is much more common than you might think, especially on film soundtracks or at Broadway shows. So, after three hundred years of development, the symphony orchestra, with its fascinating mixture of people and instruments, and its remarkable ideal of multiple individuals all collaborating to convey complex emotions, may finally have become obsolete.

A perfect example of the Twentieth-Century orchestra is Lukas Foss's Third Movement of the "Renaissance Concerto" for Flute and Orchestra. You can watch a live performance of this work in Segment 3 of your *Inside the Orchestra* CD-ROM.

The Postmodern Dolphin Hotel at Walt Disney World Resort, Florida, completed in 1990.

William Taylor/Arcaid © Disney Enterprises Inc.

Elegiac Study **by Robert Motherwell.**

Robert Motherwell, "Dedalus Sketchbook: Elegiac Study," 1982. © Dedalus Foundation Inc./Licensed by VAGA, New York, NY.

look at tonality is known as neo-tonality, or neo-Romanticism.

Other facets of Postmodernism are a tendency to quote from earlier historical styles and a deliberate cross-fertilization of the European-American tradition with the arts of other cultures. Quotation is common in Postmodernist painting and architecture as well as in music. Paintings make overt reference to well-known paintings of the past, and buildings copy famous styles of earlier eras. Compositions contain snippets or long extracts from older musical works. These references are juxtaposed in new and startling ways, and the old is embedded in a context of the new, throwing new light upon both of them. There is also a deliberate attempt to incorporate styles from other parts of the world, as the world becomes a smaller place.

Finally, Postmodernism deliberately reached out across the traditional barrier between classical and popular music. Classical music of the late twentieth and early twenty-first centuries has moved closer to rock and even rap. The dividing line between operas and musicals (such as those of Andrew Lloyd Webber) is narrowing sharply. And performing groups deliberately mix genres: A string quartet plays arrangements of Jimi Hendrix; chamber groups include electric guitars, amplification, and video in their performances; performance artists play the violin, sing, and paint their bodies on stage.

What is common to these ideas is a deliberate eclecticism (mixing of styles). The late twentieth century seemed to be a period open to all influences, past and present, local and foreign, popular and refined. Does this mean that the late twentieth century was a period without identity, the first era that had no defining artistic style of its own, only a style borrowed from other times and places? Or does it mean that the new mixture is the way of the future, in which all barriers will come down,

and "unfriendly" that few people enjoyed it. Young people turned increasingly to rock and other forms of popular music.

In the 1980s and 1990s, this profound debate affected public support for the arts. And as economies suffered, educational institutions and local and national governments cut deeply into their funding for the arts.

From the mid-1960s through today, a new movement has taken hold in music and the other arts. This new movement is known as Postmodernism. Postmodernism is a style that juxtaposes many varied elements, especially familiar ones, in new and interesting ways.

Postmodernism has many facets. The most significant aspect of the movement is a deliberate return to the past. In painting, artists returned to representation and figuration, after many years of abstractionism. In architecture, buildings once again began to display decorative structures and fantasy, after the austere (and, to some, ugly) functionalism of the mid-century. In music, the return to the past was exemplified by a return to the language of tonality, so resoundingly rejected for so many years. It was suggested that the main characteristics of tonal music—a key center, repetition, and return—correspond to basic impulses in the human brain and are therefore fundamental to human nature. This new

Classical Music Today

The first performances of new pieces are, and always have been, exciting events. People enjoy the prospect of experiencing newly created music. *Our* expectations of new music, however, are very different from those of people in the eighteenth century who listened to new works by Mozart or Haydn. The huge diversity of musical styles that now confronts us had no parallel in the eighteenth century. Classic composers were expected to conform to certain rules. Now there aren't any rules. A piece performed today in a concert hall by a screaming singer and a drummer standing on their heads with only a lighted candle and a motionless baseball player behind them on the stage would be greeted today with interest and anticipation rather than disbelief or derision. We are used to aural and visual incongruity and radical experimentation. If art mirrors life, then the diverse and complex range of music in our new century may well reflect the splintered, multifaceted nature of modern culture.

the past will be absorbed into the present, and all art will become one, in a global unity of shared experience?

We'll see.

POSTMODERN MUSIC

One of the ways in which Postmodernism first began to manifest itself in music was by quotation. In one composition entitled *Nach Bach (After Bach*, 1967), the American composer George Rochberg suspends little fragments of Bach's harpsichord music in a surrounding context of dissonance and abrupt silences. Luciano Berio's *Sinfonia* (1969) has a movement-length quotation from Mahler's Second Symphony, overlaid with readings of modern poetry, shouts, and tiny fragments of quotations from many *other* composers. And Lukas Foss's *Renaissance Concerto* (1986) is based on the music of Orfeo's lament from Monteverdi's *Orfeo*. (**See Listening Guide on page 400.**)

The return to tonality was another striking feature of Postmodern music. David del Tredici (b. 1937) is best known for a series of extended compositions based on the stories *Alice in Wonderland* and *Through the Looking Glass*. The music is wonderfully inventive and captures the tone of Lewis Carroll's quirky prose with a modern aesthetic. *Final Alice* (1976), for example, is a long symphony with a big, rich orchestra, amplified voice, and a small rock group. The harmonies are late nineteenth century, but the context is totally new, and the result is bizarre, beautiful, humorous, and touching by turns.

Tonality is mingled with Modernism in the work of the English composer Oliver Knussen (b. 1952). Knussen's setting of Maurice Sendak's children's story *Where the Wild Things Are* (1983) can be performed both as an opera and as a concert piece. It is a good way to introduce children to modern music.

Multimedia Postmodernist work is perhaps best represented by the performance artist Laurie Anderson (b. 1947). A trained violinist, Anderson is also actress, singer, poet, and storyteller. She creates works that use spoken words over rock patterns, high-tech video, and large backdrops, against which she projects her fragile-looking, razor-sharp stage personality.

The incorporation of musical elements from other

Here is a quotation from a book that quotes a book quoting a book on quoting: "Even if a text is wholly quotation, the condition of quotation itself qualifies the text and makes it so far unique. Thus a quotation from Marvell by Eliot has a force slightly different from what it had when Marvell wrote it. . . . There is a perception of something previously unknown, something new . . ."

Lukas Foss (b. 1922)
Third Movement (*Recitative*—after
Monteverdi*) from *Renaissance Concerto
for Flute and Orchestra

Date of composition: 1986
Orchestration: Solo flute and strings
  (plus "distant" small group of
  strings and flute)
Tempo: *Lento* ("Slow")
Meter: ⁴⁄₄
Duration: 5:15

Complete CD Collection: 7, track 24

*W*e have mentioned how much contemporary music tends to rely on quotation or reference. *The Renaissance Concerto* of Lukas Foss is based on several themes and snippets from earlier eras. Despite the title, most of them are from the Baroque era. Perhaps Foss meant his piece to suggest "renaissance" in its generic meaning of "rebirth," for his concerto reinterprets and brings to life many works from the past. Foss calls this approach a "handshake across the centuries."

The third movement of this concerto is based on the lament of Orfeo for Euridice from Monteverdi's great opera *Orfeo*, of 1607. Foss recaptures the atmosphere of that music in several ways. First, many repeated pitches in the solo flute evoke Monteverdi's recitative style. Notice how many of the flute's phrases (such as the one at 0:40) seem speechlike in their shape and rhythm. Second, the opening phrase, with its distinctive falling interval of a diminished fourth, is taken directly from the opening of Monteverdi's lament. And finally, the mournful, haunting quality of the music and the curious echoing effect of the "distant" flute and strings suggest a timeless other world—the other world that Orpheus vows to visit to rescue Euridice from death.

(24)	**0:00**	Diminished fourth, first chordally in strings, then melodically in flute, imitated in strings. Fade.

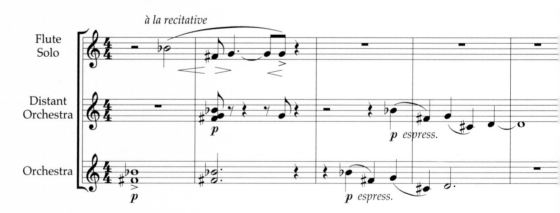

0:27	Stepwise rising idea, beginning with sliding half step that returns in final section.

0:40	Even, repeated notes on flute, then descent.

0:54	Falling diminished fourth returns in strings, then flute.
1:12	Accented repeated notes on flute; quieter.
(25) 1:25	Fast declamatory pitches on flute over high sustained string tone; flute moves higher, reaching highest pitch.
1:48	Texture thins, flute descends slowly.
2:07	Flute alone descends in slow arpeggio.
2:45	Faster ascending idea on flute, imitated on strings.
3:05	Flute: short phrases with two repeated notes, echoed in "distant" flute and strings; quieter.
(26) 3:45	Slow slide up half step, reiterated higher and louder; "distant" flute echoes clearly.

| 4:25 | Slide pushes up to a high dissonant chord; then the tension is released as the accompaniment thins and the flute unwinds with a relaxed swirl of descending notes; movement ends with a low, hollow fifth in the strings. |

cultures may be found in the works of Alan Hovhaness (b. 1911), Frederic Rzewski (b. 1938), and David Hykes (b. 1953). Hovhaness has written an extraordinary number of works, all neo-tonal and many of them influenced by Armenian and Far Eastern music. Rzewski's *The People United Will Never Be Defeated* (1975) is based on a revolutionary ballad from Chile, and his *Four Pieces* for piano (1977) use other Latin American melodies. And in the 1970s and 1980s, Hykes became fascinated with the special, "multiphonic" singing of the Tibetan monks, in which the singers produce low tones in their throats and at the same time high, floating harmonics. Hykes taught himself and several other American singers this technique and founded the Harmonic Choir, for which he has written many works, including *Current Circulation* (1984). Other influences on Postmodern music come from China, Japan, Indonesia, India, and Africa, but

Agnes Martin's minimalist painting *Trumpet* (1967).

Agnes Martin, "Trumpet," 1967. Acrylic and pencil on canvas, 72 × 72". Courtesy of Pace Wildenstein. © 1967 Agnes Martin.

also from Native America. An example of the latter is *O-Ke-Wa*, based on the Seneca people's song for the dead, and written in 1974 by the American composer Daniel Lentz (b. 1942).

The meditative, spun-out quality of music from the East has been a major contributor to New Age music, which is also neo-tonal, but with a minimal sense of drive and resolution; it is floating, gentle, calm, and without form. A newer category of New Age music is known as Space Music. Formed mostly on synthesizers, it evokes the openness, vastness, and formlessness of outer space.

The merging of popular and "serious" music is perhaps the most interesting trend in Postmodern music. Starting in the 1960s but continuing strongly into the 1970s and 1980s, a new type of music was born, which was labeled **minimalism**. Like many other musical style terms, this one came from the art world. Artists such as Frank Stella, Agnes Martin, and Robert Wilson reduced their paintings to the bare minimum, with flat surfaces, thin lines, simple shapes, and primary colors.

Minimalist music borrows from rock music the idea of harmonic simplicity and repetitive rhythm. It uses very limited materials and remains at an almost constant tempo and dynamic. The result is music that is hypnotizing in its sameness, inducing an almost trancelike state in the listener, and in this perhaps it also was influenced by music from the Far East. It changes the listener's perception of the passage of time. Many examples of minimalist music involve very slow shifts over a period of time; we have seen a similar pattern in African mbira music, in the first chapter of this book. Perhaps because of its links to rock, minimalism brought classical music back into favor again and attracted large audiences.

The central principle of minimalist music is that under the seeming changelessness there *is* change. And later minimalist compositions concentrate upon this very idea: a very slow and gradual change disguised under a surface of apparent stasis. Steve Reich (b. 1936) explored this idea in his *Piano Phase* (1967). Two pianists play a constant sixteenth-note pattern simultane-

ously. Very gradually, one of the pianists accelerates, getting "out of phase" with the other, until the notes finally coincide again ("back in phase").

Philip Glass (b. 1937) became a cult figure in the 1970s and 1980s, attracting a large following with his music. He has written lengthy operas and some fine film scores.

The most successful minimalist composer of the 1980s and 1990s was John Adams, who favors traditional orchestral and vocal forces. Adams's best-known works are his operas, which are based on contemporary political events. The first was *Nixon in China* (1987), which is set during the historic visit of President Nixon to China in an attempt to forge links between the two countries. The second, The *Death of Klinghoffer* (1991), is based on the terrorist murder of a wheelchair-bound American tourist while on a cruise ship in the Mediterranean.

FUSION

Perhaps the most important aspect of the Postmodern era is the narrowing of gaps between all types of music. The jazz trumpeter Miles Davis and others created a mixture of jazz and rock that was called fusion. There are many different kinds of fusion today, created by

The Kronos Quartet

The gradual disappearance of the traditional barriers between classical and popular music is well illustrated by a group calling themselves the Kronos Quartet. Dressed in sharp, up-to-date clothing, or jeans and flannel shirts, the musicians offer a striking contrast to the image of a traditional string quartet. They play on comfortable chairs and drape the stage with cloth. Their instruments are often amplified. The Kronos musicians are a highly trained set of instrumental virtuosos who can—and do—play Bartók or Webern brilliantly and with the most refined style and sensibility. But they have also commissioned works from the leading minimalists, performed music from Asia and Africa, and played songs of Jimi Hendrix for encores. They represent one facet of the disappearing of boundaries in the late twentieth century.

The Kronos Quartet with poet Allen Ginsberg at Carnegie Hall in 1994.

artists as diverse as Keith Jarrett, Malcolm McLaren, Yo-Yo Ma, and Eric Clapton.

One of the most fertile meeting places of the several worlds of music has been the theater. Postmodernism created a strong revival of music theater in the 1980s and 1990s. Among the most successful of these productions were those by Andrew Lloyd Webber. His works combine the style of the Broadway musical with the continuous musical settings and extended scenes of opera, the heavy beat and synthesizer-enhanced sound of rock, the sentimental lyricism of pop, and elaborate, high-tech, Postmodern stage effects.

In the modern era, as one contemporary composer and cultural commentator has written: "Multi-track, multi-layer experience becomes the norm: Ravi Shankar, John Cage, the Beatles, Gregorian chant, electronic music, Renaissance madrigals and motets, Bob Dylan, German *Lieder*, soul, J. S. Bach, jazz, Ives, Balinese gamelan, Boulez, African drumming, Mahler, *gagaku*, Frank Zappa, Tchaikovsky, ... all become part of the common shared experience."

INCLUSION

It is a commonplace of historiography (the writing of history) that the present is too close to see with any perspective. Who are the great composers of today? Will their works last? We don't know the answers to these questions.

One thing *is* clear, however. In the late twentieth century, women and minorities were gradually taking their rightful place in American music-making. In every chapter of this book, we have considered the role of women in the history of music. On the whole, with significant exceptions, it has been a history of exclusion or marginalization. One striking element of our present time has been the unraveling of this pattern and the gradual acceptance of women as full partners in the world of music. Although there are one or two orchestras in Europe that (believe it or not) still do not hire women, most European and North American orchestras contain large numbers of female musicians. There is an increasing number of conductors who are women, and some of the foremost composers of our age are women.

Representation for African-American musicians in the world of classical music still lags behind. There are a few black players in orchestras, some black conductors, and very few well-known composers.

To try to represent this picture of growing inclusiveness, we have chosen to end this chapter with the work of four contemporary American composers—three women, one African-American. These works do not claim to speak for their composers' gender or race. They are not typical of any stylistic trends. They simply show that the differences between male and female or black and white in music disappear in the individuality that human beings share. The music of a gay composer or a black composer or a woman or an Australian aborigine or a Japanese master of the shakuhachi speaks to us because it is the communication of one human being to others. All we have to do is listen.

The first work we shall listen to is *Sound Patterns* by Pauline Oliveros. Born in Houston in 1932, Oliveros has written numerous compositions, served as composer-in-residence at several colleges, and toured the country in performances of contemporary music. In

Left: Composer Ellen Taaffe Zwilich.

Middle: Composer Joan Tower.

Right: Composer Olly Wilson.

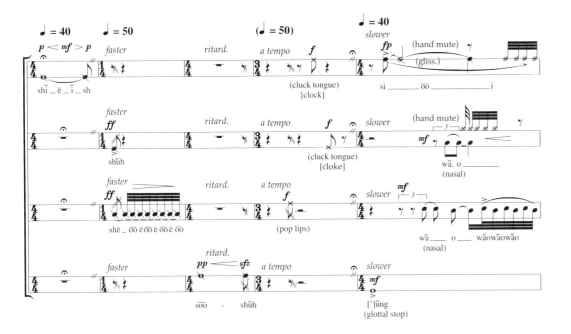

1992 she won a fellowship from the National Endowment for the Arts. She is the founder of a group of women musicians and has worked frequently with actors, dancers, and film makers. The first few measures of her *Sound Patterns* for mixed chorus are shown above.

> The awe of music never goes away. If anything, it gets more mysterious.
> —Ellen Taaffe Zwilich

LISTENING GUIDE

Pauline Oliveros (b. 1932)
Sound Patterns

Date of composition: 1964
Orchestration: Mixed chorus
Duration: 4:01

Complete CD Collection: 7, track 27

Sound Patterns is written for a mixed chorus (sopranos, altos, tenors, and basses). It involves no text. Rather, the composer calls for a huge range of nonverbal sounds from the singers, including clicking, trilling, hissing, sliding, screeching, whooping, popping, *ow*-ing, and *zz*-ing. The music mixes men and women, loud and soft, group and separate textures, high and low, all in a kaleidoscope of sound.

The work is so fascinating in its variety and so continuous that a timed Listening Guide would serve only as a distraction. Listen and enjoy!

Olly Wilson is an African-American composer who was born in St. Louis, Missouri, in 1937. He has degrees in music from Washington University in St. Louis, the University of Illinois, and the University of Iowa, and he is currently professor of music and chairman of the music department at the University of California at Berkeley. Wilson has won numerous prizes, grants, and fellowships, including a Guggenheim Fellowship that allowed him to spend a year studying music in Africa. He has published a book on black music in America. In 1995, Olly Wilson was elected to the American Academy of Arts and Letters. Wilson has specialized in electronic music, much of which was created in the Electronic Music Studio at Berkeley. (**See Listening Guide below.**)

LISTENING GUIDE

Olly Wilson (b. 1937)
Sometimes

Date of composition: 1976
Orchestration: Tenor and taped electronic sounds
Duration: 6:02

Student CD Collection: 3, track 47
Complete CD Collection: 7, track 28

Sometimes is based on the spiritual "Sometimes I Feel Like a Motherless Child." It is written for tenor and tape, and it calls for extraordinarily demanding singing. The tape uses both electronic sounds and manipulated snippets of the tenor's voice. Throughout the work, which lasts more than 15 minutes, the spiritual lends its powerful presence (even when it is absent).

47 (28)	**0:00**	Tape noises.
	0:09	Taped whispering: "motherless child."
	0:35	More activity; manipulated taped voice and electronic sounds; echoes.
	1:00	Tape noises, both screeching and low.
	1:10	Sounds like those of a bass guitar.
	1:28	Loud bass. Pause.
	1:39	Whistle sounds, feedback, clonks, ringing sounds, chimes, blips, etc. Pause.
48 (29)	**2:30**	Voice and manipulated taped voice; noises. "Sometimes . . . "; crescendo.

	3:23	"I feel ... " Tape noises; crescendo.
	3:43	"Sometimes ... " Tape noises.
49 (30)	4:08	Very high singing, "Sometimes ... "; much more activity, crescendo.
	4:33	Voice over bass tape noises.
	4:38	"I feel like a motherless child."
	4:56	"True believer ... " Whistles, blips, feedback.
	5:17	Voice and distorted taped voice ("Sometimes I feel ... ").
	5:44	Extremely high singing.
	5:58	Pause.

Joan Tower was born in New York in 1938 but was raised in South America. After returning to New York and gaining degrees at Bennington College and Columbia University, Tower founded a contemporary music ensemble in which she played the piano. She has won several composition prizes and served as composer-in-residence to the Saint Louis Symphony. In 1990 she was the first woman to win the prestigious Grawemeyer Award for Music Composition, and in 1998 she won a Distinguished American Composers award. She lives in upstate New York and is professor of music at Bard College. **(See Listening Guide below.)**

LISTENING GUIDE

Joan Tower (b. 1938)
Wings

Date of composition: 1981
Orchestration: Solo clarinet
Duration: 6:01

Complete CD Collection: 7, track 31

*T*ower has written that the image behind *Wings* is that of a falcon, at times gliding high along the air currents and at other times "going into elaborate flight patterns that loop around, diving downwards, gaining tremendous speeds." *Wings* lasts more than ten minutes; we shall hear a little more than half of the work.

(31)	0:00	Clarinet begins from no sound to a very quiet single tone.
	0:19	Change of pitch. More activity, though still quiet.
	0:53	Crescendo. Long tones mixed with faster notes.
	1:25	New melodic and rhythmic fragment.
	1:45	Excited. Trill.
	1:51	Jumpy, loud. Jumping high to low.
	2:11	Very fast. High trills.
	2:37	Low notes, running passages, high/low. Slowing down, quieter.
(32)	2:56	Even notes, tranquil. Very quiet. Pause.
	3:35	Climbing even notes. Pause.
	3:55	Quiet; climbing even notes, from very low to high.
	4:21	Low, quiet passage. Pause.
	4:45	Single note, long crescendo.
	5:01	Two octaves higher.
(33)	5:07	Gradually increasing activity, getting faster and higher.
	5:33	Quiet, "echolike."
	5:40	Frenetic; gradually calming down.
	5:55	Section ends on a single tone. Crescendo to pause.

Ellen Taaffe Zwilich was born in Florida in 1939 and studied with Elliott Carter and Roger Sessions at the Juilliard School of Music. Her music demonstrates a concern with linking the present with the past. Her Symphony No. 1, composed in 1983, won a Pulitzer Prize in music; she was the first woman to win this award. In 1996, she was appointed the first composer-in-residence at Carnegie Hall. Ellen Zwilich describes composition as "... an obsession. It is profoundly thrilling to me." In the preface to the score of her Symphony No. 1, she outlines her underlying compositional approach:

First, I have long been interested in the elaboration of large-scale works from the initial material. Second, I have been developing techniques that combine modern principles of continuous variation with older principles, such as melodic recurrence and clearly defined areas of contrast. Finally, Symphony No. 1 was written with great affection for the modern orchestra, not only for its indescribable richness and variety of color, but also for the virtuosity and artistry of its players.

PEANUTS reprinted by permission of United Feature Syndicate, Inc.

Ellen Taaffe Zwilich (b. 1939)
Third Movement (*Rondo*) from
   Symphony No. 1

Date of composition: 1983

Orchestration: Piccolo, 2 flutes, oboe, English
   horn, clarinet, bass clarinet, bassoon,
   contrabassoon, 4 horns, 2 trumpets,
   2 trombones, tuba, piano, harp, strings, and
   percussion, including timpani, cymbals,
   tambourine, bass drum (small and large),
   orchestral bells, vibraphone, tubular bells,
   snare drum, and suspended cymbals

Duration: 4:01

Student CD Collection: 3, track 50
Complete CD Collection: 7, track 34

The third movement is a rapid, energetic rondo, but the main thematic material, instead of being identical on each recurrence, is varied every time it returns. The main thematic idea is that of fast eighth notes, occurring in different ways: in the timpani as repeated pitches (A_1), as forceful rising arpeggios (A_2), and as an oscillation between two pitches (A_3). These are contrasted with a slower set of four eighth notes that rise in a jagged ascent (A_4), creating a four-against-six cross-rhythm with the driving faster eighths.

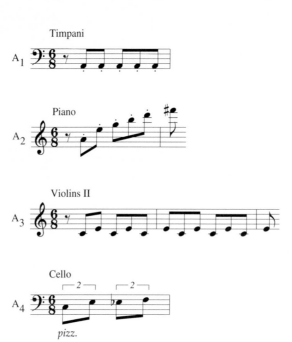

A		
50 (34)	**0:00**	Theme group A_1–A_4, featuring the strings and frequent punctuation by percussion.

B		
51 (35)	**1:07**	The chime strikes a sudden change. Sustained passage with high glassy harmonics in the violins.

A		
	1:32	Underlying timpani reintroduce the driving material.

B		
	1:47	The sustained idea returns, with chimes and an ascending violin line. This leads to:

C		
	2:16	A lyrical new melody in the oboe, with a soothing accompaniment including harp.

A		
52 (36)	**2:37**	The restless, driving A material enters again, softly in the violins, and then building in dynamics and intensity. Brass and percussion add heavy accents.

A		
	3:26	The rising arpeggio idea (A_2) predominates, pushing the violins up to a high strained register.

53 (37) **3:37** | Sustained idea, now dissonant and harsh rather than soothing, is interrupted by timpani (A₁), leading to the final, driving, accented chords.

Timpani

A₁

Conclusion

In the late twentieth century, Classical music was in a lively but anxious state. Exciting concerts of new music were still being given, and the fusion of styles, as well as the inclusion of formerly excluded voices, made the music more interesting and of wider appeal. However a large proportion of classical-music concerts even today are devoted to music of earlier centuries. Many older people grew up in the fifties and sixties, when new classical music was difficult and unappealing. These people turned backwards for their musical, emotional, and spiritual satisfaction. In the eighteenth century, almost all the classical music people listened to was new music. They were interested in the latest Haydn symphony or the newest Mozart opera, not in last year's music, and certainly not in the music of several hundred years earlier.

Today we are fortunate that the music of the past is so easily available to us, and we can find pleasure in older styles and plumb the depth of masterpieces of earlier eras. But new classical music is becoming a rarefied taste. It is not just that older people are afraid of it; young people are more attracted to music that is undemanding and gives easier and quicker gratification. This is a pity, for all worthwhile things take effort. Try listening carefully to the fascinating East/West music of Tan Dun, who won an Oscar in 2001 for the score to the film "Crouching Tiger, Hidden Dragon." Or take a few minutes and go to your music library and listen to a luminous new piece by John Corigliano or the brilliant and profound music of Osvaldo Golijov or Augusta Read Thomas. These people do not appear on Pepsi ads or on huge posters in your record store. But they have something very important to say. To you.

Stylistically, the music of the twentieth century can be divided into three periods: early (Modernism), middle (Serialism), and late (Postmodernism). The early (Modernist) period was an age of revolution, in which all the old rules were broken. The greatest representatives of musical Modernism were Debussy, Stravinsky, and Schoenberg. Debussy wrote music that was suggestive, unfocused, impressionistic. His use of the orchestra was highly coloristic, and he managed to evoke cloudy skies, turbulent seas, and rainy gardens both in his orchestral music and in his music for solo piano. Stravinsky was such an original composer he influenced the music of most of the century. He wrote big, powerful orchestral pieces in primitive style, he incorporated jazz sounds and techniques in other works, and he invented a new "neo-classic" style that borrowed from the clarity and transparency of the eighteenth century and yet was enlivened with animated, quirky, off-beat rhythms and pungent dissonances.

Perhaps the biggest revolution of Modernism was that stirred up by Schoenberg. He replaced the centuries-old system of tonality with a new system based on all twelve pitches. This twelve-tone system (or Serialism) became the basis of composition for many composers of the mid-twentieth century. It was rigid and intellectually coherent, but few major compositions written in the style have found favor with the general public.

While Schoenberg and his colleagues and followers were pursuing the acerbic, somewhat academic lure of Serialism, other, more popular musical styles were asserting themselves. In America, the sounds of jazz and Broadway infiltrated much classical music, and popular and classical music came closer together.

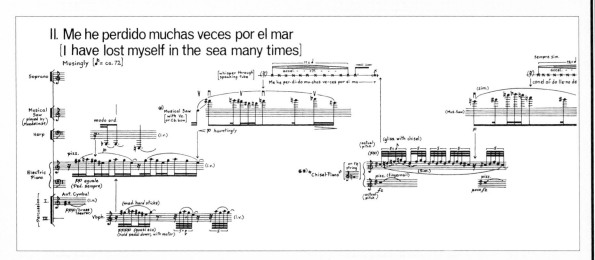

An unconventional-looking score for a twentieth-century composition.

In the last third of the twentieth century, this merging of styles culminated in the Postmodern movement. This movement drew on an eclectic variety of influences: rock, Baroque, Africa, the Middle East, politics, electronics, film. As the music became more inclusive, so did the musical world. Women finally were fully accepted as composers, performers, and conductors, and African-American, Hispanic, Asian, and other musicians became more prominent in the world of classical music.

The most notable trend at the end of the century was a return to melody, consonance, and tonality. The clashing, difficult sounds of Modernism and Serialism were replaced by compositions of great sensuous beauty and a return to a romantic quality of emotional expression. Perhaps it was no wonder that most of the music of the twentieth century had been filled with dissonance, angst, violence, and anger, for it had been so in the real world, too. A century of two world wars, Hiroshima, and the Holocaust was not likely to produce music of peace and calm. Music reflects the society that creates it, as we have said all along.

FUNDAMENTALS OF TWENTIETH-CENTURY MUSIC

- ✦ Tonality was replaced by other organizational systems, including "twelve-tone" or serial music

- ✦ Nontraditional scales are used

- ✦ Traditional instruments are deployed in startling new ways

- ✦ New instruments using electricity were invented, culminating in the synthesizer and computer

- ✦ Composers question all aspects of music making, including the length of pieces, the participation of the performers, and even the idea of a concert itself

- ✦ Popular music and the music of other cultures are blended with "classical" styles

- ✦ Music returns to tonality and attractiveness at the end of the century

THE TWENTIETH CENTURY II: JAZZ, AN AMERICAN ORIGINAL

What is jazz? Most of us recognize it when we hear it, but it's not so easy to list the essential ingredients of jazz. First of all is the rhythm. Jazz usually has a steady rhythm that continues from the very beginning of a piece to the end. That rhythm is often underscored by percussion instruments, which play a central role in the performance of jazz. The most characteristic part of jazz rhythm is syncopation: the accentuation of "offbeats," or beats that are unstressed in other types of music. The combination of these rhythmic elements contributes to what is known as "swing." Swing is the *feeling* generated by the steady rhythm and accented offbeats of the music and by the lively, spirited playing of jazz performers. Swing is what makes you want to move to the music.

Another primary ingredient of jazz is the use of "blue notes." Blue notes are notes that are played or sung lower or flatter than the pitches in a conventional Western scale. Common blue notes in jazz are the third, fifth, and seventh notes of a scale. Often, these notes are not exactly a half step low but rather indeterminate in pitch, and they can be "bent" or "scooped" by many instruments and by singers. These blue notes contribute to the expressive nature of much jazz performance.

Third, jazz often contains special sounds or conventional instruments playing in unusual ways. Trumpets playing "wah-wah" with a mute, trombones making slides, clarinets squealing in the high register — these are sounds directly associated with jazz but avoided in "straight" concert music. Jazz singers also deliberately make use of unusual sounds. A special kind of singing in which the vocalist improvises with nonsense syllables ("doo-be-doo dah," etc.) is known as "scat" singing. There are also instruments rarely used in concert music that are central to jazz. Foremost among these is the saxophone, which comes in many sizes, from the small soprano sax to the enormous contrabass. Most common in jazz are the alto and tenor instruments.

Finally, most people would say that improvisation is a necessary element in jazz. Certainly in many forms of jazz, improvisation plays a central role in the creation of the music, and some of the best jazz performers have been spontaneous and inventive improvisers. There is a difference, however, between genuine improvisation and the performance of a free-sounding melodic line that has been worked out in advance. Some of the most famous jazz performers would repeat their best solos night after night. This does not mean that they were not playing jazz. Perhaps the best approach is to say that improvisation is a typical but not an absolutely necessary ingredient of jazz.

Great jazz artists, however, are often great improvisers. This means that they are not just performers but *composers* as well.

> A jazz musician is a juggler who uses harmonies instead of oranges.
> —Jazz author Benny Green

The saxophone family (from left to right): bass, baritone, two tenors, two altos, and soprano.

Jazz combo at the Village Vanguard club in New York City.

THE HISTORY OF JAZZ

ORIGINS

Both the place and the time of the emergence of jazz can be fixed with some certainty. The place was New Orleans, the time was the 1890s.

In the late nineteenth century, New Orleans was one of the most culturally diverse and thriving cities in the United States. Its people were of African, French, Spanish, English, and Portuguese origin. There were first-, second-, and third-generation Europeans; African-Americans who were former slaves or descendants of former slaves; Haitians; Creoles; and a constant influx of new immigrants from Europe, the Caribbean, and other parts of the United States. Being a flourishing port, New Orleans also attracted sailors and visitors from all over the world.

The city had one of the liveliest musical cultures of any city in America. There was opera and chamber music. European ballroom dances were heard side by side with sailors' songs and hornpipes. Street sellers advertised their produce with musical cries. Work songs and "field hollers" mingled with the piano music of elegant salons. The bars, gambling joints, dance halls, and brothels were filled with smoke, liquor, and music.

BAND MUSIC

Everywhere in New Orleans were the bands: marching bands, dance bands, concert bands, and society orchestra bands. Bands played at weddings, funerals, parades, and political rallies, or just for the joy of it. Some of the

> Jazz is about the only form of art existing today in which there is freedom of the individual without the loss of group contact.—Dave Brubeck

Marching band in New Orleans, 1900.

Courtesy of Hogan Jazz Archive, Howard-Tilton Memorial Library, Tulane University.

The notorious Basin Street of New Orleans in the 1890s, lined with saloons and brothels.

Courtesy of Hogan Jazz Archive, Howard-Tilton Memorial Library, Tulane University.

musicians were classically trained; most could not read a note. But almost everybody played. Bands often held competitions among themselves to see which could play the best. And the sound of a band in the street was an excuse for children (and adults) from all the neighborhoods to come and join the fun.

The standard instruments in late nineteenth-century American bands were the trumpet (or cornet), clarinet, trombone, banjo, drums, and tuba. This instrumentation provided the proper balance between melody instruments, harmony instruments, bass, and percussion. All these instruments were, of course, portable. Only later, when band music moved indoors, did the instrumentation include piano and string bass.

Band music was the first of the three major musical influences on early jazz. The other two were ragtime and the blues.

RAGTIME

> Ragtime: white music, played black.—Author Joachim Berendt

Ragtime was a type of piano music (sometimes also played on other instruments) that also became popular in the 1890s. It was originally played mostly by African-American pianists in saloons and dance halls in the South and the Midwest. "Ragging" meant taking a

popular or classical melody and playing it in characteristic syncopated style. Later the style caught on, developing a form of its own, and ragtime was played by both black and white musicians to audiences all over the country.

Ragtime music is usually in duple meter and has the feel and tempo of a march. The left hand plays a steady, regular beat while the right hand plays a lively melody in syncopated rhythm. A ragtime composition usually consists of a series of related sections with a repetition pattern, most often AA BB A CC DD or something similar.

The most famous composer and performer of ragtime was Scott Joplin, whose father was a slave but who himself received a formal music education and composed classical music as well as a large number of piano rags.

Scott Joplin was born in 1868 and eventually got a job as a pianist in the Maple Leaf saloon in Sedalia, Missouri. His most famous piece, the *Maple Leaf Rag*, was published in 1899 and sold so well that Joplin moved to St. Louis to concentrate on composition. **(See Listening Guide below.)** In 1909 he settled in New York and composed a full-length opera, *Treemonisha*, which he attempted (without success) to have professionally produced. Joplin died in 1917, completely unrecognized by the musical establishment.

LISTENING GUIDE

Scott Joplin (1868–1917)
Maple Leaf Rag, **for piano solo**

Date of composition: 1899
Tempo: *Tempo di marcia* ("March tempo")
Meter: ²⁄₄
Key: A♭ Major
Duration: 3:12

Complete CD Collection: 7, track 38

Scott Joplin's *Maple Leaf Rag* sold hundreds of thousands of copies after it was published in 1899. It is typical of much ragtime music written around the turn of the century. A steady left-hand accompaniment keeps the march beat going throughout the piece while the right hand plays a lively, syncopated melody against this steady beat. The sections are repeated in the usual pattern: AA BB A CC DD. Each section is 16 measures long. The slight changes between sections, the standard but slightly irregular repetition pattern, the contrast between the rock-steady left hand and the dancing right hand—all these make for a composition of great attractiveness and help to explain the enormous popularity of ragtime in the early years of the history of jazz. In this recording, we hear a piano roll made by Joplin himself in 1916.

A			
(38)	**0:00**	Strong, steady chords in left hand; syncopated rhythm in right hand; short arpeggiated phrases.
A			
	0:21	Repeat.
B			
(39)	**0:42**	Melody begins higher and moves down; *staccato* articulation.
B			
	1:03	Repeat.
A			
	1:24	Opening section is played only once here.
C			
(40)	**1:45**	Change of key to D♭ Major (IV); rhythmic change in right hand; left-hand leaps.
C			
	2:06	Repeat.
D			
(41)	**2:28**	Return to original key; strong final cadence.
D			
	2:48	Repeat.

THE BLUES

The blues is a form, a sound, and a spirit, all at the same time. It began as a type of vocal music that crystallized in the 1890s from many elements. Among these were African-American spirituals, work songs, and street cries. The blues began as unaccompanied song but soon came to use banjo or guitar accompaniment. The common themes of early blues are sadness in love, betrayal, abandonment, and sometimes humor.

There is great variety in sung blues, but if there is a "standard" form, it is this: a series of three-line stanzas, in each of which the first two lines are the same:

> *I followed her to the station, with a suitcase in my hand.*
>
> *I followed her to the station, with a suitcase in my hand.*
>
> *Well, it's hard to tell, it's hard to tell, when all your love's in vain.*
>
> *When the train rolled up to the station, I looked her in the eye.*
> *When the train rolled up to the station, I looked her in the eye.*
> *Well, I was lonesome, I felt so lonesome, and I could not help but cry.*

(From Robert Johnson, "Love in Vain")

Each line is set to four measures, or bars, of music, so this pattern is known as **12-bar blues** (4 bars × 3 lines = 12 bars). The chord progressions in 12-bar blues are very simple, using only tonic (I), subdominant (IV), and dominant (V) chords. The overall pattern of 12-bar blues looks like this:

	MEASURE 1	MEASURE 2	MEASURE 3	MEASURE 4
LINE 1	I	I	I	I
LINE 2	IV	IV	I	I
LINE 3	V	V (or IV)	I	I

Every stanza of the song follows the same pattern. The singer may occasionally vary the accompaniment a little by introducing other chords or extra beats, but the basic pattern stays the same. Also, the singer has ample opportunity for varying the melodic line according to the expression of the text and his or her own personal feeling. The best blues singers use the rigid

structure of blues for the most subtle variations in pitch (blue notes) and rhythm. Slight shadings of the pitch, little ornaments, and especially deliberate "misplacement" and constant manipulation of the rhythm are part and parcel of blues singing. The effect is of a very flexible and very personal vocal style against a square and simple background.

The form of the blues, with its special combination of flexibility and rigidity, began to be widely used by instrumentalists in the 1920s and has strongly influenced other types of popular music and jazz ever since.

Our example of blues singing is by Bessie Smith (1894–1937), known as the "Empress of the Blues." **(See Listening Guide on page 421.)** Bessie Smith grew up in Tennessee and from an early age helped support the family by singing on street corners. After false starts as a dancer and a vaudevillian, she devoted herself full-time to singing blues.

Smith had a hit in 1923 with her very first recording. Audiences were stunned by the mature, tragic quality of her voice and by her sensitive, personal style, which seemed to speak directly to the listener. On her way to a singing session in 1937 her car crashed into the side of the road, and by the next day Bessie Smith was dead.

DIXIELAND

Dixieland jazz (sometimes known as New Orleans jazz) flourished in the city of New Orleans, especially in the red-light district called Storyville. Small bands played in the brothels and saloons, and a standard form of "combo" arose: a "front line" of trumpet, clarinet, and trombone, and a "rhythm section" of drums, banjo, piano, and bass. Every instrument in a Dixieland band has a specific function. The main melody is played by the trumpet, while the clarinet weaves a high countermelody around it. The trombone plays a simpler, lower tune. In the rhythm section, the drums keep the beat, the piano

Bessie Smith (1894–1937)
Florida-Bound Blues

Date of performance: 1925
Duration: 3:13

Student CD Collection: 3, track 54
Complete CD Collection: 7, track 42

Bessie Smith often recorded with a small ensemble, but many of her performances feature piano and voice alone. Some of the great jazz pianists of the day recorded with Smith, and this recording features pianist Clarence Williams, who was also active as a songwriter, music publisher, and record producer.

Florida-Bound Blues is a standard 12-bar blues with words and music in an AAB pattern. Listen, though, for subtle changes in the words and melody between the first two lines of each stanza. In the first stanza, for example, "North" and "South" are sung as short notes in the first line but extended in the second line.

Among Smith's many vocal trademarks found in this recording is the addition of a chromatic note before the last note of a line.

The bare-bones melody:

Bessie Smith's version:

Sometimes she makes a quick slide, but sometimes she stretches out the added note.

Another common effect is a sudden pitch drop at the end of a line, producing a more intimate spoken sound. This sort of trick was a dependable way of creating a bond with an audience that was often doing plenty of talking on its own.

Florida-Bound Blues also shows the broad, world-weary tone that permeates her work and provides glimpses of her offhand sense of humor. Above all, this recording provides a clear picture of her masterful control of pitch, rhythm, and volume.

54 (42)	0:00	Piano introduction	Piano immediately puts listener off balance before settling into a solid key and rhythm.
55 (43)	0:11	*Goodbye North, Hello South,*	Strict rhythm in piano is offset by Bessie's extra beat in the first line.
		Goodbye North, Hello South.	Vocal control: Listen to the change of volume on "North" and "South."
		It's so cold up here that the words freeze in your mouth.	Compare the heavily blued note on "words" to the centered pitch on "freeze."

56 (44)	0:46	*I'm goin' to Florida where I can have my fun,*	Piano introduces a smooth, more melodic response to vocal.
		I'm goin' to Florida, where I can have my fun.	Listen for the added chromatic note on "fun."
		Where I can lay out in the green grass and look up at the sun.	Note the piano "roll" filling in the space after "grass."
57 (45)	1:22	*Hey, hey redcap, help me with this load.*	Listen for the deliberate variety and humor in these two lines.
		Redcap porter, help me with this load (step aside).	
		Oh, that steamboat, Mr. Captain, let me get on board.	Each of the repeated notes is approached from below, creating a pulse in the line.
58 (46)	1:58	*I got a letter from my daddy, he bought me a sweet piece of land.*	Heavily blued notes on "from my daddy" ("daddy" means "lover").
		I got a letter from my daddy, he bought me a small piece of ground.	
		You can't blame me for leavin', Lord, I mean I'm Florida bound.	Bessie varies this line by not taking a breath in the middle, making the ending breathless.
59 (47)	2:35	*My papa told me, my mama told me too.*	A new ending for the melody of the first two lines.
		My papa told me, my mama told me too:	Vocal line moves up on "fool,"
		Don't let them bell-bottom britches make a fool outa you.	highlighting the punchline at the end.

The King Oliver Creole Jazz Band, 1921.

Frank Driggs Collection/Archive Photos.

and banjo play chords, and the bass plays the bass line (usually on plucked strings).

The sound of Dixieland jazz is of many lines interweaving in a complex but organized way. The effect is of collective improvisation but with every instrument having a carefully defined role. The most common musical forms are 12-bar blues and **32-bar AABA form** (the standard form of thousands of pop songs throughout the twentieth century).

The 32-bar AABA form has four eight-measure sections:

- ✧ A eight measures
- ✧ A eight measures
- ✧ B eight measures
- ✧ A eight measures

The first statement of the tune takes up the first 32 measures. Then the band plays variants of the tune or improvises on its basic chord progressions, while keeping to the 32-measure format. Each statement of the tune or the variation on it is known as a "chorus." In Dixieland jazz, a piece usually begins with the whole band playing the first chorus, and then features alternations of (accompanied) solo and collective improvisation. Some-

times everybody stops playing for two or four measures except for a single soloist. This is known as a "break."

Some of the most famous musicians and bandleaders of early jazz were Jelly Roll Morton (piano), Louis Armstrong (trumpet), Joe "King" Oliver (trumpet), Bix Beiderbecke (trumpet), Sidney Bechet (clarinet and soprano saxophone), and Jack Teagarden (trombone).

The most important figure in jazz from the 1920s was Louis Armstrong (1901–1971). After he left New Orleans, Armstrong settled in Chicago, where, with his composer and pianist wife, Lil Hardin, he made a series of groundbreaking recordings. His brilliant trumpet-playing and enormously inventive improvisations paved the way for a new focus in jazz on solo playing. Armstrong's career spanned more than 50 years in American music, and in later years, when asked to speak about his life, he would simply point to his trumpet and say: "That's my living; that's my life."

Armstrong's Chicago music brought jazz from the dense polyphony of New Orleans, with many simultaneous lines, to an era of the astonishing solo. The performance we will hear is a Hot Five recording—trumpet, clarinet, and trombone for the musical lines, and piano (Lil Hardin), guitar, and banjo for rhythm and fill-in harmony.

Hotter Than That is a remarkable performance on many levels. It might be seen as a primer on early jazz: It contains bits of the earlier polyphonic New Orleans style as well as the flashy solos that became popular in the 1920s, and it displays breaks, stop-time, and call-and-response, all standard parts of the vocabulary of early ensemble jazz. Beyond that, it is one of the first truly great jazz recordings, showing Armstrong at his exuberant best on both trumpet and vocals. **(See Listening Guide on page 424.)**

 WING

In the 1930s and early 1940s, the most popular jazz style was **swing**. The Swing Era takes its name from the fact that much of the music of the time was dance music. Because swing was usually played by large bands with as

Louis Armstrong's Hot Five, Chicago, 1925 (from left to right): Armstrong, Johnny St. Cyr, Johnny Dodds, Kid Ory, Lil Hardin.

Frank Driggs Collection/Archive Photos.

many as 15 or 20 musicians, the Swing Era is also called the Big Band Era. This period also saw the growth of much solo playing, such as that of tenor saxophonists Coleman Hawkins and Lester Young, trumpeter Roy Eldridge, and pianists Fats Waller and Art Tatum.

The most important changes from Dixieland jazz to the big bands were the larger number of performers, the use of saxophones in the band, and the use of written (composed or "arranged") music. For the first time, jazz was mostly written out, rather than mostly improvised. Swing music became extraordinarily popular during these years, and huge ballrooms would be filled with enthusiastic crowds dancing to the music. Some of the great swing bands of the time were those of Fletcher Henderson, Count Basie, Duke Ellington, and Benny Goodman.

The instruments of the big bands were divided into three groups: the saxophones, the brass section, and the rhythm section. The saxophone group included alto and tenor saxophones, and saxophone players ("reedmen") could usually also play clarinet. The brass section included both trumpets and trombones. The rhythm section included guitar, piano, bass, and drums. In addition, the bandleader (usually a pianist, a clarinetist, or a trumpeter) would often be featured as a soloist.

Visual presentation was an important element of

Hearing Louis Armstrong play, I stood silent, almost bashful, asking myself if I would ever be able to attain a small part of Louis Armstrong's greatness.—Tenor saxophonist Coleman Hawkins

Louis Armstrong (1900–1971)
Hotter Than That

Date of performance: 1927
Instruments: Trumpet, clarinet,
  trombone, piano, banjo, guitar
Duration: 3:00

Complete CD Collection: 7, track 48

Hotter Than That is built around a 32-measure tune written by Lil Hardin. The 32-measure chord pattern is repeated several times, and the performers improvise all their melodic lines over this stable chord structure. The end of each 16-measure section is played as a break: everyone drops out except the soloist, who leads the song into the next half of the chorus or into the next chorus itself. The basic structure of the performance is shown here:

Intro:	full ensemble (8 bars)
Chorus 1:	trumpet solo with rhythm section (32 bars)
Chorus 2:	clarinet solo with rhythm section (32 bars)
Chorus 3:	vocal with guitar (32 bars)
New material:	vocal and guitar duet (16 bars)
Chorus 4:	trombone solo with rhythm section (16 bars)
	full ensemble (16 bars)
Coda:	trumpet and guitar

In the third chorus, Armstrong sings instead of playing, scatting through the entire 32 bars. Pay special attention to the similarity between his trumpet-playing and his singing: he uses the same clean attack, the same "shake" at the end of a long note, the same "rips" up to a high note, and the same arpeggiated style of melody. He also builds a string of 24 equal syncopated notes, intensifying the swing in the rhythm.

After the scat chorus, Armstrong and guitarist Lonnie Johnson play a call-and-response chorus, imitating each other's notes, inflections, and rhythms. In this section, as in the whole song, every note drives the song forward, producing a work of great energy and unity.

INTRO		
(48)	**0:00**	Full ensemble, New Orleans–style polyphony. Listen for the individual instruments.

CHORUS 1		
(49)	**0:08**	Trumpet solo. Listen for Armstrong's confident rhythm and occasional "burbles."
	0:24	Break: background drops out, Armstrong "rips" to a high note.
	0:26	Armstrong improvises on arpeggios. "Shake" on long notes.

	0:42	Break: clarinet jumps in on trumpet line, prepares for solo.

CHORUS 2

(50)	**0:44**	Clarinet solo. Same tempo, but not as much rhythmic variety.
	1:00	Break: Clarinet dives into a long blued note.
	1:02	Clarinet solo continues.
	1:17	Break: Armstrong jumps in, preparing the scat chorus.

CHORUS 3

(51)	**1:20**	Scat chorus. Listen for variety of sound: jagged lines vs. smooth lines, notes hit perfectly vs. notes slid.
	1:35	Break: "rip" to high note.
	1:39	Scat in syncopation with guitar.
	1:53	Break: whining scat, preparing for:

NEW MATERIAL

(52)	**1:55**	Scat/guitar dialogue. Call-and-response.
	2:08	"Rip" to high note in voice, imitated in guitar.
	2:13	Piano transition to:

CHORUS 4

(53)	**2:17**	Trombone solo, ending with chromatic climb to:
	2:32	Break: Armstrong on an energetic climbing sequence into:
	2:35	New Orleans–style polyphony by full ensemble, Armstrong on top.
	2:43	Multiple breaks ("stop-time").

CODA

(54)	**2:47**	Full group, followed by:
	2:49	Guitar/trumpet interchange.

The Duke Ellington Orchestra, 1949.

the big bands. Similarly, the sound of the big bands of the Swing Era was smooth and polished. This was partly because of the prominence of the smooth-sounding saxophones, and partly because the music was almost all written down. The polyphonic complexity of collective improvisation had given way to an interest in a big homophonic sound, lively presentation, and polish.

One of the most important and influential composers in the history of jazz was Duke Ellington (1899–1974). He is said to have been responsible for as many as 1,000 jazz compositions. Ellington was a man of many talents, being at one and the same

LISTENING GUIDE

Duke Ellington (1899–1974)
It Don't Mean A Thing
  (If It Ain't Got That Swing)

Date of performance: 1932
Orchestration: Voice, 3 trumpets,
  2 trombones, 3 saxophones, piano,
  banjo, bass, drums
Duration: 3:09

Student CD Collection: 3, track 60
Complete CD Collection: 7, track 55

The title of *It Don't Mean A Thing (If It Ain't Got That Swing)* became a motto for an era—and has survived as a catch-phrase in the jazz world up through today. The song is an exceptionally lively and infectious number that displays numerous hallmarks of the Ellington sound at the beginning of the swing era: the unique interplay between vocals and orchestra, the growling wah-wah brass contrasted with the sultry saxophones, the driving slap of the bass, the sensational solos by Joe "Tricky Sam" Nanton on muted trombone and Johnny Hodges on saxophone, and the superb instrumental arrangement and wide palette of instrumental timbres used throughout each variation of the principal theme.

60 (55)	**0:00**	Introductory vamp between Ivie Anderson's scat improvisation and the driving bass and drum.
	0:11	Joe "Tricky Sam" Nanton plays a muted trombone solo atop a subdued chorus of saxophones and muted trumpets that blare out in brief response to each phrase of Nanton's solo. This solo elaborates on the entire tune *before* the band's initial statement.

61 (56)	**0:46**	Entry of the first chorus (see below). Blue note on "ain't." Note the call-and-response interplay between vocals and orchestra.
	0:54	Second chorus.
	1:03	Transitional section of contrasting character.
62 (57)	**1:13**	Restatement of first chorus.
63 (58)	**1:22**	Entry of Johnny Hodges's saxophone solo. Notice how Ellington's arrangement accelerates the shifts in the orchestral timbres behind Hodges. Ellington veers further and further away (in texture, harmony, and counterpoint) from the original statement of the vocal model in each variation. Notice also the prearranged backing and elaborate responses to the solo.
64 (59)	**2:43**	Scat improvisation by Anderson.
	2:52	Return to first chorus and fadeout by muted trumpets on the motive from their response.

It Don't Mean A Thing

(If It Ain't Got That Swing)

Duke Ellington

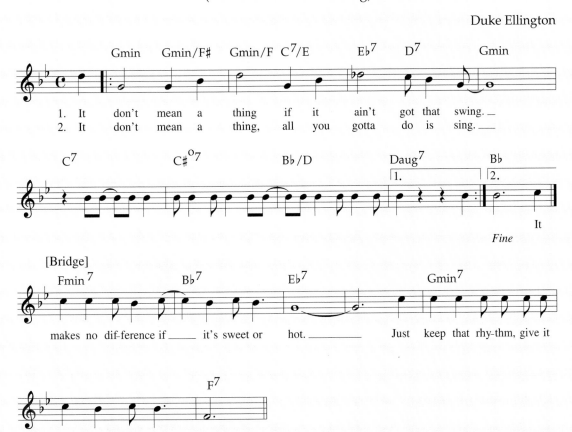

Benny Goodman in 1938, with manic drummer Gene Krupa.

time a master songwriter, an innovative composer and arranger, an imaginative and capable pianist, and an extraordinary bandleader.

Ellington was the first to make full use of the rich palette of colors available to the jazz orchestra. Similarly, Ellington's harmony was years ahead of that of his contemporaries, using extended chords, deft chromatic motion, and novel combinations of disparate sonorities. **(See Listening Guide on page 426.)**

The bandleader who did the most to popularize swing was Benny Goodman (1909–1986). Known as the "King of Swing," clarinetist Goodman led a band that was heard by millions across America on a weekly radio show, and he achieved the unprecedented in 1938 by bringing his band to Carnegie Hall, the traditional home of classical music. Goodman was also the first to break through what was then known as the "color barrier" by hiring black musicians such as pianist Teddy Wilson and vibraphonist Lionel Hampton to play among white musicians. This was an important step in what was still an officially segregated country.

Another influential aspect of Goodman's work was his formation of small groups—sometimes a trio or a quartet, most often a sextet. Goodman's sextet and his other small groups paved the way for the virtuoso solo playing and small combos of bebop.

> J**azz** is freedom. Think about that. You think about that.— Thelonious Monk

B**EBOP**

In the early 1940s, a reaction to the glossy, organized sound of some of the big bands set in. Some jazz musicians began to experiment again with smaller combos and with a type of music that was more intellectually demanding, more for listening than for dancing. This style is known as **bop** or **bebop**. The name probably derives from some of the nonsense syllables used in scat singing ("Doo-wah doo-wah, be-bop a loo-wah"). And the most frequent phrase-ending in bebop solos is ♪♪

which fits the word "bebop" perfectly. There is also a composition by Dizzy Gillespie that is called *Bebop*.

The pioneers of bebop were Charlie "Bird" Parker (alto saxophone), Dizzy Gillespie (trumpet), and Thelonious Monk (piano). In turn, these three players influenced other musicians, including Stan Getz, Miles Davis, Sarah Vaughan, and John Coltrane. In fact, it would be difficult to find a jazz musician who has not been influenced by Parker, Gillespie, and Monk.

Bebop is a very different kind of music from swing. It is harder, irregular, and less predictable. It is played by a small group (for example, saxophone and trumpet with piano, bass, and drums). The tempo is generally faster, and there is far more solo improvisation. The chord progressions and rhythmic patterns are complex and varied. Bop is generally considered the beginning of modern jazz.

With its fast pace and its emphasis on solo improvisation, bebop depended on the inventiveness, quick thinking, virtuosity, and creativity of individual musicians. Charlie Parker, Dizzy Gillespie, and Thelonious Monk began playing independently, but had a similar approach to the new music. They also performed together and developed considerable complexity in their playing. Their solo improvisations were quick and unpredictable, full of fiery fast notes, lengthy pauses, and sudden changes of direction. Although bop was still based on popular songs (AABA form) or on the 12-bar blues pattern, the simple harmonies were enriched with new and more dissonant chords, and the

Beboppers in 1948. From Left to Right: Thelonious Monk, Howard McGhee, Roy Eldridge, Teddy Hill.

known songs of the day. Beboppers avoided improvising on the melody; their solos were built strictly on the chord patterns and often made no reference to the tune. As a result, their music could sound quite different from the original song.

A distinct culture surrounded bebop. It was a music of rebellion. Swing had been accepted, and even taken over, by the white establishment, and bebop was, in a sense, a reaction to this. It was designed to be different.

For such controversial music, bebop is based on a remarkably conservative structure. Normally it begins with a 32-bar tune. Often the melody instruments play the tune in unison. Then each instrument improvises over the chords of the tune.

The great genius of bebop was Charlie Parker (1920–1955), a brilliant, self-destructive saxophonist who died at the age of 34 from alcoholism and drug addiction. His improvisations changed the way a generation

Charlie Parker and Dizzy Gillespie in 1950, with John Coltrane (tenor saxophone) and Tommy Potter (bass).

accompanying rhythms were more complex. Soloists often deliberately overran the underlying sectional patterns and began and ended phrases at unexpected and unconventional places.

Bebop musicians sometimes wrote new tunes themselves, but more often they improvised around well-

LISTENING GUIDE

The Charlie Parker Quartet
Confirmation

Date of performance: July 30, 1953
Personnel: Charlie Parker, alto
    saxophone; Al Haig, piano; Percy
    Heath, bass; Max Roach, drums.
Duration: 2:58

Student CD Collection: 3, track 65
Complete CD Collection: 7, track 60

*C*onfirmation is one of the most stunning of Parker's many extraordinary performances. The studio tapes show that the piece was recorded straight through, with no splicing, no alternative takes, and no errors. It is important to remember that although the first few measures (the initial A of the AABA form) and the third group of eight measures (the B section) have been worked out beforehand, all the rest of what Parker plays is made up on the spot. All the running notes, the rhythmic figures, the cascades of musical gestures—all these are created in the very moment of performance. Not only that, but each time Parker plays the A section—every single time—he varies it considerably. It is hard to imagine that anyone could display such rich and instantaneous creativity.

Charlie Parker's alto saxophone is accompanied by piano, bass, and drums. These serve to create a harmonic foundation and keep a consistent beat, against which Parker's ingenuity, flexibility, and expressive flights can shine. Toward the end of the piece, each of the other players gets a few measures to improvise on his own: first the pianist, then the bass player, and then the drummer. Parker wraps everything up with everyone playing together again.

The form of the piece is the favorite one of the bebop era: AABA form. Just to remind you, each section of this form lasts for 8 measures. So each statement or *chorus* of the whole form lasts for 32 measures. There are three whole choruses with Parker, then the piano plays the A section twice (= 16 measures), the bass player has 8 measures, the drummer has 8, and then Parker returns to play B and A once more (the final 16 measures). To keep your place, keep counting measures (*1*, 2, 3, 4; *2*, 2, 3, 4; etc.) all the way through (it's easier if you focus on the bass, which plays on the beat all the way through).

INTRODUCTION		
65 (60)	**0:00**	There is a brief 4-measure introduction by the piano.

CHORUS 1		
66 (61)	**0:05**	The tune is a typical bebop composition: angular, irregular, and offbeat. Yet Parker makes it sound melodic as well as deeply rhythmic. The rhythm section is rock-solid, though the drummer manages to be splashy and interesting at the same time. Although the chorus altogether contains three statements of the A section, Parker makes them sound different each time. The B section (0:25–0:34) is not as highly differentiated in this piece as it is in some bebop compositions, though its harmonies are different.

CHORUS 2		
67 (62)	**0:44**	Parker really starts to fly on this chorus (hence his nickname, "Bird"). He also plays in the lower register of the saxophone to give variety to his solo.

CHORUS 3		
68 (63)	**1:22**	The third chorus is unified by rapid, descending chromatic phrases, which in turn are balanced by arch-shaped arpeggios. A triplet turn is a common motive, and Parker plays right across the "seams" of the AABA form to make long, compelling musical statements of his own.

PIANO SOLO (AA)		
69 (64)	**2:00**	Al Haig takes 16 measures for his improvisation, which is quite musical for a normal human being, but which sounds pretty flat after listening to Charlie Parker!

BASS SOLO (B)		
	2:16	Percy Heath gets to play some different rhythms for 8 measures with hints of the tune.

DRUM SOLO (A)		
	2:28	Amazingly, Max Roach manages to suggest the melody on his 8 measures. (Try humming it along with him.)

FINAL HALF-CHORUS (BA)		
70 (65)	**2:35**	Parker repeats the B and A sections as a final half-chorus, playing with intensity but closer to the original melody. Percy Heath (who was said to be overwhelmed by Parker's playing on this recording date) gets in the last word!

thought about jazz. His playing was profound, dizzying, subtle, and complex; his phrasing unconventional and inspired; his tone edgy and intense, liquid in one line and sandpaper in the next. Parker absorbed music of all kinds, including Stravinsky and Bartók; he loved painting and dance. And he was both loyal and inspiring: Dizzy Gillespie called him "the other half of my heartbeat."

We shall listen to a remarkable performance by Parker, entitled *Confirmation*, which he recorded in 1953. Like the jazz piece *Crazeology* that we studied in the Listening chapter at the beginning of this book, Charlie Parker's *Confirmation* is based on the chord changes of Gershwin's *I Got Rhythm*, known familiarly as "rhythm changes." Also like *Crazeology*, *Confirmation* is a 32-bar AABA form. But these aspects of the piece, though they are important, pale in comparison with the extraordinary creativity and brilliance of the saxophonist. **(See Listening Guide on page 429.)**

COOL JAZZ

Cool jazz was really a subcategory of bop. It continued to use small combos, and the rhythmic and harmonic styles were similar. Cool-jazz pieces also were based on popular tunes or blues patterns. The departures from bop can be noted immediately in the overall sound of the groups and in the improvised solos. The playing is more subdued and less frenetic. Pieces tend to be longer, and they feature a larger variety of instruments, sometimes including the baritone saxophone, with its deep, full sound, and even some classical instruments, such as the French horn and the cello, which are characteristically mellow in sound.

Some groups specializing in cool jazz became quite popular in the 1950s. Miles Davis formed a group with

nine instruments; the George Shearing Quintet used piano, guitar, vibraphone, bass, and drums; and perhaps the most popular group of all (certainly one of the longest lasting) was the Modern Jazz Quartet, which featured Milt Jackson on vibraphone. The vibraphone (an instrument like a xylophone, with metal bars and an electrically enhanced, sustained, fluctuating tone) is the perfect instrument for projecting the "coolth" of cool jazz.

FREE JAZZ

At the end of the 1950s, the move away from preset chord progressions led to the development in the 1960s and 1970s of what is known as free jazz. This style depended both on original compositions and on creative improvisation. The most influential musician of this period was Ornette Coleman, alto saxophonist, trumpeter, violinist, and composer. Several pieces have been named for him, and an album of his, made in 1960 and entitled *Free Jazz*, gave its name to the whole period.

Free jazz is abstract and can be dense and difficult to follow. Besides abandoning preset chord progressions, it often dispenses with regular rhythmic patterns and melody lines as well. Drumming is energetic, full of color and activity, without a steady and constant pattern of beats. Melodic improvisations are full of extremes: very high notes, squawks and squeals, long-held tones, fragmented phrases, and sudden silences. Many free-jazz groups have experimented with the music of other countries. Idioms borrowed from Turkish, African, and Indian music appear in many free-jazz compositions, and some groups have made use of non-Western instruments, such as sitars, gongs, and bamboo flutes.

The Modern Jazz Quartet.

Bird [Parker's nickname] was kind of like the sun, giving off the energy we drew from him. In any musical situation, his ideas just bounded out, and this inspired anyone who was around.— Max Roach, jazz composer and drummer

> A jazz musician who plays fusion is selling out.
> —Wynton Marsalis

Free jazz in its purest form was not popular. It could be difficult to listen to and was often raucous and dissonant. Totally free collective improvisation must necessarily have many moments of complete chaos. (Coleman's *Free Jazz* has two bands improvising simultaneously with no predetermined key, rhythm, or melody.) Free-jazz composers responded to this problem by writing compositions that would begin and end with a set theme or melody, allowing room for free improvisation in between. Obviously, in these cases the melody provides a common basis for the intervening improvisations and eliminates the randomness of complete freedom. Also, the influence of Eastern and African music brought to free jazz a common language of drones and new scale patterns.

FUSION

Fusion is the name given to the musical style of the 1970s and 1980s that combined elements of jazz and rock music. Perhaps it was the lack of an audience for free jazz or the overwhelming popularity of rock that encouraged jazz musicians to incorporate elements of rock into their performances and compositions during this period.

Rock and jazz have some origins in common: early blues, gospel music, and popular ballads. But they developed along separate lines. Rock is largely vocal music and is based on simple and accessible forms and harmonies. Jazz is mostly instrumental music, and some forms of jazz are quite complex, ignoring popular appeal.

Fusion was the first jazz style to achieve wide popularity since the mass appeal of swing in the 1930s and 1940s. Its most influential proponent was Miles Davis, who made two records in 1969 that established the fusion style for the 1970s and 1980s: *In a Silent Way* and *Bitches Brew*.

The primary characteristics of fusion are the adoption of electric instruments (electric piano, synthesizer, and electric bass guitar) in place of their traditional ancestors, a large percussion section (including several non-European instruments such as hand drums, bells, gongs, shakers, and scrapers), and simplicity of form

Jazz singer Betty Carter performing in Carnegie Hall.

Jazz and Classical

Some of the elements of jazz—syncopation, for example—appear in classical music. Some Bach melodies are fascinating in their syncopations and cross-rhythms; Beethoven wrote some variations that sound like ragtime; and Debussy invented many of the chords used later in jazz. But jazz brought to the musical scene an art that was highly original and full of vitality. And many classical composers of the twentieth century turned to the inspiration of jazz in their own work. ✦ Jazz exerted a strong influence on Stravinsky. His first work to incorporate elements of jazz was *L'Histoire du Soldat* (1918); subsequent compositions that employ jazz techniques include *Ragtime*, of the same year, *Piano-Rag-Music* (1919), and the *Ebony* Concerto for clarinet and jazz band (1945). ✦ Ravel, Milhaud, Copland, and Bernstein were four other famous twentieth-century composers influenced by jazz. The Ravel piano concertos each contain jazzlike episodes, and his Violin Sonata has a second movement entitled "Blues." Milhaud's *Création du Monde* incorporates influences from the jazz he heard in Harlem nightclubs in the early twenties. Copland's music is full of jazzy rhythms and harmonies, as is that of Bernstein, who moved especially freely between the two worlds. ✦ The composer who most successfully brought together elements of jazz and classical music was George Gershwin. His *Rhapsody in Blue* (1924) is a perfect example of a symphonic work permeated by elements of the jazz style.

and harmony. Fusion is often based on straightforward chord progressions and highly repetitive rhythmic patterns. Over this accessible and almost hypnotic foundation, however, fusion presents a kaleidoscopic variety of sounds.

The most popular fusion group of this era was Weather Report, founded by musicians who had worked with Miles Davis on *In a Silent Way* and *Bitches Brew*. The leading light of the group was Joe Zawinul, composer and pianist, but all the members were expert musicians who worked together brilliantly. The result was a remarkable talent for true collective improvisation, with a combination of solo lines merging into a rich group sound. Other important groups were founded by Herbie Hancock and Chick Corea.

Miles Davis.

THE CURRENT SCENE

The 1990s witnessed a big jazz revival and the coexistence of many different jazz styles. Dixieland groups, big and medium-sized bands, bebop players, experimenters with electronic music, and fusion players (often with only a small proportion of jazz in the mix) all attract audiences. Many colleges and universities are adding jazz courses to the curriculum. Women were more active than ever in jazz, most of them singers, pianists, or composers. They included composers Toshiko Akiyoshi, Marian McPartland, Carla Bley, and Maria Schneider; singers Diane Schuur, Abbey Lincoln, Cassandra Wilson, and Dianne Reeves; pianists Joanne Brackeen, Eliane Elias, Geri Allen, and Renee Rosnes; singer-pianist Diana Krall; saxophonist Jane Ira Bloom; and drummer Terri Lyne Carrington. Jazz is also fast becoming an international language. It has large audiences and great performers in Japan, as well as in Western Europe (especially Scandinavia), Latin America, the Caribbean, Africa, and Eastern Europe.

In the 1990s, many of the jazz legends passed away, among them Miles Davis (1991), Dizzy Gillespie (1993), and Ella Fitzgerald (1996), but a new generation of talented young players has established itself on the mainstream jazz scene. Saxophonists Joshua Redman and James Carter, trumpeters Roy Hargrove and Nicholas Payton, pianists Eric Reed and Jacky Terrason, bassist Christian McBride, and drummer Leon Parker all display a deep knowledge of jazz tradition and a remarkable fluency in a variety of styles.

As an alternative to mainstream jazz, various blends of jazz with ethnic, pop, rap, and classical idioms continue to take place, and new musical horizons are being explored by such diverse avant-garde artists as John Zorn and Steve Coleman. A special kind of blend has been called "acid jazz" (a particularly unhelpful name). This music is a hybrid of traditional jazz and popular dance rhythms, created by manipulating "samples" of classic jazz records to form a background for new improvised solos, rap vocals, or both. Acid jazz functions primarily as dance music. A bluesy, complex, repetitive but rhythmic style of jazz called funk or groove music has also become popular. Its best-known exponents include guitarist John Scofield, saxophonist Maceo Parker, and the organ-bass-drums trio Medeski, Martin, and Wood.

In addition to the highly eclectic mixture of up-to-date jazz styles available today, a new movement has manifested itself, which might be called a "return to the past." This important movement treats jazz as a great musical repertory, as important in its way as written, "serious" classical music.

The history of jazz is an elusive one, being concerned with much music made up on the spot and compositions that are fleeting, invented in the heat of the moment. We are fortunate that some of the great improvisations of the past have been captured on recordings and even (by some determined individuals) in notation. The most recent movement in jazz has attempted to "capture" great jazz styles of past eras in clean, modern performances, enhanced by the new virtuoso instrumental techniques of young performers.

The prime exponent of this approach has been Wynton Marsalis, a superb classical trumpeter, a fine jazz improviser, and a musician with a great respect for the past. His clean, sophisticated, modern technique,

Wynton Marsalis in concert, Lincoln Center, New York City, 1991.

allied with his reverence for the jazz greats of earlier eras, has made him the most popular jazz artist in modern times. In 1997, Marsalis became the first jazz musician ever to be awarded the esteemed Pulitzer Prize.

His compositions are often focused on the history of black people in America. One of Marsalis's works, *Harriet Tubman*, is named after the runaway slave who helped hundreds of other slaves escape before the end of the Civil War in 1865. **(See Listening Guide below.)**

LISTENING GUIDE

Wynton Marsalis
Harriet Tubman

Date of performance: 1991
Personnel: Wynton Marsalis, trumpet; Marcus Roberts, piano; Joe Henderson, tenor sax; Bob Hurst, bass; Jeff Watts, drums
Duration: 7:43

Complete CD collection: 7, track 66

Marsalis describes the piece thus:

Harriet Tubman makes homage to a woman who acted as a personal agent against the slavery that so severely limited the spiritual potential of our nation and was detrimental to the fulfillment of our democracy. She and the Underground Railroad represent the same thing that the blues does, that optimism at the core of the human will which motivates us to heroic action and tells us: NO MATTER HOW BAD, everything is going to be all right.

This blues begins in the bass with a motif that speaks of the late-night mystery. Its muted bell-like quality uses bass harmonics for an allusion to the African thumb piano [mbira]. The drums come in with another meter to enhance the African underpinnings. Siren horns and a bass vamp signal the beginning of a journey on the Underground Railway, then the sound of the blues and the wash of swing identify this as a uniquely American expression. The piece ends as it begins, in the bass, reminding us that even though the journey has ended, there is still much more to do....

The underlying structure of this piece is the traditional harmonic pattern of 12-bar blues, although Marsalis adds a flexible lilt by having the bars contain six beats instead of the traditional four. Within these six beats, different groupings—3+3, 2+2+2, 2+4—are all explored.

(66)	**0:00**	Introduction: Light, percussive use of harmonics and a syncopated rhythmic pattern on the bass suggest the use of the mbira. (See p. 20 in Chapter 1.)
	0:11	Short rhythmic pattern on percussion; then short scalar pattern on piano.

	0:31	Entrance of sustained trumpet and saxophone. This section presents all the basic ideas of the piece: rhythmic polyphony and melodic material including sustained notes that lead to faster or more jagged melodies.
	1:22	Arrival at sustained notes, with pause in underlying rhythm, establishes the end of the section.
(67)	**1:34**	Marsalis (trumpet) takes the solo on the first chorus. Starts with leaps to a high note, which serves as an anchoring point for the improvisation. More conventional accompaniment, with a regular walking bass and light cymbal strokes giving a regular pulse; harmonies filled out by the piano; free melodic exploration followed by return to the same high note (2:08).
	2:18	Faster melodic fragments and scales lead to:
	2:42	Arrival of full ascending arpeggios reaching the original high note, rich chords in piano; reaching beyond that high note triggers a melodic outburst of jagged contour. Returns to high note, then descent.
(68)	**3:20**	Tenor saxophone—picks up arpeggio figure last stated by trumpet, moves to fast-moving, short, three-note ideas. Emphasis on quick flourishes, rapid sequences.
	4:25	Regular ascending notes, but slightly off the beat as emphasized by steady piano, then elaborated with virtuosic flourishes.
(69)	**5:01**	The piano takes its solo, still providing accompaniment with the left hand. It begins with short melodic fragments, then moves to a wide-sweeping longer line.
	5:16	Back to short, nervous gestures that work in a narrow range, then cascade down to a lower range.
	5:33	Short gestures are repeated insistently in right hand, while harmonies move around them.
	5:51	Repeated series of three notes with octave leap; the piano continues to alternate between very restricted gestures and freer ones.
(70)	**6:42**	Return of initial theme (sustained notes in trumpet and sax), and emphasis on off-the-beat rhythms.
	7:14	Trumpet and sax decrescendo with held notes, bass returns to its original pattern of harmonics; fade out.

America inherited many of its musical forms and styles from Europe. Jazz, however, is one of the truly original American art forms.

Jazz was forged in New Orleans from a vigorous amalgam of African-American singing and playing styles and European instruments and harmony. Its strongest early influence was band music, and to this day a jazz group is known as a band. From band music, jazz inherited its instruments: drums as the backbone, trumpet, trombone, clarinet, banjo, and tuba. These instruments could be carried while marching and were loud enough to be heard outdoors. When jazz moved indoors and became stationary, banjo and tuba were gradually replaced by piano and string bass, and later various sizes of saxophone began to dominate.

Two other early influences were the syncopated rhythms of ragtime (which was also based on march tempo, meter, and form) and the blues. The blues is simultaneously a poetic form, a harmonic template, a flexible, highly inflected sound, and a people's spirit.

Even more than in classical music, in jazz the music is strongly influenced by individual personalities. And no single person had more influence on jazz than Louis Armstrong—trumpeter, band leader, singer, actor, individualist, collaborator, and cultural ambassador. It is said, with only slight exaggeration, that he invented swing—that almost indefinable element of rhythm that gives jazz its life.

The only period in the twentieth century when jazz could genuinely lay claim to being a popular music was in the 1930s, variously known as the Swing Era or the Big Band Era. White audiences, necessarily more numerous than black, and their black counterparts embraced the new music and its exponents and danced to their radios or in dance halls all across America. Swing bands were polished, showy, and put less emphasis on individual accomplishment than on group sound. This did not stop one of the greatest band leaders, Duke Ellington, from showcasing some of the strongest individual players of the era as members of his band or from using his band to highlight his own remarkably original and sophisticated compositions.

After the Second World War changed everything, small groups led the way, concentrating on individual expression, instrumental virtuosity, and challenging improvisation. The voluble genius Charlie Parker on alto saxophone and the taciturn, oblique

Duke Ellington's own handwritten score for one of his most famous compositions.

trumpeter Miles Davis showed how the new smaller combos could be a framework for complex, profound statements.

In the 1970s and 1980s an amalgam of jazz and rock, known as fusion, attracted attention. Since that time, jazz has been blended with a large assortment of other elements, including Latin sounds and rhythms, synthesized mood music, rap, and funk. These blends are heard all over the airwaves, in nightclubs, and on recordings, though in the 1990s a "return to the real thing" movement, spearheaded by Wynton Marsalis, led to a sudden upsurge in the performance of older styles by a series of young, mostly African-American players and singers.

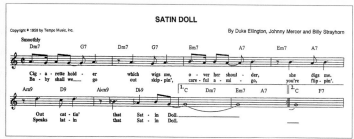

The same song in a printed score.

Purists would say (and have said) that to stay alive jazz must move forward and not back. After a flourishing one hundred years of life, is jazz dead?

FUNDAMENTALS OF JAZZ

- ✦ The three primary influences were marching bands, ragtime, and the blues
- ✦ The characteristic harmony and melodies of jazz are based on the blues scale, with variable third, seventh, and, occasionally, fifth notes in the scale
- ✦ Characteristic instrumental sounds are those of saxophone, trumpet (often muted), plucked string bass, and drum set
- ✦ Performing forces usually range from the trio to the small combo (five or so players) to the big band (about twelve to fifteen players)
- ✦ Jazz usually includes an element of improvisation
- ✦ Recent jazz has either turned backwards or become an ingredient in a blend of other styles

THE TWENTIETH CENTURY III: POPULAR MUSIC

Popular music is one of the most widespread phenomena of contemporary Western culture. Throughout the world, American popular music is a symbol of the twentieth-century success story. The music represents Western commercial and popular culture with the same force as such powerful icons as Coca-Cola, Microsoft, and Marlboro.

In addition to its associations with a technological and commercial society, popular music—especially rock—also connotes youth. Young people buy the largest share by far of tapes and CDs, and most performers are under 30. The rock phenomenon began in the 1950s and 1960s, when pop and rock music were symbols of youthful rebellion. It coincided with the post–World War II period of prosperity, when young people had more money to spend than ever before. The vast spread and commercial success of popular music are the result of a society with time on its hands and money to spend.

STYLES OF POPULAR MUSIC

By definition, popular music is designed to appeal to the widest possible audience. No formal training is required to appreciate it, and it is usually vocal, because everybody can sing (more or less). Its subject matter—usually love or sex—is attractive to all, and the style and structure of the music are simple and repetitive. Often the refrains of popular songs are very catchy:

"One, two, three o'clock, four o'clock ROCK!"
or:

"Jumpin' Jack Flash, it's a gas-gas-gas."
or:

"Are you ready for a THING CALLED LOVE?"

These refrains from successful popular songs have a rhythm that immediately suggests the music, even if you don't know the melody. Once you do know the melody, the music is so accessible, and the rhythm and melody are so molded to the words, that it is impossible to forget them. This is the same technique that advertisers use to sell their products.

The three most important elements in popular music are the words, the rhythm, and the melody. (Because harmony is one of the more complex elements of music, popular music has tended to underplay the harmony, which is usually very simple.) Different types of popular music tend to stress one or another of the three factors over the other two. For example, the most notable characteristic of rock music is the driving rhythm. In country music, the words are foremost, for they generally tell a story. In pop ballads, it is the smooth melody that creates a special atmosphere.

BEGINNINGS: 1850–1950

How did the phenomenon of popular music begin? Where did it come from?

American popular music has a long history, reaching back to the mid-nineteenth century. The first important popular songwriter was Stephen Foster (1826–1864). During his lifetime, Foster wrote some of the most enduring songs of the American tradition, including *Oh! Susanna*, *Camptown Races*, and *Old Folks at Home*.

Old Folks at Home is typical of the early popular song in three ways. First, it has a catchy melody. In fact, its first line is so catchy ("Way down upon the Swanee

Patronage and Commercialization

Throughout the history of music, financial backing has been needed to support the composition and production of musical performances. A person or an institution providing such backing is known as a patron. And patrons can support music in a variety of ways: by buying tickets for concerts, by volunteering their time to help a musical organization, or by donating funds. ¶ As we have seen, in Europe of the Middle Ages, the greatest patron of music (and all the arts) was the church. In the Renaissance, Baroque, and Classic eras, the foremost patrons were wealthy aristocrats, who employed composers and performers in their courts. In the nineteenth century, the main support for music gradually spread to the middle classes. Public concerts became common, and music was funded by ticket sales and by the sale of printed music for amateurs to perform at home. During the twentieth century, this reliance on wider support has continued to grow, until by now the central driving force behind the production of most popular music has become commercial gain. The potential profits are enormous. ¶ As the multinational corporations that produce recordings become more and more powerful, it is worth asking what really shapes the musical tastes of today's music patrons. Are their tastes being formed by their own individual preferences or by the combined forces of millions of dollars of advertising?

Stephen Foster.

Stephen Collins Foster, 1826–1864.
Watercolor by Walter L. White cf from
Ambrotype, Foster Hall Collection, Center for
American Music, University of Pittsburgh.
Source ID# 120.

W hen writing popular songs, always bear in mind that it is to the untrained musical public that you largely look for support and popularity. Therefore, do not offer them anything which in subject matter or melody does not appeal to their ears. To do so is just so much time thrown away.— Charles K. Harris

The cover of the sheet music to *Avalon* (1920).

River") that most people use it as the song's title. Second, the words are sentimental. And third, the harmony is extremely simple, using only three chords throughout.

G   G   C
Way down upon the Swanee River,
G   D
Far, far away,
G   G   C
There's where my heart is turnin' ever,
G   D   G
There's where the old folks stay.

G   G   C
All up and down the whole creation
G   D
Sadly I roam,
G   G   C
Still longing for the old plantation,
G   D   G
And for the old folks at home.

D   G
All the world is sad and dreary
C   G   D
Everywhere I roam,

G   G   C
Oh, darkies, how my heart grows weary,
G   D   G
Far from the old folks at home.

With the success achieved by Stephen Foster and other songwriters, music publishers began to realize the commercial potential of popular music. Charles K. Harris (1865–1930), a songwriter who set up his own publishing company, landed a major hit with the publication of his song *After the Ball* in 1892. Within a few years, the song had sold an unprecedented two million copies. Remember that in the era before records, radio, or television, all home entertainment was "homemade"—provided by a willing voice, a piano, and copies of songs in sheet music.

One of the most concentrated periods in the history of American popular song came in the 1920s, 1930s, and 1940s. This was the era of great songwriters such as Cole Porter, Irving Berlin, Richard Rodgers, Jerome Kern, and George Gershwin, and of popular singers such as Al Jolson, Bing Crosby, and Frank Sinatra. It was also the era of new technologies that revolutionized

Copyright and Royalties for Popular Music

For the whole of the nineteenth century and up to 1914, the laws of copyright did not cover the *performance* of a piece of music. The composer and the publisher received royalties only on sales of printed music; for all the times a piece of theirs was played or sung, they received nothing at all. This situation was remedied with the formation in 1914 of the American Society of Composers, Authors, and Publishers (ASCAP). Whenever a piece was played or a song was sung in a dance hall, nightclub, hotel, or restaurant, and whenever a record was played over the radio, the composer and the publisher received a royalty payment. By 1940, the major radio networks were paying fees to ASCAP of $4½ million a year, and these fees were distributed to ASCAP members. At this time, a rival organization called Broadcast Music Incorporated (BMI) was formed, also providing copyright protection for the composers and publishers of popular music. Today, almost everyone working in the music industry is covered by one or the other of these organizations. In the year 2000, ASCAP collected royalties of $576 million for its members, and BMI collected over $400 million.

The *Summertime* scene from a 1987 production of George Gershwin's *Porgy and Bess.*

popular music. Sound movies, radio, and the phonograph all hit their stride in the 1920s, and all three supported and fostered popular songs.

In the 1930s, George Gershwin (1898–1937) wrote the music and his brother Ira wrote the lyrics for many songs that have become American classics. They include *'S Wonderful, I Got Rhythm,* and *Love Walked In,* as well as the great songs from the opera *Porgy and Bess,* especially the enduringly popular *Summertime.*

Richard Rodgers (1902–1979) was one of the most successful songwriters of the 1930s and 1940s, writing the music for many of the era's famous shows, including *Oklahoma!, Carousel,* and *South Pacific,* as well as many songs not associated with shows. Among his hits were *Oh, What a Beautiful Morning, Some Enchanted Evening,* and *Blue Moon* (**See Listening Guide on page 444.)**

There are hundreds of other composers whose names are largely forgotten but whose music lives on in songs such as *Take Me Out to the Ball Game, Happy Birthday to You,* and *When Irish Eyes are Smiling.* All these familiar songs, numerous as they are, constitute only a brief list compared with the thousands that once swept the country but have since been forgotten. Stylistically, most of these songs conformed to the model of the sentimental ballad: lyrical melodies, simple harmonies, repetitive rhythm, and a recurring refrain (chorus).

(Note: It is almost impossible to obtain permission to copy recordings of popular music. On the other hand, the records themselves are widely available. Please borrow recordings of the songs in this chapter from friends or from your library.)

Frank Sinatra

Date of composition: 1934

Blue Moon

Music by Richard Rodgers, words by
    Lorenz Hart

From very early on, the music industry recognized the advantages of tying a popular song to a particular singer. The success of the song depended to a large extent on the degree of "stardom" of the singer. Early sheet music often had the words "as sung by" printed on the cover, or displayed a photograph of the singer.

Born in 1915, Sinatra was a pop-music phenomenon in the late 1930s and early 1940s. He toured with dance bands, and his romantic appeal and individual singing style endeared him to millions of listeners. At his concerts, teenage girls screamed and fainted in one of the earliest examples of mass adoration of a popular music figure. Sinatra's death in 1998 at the age of 82 caused a resurgence of interest in his life and in his music. A look at Sinatra's version of *Blue Moon* will demonstrate both his special style of singing and the character and structure of the pop song at this stage in its history.

This ballad follows the character of most songs from the 30s and 40s in that it is slow, lyrical, and sentimental. Sinatra's singing style beautifully conforms to the character of the song. It is relaxed, casual, and somehow intimate. He sounds very comfortable, almost as if he were talking. The sense of relaxation is conveyed particularly by the way his voice "slides" in and out of phrases.

The structure of the song is simple. It is cast in AABA form, with eight measures for each section. The music for the first section (A) is repeated for the second section (A), then there is a contrast (B: "And then there suddenly appeared…") before the return of the A section again. In this song, the pattern is very easy to follow, because all three A sections begin with the words "Blue moon…" As with many songs of the era, the B section uses more colorful chords than the A section, which emphasizes the contrast between the two.

0:00	[Instrumental introduction]

A

0:16	D♭ B♭min E♭min7	A♭7
	Blue moon!	You saw me standing a-
	D♭ B♭min E♭min7	A♭7
	lone,	Without a dream in my
	D♭ B♭min E♭min7	
	heart,	Without a love of my
	D♭ G♭ D♭ A♭7	
	own.	Blue

A

0:33

moon!	You knew just what I was
there for.	You heard me saying a
prayer for	Someone I really could
care for.	And then there

B

0:49

G♭   A♭7   D♭
suddenly appeared before me   The only

G♭   A♭7 D♭
one my arms will ever hold.   I heard some-

F♯min7   B7   E
body whisper "Please adore me."   And when I

A♭   B♭min7   E♭min7 A♭7
looked, the moon had turned to gold! Blue

A

1:06

moon!	Now I'm no longer a-
lone.	Without a dream in my
heart,	Without a love of my own.

A

A

1:23   [Saxophone solo]

B

1:56

And then there suddenly appeared before me
The only one my arms will ever hold.
I heard somebody whisper "Please adore me."
And when I looked, the moon had turned to gold!

A

2:13

Blue moon! Now I'm no longer alone,
Without a dream in my heart,
Without a love of my own—

A

2:30

[repeat]
Blue moon! Now I'm no longer alone,
Without a dream in my heart,
Without a love of my own.

Frank Sinatra is a singer who comes along once in a lifetime. But why did he have to come in *my* lifetime?—singer Bing Crosby

SOME OF THE MOST SUCCESSFUL POPULAR SONGS BEFORE 1950

TITLE	DATE	COMPOSER
Old Folks at Home	1851	Stephen Foster
When Johnny Comes Marching Home Again	1863	Louis Lambert
After the Ball	1892	Charles K. Harris
The Birthday Song	1893	Patty Hill and Mildred Hill
Bill Bailey, Won't You Please Come Home	1902	Hughie Cannon
Oh, You Beautiful Doll	1911	Seymour Brown/Nat D. Ayer
Swanee	1919	George Gershwin/Irving Caesar
Avalon	1920	Al Jolson/Vincent Rose
Tea for Two	1924	Irving Caesar/Vincent Youmans
Sweet Georgia Brown	1925	Ben Bernie/Maceo Pinkard/Kenneth Casey
Ain't Misbehavin'	1929	Fats Waller
I Got Rhythm	1930	George and Ira Gershwin
On the Sunny Side of the Street	1930	Jimmy McHugh/Dorothy Fields
Smoke Gets in Your Eyes	1933	Jerome Kern
Blue Moon	1934	Richard Rodgers/Lorenz Hart
Begin the Beguine	1935	Cole Porter
Summertime	1935	George Gershwin/DuBose Heyward
Over the Rainbow	1939	Harold Arlen
White Christmas	1942	Irving Berlin
Some Enchanted Evening	1949	Richard Rodgers/Oscar Hammerstein
Rudolph the Red-Nosed Reindeer	1949	Johnny Marks

THE FORTUNATE FIFTIES

Scene from the popular 1950s television show *Father Knows Best*.

The post-World War II period in the United States was a time of unprecedented economic prosperity. Low unemployment and high productivity combined to produce an economic boom, and relief at the ending of the war and a new optimism for the future led to what has been called the "baby boom." Middle-class families had several children, and the birthrate soared. Many Americans also had more leisure time and higher incomes than ever before.

This idyllic life was represented in the new television shows of the 1950s that pictured the perfect family, complete with working father, beautifully groomed mother, two or three kids, and a dog. A revealing insight into the social climate of the time can be obtained by watching reruns of such shows as *Father Knows Best*, *Leave It to Beaver*, or *The Donna Reed Show*.

By the late 1950s, the babies of the "baby boom" were becoming teenagers, enjoying the fruits of the new prosperity. Teenagers bought an average of two new records a month, but there were many who bought 12 or more.

Technology fueled the teenage buying spree. Long-playing (LP) records swept the country in the 1950s, replacing the old 78s. These new discs contained much more music and were able to reproduce sounds with far more accuracy. Most teenagers had access to a small record player. And radios, which had been major pieces of furniture in the 1940s, were now equipped with transistors—another scientific breakthrough. By the mid-1950s, teenagers could take their transistor radios, running on batteries and weighing little over a pound, to the park, to a picnic, or to the beach. The swamping of America with popular song had begun.

Left: Portable record player from the 1950s.

ROCK AND ROLL: THE BEGINNINGS

The early influences on rock and roll were many and varied. First and most important was the mixture of slow blues singing with a harder, more rhythmic accompaniment that became known as rhythm and blues. Early R & B artists primarily were black. They included singers such as Muddy Waters, who grew up on a Mississippi plantation, moved to Chicago "with a suitcase and a guitar," and mixed the rural sound of the blues with the electrified edge and raucous rhythms of the city streets. Rhythm and blues often expanded the personal, one-man-with-a-guitar tradition of country blues into a group of musicians. Also vital to the early growth of rock and roll were the wild, hard-driving instrumental sounds of Little Richard and Chuck Berry. Little Richard was also from the South, and he pounded rather than played the piano and screamed his lyrics like a wild man. Chuck Berry played a clean, hard guitar and wrote fast songs with an irresistible beat. A list of his hits includes some of the early classics of rock and roll: *Roll Over Beethoven*, *Rock and Roll Music*, and *Johnny B. Goode*. As one Chicago bluesman

Below: Muddy Waters.

said: "You're playing rhythm and blues. You step the stuff up, and you're playing rock and roll."

Another early influence on rock and roll was country music. Before the term "rock and roll" was widely used, the early sound of Elvis Presley and others was known as "rockabilly" ("rock" + "hillbilly"). **(See Listening Guide on page 450.)** It combined the drive of rhythm and blues with music from the rural South known as Country and Western, with its fiddle playing, guitar picking, and warm harmonies. Rockabilly stars who scored big hits at this time were Jerry Lee Lewis (*Great Balls of Fire* and *Whole Lotta Shakin' Goin' On*), Johnny Cash (*I Walk the Line*), and Carl Perkins (*Blue Suede Shoes*). All were white, poor, and from the rural South. Another rockabilly star from this time was the unlikely looking Buddy Holly, skinny and bespectacled. Buddy Holly was on the threshold of an important career when he died in a plane crash at the age of 22.

ELVIS PRESLEY

Despite strings of hits, none of these singing stars came close to the phenomenon of Elvis Presley. Presley came from a poor background in Mississippi. Born in 1935, he moved with his family to Memphis when he was 13. Elvis worked in a factory and drove a truck until he turned to music, singing with a small group. At the age of 18, he went to the local recording studio, where anyone could make a record for four dollars, and recorded a song as a present for his mother. Six months and two or three recordings later, his records suddenly began to attract attention on radio stations. Elvis took his group around the South. And on his very first tour, in the summer of 1955, the hysteria started. A country singer described the scene:

> The cat came out in red pants and a green coat and a pink shirt and socks, and he had this sneer on his face and he stood behind the mike for five minutes, I'll bet, before he made a move. Then he hit his gui-

I can't sing very well, but I'd like to try.—Elvis Presley, on first entering a recording studio

Elvis Presley in concert, 1956.

tar a lick, and he broke two strings. So there he was, these two strings dangling, and he hadn't done anything yet, and these high school girls were screaming and fainting and running up to the stage, and then he started to move his hips real slow like he had a thing for his guitar. That was Elvis Presley when he was about 19, playing Kilgore, Texas.

By 1957, Elvis mania was sweeping the country. And the new technology fueled the fire. Presley appeared on *The Ed Sullivan Show*, one of the most popular television shows of the day. Within months after his appearance, Elvis had a series of hits at the top of the charts, including *Love Me Tender*, *Hound Dog*, and *All Shook Up*. A new radio format, the Top Forty, aired Presley hits almost constantly. And Elvis appeared in

Elvis Presley's house, Graceland, in Memphis, Tennessee.

the movie *Love Me Tender* in 1956. It was the first of 31 movies he was to make during his career.

After this period, Presley began to retreat from the rockabilly sound to the more mainstream sentimental ballad that had been the staple of popular music for decades. This smoother, more acceptable Elvis appealed to an even wider audience and sold even more records. By the end of his career, Elvis Presley had sold the largest number of records in the history of recorded sound: more than 250 million. The commercial success of Elvis the singer led to the creation of an entire industry. In the late 1950s, fans could choose from a range of "Elvis products," including bobby socks, blouses, skirts, shoes, and lipstick ("Hound Dog" Orange, for example). There were also Elvis pajamas, an Elvis pillow, and a glow-in-the-dark Elvis poster. By the end of 1957, the Elvis business had grossed $55 million.

This poor-boy-made-good couldn't spend money fast enough. He bought a mansion in Memphis, called Graceland, for himself and his parents. He also bought a fleet of Cadillacs, an airplane, and hundreds of television sets. And yet his very fame eventually made his life miserable.

Elvis became depressed and sometimes violent. He retreated into drugs and alcohol. Gradually the charismatic teenage sex idol turned into an overweight, drugged parody of himself, singing ballads in Las Vegas hotels, squeezed into a sequined costume. He died in 1977 at the age of 42, a victim of the commercial world of popular music.

> I was very lucky. The people were looking for something different, and I came along just in time.—Elvis Presley

Elvis Presley
Blue Suede Shoes
Words and music by Carl Perkins

Date of performance: 1956

*L*ike a number of Presley's early hits, *Blue Suede Shoes* was written and first recorded by another artist, in this case Carl Perkins. Presley's recordings of these songs were often the principal catalyst for their immense popularity, and they became immediately associated with his name. His studio recording of *Blue Suede Shoes* didn't match the phenomenal success of some of his early No. 1 hits (*Heartbreak Hotel*, *Hound Dog*, *Don't Be Cruel*), but it did make it to No. 20 on the pop charts in 1956. There is also a recording of a mid-1950s live performance, which captures the atmosphere and intensity of the early Elvis phenomenon. The performance is swinging, rough, and exciting.

The song is essentially a basic 12-bar blues progression with a rockabilly backbeat. The 12-bar blues is an extremely common chord progression in jazz, pop, and rock music. As you know, it consists of three lines of four measures ("bars") each, in the following pattern:

I	I	I	I	(I is the tonic chord, IV is the
IV	IV	I	I	subdominant chord, and V is the
V	IV	I	I	dominant chord.)
	(or V)			

Blue Suede Shoes is in the key of B♭, so the song uses these chords throughout: B♭ (I), E♭ (IV), and F (V).

0:00	[Brief guitar riff as an introduction]
0:02	B♭[I]　　　　　B♭[I] Well it's one for the money, two for the show, B♭[I]　　　　　B♭[I] three to get ready, now go cat go,
0:06	E♭[IV]　　E♭[IV]　　　　B♭[1]　　B♭[1] But don't you step on my blue suede shoes. 　　　　F[V]　　　　　E♭[IV]　　　　B♭[1]　　B♭[1] Well you can do anything but lay off of my blue suede shoes.
0:16	You can knock me down, step in my face, slander my name all over the place. Do anything that you wanna do, but uh-uh honey lay off of my shoes.
0:26	Now don't you step on my blue suede shoes. Well you can do anything but lay off of my blue suede shoes.

0:37	Well it's blue, blue, my blue suede shoes, my baby, blue, blue, blue suede shoes, yeah, Blue, blue, my blue suede shoes, baby, blue, blue, blue suede shoes— Well you can do anything, but lay off of my blue suede shoes.
0:52	You can knock me down, step in my face, slander my name all over the place. Do anything that you wanna do, but uh-uh honey lay off of my shoes.
1:02	Now don't you step on my blue suede shoes. Well you can do anything but lay off of my blue suede shoes.
1:13	Well it's blue, blue, my blue suede shoes, my baby, [etc.]

The live performance omits the third verse, which Presley included on his studio recording:

> You can burn my house, steal my car, drink my liquor from an old fruit jar,
> Do anything that you wanna do, but uh-uh honey lay off of my shoes.
> Now don't you step on my blue suede shoes.
> Well you can do anything, but lay off of my blue suede shoes.

REBELLION

In his early years, Elvis Presley symbolized something very important for American youth. He was the symbol of freedom, of rebellion. His unconventional clothes, the messages of his music, and especially his raw sexuality appealed to the new and numerous group of American teenagers. The spirit of rebellion was in the air. James Dean projected restlessness and moody defiance in his films *East of Eden* (1953) and *Rebel Without a Cause* (1955). The young Marlon Brando appeared as a member of a motorcycle gang in *The Wild One* (1953) and as a rebel union leader in *On the Waterfront* (1954). And J. D. Salinger's novel *Catcher in the Rye* (1951), about a student at odds with society, was extremely popular with high-school students throughout the 1950s and 1960s.

This wild and rebellious spirit was captured by a song that did more to popularize the term "rock and roll" than any other. The song was *Rock Around the Clock*, and it was sung by Bill Haley and the Comets. *Rock Around the Clock* first came out in 1954, but it was re-released in 1955 and became a major hit when it was used in the opening and closing sequences of *Blackboard Jungle*, a movie of teenage

High-school dance in the 1950s.

violence and rejection. Bill Haley later described his own view of how rock and roll was born. "We started out as a country and western group, then we added a touch of rhythm and blues. We didn't call it that at the time, but we were playing rock and roll."

Rock and roll fed into the dance craze that gripped America's young people in the '50s. Dancing was a physical outlet for repressed energy, and teenagers went wild with dancing. School dances, "sock hops," picnics, and parties were soon filled with rock and roll music, and with teenagers jiving, stomping, and swinging.

Rock and roll represented a dramatic change from the smooth musical style that had dominated popular music for the previous hundred years. It was rough, raucous, loud, electric, and intense. And then, of course, there was the beat. Most of the early rock and roll songs were fast. And there was a pounding accent on the first beat of every measure. Both the sound and the lyrics were often frankly sexual.

And that's where the problem came in. The 1950s were the start of a phenomenon that has become a central force in the American social psyche: the so-called generation gap.

Adults, used to the smooth and sentimental sound of most popular music, were appalled at the suggestiveness of rock and roll. In 1956, *Time* magazine expressed the attitude of the older generation:

> There is no denying that rock 'n' roll evokes a physical response from even its most reluctant listeners, for that giant pulse matches the rhythmical operations of the human body, and the performers are all too willing to specify it.

Local police departments banned rock and roll dances. Radio disc jockeys joined together to keep the music off their shows. Speeches were made in the House of Representatives. Religious leaders sermonized against rock and roll. A distinguished psychiatrist called rock and roll "a communicable disease," and a composer described it as "acoustical pollution." Elvis Presley was the focus of the greatest concern. One minister labeled him "a whirling dervish of sex." And when

Presley appeared on *The Ed Sullivan Show*, he was filmed from the waist up, so that the television audience couldn't see the legendary gyrations of "Elvis the Pelvis." But young people knew what rock and roll did for them. A fan wrote later: "Elvis Presley turned our uptight young awakened bodies around. Hard animal rock energy/beat surged hot through us, the driving rhythm arousing repressed passions."

EARLY ROCK AND ROLL: STRUCTURE AND STYLE

Many early rock and roll songs are based on the 12-bar blues pattern. As you saw with Presley's *Blue Suede Shoes*, this pattern consists of three phrases of four measures each, with the following chord sequence:

Text:	A	A	B
Chords:	I I I I	IV IV I I	V IV (or V) I I

The lyrics to 12-bar blues often follow the pattern AAB—that is, the first line of text is repeated and then followed by another line, which usually rhymes with the first.

As a result of this limited number of chords, the harmonies are extremely limited and repetitive—insistent rather than complex. This puts more focus on the rhythm. It, too, is insistent, with a strong accent on the first beat of every measure and secondary accents on the second and fourth beats. Both the harmonic pattern and the beat continue unchanged from the beginning to the end of the song.

Early rock and roll bands usually featured a limited number of instruments: piano, bass, and drums, occasionally with an electric guitar or saxophone. Some included a string section to accompany slow songs, but heavy orchestration was largely reserved for hits directed at older audiences. Almost all songs from this time lasted $2\frac{1}{2}$ minutes, because they were designed to fit on one side of a 45-rpm record.

The lyrics of early rock and roll concentrated on a

few subjects guaranteed to appeal to teenagers: love, sex, and dancing. As rock and roll transformed the landscape of American popular music, some room was still left for the 32-measure, AABA-form slow ballad that was popular in the first half of the century. For sentimental songs always have an audience. There was a brief rash of sentimental songs that displayed a morbid fascination with death: *Teen Angel* (Mark Dinning, 1959) and *Tell Laura I Love Her* (Roy Peterson, 1960) both describe tragic deaths of young people, one by a train and the other in a car crash. But the main subject of slow songs was romance. And teenagers were quite happy to have a few ballads played at their parties for slow dancing.

EARLY ROCK AND ROLL: BLACK AND WHITE

An important social element of rock and roll was the racial integration that it helped to accomplish. The Supreme Court ruled in 1954 that equal access must be granted to all students in the nation's public schools. Rock and roll was itself a melding of black and white music: the blues plus Country and Western. Audiences at concerts began to be more mixed, and teenagers from different ethnic backgrounds bought many of the same records and listened to the same radio shows. And yet these manifestations of equality did not occur without serious setbacks. White racist organizations in the South attacked rock and roll in the press as a "plot to mongrelize America." And in 1956, the black jazz singer and pianist Nat King Cole was beaten at one of his concerts in Birmingham, Alabama. Some black singers were even banned from radio and television shows.

To prevent the racism in American society from cutting into their profits, record companies often hired white singers to "cover"—that is, copy—popular hits by black singers. Pat Boone covered many hits in the 1950s, toning down the originals both in their lyrics and in their style. The covers were smoother, less raucous and rough, with lusher instrumental accompaniment. Boone was one of a number of clean-cut, white, Northern, middle-class young people, such as Frankie Avalon, Paul Anka, Brenda Lee, and Bobby Darin, who helped make rock and roll more widely acceptable to the American mainstream. But as a result, black singers were often denied the success that was their due. Bo Diddley later complained, "With me there had to be a copy. They wouldn't buy me, but they would buy a white copy of me. Elvis got me. I don't even like to talk about it."

THE TURBULENT SIXTIES

The 1960s were a decade of profound social upheaval. The period began with optimism and excitement, as the young and charismatic John F. Kennedy was elected president of the United States. Idealistic civil rights workers, both black and white, sought to increase registration of black voters in the South and end housing discrimination in the North. The Rev. Dr. Martin Luther King attracted nationwide attention as he fought with unprecedented success (and immense dignity) to end segregation and racism in America without the use of violence.

Soon, however, the idealism and optimism were shattered. President Kennedy was assassinated in 1963. The passage of the Civil Rights Act in 1965 was regarded by many new militant black groups as "too little, too late." Riots broke out in many cities in the summers of 1965–68. And in 1968, both Martin Luther King and Robert Kennedy, the president's brother, were gunned down. But the most divisive force in American society in the 1960s was the Vietnam War.

The American presence in Vietnam had begun in the 1950s. And by the time the war ended with a

John F. Kennedy's Inaugural Address (Extracts)

In his inaugural address, John Kennedy invoked an idealism and displayed a quality of leadership more inspiring than Americans had heard, or would hear, for many, many years: ✦ "Let the word go forth from this time and place, to friend and foe alike, that the torch has been passed to a new generation of Americans, born in this century, tempered by war, disciplined by a hard and bitter peace, proud of our ancient heritage, and unwilling to witness or permit the slow undoing of those human rights to which this nation has always been committed...." ✦ "Let every nation know, whether it wishes us well or ill, that we shall pay any price, bear any burden, meet any hardship, support any friend, oppose any foe to assure the survival and the success of liberty...." ✦ "And so, my fellow Americans, ask not what your country can do for you; ask what you can do for your country. My fellow citizens of the world, ask not what America will do for you, but what together we can do for the freedom of man."

Martin Luther King's "I Have a Dream" Speech (Extracts)

Dr. King delivered this speech standing in front of the Lincoln Memorial on August 28, 1963. He was addressing more than 200,000 people, who were there for the Civil Rights March on Washington. Television cameras carried his speech around the nation: ✦ "I am happy to join with you today in what will go down in history as the greatest demonstration for freedom in the history of our nation...." ✦ "So I say to you, my friends, that even though we must face the difficulties of today and tomorrow, I still have a dream. It is a dream deeply rooted in the American dream that one day this nation will rise up and live out the true meaning of its creed: 'We hold these truths to be self-evident, that all men are created equal....'" ✦ "And when we allow freedom to ring, when we let it ring from every village and hamlet, from every state and city, we will be able to speed up that day when all of God's children—black men and white men, Jews and Gentiles, Catholics and Protestants—will be able to join hands and to sing in the words of the old Negro spiritual, 'Free at last, free at last; thank God Almighty, we are free at last.'"

Communist victory in 1975, countries counted their dead: more than 600,000 North Vietnamese, more than 200,000 South Vietnamese; 57,000 American dead and 155,000 wounded.

The Vietnam War was one of the focal points for student uprisings throughout the 1960s and early 1970s. Young people did not want to be drafted to face the possibility of dying thousands of miles from home in a war many of them didn't believe in. But the alienation of young people in the 1960s had other causes, too. Partly, it was a continuation of the generation gap of the 1950s; partly, college students began to regard their courses as irrelevant. Many young people "dropped out" of society, living in communes, wearing deliberately outrageous clothes, and taking drugs. Large numbers of young people, known as "hippies," wore beads, dressed in flowery clothes, and experimented with mind-altering or "psychedelic" substances, including LSD, which was legal until 1966.

The alienation of almost an entire generation of young people, the baby boomers, was strengthened by the events of the early 1970s. In 1973, the vice president of the United States, Spiro Agnew, resigned his office amid charges of corruption and bribery. In 1974, as a result of the Watergate scandal, President Richard Nixon resigned in disgrace.

Throughout this era, it was popular music that bound members of the younger generation together. The main performers of the 1960s were regarded as emblems of an entire social movement. They also created worldwide sensations and had an incalculable influence on pop and rock music from that time until today. Foremost among them were the Beatles, Bob Dylan, and Jimi Hendrix.

THE BEATLES

The Beatles represented the first wave in what has been called the British Invasion of America. During the 1960s, England became a world center of pop and rock music. Rock music in England was the expression of working-class frustrations. There were severe economic

"Hippies" in the 1960s.

hardships in a country that had spearheaded the defense of Western Europe during World War II. Food rationing continued until nearly 10 years after the war. There were few jobs, and with the end of the draft, young people were leaving school with no expectations and little to do. "Music was a way out," explained the Beatles' drummer, Ringo Starr. "Back then, every street had a band. We all picked up guitars and drums and filled our time with music."

All four members of the Beatles grew up in working-class backgrounds in Liverpool, an industrial city in the north of England. The group was founded in 1959. By 1962, they had completely conquered England and much of the rest of Europe. They played before the queen and scored major hits with two singles: *She Loves You* and *I Want to Hold Your Hand*. Their first album, *Please Please Me*, stayed at the top of the British charts for six months. Two years later they embarked on their first tour of the United States. In 1964, in the course of

The Beatles welcomed by a ticker-tape parade, 1964.

W*e're more popular than Jesus Christ right now.*
—John Lennon, 1966

one week, the Beatles appeared on *The Ed Sullivan Show*, played two concerts at Carnegie Hall, appeared before 8,000 fans at the Washington Coliseum, and pushed *I Want to Hold Your Hand* to the top of the American charts. In 1965, they toured the United States again, including a concert at New York's Shea Stadium before 55,000 screaming teenagers. The nationwide tour grossed more than $56 million.

The most important musical influences on the Beatles were rhythm and blues and American rockabilly. They covered some Chuck Berry songs, such as *Roll Over Beethoven*, but their main model in the early years was Elvis Presley. "Nothing really affected me until Elvis," said John Lennon. "Elvis changed my life," said Ringo Starr. "He totally blew me away, I loved him so."

With the advent of the Beatles in the early 1960s, the character of popular music changed in fundamental ways:

1. Rock music became an international activity, no longer the exclusive province of the United States.
2. Every rock group developed its own identifiable sound, and its own specific look. In the

The Beatles in concert, 1963.

early days, for example, the Beatles all wore the same clothes and had matching haircuts.

3. Rock groups became a self-contained, identifiable entity, with specific personnel, each of whom was assigned a particular role. In the case of the Beatles, George Harrison was the lead guitarist, John Lennon played rhythm guitar, Paul McCartney played bass guitar, and Ringo Starr was the drummer; Lennon and McCartney sang most of the vocals. Each member of the group stood at the same place on the stage each time they performed. Each earned his own following and had his own fan club.

Many other rock groups surfaced in the 1960s, the most famous of which was the five-member group that called themselves the Rolling Stones. Their manager described them as "the opposite of those nice little chaps, the Beatles." The song that captured the aggressive spirit of the 1960s generation more than any other was the scathing, snarling *(I Can't Get No) Satisfaction*.

The Beatles' career as a group may be divided into two periods: the public and the private. The public

The Beatles walking from their studio in Abbey Road, London, 1969.

period is represented by the first half of the decade, when they toured and made records of songs they could sing on stage. The private period, the second half of the decade, was devoted exclusively to recording, using the technology of the studio in novel ways that could not be reproduced in a live performance. During this latter period, they made several technologically advanced records—singles and albums—that had an enormous influence on recording techniques for the whole of the later history of rock music.

We shall examine two Beatles songs from the 1960s. The first one, *It Won't Be Long*, comes from what we have called the public period in the Beatles' career. The second, *Strawberry Fields Forever*, is from their private (studio) period. **(See Listening Guides on pages 458 and 459.)**

With the release of their album *Sgt. Pepper's Lonely Hearts Club Band* (also a studio production from 1967), the Beatles truly revolutionized the making of popular music records. Henceforth, the record album took on a new dimension in artistic production. Rather than

bringing together a collection of previously released hits and perhaps a few new songs, the new "concept album" was a completely integrated entity, with songs that were connected, either literally or thematically. Every aspect of *Sgt. Pepper* received special attention, including elaborate jacket and sleeve design with printed lyrics. The music is enormously varied and inventive, but the record is unified as a kaleidoscopic reflection of contemporary life, including loneliness, alienation, affection, friendship, and the new drug culture.

The Beatles were no longer constrained by many of the conventions surrounding popular music. Dancing was no longer a central focus of their audience. People could sit and listen to their songs (and analyze and discuss them), and that began to inspire more intellectual participation on the part of their listeners. The creativity of the Beatles found many outlets, including books (John Lennon's *In His Own Write*), solo performances, films (*The Magical Mystery Tour*), social and political activity, and exploration of the philosophy and music of the East, especially India. Perhaps the

The Beatles
It Won't Be Long
Music and words by John Lennon
and Paul McCartney

Date of recording: 1964

An example of the Beatles' early, public sound is *It Won't Be Long*. Notice here the prominence of the electric bass and the background vocals. Other features that are trademarks of the Beatles' early style are the "yeah, yeah, yeah" exclamations and the constant interchange between lead and background vocals. One particular element that characterized the music of the Beatles was its harmonic interest. They tended to use more interesting chord progressions and more complex harmonies than other groups. In *It Won't Be Long*, we can hear an unusual chord progression (major tonic to lowered submediant—I–♭VI—and back again) on the words of the two-line verses:

E(I)   C(♭VI)   E(I)
Every night when everybody has fun

E(I)   C(♭VI)   E(I)
Here am I sitting all on my own.

Colorful harmonies like this give added richness and depth to this song. Notice, too, how the repeated guitar riff is derived from the vocal line on "Every night…," "Here am I…," etc., and listen to the chromatic descent of the background vocals on "Since you left me…"

0:00	It won't be long yeah (yeah), yeah (yeah), yeah (yeah)
	It won't be long yeah (yeah), yeah (yeah), yeah (yeah)
	It won't be long yeah (yeah), 'til I belong to you.
0:16	Every night when everybody has fun,
	Here am I sitting all on my own.
0:27	It won't be long, etc.
0:42	Since you left me, I'm so alone,
	Now you're comin', you're comin' on home.
	I'll be good like I know I should,
	You're comin' home—you're comin' home.
0:57	Every night, the tears come down from my eyes;
	Every day, I've done nothing but cry.
1:09	It won't be long, etc.

1:23	Since you left me, etc.

1:38	So, every day we'll be happy, I know. Now I know that you won't leave me no mo'.

1:50	It won't be long, etc.

LISTENING GUIDE

The Beatles
Strawberry Fields Forever
**Words and music by John Lennon
and Paul McCartney**

Date of recording: 1967

*T*he Beatles' private, or studio, period can be represented by *Strawberry Fields Forever*, a song that originally appeared on a single with *Penny Lane* on the other side. In this song, notice the instrumental exploration (including orchestral instruments, flute sounds, and an Indian harp), the backward taping of cymbals, and the rather daring chord progression. Notice also the somewhat mysterious and elusive nature of the words. It was at this time that the Beatles began to move away from the conventional lyrics of the standard pop song.

The release of this record was almost immediately followed by a promotional video, a very new idea in the 1960s. The electronically produced studio sound makes this song a production rather than a performance. Even today, with the rapid advances in technology that have occurred since 1967, it would be difficult to render a live performance of it.

A
Let me take you down 'cause I'm going to

Em   **F#**
Strawberry Fields, nothing is real

  D   **F#**
And nothing to get hung about.

D   **A**
Strawberry Fields forever.

most controversial aspect of their constant curiosity was their widely publicized experimentation with drugs.

As a group, the Beatles lasted until 1970, when they broke up with some bitterness and acrimony. All four then began individual careers, with varying degrees of success. But the individual achievements of the four men never matched the extraordinary synergy they experienced as a group. Among all the worldwide successes the Beatles gained, the millions of dollars they made, and the controversies they caused, one achievement stands out: From 1963 to 1970, the group known as the Beatles released 13 record albums, from the early, energetic, tight-harmony *Please Please Me* to the strange and questing *Rubber Soul* to the amazingly varied *Sgt. Pepper* and, finally, *Abbey Road*. In only seven years, they changed the entire course of popular music.

BOB DYLAN

Apart from the many, many groups that sprang up in the 1960s, there were two individuals who had a powerful influence on pop and rock music during that turbulent decade. They were Bob Dylan and Jimi Hendrix.

Bob Dylan's brand of folk-inspired, intensely committed **protest song** caught the imagination and fired the spirits of millions of young people in the rebellious, activist sixties. He sang about the threat of nuclear war, about civil rights and racism, and about the power of the military-industrial complex. "There's other things in this world besides love and sex that're important," Dylan said.

Bob Dylan in concert, 1978.

The protest song was not new. American slaves used to sing songs of protest under the guise of ballads or lullabies. And from the 1920s to the 1950s, the tradition of the protest song was continued by Woody Guthrie and Pete Seeger, who composed, sang, and accompanied their own songs on the guitar.

During the 1960s, Bob Dylan captivated the popular music world with his intensity and commitment. He seemed to personify a generation constantly in search of answers to new and profound questions. The protest songs—especially those with an antiwar sentiment, such as *Masters of War* and *Blowin' in the Wind* (1963)—strongly caught the 1960s mood of bitterness and alienation. Dylan's snarling, nasal delivery and his rough guitar and harmonica playing gave bite and impetus to the music. As with many of the early black rockers, Dylan's music was too raw for most listeners and sold best when covered in versions by Peter, Paul, and Mary (*Blowin' in the Wind, The Times They Are a-Changin'*), Joan Baez (*Don't Think Twice, It's All Right, It's All Over Now, Baby Blue*), and the Byrds (*Mr. Tambourine Man*). Dylan is a restless and creative spirit, and no sooner had he made a major hit with one style than he was exploring something new and different. He was always ahead of his fans, shifting from folk ballads to protest songs to electrified rock to country.

Bob Dylan has changed his focus many times since those early days, and each time his followers have complained. Since the 1960s, he has sung Christian anthems, Jewish ballads, raucous rock, and deeply moving love songs. Many of his songs, both from the sixties and later, are so original they defy classification. One of these is the brilliant, bitter, mournful *Sad-eyed Lady of the Lowlands* (1966). **(See Listening Guide on page 461.)** Other examples among many include the exquisite *Sara* (1975), a testament of love for his wife, and the intense, slow, lustful *Blood in My Eyes* (1993). Bob Dylan continues to compose, perform, protest, release records, and experiment with expressing his mind and heart in music. His 1997 album *Time Out of Mind*, with its mature and searching reflections on the human condition, may well be the best thing he has ever done.

Bob Dylan

Sad-eyed Lady of the Lowlands

Words and music by Bob Dylan

Date of recording: 1966

*S*ad-eyed Lady of the Lowlands is an epic ballad more than ten minutes long. Like much of Dylan's music, the essence of this song is in its superb poetry and its charismatic vocal delivery. The accompaniment of Dylan's guitar and his backup group at the time, the Band, is fairly static. However, notice Dylan's subtle shifts in accent and his colorful emotive changes through each of the verses and each chorus; this is his true art as a singer of his own songs. Dylan transcends the simple framework of his songs to create a performance that is more a powerful musical-poetic reading than a mere song.

| 0:00 | [Instrumental introduction with harmonica solo] |

VERSE 1

0:17

D   F#min   Bmin   A
With your mercury mouth in the missionary times,

D   F#min   Bmin   A
And your eyes like smoke and your prayers like rhymes,

G   F#min   Emin   D
And your silver cross, and your voice like chimes,

D   Emin   A
Oh, who among them do they think could bury you?

0:51

D   F#min   Bmin   A
With your pockets well protected at last,

D   F#min   Bmin   A
And your streetcar visions which you place on the grass,

G   F#min   Emin   D
And your flesh like silk, and your face like glass,

D   Emin A
Who among them could they get to carry you?

CHORUS

1:23

Emin   G   D A
Sad-eyed lady of the lowlands,

Emin   G   D   A
Where the sad-eyed prophet says that no man comes,

D   F#min   Bmin   A   G   F#min Emin
My warehouse eyes, my Arabian drums,

Emin   A
Should I put leave them by your gate,

Emin   D
Or, sad-eyed lady, should I wait?

VERSE 2

2:11 | With your sheets like metal and your belt like lace,
And your deck of cards missing the jack and the ace,
And your basement clothes and your hollow face,
Who among them can think he could outguess you?

2:45 | With your silhouette when the sunlight dims
Into your eyes where the moonlight swims,
And your match-book songs and your gypsy hymns,
Who among them would try to impress you?

CHORUS

3:20 | Sad-eyed lady…

VERSE 3

4:06 | The kings of Tyrus with their convict list
Are waiting in line for their geranium kiss,
And you wouldn't know it would happen like this,
But who among them really wants just to kiss you?

4:41 | With your childhood flames on your midnight rug,
And your Spanish manners and your mother's drugs,
And your cowboy mouth and your curfew plugs,
Who among them do you think could resist you?

CHORUS

5:13 | Sad-eyed lady…

VERSE 4

6:01 | Oh, the farmers and the businessmen, they all did decide
To show you the dead angels that they used to hide.
But why did they pick you to sympathize with their side?
Oh, how could they ever mistake you?

6:35 | They wished you'd accepted the blame for the farm,
But with the sea at your feet and the phony false alarm,
And with the child of a hoodlum wrapped up in your arms,
How could they ever, ever persuade you?

CHORUS	
7:09	Sad-eyed lady…

VERSE 5	
7:55	With your sheet-metal memory of Cannery Row,
	And your magazine-husband who one day just had to go,
	And your gentleness now, which you just can't help but show,
	Who among them do you think would employ you?

8:29	Now you stand with your thief, you're on his parole,
	With your holy medallion which your fingertips fold,
	And your saintlike face and your ghostlike soul,
	Oh, who among them do you think could destroy you?

CHORUS	
9:03	Sad-eyed lady…

9:46	[h a r m o n i c a s o l o ; f a d e o u t]

JIMI HENDRIX

In the 1960s, Jimi Hendrix was a unique figure. He was part black and part Native American, and he played the electric guitar like a man possessed. Accompanied only by bass and drums, Hendrix sang and played high-intensity versions of other people's songs (including his own protest: a wildly distorted, lamenting, dragged-out *Star-Spangled Banner*). But he also sang and played many highly original songs of his own, including *Purple Haze* (1967), *Foxy Lady* (1967), and the remarkable *Voodoo Chile* (1968).

Hendrix plays with his hair flying from his head in electric fright, doing things to his guitar so passionate, so concentrated, and so intense that anyone with halfway decent manners has to look away.
— A critic in the 1960s

Jimi Hendrix playing his "Strat."

The guitar playing of Jimi Hendrix was loud, sometimes angry, and always brilliantly inventive. He used electronic devices such as the wah-wah pedal and the fuzz box as well as effects such as feedback to create a dizzying array of sounds, and his virtuosity on his instrument was unparalleled. He played the Fender Stratocaster, the choice of many early rockers. The "Strat" featured a vibrato bar, which, when depressed, lowered the pitch of the strings. Hendrix's modifications of this device allowed him to bend the pitch of his strings by an octave or more, creating "dive-bomb" effects. Hendrix's playing was an inspiration for the sounds later explored by many heavy-metal guitar soloists, though very few guitarists can match his brilliance even today. He used his guitar to express musical ideas of startling originality, intensity, and complexity.

ADDITIONAL NOTES TO THE SIXTIES

The amount and variety of popular music during the 1960s could take up a book by itself; here we must be content with just a few notes on some of the other musical trends of the era. Each of these was a significant force at the time and also had important consequences for the later development of popular music.

MOTOWN

Motown was the creation of Berry Gordy, a producer and songwriter who built one of America's most successful music empires. Named after the great city of the automotive industry ("Motortown" = Detroit), the

The Stratocaster

The Stratocaster is a specific model of electric guitar that was developed by Leo Fender in 1954. It was popularized some 12 years later by Jimi Hendrix, who explored the instrument's every aspect. The Stratocaster was soon adopted by Eric Clapton (who still considers it his top choice and has a model of it bearing his own name). These endorsements have inspired other manufacturers to copy the instrument as much as legally possible. The shape of the body is probably the most rec-

ognizable in all of today's popular music, because the Strat is used by players from country to rock to jazz. Modern versions retail for about $3,000, but the guitar originally sold for $229 in 1954. For an additional $20, one could purchase the instrument with the patented "synchronized tremolo," which enabled the player to incorporate vibrato effects by moving a lever. Modern tremolos have been developed by companies such as Floyd Rose, but they cost as much as $300, compared with Fender's original $20 add-on.

company created an assembly line of successful black groups, including the Supremes, the Temptations, the Miracles, the Four Tops, and the Jackson 5.

The Motown sound was distinctive—polished, smooth, heavily orchestrated, with a danceable beat, and the echoey, call-and-response quality of gospel singing. The biggest hits of the Motown groups were *Stop! In the Name of Love* and *You Keep Me Hangin' On* (Supremes), *Standing in the Shadows of Love*, and *I Can't Help Myself* (the Four Tops), *My Girl* (Temptations), and *A-B-C*, *The Love You Save*, and *I'll Be There* (Jackson 5).

Motown was responsible for launching the solo careers of Diana Ross, Stevie Wonder, and Michael Jackson. But the most important aspect of the Motown legacy was the establishment of a vital place for black entrepreneurs in the commercial world of popular music and a new and highly attractive sound to add to the many sounds of the sixties.

SURFING SONGS

Another element in the sounds of the sixties was the music of the surfer groups. Surfing became a California craze in the early 1960s, partly as a result of the movie *Gidget* (1959), which depicted a beach romance. By the summer of 1963, 100,000 teenagers were addicted to the new sport, which had connotations of sun, sand, brawn, and bikinis. "If you're a good surfer," said one California boy, "you're always in. All you've got to do is walk up and down the beach with a board and you've got girls."

Surfing songs featured a high, bright sound with close harmonies and bouncy rhythms. Formed in 1961, the kings of the surfing song were the Beach Boys, who carried their tanned, clean-cut image and distinctive multivoiced harmony around the nation with such hits as *Surfer Girl*, *California Girls*, *Fun, Fun, Fun*, and the national anthem of the surfing craze, *Surfin' U.S.A.*

FOLK

The history of folk song goes back to the early seventeenth century in America, and of course much further

The Supremes.

back than that in Europe. The subject matter touched on the fundamental themes of rural human existence: love, death, nature, parting, work. Folk songs often tell a story. The melodies are simple, often modal, without large skips or awkward intervals. They are attractive, singable, and memorable.

In the 1960s, folk music experienced an enormous upsurge of interest among young people. The Kingston Trio had scored a major hit with their recording of the traditional folk ballad *Tom Dooley* in 1958. For the next 10 years, the Kingston Trio remained one of the favorite groups in America. They sang folk songs in smooth harmonies accompanied by acoustic guitars. Other successful folk groups included the Limeliters and the perennially popular Peter, Paul, and Mary, who combined traditional songs (*Lemon Tree*) with twentieth-century American classics (Pete Seeger's *If I Had a Hammer*), as well as new songs written by themselves (the wonderfully evocative *Puff, the Magic Dragon*).

COUNTRY

Country music dates back to the 1920s, when a brand of folk music—featuring steel guitar, violin ("fiddle"), and quick rhythms—began to take on its own style. This style became known as Country and Western when, in the 1940s, songs became popular that featured the American West (*Riders in the Sky, Don't Fence Me In*). This coincided with the growing appeal of radio shows and, slightly later, TV shows that were based on cowboy legends.

Country music gained widespread appeal in the 1940s and 1950s with such singing stars as Hank Williams and Eddy Arnold. The topics were rural, down-to-earth, sentimental, or religious, and they spoke of wide-open spaces, hard work, other men's "wimmin," prison, and patriotism. The songs were delivered in a nasal twang, with an occasional sob or "catch" in the voice and accompanied by a relaxed beat. Country music is also a narrative form: The songs tell a story.

Country music caught on in a big way in the 1960s. Both Buddy Holly and Elvis Presley began their careers in country bands. Bob Dylan recorded a country album (*Nashville Skyline*) that included a duet with country-music star Johnny Cash.

It was during this period that country music began to cross over into the pop charts. One of the biggest country hits of the period was Tammy Wynette's *Stand By Your Man* (1967). Other successful country singers of the sixties were Buck Owens, Jim Reeves, Merle Haggard, and Waylon Jennings.

Country music is accessible and easy to understand. Its domain includes country swing, cowboy songs, bluegrass (with its fancy banjo and fiddle work), and sentimental ballads. Many of its stories contain old-fashioned moralistic points of view or religious convictions rooted in rural society. The songs often have repeated sections or refrains, and the words are clear and prominent. Accompanying instruments include steel guitar (sometimes a "Hawaiian" guitar that *slides* between notes), fiddle, banjo, and "honky-tonk" piano. A typical country bass line bounces from the tonic to the dominant and back again.

As the author of this book, I collect country music titles. Some of my favorites include:

"Dropkick Me, Jesus, Through
   the Goalposts of Life"
"All My Ex-es Live in Texas"
"Washed Up in Mexico, Living on
   Re-Fried Dreams"
"You Done Stomped on My Heart
   and Squished That Sucker Flat"
"Get Your Tongue Outta My Mouth
   'Cause I'm Kissing You Goodbye"
"I Cain't Get Over You 'Til You
   Get Out From Under Him"
Got any good ones to send me for the next edition of *Understanding Music*?

J.Y.

THE BRITISH BLUES REVIVAL

At the height of the Beatles' popularity, an additional musical current was evident in England. This was the British blues revival. British groups such as the Yardbirds attempted to revive old blues styles and translate them into the rock idiom. Eric Clapton was the first of a trio of brilliant guitarists who were associated with the Yardbirds. Clapton, Jeff Beck, and Jimmy Page had a lasting impact not only on the new interpretation of the blues but also on guitar virtuosity.

One group that lasted for only a short time during the sixties was known as Cream and featured Eric Clapton on guitar, Jack Bruce on bass, and Ginger Baker on drums. These players were regarded as the very best in the profession, or the "cream of the crop." As a group, they lasted only from 1966 to 1968, but what they brought to rock music had important implications.

Clapton's guitar-playing abilities and his musicianship caused him to be respected and imitated in all branches of popular music. His work contributed to the extremely high profile of the electric guitar, which became a universal symbol of rock music. But his proficiency as an instrumentalist also encouraged mastery by players of other instruments. Eric Clapton continues to be a driving force in rock and popular music.

THE 1970S AND 1980S: VARIETY, LEGACY, AND CHANGE

The story of popular music in the 1970s and 1980s is one of great diversity. Many of the musical currents that had contributed to the ferment of the 1960s remained strong. The imaginative and prolific work of the Beatles, the spread of folk and country music, the revival of the blues, the use of new recording techniques—all these paved the way for a new variety in the tempo and texture of pop and rock music. Bob Dylan's restless shifts between musical styles (and his continuing presence on the scene) added to the openness and flexibility of the music. And the legend of Jimi Hendrix, as well as the more controlled virtuosity of the members of Cream, expanded the horizons of instrumental performance throughout the field of rock music. The power of the sixties legacy can be measured by the fact that records by these performers are almost as popular today as they were in their own time.

During the 1970s and 1980s, the baby boomers grew older. The rebellious generation, whose rallying cry used to be "Never trust anyone over thirty," were now in their forties. The 1970s brought a concentration on individual accomplishment rather than on social goals. This was the era known as the "Me Decade," in which people seemed to turn their backs on the social causes of the 1960s. In the 1980s, corporate interests were buoyed up, real estate boomed, and many members of the upper class got very rich indeed. But while some individuals and businesses flourished, unemployment doubled, the standard of living dropped, and public spending was drastically cut.

During this time, popular music spread into the mainstream. Rock music became the staple sound of radio stations all over the country. It could be heard in bus stations, supermarkets, and elevators. Nostalgia for the 1960s and even for the 1950s grew as the 1980s progressed. Many radio stations began to play exclusively "golden oldies." "Oldies for the oldies" it might be called. Movies were made chronicling the life stories of pop stars from the fifties and sixties. Indeed, many of the artists from the sixties were still performing, a little grayer perhaps, but still active and still pursuing that elusive perfect song: Paul McCartney, George Harrison, Ringo Starr, Bob Dylan, Joan Baez, Joni Mitchell, the Stones, the Grateful Dead, Paul Simon, Eric Clapton. And many new groups and performers played classic hits from the sixties. In many ways, therefore, the sounds and style of pop and rock music had not changed radically.

One of the great legacies of the sixties was diversity, and diversity was the hallmark of pop and rock in the 1970s and 1980s. *Acid rock* was an outgrowth of the drug culture, "acid" being a term for the drug LSD. The most successful acid-rock groups were the Grateful Dead, the Doors, and Jefferson Airplane, later renamed Jefferson Starship. Acid rock was extremely loud; Jerry Garcia of the Grateful Dead termed it "sensory overload." It also featured songs of considerable length, with extended guitar solos, and a deliberately outspoken approach to sex. Marty Balin of Jefferson Starship said: "The stage is our bed and the audience is our broad."

Acid rock evolved into *heavy metal*, a loud, thickly textured rock style with a deeply pounding beat, based primarily on the sounds of guitars and drums, often heavily distorted and employing "power chords." Power chords use the lowest, open strings of the guitar; they are based on the root and the fifth of the chord,

Album covers of James Taylor, Carole King, and Led Zeppelin.

Tapestry album artwork © 1977 Ode Records. Courtesy Ode/Epic/Legacy Recordings. Used by permission.

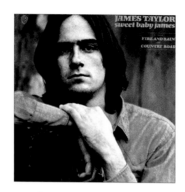

usually omitting the third. Chords in this position introduce the fewest dissonances, sounding most powerful when punched at tremendous volume. Heavymetal bands included Led Zeppelin, Black Sabbath, Metallica, and Aerosmith.

Fusion was the result of a mixture of rock and jazz. The leader of this new musical trend was the great jazz trumpeter Miles Davis, who blended the freer improvisatory sounds of jazz with the electric edge and heavy beat of rock. Other fusion bands included Weather Report, Blood, Sweat and Tears, Steely Dan, and Pink Floyd. Each of these groups scored successes with carefully produced albums, featuring the latest advances in electronic sound.

The 1970s brought a resurgence of interest in solo performers: Carole King, Joni Mitchell, Roberta Flack, Judy Collins, Carly Simon, and Linda Ronstadt were the most prominent female singers; James Taylor, Stevie Wonder, Paul Simon, and Elton John became the most popular male singers. Often their sound was in deliberate contrast to the ear-splitting levels of acid rock, with more relaxed, introspective singing, accompanied by acoustic guitars, background strings, or sometimes just a single piano.

Country music suddenly became a part of the popular mainstream in the 1970s, with singers such as Johnny Cash and Willie Nelson becoming crossovers from country into pop. Many songs in this era successfully blended the traditional country style—storytelling, acoustic accompaniment, and twangy accents—with rock elements to produce the blend known as country rock. One of the biggest stars of country rock was Willie Nelson, who produced an extraordinary string of hits starting in the mid-1970s and continuing

throughout the 1980s and into the 1990s. Nelson is an inventive and original songwriter, and his particular blend of country themes with the harder edge of rock found millions of responsive listeners throughout the country. He spoke of his music as appealing to "both rednecks and hippies."

A new fad of the 1970s, discos, originating in Europe, ushered in a special musical style and brought back the popularity of dancing. The disco sound was light, crisp, and very intense, with fast drumming, high vocals, and a solid, thumping bass. With their flashing strobes, walls of mirrors, recorded sound, and emphasis on the audience, discos reflected the narcissism of the Me Decade.

The so-called Queen of Disco was Donna Summer, whose *Love to Love You Baby* sold millions of copies. And a disco movie, *Saturday Night Fever*, simultaneously established disco as a national phenomenon and catapulted an Australian group to international stardom. The Bee Gees, who had been around since the 1960s, sold more than 30 million copies worldwide of the double-LP soundtrack to *Saturday Night Fever*.

Elaborate costumes and make-up of the rock group Kiss.

Some '70s phenomena seemed to suggest that the originality and interest had gone out of pop music. Gigantic, and in some cases grotesque, stage shows accompanied rock tours. This focus on the visual element set the stage for the music videos of the 1980s.

In the 1970s, more rock stars made more money than ever before. About the middle of that decade, it was estimated that at least 50 rock musicians were each earning more than $2 million per year. But if the musicians were making money, it was nothing compared with the profits of the record industry. In 1950, total record sales in the United States amounted to $189 million; by the late 1970s, that total had increased to $4 billion. Companies created, promoted, and sold rock groups. Music was no longer the province of the counterculture. It was the product of corporate America.

In the 1980s, an anti-establishment trend once more reasserted itself. It had begun a few years earlier with the rise of a deliberately shocking style of rock known as *punk*, which continued into the eighties.

Punk rock featured performers with outrageous costumes and nasty names. Lyrics were offensive, often violent. The titles of some songs from this time include *Slip It In*, *Killing an Arab*, and *Suicide Madness*. Punk rock was a short-lived phenomenon, though it left its mark on later rock styles.

A technological phenomenon of the 1980s revolutionized the way young people experienced popular music. Music Television, or MTV, a cable channel broadcasting nonstop music videos, was begun in 1981. Technology also influenced the sound of rock groups themselves. Synthesizers allowed the realistic duplication of sounds, which could be combined, modified, and manipulated in the most sophisticated ways.

MTV helped to create the extraordinary rebirth of Michael Jackson. Jackson had a long history as a singer. He appeared in the late 1960s at the age of 10 with his brothers in a group known as the Jackson 5 (later the Jacksons). Jackson's biggest success came during the 1980s, when his solo album *Thriller* (1982) sold more than 40 million copies worldwide. **(See Listening Guide on page 470.)** He was described as "the biggest thing since the Beatles" and as "the hottest single phenomenon since Elvis Presley."

Other singers whose careers were buoyed up on the MTV wave include Whitney Houston and Madonna. Both singers traded heavily on visual appeal. Houston was a fashion model as well as a singer, and her videos (and later her movies) pushed her albums to instant success. Madonna (Madonna Louise Ciccone) adopted a Marilyn Monroe image, and her dance training, combined with an overt sexuality, made her videos widely popular. Madonna's *Material Girl* seemed to catch the spirit of the money-making eighties. **(See Listening Guide on page 472.)** She later traded even more heavily on her body by releasing simultaneously a CD entitled *Erotica* and a book, *Sex*, displaying herself in various nude poses.

"World music" came to the fore in the 1980s, bringing into the American popular scene the sounds of many other cultures. Perhaps the most popular of these was *reggae*, which leapt out of Jamaica in the 1970s and

Punk rock is the generic term for the latest musical garbage.—Newspaper editorial

Question: "Do you think Michael Jackson has a Messiah complex?" Noel Gallagher of Oasis: "Who does he think he is? Me?"

Michael Jackson in concert, 1988.

Michael Jackson
Billie Jean
Words and music by Michael Jackson

Date of recording: 1982

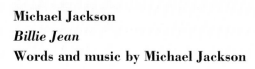ichael Jackson's album *Thriller* contains 10 songs, nine of which reached the Top Ten as singles! Perhaps the most typical of Jackson's style is *Billie Jean*. The music is fast and glossy, with a high, artificial, synthesized sound and a persistent disco beat. Jackson's voice is high, slick, and breathless. Toward the end, a little variety is introduced by means of some funky guitar tracks. The "funk" sound is produced by plucking the strings on an electric guitar a little harder than normal so that they slap against the fretboard.

Censorship in Popular Music

The idea of controlling music in society has been around for a long time. About 2,400 years ago, the Greek philosopher Plato said that the types of music people listened to should be controlled by the state. During the Middle Ages and the Renaissance, it was the Church that specified how music should be composed and performed. And in later centuries, secular rulers held a virtual monopoly over the music that was allowed in their realm. Often, composers had to submit a work to a committee before it was allowed to be published or performed. ◆ The question of censorship is still very much alive in the twenty-first century, particularly in reference to popular music. When rock and roll started, there were many people calling for it to be banned. And in the 1980s, an organization named the Parents Music Resource Center was formed, which fought successfully for the appearance of advisory stickers on certain records. ◆ No subject is taboo in rock music: There have been songs about oral sex, incest, and masturbation, as well as songs about murder, rape, and violence. Some rock songs imitate the sounds of orgasm. ◆ Should there be some controls on this kind of music? Should anybody be free to

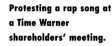

◆ Several radio stations from Los Angeles to New York adopted a policy that barred all songs promoting violence or drugs or containing degrading comments about women. And in 1993 the minister of the Abyssinian Baptist Church in Harlem held a rally at which he ran a steamroller over CDs and tapes he considered offensive. ◆ Censorship pressures can come from both sides of the political spectrum. Paul Simon, attempting to build bridges by using black musicians from South Africa on one of his records, got into trouble with liberals in America because he was accused of violating a cultural boycott against that country. And pressure from feminists persuaded the country singer Holly Dunn to have her song *Maybe I Mean Yes* banned from radio stations. Is that censorship? Or is it only censorship when it comes from conservative groups?

listen to these songs, including young children? If not, at what age do you draw the line? The Federal Communications Commission already legislates the appropriateness of certain words and subject matter on radio and television. So far, the controls on records have been voluntary; the sticker system is administered by the recording industry itself. Singers sometimes release two versions of a record. Under intense pressure, the rapper Ice-T removed the song *Cop Killer* from his album *Body Count*, so that while earlier copies of the album contained the song, later copies did not. The Artist Formerly Known as Prince released two versions of a record in 1992, one with a warning sticker, the other "cleaned up" without a sticker.

Madonna.

> I am my own experiment. I am my own work of art.
> —Madonna

spread like wildfire. Reggae has a light, infectious sound, characterized by cross-accents played by the rhythm guitar on the offbeats. The wonderfully inventive musical tradition of Africa was also discovered by musicians in the 1980s and strongly influenced singing styles and instrumental techniques in pop and rock music.

One final technological innovation of the 1980s that had an enormous impact on the spread (and the profits) of popular music was the invention of the compact disc. It was introduced in 1983 and quickly gained popularity. Gradually, CDs and the newly popular cassettes began to replace vinyl LPs. Many consumers not only bought new recordings as they came out on CD but also bought CDs to replace all their favorite old albums. It was a bonanza for the record industry. A CD cost less than a dollar to manufacture and sold for between $12 and $20. The profits were enormous. In 1987, CBS made more than $200 million in profits. In 1989, Time Warner announced profits of nearly $500 million.

LISTENING GUIDE

Madonna
Material Girl
Words and music by Peter Brown and Robert Rans

Date of recording: 1984

Material Girl was one of the principal hit singles from Madonna's phenomenally successful album *Like a Virgin*. The video to the song introduced one of Madonna's many well-known images: a Marilyn Monroe-like blonde bombshell who is being fawned over by a large chorus of male suitors (who form a robotic chorus later in the song). The song is a fairly straightforward dance-club pop number. It is based on several recurrent melodic lines or riffs and has a persistent rhythmic beat and catchy lyrics.

0:00	[dance-pop introduction with synthesized keyboards and bass, electric guitar, and drums; guitar has main riff.]

VERSE

0:28	Some boys kiss me, some boys hug me. I think they're okay. If they don't give me proper credit I just walk away.
0:42	They can beg and they can plead, but they can't see the light, that's right. 'Cause the boy with the cold hard cash is always Mr. Right.

CHORUS

0:56	'Cause we are living in a material world and I am a material girl. You know that we are living in a material world and I am a material girl.
1:09	[Guitar break of main riff with echoes of squealing pleasure sounds by Madonna.]

VERSE

1:16	Some boys romance, some boys slow dance. That's all right with me. If they can't raise my interest then I have to let them be.
1:30	Some boys try and some boys lie, but I don't let them play. (No way.) Only boys who save their pennies make my rainy day.

CHORUS

1:43	'Cause we are living in a material world and I am a material girl. You know that we are living in a material world and I am a material girl.
1:58	Living in a material world and I am a material girl. You know that we are living in a material world and I am a material girl.
2:10	[Guitar break of main riff with echoes of Madonna squealing.]
2:24	Living in a material world. (Material.) Living in a material world. Living in a material world. (Material.) Living in a material world.

VERSE

2:38	Boys may come and boys may go and that's all right, you see. Experience has made me rich and now they're after me.

CHORUS

2:51	'Cause everybody's living in a material world and I am a material girl. You know that we are living in a material world and I am a material girl.

3:06	Living in a material world and I am a material girl. You know that we are living in a material world and I am a material girl.
3:24	A material, a material, a material, a material world.
3:32	[Echoes and fades; a false ending, which returns to the main song. Robotic men's chorus.] Living in a material world. (Material.) Living in a material world. Living in a material world. (Material.) Living in a material world. [Fade out.]

THE NINETIES: RAP, RAGE, AND REACTION

In the 1990s, the world became aware that the end of the decade would bring not only the end of a century but also the turning of a millennium. On the international scene, there was staggering change. The monolithic Union of Soviet Socialist Republics splintered into many of its formerly separate components, as the largest Communist system in the world collapsed. Many other countries of Eastern Europe tentatively embraced democracy. South Africa struggled toward greater equality; Europe struggled toward economic unity; countries in the Middle East struggled toward peace.

In America there was both hope and despair. In the spring of 1992, riots broke out in Los Angeles, causing death and destruction over many city blocks. Large numbers of Americans had not benefited from the economic surge of the 1980s. Indeed, America as a whole was fast becoming aware of its limitations. The standard of living in the United States fell below that of several other nations. The illiteracy rate was soaring and, perhaps most scandalous of all, the health rate of the richest nation in the world stood at twelfth among Western nations.

Within America, too, divisions between segments of society widened rather than narrowed. Prejudice erupted in new and overt instances of anti-Semitism. Public schools and colleges became less tolerant of freedom of thought and began to enforce a new conformity of ideas known as "political correctness." And many black Americans, impatient at their lack of progress toward equality, returned to militancy and rage.

The main musical phenomenon of the nineties was **rap**. Rap is usually half-spoken, rather than sung, with a strong and complex rhythm, backed by bass, synthesizer, and percussion. Rap traded on ideas of violence, aggression, and resentment. Urban street life provided the backdrop of guns, murder, and drugs, and the messages were heavy-handed, direct, and to the point:

> Some police think
> They have the authority
> To kill the minority.

Others spoke of drug dealers, violence in the streets, legal injustice, and civil unrest.

Some rap records provoked serious controversy. The song *Cop Killer* by the rap artist Ice-T flaunted a murderous joy: it spoke of the delights of slitting a policeman's throat and watching his family mourn. Police organizations around the country called for a boycott of Time Warner, Ice-T's record company, and the vice-president of the United States publicly joined the call. The result: the record surged strongly in the charts.

There were ugly elements in rap music. Some rap songs displayed overt racism against Asians; some were offensively homophobic. But a common trait was prejudice against women. Many rap songs referred to women as "bitches" or "ho's" (whores), and some even advocated deliberate violence and brutality against women.

The public militancy of rap was partly a reflection of a divided society, but it was also partly boosted by commercial considerations. Record companies soon discovered that aggression and a militant image sold a lot of records. Bill Stephney, a rap businessman and one of the founders of the group Public Enemy, said that he had deliberately polished the group's militant image. "In many respects, that was done on purpose ... to curry favor with a white audience by showing rebellion."

Many black leaders denounced the most vicious aspects of rap. Others saw a real danger in the militant pose of much rap music, with its stereotyping of the "drug-dealin', Uzi-totin', gangsta of today." This picture seemed as prejudicial to the reality of African-Americans as the offensive, primitive picture portrayed by nineteenth-century "blackface" minstrel shows. In the meantime, many young people said they didn't listen to the words anyway!

In all the writing and hand-wringing over rap, almost nothing was said about the music. For rap was primarily a social phenomenon. It featured a repetitive, heavy bass (often produced electronically) with a hard, high drumbeat (made on a drum machine). Rapid splicing, overdubbing, and heavy engineering produced a glossy, unvarying sound that was hypnotizing in its sameness. And against this hypnotic, percussive layer, the "messages" streamed, almost without melody.

As rap settled into the mainstream, it tended to fall into two categories. The first, "gangsta rap," continued the angry image, with heavy rhythm and little or no melody or harmony. The second, sometimes called pop

The rapper Eminem.

rap, spoke more of unity than of violence, often featured female singers, and tended to incorporate more melodic interest. Creative blends of rap with rock, rap with reggae, and rap with jazz showed that the musical ferment caused by the worldwide spread of popular culture was far from over. Rap even became the medium for gospel and Christian music.

The songs of actress and rapper Queen Latifah, written from the woman's point of view, often seemed to be a response to the macho world of hard-core rap. She spoke of respect and of community. Her song *Unity* appeared in 1993 on her album *Black Reign* and won a Grammy in 1995.

After the turn of the millennium, the commercial element of popular music was its most prominent feature. Record companies became more sophisticated than ever at marketing their products, using MTV and other television programs, as well as magazines and music outlets, to give the maximum exposure to a star or a group at just the right time. Successful debut albums are followed by singles that whet fans' appetites for the inevitable blockbuster. Teenagers in the United States now number over 30 million, and a strong economy gives them massive buying power. In the year 2000, American teenagers were able to spend over $150 billion.

This format of the debut album, followed by massive exposure, followed by a single, followed by a huge hit, was utilized in the year 2000 by the companies promoting three popular-music phenomena. Britney Spears sold 1.3 million copies of her new album, the white rapper Eminem 1.7 million copies, and the pop group 'N Sync an amazing 2.4 million copies—all in the first *week* of sales. Before that year, the Backstreet

Boys had held the record with 1.1 million. Figures for first-week sales have themselves now become part of the hype.

'N Sync and Britney Spears recorded for the same company and depended upon the same upbeat pop sound, pretty looks, and smooth moves for their appeal. On their model, the pop world in the early years of the twenty-first century seemed to be full of "boy bands" and "teen queens." Eminem, however, was a different proposition: he was ironic, clever, parodistic, and often vicious.

Rappers dominated the pop charts, and the controversy continued. In one week in the year 2000, six of the top twenty albums were rap records, and every single one of them carried parental-advisory stickers. The themes were violence and sex—often the two combined—and money. Both the videos and the successful rappers flaunted obscene financial excess. And again voices were heard in the black community condemning rap's reinforcement of racial stereotypes. Maybe rap has become the new version of the nineteenth-century minstrel show.

As the twenty-first century gets underway, a serious question arises. Will the accessibility and enormous profitability of popular music swamp more delicate and financially unstable musics? Audiences at classical-music concerts, folk festivals, and jazz clubs are diminishing rapidly. Will young people grow up appreciating the diversity, complexity, and richness of older musical traditions? And, around the world, will the multiplicity of world musical cultures survive the overwhelming popularity and commercial pressures of Western pop and rock? In 20 or 30 years, we'll know the answers to these questions.

The most important requirement of popular music is that it must appeal to a large number of people. This obviously affects musical style: popular music must have catchy rhythms or an attractive melody or interesting words or some combination of all three.

By far the largest proportion of popular music is vocal. Most of us seem to like listening to singing because it makes the music more personal. From the mid nineteenth century to the present, popular music has mostly been synonymous with song. From Stephen Foster, who composed many songs that have become staples of American popular culture, through to the "boy bands," "girl singers," and rappers of today, it is the sound of singing that has the widest appeal. Perhaps that is because we can (more or less) reproduce the sound ourselves without any special training.

Popular songs usually have simple harmonies and repetitive rhythms. However, the great songs of the 1920s, 30s, and 40s have wonderful melodies and clever, literate lyrics. At that time, jazz and popular music became strong mutual influences. Popular singers like Frank Sinatra and Bing Crosby sang with jazzy inflection, and jazz bands and small combos based their music and improvisations on popular songs.

In the 1950s, a new popular music swept through England and North America. Variously known as rock and roll, rhythm and blues, and (with a country influence) rockabilly, it employed electric guitars, hard rhythms, more raucous singing, and more intense sexuality to become (with its offshoots) the most widespread form of popular music ever.

The most important reason for the popularity of rock and roll was strictly commercial. The spread of radio, television, movies, phonographs, and recordings had made popular music available in millions of homes. Commercial interests were not slow to capitalize on this.

In the 1960s, popular music became the music of the "counterculture." Rock bands with a standard format of three electric guitars and drums were wildly popular, though some individuals with prodigious talent, such as the poet-singer-songwriter Bob Dylan and the virtuoso electric guitarist and singer Jimi Hendrix, stood out. The blues were the structural basis of many of the rock and pop songs of the day. Sentimental songs, not much different from those at the turn of the century but with an updated accompanying sound, still became great popular hits.

Throughout the remainder of the twentieth century, those two formats, the small group of singers and guitarists on the one hand and the individual singer (sometimes also playing guitar) with pop or rock accompaniment on the other, remained constant. The form and content of the songs, whose subject matter can almost always be summarized in one word: love—(or sex), also stayed fairly fixed, though their length increased.

The only really new musical style of the last part of the twentieth century was rap. With its heavily synthesized, multi-track background, it depended a great deal on modern technology. Rap and all popular music at the turn of the millennium also depended on a massive machinery of corporate interests, which spent millions of dollars in advertising and generated billions of dollars in profits. Popular music equals money.

The score of John Lennon's "Strawberry Fields."

FUNDAMENTALS OF POPULAR MUSIC

- ✦ Popular music is usually less complex than classical music
- ✦ Popular music has attractive melodies, simple harmonies, and catchy rhythm
- ✦ Popular music is mostly vocal
- ✦ The subject matter is mostly love (sex)
- ✦ Rock turned popular music rougher, sometimes raucous
- ✦ Rap began angry and alienated, though it was soon assimilated into the mainstream
- ✦ By the end of the century, popular music had become an enormous, highly manipulated, international business

GLOSSARY AND MUSICAL EXAMPLE LOCATOR

(Fuller discussions of these terms may be found on the pages indicated.)

ABA or aria or da capo form   Tripartite form, found in opera arias and some slow movements of instrumental works, featuring an opening A section, a contrasting B section, and a return to the A section, which is often sung with embellishments. (See p. 149.) (Musical example: George Frideric Handel, *Giulio Cesare*, p. 150.)

Alberti bass   Accompaniment in which the chords are broken up into individual short notes played in a repeated rhythm. (See p. 163.)

arch form   Five-part form in which part one corresponds to five, part two corresponds to four, and part three is the apex. (See p. 370.)

aria   Lyrical section of opera for solo singer and orchestra, usually in ABA form. (See p. 121.) (Musical example: George Frideric Handel, *Giulio Cesare*, p. 151.)

atonality   The lack of a key system or tonal center in music. (See p. 328.) (Musical example: Arnold Schoenberg, *Madonna* from *Pierrot Lunaire*, p. 354.)

Baroque   The period in European music from about 1600 to 1750. (See p. 115.)

basso continuo   Single instrument or small group of instruments, usually including a harpsichord, playing the bass line in Baroque music. (See p. 119.) (Musical examples: Arcangelo Corelli, Trio Sonata, Op. 3, No. 7, p. 129, and Johann Sebastian Bach, *Brandenburg* Concerto No. 2 in F Major, p. 140.)

bebop or bop   Form of jazz that developed in the 1940s for small combos, with harder, more improvisatory music. (See p. 428.) (Musical examples: Charlie Parker, *Confirmation*, p. 429, and Benny Harris, *Crazeology*, p. 70.)

binary form   A form with two sections, each of which is repeated, as in the pattern AABB. (See p. 67.) (Musical examples: Wolfgang Amadeus Mozart, Minuet and Trio from Symphony No. 18 in F Major, K. 130, p. 66, and Franz Joseph Haydn, Minuet and Trio from Symphony No. 45 in F-sharp Minor, p. 177.)

bitonality   Two different keys sounding simultaneously. (See p. 341.) (Musical example: Charles Ives, "Putnam's Camp" from *Three Places in New England*, p. 378.)

blue note   Flattened or "bent" note played or sung in jazz. (See p. 416.) (Musical examples: Bessie Smith, *Florida-Bound Blues*, p. 421, and Duke Ellington, *It Don't Mean a Thing (If It Ain't Got That Swing)*, p. 426.)

bunraku   Traditional Japanese puppet theater. (See p. 15.)

caccia   Medieval Italian secular song in which two voices sing in a round. (See p. 87.)

cantata   *Chamber* cantatas were unstaged dramatic works for a single singer or a small group of singers and accompanying instruments. *Church* cantatas involved solo singers, choir, and instruments and focused on the liturgical theme of a particular day. (See p. 118.)

canzona   Renaissance instrumental work, often involving counterpoint. (See p. 108.) (Musical example: Giovanni Gabrieli, *Canzona Duodecimi Toni*, p. 110.)

castrato   Male singer castrated before puberty to retain high voice. Castratos were common in the eighteenth century. (See p. 151.)

character piece   Short programmatic piece usually for solo piano. (See p. 270.) (Musical example: Robert Schumann, *Träumerei* (*Dreaming*) from *Kinderszenen*, Op. 15, p. 270.)

chorale   A Protestant hymn sung in unison by the entire congregation in even rhythm. Often harmonized for use by church choir. (See p. 119.) (Musical example: Johann Sebastian Bach, *St. Matthew Passion*, p. 146.)

Classic   The period in European music from about 1730 to 1800. (See p. 158.)

comic opera   (Italian: *opera buffa*; French: *opéra comique*; German: *Singspiel*.) Light opera, with amusing plots, down-to-earth characters, simpler music, and spoken dialogue. (See p. 163.) (Musical example: Giovanni Pergolesi, *La Serva Padrona*, p. 164.)

concerto   Instrumental work, usually in three movements, highlighting contrast. Baroque concertos were usually written in the pattern fast-slow-fast, featuring ritornello form. A *concerto grosso* featured a small group of instruments contrasted with the whole group. A *solo concerto* featured a single instrument contrasted with the whole group. (See p. 118.) (Musical examples: Antonio Vivaldi, *La Primavera* (*"Spring"*) from *The Four Seasons*, p. 135, and Johann Sebastian Bach, *Brandenburg* Concerto No. 2 in F Major, p. 142.) Classic and Romantic concertos tended to be solo concertos, retaining the fast-slow-fast pattern, and combining ritornello form with Classic forms, such as sonata form or aria form. (See pp. 173, 259.) (Musical example: Felix Mendelssohn,

Concerto in E minor for Violin and Orchestra, Op. 64, p. 259.)

concerto form   Three movements, in the pattern fast-slow-fast. (See p. 127.)

continuo   See **basso continuo**.

courtly love   Stylized convention of poetry and code of behavior developed in the medieval courts of southern France. (See p. 81.) (Musical example: Beatriz de Dia, *A chantar*, p. 82.)

didjeridoo   Wooden wind instrument in use among the Australian aborigines. (See p. 13.)

divertimento   A chamber work meant as a "diversion"; generally lighter in style and with five, six, or more movements. (See p. 161.)

double-stopping   Playing more than one string at a time on a string instrument. (See p. 259.) (Musical example: Felix Mendelssohn, Concerto in E minor for Violin and Orchestra, Op. 64, p. 259).

Enlightenment   Eighteenth-century philosophy that favored a rational and scientific view of the world. (See p. 158.)

ensemble   Usually used to refer to opera scenes in which several individuals sing together.

étude   Solo instrumental piece focusing on a particular aspect of technique. (See p. 265.)

Expressionism   Artistic and musical movement focusing on extreme emotions, such as fear or anguish. (See p. 349.) (Musical example: Alban Berg, *Wozzeck*, Act III, Scenes 3, 4, and 5, p. 359.)

fanfare   A stirring phrase or a complete short work that is written primarily or entirely for brass instruments. (See p. 61.) (Musical examples: Paul Dukas, Fanfare from *La Péri*, p. 62, and Aaron Copland, *Fanfare for the Common Man*, p. 381.)

fugue   Highly organized contrapuntal work featuring a theme or "subject" that occurs in all the musical lines in turn until all the lines are sounding at once. (See p. 141.) (Musical example: Johann Sebastian Bach, Prelude and Fugue in E minor, p. 140.)

fusion   Music combining elements of both jazz and rock. (See p. 432.)

fuzz box   Device that adds distortion to the sound of an electric guitar. (See p. 464.)

gagaku   Ancient Japanese orchestral music. (See p. 15.)

gamelan   Indonesian musical ensemble involving mostly metal percussion. (See pp. 17–19.) (Musical example: *Gangsaran - Bima Kurda - Gangsaran*, p. 18.)

German song   A work for voice and piano set to a German text. (See p. 63.) (Musical example: Franz Schubert, *Gretchen am Spinnrade*, p. 63.)

grand opera   Spectacular type of nineteenth-century

French opera, with elaborate stage sets, ballet, and crowd scenes. (See p. 275.)

Gregorian chant   See **plainchant**.

ground bass   A phrase in the bass that is repeated over and over again. (See p. 125.) (Musical example: Henry Purcell, Dido's Lament from *Dido and Aeneas*, p. 126.)

hardingfele   Norwegian folk violin. (See p. 12.)

Impressionism   Movement in painting of the late nineteenth and early twentieth centuries in which the outlines are vague and the pictures dreamy and suggestive. Also refers to a parallel movement in music. (See p. 334.) (Musical example: Claude Debussy, *Prélude à l'après-midi d'un faune*, p. 337.)

impromptu   Instrumental piece, usually for piano, that gives the impression of being improvised. (See p. 265.)

jali   Official singer and historian of the Mandinka tribe of West Africa. (See p. 5.)

kabuki   Japanese style of traditional musical theater, involving an all-male cast. (See p. 15.)

koto   Japanese instrument plucked like a zither. (See p. 15.)

leitmotiv   Musical phrase or fragment with associations to a character, object, or idea. (See p. 295.) (Musical example: Richard Wagner, Prelude and *Liebestod* from *Tristan und Isolde*, p. 292.)

libretto   The text for an opera. (See p. 176.)

liturgical music   Music for a religious ceremony. (See p. 77.)

lute   A plucked instrument with a rounded back, short neck, and frets. (See p. 72.) (Musical example: Guillaume de Machaut, *Doulz Viaire Gracieus*, p. 88.)

lyric opera   Type of French opera midway between grand opéra and opéra comique, usually featuring plots of tragic love. (See p. 275.)

madrigal   Secular vocal work, often in Italian, for a small group of singers. (See pp. 72, 106.) (Musical example: Maddalena Casulana, *Morte, te chiamo*, p. 72.)

Magnus Liber Organi   "Great Book of Polyphony." Late twelfth-century collection of polyphonic compositions designed for the Cathedral of Notre Dame in Paris. (See p. 85.) (Musical example: Perotinus, *Viderunt Omnes*, p. 86.)

mbira   African instrument made of a small wooden box or gourd with thin metal strips attached. (See pp. 12, 20–21.) (Musical example: *Chemetengure/Mudendero*, p. 21.)

melismatic   Musical setting of text with a large number of notes to a single syllable. (See p. 78.)

Middle Ages   The period in European music from about 400 to 1400. (See p. 76.)

minimalism   Musical style of the 1960s to the 1990s involving very limited materials, constant repetition, and very gradual change. (See p. 402.)

minuet (and trio)   An instrumental work in the tempo (moderate) and meter (triple) of a favorite seventeenth- and eighteenth-century dance, in binary form. The trio is in form and structure like another minuet, but it usually has a contrast of texture, instrumentation, and sometimes key. (See p. 66.) (Musical example: Wolfgang Amadeus Mozart, Minuet and Trio from Symphony No.18 in F Major, K.130, p. 66, and Franz Joseph Haydn, Minuet and Trio from Symphony No. 45 in F-sharp Minor, p. 178.)

minuet-and-trio form   Often used for third movements of Classic instrumental works. Both minuet and trio are in two parts, each of which is repeated. The minuet is played twice, once before and once after the trio. (See p. 171.) (Musical examples: Wolfgang Amadeus Mozart, Minuet and Trio from Symphony No.18 in F Major, K.130, p. 66, and Franz Joseph Haydn, Minuet and Trio from Symphony No. 45 in F-sharp Minor, p. 178.)

Modernism   The cultural movement, stressing innovation, that dominated the first sixty to seventy years of the twentieth century. (See p. 327.)

modes   System of melodic organization used in music of the Middle Ages and early Renaissance. There are four main medieval modes, designating pieces ending on D, E, F, and G, respectively. (See p. 78.) (Musical example: Kyrie, p. 79.)

monody   Type of early Baroque music for solo voice and **basso continuo** with vocal line imitating the rhythms of speech. (See p. 119.) (Musical example: Claudio Monteverdi, extracts from *Orfeo*, p. 122.)

motet   (Renaissance) A vocal setting of a Latin text, usually sacred. (See p. 104.) (Musical example: Giovanni Pierluigi da Palestrina, *Exsultate Deo*, p. 105.)

movement   Large, separate section of a musical work.

music drama   Term coined by Wagner to refer to his operas, which involve ancient myth, resonant poetry, and rich, dramatic music. (See p. 292.) (Musical example: Richard Wagner, Prelude and *Liebestod* from *Tristan und Isolde*, p. 296.)

nationalism   A nineteenth-century movement that stressed national identity. In music, this led to the creation of works in native languages, using national myths and legends, and incorporating local rhythms, themes, and melodies. (See p. 230.) (Musical example: Bedřich Smetana, *The Moldau*, p. 302.)

neumatic   Musical setting of text with varying numbers of notes per syllable. (See p. 78.)

nocturne   Moody, introspective piece, usually for solo piano. (See p. 265.)

noh   Ancient Japanese theatrical genre, with highly stylized acting. (See p. 15.)

octatonic scale   Scale with eight notes within the octave, separated by a series of alternating whole and half steps. (See p. 333.)

opéra comique   Small-scale French nineteenth-century opera, with humorous or romantic plots. (See p. 275.)

opera seria   ("Serious opera") Italian Baroque form of opera in three acts, with conventional plots, and alternating recitatives and arias. (See p. 131.) (Musical example: George Frideric Handel, *Giulio Cesare*, Act III, Scene 4, p. 150.)

oral tradition   The practice of passing music (or other aspects of culture) orally from one generation to another. (See pp. 2 and 8.)

oratorio   An unstaged dramatic sacred work, featuring solo singers (including a narrator), choir, and orchestra, and usually based on a biblical story. (See p. 119.)

orchestral song cycle   Song cycle in which the voice is accompanied by an orchestra instead of a piano. (See p. 322.)

Ordinary of the Mass   The collective name for those five sections of the Catholic Mass (Kyrie, Gloria, Credo, Sanctus, Agnus Dei) that occur in every Mass. (See p. 97.)

ostinato   Constantly repeated musical phrase. (See p. 341.) (Musical example: Igor Stravinsky, *Le Sacre du Printemps* (*The Rite of Spring*), p. 342.)

pantonality   Term referring to the simultaneous existence of all keys in music. (See p. 332.)

Passion   Similar to the oratorio. An unstaged dramatic sacred work, featuring solo singers (including a narrator), choir, and orchestra, and based on one of the Gospel accounts of the last days of Jesus. (See p. 119.) (Musical example: Johann Sebastian Bach, *St. Matthew Passion*, p. 145.)

pentatonic scale   A scale with five notes; the most common form has the following intervals: whole step, whole step, minor third, whole step. (See p. 332.)

plainchant   Monophonic liturgical vocal music of the Middle Ages. (See p. 77.) (Musical example: Kyrie, p. 79.)

point of imitation   Section of music presenting a short phrase imitated among the voices. (See p. 98.) (Musical example: Josquin Desprez, Kyrie from the *Pange Lingua* Mass, p. 100.)

polyphony   Music with more than one line sounding at the same time. (See p. 81.) (Musical example: Perotinus, *Viderunt Omnes*, p. 86.)

polyrhythms   Different meters sounding simultaneously. (See p. 341.)

polytonality   The existence in music of two or more keys at the same time. (See p. 332.)

Postmodernism   A cultural movement of the last part of the twentieth century, involving a juxtaposition of past and present, popular and refined, Western and non-Western styles. (See p. 330.)

prelude (toccata)   Free, improvisatory work or movement, usually for organ. (See p. 141.) (Musical example: Johann Sebastian Bach, Prelude and Fugue in E minor, p. 140.)

Primitivism   Artistic movement of the early twentieth century concentrating on nonurban cultures and untamed nature. (See p. 340.)

program music   Instrumental music that tells a story or describes a picture or a scene. (See pp. 134, 241.) (Musical example: Antonio Vivaldi, *La Primavera* ("*Spring*") from *The Four Seasons*, p. 135.)

protest song   A song devoted to a social cause, such as the fight against injustice, antiwar sentiment, etc. (See p. 460.)

quartal chords   Chords based on fourths rather than thirds. (See p. 333.)

quarter tones   Pitches separated by a quarter of a step rather than a half or a whole step. (See p. 334.)

ragtime   Early jazz in which the melody is highly syncopated, usually in duple meter and march tempo. (See p. 418.) (Musical example: Scott Joplin, *Maple Leaf Rag*, p. 418.)

rap   Popular music style of the 1980s and 1990s with fast, spoken lyrics and a strong, and often complex beat. (See p. 474.)

recitative   Music for solo voice and simple accompaniment, designed to reflect the irregularity and naturalness of speech. (See p. 121.) (Musical example: Claudio Monteverdi, extracts from *Orfeo*, p. 122.)

recitative accompagnato   Dramatic recitative accompanied by the orchestra. (See p. 148.) (Musical example: George Frideric Handel, *Giulio Cesare*, Act III, Scene 4, p. 149.)

reggae   Popular music style from Jamaica, with a light, catchy sound, characterized by offbeats played on the rhythm guitar. (See p. 469.)

Renaissance   The period in European music from about 1400 to 1600. (See p. 94.)

Requiem Mass   Mass for the dead. (See p. 186.)

riff   A short, repeated, melodic phrase often found in popular music. (See p. 458.) (Musical example: The Beatles, *It Won't Be Long*, p. 458.)

ritornello   An orchestral passage in a concerto that returns several times, in the same or in different keys. (See p. 133.) (Musical example: Antonio Vivaldi, *La Primavera* ("*Spring*") from *The Four Seasons*, p. 135.)

rondo form   Often used for last movements of Classic instrumental works. A theme constantly returns, alternating with constrasting passages (episodes). (See p. 173.) (Musical example: Franz Joseph Haydn, String Quartet, Op. 33, No. 2, in E-flat Major, p. 180.)

scat   To sing with made-up syllables. (See p. 416.) (Musical example: Louis Armstrong, *Hotter Than That*, p. 422.)

secular music   Music that is nonreligious. (See p. 77.)

shakuhachi   Japanese end-blown bamboo flute. (See pp. 10, 15–16.) (Musical example: *Koku-Reibo*, p. 16.)

shamisen   Japanese plucked instrument with three strings and a long neck. (See p. 15.)

sinfonia   Three-movement instrumental introduction to eighteenth-century Italian opera. (See p. 169.)

sitar   A long-necked, resonant, plucked string instrument from India. (See p. 10.)

sonata   Baroque: A work for a small group of instruments. Sonatas include solo sonatas (one instrument and basso continuo) and trio sonatas (two instruments and basso continuo). Also divided by style into *sonata da camera* ("chamber sonata"), whose movements were based on dance rhythms, and *sonata da chiesa* ("church sonata"), whose movements were more serious in character. (See p. 119.) Classic and Romantic: Work for solo piano or piano and another instrument in three or four movements. (See p. 171.) (Musical examples: Arcangelo Corelli, Trio Sonata, Op. 3, No. 7, p. 129, and Ludwig van Beethoven, Piano Sonata in E Major, Op. 109, p. 221.)

sonata form   Organizing structure for a musical work or movement. It has three main parts: an *exposition*, in which the main themes are presented and the primary key moves from tonic to dominant; a *development* in which many keys are explored and the themes are often presented in fragments; and a *recapitulation*, in which the music of the exposition returns, usually staying in the tonic key throughout. (See p. 171.) (Musical examples: Wolfgang Amadeus Mozart, Symphony No. 40 in G minor, K. 550, p. 191, and Ludwig van Beethoven, Symphony No. 5 in C minor, p. 206.)

song cycle   Series of songs linked together. (See p. 244.)

Sprechstimme ("speechsong")   Technique of singing, halfway between speech and song. (See p. 359.) (Musical example: Arnold Schoenberg, *Madonna* from *Pierrot Lunaire*, p. 354.)

string quartet   Work, usually in four movements, for two violins, viola, and cello. (See p. 169.) (Musical examples: Franz Joseph Haydn, String Quartet, Op. 33, No. 2, in E-flat Major, p. 180, and Béla Bartók, String Quartet No. 4, p. 370.)

strophic song   Song in which all stanzas are sung to the same music. (See p. 243.) (Musical examples: Beatriz de

Dia, *A chantar*, p. 82, and Franz Schubert, *Gretchen am Spinnrade*, p. 63.)

suite A series of short pieces, usually based on various Baroque dance forms. (See p. 119.)

swing (1) The feeling generated by the regular rhythm and the syncopated accents of jazz. (See p. 416.) (2) Dance music played by jazz bands in the 1930s and early 1940s. (See p. 422.) (Musical example: Duke Ellington, *It Don't Mean a Thing (If It Ain't Got That Swing)*, p. 426.)

syllabic Musical setting of text with one note per syllable. (See p. 78.)

Symbolism Literary movement of the late nineteenth and early twentieth centuries concentrating on suggestion rather than description. (See p. 335.)

symphonic poem Programmatic orchestral work in one movement. (See p. 242.) (Musical example: Franz Liszt, *Hamlet*, p. 283.)

symphony Orchestral work, usually in four movements, the first being moderate in tempo, the second slow, the third a minuet or a scherzo, and the fourth fast. (See p. 169.) (Musical example: Ludwig van Beethoven, Symphony No. 5 in C minor, p. 206.)

thematic transformation Technique of changing or varying a theme in its different appearances throughout a work. (See p. 279.) (Musical example: Franz Liszt, *Hamlet*, p. 283.)

theme and variations Form of a work or a movement in which successive statements of a melody are altered or embellished each time. (See p. 43.) (Musical examples: Ludwig van Beethoven, *Six Easy Variations on a Swiss Tune*, p. 204, and Franz Schubert, Quintet in A Major (*The Trout*), p. 248.)

32-bar AABA form Format involving four eight-measure phrases, the first two and the last being the same. This form is very common in popular songs and jazz. (See p. 69.) (Musical example: Benny Harris, *Crazeology*, p. 70.)

through-composed song Song in which the music is continually evolving. (See p. 243.) (Musical example: Arnold Schoenberg, *Madonna* from *Pierrot Lunaire*, p. 354.)

tone color The distinctive sound of an instrument or voice. (See p. 10.)

total serialism Strict organization of all musical elements (dynamics, rhythm, pitch, etc.) of a musical composition by arranging them into series. (See p. 389.) (Musical example: Pierre Boulez, *Structures I* for two pianos, p. 391.)

troubadour Poet-musician of medieval southern France. (See p. 81.) (Musical example: Beatriz de Dia, *A chantar*, p. 82.)

trouvère Poet-musician of medieval northern France. (See p. 81.)

twelve-tone system Twentieth-century compositional technique in which the composer treats all twelve pitches as equal and uses them in a highly organized way. (See p. 332.) (Musical example: Arnold Schoenberg, Theme and Sixth Variation, *Variations for Orchestra*, Op. 31, p. 356.)

verismo Literary and operatic style featuring down-to-earth plots and characters. (See p. 275.)

virtuoso A performing musician (usually instrumentalist) who is outstandingly gifted. (See p. 221.)

Wagner tuba Brass instrument with a range between French horn and trombone. (See p. 295.)

wah-wah pedal Device for electric guitar that changes frequencies on the same note. (See p. 464.)

whole-tone scale A scale with six notes, each separated from the next by a whole step. (See p. 333.)

word-painting The technique of depicting the *meaning* of words through music. (See p. 107.) (Musical example: Thomas Morley, *Sweet Nymph Come to Thy Lover* and *Fire and Lightning*, p. 109.)

PHOTO CREDITS The author and publisher wish to acknowledge, with thanks, the following photographic sources.

ON ALL LISTENING GUIDES:
Beethoven's handwritten sketches for the Fifth Symphony. Gesellschaft der Musikfreunde in Wien.

CHAPTER 1
1 Steve Cole, PhotoDisc, Inc.
2 Pierpont Morgan Library/Art Resource, NY
3 (bottom left) Ramey/Stock Boston
3 (top right) Lisa Quinones/Black Star
3 (bottom right) Ramey/Stock Boston
4 (left) eStock Photography LLC
4 (right) Jack Vartoogian
5 (left) Jack Vartoogian
5 (right) Jack Vartoogian
6 (left) Wolfgang Kaehler Photography
6 (right) Jay Blakesberg/Retna, Ltd.
7 (left) John Lei/ Stock Boston
7 (bottom right) Steve Vidler/eStock Photography LLC
9 Jagdish Argarwal/Dinodia Picture Agency
10 Jack Vartoogian
11 (top right) Musée de l'Homme, Phototheque
11 (second from top) Culver Pictures, Inc.
11 (middle right) Paolo Koch/Photo Researchers, Inc.
11 (bottom right) Courtesy of the author.
12 (left) Musser, a Division of The Selmer Company
12 (top right) Sarah Errington/The Hutchinson Library
12 (middle right) Jitendra Arya
13 (top left) José Azel/Woodfin Camp & Associates
13 (bottom left) Wolfgang Kaehler Photography
13 (right) Lester Sloan/Woodfin Camp & Associates
14 Wolfgang Kaehler Photography
15 (left) Jack Varoogian
15 (top right) Jack Vartoogian
15 (bottom right) Jack Vartoogian
16 Jack Vartoogian
19 Steve Vidler/eStock Photography LLC
20 Marc & Evelyne Bernheim/Woodfin Camp & Associates
21 Shanachie Entertainment

CHAPTER 2
23 Ben Christopher/Performing Arts Library
44 (top right) Stephen Morley/Retna, Ltd.
44 (left) Eric Simmons/Stock Boston
44 (bottom right) UPI/Corbis/Bettmann
45 (top left) Volkman Kurt Wentzel/National Geographic Society
45 (middle right) CTK/Sovfoto/Eastfoto
47 (top) Walter H. Scott
47 (bottom) Institut Royal du Patrimoine Artistique (IRPA-KIK)
48 (top) Fritz Henle/Photo Researchers, Inc.
48 (bottom) Walter H. Scott
49 (top) Jon Blumb
49 (bottom left) Index Stock Imagery, Inc.
49 (bottom right) Tony Freeman/PhotoEdit
50 (top left) Walter H. Scott
50 (top right) Walter H. Scott
50 (bottom) Walter H. Scott
51 (top right) Walter H. Scott
51 (middle right) Walter H. Scott
51 (bottom extreme right) Walter H. Scott
51 (bottom left) John Bacchus/Pearson Education Corporate Digital Archive
51 (bottom middle) Todd Powell/Index Stock Imagery, Inc.
51 (bottom right) Robert Ginn/PhotoEdit
52 (top left) Walter H. Scott
52 (top right) Royal Ontario Museum. With permission of the Royal Ontario Museum, © ROM.
52 (bottom) Walter H. Scott
53 (left) Steinway & Sons
53 (middle) Royal Ontario Museum. With permission of the Royal Ontario Museum, © ROM.
53 (right) Steinway & Sons
54 (left) Giraudon/Art Resource, NY
54 (right) Corbis
54 (bottom right) Janet Gillies/Experimental Musical Instruments
55 (top right) Walter H. Scott
55 (bottom right) Walter H. Scott
56 Walter H. Scott
57 (top left) Walter H. Scott
57 (top right) Walter H. Scott
57 (bottom) John Abbott Photography
58 (top left) The Granger Collection
58 (right) French Government Tourist Office
58 (bottom left) Snark International/Art Resource, NY

CHAPTER 3
60 Mary Kate Denny/PhotoEdit
63 Archiv/Photo Researchers, Inc.
66 Art Resource, NY
70 Frank Driggs Collection
72 Bob Grove/National Gallery of Art, Washington, DC

CHAPTER 4
75 Lebrecht Music Collection/NL
78 AKG London Ltd.
80 Art Resource, NY
82 Fitzwilliam Museum
84 (top left) Research Center for Music Iconography, CUNY
84 (bottom left) Research Center for Music Iconography, CUNY
84 (top right) Courtesy of the Library of Congress
85 Chad Ehlers/Stone
88 Courtesy of the Library of Congress
89 Photography by Jean Bernard in "L'Univers de Chartres" Copyright Bordas, Paris 1988. Photography by Jean Bernard in *L'Univers de Chartres,* copyright Bordas, Paris 1988.
91 Steve Vidler/eStock Photography LLC
92 Handwritten score, "Introit & Kyrie, Missa for Sancti Ylarionus Abbatis." Torino, Biblioteca Nazionale Universiteria. Lucca: Libreria Musicale Italiana © 1990. Used by permission.

CHAPTER 5
93 Thomas Photos Oxford
94 (top) Siegfried Layda/Stone
94 (bottom) Courtesy of the Library of Congress
95 Erich Lessing/Art Resource, NY
96 Art Resource, NY
98 AKG London Ltd.
100 Bildarchiv der Österreichische Nationalbibliothek
105 Thomas Photos Oxford
107 Library of Congress
112 Ockeghem "Missa mi mi," by Johannes Ockeghem. Vatican City, Biblioteca Apostolica Vaticana, MS Chigi CVIII 234. Used by permission.
113 "Missa mi mi" from "Masses and Mass Sections" by Johannes Ockeghem, edited by Jaap van Benthem. Copyright 1994 Koninklijke VNM. Used by permission.

332 Man Ray/AKG London Ltd.

335 (top) Deutsches Museum

335 (bottom) AKG London Ltd.

336 Lauros-Giraudon/Art Resource, NY

340 AKG London Ltd.

341 (top) AKG London Ltd.

341 (bottom) The Museum of Modern Art

345 Equity Management Inc. (EMI)

349 Archive Photos

350 (top) AKG London Ltd.

350 (bottom) Richard Fish

351 Richard Fish

355 Arnold Schoenberg Center, Privatstiftung, Vienna, Austria Institute Archives

358 © Universal Edison

360 AKG London Ltd.

367 (left) Joan Miro, *The Migratory Bird,* from the Constellation series. Palma de Mallorca, May 26, 1941. Gouache and oil wash on paper, 18⅛ × 15" (46.1 × 39.1 cm). Private Collection, Pierre Matisse Gallery. © 2002 Artists Rights Society (ARS), New York/ADAGP, Paris.

367 (right) Corbis

369 AKG London Ltd.

372 Bildarchiv Preussischer Kulturbesitz

373 (top) Culver Pictures, Inc.

373 (bottom) Yoke Matze/Arcaid

378 Courtesy of the Library of Congress

380 Walter H. Scott

384 (top) Walter H. Scott

384 (bottom) William P. Gottlieb

389 AKG London Ltd.

392 Edwin London

398 (top) William Taylor/Disney Publishing Worldwide

398 (bottom) Eric Pollizter/Daedalus Publishing

402 Pace Wildenstein/Pace Wildenstein MacGill

403 Steve J. Sherman

404 (left) Steve J. Sherman

404 (middle) Steve J. Sherman

404 (right) Eliot Khuner

409 PEANUTS reprinted by permission of United Feature Syndicate, Inc.

413 "Me he perdido muchas veces por el mar" by George Crumb, © 1971 C. F. Peters Corporation. Used by permission.

CHAPTER 11

415 Mel Lindstrom/Photo Researchers, Inc.

416 Popperfoto

417 (top) Jack Vartoogian

417 (bottom) Howard-Tilton Memorial Library

418 (top) Howard-Tilton Memorial Library

418 (bottom) The New York Public Library at Lincoln Center

421 Corbis

422 Archive Photos

423 Archive Photos

426 Corbis

428 (top) Corbis

428 (bottom) Archive Photos

429 Corbis

431 David Gahr

432 Jack Vartoogian

433 © Bettmann/CORBIS

434 Jack Vartoogian

437 "Satin Doll" handwritten score from "Music is My Mistress" by Duke Ellington. © 1973 by Duke Ellington, Inc. Used by permission of Doubleday, a division of Random House, Inc.

438 "Satin Doll" from "Sophisticated Ladies." Words by Johnny Mercer, Duke Ellington, and Billy Strayhorn, music by Duke Ellington. Copyright © 1953, 1958 (renewed 1986) and assigned to Famous Music Corporation, WB Music Corp., Famous Music Corporation, and Tempo Music Inc. c/o Music Sales Corporation in the U.S.A. Rights for the world outside the U.S.A. controlled by Tempo Music, Inc. c/o Music Sales Corporation. International copyright secured. All rights reserved.

CHAPTER 12

439 Tony Garcia/Stone

442 (top) Center for American Music

442 (bottom) Library of Congress

443 Jim Caldwell/Houston Grand Opera

447 (top) Corbis

447 (bottom left) Corbis

447 (bottom right) MICHAEL OCHS ARCHIVES.COM

448 CORBIS/Bettmann

449 Gil Michael Photography/Elvis Presley Enterprises, Inc.

450 © United States Postal Service. Displayed with permission. All rights reserved. Written authorization from the Postal Service is required to use, reproduce, post, transmit, distribute, or publicly display this image.

451 Archive Photos

454 Ken Heyman/Black Starr

455 (top) John Launois/Black Star

455 (bottom) Frank Driggs Collection

457 Globe Photos, Inc., 2004

459 Michael Putland/Retna, Ltd.

463 Joel Axelrad/Retna Ltd.

465 UPI/Corbis

468 (top left) Warner Brothers Records/Reprise Records. Courtesy of Warner Bros. Records.

468 (top middle) "Tapestry" album artwork. © 1977 Ode Records. Courtesy Ode/Epic/Legacy Recordings. Used by permission.

468 (top right) Atlantic Records

468 (bottom) Chuck Jackson/Corbis

468 Hollis/Retna, Ltd.

471 Reuters/Corbis

472 Ian McKell/Retna, Ltd.

475 Patrick Ford/Retna Ltd.

459, 478 "Strawberry Fields Forever," words and music by John Lennon and Paul McCartney. Copyright 1967 Northern Songs Ltd. Copyright renewed. All rights controlled and administered by EMI Blackwood Music Inc. under license from ATV Music (Maclen Music). All rights reserved.